BARRISTERS IN IRELAND

Barristers in Ireland

An evolving profession since 1921

Niamh Howlin

FOUR COURTS PRESS

Typeset in 10.5 pt on 12.5 pt Ehrhardt by
Carrigboy Typesetting Services for
FOUR COURTS PRESS LTD
7 Malpas Street, Dublin 8, Ireland
e-mail: info@fourcourtspress.ie
and in North America for
FOUR COURTS PRESS
c/o ISBS, 920 NE 58th Avenue, Suite 300, Portland, OR 97213.

A catalogue record for this title is available
from the British Library.

ISBN 978–1–80151–084–4

Printed in England
by Antony Rowe Ltd, Chippenham, Wilts.

Contents

Abbreviations

ABA	American Bar Association
A.C.	Appeal Cases
A.J.L.H.	*American Journal of Legal History*
Alt. L.J.	*Alternative Law Journal*
Att. Gen.	Attorney General
B.C.L.C.	Bar Council Library Committee minutes
B.C.M.	Bar Council minutes
B.R.	*Bar Review*
Camb. L.J.	*Cambridge Law Journal*
Can. J. Ec. Pol. Sc.	*Canadian Journal of Economic and Political Science*
CCBE	Council of Bars and Law Societies of Europe
C.J.E.U.	Court of Justice of the European Union
Crim. L.Q.	*Criminal Law Quarterly*
Deb.	Debates
Dept.	Department
D.H.R.	*Dublin Historical Record*
D.I.B.	*Dictionary of Irish biography, online edition*
DPP	Director of Public Prosecutions
D.U.L.J.	*Dublin University Law Journal*
ECHR	European Convention on Human Rights
ECtHR	European Court of Human Rights
EEC	European Economic Community
E.H.R.R.	European Human Rights Reports
FLAC	Free Legal Advice Centres
F.T.C.	Report of the Fair Trade Commission, 1990.
GAA	Gaelic Athletic Association
Govt.	Government
IBA	International Bar Association
I.H.S.	*Irish Historical Studies*
I.L.T.	*Irish Law Times (new series)*
I.L.T.S.J.	*Irish Law Times and Solicitors' Journal*
Int. J. Leg. Prof.	*International Journal of the Legal Profession*
Int. L.	*The International Lawyer*
I.R.	Irish Reports
Ir. Jur.	*Irish Jurist*
Ir. Pol. Stud.	*Irish Political Studies*
J.A.B.A.	*Journal of the American Bar Association*
J. Ind. Ec.	*Journal of Industrial Economics*

J.L.E.	*Journal of Law and Economics*
J.L.P.	*Journal of the Legal Profession*
J.W.H.	*Journal of Women's History*
KC	King's Counsel
K.I.B.M.	King's Inns benchers' minutes
L.I.M.	*Legal Information Management*
Min.	Minister
M.L.R.	*Modern Law Review*
NAI	National Archives of Ireland
N.I.L.Q.	*Northern Ireland Legal Quarterly*
N.Z.L.R.	New Zealand Law Reports
ODNB	*Oxford dictionary of national biography*
PI	Personal Injuries
RTÉ	Raidió Teilifís Éireann
Sec.	secretary
TCD	Trinity College Dublin
TD	Teachta Dála
UCD	University College Dublin
UCDA	University College Dublin Archives
W.L.J.	*Women's Law Journal*
W.L.R.	Weekly Law Reports

Acknowledgments

This book would not have been conceived were it not for an approach by James O'Reilly SC, King's Inns bencher and chair of the King's Inns library committee in 2017. He suggested a twentieth-century history of the Irish Bar, and I was intrigued. After a couple of meetings between myself, James and Renate Ní Uigín, the King's Inns librarian, I resolved to take on the project. I am very grateful to James and Renate for their support, encouragement and friendship over the last six years, and I have enjoyed our regular lunch meetings and stimulating discussions.

I thank the current chair of the Bar Council, Sara Phelan SC, as well as her predecessors Maura MacNally SC and Mr Justice Micheál P. O'Higgins, for supporting and encouraging this book. I also wish to thank the library committees of the Bar Council and of the King's Inns for facilitating access to their respective archives. Staff at National Archives of Ireland, the National Library of Ireland, the UCD Archives and the libraries at University College Dublin, Trinity College Dublin and the King's Inns were always helpful. In particular, Nuala Byrne, John Duffy, Damien Grenham and Louis Connaire in the Law Library and of course Renate Ní Uigín in the King's Library went beyond the call of duty. Cormac Ó Culáin from the Bar Council has also been extremely helpful.

The academic community in Ireland is small, and the legal history community is even smaller. I have been fortunate to have been able to call on the expertise and advice of other scholars who have published histories of the Irish legal professions: Kenneth Ferguson, Colum Kenny, Daire Hogan, Liz Goldthorpe and the late Tony Hart were all generous with their time over the past number of years. I am grateful to my UCD colleagues for their helpful suggestions and feedback at different stages of this project. In particular, I would like to thank Dr Kevin Costello, Tony Kerr SC, John O'Dowd, Dr Tom Mohr, Dr Mark Coen, Dr Cliona Kelly, Dr Noel McGrath and Dr Maebh Harding. I am also grateful to John Lynch, Rory Clarke, Greta Jursys and Rachel Minogue for providing research assistance, and to Siobhan Gaffney for her transcription work. I wish to acknowledge the UCD Sutherland School of Law, for facilitating two research sabbaticals to work on the project, and I'd like to thank current and former Deans of Law, Professors Imelda Maher and Laurent Pech, for their support.

A publication such as this would not be possible without financial support, and I gratefully acknowledge the generous funding provided by the UCD Sutherland School of Law, the UCD Seed Funding scheme, the Bar of Ireland and The Honourable Society of King's Inns.

I am very grateful to the twenty-nine people who agreed to be interviewed for this book and who spoke so candidly about their experiences. We met in offices and chambers, in city suburbs and in country houses. Some took trains across the country or made the trek out to Belfield, while others welcomed me into their homes and plied me with tea and biscuits. I am grateful for their time, for their honesty and openness, and for their willingness to entertain this project. Much of what they had to say is presented in this book, but there was always a proportion of the stories over which a veil of discretion had to be drawn. In keeping with the Bar's oral storytelling tradition, I was thoroughly entertained by these past and present members of the Bar.

In Plain Sight, a joint initiative of the Bar of Ireland and the King's Inns, provides financial support for artists to produce portraits of prominent female barristers or judges. Emma Stroude was selected as the 2022 *In Plain Sight* commissioned artist, and her portrait of Frances Kyle BL and Averil Deverell BL, the first women called to the Irish Bar in 1921, has been used as the cover image for this book. I would like to thank the *In Plain Sight* committee for allowing the use of this striking portrait as a cover image. The original piece hangs in the King's Inns. I wish to thank David Nolan SC for his help sourcing images in the Bar of Ireland Digital Archive for this book. I would also like to acknowledge the RTÉ Archives, the Honorable Society of King's Inns, the Irish Architectural Archive, British Pathé, the Irish Newspaper Archive and the Irish Photographic Archive for permission to use images from their respective collections.

Once again, it has been a pleasure to work with Four Courts Press, a publishing house that combines high editorial and production standards with good humour and flexibility. While everyone on the team has contributed towards this endeavour, I would like to note my particular thanks to Martin Fanning. Thanks also to Julitta Clancy for the excellent index which helps to make this book a useful work of reference.

Thank you to my husband, Robert Fitzpatrick, who has fielded many questions about the inner workings of the Bar and has provided unlimited intellectual, moral and practical support during the life of this project. Finally, thank you to our daughters, Louise and Neasa, for all the patience, encouragement and fun.

Foreword

There is nothing permanent except change

Heraclitus

This book serves as an important way marker in the continued development of the Bar and the barrister profession and indeed provides an insight into social history between 1921 and 1999. What emerges in this book is the nature of change, response and leadership. Dr Howlin has expertly plaited together the rich seam of literature and research on the nuances of the barrister profession, with contemporary interviews and testimonies of those who practiced, and continue to practice, each side of the new twenty-first century.

The footnotes alone serve as a fascinating *tour de force* of the uniqueness of the profession – and the degree to which it is of interest to others. The documentary research, drawing from the archives of the Honorable Society of Kings Inn's, the Bar of Ireland, universities and state papers, indicates that the profession has contributed to – and caused – some fascinating discussions which have a wider societal and political impact. As Dr Howlin states, many barristers 'were at the forefront of the foundation of the state and displayed both innovation and resourcefulness'.

Dr Howlin's work reflects a society in change – gender and diversity, work life balance, public perception to name but a few. Just as the Bar in 1921 differed greatly from the Bar of 1999, so too has great change arisen between 1999 and the Bar of today – 2023. Thirty-two people were called to the Bar in 1921, and by 1999 membership of the Law Library had risen to 1,185. Today, the Bar Council oversees and delivers for a membership of approximately 2,100. So what has changed? The context has changed and membership profile has changed. One significant profile change is that of gender: the Bar is now comprised of 36 per cent female; 64 per cent male members. Much work has been done. Much more work remains to be done across many fronts. Services delivered today – both at the Bar of Ireland and at the Honorable Society of King's Inns – include a formal professional development programme, embodying a recognition of the complexity of practice through a number of mentoring, practice management and resilience initiatives. In addition, the issue of specialisation and marketing of members increasingly comes to the fore and is being responded to by the development of specialist Bar associations and general professionalisation of supports and resources. Both organizations continue to extend pathways to the profession and attract a diverse and talented range of entrants, through part-time access routes, bursaries and fellowships. Graduates from disciplines other than law increasingly figure as applicants.

So the Bar today is already much different than the Bar of 1999. And so it should be. The next tome of this publication, if we are to keep to the arc of time considered by Dr Howlin – 2000 to 2080 – will record developments we cannot possibly conceive of today. But it will record our success in responding to the use of technology in advocacy, legal research and services generally, competition from traditional and non-traditional sources, the direction of regulation and the impact of internationalization.

Thankfully, some things remain the same, regardless of the epoch. As this publication captures, the Bar is home to all of humanity, our frailties, our qualities, our fears and our strengths. The variety of experience, the challenges of practice and 'getting on', and the importance of collegiality are also immutable.

Clearly the position has been, and continues to be, that barristers occupy a unique position between the citizen and their access to justice. That position is one that requires careful attention and vigilance, and should call upon us all, how can we shape a positive legacy for the future citizen and future barrister?

Sara Phelan SC
Chair of the Council of
The Bar of Ireland

Hugh Mohan SC
Chair of the Council of
The Honorable Society of King's Inns

CHAPTER ONE

Introduction

'Lawyers are history buffs, much enamoured with the traditions
of their profession.'[1]

The study of legal professions

The Irish Bar is replete with anecdotes, legends, memoirs and reminiscences.
Stories are exchanged between colleagues and passed down to junior members
of the Bar, in both formal and informal settings; over dinners and drinks, waiting
outside courtrooms, in the Law Library and in the barristers' tea rooms. Some
stories are told as advice or context for those new to the profession; some are told
to entertain; many are comedic. Such anecdotes focus on individual actors,
usually well-known advocates and orators. Both the content of the stories and
their mode of delivery are important; re-enactment, mimicry and dramatic
timing all play a part. There are as many anecdotes about those perceived to be
at the top of their profession as there are about those struggling on the margins.

In 2016, the Canadian scholar Wesley Pue described lawyers as 'energetic
purveyors of historical myth.'[2] This is true of lawyers in various common law
countries, including those in Ireland. Such 'myths'[3] are not untruths, but rather
narratives about the development of the legal professions, their roles in society
and public life, and the traditions, controversies and personalities associated with
them. Many of these myths or narratives are passed down as part of the Bar's
strong oral tradition. Some are reproduced in first-person written accounts of
life at the Bar,[4] while others appear in legal biographies, institutional histories
and official publications. So strong is the storytelling tradition at the Bar, that
when asked about their personal experiences at the Bar during the interviews
conducted for this book, several reverted to relaying tales about other barristers;
passing on the myths and 'lore' of the profession.[5] Upon being told that a
twentieth-century history of the Bar was in preparation, many members of the
profession have generously offered up their anecdotes or recommended that
I speak with individuals who were known to have 'good stories'. While
acknowledging the richness of the narrative tradition at the Bar, this book seeks

1 W. Wesley Pue, *Lawyers' empire: legal professions and cultural authority, 1780–1950* (Vancouver,
2016), p. 3.   2 Pue, *Lawyers' empire*, p. 4.   3 Peter Fitzpatrick, *The mythology of modern law*
(London, 1992), p. i, argues that 'myth is vibrantly operative in modernity.'   4 See further below
for a discussion of various written memoirs and biographies.   5 This is common in both folklore
and oral history; '[s]tories told in an interview often involve a retelling of something the interviewee

to go beyond a simple retelling of these stories. It is an attempt to move away from the focus on the individual to tell a more collective story about life at the Bar. As Pue observes, '[b]ridging the gap between historical research and professional rhetoric is essential if we are to develop a perspective on the legal profession, its history, and its role in contemporary ... society'.[6] This book attempts to move beyond 'professional rhetoric' and the 'myths' of the profession in an Irish context. It seeks to get behind the entertaining stories to understand barristers' motivations, anxieties and conflicts.

Since the twentieth century, scholars in different fields have focused on professions, including legal professions, through a variety of lenses. Economists, for example, have focused on competition,[7] lawyers' earnings,[8] regulation[9] and issues of supply and demand.[10] Political scientists have tended to be more interested in professions' power, autonomy[11] and relationship with the state.[12] The professions have also been a rich source of study for sociologists.[13] Until the 1960s, many sociologists viewed professions in terms of public service,[14] 'through the schooled application of their unusually esoteric knowledge and complex skill'.[15] There was a strong disciplinary focus on the control and deployment of expert knowledge.[16] Subsequent sociological studies of professions were more critical.[17] Scholars like Foucoult focused on the social control function of lawyers,[18] while Weber examined the education of lawyers,[19] and their role in creating law.

heard from someone else or has previously told to others.' Donald Richie, *Doing oral history* (Oxford, 2014), p. 25.   **6** Pue, *Lawyers' empire*, p. 26.   **7** E.g., John Schroeter, Scott L. Smith and Steven Cox, 'Advertising and competition in routine legal service markets: an empirical investigation', *J. Ind. Ec.* 36 (1987), 49. On the monopolistic nature of professions more generally, see M. Friedman, *Capitalism and freedom* (Chicago, 1962), pp 137–60.   **8** E.g., Steven Cox and William Canby, 'Consumer information and the pricing of legal services', *J. Ind. Ec.* 30 (1982), 305; Sherwin Rosen, 'The market for lawyers', *J.L.E.* 35:2 (1992), 215.   **9** E.g., George J. Stigler, 'The theory of economic regulation', *Bell J. Econ. & Management Science* 2 (1971), 3.   **10** E.g., B. Peter Pashigian, 'The market for lawyers: the determinants of the demand for the supply of lawyers', *J.L.E.* 20:1 (1977), 53.   **11** E.g., Eliot Freidson, *Profession of medicine: a study of the sociology of applied knowledge* (Chicago, 1988).   **12** E.g., C.L. Gilb, *Hidden hierarchies: the professions and government* (New York, 1966); Terry Johnson (ed.), *Professions and power* (London, 1972); P.J. Corfield, *Power and the professions in Britain, 1700–1850* (London, 2000).   **13** E.g., Brian Abel-Smith and Robert Stevens, *Lawyers and the courts: a sociological study of the English legal system, 1750–1965* (London, 1967). Although, as Halpérin points out, '[f]or a long time, legal historians have neglected or under-evaluated the teachings of sociologists regarding lawyers': Jean-Louise Halpérin, 'For a renewed history of lawyers', *A.J.L.H.* 56:1 (2016), 53, at 54.   **14** E.g., T.H. Marshall, 'The recent history of professionalism in relation to social structure and social policy', *Can. J. Ec. Pol. Sc.* 5 (1939), 325: 'professionalism is not concerned with self-interest by with the welfare of the client'.   **15** E.g., Eliot Freidson, 'The theory of professions: state of the art' in Robert Dingwall and Philip Lewis (eds), *The sociology of the professions: lawyers, doctors and others* (London, 1983), p. 19.   **16** Dietrich Rueschemeyer, 'Professional autonomy and the social control of expertise' in Dingwall and Lewis (eds), *The sociology of the professions*.   **17** See, for example, Dietrich Rueschemeyer, 'Professional autonomy and the social control of expertise' in Dingwall and Lewis (eds), *The sociology of the professions*, p. 38. See also Magali Sarfatti Larson, *The rise of professionalism: a sociological analysis* (Berkeley, 1977).   **18** Michel Foucault, 'Intellectuals and power' in D.F. Bouchard (ed.), *Language, counter-memory, practice: selected essays and interviews by*

The contemporary study of legal professions has seen considerable growth in recent decades, and the vast body of work produced includes studies focusing on their organisation[20] and regulation,[21] and the impact of technology.[22] Recent scholarship, particularly in the UK, has also examined gender,[23] diversity[24] and elites.[25] Political historians have frequently considered the role and impact of the legal professions and of individual lawyers[26] on key historical events, periods and

Michel Foucault (Oxford, 1977). **19** Max Weber, *Economy and society* (Cambridge, 1969). **20** E.g., Jerry Van Hoy (ed.), *Legal professions: work, structure and organization* (Bradford, 2001); Atalanta Goulandris, *The enterprising barrister: organisation, culture and changing professionalism* (Oxford, 2020). **21** E.g., Michael J. Trebilcock, *Paradoxes of professional regulation: in search of regulatory principles* (Toronto, 2022), ch. 7; Camille Chaserant and Sophie Harnay, 'Self-regulation of the legal profession and quality in the market for legal services: an economic analysis of lawyers' reputation', *European J.L. & Economics* 39:2 (2015), 431; Richard Abel, 'Lawyer self-regulation and the public interest: a reflection', *Legal Ethics* 20:1 (2017), 115; Richard F. Devlin, 'Regulating lawyers: North American perspectives and problematics', *The International Lawyer* 50:3 (2017), 401; Maeve Hosier, 'The legal profession in troikaland: before and after the Irish bailout', *Int. J. Leg. Prof.* 22:2 (2015), 193; R. Deech, 'How the Legal Services Act 2007 has affected regulation of the Bar', *L.I.M.* 11 (2011), 89; M. Mason, 'UK: room at the inns – the increased scope of regulation under the new Bar Standards Board handbook for England and Wales', *Legal Ethics* 17:1 (2014), 143; Edward Shinnick, Fred Bruinsma and Christine Parker, 'Aspects of regulatory reform in the legal profession: Australia, Ireland and the Netherlands', *Int. J. Leg. Prof.* 10:3 (2003), 237. **22** Paresh Kathrani, 'An "existential" shift? Technology and some questions for the legal profession', *Legal Ethics* 20:1 (2017), 144; Daniel N. Kluttz and Deirdre K. Mulligan, 'Automated decision support technologies and the legal profession', *Berkeley Technology L.J.* 34:3 (2019), 853. **23** E.g., Patrick Polden, 'Portia's progress: women at the Bar in England, 1919–1939', *Int. J. Leg. Prof.* 12:3 (2005), 293; Erika Rackley, *Women, judging and judiciary: from difference to diversity* (London, 2013); Ulrike Schultz and Gisela Shaw (eds), *Women in the world's legal professions* (Oxford, 2002); Ivana Bacik, Cathryn Costello and Eileen Drew, *Gender injustice: feminising the legal professions?* (Dublin, 2003); Hilary Sommerlad, 'The myth of feminisation: women and cultural change in the legal profession', *Int. J. Leg. Prof.* 1:1 (1994), 31; Suzanne Carthy, 'Inequality regimes and long hours: a mixed methods study of gender inequality in the solicitors' profession in Ireland' (PhD, UCD, 2018); Rosemary Hunter, 'Discrimination against women barristers: evidence from a study of court appearances and briefing practices', *Int. J. Leg. Prof.* 1 (2005), 123; Natasha S. Madon, 'Early departure: factors associated with the flight of women from the private practice of criminal law', *Criminal Law Quarterly* 65:3–4 (2018), 395; Mary Jane Mossman, *The first women lawyers: a comparative study of gender, law and the legal profession* (Oxford, 2006). **24** E.g., Steven Vaughan, '"Prefer not to say": diversity and diversity reporting at the Bar of England & Wales', *Int. J. Leg. Prof.* 24:3 (2017), 207; Louise Ashley, 'Making a difference? The use (and abuse) of diversity management at the UK's elite law firms', *Work, Employment and Society* 24:4 (2010), 711; M. Suresh, *Mapping and evaluating the formal and informal lesbian, gay and bisexual networks in the legal profession in England* (London, 2014); Lizzie Barmes and Kate Malleson, 'The legal profession as gatekeeper to the judiciary: design faults in measures to enhance diversity', *M.L.R.* 74:2 (2011), 245; John M. Conley, 'Tales of diversity: lawyers' narratives of racial equity in private firms', *Law & Social Inquiry* 31:4 (2006), 831; M. Blackwell, 'Taking silk: an empirical study of the award of queen's counsel status, 1981–2015', *M.L.R.* 78 (2015), 971; Hilary Sommerlad, Lisa Webley, Liz Duff, Daniel Muzio and Jennifer Tomlinson, *Diversity in the legal profession in England and Wales: a qualitative study of barriers and individual choices* (London, 2010); Justine Rogers, 'Representing the Bar: how the barristers' profession sells itself to prospective members', *Leg. Studies* 32:2 (2012), 202. **25** E.g., Fernanda Pirie and Justine Rogers, 'Pupillage: the shaping of a professional elite' in Jon Abbink and Tijo Salverda (eds), *The anthropology of elites: power, culture and the complexities of distinction* (New York, 2013). **26** E.g., Marianne Elliott, *Theobald Wolfe Tone* (2nd ed., Liverpool, 2012); Patrick Geoghegan, 'Daniel O'Connell and the law' in Felix M. Larkin and Norma M.

movements.[27] The legal professions have also long been a subject of interest for legal historians. The early history and development of the English legal professions have been well documented,[28] while the twentieth-century Bar has also recently attracted attention.[29] Scholarship has included the medieval[30] and early modern professions,[31] as well as developments in the eighteenth[32] and nineteenth centuries.[33] The evolution of the legal professions in Ireland,[34] the education of lawyers,[35] the development of distinct legal professions,[36] cultures

Dawson (eds), *Lawyers, the law and history* (Dublin, 2013); Patrick Geoghegan, 'Daniel O'Connell and the Magee trials, 1813' in M. Brown and S.P. Donlan (eds), *The laws and other legalities of Ireland, 1689–1850* (Farnham, 2011); Leslie Hale, *John Philpot Curran: his life and times* (London, 1958). **27** E.g., Patrick M. Geoghegan, *1798 and the Irish Bar* (Dublin, 1998); Sean Enright, *After the rising: soldiers, lawyers, and trials of the Irish Revolution* (Dublin, 2015). Enright, p. 1, comments that a 'unique feature of this revolution was the extent to which the conflict centred on law and the legal institutions which kept the status quo in place.' See also Sean Enright, *Easter Rising 1916: the trials* (Dublin, 2014). **28** E.g., John Baker, *The legal profession and the common law: historical essays* (London, 1986). **29** E.g., Ren Pepitone, 'Gender, space, and ritual: women barristers, the inns of court, and the interwar press', *J.W.H.* 28:1 (2016), 1016. **30** E.g., James A. Brundage, *The medieval origins of the legal profession: canonists, civilians, and courts* (Chicago, 2008); Paul Brand, *The origins of the English legal profession* (Oxford, 1992); Paul Brand, 'The early history of the legal profession of the lordship of Ireland, 1250–1350' and Katharine Simms, 'The brehons of later medieval Ireland' both in Daire Hogan and W.N. Osborough (eds), *Brehons, serjeants and attorneys: studies in the history of the Irish legal profession* (Dublin, 1990); Paul Brand, 'The birth and early development of a colonial judiciary: the judges of the lordship of Ireland, 1210–1377' in W.N. Osborough (ed.), *Explorations in law and history* (Dublin, 1995). **31** E.g., Wilfred Prest, *The rise of the barristers: a social history of the English Bar, 1590–1640* (Oxford, 1986); Wilfred Prest, *Lawyers in early modern Europe and America* (London, 1981); Michael Lobban, Joanne Begiato and Adrian Green, *Law, lawyers and litigants in early modern England: essays in memory of Christopher W. Brooks* (Cambridge, 2019); Jessica Winston, *Lawyers at play: literature, law and politics at the early modern inns of court* (Oxford, 2016); Christopher Brooks, *Lawyers, litigation and English society since 1450* (London, 1998). **32** Daniel Duman, 'The English Bar in the Georgian era' in Wilfrid Prest (ed.), *Lawyers in early modern Europe and America* (London, 1981); Simon Devereaux, 'Arts of public performance: barristers and actors in Georgian England' in David Lemmings (ed.), *Crime, courtrooms and the public sphere in Britain, 1700–1850* (London, 2012). **33** E.g., Raymond Cocks, *Foundations of the modern Bar* (London, 1983); Brooks, *Lawyers, litigation*, ch. 3–6. **34** E.g., Hogan and Osborough, *Brehons*, which includes W.N. Osborough, 'The regulation of the admission of attorneys and solicitors in Ireland, 1600–1866'; Jacqueline Hill, 'The legal profession and the decline of the ancien regime in Ireland, 1790–1840' and T.P. Power, 'Conversions among the legal profession in Ireland in the eighteenth century'. **35** E.g., David Barker, *A history of Australian legal education* (Australia, 2017); Conor Mulvagh, *Irish days, Indian memories: V.V. Giri and Indian law students at University College Dublin, 1913–1916* (Dublin, 2016); A.R. Hart, *A history of the Bar and inn of court of Northern Ireland* (Belfast, 2013); Colum Kenny, *The Honorable Society of King's Inns, 1541–2016* (Dublin, 2016); Colum Kenny, *Battle of the books, 1972: cultural controversy at a Dublin library* (Dublin, 2002); Colum Kenny, *Tristram Kennedy and the revival of Irish legal training, 1835–1885* (Dublin, 1996); Colum Kenny, *King's Inns and the kingdom of Ireland: the Irish 'inn of court' 1541–1800* (Dublin, 1992); J.A. Bush and A. Wijffels (eds), *Learning the law: teaching and the transmission of law in England, 1150–1900* (London, 1999). **36** E.g., Eamonn G. Hall and Daire Hogan, *The Law Society of Ireland, 1852–2002: portrait of a profession* (Dublin, 2002); Kenneth Ferguson, *King's Inns barristers, 1868–2004* (Dublin, 2005); A.R. Hart, 'The king's serjeants at law in Ireland: a short history' in Osborough (ed.), *Explorations*; A.R. Hart, *A history of the king's serjeants at law in Ireland: honour rather than advantage?* (Dublin, 2000); Hogan and Osborough, *Brehons, serjeants and attorneys* (Dublin, 1990); Daire Hogan, *The legal profession in Ireland 1789–1922* (Dublin, 1986). **37** E.g., James G. McLaren, 'A brief history of wigs in the legal profession',

and practices,[37] and the role of lawyers in colonialism[38] have all attracted significant scholarship. Recent years have seen a number of oral history projects focusing on twentieth-century Bar histories.[39] Pue and Backhouse have produced a significant body of work on the history of the Canadian legal profession over the past couple of decades,[40] and smaller Bars have also been examined, including those of the Isle of Man,[41] Palestine,[42] Scotland[43] and Northern Ireland.[44] Broad historical surveys of European lawyers have accelerated our comparative understanding of how different legal professions and elites have evolved.[45]

Sources and methodology

This book builds upon a strong tradition of scholarship on the Irish legal professions.[46] Scholars such as Hogan and Osborough have taken a wide view of

Int. J. Leg. Prof. 6:2 (1999), 241; William Norman Hargreaves-Mawdsley, *A history of legal dress in Europe until the end of the eighteenth century* (Oxford, 1963). **38** E.g., Pue, *Lawyers' empire*; D. Duman, *The English and colonial Bars in the nineteenth century* (London, 1983); Jarlath Ronayne, *First fleet to federation: Irish supremacy in colonial Australia* (Dublin, 2002); Helen O'Shea, *Ireland and the end of the British empire: the republic and its role in the Cyprus emergency* (London, 2020). **39** E.g., the New South Wales Bar Association oral history: https://nswbar.asn.au/the-bar-association/bar-history/oral-history#/; Victorian Bar oral history project: www.vicbar.com.au/public/about/about-victorian-bar/our-history and the Ontario Bar oral history interviews: https://lso.ca/about-lso/osgoode-hall-and-ontario-legal-heritage/collections-and-research/online-resources-and-finding-aids/oral-history-interviews. Oral histories of judges include the New Zealand *Women judges oral histories* project: Elizabeth Chan, 'Women trailblazers in the law: the New Zealand women judges oral histories project', *Victoria University of Wellington Law Review* 45 (2014), 407; and the Australian *Trailblazing women and the law* project: Hollie Kerwin and Kim Rubenstein, 'Reading the life narrative of Valerie French, the first woman to sign the Western Australian Bar roll' in F. Davis, N. Musgrove and J. Smart (eds) *Founders, firsts and feminists: women leaders in twentieth-century Australia* (Melbourne, 2011). **40** E.g., Constance Backhouse and W. Wesley Pue (eds), *The promise and perils of law: lawyers in Canadian history* (Toronto, 2009). See also Joan Brockman and Dorothy E. Chunn, 'New order of things: women's entry into the legal profession in British Columbia', *The Advocate* 60:3 (2002), 385 and George Blaine Baker and Jim Phillips (eds), *Essays in the history of Canadian law: in honour of R.C.B. Risk* (Toronto, 1999); Philip Girard, *Lawyers and legal culture in British North America: Beamish Murdoch of Halifax* (Toronto, 2015). **41** Peter W. Edge, 'Lawyers' empires: the anglicisation of Manx Bar and judiciary', *J.L.P.* 19 (1994–5), 29. **42** E.g., Mutaz M. Qafisheh, 'A century of the law profession in Palestine: quo vadis?', *Int. J. Leg. Prof.* 25:2 (2018), 175. **43** E.g., John Cairns, *Law, lawyers, and humanism: selected essays on the history of Scots law, volume 1* (Edinburgh, 2015), ch. 11–13. **44** E.g., Hart, *A history of the Bar.* See also Robert Carswell, '*Eheu fugaces*: fifty years in the Northern Ireland courts' in Hogan and Kenny (eds), *Changes in practice*; Lord Carswell, 'Founding a legal system: the early judiciary of Northern Ireland' in Larkin and Dawson (eds), *Lawyers.* Work on the solicitors' profession in Northern Ireland includes Alan Hewitt, *The Law Society of Northern Ireland: a history* (Belfast, 2010) and Alan Hewitt, 'The regulation and education of the solicitors' profession in Northern Ireland, 1976–2002' in Hogan and Kenny (eds), *Changes in practice.* **45** E.g., Maria Malatesta, *Professional men, professional women: the European professions from the 19th century until today* (tr. Adrian Belton, London, 2011); James Albisetti, 'Portia ante Portas: women and the legal profession in Europe, ca. 1870–1925', *Journal of Social History*, 33:4 (2000), 825. **46** E.g., Kenny, *The Honorable Society*; Kenny, *Battle of the books*; Kenny, *Tristram Kennedy*; Kenny, *King's Inns and the kingdom of Ireland*; Edward Keane, Beryl P. Phair, Thomas U. Sadleir (eds), *King's Inns admission papers, 1607–1867* (Dublin, 1982); Colum Kenny, 'Not every judge a phoenix: King's Inns under Cromwell' in

the professions over a number of centuries,[47] and have done much to advance our knowledge of the evolution of the legal professions in Ireland. Other scholarship has focused on discrete aspects of the Irish Bar, such as the impact of First World War[48] and the evolution of circuit traditions.[49] The history of the King's Inns has been thoroughly examined by Kenny over the past three decades.[50] Ferguson's *King's Inns barristers, 1868–2004* has been an invaluable source of reference, and continues to be the first port of call for genealogical research into barristers in the twentieth century.[51] His essay on the Irish Bar, 1868–1968, paints a picture of the Bar undergoing changes on a number of fronts in the early twentieth century. In recent years there has also been some work on the barristers' profession in Northern Ireland from 1921; notably the late Tony Hart's work,[52] which provides a detailed history of the Bar of Northern Ireland. More recently, attention has been focused on the place of women in the legal professions, particularly since the centenaries of the first women lawyers in Ireland.[53]

There is a strong tradition in Ireland of producing and publishing full-length and short-form biographies[54] of judges,[55] barristers[56] and solicitors[57] as well as

Coleman Dennehy (ed.), *Law and revolution in seventeenth-century Ireland* (Dublin, 2019); Colum Kenny, 'The records of King's Inns, Dublin' in Daire Hogan and W.N. Osborough (eds), *Brehons, serjeants and attorneys: studies in the history of the Irish legal profession* (Dublin, 1990); Colum Kenny, 'King's Inns and Henrietta Street chambers', *D.H.R.* 47:2 (1994), 155–68; Ferguson, *King's Inns barristers*; Hart, *A history of the Bar*; Daire Hogan, *The legal profession in Ireland, 1789–1922* (Dublin, 1986); Daire Hogan and W.N. Osborough, *Brehons, serjeants and attorneys: studies in the history of the Irish legal profession* (Dublin, 1990); A.P. Quinn and John Bowman, *Wigs and guns: Irish barristers in the Great War* (Dublin, 2006); Charles Gamble, *Solicitors in Ireland: 1607–1921: the Incorporated Law Society's work* (Dublin, 1921); Hall and Hogan, *The Law Society*; Colum Kenny, 'The exclusion of Catholics from the legal profession in Ireland, 1537–1829', *I.H.S.* 25:100 (1987), 337. **47** Hogan, *The legal profession*; Hogan and Osborough, *Brehons*. **48** Quinn and Bowman, *Wigs and guns*. **49** Hugh Geoghegan, 'The changing face of the circuits during the past twenty-five years' in Hogan and Kenny (eds), *Changes in practice and law*. **50** See for example Kenny, *King's Inns 1541–2016;* Kenny, *Battle of the books, 1972;* Kenny, *Tristram Kennedy;* Kenny, *King's Inns and the kingdom of Ireland*; Kenny, 'Not every judge a phoenix'; Kenny, 'The records of King's Inns, Dublin'; Kenny, 'King's Inns and Henrietta Street'. **51** Ferguson, *King's Inns barristers*. **52** Hart, *A history of the Bar*. See also Neil Faris, 'The Bar in Northern Ireland and the royal commission on legal services', *NILQ* 39:3 (1988), 284. **53** E.g., Liz Goldthorpe, 'First woman to practice as a barrister in Ireland and the (then) United Kingdom, Averil Deverell, 1921' in Erika Rackley and Rosemary Auchmuty (eds), *Women's legal landmarks: celebrating the history of women and law in the UK and Ireland* (Oxford, 2019); Colum Kenny, 'You just have to get on with it: the advance of women in the legal profession, 1910–2012' in Hogan and Kenny (eds), *Changes in practice;* Emma Hutchinson, 'First woman professor of law in Ireland, Frances Moran, 1925' in Rackley and Auchmuty (eds), *Women's legal landmarks*; J. Bourne and M. Mossman, *Helena Normanton and the opening of the Bar to women* (Hampshire, 2016); Lucinda Acland and Kate Broomfield, *First: 100 years of women in law* (London, 2019). For a discussion of how the Irish Bar marked the centenary of the first women lawyers, see Vanessa Curley and Sarah Foley, 'Celebrating a century of women in the law: using historical exhibitions to enhance user engagement and promote a library service', *L.I.M.* 21:1 (2021), 36. These issues are explored further in ch. 2 and ch. 9. **54** E.g., Charles Lysaght, 'The life of Cecil Lavery', *B.R.* 17:4 (2012), 83; R.V.F. Heuston, 'Frances Elizabeth Moran', *D.U.L.J.* 11 (1989), 1. Many legal lives are also captured in the *Oxford dictionary of national Biography* and, since 2009, in the *Dictionary of Irish biography*, and by obituaries in the *Irish Law Times* and the national press. Both the *Irish Law Times* and the *Bar*

Festschriften in honour of senior legal figures.[58] Political biographies are also common, and public figures who had fleeting legal practices or legal training also provide insights into the professions.[59] Self-penned memoirs by lawyers provide a useful and often colourful snapshot of the profession at a particular point in time, and tell us much about legal culture and traditions.[60] A number of barristers' memoirs and anecdotes published around the early 1990s[61] shed light on the practice of law from the 1930s onward. Older Bar memoirs[62] and

Review have published interviews with members of the Bar when they reached milestones such as fifty years of practice: e.g., Garrett Edward Gill, 'A half-century in the Law Library', *I.L.T.* (ns) 10 (1992), 46 and 'Ralph Sutton, SC, called to the Bar, July 1948', *B.R.* 4:3 (1999), 152.   **55** E.g., Aidan Carl Matthew (ed.), *Immediate man: cuimhní ar Cearbhall Ó Dálaigh* (Dublin, 1983); Colum Kenny, 'Irish ambition and English preference in chancery appointments, 1827–1841: the fate of William Conyngham Plunkett' in Osborough (ed.), *Explorations*; Daire Hogan, 'Arrows too sharply pointed: the relations of Lord Justice Christian and Lord O'Hagan, 1868–74' in John McEldowney and Paul O'Higgins (eds), *The common law tradition* (Dublin, 1990); G.M. Golding, *George Gavan Duffy, 1882–1951* (Dublin, 1992); Patrick C. Kennedy, *Hugh Kennedy: the great but neglected chief justice* (Limerick, 2005); Tom Daly, 'Hugh Kennedy: Ireland's (quietly) towering nation-maker' in Rehan Abeyratne and Iddo Porat (eds), *Towering judges: a comparative study of constitutional judges* (Cambridge, 2021); Hugh Geoghegan, 'Three judges of the Supreme Court of the Irish Free State: their backgrounds, personalities and mindsets' in Larkin and Dawson (eds), *Lawyers.*   **56** E.g., Terence de Vere White, *The road of excess, a life of Isaac Butt* (Dublin, 1946); V.T.H. Delany, *Christopher Palles, lord chief baron of her majesty's court of exchequer in Ireland 1874–1916* (Dublin, 1960); C.E.B. Brett, 'Two eighteenth-century provincial attorneys: Matthew Brett and Jack Brett' in Hogan and Osborough (eds), *Brehons;* Eugene Broderick, *John Hearne: architect of the 1937 constitution of Ireland* (Dublin, 2017); Geoffrey Lewis, *Carson: the man who divided Ireland* (London, 2005); David McCullagh, *The reluctant taoiseach: a biography of John A. Costello* (Dublin, 2011); Eda Sagarra, *Kevin O'Shiel, Tyrone nationalist and state builder* (Dublin, 2013); Robert Marshall, 'Lieutenant W.E. Wylie KC: the soldiering lawyer of 1916' in Larkin and Dawson (eds), *Lawyers.*   **57** E.g., Jasper Ungoed-Thomas, *Jasper Wolfe of Skibbereen* (Cork, 2008); A. Keller, *A personal history of Whitney Moore and Keller solicitors: from 1882 to 1985* (Dublin, 1992); Eugene McCague, *Arthur Cox 1891–1965* (Dublin, 1994); Peter Connell, *Eamon Duggan, counsel to the revolution* (Meath, 2021); Daire Hogan, *McCann Fitzgerald: origin and fifty years* (Dublin, 2016).   **58** E.g., James O'Reilly (ed.), *Human rights and constitutional law: essays in honour of Brian Walsh* (Dublin, 1992); Bláthna Ruane et al. (eds), *Law and government: a tribute to Rory Brady* (Dublin, 2014).   **59** E.g., Terence de Vere White, *Kevin O'Higgins* (London, 1986); Mary Robinson, *Everybody matters: a memoir* (London, 2013); A.J. Jordan, *Sean MacBride: a biography* (Dublin, 1993).   **60** E.g., Terence de Vere White, *A fretful midge* (London, 1957). Kenneth Deale's collection of stories of infamous murder trials also illustrates aspects of trial practice and includes concise descriptions of the barristers involved: Kenneth Deale, *Beyond any reasonable doubt? A book of murder trials* (Dublin, 1971).   **61** These include Gerard A. Lee, *A memoir of the South-Western Circuit* (Dublin, 1990); Charles Bewley, *Memoirs of a wild goose* (Dublin, 1989); Patrick MacKenzie, *Lawful occasions: the old Eastern Circuit* (Cork and Dublin, 1991); Rex Mackey, *Windward of the law* (2nd edn, Dublin, 1991); Patrick Lindsay, *Memories* (Dublin, 1992); Thomas F. O'Higgins, *A double life* (Dublin, 1996); James Comyn, an Irish barrister who emigrated to England and practised there, produced four volumes of memoirs and anecdotes in the early nineties, following three earlier volumes published in England in the preceding decades: James Comyn, *Their friends at court* (Chichester 1973); James Comyn, *Lost causes* (London, 1982) James Comyn, *Irish at law: a selection of famous and unusual cases* (London, 1983); James Comyn, *Summing it up: memoirs of an Irishman at law in England* (Dublin, 1991); James Comyn, *Watching brief: further memoirs of an Irishman at law in England* (Dublin, 1993); James Comyn, *Leave to appeal: further legal memoirs* (Dublin, 1994) and James Comyn, *If your lordship pleases: legal recollections* (Dublin, 1996).   **62** E.g., Maurice Healy, *The old Munster Circuit: a book of memories and traditions* (Dublin, 1939); John Ross, *The*

biographies[63] from the nineteenth[64] and early twentieth century[65] have also been useful in painting a picture of the profession. Of course, the limitations of self-penned memoirs as historical sources must be borne in mind. They represent personal experiences and opinions, and their focus may not be aligned with that of the researcher using them. For example, there is often an emphasis on humorous anecdotes, or stories that present the author in a certain light, and they often presume a level of insider or institutional knowledge on the part of the reader. Nevertheless, these sources complement the interviews conducted with twentieth-century barristers.

The empirical research for this book involved twenty-nine semi-structured, face-to-face interviews, with practising and former members of the Bar.[66] The purpose of the interviews was to access information that was not available in print. This included first-hand accounts of experiences of life at the Bar, where there has always been a rich oral tradition. Barristers in other jurisdictions have quite frequently been interviewed about aspects of their work,[67] and there also are a number of Irish studies which have employed interviews,[68] focus groups[69] and questionnaires.[70] Various challenges present themselves when interviewing

years of my pilgrimage: random reminiscences (London, 1924) and John Ross, *Pilgrim scrip: more random reminiscences* (London, 1927). **63** E.g., Edward Marjoribanks, *The life of Lord Carson*, vol. 1 (London, 1932). **64** E.g., A.M. Sullivan, *Old Ireland: reminiscences of an Irish KC* (London, 1927); A.M. Sullivan, *The last serjeant* (London, 1952); George Hill Smith, *The north east Bar. A sketch, historical and reminiscent* (Belfast, 1910); Thomas Lefroy, *Memoir of Chief Justice Lefroy* (Dublin, 1871); Henry Grattan, *Memoirs of the life and times of the Rt Hon. Henry Grattan* (London, 1839); J.R. Flanagan, *The Munster Circuit: tales, trials and traditions* (London, 1880); Richard Lalor Sheil, *Sketches of the Irish Bar* (Dublin, 1854). **65** E.g., Ernest Bowen-Rowlands, *Seventy-two years at the Bar: a memoir* (London, 1924); Eugene Sheehy, *May it please the court* (Dublin, 1951); J.C. MacDermott, *An enriching life* (Belfast, 1980); John Adye Curran, *Reminiscences of John Adye Curran KC, late county court judge and chairman of quarter sessions* (London, 1915); M. M'Donnell Bodkin, *Recollections of an Irish judge: press, Bar and parliament 1850–1933* (London, 1914). **66** The flexibility of the semi-structured interview facilitated exploration of unanticipated and unexpected topics which arose. Interviews were typically ninety minutes in length, each generating around thirty pages of typed text upon transcription. The interview transcripts were coded using the NVivo software. Ethical approval for the interviews was granted by University College Dublin's Research Ethics Committee. **67** E.g., Goulandris, *The enterprising barrister*; Rosemary Hunter, 'Discrimination against women barristers: evidence from a study of court appearances and briefing practices', *Int. J. Leg. Prof.* 12:1 (2005), 3, involved interviewing barristers in Victoria, Australia; John Flood and M. Hviid, *The cab rank rule: its meaning and purpose in the new legal services market* (London, 2013); John Flood and Avis Whyte, 'Straight there, no detours: direct access to barristers', *Int. J. Leg. Prof.* 16:3 (2009), 131. **68** E.g., John Morison and Philip Leith, *The barrister's world and the nature of law* (Berkshire, 1992) interviewed barristers practising at both the Irish and the Northern Irish Bar. Mark Coen, Niamh Howlin, Colette Barry and John Lynch, *Judges and juries in Ireland: an empirical study* (Dublin, 2020) interviewed practising criminal barristers (as well as judges); Alpha Connolly and Betty Hilliard, 'The legal profession' in Alpha Connolly (ed.), *Gender and the law in Ireland* (Dublin, 1993) interviewed women working in different legal professions. Jennifer Caroll McNeil *The politics of judicial selection in Ireland* (Dublin, 2016) included interviews with 'key political protagonists', many of whom were former barristers (including judges and former attorneys general). **69** E.g., Ivana Bacik, Cathryn Costello and Eileen Drew, *Gender injustice: feminising the legal professions?* (Dublin, 2003) involved focus groups with barristers, as well as with King's Inns students. **70** E.g., ibid. Mary Bourke, 'The education of the Irish barrister', *Justice –*

barristers. These include potential misunderstandings between the interviewee and interviewer,[71] as well as practical problems.[72] In a performative profession such as the Bar, where success is to be projected,[73] barristers might struggle to honestly articulate frailties or anxieties. Morison and Leith captured some of these potential difficulties in their 1992 project *The barrister's world*.[74] They acknowledged that it might be difficult for barristers to give frank and truthful answers to their questions, and they identify some possible reasons for this: 'they might wish to express (and, perhaps, believe in) the professional ideology; they might be suspicious of our intentions; they might simply misinterpret the questions asked of them.'[75]

The interviewees for this book were people who had been in practice in the second half of the twentieth century, from the 1950s onward. In selecting interviewees, I sought individuals based on specific attributes: men and women[76] in different practice areas (family, crime, judicial review, personal injuries, etc.), with both Dublin-based and circuit practices. Some interviewees had very large, busy practices while others had more modest practices. Some practised mainly in the superior courts, while others were largely based in the Circuit Court. Some came from families where there were already barristers, solicitors or judges, while others were from backgrounds where there were no other lawyers or where they did not have the same level of financial cushioning or social capital. Some had gone on to take silk, or were appointed to the bench, while others remained as junior counsel. Different religious, political and educational backgrounds were represented, and the sample also included some diversity in terms of disability and sexuality. The barristers selected are not intended to be statistically 'representative' of the profession as a whole,[77] but purposive

---

Irish Student Law Review (1966), 16, conducted a survey of King's Inns students.   **71** There is the risk that potential interviewees might see no value in the research, the purpose of which might not clearly be communicated. There might, even, be some mistrust between the profession and the academic researcher. In line with best practice for this kind of research, all interviewees were provided with 'participant information sheets' explaining the scope and purpose of the study, and the purpose of the interviews. Follow-up questions or queries were encouraged, and at least one participant phoned or emailed after their interview to add further comments or context. One interviewee declined to be audio-recorded, and the account of that interview is based on handwritten contemporaneous notes. Several requested and were provided with typed transcripts of their interviews, and once or twice an interviewee requested that a statement be removed or redacted. This was done unreservedly. To avoid misinterpretation of the questions, a semi-structured format was used, which allowed for follow-up and clarificatory questions. Any interviewee who requested to see the question topics in advance was facilitated. Interviews took place at times and in locations chosen by the interviewees in order to ensure their comfort and, as far as possible, avoid distractions.   **72** Barristers may live or work anywhere in the country; if still in practice, they are likely to be very busy professionals with limited time to spare; conversely, those who are retired may be vulnerable, or suffer from ill-health.   **73** See ch. 7.   **74** Morison and Leith, *Barrister's world*, p. 14.   **75** Ibid. On the issue of access, see E. Nir, 'Approaching the bench: accessing elites on the judiciary for qualitative interviews', *Int. J. Social Research Methodology* 21:1 (2018), 77.   **76** One-third of the interviewees were women, which aligns with the proportion of women at the Bar by the late twentieth century.   **77** See Mario Luis Small, 'How many cases do I

sampling means that a diversity of experiences has been captured.[78] The interviews have proved to be an extremely rich source about the inner lives of barristers, and about some of the hidden aspects of working at the Bar.[79]

Although the focus of the interviews was on the working lives of barristers, inevitably sensitive topics arose, including stress, mental health, alcoholism, suicide, sexuality, discrimination, bullying and financial insecurity. Interviewees sometimes spoke in very personal terms about their fears and anxieties, about their family situations and their emotions. Some gave very detailed information about their earnings, or about the clients they represented. Others spoke candidly about their colleagues, specific solicitors' firms or members of the judiciary. To ensure that they could speak freely and frankly, anonymity was assured, and their identities will not be revealed in this book. A number of those who were interviewed hold or have held senior public offices or positions of authority in the state, and there is a particular sensitivity about ensuring their anonymity.[80] It will be seen in subsequent chapters that they are generally referred to by code numbers in the book, such as B1, B2 etc.[81] When interviewees spoke about other individuals, I used my discretion in redacting their names and replacing with '[X]' or '[Y]', particularly where very negative comments were made.

Interviews with barristers have frequently been used in oral history projects in other jurisdictions.[82] One description of oral history is collecting 'not what is

need? On science and the logic of case selection in field-based research', *Ethnography* 10:1 (2009), 5. Small makes the point, at 15, that 'there is a place for a small interview study to make meaningful contributions to knowledge.' 78 See further Esra Bakkalbasioglu, 'How to access elites when textbook methods fail: challenges of purposive sampling and advantages of using interviewees as "fixers"', *The Qualitative Report* 25:3 (2020), 688. 79 Themes identified and discussed in early interviews were then further explored in subsequent interviews. Interviews were loosely structured, allowing interviewees to introduce topics which they considered important or relevant, rather than adhering rigidly to a list of questions. 80 Members of the legal professions are generally considered to be 'elites', and there is a considerable body of literature which addresses some of the challenges and considerations for researchers who interview such groups; e.g., Nir, 'Approaching the bench'. Some social scientists argue that 'elite' groups are more difficult to penetrate than other types of groups: e.g., A. Cochrane, 'Illusions of power: interviewing local elites', *Environment and Planning A* 30:12 (1998), 2121 and Margaret Desmond, 'Methodological challenges posed in studying an elite in the field', *Area* 36:3 (2004), 262. Katherine E. Smith, 'Problematising power relations in 'elite' interviews', *Geoforum* 37 (2006), 643 however, argues that many of the claims made in relation to 'elite' interviews are equally applicable to other types of interviews. She also questions, at 645, the use of the term 'elite', which rests on 'the rather simplistic idea that there is a dichotomy between "powerful elite" and "powerless others"'. 81 It will be seen that sometimes no code number is attributed to a comment, because of the possibility of identification or attribution by cross-referencing with other comments made. Similar concerns about identifiability were outlined by Carthy, *Inequality regimes*, pp 87–8. 82 See above, and in the United Kingdom, the British Library National Life Stories, 'Legal lives': www.bl.uk/projects/national-life-stories-legal-lives; the ongoing Oxford Centre for Socio-Legal Studies project, 'Enhancing democratic habits: an oral history of the law centres movement': https://gtr.ukri.org/ projects?ref=AH%2FT 007710%2F1. See also the London School of Economics, 'Legal biography project: judicial interviews': www.lse.ac.uk/law/legal-biography-project/judicial-interviews.

already known but information, observations, and opinions unavailable elsewhere',[83] and in that regard, the testimonies recorded for this book resemble oral histories. However, according to Ritchie,

> An interview becomes an oral history only when it has been recorded, processed in some way, made available in an archive, library, or other repository, or reproduced in relatively verbatim form for publication. Availability for general research, reinterpretation, and verification defines oral history.[84]

The recordings and transcripts of the interviews conducted for this book will remain confidential and cannot therefore be said to constitute an oral history project. The approach taken is closer to that of a social scientist than an oral historian.[85]

The archival materials consulted in the course of researching this history of the Bar were drawn from various sources. The National Archives of Ireland hold a range of relevant materials from different government departments, dealing with different aspects of the Irish Bar. These include papers from the Attorney General's Office;[86] the Department of Justice;[87] the Department of Foreign Affairs;[88] the Department of Finance[89] and the Department of the Taoiseach.[90] Between them, these sources shed light on the Bar's international relations,[91] reform and regulation,[92] as well as individual experiences,[93] applications for patents of precedence,[94] judicial appointments[95] and certification for calls to other Bars.[96] The UCD Archives house a number of deposited collections from individual barristers, including most notably John A. Costello,[97] Hugh Kennedy,[98] Cearbhall Ó Dálaigh,[99] George Gavan Duffy,[100] Declan Costello,[101] P.J. McEnery[102] and John Hearne.[103] These have illustrated personal experiences of practice, as well as showing how careers at the Bar were combined with public service; in addition to being barristers, these people were judges, politicians, attorneys general, taoisigh and presidents.

I have also made extensive use of the minutes of the Bar Council and general meetings of the Bar; the King's Inns benchers' minutes and other records of the King's Inns, and I am grateful to both the Bar Council and the benchers for

83 Richie, *Doing oral history*, p. 35.   84 Ibid., p. 8.   85 Ibid., p. 24 notes that '[o]ral historians, folklorists, ethnographers, cultural anthropologists, sociologists, and linguists, all interview but have different objectives that influence their methodologies.'   86 E.g., NAI 2003/4/7; NAI 2011/17/871.   87 E.g., NAI JUS/90/113/4.   88 E.g., NAI DFA/6/408/222 I; NAI DFA/1/GR/1100; NAI DFA/5/316/1/47. Previously the Department of External Affairs.   89 E.g., NAI FIN/1/665; NAI FIN/1/3873.   90 E.g., NAI TSCH/3/S16108 A; NAI TSCH/3/S13867.   91 E.g., NAI JUS/90/113/4.   92 E.g., NAI TSCH/3/S13867; NAI TSCH/3/S6694 B/62; NAI TSCH/3/S8613.   93 E.g., NAI 2008/117/607 and NAI PRIV1367/11.   94 E.g., NAI 2003/4/7.   95 E.g., NAI 2005/159/81.   96 E.g., NAI 2009/74/742.   97 UCDA P190.   98 UCDA P4.   99 UCDA P51.   100 UCDA P152.   101 UCDA P237.   102 UCDA P74.   103 UCDA P291.

facilitating access to these records.[104] These sources are a mine of information about how the Bar self-regulated and how it viewed its role in society, as well as how the organisations themselves functioned and related to individual members of the profession. The twentieth century is very recent history, particularly in a profession where there is no compulsory retirement age and long careers are not unusual.[105] I have refrained from naming individuals mentioned in the benchers' and Bar Council minutes, particularly in relation to the later decades of the twentieth century.

Scope of this book

This book examines barristers in Ireland from 1921 until 1999. These start- and end-dates were chosen for a number of reasons. First, 1921 represents the first time that women were called to the Bar, and the first call-date since the partition of Ireland. These changes frame the project, which seeks to establish how the profession has evolved over a century. Second, there is now a substantial body of historical scholarship examining the two branches of the Irish legal profession up to the early twentieth century.[106] While it may seem like an arbitrary cut-off, the eve of the new century was a time of significant change in the legal profession. The 1990s saw several significant developments at the Bar, including changes to regulation,[107] physical space,[108] the gender balance,[109] technology[110] and practice generally.[111] For an institution often criticised for being slow to evolve, it is remarkable to compare the 1921 Bar with the Bar which existed eighty years later. As will be demonstrated in chapter five, the typical new barrister in 1921 was a 21-year-old, middle class, Protestant, Dublin man, who worked at a desk in the Four Courts Law Library. By 1999 the typical new barrister was a Catholic in his or her early twenties, working in a satellite building near the Four Courts, who was more likely than their 1921 counterpart to be from outside of Dublin.

The first substantive chapter in this book sets the scene for the Bar as it existed in the early twenties. In the chapters which follow, this book considers barristers' typical career path (including devilling[112] and taking silk),[113] as well as their working lives,[114] and the various factors that might affect success (or apparent success). It asks who the typical barrister was, and traces how this changed over the course of eighty years.[115] This book also examines the changing workplace, infrastructure and working conditions for barristers,[116] and the peculiarities of circuit practice in the twentieth century, which was in many ways more ritualised than Dublin-based practice.[117] It considers how the practise of

---

104 The minutes of the Bar Council dating back to 1815 have been digitised; on the background to this, see Curley and Foley, 'Celebrating a century'. 105 See further ch. 4. 106 See above; particularly the work of Kenny, Hogan and Ferguson. 107 Ch. 16. 108 Ch. 11. 109 Ch. 9. 110 Ch. 5 and 11. 111 Ch. 11. 112 Ch. 3. 113 Ch. 4. 114 Ch. 6. 115 Ch. 5. 116 Ch. 11. 117 Ch. 10.

law and advocacy changed over eighty years.[118] The changing position of women at the Bar from 1921 until the end of the century is also examined; not only the recitation of 'famous firsts', but also the everyday lived experiences of women navigating what had hitherto been a male domain.[119] It asks how new barristers were socialised into the profession, and the different ways in which institutional knowledge, acceptable practises and professional ethics were shared.[120] It considers the paradox of the 'collegiate' Bar and its oft-cited 'camaraderie', where nevertheless every individual was a sole practitioner, in competition with their peers.[121] The role of the King's Inns and the Bar Council in regulating the profession is considered, as well as increasingly frequent attempted incursions by the state in the late twentieth century.[122] This book looks at the contributions made by Irish barristers to the state and to international law and politics.[123] It considers both how the Bar was connected externally, to other professions and other Bars,[124] and asks how the profession was perceived from the outside.[125]

* * *

Although the Law Library may at times have been described as insular, the barristers' profession was far from immune to social, political and economic developments. The second chapter of this book considers the position of the Bar in the 1920s – a turbulent decade that saw a new constitution, new courts systems, the appointment of a new judiciary, the physical destruction of the barristers' place of work, the arrival of women barristers, the split with the Bar of Northern Ireland and the development of new customs and work practises. The following decade saw the introduction of another new constitution,[126] followed soon afterwards by the outbreak of the Second World War. The 'emergency' impacted on barristers in different ways; travelling on circuit was slow and difficult, incomes dropped, and the general deprivation around the country affected the types of cases coming before the courts.[127] Economic decline and relative isolation characterised the decade after the war.

Taking its seat on the United Nations in 1955 marked a turning point in Ireland's international relations following several decades of relative isolation. Members of the Bar were to the fore in this, both within Ireland and abroad.[128] The Bar also contributed significantly to what can broadly be termed 'the European project', and was represented on such bodies as the organisation for European Economic Cooperation, the Council of Europe, the European Commission on Human Rights and the European Court of Human Rights. Its members also contributed to drafting the European Convention on Human Rights and Fundamental Freedoms. When Ireland joined the EEC in 1973 the

118 Ch 6. 119 Ch. 9. 120 Ch. 12. 121 Ch. 7. 122 Ch. 16. 123 Ch. 14. 124 Ch. 13. 125 Ch. 15. 126 Bunreacht na hÉireann 1937. 127 E.g., Lee, *Memoir*, p. 2. 128 Ch. 14.

Bar had to grapple with what this meant for the profession, and it presented new opportunities for individual practising barristers.[129] The outbreak of violence in Northern Ireland in the mid-century had a significant impact on the legal professions there, and members of the Irish Bar sought to reach out and show solidarity.[130] The 1980s saw record numbers of people joining the Bar, and the opening of the international financial services centre in Dublin was symbolic of a changed business environment that led to an increase in high-value commercial transactions and litigation. By the 1990s there was an atmosphere of increasing professionalism, specialisation and modernisation, which led to the development of new, modern facilities for the Bar, as well as an increasing focus on professional regulation.[131]

It will become evident in the ensuing chapters that 'the Bar' was not a monolithic entity. Even when it appeared to be a homogenous group of middle-class, university-educated and Dublin-based men in the early years of this study, 'the Bar' was made up of individuals, with individual practices. No two barristers had identical experiences. Two phrases that were used by almost every barrister who was interviewed for this book were 'independent sole trader' and 'camaraderie.' This underlines one of the paradoxes of the Bar; the relative isolation and self-reliance that existed alongside strong social networks and a fairly cohesive professional identity. This is one of many contrasts which will present itself in this book.

Another theme that emerges is that of constant (albeit gradual) change. The Bar has been criticised on occasion for intransigence; for being slow to respond to social changes or other external pressures. However, as this book demonstrates, the Bar was not immune to social, technological or political change. The Bar in the year 2000 was in many ways very different to the Bar in 1921, which in turn differed from the Bar of the 1840s. Many of the rituals, symbols and practises at the Bar give the impression of being immutable and dating from time immemorial; however, in reality, many are relatively recent developments, or have been altered over time to suit the prevailing circumstances.

It will also be demonstrated that the Bar was both well-connected and influential. Practising and non-practising members of the Bar were to be found in many spheres of Irish life. Individually and collectively, barristers had considerable influence on twentieth-century Irish politics and society, as well as within the confines of the legal system. The Bar was also, in many ways, outward-looking, both individually and collectively. It will be seen that it frequently liaised with other legal professions, both nationally and internationally.

In the course of one of the interviews conducted for this book, one barrister spoke about managing the volume of work as a busy senior counsel:

129 Ch. 14.   130 Ch. 13.   131 Ch. 16.

You never feel like you have enough time to do all the work because there's an endless amount of reading you can do, there's an endless amount of research and one of the skills is being able to do the triage and say 'we've only so much time'.[132]

This might equally apply to someone putting together a book on the profession itself. The sources available to tell the twentieth-century history of the Bar are seemingly endless, and it has been necessary to 'do the triage' or risk never reaching the end of the project. Thus, there will inevitably be those with lived experience of the Bar during the relevant time period who will recall anecdotes, motivations and controversies that are not represented here. Given the size of the profession and the length of time covered by the book, this is to be expected, but it is hoped that this book will spark conversations and reminiscences, as well as bringing forth hitherto obscured or hidden narratives, details and perspectives.

132 B26.

CHAPTER TWO

The Bar in the twenties

Introduction

This story begins in the early 1920s. Before moving on to the thematic analysis of the Bar, it is worth pausing to consider some of the realities facing the profession at the birth of the new state. It was a turbulent period for Irish society and for the profession. At a personal level, it was a time of considerable uncertainty and unpredictability. For those involved in the administration of justice, there were challenges of authority and legitimacy, as well as professional ambitions and practical considerations. There was a crisis of identity, reflected in debates over professional attire and the Irish language, and there was bitter divisiveness as the realities of the impact of partition on the Bar became apparent. The early twenties were also a transformative period for the composition of the Bar, with the arrival of women and the departure of the barristers of Northern Ireland.

The Bar in the revolutionary years

Following the declaration of a truce in the War of Independence in July 1921[1] the Anglo-Irish Treaty was signed in December 1921.[2] The Government of Ireland Act 1920 had already created the separate state of Northern Ireland, which remained firmly part of the United Kingdom. Its separate existence was strongly resented by nationalists north and south. The Anglo-Irish Treaty gave considerable autonomy to the new Irish Free State, but it reinforced the border with Northern Ireland. The period 1922–3 saw Ireland descend into a short but bitter civil war,[3] fought 'between two blocs of the republican movement over a

---

1 Recent scholarship on the revolutionary period which provides useful background reading includes Diarmaid Ferriter and Susannah Riordan (eds), *Years of turbulence: the Irish Revolution and its aftermath* (Dublin, 2015); Thomas Earls FitzGerald, *Combatants and civilians in revolutionary Ireland, 1918–1923* (London, 2021); Patrick Mannion and Fearghal McGarry, *The Irish Revolution: a global history* (New York, 2022). 2 Recent re-examinations of the Treaty include John Gibney and Zoë Reid, *The Treaty: records from the archives* (Dublin, 2021); Gretchen Friedmann, *The Treaty: the gripping story of the negotiations that brought about Irish independence and led to the Civil War* (Dublin, 2021); Colum Kenny, *Midnight in London: the Anglo-Irish Treaty crisis, 1921* (Dublin, 2021); Fiona Murray and Eda Segarra, *The men and women of the Anglo-Irish Treaty delegations, 1921* (Dublin, 2021). For a discussion of contemporary legal analysis of the Treaty, see Thomas Mohr, 'The Anglo-Irish Treaty: legal interpretation, 1921–1925', *Ir. Jur.* 66 (2021), 1. 3 Recent scholarship on aspects of the Civil War includes Diarmaid Ferriter, *Between two hells: the Irish Civil War* (London, 2021); Síobhra Aiken, *Spiritual wounds: trauma, testimony and the Irish Civil War*

treaty that had fairly broad public support'.[4] The conflict resulted in an estimated 1,300 casualties, and its fallout dominated Irish public discourse and politics for decades.[5]

The early 1920s were thus a time of great upheaval. From the perspective of the legal professions, there was a new state, a new constitution and a new system of justice to be carved out against a backdrop of continued violence, political uncertainty and professional risk.[6] As Enright has pointed out, there were in effect three competing and overlapping systems of law and order operating: the established criminal justice system, the courts-martial system established under the Restoration of Order in Ireland Act 1920, and the Dáil Courts.[7] Barristers were involved, to a greater or lesser degree, with each of these legal regimes.[8] One barrister later recalled,

> We had two of everything … We had the British High Courts in the Four Courts, we had Dáil Éireann High Courts; we had British High Court judges and county court judges and Dáil Éireann High Court judges and county court judges; British RMs (Resident Magistrate) and JPs (Justices of the Peace), Dáil Éireann magistrates …[9]

The system of alternative courts, known first as arbitration courts or Sinn Féin courts, had evolved from informal 'small groups of influential men [who] offered their services as mediators'.[10] Foxton describes 'the establishment of a

(Newbridge, 2022); Bill Kissane, 'The geographical spread of state executions during the Irish Civil War, 1922–23', *Social Science History* 45:1 (2021), 165; Gemma Clarke, 'Violence against women in the Irish Civil War 1922–3: gender-based harm in global perspective', *I.H.S.* 44:165 (2020), 75; Gavin Foster, *The Irish Civil War and society: politics, class, and conflict* (Basingstoke, 2015). For a multi-faceted consideration of the year 1922, see Darragh Gannon and Fearghal McGarry (eds), *Ireland, 1922: independence, partition, civil war* (Dublin, 2022). On the British withdrawal from Ireland, see John Gibney and Kate O'Malley, *The handover: Dublin Castle and the British withdrawal from Ireland, 1922* (Dublin, 2022). 4 Ferriter, *Between two hells*, p. 1. 5 See Bill Kissane, *The politics of the Irish Civil War* (Oxford, 2005). 6 This included participating in courts martial in 1920, for example. When a number of English barristers arrived in Dublin to appear at the courts martial, the *Irish Law Times* commented that this was in spite of the fact that there was 'no lack of Irish counsel who are willing to undertake this work.' It expressed a hope that the matter would be 'rectified at once.' *I.L.T.S.J.* 280 (20 Nov. 1920). Bewley recalled meeting English counsel who had newly arrived, and who travelled by armoured car. 'They were inclined to start at any sudden noise: one could see that only a strong sense of duty, a proportionate fee and the prospect of speedy promotion could have induced them to accept so perilous a task.' Charles Bewley, *Memoirs of a wild goose* (Dublin, 1989), p. 56. 7 Sean Enright, *After the rising: soldiers, lawyers, and trials of the Irish Revolution* (Dublin, 2015), p. 2. He describes a fourth regime introduced in the summer of 1920 with the declaration of martial law in the west of Ireland and the introduction of military courts: 'It was intended that trials and executions should take place swiftly and without recourse to law but the families of prisoners sought writs of habeas corpus to prevent the executions and this set in motion a series of legal challenges which eventually led to the courts ruling that these tribunals were unlawful', p. 2. 8 E.g., Bewley, *Wild goose*, p. 56 recalled defending prisoners at courts martial in 1920. 9 P.J. McEnery, 'Ireland, 1900–50. Glimpses in retrospect', UCDA P174/1, p. 54. 10 Mary Kotsonouris, *Retreat from revolution: the Dáil Courts, 1920–24* (Dublin, 1994), pp 11–12.

rival court structure, and a boycott of the "enemy" legal institutions' as a key element of the Sinn Féin programme.[11] People began to bring all sorts of civil disputes to these courts. In June 1919 the Dáil decreed 'the establishment in every county of national arbitration courts'.[12] By this stage, the arbitration or Sinn Féin courts were functioning effectively and had popular support.[13] A barrister writing in 1920 observed that

> In hardly more than three months since their first inception, we have seen the regular Irish county courts practically deserted, and the cases already heard by them and awaiting appeal to his majesty's judges of assize withdrawn from the record.[14]

This was despite the challenges of 'harassment by the crown forces, lack of suitable buildings, sources, and the shortage of trained legal personnel.'[15] While mainly dealing with civil disputes (land disputes in particular),[16] they also exercised some criminal jurisdiction.[17] Local and national newspapers reported on the proceedings in the informal courts, lending them further credibility and authority.[18] One commentator has described these courts as 'one of the most extraordinary phenomena of any contemporary European nationalist movement.'[19] Garvin notes that the Dáil Courts frequently administered 'an inexpensive, even-handed and sensible arbitration in everyday civilian disputes'.[20] In many cases the alternative courts were almost as formal as the official courts, with rules of procedure, evidence, judges and juries, and of course, lawyers. Maguire recalled that '[e]xcept for the absence of judicial robes, the courts were carried on exactly as were our opposite numbers of the established British system.'[21]

11 David Foxton, *Revolutionary lawyers: Sinn Féin and crown courts in Ireland and Britain, 1916–23* (Dublin, 2008), p. 23. 12 Fourth session (day 2), 18 June 1919. *Miontuairisc an chead Dála, 1919–1921: Minutes of proceedings of the first parliament of the Republic of Ireland 1919–1921* (Dublin, 1922), p. 122. See James Casey, 'The genesis of the Dáil Courts', *Ir. Jur.* 9:2 (1974), 328, at 328. On Dáil decrees see Brian Farrell, 'The legislation of a "revolutionary" assembly: Dáil decrees, 1919–1922', *Ir. Jur.* 10:1 (1975), 112 and Thomas Mohr, 'The strange fate of the Dáil decrees of revolutionary Ireland, 1919–22', *Statute L. Rev.* 43:1 (2022), 120. 13 For a first-hand account of the courts in Mayo, see Conor A. Maguire, 'The republican courts', *Capuchin Annual* (1939), 378. He writes, at 378, '[t]o our surprise we found it comparatively easy to persuade litigants and solicitors to bring their cases before the new tribunals'. 14 W.H. Brayden, *Republican courts in Ireland* (Chicago, 1920), pp 3–4 (reprint of W.H. Brayden, 'Sinn Féin courts in operation', *J.A.B.A.* 6:4 (1920), 8). 15 Ronan Keane, 'The voice of the Gael: Chief Justice Kennedy and the emergence of the new Irish court system 1921–1936', *Ir. Jur.* 31 (1996), 205, at 207. 16 See Cahir Davitt, 'The civil jurisdiction of the courts of justice in the Irish republic 1920–1922', *Ir. Jur.* 3:1 (1968), 121 and James Casey, 'Republican courts in Ireland 1919–1922', *Ir. Jur.* 5:2 (1970), 321. 17 Maguire, 'Republican courts', at 279. 18 E.g., 'Dunsaughlin Sinn Fein court', *Drogheda Independent,* 14 Aug. 1920, p. 2; 'Sinn Fein courts. Police and military watch Ballinamore proceedings', *Belfast News Letter,* 9 Aug. 1920, p. 5; 'Sinn Fein Court', *Cork Examiner,* 19 May 1920, p. 5. 19 Eda Sagarra, *Kevin O'Shiel: Tyrone nationalist and Irish state-builder* (Kildare, 2013), p. 130. 20 Tom Garvin, *1922: The birth of Irish democracy* (Dublin, 1996), p. 170. 21 Maguire,

By the summer of 1920 the Dáil had established a full parallel court system. The volume of business at the regular courts dipped dramatically, as litigation was increasingly being transferred to the alternative courts.[22] This was the case on every circuit except the North-East. So much was dealt with by the informal courts that white gloves were frequently presented at the regular sessions,[23] which symbolised that there was no serious crime to consider. Members of the judiciary were aware of the likely reality, however; when Justice Dodd was presented with white gloves at the Longford assizes in spring 1920, he remarked to the grand jury that 'perhaps where crime had been discovered the criminals had been removed for trial to other venues'.[24] Other judges were more explicit in their statements on the white gloves, and either refused to accept them[25] or commented that they had lost their significance.[26]

The Irish legal profession had an ambivalent relationship towards these alternative courts. Rules for the Dáil Courts were drawn up in 1920 by a committee that included Conor A. Maguire, James Creed Meredith, Arthur Clery,[27] Diarmuid Crowley[28] and Hector Hughes.[29] When the benches of the new Dáil Courts were populated,[30] Clery and Creed Meredith were appointed to the bench of the Dáil Supreme Court, while Crowley and Cahir Davitt[31] were appointed to the Dáil Circuit Court.[32] However, on the whole, the involvement of the Irish Bar was quite limited.[33] Austin Stack commented that there were scarcely half a dozen barristers involved,[34] and Kotsonouris' work suggests that there were perhaps a dozen or more.[35] Charles Bewley claimed to be the first barrister to appear in the Dáil Courts.[36] He describes how 'most of the sittings were held in school-houses or deserted dwellings or presbyteries,'[37] and provides a detailed account of how he and a colleague had received a number of briefs in a western county. They travelled by train and were advised to alight at a small

'Republican courts', at 379.   **22** Ibid., at 380, describes a boycott of local county courts. **23** Kotsonouris, *Retreat*, p. 22. Newspapers started reporting on cases decided in the 'Dáil Courts' in 1920.   **24** 'White gloves for the judge. Extraordinary military precautions', *Irish Examiner*, 3 Mar. 1920, p. 8.   **25** 'White gloves refused. Assize judge rejects sub-sheriff's gift at Tullamore', *Freeman's Journal*, 6 July 1921, p. 8 (Wylie J). See also 'Leitrim assize. Judge Pim and white gloves', *Examiner*, 6 July 1920, p. 8. Judge Pim described the ceremony as 'a mockery and an insult'. **26** 'State of Tyrone. White gloves no index', *Fermanagh Herald*, 25 Mar. 1922, p. 8 (Linehan J). **27** Called in 1902; professor of law at UCD. See Ferguson, *King's Inns barristers, 1868–2004* (Dublin, 2005), p. 157.   **28** Called in 1916 as Jeremiah Crowley; see ibid., p. 167 and Pauric Dempsey, 'Crowley (Ó Cruadhlaoich), Diarmuid', *D.I.B.*   **29** Called in 1915; see Ferguson, *Barristers*, p. 210.   **30** All of those appointed to the Dáil Court judiciary in the higher courts were barristers. Some barristers and solicitors were also given temporary commissions 'when extra circuit sittings were needed.' Kotsonouris, *Retreat*, p. 31.   **31** Called in 1916 as 'Cathar Davitt'; see Ferguson, *Barristers*, p. 171.   **32** Conor A. Maguire, who was later called to the Bar, and Kevin O'Shiel were appointed as land commission judges. Kevin O'Shiel had advised Arthur Griffith about setting up Dáil Land Courts, and Art O'Connor, the minister for agriculture, gave O'Shiel a warrant to set up a special judicial commission to hear and determine disputes over land. He began hearing cases in May 1920: Sagarra, *Kevin O'Shiel*, p. 131.   **33** See Foxton, *Revolutionary lawyers*, p. 28.   **34** Quoted in Hogan, *The legal profession*, p. 152.   **35** Kotsonouris, *Retreat*.   **36** Bewley, *Wild goose*, pp 67–8.   **37** Ibid.

country station rather than in the county town. They were met by a driver who saluted them in military fashion, and drove them by various country roads and lanes and through some fields until they reached an eighteenth-century country house:

> In the centre of the great hall was a long deal table looking like a kitchen table, and around it deal chairs which were evidently kitchen chairs ... Now they were occupied by the republican judge, who in private life was the village schoolmaster, and valuers and auctioneers; the republican police with rifles and bandoliers stood around the walls, and the litigants and witnesses strolled about among the statues, and smoked their pipes and cigarettes, and from time to time spat furtively on the floor. My colleague and I took the places reserved for us at the table: we were no less essential a part of the picture than the others.[38]

In the summer of 1920, the Bar Council was asked to make a ruling[39] on members of the Bar acting in such courts,[40] and it ruled that it amounted to professional misconduct, rather than a breach of professional etiquette. The matter arose again in November 1920 at a meeting of the General Council of the Bar. Tim Healy KC argued that the Bar Council had no authority to pass judgment on the conduct of any member of the Bar, and that only the benchers of the King's Inns had that right.[41] Another silk's comment that '[t]hey had all been a happy family in the Library, and it would be a pity to introduce anything that would cause friction or disagreement',[42] was quite representative of the Bar as a place where political and ideological differences were generally put to one side.[43]

Hogan suggests that one reason for the Bar's limited representation in the Dáil Courts was because of the nature of their business; usually a solicitor sufficed.[44] He adds that 'participation by a barrister would have been more formal and noticeable than in the case of a solicitor.'[45] Another deterrent was the danger involved. For example, Kevin O'Shiel, on being instructed by Collins to avoid capture by the Black and Tans or the Auxiliaries, disguised himself as a travelling salesman while going around the country to hear cases.[46] Conor A. Maguire was said to have disguised himself with a sports suit and a set of golf clubs,[47] while Charles Bewley recalled circuitous and clandestine journeys in

---

38 Ibid., p. 70. 39 See pp 339–40. 40 (1920) 54 *I.L.T.S.J.* 152 (26 June 1920) and 'Sinn Fein courts. Action of Irish Bar Council', *Skibbereen Eagle*, 26 June 1920, p. 8. 41 For further discussion of the responsibility for disciplinary matters see ch. 16. 42 (1920) 54 *I.L.T.S.J.* 272 (6 Nov. 1920). 43 See further ch. 5. 44 At a sitting in Mullingar on 2 July 1920, most of the local solicitors attended, 'plus a few barristers'. Sagarra, *Kevin O'Shiel*, p. 141. 45 Hogan, *The legal profession in Ireland*, p. 152. 46 He carried with him all of the equipment needed for selling an ointment called Gitsol, including samples, notebooks and files. At one point he put on an English accent and offered to supply the ointment to the 'bored, drunken Black and Tans' on a train. Later said to have quipped, 'I can bore for Ireland if my country needs me to.' Sagarra, *Kevin O'Shiel*, p. 242. 47 Ibid.

order to appear at sittings.[48] In January 1921, barrister Diarmuid Crowley was tried before a court martial in Galway, having been found in possession of various papers and files relating to Dáil Courts.[49] He admitted to being a judge in the republican courts, and was found guilty.[50] In October 1922 the *Irish Law Times* reported that, despite the continuing Civil War, local courts were now functioning normally in most counties,[51] although the burning of courthouses continued.

When the Anglo-Irish Treaty was signed, these informal courts were retained 'to save face' as they were so popular, and 'no attempt was made to curtail their jurisdiction nor to rehabilitate the statutory courts that had been all but obliterated.'[52] Within weeks of the outbreak of the Civil War, however, a decision was taken to close them down,[53] and there followed what Kotsonouris describes as 'a year of confusion, anger and frustration'.[54] There had been no prior warning, and both the public and the legal profession worried about how ongoing litigation was to proceed. In 1923, a judicial commission was established to wind up the Dáil Courts.[55] This was, in Kotsonoris' view, in effect an 'extraordinary admission' that the original hasty decision to shut down the courts without having a coherent plan for their replacement had been ill-advised.[56] James Creed Meredith, who had been the president of the Dáil Supreme Court, was the chief commissioner, working alongside Diarmuid Crowley and St Lawrence Devitt.[57] Other barristers who served on the commission included Charles Stewart Kenny,[58] Joseph Patrick Kenny,[59] Charles Stewart Wyse Power[60] and Eugene Sheehy.[61] The commission was dissolved in 1925.

The creation of a new state

The Anglo-Irish Treaty was signed on 6 December 1921[62] and was due to come into force a year later. The second Dáil met on 14 December to discuss it, and

---

48 Bewley, *Wild goose*, pp 68–70. 49 'West Cork barrister tried. Possession of Dáil Court documents' *Skibbereen Eagle*, 22 Jan. 1921, p. 1. 50 Crowley was sentenced to two years' hard labour and was released shortly before the Treaty. After 1924, he sought the continued payment of his full judicial salary, on the grounds that his appointment had been for life. In 1925 the Dáil Supreme Court (Pensions) Act was passed, providing the former judges with a pension of £500. Crowley later pursued litigation against the state, *O'Crowley v. The Minister for Justice and the Minister for Finance* [1935] I.R. 536. See Pauric Dempsey, 'Crowley (Ó Cruadhlaoich), Diarmuid', *D.I.B.* and Ferguson, *Barristers*, p. 167. 51 (1922) 56 *I.L.T.S.J.* 252 (21 Oct. 1922). 52 Kotsonouris, *Retreat*, p. 13. 53 See Thomas Mohr, 'British involvement in the creation of the constitution of the Irish Free State', *D.U.L.J.* 30 (2008), 166. 54 Mary Kotsonouris, *The winding-up of the Dáil Courts, 1922–1925: an obvious duty* (Dublin, 2004). 55 See generally Kotsonouris, *Winding-up*, and Dáil Éireann Courts (Winding Up) Act 1923; Dáil Éireann Courts (Winding Up) Act 1923 Amendment Act 1924 and Dáil Éireann Courts (Winding Up) Act 1925. See also Thomas Mohr, 'Law and the foundation of the Irish state on 6 December 1922', *Ir. Jur.* 59 (2018), 31, at 37. 56 Kotsonouris, *Winding-up*, p. 5. 57 Called in 1901: Ferguson, *Barristers*, p. 173. 58 Called in 1911: ibid., p. 220. 59 Called in 1909: ibid., p. 220. 60 Called in 1913: ibid., p. 284. 61 Called in 1910: ibid., p. 297 and Eugene Sheehy, *May it please the court* (Dublin, 1951). 62 For an account of the Treaty negotiations see Diarmaid Ferriter, *A nation and not a rabble: the Irish Revolution,*

there followed fifteen days of intense debate[63] before it was accepted by a vote of sixty-four in favour to fifty-seven against.[64] Almost immediately, one of the first tasks facing the government was the creation of a new, written constitution for the Irish Free State. For this, a committee was established by Michael Collins. As Mohr observes, 'there was no shortage of legal and administrative talent on the constitution committee'.[65] Four of the ten committee members were barristers: Hugh Kennedy,[66] John O'Byrne,[67] Kevin O'Shiel,[68] and James Murnaghan.[69] Two members of the secretariat were also barristers: Edward (or 'Ned') Millington Stephens[70] and Patrick Albert O'Toole.[71] While Michael

1913–1923 (London, 2015), pp 245–52.   63 For detailed analysis of the debates, see the contributions in Liam Weeks and Mícheál Ó Fathartaigh, *The Treaty: debating and establishing the Irish state* (Newbridge, 2018).   64 Weeks and Ó Fathartaigh argue that these debates were a critical moment in modern Irish history: Liam Weeks and Mícheál Ó Fathartaigh, 'Introduction' in Weeks and Ó Fathartaigh, *The Treaty.*   65 Mohr, 'British involvement', at 169.   66 Kennedy was called to the Bar in 1902 and was made a KC in 1920. He was the most senior and experienced lawyer on the committee, and was known by some acquaintances as 'the Brehon'; Ailsa C. Holland, 'The papers of Hugh Kennedy', *Ir. Jur.* 24 (1989), 290. Curran later described his 'firmly held opinions, and the patient, exact thoroughness in which he carried through all he then conceived and undertook'. C.P. Curran, *Under the receding wave* (Dublin, 1970), p. 122. See also Thomas Mohr, 'The influence of Chief Justice Hugh Kennedy'; Ronan Keane, 'Kennedy, Hugh', *D.I.B.* and Geoghegan, 'Three judges of the Supreme Court of the Irish Free State, 1925–36' in Larkin and Dawson (eds), *Lawyers*, pp 32–8.   67 Before being called to the Bar O'Byrne had worked as a civil servant in London, and in the Irish Land Commission. He was called to the Bar in 1911 and practised on the Leinster Circuit. In 1921 he served as a legal adviser to the Dáil delegation in the negotiations leading to the Anglo–Irish Treaty. He also later sat on the judiciary committee. In June 1924 he became a KC and was then appointed as attorney general. He was appointed a judge of the High Court in 1926 and joined the Supreme Court in 1940. Gerard Hogan, 'O'Byrne, John', *D.I.B.* 68 O'Shiel was called to the Bar in 1913 and practised on the North-Western Circuit. During the First World War, O'Shiel began to combine his work at the Bar with political journalism. He published *The birth of a republic* in 1920, described by Garvin as 'a competent popular history for Irish readers of the birth of the American republic'. Garvin, *1922*, p. 148. In 1920 he advised Arthur Griffith about the setting up of the Dáil Land Courts, where he then served as a judicial commissioner. By 1922, he had a solid reputation and was appointed assistant legal advisor to the provisional government. After the constitution committee finished its task, he worked on the Boundary Bureau. He then worked as a land commissioner from 1923 until his retirement in 1965. Sagarra, *Kevin O'Shiel*, p. 151. See also Bureau of Military History, 1913–1921, Statement by witness. Commissioner Kevin R. O'Shiel B.L.   69 Murnaghan was called to the Bar in 1903 and practised on the Northern and Midland Circuits. He was appointed as a part-time professor of jurisprudence, Roman law, and international law at UCD in 1908, and retained his practice at the Bar. Hugh Geoghegan characterises Murnaghan as 'primarily, an academic', with a practice that was 'solid but modest'; Geoghegan, 'Three judges of the Supreme Court', p. 42. Murnaghan was also professor of jurisprudence at UCD. See Ronan Keane, 'Murnaghan, James Augustine', *D.I.B.*. Unusually for someone who had not yet taken silk, Murnaghan was appointed a judge of the new Supreme Court in 1924 and remained in office for twenty-eight years. Keane characterises Murnaghan's written judgments as 'carefully reasoned and erudite', and Geoghegan in 'Three judges of the Supreme Court', p. 42, writes that he was 'nobody's poodle'.   70 Stephens had been called to the Bar a decade before, in 1912. He had accompanied Collins as a legal draughtsman during the Treaty negotiations in London in 1921. At Collins' behest, he was then seconded from his civil-service position to serve the constitution committee. Afterwards he served as secretary to the North-Eastern Boundary Bureau from 1922–6, and as an assistant parliamentary draughtsman. He was later assistant registrar of the Supreme Court, and registrar of the Court of Criminal Appeal.   71 O'Toole was called to the Bar in 1913. George Gavan Duffy, who was not on the

Collins was nominally the chair of the committee, in practice this fell to Darrell Figgis, the deputy chairman.[72] The committee began its work on 24 January 1922, and by 27 May a draft was ready to be brought by Michael Collins and Arthur Griffith to London. The committee met twenty-seven times[73] and evidently worked at a pace – Hugh Kennedy's diaries suggest that he was attending for forty hours per week in February 1922, despite his other commitments. The nature of the contribution made by the barristers on this committee is explored further in chapter ten. Garvin, writing about democracy in the Free State, notes that

> The fact that the new politicians were, by and large, veterans of guerrilla warfare weakened their claim to political legitimacy. 'Law' offered the pro-Treatyites a way out, a psychological defence against the ideological arguments of the anti-Treatyites. 'Law' could, of course, only be supplied by lawyers.[74]

He says that this accounts for 'the rapid post-Treaty political ascent of lawyers such as Patrick McGilligan, Hugh Kennedy and Kevin O'Shiel. The relative absence of lawyers in the pre-Treaty elite and their conspicuous presence in the early Free State elite is a crucial contrast; lawyers knew how to build law-bound states.'[75]

The Irish Free State came into existence on 6 December 1922,[76] when the constitution took effect.[77] One of the first important areas of reform was the courts system.[78] While the constitution provided for local courts, a High Court and a Supreme Court, it was silent as to the detail of how these new courts would function.[79] A commission known as the judiciary committee was established, 'to

---

constitution committee, may have indirectly influenced the drafting of the constitution. He was in regular correspondence with Douglas regarding the drafting. Brian Farrell, 'The drafting of the Irish Free State constitution: I', *Ir. Jur.* (ns) 5:1 (1970), 115 at 130. Another lawyer on the committee was Clemens J. France, a US attorney. Michael Collins chaired the committee and well-known literary figure Darrell Figgis was vice-chairman. Also on the committee were James Douglas (a nationalist Quaker and a businessman); James McNeill (a former civil servant); Professor Alfred O'Rahilly (a UCD professor) and Darrell Figgis, author of *The Gaelic state in the past and future* (Dublin, 1917). Other people who were either invited or suggested were Labour leader Thomas Johnson; American lawyer Michael Francis Doyle; academic Ernest Henry Alton and Lord Justice James O'Connor, as well as some members of the clergy.   72 Farrell, 'The drafting', at 117.   73 Bill Kissane, 'Defining independence' in Gannon and McGarry (eds), *Ireland 1922*, p. 299.   74 Garvin, *1922*, p. 159.   75 Ibid.   76 See Mohr, 'Foundation of the Irish state', at 31–58.   77 See Laura Cahillane and Donal Coffey (eds), *The centenary of the Irish Free State constitution: constituting a polity?* (London, 2023).   78 Garvin, *1922*, p. 169 considers the courts system to have been 'an early object of Free State leaders' reformist energies.'   79 A significant amount of new legislation had to be drafted to reflect the administration and enforcement of a new legal system, and members of the Bar played an active role in such drafting. These included, for example, the County Courts (Amendment) Act 1923; the District Justices (Temporary Provisions) Act 1923; the Solicitors (Ireland) Act 1898, Amendment Act 1923; the County Court Appeals Act 1924; the Court

advise the government on matters judicial.'[80] In his letter to each of the committee members, Cosgrave wrote:

> There is nothing more prized among our newly won liberties than the liberty to construct a system of judiciary and an administration of law and justice according to the dictates of our own needs and after a pattern of our own designing.[81]

The committee was chaired by Sir James Campbell (Lord Glenavy), the former lord chancellor. Several barristers were appointed, including John O'Byrne, Hugh Kennedy, Timothy Sullivan, William J. Johnston, James Creed Meredith and Cahir Davitt. After 'many protracted sittings and full and anxious consideration',[82] the proposed new courts system was set out in the Courts of Justice bill 1923.[83] New Circuit Courts would replace county courts as well as much of the jurisdiction of the centralised High Court.[84] District Courts would be staffed by salaried, professional judges.[85] Other reforms included a system of criminal appeal to the Court of Criminal Appeal.[86] There were to be six judges of the High Court[87] and three in the Supreme Court,[88] and the most senior judge would be the chief justice.[89] A compulsory retirement age for judges was introduced for the first time.[90] The Courts of Justice Act 1924 was signed into law in April 1924,[91] and three months later the names of the new members of the judiciary were announced. Hugh Kennedy was appointed chief justice and Timothy Sullivan became the president of the High Court. The new senior judiciary included two serving judges from the previous regime,[92] with the rest being newly promoted. They were a mix of Catholic and Protestant, nationalist and unionist, reflecting the political and religious diversity of the Bar itself.[93]

Officers (Temporary Appointments) Act 1924; the Criminal Justice (Administration) Act 1924; the Criminal Justice (Evidence) Act 1924; the Juries (Amendment) Act 1924; the Enforcement of Law (Occasional Powers) Act 1923; the Gárda Síochána (Temporary Provisions) Act 1923; the Dublin Police Act 1924; the Electoral Act 1923; the Prevention of Electoral Abuses Act 1923; the Defence Forces (Temporary Provisions) Act 1923. See Aengus Fallon, 'Statute law and the foundations of the Irish Free State (1922–1926)' (PhD, UCD, 2019) and Aengus Fallon, 'The foundational legislation of the Garda Síochána (1922–1926)', *Ir. Jur.* 62 (2019), 119. **80** See Dáil Éireann deb., vol. 2, col. 22 (30 Jan. 1923) (William T. Cosgrave); see also Kotsonouris, *Retreat*, p. 109. Detailed records of the commission can be found in the Hugh Kennedy papers UCDA P4, and the John A. Costello papers, UCDA P190. See also Brice Dickson, *The Irish Supreme Court* (Oxford, 2019), pp 12–13. **81** Copy of letter from President W.T. Cosgrave to each member of the committee, 29 Jan. 1923, UCDA P190/41. **82** Glanavy to Cosgrave, enclosing report of the committee (undated), John A. Costello papers, UCDA P190/41. **83** Ch. 14 further considers the contribution of barristers, both on the committee itself and in shaping the final legislation. **84** Courts of Justice Act 1924, pt. 2. **85** Ibid., pt. 3. **86** Ibid., s. 8, ss 28–30. **87** Ibid., s. 4. **88** Ibid., s. 5. **89** See Donal Coffey, 'The judiciary of the Irish Free State', *D.U.L.J.* 33:1 (2011), 61. **90** Courts of Justice Act 1924, s. 12. **91** Its provisions commenced at different dates in June and August 1924. See Dickson, *The Irish Supreme Court*, pp 19–21. **92** W.E. Wylie and Sir Charles O'Connor. **93** See Ronan Keane, 'The voice of the Gael'.

An attempt was made to make visible changes with regard to the professional attire worn by judges and barristers in the new state, something which is discussed further in chapter six.[94] Overall, however, the practise of law continued much as it had before. A barrister who had experienced the courts both immediately before the 1924 Act, and afterwards, commented:

> Pleading, practice and general procedure were substantially the same in both regimes ... the wig and bands and stuff gown remained the garb of the junior Bar, the wig and bands and silk gown remained the garb of the inner Bar ... Litigation continued as before and the procedure substantially remained the same as in the old regime.'[95]

In many respects, the practise of law continued along similar lines and with minimal disruption after 1924, but the Bar was undoubtedly undergoing a period of change on several fronts.

The impact of partition

The partition of Ireland had a profound effect on Irish society in the 1920s and, in the words of one scholar, it represented 'the most fundamental change in twentieth-century Ireland.'[96] Until the 1920s, the Bar had been an all-island body. The Government of Ireland Act 1920 provided that after the Northern and southern judiciaries were set up, members of the Irish Bar who had already been called should have an equal right of audience in courts north and south.[97] No legislative provision was made for those who were subsequently called to the Bar, and this was left to the judiciaries. After the Act came into effect on 1 October 1921, those who graduated from the King's Inns and wished to practise at the Northern Bar had to travel to Belfast to be called a second time.[98] Many barristers practising on the North-Eastern[99] and North-Western[100] Circuits effectively had to choose which jurisdiction in which to concentrate. Some who

94 Alan Hanna, *Poetry, politics, and the law in modern Ireland* (New York, 2022), ch. 2, discusses Yeats' proposed new robes and mentions, p. 33, his 'deep appreciation of law as both force and symbol'. 95 P.J. McEnery, 'Look back in love: conversations by an English fireside', UCDA P74/2, pp 64–9. 96 Robert Lynch, *The partition of Ireland, 1918–1925* (Cambridge, 2019), p. 5. He also notes, p. 6, that, until relatively recently, the partition of Ireland was a relatively under-researched topic: '[p]artition certainly occupies an uncertain place in historical narratives of the period, even for historians whose primary focus is on the north-east.' 97 Government of Ireland Act 1920, pt. 3, s. 4. 98 The first post-partition Dublin call took place on 1 November 1921. The first Belfast call was on 8 November. Two of the twenty who had been called in Dublin made the journey to Belfast; these were Frances Kyle (the first woman called to the Irish Bar) and J.C. MacDermott (a future lord chief justice of Northern Ireland). They were called to the Northern Bar by Denis Henry, the first lord chief justice of Northern Ireland. See A.D. McDonnell, *The life of Sir Denis Henry, Catholic unionist* (Belfast, 2000). The call was also recalled in J.C. MacDermott, *An enriching life* (Belfast, 1980), pp 152–3. 99 See George Hill Smith, *The north east Bar: a sketch, historical and reminiscent* (Belfast, 1910). 100 See John Ross, *The years of my pilgrimage. Random*

came from the Northern counties chose not to pursue their career in Northern Ireland and were soon appointed to the bench in southern Ireland.[101] Others chose to practise in Northern Ireland,[102] even where this involved uprooting their families from Dublin to Belfast.[103]

In late October 1921 the King's Inns benchers made a number of unanimous resolutions concerning the relationship between the two Bars and the resourcing of training and library facilities for those intending to practise in Northern Ireland. It was resolved to make arrangements 'for the giving of lectures and holding examinations, other than the final examination, in Belfast by a professor of the King's Inns.'[104] A 'branch library' of the King's Inns was to be formed, by sending to Belfast 'such books as the library committee may recommend and the judges of Northern Ireland may desire.' It was also resolved that students who were awarded the degree of Barrister-at-Law by the King's Inns should be granted audience in the courts both north and south.[105] In addition, the benchers resolved that a sub-committee of benchers be nominated to deal with Northern matters, including education and discipline.[106]

In January 1922 arrangements were made for the transfer of books to Belfast, to 'form a nucleus for a library',[107] and the first meeting of the Northern committee of the benchers of King's Inns was held.[108] This committee comprised benchers who were members of the Northern bench and Bar, and could exercise most of the powers of the King's Inns, save for the power to disbar or suspend a member of the Northern Bar.[109] The educational arrangements worked well, with the King's Inns providing the training for students who wished to join the Northern Bar. Such students divided their time between Dublin and Belfast, and part of the fees they paid to the King's Inns paid for a law professor to provide lectures in Belfast.[110] As Hart points out, the arrangements 'effectively gave the Northern committee almost complete autonomy'.[111] Reciprocal arrangements were also made for the use of dressing-rooms and libraries.[112] The year 1922 saw the establishment of a library committee, a circuit of Northern Ireland and the Northern Ireland Bar Council,[113] which oversaw the general governance of the Northern Ireland Bar.

reminiscences (London, 1924).   101 E.g., James Murnaghan (from Co. Tyrone; see Ferguson, *Barristers*, p. 261) and Henry Hanna (from Belfast; see ibid., p. 200).   102 E.g., Robert Dick Megaw (from Co. Armagh: ibid., p. 253. He was later elected MP for Co. Antrim).   103 E.g., Anthony Babington (from Co. Derry: ibid., p. 133). Before leaving Dublin, he had been a lecturer at the King's Inns: Pauric J. Dempsey, 'Babington, Sir Anthony Brutus', *D.I.B.* He was appointed attorney general of Northern Ireland in 1925.   104 K.I.B.M., 31 Oct. 1921.   105 Ibid.   106 Ibid. 107 B.C.L.C., 21 Dec. 1921. See also K.I.B.M., 11 Jan. 1922 and B.C.L.C., 19 Dec. 1921, 16 Jan. 1922. The Northern committee later expressed their gratitude 'for the loan of many valuable books to the Bar library in Belfast': K.I.B.M., 20 Apr. 1922.   108 K.I.B.M., 18 Jan. 1922.   109 The *Irish Law Times* noted the establishment of the 'circuit of Northern Ireland' in 1922, as well as noting the names of the members of the Circuit Committee and the Bar committee: (1922) 56 *I.L.T.S.J.* 24 (21 Jan. 1924).   110 K.I.B.M., 17 May 1922.   111 Hart, *History of the Bar*, p. 96. 112 B.C.M., 9 Mar. 1922.   113 Hart, *History of the Bar*, p. 176.

The friendly relations and reciprocity between north and south are evident from the minutes of both the benchers and the Bar Council around this time.[114] In June 1922 the amended rules of the King's Inns were formally adopted, to take account of the various changes described above.[115] The two Bars remained on good terms until the mid-1920s. However, this harmonious relationship was not to last. By 1924, 'the tensions inherent in the attempt by King's Inns to preserve a single governing body for the Bars of two distinct and politically hostile entities became impossible to ignore and increasingly difficult to resolve'.[116] The first indication that relations between the two Bars might be under strain came about in 1925, and things became very bitter very quickly.

After the First World War, some students of the King's Inns had been granted exemptions in relation to their examinations or their course of study, on the basis of military service. This practice continued into the 1920s,[117] and a number of the exemptions granted in 1923 and 1924 'were a source of great concern to the Northern committee, and set in train the events that led to the rupture between King's Inns and the Northern committee'.[118]

Michael Hayes, the ceann comhairle of Dáil Éireann was 'exempted from attendance on lectures and be permitted to proceed to his call to the Bar, upon the honours examination only'.[119] In response, the Northern committee wrote a letter on 7 November stating that no Free State barristers would in future be called to the Bar of Northern Ireland, and that they wished to be in a position to retain the reciprocity with the English inns of court. Unfortunately, for reasons unknown, the King's Inns benchers did not see this letter until six months later.[120] In the meantime, minister for justice (and qualified solicitor) Kevin O'Higgins had also been granted an exemption.[121] Despite never having taken any classes or undertaken any exam at the King's Inns, his exemption was granted on the basis of 'his educational attainments and the experience in legal matters acquired by him therein and elsewhere'.[122] The granting of O'Higgins' exemption, along with the apparent ignoring of the letter of 7 November, seems to have caused both offence and irritation.

Another divisive issue was the increasing legislative divergence between the two jurisdictions: a comment was made around this time that 'a new system of jurisprudence differing largely between north and south is steadily growing up'.[123] Furthermore, Chief Justice Kennedy's proposal in relation to making the

---

114 Ibid. 115 K.I.B.M., 14 June 1922. 116 Hart, *History of the Bar*, p. 93. 117 E.g., K.I.B.M., 27 May 1921. 118 Hart, *History of the Bar*, pp 100–1. 119 K.I.B.M., 25 Oct. 1924. See Ferguson, *Barristers*, p. 202 and Diarmaid Ferriter, 'Hayes, Michael', *D.I.B.* Hayes had both a BA and an MA from UCD. 120 K.I.B.M., 11 May 1925. 121 Ibid., 19 Jan. 1925. 122 Ibid. O'Higgins had an LLB qualification, had undertaken training at the Law Society, had been apprenticed to Maurice Healy and had served as both minister for home affairs and minister for justice. It is worth noting that most of the detail regarding the reasons for the exemption appears to have been subsequently added to the margins of the minutes at a later date, perhaps to justify what proved to be a significant and controversial decision. 123 *The inn of court of Northern Ireland: a*

Irish language compulsory for a call to the Bar also caused some disquiet, both north and south.[124] In October 1925, Kennedy proposed that a sub-committee of the benchers be established to consider 'what rules would need to be changed so that 'no one should be admitted to the degree of Barrister-at-Law without possessing a competent knowledge of the Irish language, Irish history and of the constitution and government of Ireland'.[125]

The Northern committee established a sub-committee to consider its future relationship with the King's Inns, and it concluded that a split was inevitable.[126] The Northern committee wrote to the King's Inns in April 1925.[127] After a fairly robust exchange of letters, on 30 July 1925 the Northern committee resolved to establish an inn of court for Northern Ireland.[128] The *Irish Law Times* lamented the development: '[a]ll who loved and admired the Bar of Ireland will regret that circumstances have resulted in its separation into two bodies.'[129] Writing in 1929, A.M. Sullivan reflected on partition's impact on the Bar:

> The division of the country meant the end of the old Irish Bar. There were set up in Ireland two totally different systems of law and administration, and it was to one whose heart and soul were buried in the practise of his profession a great loss and a great misery.[130]

This misery was undoubtedly shared by others in the profession. The relations between the two Bars post-1926 has been described as 'extremely frosty',[131] and are examined further in chapter nine. As the two states drifted further apart, both in politics and in law, the split became entrenched, despite the earnest hope expressed by the *Irish Law Times* in 1926 that 'there may be frequent occasions on which the two inns in Ireland will act in common'.[132]

The arrival of women

The Sex Disqualification (Removal) Act was passed in 1919 and removed the legal barrier to women entering the legal professions. This followed fifty years of campaigning,[133] with the First World War acting as a catalyst for

report of the proceedings at a meeting of the bench and Bar in Northern Ireland, held at the law courts, Belfast, on Monday 11th January 1926, at which the inn of court was established (Belfast, 1926), per Lord Chief Justice Moore, p. 8.   **124** E.g., pamphlets containing protests at the imposition of compulsory Irish language examinations were published in full by the *Irish Law Times*: e.g. (1929) 63 *I.L.T.S.J.* 58–9.   **125** K.I.B.M., 26 Oct. 1925. See ch. 5.   **126** See Hart, *History of the Bar*, pp 103–4.   **127** K.I.B.M., 23 Apr. 1925.   **128** Hart, *History of the Bar*, citing the Northern committee benchers' minutes, 30 July and 4 Aug. 1925.   **129** (1926) 60 *I.L.T.S.J.* 19 (20 Feb. 1926).   **130** A.M. Sullivan, 'The last forty years of the Irish Bar', *Camb. L.J.* 3:3 (1929), 365, at 375.   **131** Conversation with Sir Anthony Hart, 21 June 2019.   **132** (1926) 60 *I.L.T.S.J.* 19.   **133** For a short summary of the background to the 1919 Act, see Brenda Hale, '100 years of women in the law: from Bertha Cave to Brenda Hale', delivered 20 Mar. 2019, King's College London: www.supremecourt.uk/docs/ speech–190320.pdf and Patrick Polden, 'Portia's progress: women at

change.[134] In 1921 Frances Kyle[135] and Averil Deverell[136] were the first women to be called to the Irish Bar.[137] At the opening of the new legal term in January 1922, the *Irish Law Times* described Deverell as 'an interesting figure amongst the members of the Bar'.[138] In the context of the centenaries of 1919 and 1921 the experiences of these early women lawyers have recently been documented, both in Ireland and in the United Kingdom.[139] Their entry into the professions has also been commemorated by the professions themselves.[140]

As will be demonstrated in chapter four, the number of women joining the Bar in the first decade or so after the Sex Disqualification (Removal) Act 1919 remained low. It was not the case that once the first women were called, there followed a rising wave of women eager to pursue careers at the Bar. It would take many decades before women joined the Bar in significant numbers. The reasons for this, and the attrition rates for women, are explored further in chapter nine. The *Irish Law Times* surmised in 1930 that '[s]ome retire when they marry, while others carry on in the face of opposition from solicitors who regard giving briefs to women as only worth while when the most brilliant male advocate could not win'.[141] Although they came in small numbers, the arrival of women at the Bar was a significant development in the early 1920s. It signalled another way in

the Bar in England 1919–1939', *Int. J. Leg. Prof.* 12:3 (2005), 293. Polden also notes, at 295, that there were several women from the Irish Free State admitted to the inns of court in London, along with women from all corners of the commonwealth.   134 Erika Rackley and Rosemary Auchmuty (eds), *Women's legal landmarks: celebrating the history of women and law in the UK and Ireland* (Oxford, 2019).   135 See A.R. Hart, 'Kyle, Frances (Fay) Christian', *D.I.B.*   136 See Maria O'Brien, 'Deverell, Averill Katherine Statter', *D.I.B* and Liz Goldthorpe, 'Deverell, Averil Katherine Statter (1893–1979)', *O.D.N.B.*   137 The *Irish Law Times* noted that the call was of 'great and unusual interest to the profession and to the public, as ladies were called for the first time in the history of the Irish Bar' (1921) 55 *I.L.T.S.J.* 272 (5 Nov. 1921). The first women solicitors were admitted in 1923 (Mary Dorothea Heron and Helena Mary Early), followed by Dorothea Mary Browne in 1924. See John Garahy, 'A Trinity of women: the first women solicitors in Ireland', First 100 years project: https://first100years.org.uk/a-trinity-of-women-the-first-women-solicitors-in-ireland/; John Garahy, 'Heron (Mary) Dorothea', *D.I.B.* and Mary Redmond, 'The emergence of women in the solicitors' profession in Ireland' in Hogan and Hall (eds), *The Law Society of Ireland.*   138 (1922) 56 *I.L.T.S.J.* 11 (14 Jan. 1922).   139 E.g., Liz Goldthorpe, 'First woman to practice as a barrister in Ireland and the (then) United Kingdom, Averil Deverell, 1921' in Rackley and Auchmuty, *Women's legal landmarks*; Emma Hutchinson, 'First woman professor of law in Ireland, Frances Moran, 1925' in Rackley and Auchmuty (eds), *Women's legal landmarks*. See also the First 100 years project, with individual biographies: https://first100years.org.uk/ digital-museum/biographies/; Ivana Bacik, 'Averil Deverell', Trinity Monday Memorial Discourse, 25 Apr. 2022, Trinity College Dublin; Brenda Hale, '100 years of women in the law: from Bertha Cave to Brenda Hale', 20 Mar. 2019, King's College London.   140 E.g., in April 2018 the King's Inns hosted an exhibition on Averil Deverell to mark the acquisition of the Deverell archive, and the Irish Legal History Society's spring discourse 2019 was delivered by Liz Goldthorpe on the topic of Deverell's legal career; see further ch. 9. In 2020 the Law Library of Ireland curated an online exhibition of the first 100 women called to the Bar in Ireland: www.lawlibrary.ie/News/Campaigns/Trailblazers–100-Years-of-Women-at-the-Bar.aspx. The cover image for this book is a portrait commissioned from artist Emma Stroude by the King's Inns and Bar Council under the 'In Plain Sight' initiative: www.lawlibrary.ie/portrait-of-first-female-barristers-unveiled/.   141 (1930) 64 *I.L.T.S.J.* 161 (5 July 1930).

which the 'old order' at the Bar had to make way for new members, and it was the beginning of a long, slow process of transformation in the composition of the Bar.

The destruction of the Law Library

In 1921, members of the Irish Bar worked out of the Law Library, a communal workspace[142] in the east wing of the Four Courts complex on Inns Quay.[143] Around this time, there were concerns for the safety of the complex. In June 1921 many of the public entrances were closed and only those with business to attend to were allowed in through the main gates. Uniformed and plain-clothes police were on patrol.[144] On 14 April 1922, a few days before the start of the Easter term, a group of soldiers opposed to the Anglo-Irish Treaty, under Major General Rory O'Connor, entered the complex, locked up the guard and opened the gates to allow a convoy of lorries into the courtyard.[145] They remained in occupation for several weeks, using the Four Courts as their new headquarters. There was minimal press coverage of the occupation, no military cordon was established around the complex and people were relatively free to come and go. Clerical staff, for example, frequently visited the Four Courts Hotel next door for lunch,[146] and the business of the courts continued much as usual.

Fighting in the Civil War began on 28 June and lasted for three days. The battle has been well documented, notably by Fewer,[147] who describes in detail the various explosions and the damage they caused. The biggest explosion, on 28 June, sent legal documents and books around the north city:[148]

A great shower of papers, legal documents and records of all kinds from the headquarters block was thrown hundreds of feet into the air in the explosion, and, lifted north-eastwards by the wind, began in time to fall to earth, like giant confetti, over a large area of the north inner city. Sackville St was not yet the battleground it would become within days, and people there gathered the sheets of paper that snowed down from the sky. Half an

---

142 See further ch. 11.   143 For background on the physical location and structure of the Four Courts, see Edward McParland, 'The old Four Courts, at Christ Church'; Colum Kenny, 'On holy ground: the benchers and the site of the present Four Courts before 1796' and Tomás Clancy, 'The Four Courts buildings and the development of an independent Bar of Ireland', all in Caroline Costello (ed.), *The Four Courts: 200 years* (Dublin, 1996).   144 (1921) 55 *I.L.T.S.J.* 140 (4 June 1921).   145 Michael Fewer, *The battle of the Four Courts: the first three days of the Irish Civil War* (London, 2018), p. 37.   146 Ibid., p. 57.   147 Ibid.   148 Ibid., pp 231–2. In 2022 the Courts Service of Ireland commemorated the events of 1922 through their 'Four Courts 100' project. This included a series of lectures, a photographic exhibition, guided walking tours of the Four Courts complex and the launch of an app for self-guided tours and historical background: www.courts.ie/acc/alfresco/7eea56a7–90ff–4782–9e22–56d7b2e87fd6/CourtsDecadeof CentenariesCommemorationsPosters.pdf/pdf#view=fitH. Many of the public lectures can be viewed at https://courts.ie/four-courts–100-lecture-series.

hour after the explosion, charred pages from law digests and law reports were still falling in the Dollymount area, 4.5 miles (7.2 km) away from the Four Courts.[149]

The dust had barely settled and the fires had not yet been extinguished when Hugh Kennedy, the law officer, wrote to Constantine Curran, registrar of the Supreme Court of Judicature.[150] At Kennedy's request, Curran visited the site to conduct a preliminary survey, and produced a written report detailing the state of the various buildings. He found that the round hall was 'in complete ruin,' with the courts leading off it 'not recognisable'. The east wing, which housed the two-storey Law Library, was 'completely gutted'. However, some parts of the complex were relatively unscathed, such as the lord justice's chamber in the north-east corner of the central hall. The cellars beneath the main block had flooded, but a large number of affidavits and judgments dating from the previous 20 years were only partially damaged. The site was still clearly a place of potential danger as Curran completed his inspection, as firemen were still working on the land registry, and he saw an unexploded mine in the record office.[151]

The courts and the Law Library had by this stage been operating out of the King's Inns for several weeks,[152] with solicitors being advised to call on members of the Bar at the King's Inns library.[153] By July, members of the legal professions were 'quite keenly interested'[154] in the question of accommodating the courts, the judges and the barristers. Lord Chief Justice Molony made available rooms in his Fitzwilliam Square home for the lunacy and minors courts.[155] Such public-spiritedness certainly eased the pressures of the beleaguered justice system, but these arrangements were not sustainable in the longer term. The *Irish Law Times* listed the 'chief requirements' of a replacement for the Four Courts as:

> Courts, accommodation for the judges, offices for the various departments, connected with the courts, a law library, and dressing rooms for the Bar, premises for the Incorporated Law Society and its officers. Storage for documents is also urgently required. It is absolutely essential that premises

---

149 Fewer, *Battle of the Four Courts*, p. 233. See also Ronan Keane, 'A mass of crumbling ruins: the destruction of the Four Courts in June 1922' in Costello (ed.), *The Four Courts*.   150 Kennedy to Curran, 3 July 1922, NAI AGO/2002/16/475.   151 Kennedy to chairman, provisional govt., 4 July 1922, enclosing Curran's report, NAI AGO/2002/16/475.   152 The *Irish Law Times* noted that 'the legal profession including barristers, solicitors, and a vast number of 'clerks', had a right to work like other members of the community.' (1922) 56 *I.L.T.S.J.* 103 (22 Apr. 1922). McEnery describes attending the courts in the King's Inns: P.J. McEnery, 'Ireland, 1900–50. Glimpses in retrospect', UCDA P174/1, p. 92. During the Covid-19 pandemic, the courts once more sat in the King's Inns, this time due to the need for social distancing: Mary Carolan, 'Supreme Court to rule later on "important and difficult" climate case', *Irish Times*, 23 June 2020.   153 (1922) 56 *I.L.T.S.J.* 104 (22 Apr. 1922).   154 (1922) 56 *I.L.T.S.J.* 171 (15, 22 July 1922).   155 Ibid.

for all the purposes we have mentioned should be, as formerly was the case at the Four Courts, closely connected with one another.[156]

It emphasised the urgency of the need to relocate, noting that 'the administration of the legal system in a country is as essential to its proper progress as its proper government – indeed it is part of it'.[157]

The minutes of the Bar Council record the destruction of the Four Courts in muted terms. On 14 July 1922, the Council met at the King's Inns, and it was simply noted that 'owing to the destruction of the Four Courts, the minutes of the last meeting were neither read nor signed'.[158] It was resolved to make representations to the provisional government regarding arrangements 'for carrying on the business of the courts and to see that proper accommodation is provided for the Bar'.[159]

The destruction affected members of the Bar in a number of ways. First, they had lost their communal workspace. Barristers needed a base from which to work, and where they could be contacted by solicitors. Second, they had lost one of the library's principal resources – its books. Third, they had lost their professional attire – their wigs and gowns.[160] Fourth, the paperwork and files relating to thousands of 'live' cases had been lost. And fifth, it is likely that the destruction had a less tangible, but no less significant impact on morale.

These problems had to be addressed, and the Bar Council was anxious to ensure that arrangements for carrying on the business of the courts should also cater for the needs of barristers.[161] One of the first matters to be dealt with was the issue of workspace. On 24 July, Hugh Kennedy wrote to the Department of Finance to point out that

> The business of the courts has been carried on since Easter in the buildings of the King's Inns, Henrietta Street, which were lent to the government for this purpose by the benchers of the King's Inns. This arrangement barely enabled the business (much reduced in volume owing to the general but temporary situation) to be carried on and that with very great inconvenience to everyone concerned. Nothing but sheer necessity made it tolerable even as a temporary expedient. It really could not continue.[162]

It was soon decided to relocate the courts, offices and Law Library to Dublin Castle,[163] which was deemed 'convenient for all concerned'.[164] The courts and

---

156 Ibid. 157 Ibid. 158 B.C.M., 14 July 1922. 159 Ibid., 9 Oct. 1922. 160 See, e.g., (1922) 56 *I.L.T.S.J.* 161 (1, 8 July 1922). 161 B.C.M., 14 July 1922. 162 Kennedy to Gregg, 24 July 1922, NAI AGO/2002/16/475. He was quick to add: 'I hope that the enquiries which I hear have been made do not indicate any intention to encroach upon the existing accommodation of the law department in the Castle. It has nothing to spare at present.' 163 This had also been suggested by the *Irish Law Times* as a suitable alternative venue: (1922) 56 *I.L.T.S.J.* 171 (15, 22 July 1922). 164 (1922) 56 *I.L.T.S.J.* 240 (23 Sept. 1922).

Bar continued to operate out of Kings Inns until the new library in St Patrick's Hall was ready for them.[165] The *Irish Law Times* reported that when the new legal year commenced in October, '[t]here was some disappointment that the larger and more convenient premises were not available, still, in view of the early removal to the promised courts at the Castle, there was a disposition to make the best of things and to carry on'.[166]

The next challenge stemmed from the destruction of the library's books. Without access to printed volumes of law reports, statutes and legal treatises, the work of the barrister would be challenging, to say the least. Kennedy was keenly aware of this, and quickly took steps to ensure that the Law Library could be restocked as soon as possible.[167] The third issue was professional attire. As reported by the *Irish Law Times*, 'barristers have lost their wigs and gowns and other possessions'.[168] For a period of time, barristers appeared wigless in court.[169] At one of the Bar Council's first meetings after the destruction of the Four Courts, a motion was discussed that 'members of the Bar should assume the wearing of a forensic costume as soon as possible'.[170] At a general meeting of the Bar in February 1923, a motion for the 'resumption of Bar costume'[171] was proposed. There is no indication of what they wore in the interim. By 1924 it was agreed that government compensation would cover the cost of replacing the wigs and gowns destroyed.[172] The costs of this could have been prohibitive for individual barristers, particularly those who were in the early stages of their careers.

Another problem stemming from the destruction was the loss of paperwork,[173] which also impacted various government departments. This was referred to by the *Cork Examiner* in an article in which the lord chief justice was described as feeling 'very keenly' 'the destruction of the documents relating to the care of the 1,100 lunatics under his care as the King's direct representative'.[174] The same newspaper also speculated that '[t[he destruction of purely legal documents in other parts of the Four Courts must lead to something approaching chaos in the administration of law for some years to come'.[175] An appeal published in the *Freeman's Journal* asked members of the public to turn in 'any documents or parts of documents, however fragmentary' that came into their possession.[176] A notice in the *Irish Law Times* in August 1922 repeated the

---

165 See ch. 11.   **166** (1922) 56 *I.L.T.S.J.* 259 (28 Oct. 1922).   **167** See pp 215–17.   **168** (1922) 56 *I.L.T.S.J.*161 (1, 8 July 1922).   **169** There was precedent for this: in 1920, the disruption to the rail network meant that barristers had to travel to the Munster Circuit in shared motor cars. Given the cramped conditions, they were given permission to forego their wigs and gowns. (1920) 54 *I.L.T.S.J.* 163 (10 July 1920).   **170** B.C.M., 9 Oct. 1922.   **171** B.C.M., 2 Feb. 1923.   **172** Reported in the *Examiner*, 7 Feb. 1924, p. 7.   **173** Even before the destruction of the Four Courts, in June 1922, the *Irish Law Times* noted that 'many cases have been held up owing to the fact that necessary documents relating to them are locked up in the Four Courts': 'Trinity term opened' (1922) 56 *I.L.T.S.J.* 144 (10 June 1922).   **174** *Examiner*, 3 July 1922, p. 6.   **175** Ibid.   **176** *Freeman's Journal*, 29 July 1922, p. 5.

appeal to the public to return documents or fragments of documents which they may have had in their possession following the explosion.[177] It noted that Herbert Wood, the deputy keeper, had written to the press pointing out that 'the documents belong to the nation, and that their detention may prevent persons from obtaining their rights through the absence of documentary evidence'.[178]

Finally, there was the impact of the destruction on morale, which was less tangible than the other problems recounted above. As the *Irish Law Times* observed, '[t]he legal profession has suffered a blow from which it will not recover for many years to come'.[179] While the response in this publication was rather low-key, there was some wailing in the press. Someone described as 'a distinguished member of the Bar' commented: 'some of my brethren are very pessimistic about the future of the Irish Bar'.[180] However, this admission of pessimism and negativity was accompanied by a more optimistic, cheering outlook. Outwardly at least, the prevailing attitude appears to have been one of making the best of things and getting on with the work.

＊＊＊

It would be wrong to suggest that the barristers' profession was entirely remote or cut off from the realities of the turbulent 1920s. The destruction of the courts, the beginnings of a changed social and professional role for women, the crafting of a new state and the navigation of its relationship with the other new state in the north all impacted upon, and were in turn impacted by, the Irish Bar. Lawyers, and barristers in particular, played a significant role in the development of the new state and the new national identity.[181] The 1920s Bar was also grappling with its post-independence identity, as evidenced by the sometimes fractious debates over professional attire[182] and Irish-language requirements for practising barristers.

---

177 (1922) 56 *I.L.T.S.J.* 193 (12 Aug. 1922).   178 Ibid.   179 (1922) 56 *I.L.T.S.J.* 161 (1, 8 July 1922).   180 *Irish Independent*, 7 July 1922.   181 See ch. 14. For an examination of the role of lawyers in the earlier revolutionary period, see Foxton, *Revolutionary lawyers*. Foxton describes the courtroom as another 'front' in the struggle, p. 14.   182 See pp 97–100.

CHAPTER THREE

Early careers at the Bar

Introduction

A barrister's career usually consisted of a number of phases, and in the twentieth century, the early stages were common to almost all. Those who were awarded a Barrister-at-Law degree by the King's Inns[1] were then called to the Bar in a formal ceremony. They often undertook a period of unpaid apprenticeship known as devilling, and then spent several years developing their practice, whether general or specialised, on circuit or in Dublin. Established junior counsel usually took on devils. This chapter examines the early years of a career at the Bar, and considers the motivations, pressures and expectations that led to certain career decisions. It questions the significance of having (or not having) family or professional connections. It also looks at how new barristers learned the professional culture, rules and expectations, and considers the role of serendipity in establishing a successful career.

Motivations

People had various motivations for joining the Bar. While some were following in a family tradition,[2] not everyone had family connections,[3] and those who did not considered themselves 'fortunate'[4] if they succeeded nevertheless.[5] Some had friends or met people who were barristers and who made it seem like an appealing career choice.[6] Several had been interested in debating at school or university.[7] Some turned to the Bar as a somewhat extreme reaction to exposure to the possibility of working in a solicitor's firm, for example:

> I was brought in to meet the family solicitor ... He was a very, very old tradition style solicitor. I think I probably lost interest when he said to me that I could apprentice to him and that all going well that when I qualified, I'd earn seven pounds a week ... I'd had summer jobs where I'd earned multiples of that, so I felt that maybe being a solicitor's apprentice wasn't

---

1 See the many valuable publications by Colum Kenny listed in the bibliography. See also Daire Hogan, *The legal profession in Ireland 1789–1922* (Dublin, 1986); Mary Finlay Geoghegan, 'The Honorable Society of King's Inns: developments in legal education, 1988–2013' in Daire Hogan and Colum Kenny (eds), *Changes in practice and law: a selection of essays by members of the legal profession to mark twenty-five years of the Irish Legal History Society* (Dublin, 2013). 2 E.g., B14, B15, B11, B26. 3 E.g., B12. 4 B17. 5 See pp 246–7. 6 E.g., B25. 7 B9, B10, B27.

quite for me. So I decided that the Bar was what I wanted to do and that's what I went for.[8]

I spent three months in a solicitor's office before I did the Bar and I walked out one day and said, 'oh my God, is this what they're doing?' They were talking about wills and conveyancing ... to me a nightmare.[9]

Very, very short experience of one day in a solicitor's office ... just one day. Less than a day.[10]

Some were steered towards the Bar by family members. One barrister who was called in the 1920s recalled that he had considered studying medicine, but while he was still in school his mother said that after a discussion with his father, she

Thought I would make a very good barrister. She asked me had I ever thought of that and I said I hadn't, because all I knew about the Bar was what I had read in books or seen on newspapers.[11]

He described finding out how to go about qualifying as a barrister:

The university authorities told me that one became a barrister-at-law through King's Inns Dublin and not through the university but that one could be a law student at King's Inns and also a student at the university at the same time and that in fact my first year of studies as a King's Inns student could be done in one of the Dublin universities, University College (UCD) or Trinity College (TCD), which ever the student preferred.[12]

While some barristers studied law at university, others had diverse educational backgrounds, with degrees in such disciplines as arts, mathematics, commerce, architecture, medicine or veterinary medicine. Some had either disliked or failed in these disciplines,[13] and found their way into law as a second choice.[14] Others were attempting to escape from a family business, or a career path that had been set out by their family.[15]

Not every barrister went through the King's Inns. An alternative pathway into the career was for a practising solicitor to be called to the Bar.[16] One such

---

8 B12.   9 B20.   10 B23.   11 P.J. McEnery, 'Look back in love: conversations by an English fireside', UCDA P74/2, p. 48. Aspiring King's Inns students had to be proposed by an established practising barrister, and McEnery recalled, p. 49: 'I did not know any practising barrister of ten years standing but I wrote to my former teacher of the old Knockbeg days ... she had become Mrs Kevin O'Higgins and her husband was Minister for Justice in the government. She immediately put me in touch with Mr John O'Byrne who was a well-known barrister of over ten years standing and he was very pleased to act as my proposer and I arranged to meet him.'   12 Ibid., p. 48.   13 E.g., B20.   14 B16.   15 E.g., B9, B5, B14.   16 E.g., James Geoghegan was called in 1915

barrister recalled being 'allowed to transfer relatively easily'. Another path to the Irish Bar was by way of a reciprocal call. From time to time, members of foreign Bars would contact the King's Inns asking to be called to the Irish Bar.[17] The King's Inns tended only to grant this to lawyers from jurisdictions with similarly divided professions, and not, for example, to American lawyers.[18] In many instances, the reciprocal call was a matter of courtesy, and there was no expectation of such barristers actually practising at the Irish Bar.[19] The situation might be different when it came to members of the English and Northern Irish Bars, who might have needed to appear in the Irish courts on occasion.[20]

The call to the Bar

New barristers were called to the Bar of the Supreme Court in order of merit, based on their performance in their final exams at the King's Inns. In the first decades after 1922, the number of barristers being called on a particular day could be quite low,[21] but there was nevertheless a sense of occasion. A barrister who was called in 1926 recalled the procedure:

Now the student who is awaiting his call … remains seated in the Supreme Court until he hears his name called out by the chief justice. That call (which is his 'call' to the Bar) is the signal for him to rise and hear what the judge has to say to him. The judge, addressing him both in Irish and English, informs him that 'the benchers of the Honourable Society of the King's Inns having been pleased to admit you to the degree of barrister-at-law, I now admit you to practise in the courts of Ireland and you will take your place accordingly'. The judge then asks him: – 'Do you move anything?' In putting that question the judge is both acknowledging the barrister's newly-acquired right of audience and is also inviting him to exercise that right by proposing a motion for the consideration of the court. The answer to that question is so obvious that, in practice, it is not answered. Instead the barrister bows his head before the judge as if to say: 'Have I your Lordship's permission to retire from the court?' The judge, of course, acknowledges the bow; and the young barrister withdraws from the court having exercised, for the first time in his life, his right of

having already qualified and practised as a solicitor. See Ferguson, *Barristers*, p. 192 and Pauric J. Dempsey, 'Geoghegan, James', *D.I.B.* 17 Some foreign lawyers wrote to the Department of Justice, the Department of Foreign Affairs or even the president: NAI JUS/90/113/4. 18 The benchers tended to keep themselves informed of what the requirements were for Irish barristers to be called to other common law Bars; whether, for example, there were residency or intention to practise requirements: e.g., K.I.B.M., 12 Jan. 1976. See further ch. 13. 19 In the 1980s, for example, the Bar Council considered whether it would be 'desirable that a great many Australians from the state of Victoria should be called in Ireland because they wish to do so for sentimental reasons.' B.C.M., 19 Oct. 1986. 20 See ch. 13. 21 See ch. 5.

audience before a judge, and in the highest court of the land, the Supreme Court.[22]

Most barristers recalled the sense of occasion on the day of their call; for example,

> It was a big day for me ... I thought I was lucky to get through most of my exams pretty well, and obviously my parents were as proud as punch.[23]

> We were all dressed up. I think I had borrowed my cousin's clothes, court clothes, which of course were much too big for me.[24]

For many, it was a family occasion; one barrister who was called in the 1950s remembered his mother and 'some of the other relatives' travelling to Dublin for the ceremony,[25] while another recalled a 'big day out' with cousins, aunts and uncles.[26]

A barrister who was called in 1938 recollected that the ceremony '[made] much of the new barrister's first day wearing the wig and gown'.[27] These were the trappings of the profession, along with a dark suit or skirt, white bands or tabs and a brief-bag.[28] Some barristers describe feeling conscious of the newness of their 'glossy white'[29] wigs at the start of their careers, and others actively sought second-hand items.[30] Lindsay, for example, describes the wig he acquired in the 1940s as

> A very old horse hair wig, a genuine article, very dirty, very stained ... The wig was of vital importance but it was also important to get it as cheaply as possible. This particular wig lasted for nearly forty years. It didn't look great, but it looked experienced.[31]

Barristers' professional attire is considered in more detail in chapter six.

Devilling

After being called to the Bar, a new barrister usually entered into a period of pupillage or 'devilling' with a more established junior counsel, known as a master, who generally had at least seven years' experience at the Bar.[32] Because so little time was spent on studying practice and procedure at the King's Inns, it

---

22 Bernard Shillman, 'Every journey has an end', NAI PRIV1367/11, pp 6–7. 23 B9. 24 B10.
25 B19. 26 B26. 27 T.F. O'Higgins, *A double life* (Dublin, 1996), p. 70. 28 See pp 94–100.
29 O'Higgins, *Double life*, p. 88. 30 In 1969, Oliver J. Flanagan commented, 'I have seen some counsel in court wearing gowns which must also have been worn early in the last century. They have turned green with age': Dáil Éireann deb., vol. 243, no. 1 (2 Dec. 1969). 31 Patrick Lindsay, *Memories* (Dublin, 1992), pp 98–9. 32 E.g., B11, B12. Sometimes masters took on devils sooner than this, particularly when there was a large influx of new barristers.

was essential that the new barrister learn 'on the job'. Reflecting on his early career in the 1930s, Mackey wrote:

> It is conceivable that on the completion of his studies [a new barrister] would be qualified to hold a junior brief in one case in a hundred in the Supreme Court ... It is almost certain that he will never have seen a brief for counsel, or know the difference between a summary summons and a civil bill, both of which he will meet every day of his practising life. It is absolutely certain that he will not have the faintest idea how to cross-examine a reluctant witness or, what is far more artistic and difficult, how to examine a garrulous one.[33]

Devilling provided the new barrister with a chance to learn 'some of the tricks of the trade',[34] as well as opportunities to begin to develop his or her own professional network. The importance of securing a 'good' master was emphasised by several interviewees:

> Your choice of master is very important ... you can still make a mess of it if you have a good master but if you have a bad master or an unsuitable master it is troublesome.[35]

> If you have a bad master you're off to a very bad start and that's the reality of it and there are some masters who will never recommend you for anything. They'll never say 'why don't you try your man? give him a bit of business'.[6]

There were several features of a 'bad' master mentioned by interviewees, including a failure to give the devil work, a failure to explain things adequately, a failure to introduce the devil to solicitors, or:

> Somebody who had no work or very little work, I don't mean they would be unkind but they would have nothing for you to do ... a bad master would be someone who doesn't prepare you properly, who doesn't give you sufficient details, who doesn't ... warn you about you know the possible pitfalls.[37]

Of course, the newly called barrister did not always know what would make a good master, and furthermore, was not in a position to be choosy. First, potential masters were not always willing to take on devils, given the time it required.[38] Some would-be masters were reluctant to take on devils because they felt that

---

33 Rex Mackey, *Windward of the law* (2nd ed. 1991, Dublin), p. 22. 34 O'Higgins, *Double life*, p. 74. 35 B21. 36 B20. 37 B21. 38 O'Higgins, for example, describes approaching several people as potential masters, only to be rebuffed. Eventually, Paddy McGilligan, who had taught him

they did not have sufficient court work for them. For example, one former master ascribed this reluctance to 'devils sitting in the coffee room complaining about how "so and so is never in court."'[39] In their opinion, people did not 'want to be bad-mouthed by some devil harping on about how they're not busy enough'. A Cork-based barrister who was called in the late forties said that at that time, 'no one ever devilled in Cork', and for this reason he never took on devils.[40] Some potential masters placed barriers in the way of potential devils; for example, Hugh Kennedy was said to have insisted that someone who wished to devil with him 'should first take lessons from a writing master'.[41] The practice of charging devils is considered in a later section below.

Second, having a network was important, something considered in more detail in chapter twelve. Those without family connections sometimes found it 'very hard'[42] to find a master, while those with connections fared better, and interviewees cited parents, uncles and siblings who were quite easily able to secure masters for them.[43] One interviewee recalled a potential master who 'went around asking people did they know me', and because some had known the interviewee's father, the master agreed. Similarly, having friends already at the Bar[44] or friends who were solicitors[45] was generally very helpful. Having a strong connection with a political party could also be helpful; one interviewee recalled asking their local TD to set them up with a master. These networks and referrals worked informally, which meant that there were no official guidelines and no easily-accessible directory of eligible masters. In many cases, it was a matter of writing to, faxing or telephoning a relative stranger, perhaps based on a recommendation from a 'friend of a friend'. For example:

> I spoke to a guy that was in my class in the Inns and he devilled with a very nice woman ... I just sent her a fax ... I rang her then and said, you know, 'can I devil for you?' and she said 'well you'd have to come and see me. We'll have to see if we get on'. So, I thought, okay, fine. So, I trotted off duly out to her house.

> I had a vague connection through a friend of mine. A friend of mine was related to a senior counsel ... And he knew a junior counsel on my circuit, ... and he thought he would be a brilliant master, but he hadn't had a previous devil, so he had to convince him to take on a devil ... X eventually agreed and he was brilliant. He was also very nice and extremely knowledgeable.[46]

constitutional law at UCD, agreed to take him on. O'Higgins, *Double life*, p. 76. As it turned out, O'Higgins had received a brief on the Midland Circuit in the meantime and decided to focus on circuit work instead of devilling. Other people were much more accessible as masters, and would accept anyone who asked; e.g., B2. 39 B10. 40 'Ralph Sutton, SC, called to the Bar, July 1948', *B.R.* 4:3 (1999), 152. 41 C.P. Curran, *Under the receding wave* (Dublin, 1970), p. 120. 42 B8. 43 B15, B10, B25, B26. 44 B17, B23. 45 B5. 46 B18.

I went to my course tutor … he looked at his list of former students and he said 'the man that we get you to meet is X, criminal law, and you'll do criminal and constitutional law and protect the rights of the oppressed'. So I went down and I met with X who said 'what a load of cobblers'. He said 'if you have sense and you're a country boy … you'll devil with Y who is one of the leading members of the Midland Circuit … forget all the romantic notion of defending the criminals and doing constitutional cases; get down and get a solid practise on circuit where you get a full exposure to criminal law, civil law, family law, all and everything …' And that's what I did.

When women at the Bar were a rarity, they sometimes faced additional challenges in securing a master. Reflecting on her early career at the Bar, Mary Robinson recalled some of the difficulty:

The choice of who would be my master was a big issue because I was one of only a tiny handful of women barristers at the Bar. The idea of having a young female barrister on the somewhat chauvinistic, conservative Western Circuit, where I would plead cases in the courts in the main towns of Galway and Mayo, seemed like a joke in itself as far as some of the men were concerned.[47]

Sometimes, having secured a master, the arrangements fell through, perhaps because the master took silk or was appointed to the bench.[48] Even worse were instances where the potential devil was dropped by the master; one barrister recalled: 'X was basically better connected so I got dumped'.[49]

Once the devil had been called to the Bar and the relationship formally commenced, he or she could shadow their master, read their briefs and other documents, help with simple drafting and appear in court on the master's behalf for straightforward motions and applications, such as uncontested adjournments. O'Higgins described how a devil might learn through observation 'how to examine a witness and how to present evidence'.[50] While some masters involved their devils as much as possible, others took a very hands-off approach.[51] For example, O'Higgins' prospective master had told him:

That while he would not accept any responsibility toward me as a regular master, I could nevertheless look through his brief-bag, read any briefs I thought interesting, familiarise myself with pleadings and ask him any relevant questions which, if he had time, he would endeavour to answer. It was not everything, but it was something.[52]

47 Mary Robinson, *Everybody matters: a memoir* (London, 2013), p. 56.   48 E.g., B5.   49 E.g., B10.   50 O'Higgins, *Double life*, p. 74.   51 See further pp 47–8.   52 O'Higgins, *Double life*, p. 76.

Devilling could sometimes be a very negative experience. Most barristers reflected that they learned a lot during their year as a devil, but many said it was stressful,[53] with various descriptions of masters as 'a tyrant'; 'a most intimidating individual' and 'a serious task master'. One recalled a very stressful encounter:

> I definitely and distinctly remember crying one day, breaking into tears … when for the umpteenth time he took a pen from his pocket and ran it through a civil bill indorsement I had drafted and I thought this was word perfect because he had already scratched it four or five times … I just really felt humiliated.

Some devils found that they disliked the type of practise that their master had,[54] or found that their masters were too busy to spend time with them.[55] Sometimes the master and devil simply did not get along.[56] As one barrister said,

> It just sometimes breaks down. It just doesn't work. Sometimes just because it is a complete personal clash. Sometimes because the master isn't very good at teaching, doesn't explain or the master's practice is very busy … the devil would be kind of thrown in and expected to do things. The master would be elsewhere, and the devil doesn't really know what they're doing or doesn't have the confidence, gets bitten by a judge once or twice and loses confidence.[57]

Those who had positive experiences of devilling cited various reasons for this. Some got along very well with their master on a personal level.[58] Some were very interested in the type of work their master did.[59] Some were impressed by their master's knowledge[60] or their work ethic.[61] Some appreciated being introduced to solicitors who might later brief them,[62] and being given work to do.[63] For example, one said of their master,

> He gave me a lot of work to do and gave me a lot of exposure which a lot of masters didn't do. They're always afraid to give their devils work … in case the devils would … take off their practice.

Another recalled feeling very supported when, during their first motion, the master stood in court 'and was prompting me from the wings'.[64]

One of the perceived advantages of devilling was the mentoring provided by the master.[65] Masters taught substantive law and procedure, but they also taught their devils the relevant professional norms and etiquette, how to navigate the politics of the Bar and how to conduct themselves professionally. Usually they

53 B13.　54 B4.　55 B7.　56 B10.　57 B10.　58 B17, B3.　59 B1.　60 B2, B9.　61 B3.
62 B17.　63 B13.　64 B22.　65 O'Higgins, *Double life*, p. 74.

made introductions for their devils to help them develop their professional networks.[66] Some devils were conscious of the slight conflict of interest here for their masters: 'I was always very fortunate in getting along with the solicitors but I made sure at the same time by not treading on the corns of my "master" by getting in too quickly with his favourites.'[67] One barrister recalled that their master 'taught me the Law Library',[68] and another said that devilling 'definitely gives you a close up insight into the network that is the whole Library and how it works'.[69] In some cases the mentoring provided by the master extended beyond the year or so of devilling, and some masters and devils maintained strong professional links for the duration of the devil's career. One barrister described the ongoing role of the master as being 'the go-to person if you have a problem'.[70] One interviewee said they continued to receive advice and mentorship from their master throughout their whole career.[71] Others had similar experiences, for example:

> We stayed on very good terms and he's … somebody I still get on with … we don't tend to work in the same field anymore because of the way things panned out but he would be a good friend and colleague.[72]

Sometimes these relationships developed into sexual or romantic relationships, and this was alluded to by some interviewees.

All of the persons who devilled for a particular master were known as a devil-family, consisting of devil-brothers, -sisters, -mothers and -fathers as appropriate. Some of these families even went so far as to include second-generation devils (the devil's devil). This was an important support network for barristers; members of the same devil-family looked out for one another, and the relationships were horizontal as well as vertical.[73]

The parameters of the devilling arrangement changed over the course of the twentieth century in several respects. First, by the close of the twentieth century it was obligatory for a new barrister to spend a minimum of one year devilling. In the nineteenth century, the decision whether or not to devil was a personal one, and not everyone did it. By the early twentieth century devilling had become the norm,[74] though it was still done on a voluntary basis. There was generally a lack of uniformity when it came to devilling,[75] and in the early eighties the chairman of the Bar acknowledged that 'it had been apparent for some time that the system

---

66 B2. 67 McEnery, 'Look back', p. 74. 68 B7. 69 B24. 70 B27. 71 B11. 72 B10.
73 B24. 74 In the early 1960s, the benchers of the King's Inns requested the Bar Council's opinion as to whether graduates of the Inns ought to be required to undergo a period of pupillage either before or after their call to the Bar. It was decided to set up a sub-committee to discuss the matter and report back to the council: Bar Council minutes (B.C.M.), 3 May 1963. 75 The Fair Trade Commission was quite critical of this in the 1980s. It noted that there was 'no formal routine control by the Bar Council over, or monitoring of, the progress of the pupillage; it is left to the master to ensure that each pupil benefits appropriately'. Fair Trade Commission, *Report of study*

of pupillage at the Bar was not working'.[76] With the support of the chief justice, the attorney general and the Bar Council's education committee, the Council passed a resolution that both pupillage and 'mastership' be made compulsory'.[77]

Second, by the late twentieth century, some people opted for a second year of devilling, with a different master.[78] Often this was to gain experience in different areas; for example, someone whose master only did criminal work might have wanted to try out some civil work.[79] There is some indication that barristers earlier in the century may have devilled for more than one master, but this would have been exceptional.[80]

Third, by the close of the century it was becoming common for masters to pay a small stipend to their devils, or allow them to keep the fees for their motions.[81] However, in the past people had paid for the privilege of being allowed to devil. In the 1920s, the standard rate was said to be around fifty guineas,[82] while in the 1930s it was around a hundred pounds.[83] This practice seems to have persisted for several decades, but someone who recalled a master doing this in the mid-eighties said it was unusual at that stage and was considered 'just bloody mean'.[84]

Early career experiences

Whether or not they devilled, many barristers recall feeling nervous when they were 'very raw and innocent'[85] at the start of their career. They described it as 'daunting'[86] or 'really frightening'.[87] Some felt ill-prepared, and this exacerbated their anxiety:

> You could be hired to defend a murderer theoretically on your first day ... the likelihood of that happening was nil but at the same time ... you were being thrown on the open market without any experience really.[88]

A barrister who was called in the 1940s said 'when I came into the Law Library I didn't know what a writ was, or a civil bill. I knew nothing about pleadings.'[89]

---

into restrictive practices in the legal profession (Dublin, 1990), para. 7.27.   76 B.C.M., 5 Jan. 1982. 77 B.C.M., 15 Apr. 1983. In 1983, the chairman suggested that a panel of masters be drawn up and that 'intending entrants should be interviewed as to their interests on circuits, specialisation etc. in order to match them to a Master.' B.C.M., 11 June 1983. However, this probably proved to be too labour-intensive and by 1988 it had not yet been carried out. B.C.M., 12 Mar. 1988.   78 A newspaper article in 1990 noted that most barristers devilled for two years. Harry Browne, 'Sitting at the feet of the master – or exploitation?', Irish Times, 9 Nov. 1990, p. 2.   79 E.g., B24.   80 In a letter asking for certification to be called to the English Bar, a barrister who had been called in 1957 named three people for whom he had devilled. Letter dated 28 Feb. 1967, NAI 2009/74/742. 81 B23.   82 McEnery, 'Look back', p. 74.   83 O'Higgins, Double life, p. 74.   84 B7. 85 McEnery, 'Look back', p. 70.   86 B3.   87 B15. B5 said that their early negative experiences affected them for years: 'I was damaged and hurt, and the experience of the young counsel ... who is doing advocacy who has got the brunt of criticism from either his colleagues or from the court is forever.'   88 B15.   89 Lindsay, Memories, p. 97.

Another recalled having 'some ghastly experiences ... Because, you know, I was doing cases I knew nothing about.' Barristers described the sometimes excruciating and often tedious experience of waiting around for briefs in the early stages of their career:

> It was just boring and frustrating ... You have to sit there for years and wait. And it was difficult.[90]

> I was rather like the substitute on the sideline at a football match, who watches the game but whose services are never in fact required.[91]

> There is no greater trial in life than to be a young barrister, with youthful brains and energy, eager to work, but obliged to wait around in the back seats of a courtroom, listening to performances of little skill and waiting for solicitors to come up with a brief.[92]

In their first year or so of practice, hundreds of hours might be spent sitting in courtrooms observing the advocacy of others. A considerable amount of informal learning took place in this manner. On circuit, the received wisdom was that in order to be briefed, one had to be frequently seen:

> Being a devil or a junior barrister is like a chicken and egg. Until you get briefed solicitors don't know how good you are, they won't give you a brief until they find out how good you are.[93]

Very junior barristers who were anxious to start their careers would usually accept any work that was available; one recalled 'doing whatever I could get my hands on'.[94] This was partly to be 'seen to be working'[95] and also to gain important experience: 'You learn on your feet, literally.'[96]

Becoming established

Morison and Leith describe the 'compulsory chapter' in most barristers' biographies 'about how the famous advocate nearly relinquished the unequal struggle to survive and prosper at the Bar'.[97] That narrative was certainly evident in some of the interviews for this book, as well as in some of the published and unpublished biographies and memoirs considered. Morison and Leith further observe that '[t]he initial problem of finding work of any sort usually disappears for the successful barrister: if it does not, the unsuccessful barrister disappears.'[98]

---

90 B4.   **91** O'Higgins, *Double life*, pp 87–8.   **92** Patrick MacKenzie, *Lawful occasions: the old Eastern Circuit* (Cork, 1991).   **93** B20.   **94** B21.   **95** B21.   **96** B3.   **97** John Morison and Philip Leith, *The barrister's world and the nature of law* (Berkshire, 1992), p. 24.   **98** Ibid.

Various factors might combine in the early years of a barrister's practice for them to deem themselves (or for others to consider them) successful. First, many ascribed their success to having worked very hard in their early years. For example,

> I worked very hard, but I didn't mind working hard ... I worked very, very hard ... And that is why I continued getting the work ... when you produced it you got another brief.[99]

The culture of working long hours and weekends is discussed further in chapters six and seven. This was a common feature of many barristers' practices, especially in their early years. For example:

> Every night I'd be drafting things and I'd spend three or four hours ... just doing paperwork at night ... You could do three different types of case in the one night and ... you might draft an equity civil bill, you might do the proofs for a common law civil bill just to prove it at a trial and you might draft an answer, say, in a landlord and tenant matter for something for a tenant. So, you know, you were doing an awful lot of different work.[100]

Second, several barristers cited serendipitous encounters that gave them their first 'break'. One barrister said that early in their career they got work for one insurance company through 'an extraordinary mixture of haphazard luck' and then suddenly they were very visible to other insurance companies. Soon they were being briefed by all of the major insurance firms. Another recalled being briefed by someone who worked in an insurance company because they knew the barrister's mother. McKenzie wrote that he got his first case because the barrister who was supposed to take it was absent.[101] Some barristers got their first briefs by virtue of geographical good fortune; for example, McEnery recalled sitting in the Bar room on his first day on circuit when a solicitor came in and said 'You're young McEnery, a Ballyhale man like myself, I want to give you a brief'.[102]

Third, some barristers developed a reputation for having expertise by publishing books and articles. One who had published in a relevant area said that this 'generated some interest and some work.'[103] Similarly, Shillman recalled:

> My immediate objective, as soon as I became a member of the Law Library in January 1934, was to put the finishing touches to the manuscripts of the

---

99 B1. 100 B5. 101 MacKenzie, *Lawful occasions*, p. 23. 102 McEnery, 'Look back', p. 70.
103 B17.

treatise I was then preparing for the press on the law relating to employers' liability and workmen's compensation.[104]

His book was published in August 1934,[105] just as the Workmen's Compensation Act 1934 came into force:

> I, who was then a relatively unknown junior barrister, found that my book had already begun to pay dividends. From all parts of the country, I received from solicitors cases to advise them in regard to accidents which had just occurred to workmen.[106]

Finally, there were sometimes other qualities which barristers considered key to their success. One said, for example,

> I pretty quickly got into a criminal practice and … I developed a very good criminal practice, I think largely because I wasn't afraid of people and I would shout at judges, at the witnesses and be rude to the judges and that was the qualification to build up a practice.

Whatever led to them receiving their first big brief, there was often a clear snowball effect, where one chance encounter led to subsequent briefs, or to the development of a key relationship and the beginnings of a reputation.

There was a general expectation that one would take on devils after being in practice for six to eight years.[107] Some were put off accepting devils because they did not consider themselves to have the right type of practice;[108] for example, they may not have had much courtroom work:

> When you have a devil you kind of feel like you have to be putting them in the way and doing all the things that a master should do to make their career work and I didn't think I was necessarily in that place.[109]

> I was slow to take on a devil and in fact, ultimately, I had my arm twisted by a colleague who was on the Bar Council who said I should be taking a devil … I felt somebody would devil with me and there wouldn't be an immediate stream of work for them … I had sort of felt I didn't have a devil-friendly practice and then I was kind of frogmarched into taking devils. So, I had about five in the end.

---

104 Bernard Shillman, 'Every journey has an end', NAI PRIV1367/11, p. 15. 105 Bernard Shillman, *The law relating to employers' liability and workmen's compensation in the Irish Free State* (Dublin, 1934). This book was reviewed as far away as the United States: Samuel B. Horovitz, 'Employers' liability and workmen's compensation in Ireland. Second edition by Bernard Shillman' *J.A.B.A.* 32:2 (1946), 105. 106 Shillman, 'Every journey', p. 39. 107 B27. 108 B22. 109 B24.

Asked to evaluate their experience as a master, one barrister said:

> It's a very odd relationship because it is very personalised. You're with somebody constantly or they're with you constantly … They're working with you, for you – or a lot of the time they're not working; they're just there.[110]

Most masters described taking on devils as a help rather than a hindrance:[111]

> It meant also that when you were on circuit that motions and straightforward matters they could handle on your behalf in Dublin. They could also do some research for you, do draft pleadings and as you got busier; that was important. And also, it was enjoyable being able to give them some help or some steer in relation to their work.[112]

Those who took on devils fell into two camps. Some felt a strong sense of responsibility towards their devils, and actively helped them:

> You felt that they wanted to learn and you should make it possible for them to learn as much as they possibly could.[113]

> I'd ask them to do a draft for instance and I would then independently do my own pleadings and then I would give them sight of what I'd drafted, and then I might correct their draft – but I never used their draft.

> You're trying to teach them for the first year and making sure you're explaining things properly and then you're trying to look for opportunities to introduce them to people, bring them to social events so they learn how to network and then afterwards trying to put in a word for them with different people to see if you can get them onto panels … you know, try and make them visible.[114]

Others took a more relaxed approach: 'I didn't think it onerous at all. Basically, they sort of tagged along, you know. They could look at all your papers.' Similarly, another recalled, 'I just kind of kept a running commentary as we walked up and down the stairs'. This again highlights how difficult it might be for an incoming barrister to evaluate a prospective master.

* * *

Generalisations about 'typical' careers at the Bar cannot reflect all the myriad experiences of barristers in the twentieth century. There were as many career

110 B10.   111 B12.   112 B23.   113 B1.   114 B24.

variations as there were practising barristers. However, this chapter identifies some common themes from barristers' accounts of their own experiences, and finds commonalities as well as divergences. In the twentieth century, most people devilled, but some had quite negative experiences of this. The typical barrister found that their career got off to a slow start, but there were always the exceptional few who, for various reasons, found themselves getting relatively busy at an early stage. Unsurprisingly attitudes, expectations and practises relating to early careers at the Bar evolved over an eighty-year period. The importance of the collegiality so emphasised by barristers will be further explored in chapter twelve. It will also be seen that this pressure to keep up appearances could be a significant source of stress for barristers.[115]

115 Ch. 7.

CHAPTER FOUR

Taking silk and beyond

Introduction

The previous chapter considered the early stages of the barrister's career, including devilling, the early years in practice, and becoming established. At a certain point, some barristers contemplated applying to join the inner Bar as senior counsel. This was a significant decision in the professional life of a barrister. The process was known as 'taking silk', because of the fabric of their robes. Motivations for taking silk varied, but the impact was generally perceived as being positive. This chapter also looks at the procedures and processes to be involved in taking silk. Some barristers later became judges or served as attorneys general, while others moved on to different careers beyond the Bar. Not everyone chose this path, and many barristers elected to remain at the junior, or outer Bar.

The significance of taking silk

A patent of precedence was granted by the government to enable a barrister to practise at the inner Bar, or senior Bar, as it was sometimes known. Charles Gavan Duffy, when he was president of the High Court, described senior counsel as 'lawyers of special ability and men of experience ... a group apart.'[1] There were both performative and practical aspects to being a member of the inner Bar. As Dawson writes,

> One step closer to the bench, physically and perhaps also in professional aspiration, the elite members of the inner Bar are clearly visible from the arrangement of the court and from the fact that, by virtue of an unwritten sumptuary rule, queen's counsel wear silk while juniors wear 'stuff' gowns.[2]

---

1 Gavan Duffy, 'Memorandum in favour of the amalgamation of barristers and solicitors, June 1946', NAI TSCH/3/S13867, p. 12. He wrote, p. 13, that they 'should be an asset to the nation.' 2 N.M. Dawson, 'The rank of queen's counsel: judicial perspectives', *King's L.J.* 24 (2013), 38, at 38. See also J.H. Baker, *The common law tradition: lawyers, books and the law* (London, 2000), ch 7. Dawson traces the evolution of the rank of Queen's (or senior) counsel from the time of Elizabeth I's appointment of Bacon. She notes, at 39, that '[i]nitially, this was the device used by the monarchy to ensure the speedy despatch of crown litigation, but when queen's/king's counsel became simply a promoted rank within the Bar, the patent right of precedence and pre-audience gained

Barristers being called to the inner Bar wore a full-bottomed wig, rather than the short wig worn by junior counsel.[3] So, outwardly there was new professional attire, a new physical location within the courtroom, and precedence in the listing of cases. Practically, it meant more courtroom advocacy and less paperwork; larger fees,[4] and a greater likelihood of eventual appointment to the bench.

In the early years of the Free State, members of the inner Bar were still known as 'king's counsel' or KCs.[5] The only king's counsel actually called in the Irish Free State was John O'Byrne, in a special ceremony in June 1924, just after his appointment as attorney general.[6] The following month, the first group of new silks were called in a revised ceremony at Dublin Castle. The *Irish Law Times* noted that the barristers were 'not called "king's counsel", but are merely called "within the Bar"'.[7] The chief justice called the barristers' names first in Irish, then in English.[8] The patent of precedence granted the new silks the right of 'precedence and pre-audience ... to rank immediately after those who are now King's counsel'.[9] Some resented the change, and a commentator in the *Irish Law Times* complained in 1924 that no explanation had been given for the decision to create the title of 'senior counsel'.[10] Although members of the inner Bar were no longer officially called king's counsel, many retained the appellation for years afterwards.[11]

Deciding to take silk

The decision to take silk was not without its risks; the barrister left behind their existing, presumably successful, practice and essentially began anew. Delany described it as 'that step in the career of every established junior which may end in the glory of success or in the extinction of mediocrity'.[12] The Bar Council remarked in its evidence to the Fair Trade Commission in the 1980s that

> The decision to take silk was the biggest in the life of a barrister, even bigger than the initial decision to join the Bar. Their original very

professional significance'.   3 See pp 94–7.   4 Hogan, *The legal profession in Ireland*, pp 80–1. 5 Hogan, however, notes that the term 'senior counsel' was 'in use long before it was formally adopted in the Irish Free State as an individual designation': ibid., p. 78.   6 (1924) 58 *I.L.T.S.J.* 152 (14 June 1924).   7 (1924) 58 *I.L.T.S.J.* 180 (19 July 1924).   8 These were Ernest Phelps, Vincent Rice, John Fitzgerald, William Carson, Joseph O'Connor, William Shannon and Kenneth Dockrell: (1924) 58 *I.L.T.S.J.* 152 (14 June 1924).   9 (1924) 58 *I.L.T.S.J.* 180 (19 July 1924). 10 Ibid. See Eamonn Hall, 'Mr Solicitor', *L. Soc. Gazette* 99:3 (April 2005), 14.   11 Hugh Geoghegan, 'The relationship of the attorney general to Bar and bench' in Blathna Ruane et al. (eds), *Law and government: a tribute to Rory Brady* (Dublin, 2014), p. 68. In 1949 the issue of John A. Costello continuing to use the appellation 'KC' was raised: Dáil Éireann deb., vol. 114, no. 4 (24 Feb. 1949). As late as 1958 the use of the designation 'QC' was being debated by the Council for Law Reporting: Eamonn G. Hall, *The superior courts of law: 'official' law reporting in Ireland 1866–2006* (Dublin, 2007), p. 191.   12 V.T.H. Delany, *Christopher Palles, lord chief baron of her majesty's*

successful and high income practice disappeared overnight and, while many were successful as seniors, others were not and suffered a severe drop in income.'[13]

One of the barristers interviewed for this book recalled:

> I had gone from rags to riches really, relatively speaking and so ... if I chip in and become a senior counsel ... I'm not going to be the big senior counsel. I'm going to be at the bottom of the heap. I'm going from the top of the heap to the bottom of the heap.

A number of interviewees spoke of mulling over the decision for some time. Many found it to be a stressful decision to take, and spoke of being 'absolutely terrified.' They mentioned 'soul searching' and 'hesitation'. A significant cause of worry was the potential financial hit:

> You're always worried of course that if you took silk if you had a busy junior practice that was remunerative in sustaining you, in taking silk you're in effect starting off again.[14]

> I think it depends on your financial commitments as well and your desires around money.[15]

Barristers cited different reasons for making the decision to take silk. One common theme was the desire to achieve a more balanced workload,[16] and reduce 'the volume of paperwork as a junior'.[17] Another summed this up as follows:

> In truth you're driven to do it you know by just too many late nights and too much paperwork ... you can't handle the stuff any longer, as I say the late nights, early mornings and the drudgery of paperwork ... just feeling you're being pulled in a hundred directions.

Some sought a better work–life balance,[18] while others came to realise that they simply felt ready for the change because of longevity; for example, feeling like it was 'the right time ... a logical next step'[19] after fourteen or sixteen years of practice. Others were being led by silks who they did not regard as significantly more senior to them, and

> They say that if, as a junior, you start a lot of the gown pulling and tugging to tell people what you think they should be saying, that that's the time to take silk.[20]

Court of Exchequer in Ireland 1874–1916: his life and times (Dublin, 1960), p. 47.   13 Fair Trade Commission, *Report of study into restrictive practices in the legal profession* (Dublin, 1990), para. 7.110. 14 B23.   15 B13.   16 E.g., B23.   17 B11.   18 B11. Also B9, B13 and B19.   19 B1.   20 B11.

I wanted to lead. You get to a point when you're a junior counsel and you're sitting behind somebody and you're thinking about the ten questions that they haven't asked that you would have asked and you're sort of saying 'God, I wish I could get at this case and control it' ... I was ready to just try and move into the driver's seat rather than being, you know, the passenger or the co-pilot ... I wanted to take over the running of the case.[21]

I want to be the one running the show. I'm good enough now. I have enough experience. I can do this ... I don't want to just sit behind.[22]

Others were simply frustrated ('I was learning nothing new'[23]) and felt 'a desire to change and a desire for a new challenge'.[24] One relished the thought of taking on more 'interesting work'.[25] A barrister who took silk in the 1980s recalled that a number of senior silks were appointed to the bench in a relatively short period, and consequently there was perceived to be a need for more people to take silk around that period.[26]

Most barristers who were interviewed for this book characterised the decision to apply for silk as a risky one. However, not everyone agonised over the decision, for example:

I never really thought that I could take silk and that it wouldn't work out ... I never really was in that mindset. I always assumed that if you work hard enough and you provide a good enough service people will come back, you know, and I didn't see it really as a risk.

Possibly slightly naively, I was prepared to take that risk because the consequences to me of total failure or something didn't seem as high as they might be for other people.

Another was sanguine about the decision: 'I felt it was a good thing to do. It's something you know yourself ... I just felt the time was right.'[27] Others highlighted ways that the risk could be mitigated:

There was a cushioning effect of the two senior-rule[28] at the time. Every case had two seniors in it because the senior who opened to the jury was not supposed to close to the jury so you would come in as a second silk and that's much easier and you learn the trade that way and it was easily got over in fact.[29]

I was lucky I was sufficiently broadly-based I think with my solicitors. I got good support from the circuit.[30]

21 B16. 22 B13. 23 B18. 24 B13. 25 B23. 26 B27. 27 B17. 28 See further ch. 6 and 8.
29 B15. 30 B23.

One interviewee said the decision to take silk was made easier by the fact that they had no children and no large mortgage to worry about.[31] Emotional support was also important for some, and those who were in relationships often credited their partner with providing this; for example:

> My wife [said], 'you've always wanted to go in there and be called to the inner Bar', and I thought 'oh I think she's right, I'll chance it.' And she says, 'I supported you when you had nothing … listen, we'll manage, don't worry about it.'

Some were encouraged by colleagues: 'I was sort of getting a reputation among some of the more senior silks and some of them [said] "you should think of taking silk", and I was only too delighted'.[32] The decision was also sometimes precipitated or hastened by other colleagues' professional advancement. There was often a carefully-observed order of precedence for taking silk:

> At one stage the view was that each person in seniority had the election of taking silk or not and so therefore you waited until the persons more senior to you took silk, you shouldn't be seen to be … peremptory and decide that 'I want to go earlier and ahead of more senior colleagues'.[33]

> I remember a colleague saying to me, 'X is taking silk now and she came in a term after you. What are you going to do about it?' Just someone pulling my leg.[34]

> X was made a High Court judge so there was a natural gap for an extra person and Y was ahead of me. Y said to me at that stage he had decided to live on circuit. The rules were getting a bit more lax and he had decided to live on circuit and he said 'I'm not taking silk so you've got to take it, right?'

> Well you have to … move up, you know. Because … you're almost a silk and … most of your peers are up there and you're the next in line.[35]

> One of my friends was doing it and I kind of said 'well, if he's doing it, I probably should be doing it,' because there's a feeling at the Bar that if you stay a junior too long you get left behind you know. If you leave it too late there, I don't know whether it's true or not, but there's a sense that you could be left behind.[36]

In 1954, a 'serious contretemps' arose when one member of a circuit, X, discovered that a slightly more junior colleague was about to take silk and would thereby take precedence over X. The chief justice told the attorney general how

31 B10.   32 B2.   33 B12.   34 B17.   35 B3.   36 B21.

X had been able to save face: '[t]he position was saved by [X] putting in at the last-minute application for silk, and despite the difference in the date of the patents, I called [X] first.'[37]

The procedure for applying for silk

For most of the twentieth century, the procedures for applying to join the inner Bar were not clearly set down, and nor were the criteria to be applied when assessing applications. Although writing about England and Northern Ireland, Dawson's summary is also apt for Ireland: there were 'secret soundings' of judicial and professional opinion. There were no published guidelines, and the sense of 'having done enough' was all-important in guiding a personal decision to apply.[38] It is evident from papers in the National Archives, the minutes of the Bar Council and the interviews conducted for this book that the procedures and criteria were opaque for most of the century. Prospective applicants did not know what was required of them. For example, one applicant wrote, in 1948, 'I am unfamiliar with how I should frame my request, and I would take it as a great kindness on your part if you would let me know whether I should give you any further particulars as to my practice.'[39] The lack of explicit guidance led to some prospective silks sending in applications that were extremely brief, as will be seen further below. Barristers were simply expected to know what to do and how to proceed, which highlights the importance of connections and social capital – the informal passing on of essential professional knowledge. P.J. McEnery, who in 1939 was contemplating applying for silk, wrote that 'a recommendation from the attorney general is ninety per cent of the way'.[40]

The general practice was for a junior counsel to canvass some close colleagues for their opinions before proceeding. This practise was not, however, universal; one potential silk wrote to the attorney general, Cecil Lavery, in the 1940s: 'I have not discussed the subject of this letter with any of my barrister colleagues as I think such a matter is a private one for every individual member of the Bar.'[41] In 1967, Attorney General Colm Condon expressed the view that the practice of consultation had died out, but other members of the Bar Council were of the opinion that intending silks still consulted their colleagues. They said that 'the purpose of such consultation was to apprise other members of the circuit who might be affected or whose own arrangements might be influenced by the decision'.[42] One barrister who was in practice from the early seventies recalled that 'some people would have come to me over the years ... and said to me, "you know I was thinking of taking silk".'[43] Another barrister, who took silk in the

---

37 Letter to att. gen., 8 Nov. 1954, NAI 2003/4/7.   38 Dawson, 'The rank of queen's counsel', at 56.   39 Letter to sec. exec. council, 20 Jan. 1948, NAI 2003/4/7.   40 McEnery, 'Look back', p. 190.   41 Letter to att. gen., 9 Aug. 1948, NAI 2003/4/7. Emphasis in original.   42 B.C.M., 27 Oct. 1967.   43 B18.

eighties, mentioned 'the curious reticence at the Bar about people taking silk …
the day before it happens people denied it.'[44] As one of the interviewees for this
book commented,

> It was informal. You informed the attorney general and you informed the
> leader on your circuit with the idea that if the leader said to you, 'you
> shouldn't be doing it' or 'you're not ready for it yet' that you would listen
> to that. It wasn't in any way binding and the leader wouldn't necessarily say
> it but, you know, I think if the leader of the circuit thought that it was
> actually inappropriate, they would say it to you. So, it was a much more
> informal procedure in those days.[45]

Certainly in the early decades of the century, there was an unwritten
expectation that an applicant would consult the chief justice before formally
applying.[46] One barrister recalled such an encounter:

> You had to go to the chief justice, which was a fairly intimidating process
> … I popped down to see the chief justice … he was a gruff aul fellow. I
> mean he was alright, decent enough and so on … I forget exactly what the
> encounter was but there wasn't much of an encounter.

In one instance the chief justice hinted at some irritation when asked by the
attorney general for his views on an applicant who had not consulted him:

> I am in the difficulty that the applicant has not called upon me, nor do I
> know him personally. I know nothing of his standing at the junior Bar and
> I am wondering if you would be so good as to let me know what your views
> are about the applicant and also whether you would inform him that he
> should call upon me … If in your opinion this man has sufficient standing
> at the junior Bar I would not like to stand in his way, but I think he might
> at least have the courtesy to approach me directly.[47]

When P.J. McEnery wished to take silk, he mentioned to Attorney General
Patrick Lynch, 'if there was a chance of getting silk I'd be glad to have it.' Lynch
said that he could not recommend just one barrister for silk, and asked McEnery
to suggest additional names of people who might be interested. 'I mentioned a
few other names in the Law Library who might be suitable silks but Pat turned
them down.' Finally, Lynch agreed with one of McEnery's suggestions, saying
'Yes, he's the man, if he wants silk I'll recommend the two of you, have a word

---

44 B27.   45 B23.   46 E.g., letter to att. gen., 23 Nov. 1947 and letter to sec. executive council, 20
Jan. 1948, NAI 2003/4/7.   47 Chief Justice Conor A. Maguire to att. gen. Charles Casey, 29 Mar.
1951, NAI 2003/4/7.

with him about it and let me know.'[48] McEnery called to this colleague's house that same evening to tell him about the conversation, and 'he was almost bewildered at the news I had for him because he hadn't been thinking of silk but the more we discussed it the more he inclined to the proposition.' They informed the attorney general that they both wished to apply, and he told them 'the government would require a recommendation also from the chief justice and that we should also see the chief justice for this purpose. We saw the chief justice in his room and he gave us his blessing.'[49]

Not only were the general procedures and qualifications unclear; many potential silks did not even know to whom they should address their letter of application. The letters in the National Archives are variously addressed to the secretary to the government;[50] the attorney general;[51] and the secretary of the Department of the Taoiseach.[52]

The procedures and criteria were opaque not only for members of the Bar; but also, at times, for the attorney general and the chief justice. In 1959, for example, Attorney General Aindreas Ó Caoimh reported to the Bar Council that he had checked the files of his office to ascertain the position in regard to the granting of silk. He said that 'it was quite clear that it was a matter entirely within the discretion of the government whether a patent of precedent should be made but that there was a practice that both the attorney general and the chief justice should be consulted before any grant was made.'[53] The attorney general and the chief justice did not always agree as to the criteria to be applied when deciding whether to grant silk. For example, in one incident in the 1940s, Chief Justice Maguire did not think a particular applicant merited a patent of precedence given their relatively limited practice at the Bar. However, he was prepared to allow it if the attorney general considered that 'he might be considered having regard to his published work.'[54] Ultimately, silk was granted in that case.[55]

The lack of official guidance led to some extremely short letters of application being sent. For example:

> Dear Sir, I beg to apply for a call to the inner Bar, and for the privilege to be allowed to practise thereat. I remain, Yours faithfully, X.[56]

> I hereby apply to the government for permission to be called to the inner Bar.[57]

> I have been considering making an application for silk for some time and I do not like to postpone it any longer.[58]

48 Ibid.   49 McEnery, 'Look back', p. 190.   50 E.g., letter to sec. govt., 19 Oct. 1943; 20 and 23 Feb. 1948; Oct. 1963, NAI 2003/4/7.   51 E.g., letters to the att. gen., 23 Nov. 1947; 30 Aug. 1967, NAI 2003/4/7.   52 E.g., letter to sec. Dept. Taoiseach, 22 Jan 1948, NAI 2003/4/7.   53 B.C.M., 27 Feb. 1959.   54 Chief justice to att. gen., 23 Feb. 1948, NAI 2003/4/7.   55 Att. gen. Lavery to sec. Dept. Taoiseach, 27 Feb. 1948, NAI 2003/4/7.   56 Letter to sec. govt., 12 Mar. 1951, NAI 2003/4/7.   57 Recipient unknown; letter dated 3 Feb. 1953, NAI 2003/4/7.   58 Letter to att.

Most letters specified, at the very least, the applicant's call date and their circuit membership.[59] Others listed various accomplishments, such as books they had published.[60] One applicant who was turned down, wrote again listing what he considered further relevant qualifications, including membership of the English Bar and membership of their local parish council.[61] From the 1950s, longer letters of application were more common, with some applicants setting forth the details of their entire careers to date.[62] A more modern curriculum vitae was evident in some applications from the 1960s.[63] By the 1980s, the application was still by way of a short letter, but the procedures had become more formalised. One barrister recalled:

> You just wrote a letter to a committee ... I think you wrote a letter to the secretary of the government and then there was a committee which comprised the chief justice ... the attorney general ... and the chairman of the Bar Council.[64]

Despite the growth in numbers at the Bar in the seventies, it was still considered small enough for the attorney general and chief justice to know something about those who were applying. As one barrister explained it,

> We were still a small Bar and the attorney and the chairman of the Bar and the chief ... would have known ... a lot of the people who were proposing to take silk and if he didn't know them personally the attorney and the chairman of the Bar would have known them personally.[65]

The Fair Trade Commission commented on the lack of transparency regarding senior counsel appointments in its 1990 report:

> The appointment of senior counsel is not based upon obvious merit and certainly not upon qualifying tests of any sort. The appointment procedure is not transparent, and the fact that the appointment is made by the government in a profession which proudly maintains its independence, and is not regulated by statute, appears to be highly anomalous.[66]

The commission suggested quite significant reforms in relation to senior counsel, and these are discussed in more detail in in chapter sixteen.

gen., 22 Feb. 1948, NAI 2003/4/7. **59** E.g., letter to att. gen., 23 Nov. 1947, NAI 2003/4/7. **60** E.g., letter to sec. govt., 19 Oct. 1943, NAI 2003/4/7. **61** Letter to sec. Dept. Taoiseach, 22 Jan. 1948, NAI 2003/4/7. **62** E.g., letter to sec. govt., 7 Nov. 1952, NAI 2003/4/7. **63** E.g., letter to sec. govt., 4 Oct. 1963, NAI 2003/4/7. **64** B11. B18 recalled that when he wanted to follow up on his letter of application, 'I had to ring the attorney general's office from a pay phone ... I didn't want him to know that.' **65** B2. **66** F.T.C., para. 1.157.

Granting silk to non-practising barristers

Sometimes non-practising barristers applied to be made senior counsel,[67] and the practice in relation to this varied. For example, in 1948, an application was made by someone who had been called to the Irish Bar, but who practised in Tanganyika. Attorney General Cecil Lavery wrote to Chief Justice Maguire in unequivocal terms: 'I do not think we ought to entertain for a moment a proposal to give a patent of precedence to a non-practising member of the Bar.'[68] In the same year, a District Court judge wrote to the attorney general that he had 'for ages been toying with the idea of asking for silk', and added that when he had been at the Bar he had had 'quite a decent practice and should be entitled to silk quite as much as many who came after me.' He distinguished his position from that of a senior counsel who takes up a judicial position.[69] Lavery wrote in response that it might be 'inappropriate' for a judge to take such a step, pointing out that some judges in the Circuit and Supreme Courts were juniors.[70] The attorney general wrote:

> It is for consideration whether a member of the bench of any court is to be considered as continuing his membership of the Bar with a right of audience in any court. If they have not such a right of audience, it would be absurd to grant a patent of precedence.[71]

He later followed up, having consulted with the taoiseach, who agreed that 'the call to the inner Bar is now definitely a matter of giving precedence to practising members of the Bar and is an inappropriate distinction to bestow on judges of whatever degree.'[72]

In response to a query from Attorney General Aindrais Ó Caoimh, the Bar Council ruled in 1959 that the chief justice and the attorney general 'should not give their assent to the granting of silk to anyone other than a practising barrister except in very exceptional circumstances'.[73] The issue arose again four years later when a barrister who had qualified in Ireland, but who practised in England, applied to take silk in Ireland. Ó Caoimh wrote that while a 'rather liberal view' had over the years been taken in relation to what was meant by 'the practice of law', he did not 'know that any case has been recently considered in which it was thought desirable to grant a patent of precedence to a person not actually engaged in the practice of law in this country.'[74] This was followed by extensive

---

67 In 1959 the attorney general made the point that this had been a regular occurrence even before 1922: B.C.M., 27 Feb. 1959. 68 Att. gen. to chief justice, 19 Aug. 1948, NAI 2003/4/7. Similarly, an application by someone who had practised in Ghana and was currently working as a diplomat in Eastern Europe was refused in 1967; letter to att. gen., 30 Aug. 1967, NAI 2003/4/7. 69 Letter to att. gen., 9 Aug. 1948, NAI 2003/4/7. 70 Letter from att. gen., 12 Aug. 1948, NAI 2003/4/7. 71 Ibid. 72 Letter from att. gen., 25 Oct. 1948, NAI 2003/4/7. 73 B.C.M., 27 Feb. 1959. 74 Letter from att. gen., 26 Nov. 1963, NAI 2003/4/7.

correspondence between the applicant and the attorney general for several months, with the applicant citing his family connections in Ireland, the positions held by members of his family, and the nature of his work in England. Among other things, he pointed out that he sometimes appeared in the Irish courts and that it was 'embarrassing to everybody concerned' if he had to plead as a junior counsel in Ireland, when he was a King's counsel in England.[75]

The issue arose periodically during the late sixties and seventies. In 1967, Attorney General Cecil Lavery sought the Bar Council's guidance on the matter, pointing out that because silk had in the past been granted to non-practising barristers, 'it would now be very difficult to draw the line'.[76] This was in the context of a controversy that arose when a non-practising member of the Bar, who had been in business for some years, wrote to the attorney general signalling an intention to return to practice and to take silk. He was called to the inner Bar without having discussed the matter with members of his circuit or with the Bar Council, as requested by the attorney general.[77] In 1982, members of the Bar Council met with Chief Justice O'Higgins to discuss the criteria on which silk should be granted. While the council was of the view that it should only be awarded for 'professional eminence', the chief justice thought that it might also be granted to 'those in high positions connected with the law.' It was reported that 'no criteria for the granting of silk had resulted from the discussions, though it was desirable that they should exist.'[78]

The work of a senior counsel

As well as a mark of seniority, and a right to precedence in court, the work itself was quite different for those called to the inner Bar. As the Bar Council described in the 1980s, once a barrister took silk, 'he would tend to do much less preparatory and paper work and would be able to devote himself to the presentation of cases in court and to more interesting paper work.'[79]

> The withdrawal of work which by custom and practise of the Bar is reserved for junior counsel is another attraction, both for silks who escape the drudgery of mundane (but lucrative) work and for juniors who benefit from the redistribution of work within the Bar, secure in the knowledge that there can be no return from the front row.[80]

Several barristers have commented on the different types of work conducted by senior counsel. As discussed above, a common motivation for taking silk was to get away from 'low level paperwork',[81] referred to as donkey work'[82] by one

75 Letter to att. gen., 17 Jan. 1964, NAI 2003/4/7. 76 B.C.M., 27 Oct. 1967. 77 B.C.M., 20, 27 Oct. and 10 Nov. 1967. 78 B.C.M., 12 Feb. 1982. 79 F.T.C., para. 7.109. 80 Dawson, 'The rank of queen's counsel', at 49. 81 B6. 82 B6.

barrister. Another reflected that there was 'less drudgery on Sundays.' Most spoke about the new focus on advocacy in a very positive way, for example:

> It was a better line of work ... I found it a lot easier. Advocacy I really liked. I liked going in and I was a good cross examiner ... I always enjoyed cross examining and I always enjoyed pitching stuff at judges.

> It's wonderful to get away from the paperwork ... suddenly you're in the front line.[83]

> Well, it's a different job to some extent ... I think by and large the skills are transferable but maybe there are some people for whom they aren't transferable.[84]

Another barrister commented that instead of 'soul destroying' 'replies to particulars and updated particulars of injuries, loss and damage' ... you were doing opinions, advices on proofs and turning up in court so that was different and more appealing.'[85] A minority were less positive about the change, for example:

> It's a whole new practice ... you don't bring your junior practice with you at all, you're lucky if you can. So, you really have to start all over again more or less and again, you take anything for money and I took trials all over the country, dreadful stuff.

Some commented on other, practical ways in which their work practise changed. For example, a barrister who took silk in the late seventies explained:

> When you took silk traditionally you had to move from your circuit. You had to have a residence in Dublin or whether it was a convention – well obviously there was no absolute rule – but ... if you were in Galway, Cork: you took silk; you moved.[86]

Another, who took silk around the turn of the century, noted that seniors were 'entitled to practise on any circuit'.[87] Some who were called to the inner Bar were aware of being treated differently as a result. One recalled getting 'slightly more' respect once they were called to the inner Bar in the early nineties.[88] Another, who took silk in the forties, described the change as follows:

> One is accorded a sort of deference by the solicitors and the juniors and an acceptance of your equality with them by your fellow silks and the judges

83 B25. 84 B27. 85 B21. 86 B9. 87 B3. 88 B20.

appear to pay more attention to what you say and to what you argue than when you were a junior.[89]

Asked how the decision to take silk had impacted on them, one barrister, who took silk in the early eighties, commented that while they continued to do a lot of criminal work, with which they were very comfortable, perceptions of them had changed: 'from being a sort of country bumpkin' to 'being some kind of genius'.[90] A small minority said that taking silk had not meant much for them, and that 'everything was much the same'.[91] One who took silk in the seventies said it did not make 'a hell of a lot of difference', although 'for some of the years it was nice'.[92] One barrister who took silk in the late sixties said

> It was a tremendous upheaval and I was very disinclined to do it ... To take silk then, you had to move to Dublin lock, stock and barrel and that was very traumatic.[93]

Some barristers interviewed for this book evaluated their senior practice as having been more successful than their junior practice.

Deciding not to take silk

Of course, not everyone at the Bar chose to become a senior counsel. In 1930 the *Cork Examiner* pointed out that '[m]any aged practitioners do not seek the honour of silk. By some it is regarded as a perilous promotion from the point of view of business.'[94] As one barrister said,

> In my day you had some very good juniors who for one reason or the other didn't take silk. You particularly had it with juniors who were based in Cork, because taking silk in those days almost inevitably meant moving to Dublin and ... people had families growing up and for family reasons they didn't want to move and so you had a tradition in Cork of very, very good barristers who just never took silk, didn't want the responsibility and were happy with what they were doing, perhaps more freedom as a junior.

Some continued as juniors because they had modest practices, and were unlikely to have been successful in their application. Others were satisfied with the work they were doing and did not seek a change. And, of course, there were those whose applications were unsuccessful.[95]

---

89 McEnery, 'Look back', p. 194. 90 B18. 91 B1. 92 B19. 93 'Ralph Sutton, SC, called to the Bar, July 1948', *B.R.* 4:3 (1999), 152. 94 *Examiner*, 25 June 1930, p. 10. The paper also reported that the number of senior counsel was 'considerably reduced' in recent times; see further ch. 4 and 10. 95 NAI 2003/4/7.

Serving as attorney general

At the head of the barristers' profession was the attorney general, the 'adviser of the government in matters of law and legal opinion'.[96] In his biography of Kevin O'Higgins, de Vere White notes that O'Higgins disliked legal careerists who took up politics in order to advance in the legal profession. He 'wished to establish the practice of appointing, as law adviser to the government, a barrister who had no seat in the Dáil to think about and who could give a detached opinion, as though he were advising a private client.'[97] However, as Casey points out, 'the early history of the Free State was inimical to the development of any such practice'.[98] Attorneys general Hugh Kennedy, Conor A. Maguire, James Geoghegan, Patrick McGilligan and Declan Costello were all Dáil deputies, and Cecil Lavery was a senator. According to Casey's analysis, another nineteen attorneys general up to the mid-nineties were associated with the party or parties in office, even if they themselves were not elected representatives.

Casey argues that aside from the fact of their political allegiance, gender and membership of the Bar, the appointees up to the mid-nineties 'manifest the greatest diversity'.[99] However, this argument is difficult to sustain; for example, 23 out of 27 attorneys general in the twentieth century attended UCD and most had been educated in well-known fee-paying or private schools. It is true to say, however, that there was considerable variation in the ages of those appointed; they ranged from 34 to 73 years. Usually, the attorney general was appointed from the ranks of the inner Bar, but this was not always the case; for example, John O'Byrne, Conor A. Maguire, John Kelly and John Rogers were all appointed when they were junior counsel.[100]

Geoghegan observes that attorneys general were always regarded as practising members of the Bar,

> And indeed were, in fact, members of the Law Library. This was so irrespective of whether they ever exercised their right to conduct a case in court which some of them did and some of them did not ... Most importantly of all from the Bar's point of view is that all attorneys general have enjoyed the informal title of 'leader of the Bar.'[101]

96 1937 Constitution, art. 30. Before 1937, the attorney general had a legislative basis in s. 6 of the Ministers and Secretaries Act 1924. This similarly set out the function of the attorney general as 'advising the executive council and the several ministers in matters of law and of legal opinion.' 97 Terence de Vere White, *Kevin O'Higgins* (Tralee, 1966), p. 180. 98 James Casey, *The Irish law officers* (Dublin, 1996), p. 242. 99 Ibid. 100 Geoghegan, 'The relationship of the attorney general', p. 67, writes that John O'Byrne was appointed four days before taking silk and became the last ever KC, 'at his own request'. Geoghegan also notes that Kelly took silk a day before appointment and Rogers took silk on the same day. 'History or legend has it that Conor Maguire was called out by announcement from the old Grafton Cinema and informed on May 10, 1932 that he had been appointed attorney general and that he was expected to become senior counsel the following day.' 101 Geoghegan, 'The relationship of the attorney general', p. 69.

Personal appearances in court by the attorney general were common before independence,[102] and there are some examples of appearances by Hugh Kennedy, John Costello and Conor A. Maguire in the early years of the Free State. However, from the mid-century, they tended to appear only in cases of considerable constitutional importance. Controversy attached to the office from time to time; for example, the judicial appointment and subsequent return to the Bar of Harry Whelehan in the mid-nineties[103] and the case of Malcolm Macarthur,[104] which led to the resignation of Patrick Connolly in 1982.[105]

A number of former attorneys general were interviewed for this book, and almost all had a broadly positive experience in the office. One said that they were 'delighted to be asked' and another described it as a 'wonderful' job. All recalled working hard in the role,[106] and found satisfaction both in the legal work and in the political side, for example:

> In England the attorney doesn't sit at the cabinet table. He is called in for things but here the attorney sits at the cabinet table. Now about two-thirds of the stuff has nothing to do with you … but to sit every Tuesday at the cabinet and see the country being fixed or made a bit of a balls of … that was a fairly good entertainment.

102 Casey, *Law officers*, p. 248.   103 Former Attorney General Harry Whelehan was appointed as president of the High Court in November 1994 and resigned shortly thereafter and sought to return to practise at the Bar. As president of the High Court, he had been *ex officio* a member of the Supreme Court, and could not, under the existing Bar Council rules, have subsequently practised in any court. Following a special meeting of the Bar Council (B.C.M., 2 Dec. 1994), the issue was put to members of the Bar. John Maher, 'All members of the Bar to be polled on Whelehan issue: decision disappoints Bar Council, *Irish Times*, 3 Dec. 1994, p. 5. After a lengthy meeting, an overwhelming majority (570 to 108) voted in favour of allowing him to practise: 'Barristers vote agrees to allow Whelehan to practise', *Irish Times*, 14 Dec. 1994, p. 8 and Alison O'Connor, 'Acrimony denied at Whelehan Law Library meeting', *Irish Times*, 6 Dec. 1994, p. 8. See further Casey, *Law officers*, pp 192–206 and Carroll MacNeill, *The politics of judicial selection in Ireland*, pp 65–9.   104 Macarthur was arrested at the home of the attorney general after committing two murders. For a brief overview, see Conor Lally, 'Then and now: Malcolm Macarthur', *Irish Times* 28 June 2011. The affair is examined in detail in Mark O'Connell, *A thread of violence* (London, 2023). It led to the coining of the acronym 'GUBU' by Conor Cruise O'Brien following Taoiseach Charles Haughey's description of the events as 'grotesque, unbelievable, bizarre and unprecedented': Conor Cruise O'Brien, 'Unsafe at any speed', *Irish Times*, 24 Aug. 1982, p. 10. 105 Connolly returned to practise at the Bar. See obit., 'AG whose life changed after Macarthur entanglement', *Irish Times*, 30 Jan. 2016, p. 14.   106 By the mid-nineties, the volume of work in the attorney general's office had increased significantly. It was estimated in 1995 that there had been a 37% increase since the previous year, and about 42% compared with the three previous years. *First six-month report on implementation of report of the review group on the Office of the Attorney General* (Sept. 1995), p. 6. This report, along with a second report in Apr. 1996, were issued following the publication of a report by a review group established in Nov. 1994 and published on 21 Feb. 1995. The review group's remit was 'to review and make recommendations on the relevant organisation structure, systems, procedure and staffing arrangements in the Office of the Attorney General.' From 1996 on, the office produced annual reports: Office of the Attorney General, *Annual report 1996–7* (Dublin, 1997).

Another said they had enjoyed being at the centre of things. Every government department had legal issues that came across his desk and he found it very rewarding to be involved in so many aspects of government. Another said that he had 'really, really enjoyed' the role, partly because of the novelty:

> It was like a real breath of fresh air ... still doing legal work but doing it in a different context, doing it with people I didn't know ... so that was fantastic.

Having completed a term as attorney general, one could return to practice at the Bar. One described the return as 'Fine ... I was very fortunate I fitted in quickly again and it wasn't a problem, so I was fortunate.' Some found that having served a term as attorney general was beneficial to their practice:

> I was very lucky, people thought that I could do any sort of case. If you have been attorney general, you can sort of expect people to think that. If the government were relying on that young fellow, he must have had something.

Not all attorneys general returned to practice. Of the twenty-seven attorneys in the twentieth century, sixteen were subsequently appointed to the bench,[107] while others went on to play significant roles in public life.[108]

Appointment to the bench

Most appointees to the senior judiciary in the twentieth century came from the Bar. Some of the interviewees for this book reflected on their transition from the Bar to the bench, and said that they missed the collegiality and the close friendships. Life on the bench was a much more solitary existence by comparison:

> You'd imagine you'd be part of a new group that had huge intimacy the same as the Bar had, and it doesn't. The relationship, judges' relationship is different from barristers' relationship ... every so often I was driving out ... of [the] courthouse to go back to the hotel, sunny afternoon, I think in July, and a few guys, pals, are standing outside, I don't know, having a smoke or whatever it is and I'm thinking 'oh yes I want to be there'.

---

107 Delany wrote in 1975 that it was 'a matter of tradition' that an attorney general had 'first refusal' on any judicial vacancies which arose during their period of office: V.T.H. Delany, *The administration of justice in Ireland* (Dublin, 1975), p. 76. See also Paul C. Bartholomew, *The Irish judiciary* (Dublin, 1971), p. 33. 108 See further ch. 14.

You missed the camaraderie, you missed the bit of fun, the sort of uncertainty, the fact that you meet up somebody and they're interesting, I didn't realise how solitary this ... sorry everyone says it's solitary, you don't realise what that means, what that really means. Solitary.

When Tom O'Higgins was invited to join the High Court bench, he was somewhat reluctant to do so, in part because of the loneliness and isolation of becoming a judge.[109] Another deterrent was the comparatively low pay for judges;[110] one interviewee described 'a fourfold drop in income',[111] and another described the 'dramatic difference' between a barrister's income and a judicial salary.[112]

One interviewee emphasised the secrecy surrounding judicial applications:

You might tell a very close friend ... that you were thinking about it or what the position was. You might ask a friend of yours who was on the bench ... basically you would keep that totally silent. Now, it somehow leaks out. Well one of the things that leaks out is who is likely to be applying, so you'd know roughly who is that sort of person who would be in line to be appointed.[113]

While barristers may have been reticent about expressing their judicial aspirations to one another, this did not mean that such ambitions did not exist. One interviewee, for example, admitted that 'I sort of always wanted to be a judge if I had a chance,' while another told of applying unsuccessfully for a judicial appointment.

Beyond retirement

Aside from judicial appointments, many qualified barristers left the Bar and had very successful careers elsewhere.[114] Some were voluntarily disbarred by the

---

109 O'Higgins, *Double life,* pp 265–6. Ralph Sutton SC was said to have declined a High Court judgeship offered to him in 1985 because he could not have afforded to keep his Cork home. Obit., 'Exemplar of courtly behaviour at the Bar', *Irish Times,* 4 Dec. 1999, p. 8. See Dickson, *The Irish Supreme Court,* pp 81–6. By contrast, Healy wrote that 'incomes at the Irish Bar were so small that the salary of a judge, whether county court or High Court, was a great attraction; the appointment did not, as in England, mean a loss of income; men gained by their promotion.' Healy, *The old Munster Circuit,* p. 261.   110 By contrast, in the late nineteenth and early twentieth century, a judicial salary was 'at least comparable to, and perhaps greater than, the income which a Queen's Counsel might expect to earn.' Hogan, *The legal profession,* p. 82. Incomes for senior counsel had fallen during the nineteenth century: ibid., p. 83.   111 These transitional difficulties, and others, were articulated in the 1980s by Alan Paterson, 'Becoming a judge' in Robert Dingwall and Philip Lewis (eds), *The sociology of the professions: lawyers, doctors and others* (London, 1983), pp 278–83.   112 B26.   113 B18.   114 Indeed, many graduates of the King's Inns did not practise at all. B5 recalled Cearbhaill Ó Dálaigh was 'actively encouraging' civil servants to do the B.L. degree, and said many King's Inns classmates went into business.

King's Inns benchers, and went on to practise as solicitors.[115] Others went on to take religious vows,[116] pursue literary or artistic careers,[117] work in business[118] or join the public service.[119] Different factors affected the attrition rate at the Bar; for example, the rate was higher for women than for men.[120] One barrister recalled,

> The attrition rate for the non-graduate barrister was much higher than the attrition rate for those of us who came through Trinity and UCD and UCG ... I suspect we were younger, we were more in a position to withstand five years without earnings. Possibly I suspect we had a better legal education behind us because we'd come through the universities and not through the King's Inns you know we'd be better equipped to do legal research and write opinions and stuff like that.[121]

As self-employed individuals, barristers (unlike judges) had no compulsory retirement age, and many continued practising into their seventies and eighties.[122] This seems to have been common throughout the period; for example, in 1931 it was reported that Alexander Blood, KC, aged 78, was 'still working hard'[123] after fifty-four years in practice. At that time, the 'father of the Bar,' Robert D. Murray, aged 80 and in practice for fifty-eight years, was still considered active.[124] Many barristers found the work rewarding and had no wish to stop.[125] The comment of one barrister, in practice for around forty years, may have resonated with many: 'I could stop work now, but what on earth would I do?' Another reason not to retire was that a self-employed barrister might not have had sufficient financial security.[126] As one barrister explained,

> Professional people in Irish society in those days just ... didn't have pensions ... most people didn't earn enough to put away in a pension ...

115 E.g., K.I.B.M., 31 Oct. 1969; 11 Jan. 1971; 29 Jan., 19 July 1974; 6 Feb. 1975; 12 Feb. 1982; 6 Oct. 1986; 12 Jan. 1987; 24 May, 18 July 1989. In 1985 it was reported that a number of disbarred persons listed in the register of solicitors in the law directory had 'BL' after their names. The benchers wrote to them warning them not to use the letters 'BL' after being disbarred. Some of them wrote back to say they had thought the 'BL' referred to their degree, not the call to the Bar. K.I.B.M., 11 Feb. 1985.   116 E.g., Noreen Mackey, *The secret ladder* (London, 2005).   117 See ch. 14 and 15.   118 See p. 302.   119 See pp 298–300.   120 See pp 178–81.   121 Bio.   122 E.g., former Attorney General Patrick Connolly practised until the age of 82. Oliver Duane Gogarty, called in 1931, practised for over sixty years. Obituary, *Irish Times*, 14 Feb. 2000, p. 17 and Ferguson, *Barristers*, p. 194.   123 *Sunday Independent*, 15 Mar. 1931, p. 6; Ferguson, *Barristers*, p. 141. Blood also worked as a solicitor and barrister in New Zealand from 1878–83. See obit., *Irish Times*, 14 June 1933, p. 8.   124 *Cork Examiner*, 25 June 1930; Ferguson, *Barristers*, p. 263.   125 In 1999 Ralph Sutton SC, aged 75, marked fifty years at the Bar in an interview published in the *Bar Review*: 'Ralph Sutton, SC'. See obit., 'Exemplar of courtly behaviour at the Bar', *Irish Times*, 4 Dec. 1999, p. 8.   126 The Bar introduced a contributory pension scheme in the eighties, and the Bar Council encouraged members to join the scheme; see, e.g., John Dowling, 'Why you should consider your pension requirements now', *B.R.* 2:2 (1997), 67.

certainly people weren't in the habit of putting money into a pension fund, so barristers continued much longer, also an incentive at the appropriate time to become a judge because that did give you a pension.[127]

In a humorous anecdote, Terence de Vere White recalled an older barrister musing about the benefits of paid employment:

> 'There were some splendid jobs in the old days', he mused. 'The Indian Civil Service, now. That was splendid employment. And a nice pension too. A nice pension is the thing to look for. I made a mistake in sticking at the Bar. Unless one becomes a judge, there is no prospect of a pension.' The word pension had some hypnotic effect: by this time, seemingly, he had forgotten my presence and began to chant 'pension ... pension ... pension' to himself, until at last the words ran together, sank and rose again, no longer as words, but rather as a sigh which merged at last – after a preliminary grunt and whistle – into the soothing susurration of a snore.[128]

* * *

Whether or not to apply for silk was a personal decision that rested on many factors. Many barristers chose not to apply, and there were also those who applied unsuccessfully. Throughout the century, the inner Bar was much smaller than the outer or junior Bar, and, with some notable exceptions towards the end of the century, it remained a male domain.[129] There were other career opportunities available to those at the top of the profession, including appointment to the senior bench and appointment as attorney general. The well-defined career stages at the Bar could present opportunities for transformation:

> You can really reinvent yourself every now and then ... A senior job is very different to a junior job I think by and large ... to become a judge, that's different again.[130]

As Morison and Leith point out, '[e]llevation in the profession – securing better work, attaining senior counsel status or being appointed to the bench – depends on the good opinion of one's colleagues and particularly on the judiciary'.[131] The importance of maintaining the good opinion of one's colleagues is further explored in chapter twelve.

---

127 B23.   **128** De Vere White, *A fretful midge*, p. 90.   **129** See ch. 9.   **130** B27.   **131** Morison and Leith, *Barrister's world*, p. 18.

CHAPTER FIVE

Who was at the Bar?

Introduction

In the 1920s a person entering the barristers' profession was likely to be male, Trinity-educated, Protestant and middle class. They would be part of a small cohort graduating from the King's Inns, aged in their early twenties. Their parents were probably Dublin-based lawyers or other professionals, and they were likely to have several lawyers in their wider family network. By the late 1990s, this was no longer necessarily the case; for example, forty per cent of new entrants were women, and new members were more likely to have been educated at UCD than at Trinity. They graduated in larger numbers from the King's Inns and were more likely than before to have attended a non-elite secondary school.

This chapter examines the age, gender, religion, education, family connections and socio-economic background of Irish barristers since 1921. It also considers issues such as ethnicity, disability and sexual identity, which received little attention in the twentieth century, but which are increasingly to the fore in international studies of legal professions.[1] It considers the experiences of barristers who perceived themselves as being in a minority, as well as those who considered themselves 'typical'. It also considers diversity and inclusivity at the twentieth-century Bar. Ferguson's *King's Inns barristers*[2] is an invaluable source for piecing together the demographics of the twentieth-century Bar. He has synthesised various sources, including call-lists and benchers' minutes, in order to present a list of those who were called to the Bar in each year up to 2004, with detailed biographical information for those called up to 1968. Supplementing these statistics are various qualitative sources including memoirs and interviews with people who were in practice during every decade from the 1920s to the 1990s.

The size of the Bar

For a profession whose make-up remained more-or-less constant for several hundred years, the twentieth century saw a remarkable transformation, not only

---

1 E.g., Steven Vaughan, 'Prefer not to say': diversity and diversity reporting at the Bar of England & Wales', *Int. J. Leg. Prof.* 24:3 (2017), 207; Lizzie Barnes and Kate Malleson, 'The legal profession as gatekeeper to the judiciary: design faults in measures to enhance diversity', *M.L.R.* 74:2 (2011), 245; Hilary Sommerlad, Lisa Webley, Liz Duff, Daniel Muzio and Jennifer Tomlinson, *Diversity in the legal profession in England and Wales: a qualitative study of barriers and individual choices* (London, 2010).   2 Kenneth Ferguson, *King's Inns barristers 1868–2004* (Dublin, 2005).

in terms of the gender and socio-economic background of barristers, but also in terms of the number of people practising. While there were 34 people called to the Bar in 1921, there were 114 called in 1999. As fig. 5.1 demonstrates, there had been little or no change to the number of people being called until the mid-1960s, with an average of 24 people per year being called.[3] From the mid-sixties to the mid-eighties, there were on average 71 people called per year, and from the mid-eighties until the end of the century, there was an average of 125 per year.

Figure 5.1. Number of barristers called per year

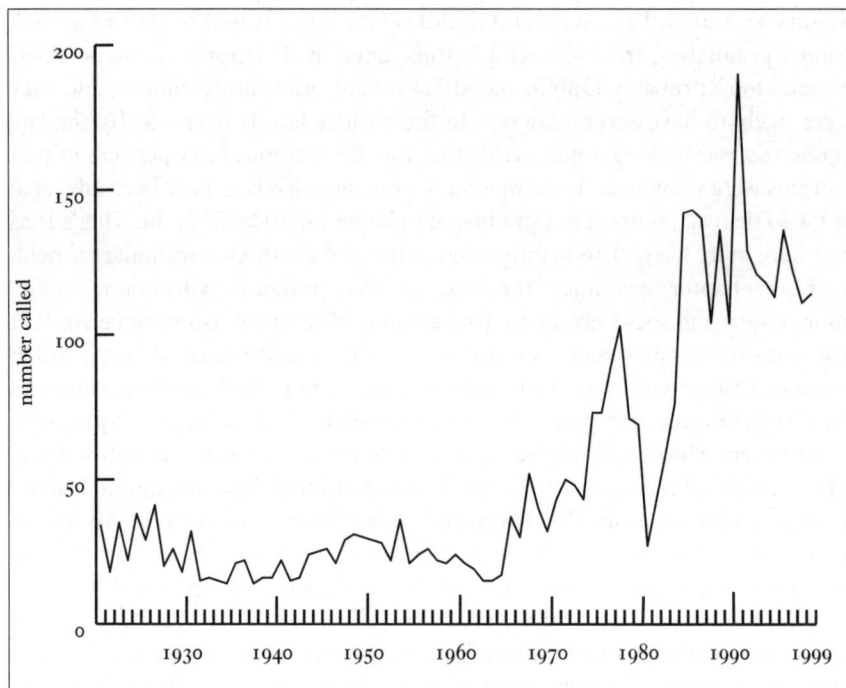

A significant increase is evident in the 1970s. There was, in the words of Senator Mary Robinson, 'an explosion of numbers seeking to study law either at the universities or at other third-level institutions'.[4] She pointed out in 1982 that there were approximately 480 practising barristers; more than double the number practising in 1973. As will be seen below, in the 1980s, the King's Inns introduced various measures to control the number of people graduating with BL degrees. These figures are not representative of the number of Law Library subscribers in a given year, as they do not take account of the number of people actually joining the Law Library and going into practice, the number of people

3 Based on data from ibid.   4 Seanad Éireann deb., vol. 101, no. 2 (22 June 1983).

leaving or the impact of things like reciprocal calls.[5] However, as Ferguson points out, '[t]he number of subscribers to the Law Library fluctuated in sympathy with the trend in numbers called to the Bar'.[6] Figure 5.2 indicates the number of subscribers to the Law Library, and it can be seen that membership was increasing from the 1970s.

Figure 5.2. Number of barristers at the Law Library

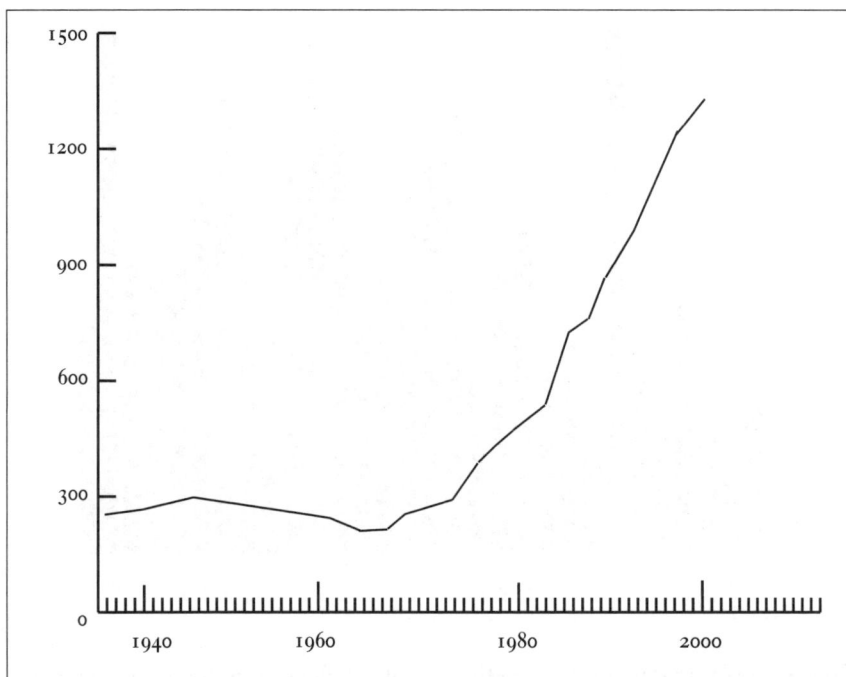

The figures indicate a profession that was growing in popularity and accessibility as the century progressed, and it will be seen in chapter eleven that these growing numbers placed a strain on the physical workspace.

Age

Unlike in the public sector, there was no upper age limit for practising barristers. As noted in chapter four, this led to many barristers working beyond the statutory age of retirement. At the other end of the age spectrum, one had to be at least twenty-one years old to be called to the Bar.[7] As can be seen from

5 In 1989, for example, of the 189 called, 25 were members of the Bar of Northern Ireland and 8 were Australian barristers. In 1990, there were 10 English barristers, 2 from Northern Ireland, 6 from Australia and one from Malaysia.   6 Ferguson, *Barristers*, p. 115.

figure 5.3, the proportion of the newly-called aged in their early twenties generally increased from 1921 onward.[8] By the 1940s they represented between sixty and eighty per cent of new entrants.

Figure 5.3. Percentage of barristers aged 21–24 at call

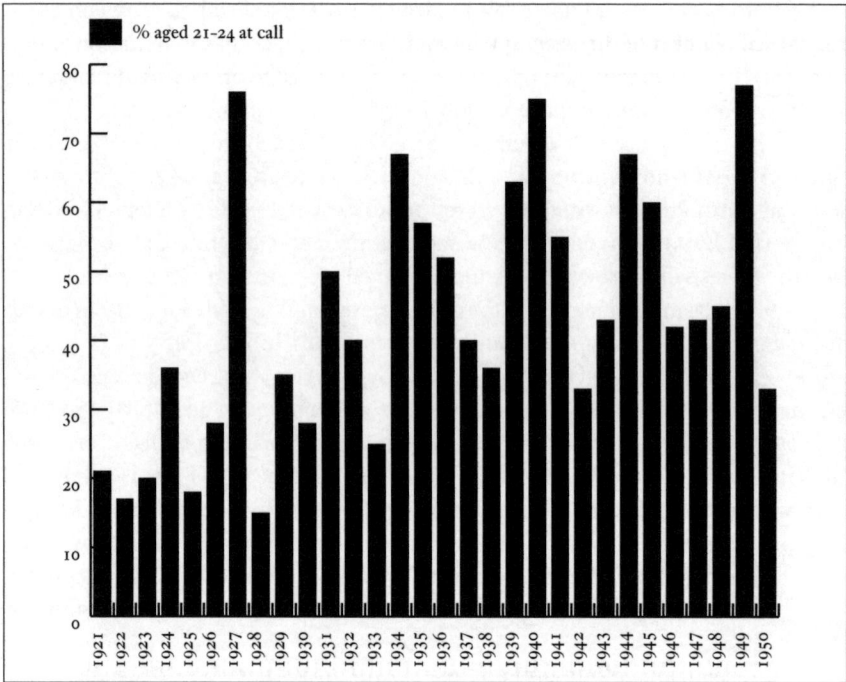

Given the young starting age and the lack of a defined retirement age, there was quite a spread of ages at the Bar. One barrister who was called in the early seventies recalled colleagues at that time who were 'young middle-aged, early old age … they were vibrant.'[9]

There was always a proportion of those called to the Bar who were slightly older. Those called in their thirties, for example, tended to make up between twenty and thirty per cent of each cohort called to the Bar until the late 1960s.[10] They tended to have previously worked in other fields, particularly the civil service and some continued to do so after their call.[11] Many did not subsequently practise at the Bar. Others in this age group went on to have successful practices at the Bar; Catherine McGuinness famously was not called to the Bar until the

7 The youngest person called to the Bar in the twentieth century appears to be Arthur Burke Kelly in 1913, aged 21 years and a day. See ibid., p. 217.   8 Based on information presented in ibid. 9 B1.   10 Based on information presented in Ferguson, *Barristers*.   11 E.g. Gretta Flood (called in 1926: ibid., p. 189); Onora Ní Shúilleabháin (called in 1972: ibid., p. 364) and Mary Murphy (called in 1972: ibid., p. 364). See further ch. 14.

age of 42, and Maurice Gaffney was aged 37.[12] Another barrister who was called at a slightly older age said that they found it advantageous to have worked in other areas before joining the Bar.

A barrister who was called in the late eighties said this period was 'the beginning of having more junior barristers who were much older'.[13] The issue of older individuals being called to the Bar and admitted to practise remained contentious in the eighties and nineties, with some members of the Bar resentful of those who were considered to be pursuing a second or part-time career at the expense of those trying to make a living:

> Some people who came in were not just second career but they were post-retirement people almost, and every brief they got was seen as a brief that wasn't going to somebody who was trying to make it on their own, so there was a little bit of resentment around that.[14]

> We used to give out in the Library in the seventies when someone came in who had retired from another job, we used to call them 'crumblies'.

> There were a number of crumblies in our year ... These were retired, sometimes retired civil servants or people coming with practices, with pensions, and while it was nice to have older people, in a real sense, if you got in there, you're going to steal the bread out of my mouth.

The number of people joining the Bar increased significantly in the 1970s, as indicated above in figure 2. As part of efforts to control these numbers,[15] the King's Inns, with the support of the Bar Council, imposed an age limit in the 1980s on those who could study for the degree of Barrister-at-Law.[16] Minister for Justice Ray Burke commented in the Dáil that this was discriminatory against mature students, 'many of whom have obtained the qualification of barrister-at-law in the past without intending to practise at all.'[17] The Fair Trade Commission considered criticisms of the age limit to be valid.[18] The Bar Council also distinguished on grounds of age when it came to Library fees. In the late eighties, it estimated that the realistic cost of providing a new entrant with a desk in the Library was £3,000. This entrance fee was imposed on persons aged over

---

12 See 'Maurice Gaffney SC – 1916–2016', *B.R.* 21:6 (2016), 187.   13 B13.   14 B13, called in the late eighties.   15 It had also limited the number of places on the degree course some years before; see further below.   16 The Bar Council had originally proposed a limit of forty-five years (B.C.M., 13 Feb. 1988), but the benchers were of the view that thirty-five was more appropriate: B.C.M., 27 Feb. 1988. The imposition of an age limit required the Bar Council to come up with interim measures for individuals who exceeded the limit but were already enrolled at the Inns; it also had to consider persons who had been called years before but who had yet to join the Library. B.C.M., 3 Dec. 1987.   17 Dáil Éireann deb., vol. 392, no. 9 (9 Nov. 1989).   18 Fair Trade Commission: *Report of study into restrictive practices in the legal profession* (Dublin, 1990), para. 7.141.

thirty who joined the Bar,[19] but a reduction was applied for those who were aged under thirty. This was essentially subsidised by older and more senior members of the Bar. The intention was to support those for whom the Bar would be their full-time and permanent career, as opposed to those who joined the Bar as a second career or as a part-time endeavour. Indeed, the Bar Council issued a ruling in 1988 stating that it rejected 'the notion of a part-time barrister'.[20] This was challenged on occasion by newly qualified barristers who felt they should be entitled to the lower fee.[21]

Gender

Although there were women barristers from 1921 onwards, for several decades they represented a tiny minority of those at the Bar. As figure 5.4 shows, the number of women being called remained low for the first fifty years, and did not begin to rise until the 1970s. Rarely did women exceed ten per cent of those called in a given year, and in many years there were no women called to the Bar at all. One of the interviewees for this book recalled that there were no women called in his year in the sixties, for example.

Figure 5.4. Number of men and women called

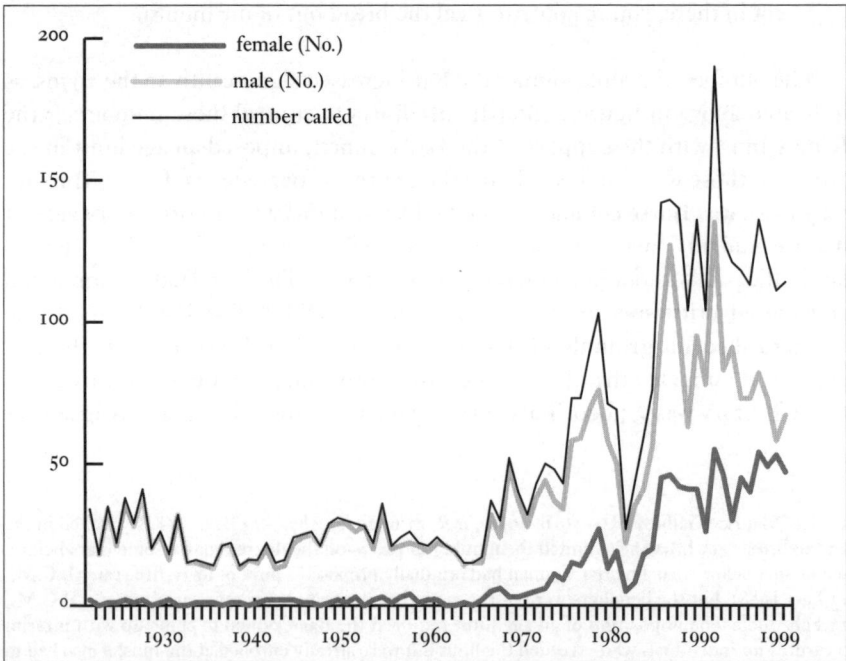

19 B.C.M., 28 Nov. 1986; K.I.B.M., 6, 16 Nov. 1987, 11 Jan. 1988.   20 B.C.M., 4 Mar. 1988.
21 B.C.M., 28 Nov. 1986; 3 Oct. 1987.

Not all of those who were called to the Bar actually practised, and chapter nine will examine in more detail the attrition rate for those women who began practising at the Bar. The small number of women in practice was reflected in the interviews for this book; a barrister called in the fifties said there were 'hardly any in the fifties and the sixties'.[22] Another, who was called in the mid-sixties, said there were only about three or four practising women barristers when he came down.[23] There were still 'surprisingly few'[24] in the early seventies; one interviewee recalled women 'not on circuit. Not anywhere. I mean at the Bar we had a tiny number of women.'[25] Another estimated that there were twelve women barristers practising in 1970.[26]

Religion

In the years immediately following independence, a large proportion of the Bar came from the various Protestant denominations, including the Church of Ireland, Methodist and Presbyterian churches.[27] A barrister who was called in 1925 recalled older, Protestant men 'who seemed to belong to a different world.'[28] The Protestant majority declined considerably in the following decades, and the number of Catholics grew. However, throughout the century the Bar was frequently characterised as a place where religious differences did not generally cause difficulties. This sentiment was expressed by a barrister who was called to the Bar in the 1920s:

> Notwithstanding the very national and Gaelic character of the new state there was never at any time the slightest trace of discrimination or intolerance against anybody native or visitor on the grounds of religious or political beliefs.[29]

The same barrister, describing his close friendship with another member of the Bar, said '[w]e were of similar age but he was as definitely of the Protestant culture as I was of the Catholic culture'.[30] This is not to say that people were unaware of religious distinctions. A barrister who was called in the sixties said that in that decade it was easy to know other people's religion, partially because the Law Library was so small; he spoke of recalling 'elderly gentlemen with Protestant names.'[31] He said 'one was always conscious' of the religious

---

22 B19.   23 B6.   24 B16.   25 B18.   26 B11.   27 Ferguson, *Barristers*, records over one hundred barristers whose fathers were ministers of different denominations, including John Sydney Cole (called in 1935: ibid., p. 158).   28 P.J. McEnery, 'Look back in love', UCDA P174/1 p. 114.   29 P.J. McEnery, 'Ireland, 1900–50. Glimpses in retrospect', UCDA P174/1, pp 101–2. The *Irish Law Times* noted that there was little evidence of changed practice in 1924: '[g]oing into any of these courts it was hard to realise the change that had taken place. The work was proceeding with the utmost regularity and expedition.' (1924) 58 *I.L.T.S.J.* 149 (14 June 1924).   30 McEnery, 'Look back in love', UCDA P174/1, p. 88.   31 B6.

distinctions. Another said that in the seventies, Protestant barristers were 'very identifiable.'[32] John Kelly was able to observe in 1977 that there was 'still a very strong representation at the Bar of the minority religious and cultural sections of the community'.[33]

Religious services to mark the beginning of the legal year were held for the Roman Catholic, Church of Ireland and Jewish legal communities.[34] Members of the Bar received individual formal invitations to these religious services.[35] In 1977 the Bar Council decided that organising the votive Mass at the start of the legal year was a task outside its scope, but that 'nevertheless something would have to be done to maintain the occasion'.[36] The tradition continued, and a couple of years later, a member of council even went so far as to invite the Pope to say the next Mass.[37] Pope John Paul II undoubtedly had a full itinerary when he visited Ireland for three days on 29 September 1979, and saying Mass for the bench and Bar did not ultimately form part of this. In 1980, representatives from the solicitors' profession wrote to the Bar Council suggesting that the annual Mass be replaced with an ecumenical service and the Bar Council interpreted this as 'an attempt to take over these proceedings from the Bar'.[38]

Aside from representation at the Bar, there was also the issue of briefing practices which took place along religious lines. Several interviewees mentioned the tacit acceptance that there were certain firms of solicitors known as Protestant firms and they would tend to brief Protestant solicitors.[39] One barrister called in the early eighties described this as follows:

> The Trinity cohort were always a closed court and some of them would have been in what might loosely be termed the Protestant offices and undoubtedly you would see instructions flowing in from the so-called Protestant offices to people who had certainly been through Trinity and probably the majority of them were Church of Ireland.

Another barrister recalled:

> X told me that when he qualified, now that would be back in the fifties, that the Protestant law firms only briefed Protestant barristers and they wouldn't give one to a Catholic barrister.[40]

---

32 B15.   33 Dáil Éireann deb., vol. 298, no. 8 (20 Apr. 1977). The representation of both Protestants and Roman Catholics in judicial appointments remained a feature throughout the twentieth century. There was also some Jewish representation on the superior courts, though a barrister called in the late sixties, B8, reflected that, for most of the century, 'there weren't enough Jews there.'   34 E.g. (1931) 65 *I.L.T.S.J.* 249 (17 Oct. 1931).   35 B.C.M., 27 June 1977.   36 Ibid. 37 B.C.M., 3 July, 27 Aug. 1979. There were plans to invite 'a large delegation of foreign lawyers'. 38 B.C.M., 23 Jan. 1980.   39 E.g., B6, called in the mid-sixties.   40 B20.

However, at least one Protestant barrister (from 'a very religious background'), who was called in the early sixties, was sceptical that their being briefed by Protestant firms had anything to do with religion. They said that most of their work came from other, non-Protestant firms. Furthermore, several Catholic barristers who were interviewed recalled being briefed by Protestant firms, in the late sixties and early seventies. One said:

> I also did work for the so-called Protestant offices too and I don't think any of them would have consciously instructed on a religious basis, that would have been very very exceptional if that happened at all.

This idea of religion being tangential to other types of connection was also raised by another barrister:

> I don't think religion per se was an issue. I don't think people really cared in that way. Religion came into it where your links were.[41]

Aside from the existence of 'Protestant firms', most interviewees did not consider religion to have been an important factor at the Bar in the second half of the twentieth century. One barrister, who began in the seventies, mentioned 'one judge who probably wasn't that fond of Protestants', but this was the only example given of sectarianism.

Catholics and Protestants were not the only religious congregations represented at the Bar. Rivlin, writing about the twentieth century, claimed that '[a]fter medicine, the chosen profession for ambitious Jews in Ireland was the law.'[42] Bernard Shillman, called in 1926, claimed to be the first Jewish barrister called in the Irish Free State,[43] and his unpublished memoir sheds light on the experiences of Jewish members of the Irish Bar.[44] Particularly from the seventies, members of the Jewish community were increasingly involved in law and politics, to which, in the words of Keogh, the community 'contributed disproportionately to its numbers.'[45] Jewish members of the Bar were represented at all levels of the profession.[46] Interestingly, a Jewish barrister described the Bar as

41 B13.   42 Ray Rivlin, *Shalom Ireland: a social history of the Jews in modern Ireland*, p. 154. A similar argument is made by Lachs in relation to nineteenth-century Jewish barristers in England: Phyllis S. Lachs, 'A study of a professional elite: Anglo-Jewish barristers in the nineteenth century', *Jewish Soc. Stud.* (1982) 44:2, 125.   43 Shillman was called in 1926 but did not begin practising until 1934. His King's Inns memorial was signed by Lionel H. Rosenthal KC, who was a member of both the English and Irish Bars and was said to be the first Jewish Irish KC. In his unpublished memoir, Shillman wrote 'Lionel Rosenthal was a very popular figure when he was in practice at the Irish Bar and was affectionately known as "Rosie" by all his colleagues at the Law Library.' Shillman, 'Every journey has an end', NAI PRIV 1367/11, p. 3. Shillman was called to the English Bar in 1946 and took silk in 1948. Ferguson, *Barristers*, p. 298.   44 He also details briefs from some Jewish solicitors, and cases involving Jewish clients. One observation made by Shillman was the similarity between the call to the Bar and the Jewish Bar-mitzvah: 'Every journey', p. 9.   45 Dermot Keogh, *Jews in twentieth-century Ireland: refugees, anti-semitism and the Holocaust* (Cork, 1998), p. 238.   46 For

A very Catholic place ... 99% Catholic ... They had a Mass at the beginning of the year you know and I think on other occasions when there were services attended. They had Christmas carols.

This suggests that to a non-Christian, the division between Catholic and Protestant at the Bar was fairly indistinct.

Politics

It was relatively common for members of the Bar to be actively involved in party politics, and the importance of these political networks for career progression is discussed further in chapter twelve. Chapter fourteen also gives examples of individuals at the Bar who were elected representatives for the main political parties. As Mohr notes, in the early years of the twentieth century, 'the Protestant and unionist traditions remained strong in the Irish legal professions'.[47] In the early years after independence, such political affiliation was more likely to be with Cumann na nGaedhal, later Fine Gael.[48] However, there were also members of the Bar who were prominent in Fianna Fáil[49] and Labour.[50] Mac Cormaic comments that '[i]f the Law Library was a Fine Gael citadel, then by the 2000s Fianna Fáil had begun to breach the ramparts.'[51]

There was a perception that members of the Bar were more likely than not to be politically active, for example:

Everybody who studied for the Bar was steeped in politics ... most of my colleagues who were studying law to go to the Bar, a lot of them had long established family histories mostly in Fine Gael, much more in Fine Gael than in Fianna Fáil.[52]

example, Henry Barron, called in 1951, who was appointed to the High Court in 1982 and the Supreme Court in 1997. See Ferguson, *Barristers*, p. 135. Joshua Baker (called in 1932) was Reid professor at Trinity College from 1935–40 and was a bencher of the King's Inns, see ibid., p. 133 and Rivlin, *Shalom Ireland*, p. 158. Raphael Victor Siev (called in 1960) served as the deputy legal advisor in the Department of Foreign Affairs, Ferguson, *Barristers*, p. 299. **47** Thomas Mohr, 'Irish law journals and the emergence of the Irish state, 1916–22', *J. Eur. Periodical Stud.* 3:1 (2018), 29 at 33. **48** See ch. 14. Examples include James FitzGerald-Kenney (called in 1899: Ferguson, *Barristers*, p. 274); John Lymbrick Esmonde; James Dillon (called in 1931, ibid., p. 174); Fionán Lynch (called in 1931, ibid., p. 275); Liam Cosgrave (called in 1943: ibid., p. 163); Tom O'Higgins (called in 1938, ibid., p. 274); Stephen Barrett (called in 1946: ibid., p. 134); Patrick Lindsay (called in 1946: ibid., p. 229); Declan Costello (called in 1948: ibid., p. 163); John Maurice Kelly (called in 1957: ibid., p. 218); Seán O'Leary (called in 1980: ibid., p. 370). **49** See ch. 14. Examples include James Geoghegan (called in 1915, Ferguson, *Barristers*, p. 192); Eoin Ryan (called in 1945: ibid., p. 277); Cearbhall Ó Dálaigh (called in 1934: ibid., p. 271); Brian Lenihan (snr) (called in 1952: ibid., p. 229); David Andrews (called in 1961: ibid., p. 131). **50** See ch. 14. Examples include Mary Robinson (called in 1967, Ferguson, *Barristers*, p. 142); Dick Spring (called in 1975: ibid., p. 366). **51** Ruadhán Mac Cormaic, *The Supreme Court* (Dublin, 2016), p. 353. **52** B16.

Mac Cormaic writes that '[i]n the 1970s, when the Law Library was a relatively small place it had been possible to identify almost everyone's party affiliation. As the numbers of practising barristers rose – by the 2000s there were about 2000 members – that became much more difficult.'[53]

As with religious differences, political differences were not generally problematic at the Bar. As independent sole traders, members of the Bar had to be able to work alongside or opposite one another, regardless of personal or political views. One barrister observed that, in any case, political differences in Ireland were fairly minimal:

> The country is small; so people know each other and probably the ends of the political spectrum are not as extreme as they are in some other countries ... Labour is kind of soft labour, Fine Gael is soft conservative, Fianna Fáil is kind of social democratic and basically we're all clustered at different sides of the centre. And you know, the politicians also get on.[54]

The political diversity at the Bar meant that barristers were generally used to dealing with people who did not share their beliefs. One barrister commented on the positive effect of this: 'finding that people who you had been programmed to think were great weren't; people who you had been programmed to think were awful had actually something to be said for them.'[55]

Social and economic background

Using the records of the King's Inns, along with other sources such as obituaries, Ferguson has been able to identify the parental occupations of some of those called to the Bar up to 1968.[56] This information is patchy, however, and in the majority of cases, details about barristers' parents are unavailable. Where they are available, they indicate that many of those called to the Bar had parents who were members of legal and other professions. For example, in the 1920s, the available details suggest that on average forty-one per cent of those called to the Bar had parents who were lawyers. In the 1930s, it was around thirty per cent. If we take legal and other professions together, this represents about fifty per cent of those for whom details are available in the twenties. For the 1930s, it was around fifty-four per cent. Slightly less common, but also listed as parental occupations during these decades were civil servants. Most of those for whom details are available were from Dublin or other cities or major towns. For most of the early twentieth century, on average one-third of those called were from rural areas. Many barristers received their secondary education at well-known private

---

53 Mac Cormaic, *The Supreme Court*, p. 354.   54 B10.   55 B26.   56 See generally, Ferguson, *Barristers*, pp 127–324.

or fee-paying schools. Overall, it is possible to generalise that most of those joining the Bar in the early twentieth century were from middle-class and professional backgrounds. Reflecting on what this meant, one barrister opined that:

> The Bar was the pinnacle of a social class structure in Ireland if you think about it ... there was a social reality to the Bar which assumed an economic capacity to survive. The idea that anybody would go to the Bar who wasn't a gentleman just didn't arise. And if you were a gentleman you were able to support yourself because your family circumstances were such that you had your own private income ... the idea of struggling at the Bar didn't arise.[57]

Lindsay similarly described the Bar as 'a group that would regard themselves as a superior class.'[58]

For most of the twentieth century, the Bar was considered to be socio-economically homogenous. A barrister who was called in the nineties said there was 'practically no diversity ... I mean I can think of maybe one or two people from a working-class background ... it really was very middle class.'[59] The perceived lack of social diversity at the Bar was commented upon in the Dáil on several occasions in the late twentieth century. For example, in 1977, John Kelly admitted that there may have been 'a concealed social bias' that led to fewer children from 'socially underprivileged families' entering the profession.[60] Liam Skelly,[61] who identified as working class, claimed to have struggled to find a barrister of ten years' standing to sign his King's Inns memorial, saying 'I was rejected because I was a member of the working class'.[62] He was also critical of the tradition of dining at King's Inns, which operated as an economic barrier to students from lower socio-economic backgrounds:

> I have seen my fellow students compelled to borrow money that they could not afford in order to buy themselves suits of clothes to go up and eat dinners that they could not afford to eat in order to fulfil the regulations as laid down by the honourable society of King's Inns.'[63]

Speaking in 1995, Derek McDowell said in the Dáil

> A large number of people in the barristers' profession come from one specific social class and reflect a specific set of values. This does not necessarily mean that they cannot represent society or that they cannot

---

57 B14.   58 Patrick Lindsay, *Memories* (Dublin, 1992), p. 101.   59 B24.   60 Dáil Éireann deb., vol. 298, no. 8 (20 Apr. 1977).   61 Called in 1973: Ferguson, *Barristers*, p. 365.   62 Dáil Éireann deb., vol. 367, no. 6 (5 June 1986).   63 Ibid.

implement the law properly, but it should invite us to look at the matter in a somewhat jaundiced way from time to time.'[64]

Several barristers commented on the dynastic element to the Bar in the twentieth century; a number of families had multi-generational success across the legal professions.[65] The Bar was not, however, entirely socially homogenous. There were always individuals who did not conform to the typical middle-class Dublin-based profile. As one put it, 'there was diversity – to a certain extent – of class.'[66] Barristers who were interviewed for this book came from a range of socio-economic backgrounds. Some had parents who had legal careers, while others had no such family tradition.[67] They listed parents who were farmers, doctors, builders, civil servants, small business owners and skilled tradespersons. One said that their parent 'would have liked to have studied law but didn't have the opportunity'. They expressed different views about the social mix of colleagues at the Bar.[68]

Several who identified themselves as coming from relatively modest backgrounds or who did not have a family tradition of working in law were sometimes conscious of difference when they joined the Bar. One was self-described as having 'a rougher edge' than people who came straight from university in the sixties, while another, who joined in the early nineties, experienced the Bar as 'a private school, male, Dublin 6 or Foxrock-type environment.' This barrister described

A sense of wealth ... I just thought 'these people are living on a different planet to me', and suddenly I was seeing all these Mercs and BMWs and flash cars ... the sense of wealth and money was something I just had never grown up with ... for me that was kind of shocking, the sort of the nonchalance around money, the spending of money, the assumption of money and various other sort of attitudes. It was a huge culture shock to me from a value system point of view.

A barrister recalled a colleague complaining on a social occasion that they hadn't been briefed because their father was a postman, and saying 'if my father was like an academic or fancy senior counsel or judge I would get work but I'm not getting it because of my background'.[69]

---

64 Dáil Éireann select committee on legislation and security (5 Dec. 1995). 65 E.g., B16, B10. Families mentioned in this regard included the Bourke, O'Higgins, Comyn, Blayney, Finlay, Geoghegan, Lenihan, Maguire and Costello clans. Ferguson, *Barristers,* also identifies some families who were prominent at the Bar in the late nineteenth and early twentieth century, in particular the Sullivan clan. 66 B13. 67 One said: 'My family weren't lawyers. There was no lawyers in my family at all.' 68 B27. 69 B20.

One barrister commented that by the early eighties, people at the Bar were 'less conscious' of 'what people's backgrounds were ... I just didn't get the sense that anybody really worried whose anybody's parents was or where they had gone to school.'[70] Similarly, by the 1990s, a barrister from a modest background felt that 'there were plenty of people like me coming in at the time so I wasn't on my own.'[71] Mac Cormaic has also suggested that the enormous increase in work available at the Bar in the late nineties 'helped to dilute the social homogeneity of the Law Library dominated as it had been for so long by middle-class men who had gone to the same schools and universities.'[72] In his words, 'there was only so much work that the big names or the sons or daughters of legal bigwigs could take on.'[73]

Educational background

A preponderance of twentieth-century barristers attended private or fee-paying secondary schools. One interviewee recalled:

> When I came to it there were a lot of public schoolboys, there was a lot of Clongowes, Glenstal, Belvedere, all protected, straight from public school into the Bar, soaking up all the tradition.[74]

In his 1996 study of the office of attorney general, Casey analysed the secondary schools attended by former attorneys. Of the twenty-five individuals he studied, four were educated by the Christian Brothers and most of the rest were educated in well-known private or fee-paying schools.[75] The private or elite school experience tended to be quite gendered; for example, in their 2003 study, Bacik found that male lawyers were 'significantly more likely to have attended private school than were their female colleagues.'[76] However, girls' private schools, whether Church of Ireland or run by orders such as the Dominicans and the Loreto sisters, also prepared their pupils for professional life: '[t]he elevated special ranks which those females were expected to reach meant that subjects such as debating also featured on the curriculum.'[77]

In the later decades of the century, it became increasingly likely that a barrister had gone to a non fee-paying secondary school. In 1967, free secondary education was introduced,[78] a development which has been described as 'one of

---

70 B23.   71 B24.   72 Mac Cormaic, *The Supreme Court*, pp 353–4.   73 Ibid., p. 354.   74 B20. 75 James Casey, *The Irish law officers* (Dublin, 1996), p. 243.   76 Ivana Bacik, Cathryn Costello and Eileen Drew, *Gender injustice: feminising the legal professions?* (Dublin, 2003), p. 142.   77 Tom O'Donoghue and Judith Harford, *Piety and privilege: Catholic secondary schooling in Ireland and the theocratic state, 1922–1967* (Oxford, 2021), p. 102.   78 See Audrey Bryan, '(In)equality of opportunity and educational reform in Ireland in the sixties' in James Kelly and Susan Hegarty, *Schools and schooling, 1650–2000: new perspectives on the history of education – the eighth Seamus Heaney lectures* (Dublin, 2017).

the most important developments in the history of independent Ireland'.[79] Up to that point, 'only a minority of young people went on to participate in post-primary schooling, with fewer still going on to third-level education.'[80] Some barristers interviewed for this book cited the opening up of secondary education as having contributed to a situation where 'there were many people who weren't completely linked to ... private schools ... but had made their own way.'[81]

> The early eighties and late seventies had probably reflected an emerging group of people coming into the Bar who would come from free schools ... the change in secondary education that opened up and gave free education across the country. That had signalled a massive change.[82]

> One of the great pieces of legislation was in 1966, it gave free education so lots of people had a chance, if you were bright, you could do it.[83]

Another observed that the introduction of free secondary education 'had profound effects but it took a while.'[84]

In 1968, a university grants scheme was introduced, increasing the number of students in full-time higher education by around 127% by the late seventies.[85] By 1980, 20% of those at school leaving age were admitted to higher education. This figure rose to 36% in 1992 and 54% in 2003.[86] Undergraduate university fees were abolished in 1996, which further opened up educational opportunities to a new cohort.

In the early decades after independence, the Bar continued to be dominated by people who had been educated at Trinity College Dublin. However, this too changed over the course of the century, as increasing numbers of UCD graduates were called to the Bar. For example, a barrister who was called in the mid-seventies said, 'the Library was incredibly UCD-orientated.'[87] Graduates also came, of course, from the other universities, but in much smaller numbers.[88]

As noted in chapter three, not everyone came to the Bar with a bachelor's degree in law from one of the universities. Many had degrees in other disciplines, or had taken law subjects as part of a BA course. Writing in the mid-sixties, Delany pointed out that the fact that the legal professional bodies granted exemptions to university graduates 'might serve to indicate that these bodies give

---

79 J.J. Lee, 'Foreword' in Judith Harford (ed.), *Education for all?: the legacy of free post-primary education in Ireland* (Oxford, 2018), p. ix. See also P. Clancy, *College entry in focus: a fourth national survey of access to higher education* (Dublin, 2001). 80 Judith Harford, 'Introduction' in Harford (ed.), *Education for all?*, p. 1. 81 B13. 82 B13. 83 B20. 84 B27. 85 John Coolahan, 'The impact and aftermath of the free education policy initiative' in Harford (ed.), *Education for all?*, p. 89. 86 Kevin Denny, 'What did abolishing university fees in Ireland do?', UCD Geary Institute discussion paper series, May 2010: www.ucd.ie/geary/static/publications/workingpapers/geary wp201026.pdf. 87 B25. 88 E.g. Ralph Sutton (called in 1948: Ferguson, *Barristers*, p. 306) John Gleeson (called in 1941: ibid., p. 193) and Dermot Gleeson (called in 1970: ibid., p. 263) were all

tacit recognition that the universities alone are competent to impart a scientific training in law. Since this exemption is granted for degrees in arts as well as law, however, there is little force in the argument'.[89] In 1973, the King's Inns proposed to change its admission requirements so that only those accepted to study in one of the university law faculties could enter the King's Inns. The Bar Council was concerned that this amounted to handing over control of entry to the profession to the universities.[90] This had arisen because of the universities' refusal to accept all students that had been admitted by the Inns.[91]

Until the early eighties, people without law degrees could gain admission to the King's Inns Barrister-at-law degree by sitting entrance exams.[92] They then spent two years on the BL degree course, attending classes in the evenings. In 1982 this was replaced by a requirement that non-law graduates complete a two-year diploma course before gaining admission to the BL degree. These classes also took place in the evenings,[93] and covered the core law subjects. Although the Fair Trade Commission later questioned whether the King's Inns diploma provided the same standard of education as a university degree,[94] members of the Bar expressed positive views of this development:

> It was great because they were people who may not have had the opportunity to do a law degree first time around or any degree first time round or certainly couldn't have afforded to have studied for those extra years and had gone into work in whatever occupation and then out a desire to become a barrister had spent a lot of time and effort getting their relevant Kings Inns qualification and came into the Bar and again that was really opening it up.[95]

By the mid-nineties, it was observed that a large number of those entering the King's Inns had primary degrees in law.[96]

UCC graduates. **89** V.T.H. Delany, *The administration of justice in Ireland* (2nd ed) (Dublin, 1965), p. 81. He also observed, p. 82, that the universities 'attempt to fulfil a dual role': both teaching law as an academic exercise, and providing law schools for the professional bodies. As a result, 'they have fallen between two stools'. **90** B.C.M., 6 Mar. 1973. **91** B.C.M., 7 May 1973. **92** They often undertook short preparatory courses before taking these exams, for example at the Rathmines College of Commerce, or the Regional Technical Colleges. **93** See Christina Murphy, 'King's Inns move to limit admissions to the Bar', *Irish Times*, 5 June 1982, p. 4. Other changes introduced at this time were the limiting of overall places on the BL course to 100; 50 of which were reserved for university law graduates; 40 for diploma graduates and 10 which were 'reserved'. The publication of this article was noted in the K.I.B.M., 9 June 1982. Kadar Asmal of Trinity College Dublin and Senator Mary Robinson were critical of these changes; see Christina Murphy, 'King's Inns decision opposed', *Irish Times*, 12 June 1982, p. 5. Robinson sought the establishment of an independent working party to carry out a comprehensive assessment of access to legal education and the provision of legal services. Seanad Éireann deb., vol. 101, no. 2 (22 June 1983). **94** F.T.C., para. 7.46. **95** B13. **96** Tom O'Malley, 'Legal education and training in Europe: Ireland', *Int. J. Leg. Prof.* 2 (1995) 63, at 71.

The university law schools were, unsurprisingly, critical of the developments in the eighties. Their views were that 'the fact that possession of a law degree no longer guaranteed a student a place in the vocational stage of training was unsatisfactory, retrograde, and a cause of general complaint among students.'[97] University law graduates needed to achieve high grades in their primary degrees in order to be admitted to the Inns. The universities were also critical of the fact that King's Inns students sometimes had to re-take subjects which they had already studied at university.[98] O'Malley suggested in 1995 that subjects such as administrative law, labour law and commercial and insolvency law 'would seem more appropriate at the academic stage of legal education.'[99]

Sexual identity

From the mid-twentieth century at least, the Bar was said to have been 'always far more tolerant'[100] of homosexuality than society more generally.[101] Interviewees tended to view the twentieth-century Bar as having been 'very tolerant',[102] and 'probably quite a friendly place for gay people'.[103]

> We did have quite a number of not necessarily 'outed' or 'declared' but known … people who were of a different interest … So, it was fully accepted … without going into names there were some very, very talented practitioners who were quite manifestly gay or homosexual. It was primarily the men at that stage, and no one paid a blind bit of difference. They were fabulous on their feet.[104]

Certainly the existence of LGBTQ barristers seems to have been generally accepted; there were said to be 'plenty of gay people',[105] and men who were 'obviously gay':[106]

> In the 1990s there were one or two people who were very obviously openly gay and then a number of others who were, it was kind of accepted they were gay but it wasn't a discussion.

However, one interviewee who was gay was rather less effusive about how tolerant the Bar was, suggesting that its acceptance of gay men did not extend to gay women:

---

97 F.T.C., para. 7.40.   98 This duplication was also referred to by interviewee B22. The King's Inns disputed this in its submission to the commission: F.T.C., para. 7.90.   99 O'Malley, 'Legal education', at 71–2.   100 B12.   101 Decriminalisation of homosexual acts was not completed in Ireland until 1993. A number of gay rights groups emerged in Ireland in the 1970s, many of which included barristers among their members.   102 B16.   103 B10.   104 B12, called in the late seventies.   105 B22.   106 B13.

> While it could be accepting of certain gay men it just had very little truck with the lesbian women ... there were very few gay people, and who they were were men.

While a few high-profile LGBTQ members of the Bar were known and accepted, there were undoubtedly many more who were unable to be open about their sexualities. It is also quite possible that the perception of tolerance is partly retrospective. Someone who was interviewed twenty years ago, for whom the twentieth-century Bar was much more recent history, commented that there was 'a culture of homophobia towards gay and lesbian members of the Bar with the result that most gay and lesbian barristers are completely 'in the closet'.[107] Attitudes differed even when speaking about specific individuals. For example, one interviewee said, 'There were gay barristers. X was well understood to be gay and nobody ever had any issue about that.'[108] However, speaking about the same individual, another barrister said 'X was gay and that wasn't acceptable.'[109] This suggest a certain ambivalence about whether or not the Bar was accepting of sexual differences.

Whether or not the Bar was tolerant, there is some suggestion that one's sexual identity may have affected one's practice. One barrister said, 'I have seen discrimination on homosexual grounds',[110] and that this related to briefing practices by 'certain solicitors, not wanting to brief people that they perceived were openly gay.' Conversely, another barrister commented that

> There was a view at one stage ... that certainly gay solicitors briefed gay barristers ... if you were a gay barrister you certainly had a very distinct coterie of gay solicitors who were briefing whereas the same didn't necessarily apply the other way ... and also what I would have found was that ordinary solicitors didn't worry about what sexual orientation somebody was. That wasn't of concern to them.[111]

The Bar was far from a utopia for gay people in the twentieth century, but the interviews here certainly suggest that it may have been a less hostile environment than other workplaces.

Disability

In the twentieth century there was very little representation of people with physical disabilities at the Bar, as was the case with most occupations and

---

107 Quoted in Bacik, Costello and Drew, *Gender injustice*, p. 301. In England, the Bar lesbian and gay group (BLAGG) was established in 1994. In 1997 the president of this group estimated that there were some 600–900 gay and lesbian barristers, many were still fearful of coming out as it might adversely affect their career development. Richard L. Abel, *English lawyers between market and state* (Oxford, 2003), pp 127–8.   108 B23.   109 B9.   110 B7.   111 B12.

professions. According to Conroy, a 'very carefully organised form of disability apartheid functioned, which separated and segregated people with disabilities into separate schools, separate training programmes, institutions, residential centres and a few segregated employment outlets.'[112] In a study of people with physical disabilities in the mid-nineties, Tubridy noted that only a minority were involved in any kind of paid work.[113] She found that 'the level of education was more important than severity of disability when it came to employment', and that those with third-level qualifications were most likely to be in paid work.[114] There were some barristers with disabilities in the twentieth century. Some of those interviewed for this book mentioned barristers who had disabilities such as blindness[115] or physical impairment.[116] They recalled guide dogs in the Law Library being well tolerated[117] but controversies over accommodating wheelchair users.[118]

There were also undoubtedly those with invisible or less obvious disabilities. An English newspaper in 1997 suggested that many barristers who developed disabilities tried to keep these hidden, given the competitive nature of the English Bar,[119] and it is likely that the same could be said of the Irish Bar. At least one barrister interviewed for this book had a learning disability, for example, which may not have been disclosed to colleagues. By the end of the century, societal attitudes and public policy relating to persons with disabilities were changing, and the Employment Equality Act 1998 required employers to accommodate workers with disabilities. While this was a positive step in recognising the problem of disabling environments rather than individual impairments, it did not apply to those who were self-employed, such as members of the Bar.

Ethnicity and nationality

Mulvagh has examined the arrival of Indian students in twentieth-century Ireland,[120] and describes the arrival of groups of Indian law students, particularly from about 1913.[121] Indian students at the King's Inns were relatively

---

112 Pauline Conroy, 'Employment policy' in Suzanne Quin and Bairbre Redmond (eds), *Disability and social policy in Ireland* (Dublin, 2003), p. 45.   113 Jean Tubridy, *Pegged down: experiences of people in Ireland with significant physical disabilities* (Dublin, 1996), p. 67. She also found that those who were self-employed considered this to be 'less desirable than being employed by someone else but felt that it was really the only option open to them.'   114 Ibid., p. 79.   115 E.g., B4, B6, B22. The *Irish Law Times* reported on blind solicitors and barristers in England on a number of occasions, e.g. (1927) 61 *I.L.T.S.J.* 15 (15 Jan. 1927); (1934) 68 *I.L.T.S.J.* 109 (28 Apr. 1934); 'First blind woman solicitor' (1955) 89 *I.L.T.S.J.* 27 (22 Jan. 1955). See also 'Blind barrister called to Bar; legal diary.' *The Times*, 12 Oct. 1999, p. 23; Richard Ford, 'Blind student memorises law to train as barrister; Lee Blakey', *The Times*, 12 Aug. 1995, p. 5 and Frances Gibb, 'A barrister with blind ambition; Millennium Bar conference', *The Times*, 10 Oct. 2000, p. 12.   116 E.g., B9, B13.   117 B6, B22.   118 B13. In England, a Bar disability panel was set up in 1992.   119 Jenny Knight, 'When justice is blind – or comes to court in a wheelchair' *The Independent*, 24 Sept. 1997, p. 25.   120 Conor Mulvagh, *Irish days, Indian memories: V. V. Giri and Indian law students at University College Dublin, 1913–1916* (Kildare, 2016).   121 Mulvagh, *Irish days*, p. 28.

common,[122] but the numbers declined in the early years of the Free State. For example, in 1916 nine Indian students, including future Indian Prime Minister V.V. Giri, were called to the Irish Bar;[123] the following year there were twenty-nine,[124] and in 1918 there were twenty.[125] By contrast, there was only one Indian student in the class of 1921, one in 1924 and one in 1927. Throughout the twentieth century there were qualifying barristers from Commonwealth countries including Nigeria, Sierra Leone and South Africa.[126] As these states gained independence, there was nowhere for aspiring barristers and judges to study locally, so many were called to Bars elsewhere.[127] Students also came in smaller numbers from other African states, and occasionally from parts of Asia and the Middle East.[128] In the eighties and nineties, students came from Malaysia.

However, while it was not uncommon for students from other jurisdictions to study at the King's Inns and qualify as barristers, few of them established practices in Dublin. They generally either returned to their home jurisdictions or emigrated elsewhere in the commonwealth.[129] For example, Crispin Beda Nagillah, from Kenya, was called in 1979 and is recorded in the *Kenya Gazette* 1982 as having completed his pupillage.[130] Anthony Oye Chukwurah,[131] from Nigeria, was called in 1961, having completed his studies in Dublin, and later took up an academic post at the University of Lagos. A barrister who qualified in the sixties said that he presumed that those who travelled from abroad to study in Ireland returned to their home countries to practise, which appears to have been the case.[132]

The number of foreign or ethnic minority barristers was always extremely low. Another barrister called in the sixties recalled 'a few Africans' at the Bar,[133] while someone else recalled 'one guy from Nigeria' in the late seventies.[134]

---

122 See e.g., Mulvagh, *Irish days*, p. 31 and Ferguson, *Barristers*, p. 118. In 1928, Minister for Justice Fitzgerald-Kenney commented that 'a great number, almost fifty per cent. of the students at one time, were not Irish born; a great many of them were Hindoos, and there is still a considerable number of such students at the King's Inns': Dáil Éireann deb., vol. 26, no. 9 (26 Oct. 1928). 123 This was out of a total of 27 barristers called. 124 Out of a call of 45. 125 Out of a call of 33. 126 See Ferguson, *Barristers*, p. 118. In 1928, the minister for justice made reference to 'a native of the State of Uganda, who was called to the Bar here and who had not a competent knowledge of English.' Dáil Éireann deb., vol. 26, no. 9, 26 Oct. 1928. 127 Anthony Allott, 'The *Journal of African Law*, 1957–96: then and now', *J. African L.* 40:2 (1996), 143 at 145. 128 In 1964, Trinity graduate Suad bint Mohammed al Lamkiya, from Oman, was called to the Bar and later went on to become a legal advisor, public prosecutor and judge in Oman. 129 As noted in ch. 6, the Legal Practitioners Qualification Act 1929 required competency in the Irish language, but this does not appear to have presented a barrier to aspiring barristers from other jurisdictions. 130 *Kenya Gazette*, 12 Feb. 1982. 131 Called in 1961, Ferguson, *Barristers*, p. 360. He completed a PhD at Manchester in 1964 and published *The settlement of boundary disputes in international law* (Manchester, 1965). 'Directory of law teachers in Nigeria', *Nigerian L. J.* 1 (1964–5), 346. Jerome Herbert Chukwulozie Okolo, called in 1960, was appointed assistant lecturer at the faculty of law, University of Nigeria at Nsukka. 'Directory of law teachers', at 348. Ferguson, *Barristers*, p. 275. 132 B6. 133 B4. 134 B23.

Kibeka Sibeta,[135] originally from Zambia, practised at the Irish Bar for a short time in the early eighties before returning to Zambia. Someone called in the early eighties said that there were 'one or two stand out people who would originally come from other countries but had been at the Bar for quite a while ... both practised in the criminal side of things. But in general no, we were a homogenous group.'[136]

Aside from people who came from overseas to qualify and practise, there were also occasionally barristers from minority ethnic backgrounds, although their visibility at the Bar seems to have varied. One barrister called in the early nineties said 'I don't remember seeing anyone that wasn't white Irish',[137] while another called around this time recalled someone from a minority ethnic background being referred to by a derogatory term. This was done 'to his face', and the interviewee found this to be 'really offensive', even though 'they thought it was funny and he thought it was funny and nobody thought anything of it'.[138]

Diversity at the Bar

Several barristers interviewed for this book commented on the relatively homogenous nature of the twentieth-century Bar. One, who was called in the eighties, reflected:

> I would say I was pretty typical. I was middle class, white, son of a professional, south Dublin; fairly standard I would have thought ... there were no Travellers, there were two coloured people in the Library, I think, maybe three, out of five hundred ... there were very, very few women.

Another, called in the late seventies, made similar observations:

> It wasn't a diverse Bar. It certainly was male-dominated in those days. You didn't have very many young ladies ... and in terms of ethnicity, it was nearly all Irish.[139]

A barrister who was called in the nineties commented that diversity 'from a race and ethnic point of view ... was practically zero'.[140]

While the twentieth-century Bar had limited gender, ethnic or socio-economic diversity, it was, however, diverse in other ways. On the late eighties and early nineties, one barrister mused:

135 Called in 1981: Ferguson, *Barristers*, p. 371.   136 B11.   137 B22.   138 B24, called in the 90s.
139 B23.   140 B24.

It depends on what you're calling diversity … there was diversity to a certain extent of religions … there were male and female coming in, there was diversity to a certain extent of class. Diversity in age as well [but] there were very few people who weren't white, all of whom were easily identifiable … there weren't travellers. There were very few gay people.[141]

Members of the Bar often held and expressed very different religious and political beliefs, but this generally did not get in the way of professional relations and the strong networks at the Bar. One barrister observed that at the Bar,

People can have very strong opinions, but they have space for other opinions … I'd actually say there is an enormous amount of tolerance and there is an awful lot of appreciation of other people's difficulty.[142]

Another characterised barristers as being 'more liberal, and I think they're more philosophical in their heads … more open in their heads'[143] than other groups. They reflected that one reason for this might be that

You lose some days, you win some days. You're constantly changing every day in what you're being asked to do and maybe you're just opened up to more diversity because of what you do.[144]

There certainly appears to have been an appreciation for the more nuanced diversity at the Bar:

From the outside the Library looked to be old men, most of them had gone to UCD and most of whom seemed to be either Fine Gael or Fianna Fáil or something like that. Actually, underneath it I think it was a lot more diverse.[145]

This quote, from a barrister called in the mid-seventies, typifies many barristers' opinions that the Bar in the twentieth century was a profession with an openness or a tolerance for different kinds of 'characters' or 'eccentrics':

There was always room for people who could plough their own furrow and do their own thing … it was and is an institution that is set up that … It's a strange institution, housing as it does some of the most remarkable brains in the country, really clever people and really dynamic people. It also houses quite a lot of eccentric people which is great and there is that sense of diversity in it … a home for those who might have no other place to be.[146]

141 B13.   142 B5.   143 B16.   144 B16.   145 B25.   146 B13.

It's a kind of broad church, it's quite good at waifs and strays ... There's always been kind of oddish people attracted to it and in it.[147]

I think if you're an outlier in society you have probably a better chance of being tolerated at the Bar than you would for example in a school or in an office. There are a lot of people in the Library who have quirky personal characteristics who might struggle or might not get the recognition that they deserve in other walks of life.[148]

The Law Library was full of people with outstanding personalities and with the correct modicum of eccentricity, combining a strong capacity for humorous observation.[149]

As the century progressed, women were increasingly joining the Bar and remaining in practice. There was some tolerance of difference in relation to opinion, sexuality and, to a limited extent, disability, at a time when such tolerance was not the norm in Irish society. Members of the Bar appear to have embraced differences when it came to mental health, disabilities, sexuality and neurodiversity (although people did not have the language with which to refer to such differences), and tended to characterise them all as 'eccentricities'. However, this tolerance of difference appears to have related more to personality types than to what would, in the twenty-first century, become protected categories. As one barrister expressed it,

I suppose there were certain eccentricities the Bar could cope with, but it couldn't cope with certain other ones.[150]

It is also worth pointing out that even this acceptance of difference was quite gendered; all of the examples given of 'eccentric' characters at the Bar were men. Nonconformity by women may not have been as readily accepted.

Belonging at the Bar

A number of interviewees described what it was like to be a minority at the Bar in the twentieth century – in terms of, for example, gender, religion, sexual identity and place of origin. Speaking to men and women who had worked at the Bar in the 1970s about the impact of gender was enlightening. While some women gave specific examples of how their gender negatively impacted upon their careers, others (both men and women) were adamant that such things did not really happen, or that they had never heard of anything untoward. This is explored further in chapter nine.

147 B10. 148 B21. 149 Patrick MacKenzie, *Lawful occasions: the old Eastern Circuit* (Cork, 1991), p. 15. 150 B13.

When asked whether they found the Bar to be a 'good fit' for them, many of the barristers interviewed for this book agreed enthusiastically. However, there were also those who, for one reason or another, felt like outsiders. Sometimes this had to do with gender or sexual identity; in other cases, it related to socio-economic background, whether one came from Dublin, the countryside, or Northern Ireland, where one had gone to school, or one's political views. For example,

> In the seventies and eighties I would have taken sort of political positions which wouldn't have been part of the mainstream and ... sometimes actually that would sort of be slightly difficult.[151]

Others were more ambivalent:

> I don't think I've ever felt totally 'in' at the Bar but I've never felt a complete outsider either ... It was a great place to be if you were on the inside and everything was absolutely perfect for you ... it was clearly a much more comforting place if you fit the norm. If you were male, usually if you had gone to one of the fee-paying schools or were sufficiently 'in' for other reasons.

> I felt like an outsider, you know, from the socioeconomic and gender point of view but I was made very welcome by some people and that was, I suppose, because they perceived me as smart and there was a lot of value given to that. So some people made me very welcome.

> It wasn't a very welcoming place in my view. But ... society wasn't welcoming ... much of this is not something that can be thrown solely at the Bar.

One barrister who was in practice in the fifties and sixties said:

> They 'type' you ... I never wanted to become an insider at the Bar you know because you're too bound ... by group thinking and all of that.

Interviewees for this book were asked about their experiences of bullying or discrimination while at the Bar. As with the discussion of sexual harassment in chapter nine, the answers given depended on whether someone belonged to a minority. For example, a barrister who was from a religious minority, said '[t]here was a bit. I did experience a little bit of it.' By contrast, a male barrister who was not part of an identified minority said 'I never saw any, I never saw that'.

151 B5.

A barrister who practised at both the English and Irish Bars commented that although there was camaraderie in England, 'it was not so all embracing and tolerant in character. It is confined largely to chambers and your circuit and your inn of court and the type of legal work you are accustomed to engage in.'[152]

* * *

Evidently the Bar was socio-economically quite homogenous in the early twentieth century, mainly drawing people from the Irish middle classes. But diversity at the Bar was apparent in other ways, including religion and politics, and there is some evidence that the Bar was considered to be an open profession for many people who identified as somehow 'different.' McEnery observed in his unpublished memoir,

> There might on paper seem to be clear cut divisions of age and rank and class but that would be entirely wrong. The Law Library was welded into one body in which the youngest and most recent member had equality with the oldest and most respected, and inside the walls of the Law Library we were all like a peculiar assortment of school boys in which all were in the same class. It was a pure democracy and every member whether young or old, learned or pedestrian, fashionable or briefless, bencher or devil, Catholic or Protestant, tory or republican had and enjoyed equal rights.[153]

The barristers interviewed for this book came from a variety of backgrounds. Although some felt like outsiders, the emphasis on professional networks, camaraderie and socialising,[154] combined with certain norms and rules of etiquette[155] meant that most developed a sense of identity and felt that they belonged.

152 McEnery, 'Look back', p. 18.   153 Ibid., p. 115.   154 See ch. 12.   155 See ch. 16.

CHAPTER SIX

The working lives of barristers

Introduction

This chapter considers what it meant to be a self-employed barrister in the twentieth century. It starts by picking up on two issues raised in chapter two: judicial attire and the position of the Irish language. The types of practice that people had varied; some were generalists, while others developed more specialist or niche practices. Their work could involve petty or serious criminal prosecutions, high-value commercial disputes, personal injuries, significant constitutional challenges or more routine Circuit Court work. Some areas of practice were considered to be particularly glamorous or prestigious, while others were thought of in quite gendered terms. The nature of work at the Bar changed as the century progressed, with new areas of practice such as European Union law and family law eplacing areas such as malicious injuries or workmen's compensation. Practice was also affected by external social, political and economic developments in the country, such as the economic war in the thirties, the 'Emergency' years of the Second World War and the accession to the EEC in the early seventies.

Professional attire

As noted in chapter two, in the early twentieth century, barristers wore wigs, gowns and bands in court.

Wigs

The abolition of mandatory horsehair wigs for barristers was considered on several occasions in the context of Kennedy's proposals relating to judicial attire.[1] In the 1920s, and again in the 1930s, he sought to abolish the judicial wig. In defence of retaining the traditional wig for barristers, Magennis said in the Dáil:

> Everyone who has any experience of the Bar practice is well aware that the country litigant feels he has got a great deal more value for his money when the argument was conducted by a man with a wig on his head before

1 See p. 25.

another man with a bigger wig on his head. That may be very faulty, very lamentable, and very regrettable, but it is incident to human nature. It is a psychological fact that people are impressed by costume.[2]

In 1936 he wrote to the minister for justice,[3] who agreed in principle, though Attorney General Conor A. Maguire was certain that such a proposal 'would arouse a storm of protest amongst members of the Bar and would be likely to give rise to a fierce controversy.'[4] The 1926 rules of the superior courts specified what barristers should wear in the High and Supreme Courts, but there were no such stipulations in the rules of the District Court.[5]

Interestingly, a report in the *Irish Times* in the forties suggested that the London-based wig manufacturers, Ede and Ravenscroft, were increasingly being asked 'to add more black hairs to give that well-used look', because 'the newly called men do not like their wigs to look too fresh.'[6] In the same decade representations were made on behalf of junior barristers who found the expense of buying new wigs and gowns to be prohibitive in the context of wartime rationing. John A. Costello highlighted that barristers' clothing coupons were 'all swept away buying wigs and gowns', adding that the attire was 'as necessary for us in earning our living as a knowledge of law is.'[7] New wigs could not be procured in Ireland and had to be imported, which added to the cost. According to the Bar Council, the cost of a new wig was £16 16s., and there was an import duty of £2 14s. 8d. on each wig.[8] Increased import levies in the 1950s further drove up the price.[9]

Wigs were quite valuable items, and theft was not unheard of. For example, in October 1969 the Garda Síochána had to be informed when several wigs, along with some gowns, were stolen from the Four Courts. Advertisements were placed in the *Times* of London in case the wigs appeared for sale in the neighbouring jurisdiction. However, the wigs were not recovered, and the Bar Council agreed to compensate those whose wigs had been stolen.[10] Two years later, robing master Sam Kelly tracked down a wig being auctioned in Dublin.[11] The secretary of the Bar Council went to the auction rooms and advised the auctioneers that the wig was stolen property and that they ought not to sell it. The Gardaí discovered that

2 Dáil Éireann deb., vol. 5, no. 6 (11 Oct. 1923).   3 Memorandum from dept. justice to the exec. council, 1 Feb. 1936, NAI TSCH/3/S8613.   4 The executive council decided that amendments should be introduced to the Courts of Justice bill to make the wearing of wigs optional. The chief justice had also suggested a new mode of address, and this was also put forward. Dept. of the pres. exec. council to the min. justice, 8 Feb. 1936, NAI TSCH/3/S8613.   5 See (1931) 65 *I.L.T.S.J.* 55 (7 Mar. 1931).   6 'London letter', *Irish Times*, 10 Dec. 1945, p. 5. The writer also added that Irish barristers had apparently larger heads than their English counterparts.   7 Dáil Éireann deb., vol. 87, no. 16 (26 July 1942).   8 The council wrote to the minister for finance asking for the import tax to be removed; B.C.M., 15 Oct. 1948 and 5 Nov. 1948. In January 1949 it was announced that a certain number of wigs could now be imported without payment of duty: B.C.M., 21 Jan. 1949.   9 New import levies meant that the price of a wig rose to £28: B.C.M., 9 Oct. 1956.   10 B.C.M., 7, 28 Nov. 1969.   11 B.C.M., 29 Jan. 1971.

this and another wig had been pawned at a Marlborough Street pawnbrokers. The secretary of the Bar Council accompanied Mr Kelly to the pawnbrokers, where they were told that several wigs and gowns had been pawned there by a member of the Bar who no longer practised in Ireland. The Bar Council wrote to this barrister, who denied the theft and claimed that the wigs had been provided by Mr Kelly. Unsatisfied with this, the Bar Council referred the matter to the King's Inns benchers, whose consideration of the case is further discussed in chapter sixteen.[12] Another theft of wigs arose in 1972 when two wigs were stolen 'from the downstairs restaurant' in the Four Courts.[13] In 1981, it was found that of eight full-bottomed wigs previously in the care of Sam Kelly, then recently deceased, only two could be found.[14] These were insured for £350 each. A third wig, belonging to a judge, was also located.[15] At a call to the inner Bar the following year, it was necessary to borrow some full-bottomed wigs from Northern Ireland.[16]

The universal wearing of wigs by barristers began to be eroded in the last decades of the century. From 1989, barristers and judges in family law proceedings wore neither wigs nor gowns.[17] In the Dáil debates over what became the Criminal Evidence Act 1992, Coen notes that the issue of barristers' attire attracted strong opinions:

> Members of the Dáil derided 'people who dress abnormally' and 'act theatrically' wearing 'ridiculous outfits more suitable to pantomime' that were 'a hangover from the colonial days of British rule'.[18]

Although the focus of this Act was the giving of evidence by vulnerable witnesses via live link, several TDs, including Alan Shatter, sought to abolish the wearing of wigs more generally.[19]

One barrister who had practised in the family courts later said that while she had been 'initially horrified at the proposals in the legislation', she had found herself functioning 'perfectly well without the wig and gown.'[20] The early nineties saw much internal debate among members of the Bar[21] over the continued

12 B.C.M., 26 Feb., 27 Mar., 30 Apr. 1971.   13 B.C.M., 28 Jan. 1972.   14 B.C.M., 16 Feb. 1981. 15 B.C.M., 9, 28 Mar. 1981.   16 B.C.M., 4 Oct. 1982.   17 Judicial Separation and Family Law Reform Act 1989, ss 33(1) and (4). The Bar Council had noted in 1988 that it was not the usual practice for counsel to wear wigs in the children's court: B.C.M., 1 Mar. 1988. In debating the Criminal Evidence bill 1992, Alan Shatter TD commented 'if I had my way, I would ban outright the wearing of wigs and gowns *in toto* for all court proceedings.' Dáil Éireann deb., vol. 416, no. 6 (3 Mar. 1992). Section 13(3) of the Criminal Evidence Act 1992 provided that wigs and gowns were to be worn when evidence was given via video link by a vulnerable witness.   18 Mark Coen, '"Radical reforming legislation" or "the politics of illusion"?: enacting the Criminal Evidence Act 1992', *D.U.L.J.* 43:1 (2022), 85, at 95–6.   19 Ibid., at 96.   20 B.C.M., 20 July 1991.   21 In 1992 a special committee of the Bar Council considered the wearing of wigs. See further ch. 11. See also 'Wigs and gowns', *Irish Law Times* 10 (1992) 177, an editorial in which the *Irish Law Times* supported the retention of the wig and gown. It added that '[t]he argument for the removal of wigs and gowns is often promoted by those whose real agenda is the abolition of the Bar and the wig and

wearing of wigs. At a general meeting of the Bar in 1991, one described them as 'an outward symbol of our independent profession,' while another argued that 'the formality and so on associated with wig and gown may encourage the telling of the truth.' Another barrister said the wig gave 'a certain indeterminate air about one's age.' Expressing the matter quite forcefully, one barrister said

> The Bar should say to the ignorant and those who wish to harm the Bar – No! We shall continue to wear our wig from here to eternity![22]

The Court and Court Officers bill 1995 sought to do away with mandatory wigs. This provoked another fairly strong reaction from the Bar, and one barrister expressed the view that these proposals were 'purely symbolic':

> This wasn't going to make a jot of a difference to anybody in the legal system, this was a symbolic gesture. It was the state, it was the government telling barristers 'we can regulate you'. This is not about a piece of horsehair. This is about a principle.[23]

Section 49 of the Courts and Court Officers Act 1995 provided that barristers were no longer required to wear 'a wig of the kind heretofore worn or any other wig of a ceremonial type.' Nevertheless, there remained some judges who insisted that they still be worn,[24] as well as barristers who preferred to continue wearing them; one interviewee said that they 'never went into a court without wearing one'.[25] In 2003 Bacik et al. noted that

> Some judges have even let it be known that they disapprove of counsel appearing before them without wearing wigs; this inevitably instils fear of going wig-less among many junior barristers, and so wigs continue to be worn widely in the courts in practice.[26]

The barristers interviewed for this book, who were in practice from the 1950s on, were generally quite positive about the wearing of wigs, particularly in their early careers.[27] One felt that it gave 'some element of dignity'.[28]

Robes

The other part of the barrister's attire was the robe or gown. The Courts of Justice bill 1923 purported to remove decision-making about legal attire from

gown is seen as the "Rock of Gibraltar" of the Bar.' **22** B.C.M., 20 July 1991. **23** B14. **24** The Court of Criminal Appeal noted in *D.P.P. v. Barnes* [2006] IECCA 165 that the trial judge had 'twice made somewhat arch and oblique comments about the fact that neither senior nor junior counsel for the defence was wearing a wig.' The court was of the view that '[t]he remarks, though plain as a pikestaff to any lawyer, were obliquely couched and cannot have meant anything to the defendant.' **25** B14. **26** Bacik, Costello and Drew, *Gender injustice*, p. 69. **27** E.g., B6. **28** B9.

the courts' rule-making committees and vest it in the minister for home affairs. This provoked strong opposition in the Dáil and from the Bar.[29] When Chief Justice Kennedy later presided over the courts' rule-making committee, he sought to introduce new judicial robes.[30] Bewley described the designs as 'extremely artistic ... The worst that could be said of them was that they were possibly too reminiscent of a scene in the Russian ballet to be entirely suitable to the prosaic atmosphere of a Dublin courthouse'.[31] The proposals were discussed at length by the bench and Bar and in the Dáil.[32] A majority opposed the new mode of dress and to Kennedy's chagrin, the new designs were not ultimately adopted. According to Bewley, the reason for the rejection was the financial burden on junior members of the Bar, who had already purchased wigs and gowns.[33] The rules of the superior courts provided that barristers should appear in court 'habited in a dark colour, and in such robes and bands and with such wigs as have heretofore been worn.'[34] Junior barristers continued to wear stuff gowns, while senior counsel wore silk gowns.[35] The gowns were black, and were obligatory attire only for court, but many barristers wore them in the Law Library and at consultations with clients and solicitors.[36] Mackenzie even recalled a colleague who was so enamoured of his wig and gown that he wore it visiting his wife and new-born child in a Dublin nursing home:

> He would come on to see her at night, bring his work with him, sit down and do it at a table. The nurses used to come in and watch the spectacle. He was not just sitting there busily writing away, but he was wearing his wig and gown. Thus attired, he solemnly laboured away.[37]

Discussions about whether to retain the gown were generally subsumed into the broader debate over wigs, but their use rarely caused much consternation or division. Public criticisms of barristers' attire were aired from time to time during the century. For example, in 1961, Noel Browne referred to

29 E.g., Dáil Éireann deb., vol. 5, no. 6 (11 Oct. 1923). Captain Redmond commented, 'I really cannot understand what the minister for home affairs has to say to what costume is worn by members of the Irish Bar.' 30 Ronan Keane, 'The voice of the Gael: Chief Justice Kennedy and the emergence of the new Irish court system 1921–1936', *Ir. Jur.* 31 (1996), 205, at 221–2. Designed by Charles Shannon, with the support of W.B. Yeats, the proposed new robes were more colourful, and were evocative of the clothing supposedly worn by the judges of old Gaelic Ireland. UCDA P4/1163–1169. 31 Bewley, *Memoirs of a wild goose*, p. 90. 32 Brian Farrell comments in the foreword to Kotsonouris' book on the Dáil Courts that '[t]he rigmarole of wigs and gowns was only the outward manifestation of the innate conservatism of the legal and political establishment of the Irish Free State.' Kotsonouris, *Retreat from revolution*, p. 3. In 1925 the Bar Council noted 'the unanimous desire of the Bar to retain their present costume': B.C.M., 10 Feb. 1925. The following year, Kevin O'Higgins reported in the Seanad that 95% of practising barristers were opposed to a change to their court attire. Seanad Éireann deb., vol. 7, no. 17 (22 July 1926). 33 Bewley, *Wild goose*, p. 91. 34 Rule 3 of order 30. 35 See ch. 4. 36 The question of solicitors wearing robes in court was raised in 1931: (1931) 65 *I.L.T.S.J.* 55 (7 Mar. 1931) and (1931) 65 *I.L.T.S.J.* 59 (7 Mar. 1931). The *Irish Law Times* noted, with horror, that some solicitors wore robes over their overcoats, 'a sartorial outrage which no expediency can justify.' 37 Patrick MacKenzie, *Lawful occasions: the*

These old men who should have more sense going round in these absurd garments, lawyers and members of the judiciary, wearing these extraordinary clothes which would get them locked up if they were seen wearing them in Grafton Street.[38]

In 1986, David Andrews suggested that the gown could be justified 'on the basis of protecting one's clothing, acting as an overall in the to-ing and fro-ing in the courts, consultations, referring to law books on a daily basis'.[39] One interviewee recalled a suggestion in the 1990s that the gowns be changed to something along the lines of the simpler French or civil law gown, but nothing came of this.[40]

Gowns were generally worn over a dark business suit or skirt, in accordance with the rules of court, and very little changed in this regard from the 1920s to the 1990s. Unusually, barrister Dubhglas Mac Fhionnlaoich[41] was known for wearing a dark green kilt under his robes in court;[42] when he was called to the Bar in 1930, the *Cork Examiner* commented on this 'touch of novelty'.[43] When women joined the Bar, there was some discussion over what attire would be appropriate for them.[44] For several decades there was an expectation that women barristers would wear skirts rather than trousers, and sometimes this was informally enforced by other barristers (male and female), or by judges.

Along with the gown, wig and suit, the barrister also wore white bands or tabs in court. For many years, bands were supplied as part of the Library subscription and freshly laundered bands were supposed to be available in the robing rooms in the Four Courts.[45] Many barristers also carried a traditional red-tasselled brief bag, colourfully described by O'Higgins:

> The brief-bag is very much part of the uniform of the new barrister. It is black in colour, and made of a stout sacking material intended to last a lifetime. It is secured by a strong red fluffy rope, which is partly encased in the top of the bag, by means of which the bag is opened and closed. The initials of the owner are inserted in strings of strong red lisle along the centre; and the barrister with his brief-bag, rushing to catch his train or whatever, often appears, in silhouette, rather like a city-dressed Santa Claus embarked upon a mission of goodwill.[46]

old Eastern Circuit (Cork, 1991), p. 60.   **38** Dáil Éireann deb., vol. 187, no. 8 (22 Mar. 1961). See also M.P. Murphy, who referred to wigs and gowns as 'tomfoolery' and 'nonsense': Dáil Éireann deb., vol. 159, no. 5 (11 July 1956). Jim O'Keefe referred to barristers parading in fancy dress,' Dáil Éireann, select committee on legislation and security deb. (27 Apr. 1994).   **39** Dáil Éireann deb., vol. 368, no. 2 (18 June 1986).   **40** B6 and B.C.M., 20 July 1991. See a general defence of robes at 'Robes' *Irish Law Times* (ns) 6 (1988), 14.   **41** Mhac Fhionnlaoich (called in 1930; Ferguson, *Barristers*, p. 233) was active in the Gaelic League and a competitive Irish dancer.   **42** E.g., he was reported as being 'as usual, attired in full Irish costume': *Donegal Democrat*, 27 Sept. 1930, p. 7. **43** 'Called with the kilt', *Cork Examiner*, 21 Jan. 1930, p. 8.   **44** See further pp 175–8.   **45** See further p. 226.   **46** T.F. O'Higgins, *A double life* (Dublin, 1996), p. 78.

Brief bags, while not compulsory, were popular with many barristers both for their symbolism and for their utility.

Barristers and the Irish language

It was noted in chapter two that in 1925, Chief Justice Kennedy proposed the establishment of a sub-committee of King's Inns benchers to consider, inter alia, whether 'a competent knowledge of the Irish language' should be compulsory for those called to the Bar.'[47] Within a couple of years of the split between the Northern and southern Bars, the legal practitioners qualification bill 1928 was proposed.[48] This was debated in the press[49] as well as in the Oireachtas and by the professions.[50] One TD wrote to the *Irish Times*, outlining his various reasons for voting against the bill, one of which was that

> An assembly like the Dáil, where not ten per cent of members are capable of conducting an intelligent debate in Gaelic for ten minutes, should impose such a language on defenceless citizens is the last word in audacity.[51]

The Bar Council was doubtful about the practicability of the proposed legislation.[52] It was suggested that it would take many years before there were lawyers able to 'thoroughly' conduct cases in Irish. However, it was pointed out that the bill did not go so far as to require that cases be conducted through Irish. The Bar Council resolved that:

> Until Irish has become a language in more general use in Saorstát Éireann than at present, it is injurious to the interests not only of the legal profession but also of the public that any statute should be enacted making such knowledge of the language as is required by the legal practitioners

---

47 K.I.B.M., 26 Oct. 1925.   48 Osborough writes that this move had been predicted some years earlier, citing a *Memorandum on the position of the southern Irish judges under the Treaty and the Irish constitution* (1922), a copy of which was held in the Thomas Molony papers. Language issues were discussed in the *Irish Law Times* on several occasions including in March 1923 when the master of the rolls had to decide whether an affidavit could be accepted if it was wholly in the Irish language. (1923) 57 *I.L.T.S.J.* 68 (17 Mar. 1923). In October 1924 the chief clerk in the Dublin District Court refused to check a document in a civil case because it was in Irish. (1924) 58 *I.L.T.S.J.* 246 (4 Oct. 1924). In *The King (Little and Ó hUadhaigh) v. Cooper*, a *mandamus* was sought to compel a district justice to sign a decree in Irish. Sullivan J. in the High Court ruled that a litigant in the District Court could prepare court documents in the Irish language: (1924) 58 *I.L.T.S.J.* 316 (27 Dec. 1924), and (1924) 59 *I.L.T.S.J.* 21 (24 Jan. 1925).   49 *Irish Independent*, 2 May 1929, p. 7.   50 The Incorporated Law Society convened a general meeting and published a pamphlet outlining its views, which was reproduced in the *Irish Law Times*: (1929) 63 *I.L.T.S.J.* 58 (9 Mar. 1929). 51 Letter from Dr Hennesy, reproduced at (1928) 62 *I.L.T.S.J.* 258.   52 It was thought that Irish-speaking judges and juries would also be needed.

qualification bill 1928 a condition precedent for admission to practise at the Irish Bar.[53]

Other arguments against the bill included that there were no Irish-language law textbooks and no Irish legal terminology.[54] However, despite opposition from the profession, the legislation was passed in June 1929.[55] It required barristers and solicitors to have

> Such a degree of oral or written proficiency in the use of the language as is sufficient to enable a legal practitioner efficiently to receive instructions, to advise clients, to examine witnesses and to follow proceedings in the Irish language.[56]

The minister for home affairs, Fitzgerald-Kenney, supported the bill and hoped that the required standard of Irish would be high.[57] However, this proved not to be the case. In the 1960s, Patrick McGilligan told the Dáil that 'no foreign student has ever yet failed to pass the test in Irish'. He asked, 'Is that not nonsense?'[58] Some years later, the King's Inns admitted that 'the Irish examination was very easy many years ago, being simply an oral examination'. However, in its submission to the Fair Trade Commission in the 1980s, it pointed out that the standard of Irish was by that stage assessed by 'a written examination and was taken seriously.'[59] The King's Inns favoured abolishing the Irish-language requirement.

The number of Irish-speaking barristers remained low for some years following the 1929 Act, although media reports may have exaggerated the deficit. For example, in 1930 Dubhglas Mac Fhionnlaoich was wrongly reported to be the only Irish-speaking lawyer in Ireland.[60] As the status and use of the language improved, some barristers, began using the Gaelicised versions of their names; for example, Carroll O'Daly became Cearbhaill Ó Dálaigh; Patrick Augustine Sheehan became Pádraig A. Ó Síocháin.

The Gaelic League sought in 1934 to increase the use of Irish in the courts.[61] One of its suggestions was to assemble a committee to compile an Irish law

---

53 B.C.M., 8 Feb. 1929.   54 E.g., Samuel Lombard Brown, a KC and a senator, told the Seanad that he was 'strongly opposed' to the bill, and that 'it would be quite impossible to put into the Irish language a great many of the legal ideas with which we are concerned in our law.' Seanad Éireann deb., vol. 12, no. 6 (1 May 1929). Speaking to members of the Law Society in 1932, Chief Justice Kennedy said that 'a technical vocabulary of law in Irish' still remained to be undertaken. (1932) 66 *I.L.T.S.J.* 27 (13 Nov. 1932).   55 Many of the contributors to the parliamentary debates over the legal practitioners (qualification) bill 1928 spoke in Irish.   56 S. 3.   57 Dáil Éireann deb., vol. 26, no. 9 (26 Oct. 1928).   58 Dáil Éireann deb., vol. 211, no. 5 (24 June 1964).   59 Fair Trade Commission, *Report of study into restrictive practices in the legal profession* (Dublin, 1990), para. 7.94.   60 *Donegal Democrat*, 11 Oct. 1930, p. 6; *Meath Chronicle*, 27 Sept. 1930, p. 3. By the mid-thirties, a considerable number of Circuit Court cases were being heard in Galway entirely through Irish, but the Courts of Justice Act 1936 made no provision for the language.   61 (1934) 68 *I.L.T.S.J.*

dictionary. Two years later, a member of the Bar bemoaned the continuing lack of Irish language textbooks, adding that 'there were a lot of young men with a good knowledge of Irish and knowledge of the law'.[62] The issues of textbooks and legal terminology were addressed as the century progressed. The Irish Legal Terms Act 1945 provided for the establishment of an advisory committee, to include judges and barristers, which would assist the minister for justice making declarations 'that the equivalent in the Irish language of any specified term shall be such word or words as he thinks fit.'[63] This led to the publication of official *téarmaí dlí* or Irish legal terms.[64] In the 1960s Pádraig Ó Síocháin published Irish-language textbooks on criminal law and evidence.[65]

Self-employed sole traders

As discussed in chapter eleven, barristers worked out of the communal Law Library for most of the twentieth century. They were independent and self-employed, and many barristers valued this independence, for example:

> There is a certain amount of flexibility about it because no solicitor owns you ... You can not be available, and they don't know why.[66]

> You make your own way, you stand or fall on your own feet, you get the rewards ... if you're successful, you have the failures at your door.[67]

However, being self-employed meant a lack of paid holidays or paid leave for sickness or maternity. If a barrister fell ill and was unable to work, they often depended on the altruism of colleagues who might run their cases and disclaim the fees.

As independent, sole practitioners, barristers were not permitted to conduct themselves as partners or groups of associates.[68] The Bar Council raised the issue of chambers in Ireland in the seventies, but this was rejected by members.[69] The issue was raised again in the eighties, and the chairman said that while at one

---

168–9 (23 June 1934). **62** (1936) 70 *I.L.T.S.J.* 103 (18 Apr. 1936). **63** S. 3. The Act also provided for publication of Irish versions of legal forms and precedents of legal instruments. John A. Costello was lukewarm about the proposed bill, saying 'It may possibly do some good, and I do not think it will do any harm.' He added, however, that 'one possibly useful aspect of the bill 'may be that unfortunate law students who are harassed at the moment in trying to pass the examinations required by the Legal Practitioners Qualification Act may have some sort of standard to guide them in their effort to pass their Irish examination.' Dáil Éireann deb., vol. 96, no. 7 (11 Apr. 1945). **64** E.g., *Liosta de théarmaí dlíthiúla a bhaineas le dlí conradh, maraon lena n-iontamhail sa Ghaeilge* (Dublin, 1950) and *Téarmaí dlí; Béarla-Gaeilge, Gaeilge-Béarla* (Dublin, 1959). **65** P.A. Ó Síocháin, *Dlí coiriúil na hÉireann* (Dublin, 1964) and P.A. Ó Síocháin, *Dlí na fianaise in Éirinn* (Dublin, 1962). **66** B22. **67** B26. **68** Rule 8.18 of the code: 'Barristers shall not carry on their practices as partners or as a group of associates or in such a way as to lead solicitors and others to believe that they are partners or members of a group or associates.' Rule 8.1: 'The Law Library is the central and primary place of practice for the Bar of Ireland.' **69** F.T.C., para. 11.17.

time he had 'been involved in a proposal to set up chambers, he was now firmly convinced that the Law Library system was by far the best if it could be maintained, and he felt that everything should be done to preserve it.'[70] Fearful that a system of chambers might be established by stealth, the Bar Council attempted to regulate any attempts by members to set up external offices. In 1975 it ruled that it was inconsistent with membership of the Library for two or more barristers to conduct their practice from chambers or offices in association with each other without the consent of the Bar Council.[71]

The Library subscription fee ensured a basic workspace (albeit overcrowded at times) and access to resources such as law reports, phones and sometimes paid-for secretarial services such as a typing pool. As demonstrated in chapter eleven, barristers also tended to work from home outside of the Library hours,[72] and in later years, overcrowding and the changing nature of practice led many to rent office spaces.

Being self-employed meant that each individual barrister was responsible for all aspects of their practice, including correspondence, filing, researching, typing (or later, word-processing), keeping accounts, chasing fees and paying taxes. By the seventies and eighties, barristers were expected to pay and be registered for VAT, which was variously described as 'hard work'[73] or something to be initially avoided.[74] When the possibility of requiring the profession to charge VAT was raised in 1976, the Bar Council anticipated that it 'would cause terrible confusion at the Irish Bar, and would require the keeping of account-books.'[75] However,

> It actually came to the stage where solicitors and clients were not happy to brief you if you weren't registered for VAT because they were able to get the VAT back and clients were able to claim the VAT back so there was an actual benefit, it was nearly a marketing benefit to actually be VAT registered.[76]

Running an independent practice became ever more complex, and barristers received no formal training on these matters. As one said succinctly, 'we didn't even know how to keep a set of books.'[77] Another mused, 'I really could have done with a practical course on how to run your practice'.[78] Unlike in England, a barrister could not rely on the practical support of a chambers clerk to deal with administrative matters. Some barristers engaged professional accountants,[79]

---

70 B.C.M., 7 Sept. 1982.   71 B.C.M., 14 July 1975.   72 E.g., in 1976, the council received a request from a barrister who wished to take two offices in a building near the Four Courts, because it was 'increasingly difficult' to carry on his practice in the Library or his home. B.C.M., 16 Feb. 1976.   73 B1.   74 B7. One barrister wrote to the *Irish Law Times* in 1989 describing the imposition of VAT on legal services as 'a wicked tax' which was 'probably unconstitutional'. Letter to the editor, *Irish Law Times* (ns) 7 (1989), 147.   75 B.C.M., 25 Mar. 1974.   76 B7.   77 B22. See ch. 8.   78 B29.

typists[80] or secretaries[81] to assist them, and one commented that ideally, for a busy practice, one would have needed a staff. In the absence of staffing supports, people developed their own ways of working.[82] One who had previously worked in an office environment before joining the Bar said they found this to be helpful:

> I had worked for nearly six years … in an office environment, you were meeting deadlines, you were preparing documents, … you were dealing with people, your clients … people working with you, colleagues, staff working for you, that, all of that, gave me a huge experience.

An independent referral Bar

The 'cab rank rule' meant that clients, via their solicitors, should be able to avail of the services of any available qualified barrister.[83] Any country solicitor whose client was a private individual could theoretically avail of the same expertise as a solicitor in a large firm representing a wealthy corporate client. Even the least sympathetic clients were guaranteed legal representation. One barrister described the system as meaning 'the services of the … most miniscule to the mightiest are available to every citizen.'[84] Conventions such as this, coupled with a tradition at the Bar of representing poorer clients for little or no fees, meant that barristers were accessible to litigants and defendants of all kinds. Barristers were generally proud of these traditions, and cited them as examples of the public service ethic at the Bar. For example:

> There's no doubt about it, you get cases brought in this jurisdiction and argued, really, in a highly professional and highly expert way that I don't think you get elsewhere and that's because the solicitors down the country are able to ring any barrister and get them.[85]

The Bar Council generally resisted attempts to erode the independent nature of the Bar.[86] The secretary of the Connaught Bar wrote to the Bar Council in April 1950 with concerns about a resolution passed by the Mayo solicitors' Bar Association. The latter sought to prevent its members from briefing any counsel who had accepted work from a Mayo–based solicitor who was not a member of the Mayo solicitors' Bar Association. A deputation from the Connaught Bar addressed the Bar Council and the matter was discussed, with the council concluding that the Mayo solicitors' proposal would be in breach of the principle of the independence of the Bar.[87]

---

79 E.g., B7. 80 See ch. 11. 81 B1. 82 B7. 83 On the operation of the cab rank rule in England see Andy Boon and John Flood, 'Trials of strength: the reconfiguration of litigation as a contested terrain', *L. & Soc. Rev.* 33:3 (1999), 595. 84 B12. 85 B23. 86 E.g., see ch. 8. 87 B.C.M., 21

Types of practice

No two barristers' practices were exactly alike. There was a multitude of practice areas, and these could differ between Dublin and the circuits. Even within defined practice areas, there were variations in the cases, the clients and the solicitors. Being briefed by the state was generally seen as a very positive development in one's career. John Kelly commented in 1977,

> Quite apart from judicial appointments, which are the ones which get the most attention, a far more lucrative source of revenue for the legal profession is state work, employment as a prosecutor or counsel for the state in the various forms of civil or non-criminal action in which the state is involved. The value of that legal work now amounts to almost £1 million a year.[88]

The kinds of state work described by interviewees included constitutional cases, 'buying and selling for the state',[89] as well as criminal prosecution.[90] As discussed in chapter twelve, receiving state work was often, but not always, a matter of political patronage. This brought its own risks; for example,

> Even with a good state practice if there's a change of government you could be screwed.[91]

As jurisprudence evolved, some types of work died out while new fields emerged. For example, Charles Bewley recalled doing a lot of compensation cases in the early twenties following the destruction that had been wreaked during the War of Independence.[92] Eugene Sheehy reflected on the type of cases common around the same period:

> My guess is that were it not for the Malicious Injury Acts, culminating in the Damage to Property Act 1923, most members of the Irish Bar would have passed away into genteel poverty, with empty wine glasses possibly retained as poignant souvenirs of happy nights on circuit.[93]

Mackenzie similarly described workmen's compensation and malicious injury cases as 'the bread and butter of the Bar' in the forties.[94]

Writing about the early forties, Lee recalled that '[c]ertain types of case came frequently before the court as a result of the war. Ejection cases were common and they were often decided on the question of where the greater hardship lay.

Apr. 1950.   **88** Dáil Éireann deb., vol. 298, no. 8 (20 Apr. 1977).   **89** B1.   **90** E.g., B24.   **91** B22.
92 Bewley, *Wild goose*, pp 93–4.   **93** Sheehy, *May it please the court*, p. 64.   **94** MacKenzie, *Lawful occasions*, p. 8.

Due to the shortage of coal, timber and turf which constituted the principal source of heat, the trees on boundary fences became valuable'.[95] Lindsay, who began practicing in the late forties, similarly described the demise of many property actions:

> Land rows have, in the main, gone. In fact the craving for land seems to have gone altogether. When I first started in practice, the title action was a regular feature of every Circuit Court. People were fighting over two square yards of a little path or kesh, or a path to a well, or a mass path, or setting aside deeds.[96]

He also wrote that since the passing of the Succession Act 1965,

> The old days of cutting the wife off without a shilling, or threatening that if she remarried she would have to give up her life tenancy, that kind of thing is all gone.[97]

In the late nineties, getting onto a tribunal or even representing a third party before a tribunal was also likely to be very well remunerated, as discussed in chapter eight. Although tribunal work could be seen as lucrative, barristers who had been involved commented on the stressful nature of this work:

> Pretty heavy, heavy, heavy going. An awful lot of work in every sense of the word. An awful lot of paperwork in it. A lot of focus on you and your performance and on what you say and what you don't say and what you say on his behalf and what you tell him to do or not to do and all that sort of stuff, you know. That was really stressful.

Another interviewee commented that tribunal work had a negative effect on the barristers involved:

> The people who did the tribunals ... they all regretted it. They all will tell you. A life-changing experience for the worse ... I have never found a single barrister who said, well, they're lucky to get a tribunal. Exact opposite, they say.[98]

Another who was involved in a tribunal said that because of it, they lost all of their other work. However, at least one interviewee said that they had enjoyed tribunal work, 'even though it was heavy going.'

95 Gerard A. Lee, *A memoir of the South-Western Circuit* (Dublin, 1990), p. 9.   96 Lindsay, *Memories*, p. 123.   97 Ibid.   98 B20. The same barrister recalled a colleague who accepted work on the Moriarty tribunal, thinking that this would be a six-month break from other work – and was

Specialised or generalist practice?

In the early twentieth century it was typical for barristers to have quite generalised practices, particularly in their early years. McEnery wrote that this contrasted with the English Bar, where people were more likely to specialise.[99] In Ireland, 'the vast majority would be glad to go into any court of any character on any case provided there was a fee at the end of it'.[100] Many of the interviewed barristers recalled having quite broad practices, partially as a result of their aversion to saying 'no' to any potential work. One said they did 'anything that came my way'.[101] Another recalled their master's advice: 'never turn a brief down'.[102] Others made similar observations:

> You just accept it. If you were lucky enough to get the work you weren't going to say no.[103]

> There's always that fear I think for members of the Bar that goes on and part of that fear then feeds into people having to take on all the work and never being able to say 'no' … I got into that situation that it was really stressful, you know, to keep on answering that phone, to keep on saying 'yes send that to me, I'll get back to you' and never ever to be able to say 'actually, I can't do that now'.[104]

Only a minority appear to have been more selective. For example,

> I was one of the very few people I know who said no to things … a lot of the time I would say 'no, I'm not doing that'.[105]

Some barristers sought to avoid practising in certain areas, for example conveyancing[106] or family law.[107] Chancery work was considered by many to be prestigious; McEnery, who began practising in the late twenties, described it as 'high class stuff'.[108]

When there were fewer barristers, in the sixties and seventies, people practised across a variety of areas.[109] One barrister stated his practice had included constitutional law, company law, administrative law, land law, PI (personal injuries) and crime. Others similarly described the variety of their practices in the 1970s:

> Dance hall fights, personal injury stuff which was sort of meat-and-drink, rent restrictions … drunken driving … crime.[110]

---

still working on it eight years later. **99** P.J. McEnery, 'Look back in love: conversations by an English fireside', UCDA P74/2, p. 118. **100** Ibid. **101** B16. **102** B15. **103** B9. **104** B13. **105** B24. **106** B15. **107** B7. Both of these areas, incidentally, were viewed by many as women's areas; see ch. 9. **108** McEnery, 'Look back', p. 91. **109** B6. **110** B2.

A little bit of personal injuries work, a little bit of banking work.[111]

Some defamation … state work, crime (prosecuting and defending) … a reasonable stream of work from the state on judicial review … title work and quite a lot of written work.[112]

A similar level of generalisation was evident in the eighties:

I did a lot of different things … I wasn't exclusively personal injuries. I wasn't exclusively commercial. I wasn't exclusively insolvency … I wasn't exclusively crime. So, I did bits of everything.[113]

I did other work as well, not just PI. I did probate … a little bit of family … I did a little bit of crime … I did a fair bit of landlord and tenant.[114]

Several barristers spoke of the value of generalised practice:

I suppose I ended up doing every type of work and I think I got stuck with the idea that there is no such thing as a barrister unless he is an all-rounder.[115]

There is no doubt that in general those who have engaged in criminal law, defence and prosecution, would generally be somewhat sharper on the cross examination, sharper on the points.[116]

In particular, working on circuit meant that one was exposed to a broader range of practice areas:

An advantage that we had over Dublin practitioners was that you would have had right across the board experience. So, you'd be available to do non-jury work and land law work and criminal work.

A good circuit practitioner would know great landlord and tenant, would know all the probate stuff, he would know family law … he would turn his hand to anything, construction, any area.

Barristers who had criminal practices generally took on both defence and prosecution work, and few specialised exclusively as prosecutors.[117] As one commented:

I suppose it's part of the adaptability that it is expected of people at the Bar, that you're able to be for the defendant one side and the plaintiff the next and so on.[118]

---

111 B16.   112 B25.   113 B21.   114 B7.   115 B5.   116 B12.   117 B13.   118 B21.

Some people sought to make a name for themselves in particular areas of practice; for example, Shillman wrote that he tried to gain a reputation in workmen's compensation cases, and soon found that he was being briefed by solicitors in this area.[119]

Practising in the various courts

Some of one's experiences at the Bar depended on the court in which one appeared. Some barristers began their careers doing relatively straightforward criminal work in the District Court. These would have been short cases, such as dangerous driving prosecutions, and the fees were low. One barrister jokingly described this kind of work as 'the lowest form of life'. As discussed in chapter ten, Circuit Courts had their own peculiarities, and were often very much shaped by the presiding judge. The nature of work differed between the Circuit and High Court; for example,

> In Dublin if you're working in the High Court, the junior's role is to do a lot of … much more paperwork that has to be done than you would have on circuit and you're less on your feet.[120]

Both the Circuit and the High Court could involve lengthy trials, including jury trials, as well as short applications. The same barrister pointed out that High Court and Supreme Court advocacy were very different:

> In the High Court you always had to keep your eye on the possibility of the appeal … a High Court judge has a particular point of view about a case and for example is saying 'well there's no need to call evidence on that, no need, it's obvious and blah blah' and you're concerned that his or her point is not a great point and you really feel that you need to get in the evidence to support another point that might be successful in the appeal … how you diplomatically – without alienating the High Court judge who may be in your favour – try and make sure that you at least get in the evidence which will allow you pursue the other point on appeal.[121]

Some barristers appeared in the Supreme Court on their own as junior counsel once they had reached a certain level of seniority,[122] while most associated Supreme Court work with having taken silk. One recounted a situation where they ended up in the Supreme Court as a devil in the absence of their master:

---

119 Bernard Shillman, 'Every journey has an end', NAI PRIV1367/11, p. 39. 120 B11.
121 B11. 122 B11.

He was missing somewhere else and this was some application in front of
the Supreme Court and I went in as the devil into the Supreme Court and
in fairness, counsel on the other side … said 'well look, I'll, you know, I'll
put it back to two o'clock.' So the five Supreme Court judges came out and
said 'well, where is Mr X?' And I said, 'he's … indisposed', which was kind
of a crazy thing to say, and [opposing counsel] said 'well, I have no
objection to putting it back to two o'clock' and 'well,' the chief justice said,
'I'll put it back to two o'clock and I hope Mr X is here at two o'clock' and
before the words were out of my mouth I heard myself saying '… and so
do I!'[123]

Appearing before multiple judges could be tricky:

You were appearing before three or five judges … and you knew that there
were differing points of view and perhaps one [judge] a bit in your favour
and the thing was to try and play which one you were going to try and
move along and then keep an eye on the remainder who were perhaps more
silent to see where they were.[124]

In the Supreme Court you'd need to know which judge really understood
this, which judge hated American precedents, which judge loved them …
just pitching it at the judge is the key thing, trying to keep their
attention.[125]

As one barrister pointed out, 'if you're in the Supreme Court, you know, people
are asking hard questions.'[126] It was undoubtedly challenging:

I remember the very first case I did in the Supreme Court and it went on
for about a day and a half and I remembered I was so drained like I went
home at lunchtime when it finished on day two and went to bed … It just
had taken a lot out of me.[127]

The appellate work is really challenging because this is before submissions,
the point is five minutes in they might say 'but why do you say that?' and
you can't say 'oh God ask me that after lunch.'[128]

One interviewee recalled two colleagues who, disgruntled with a decision of the
Supreme Court, hung a poster saying 'Down with the gang of five' from the
balcony of the Law Library.[129] The interviewee added, 'I didn't hear any member
of the Law Library say "take it down" – it was a member of the Library staff who
suggested that it be removed after a few hours'.

123 B21.   124 B11.   125 B2.   126 B26.   127 B27.   128 B25.   129 B5.

From the mid-century on, Irish barristers appeared before the European Court of Human Rights in Strasbourg and the European Court of Justice in Luxembourg. One barrister described this work as 'interesting but quite frustrating', because of the limited speaking time in court. The oral hearing as 'the icing on the cake':

> You have a real sense that while [the judges] enjoy the oral hearing they are largely looking at the submissions and even looking behind that at their own researchers and their own issue.

They describe being unused to the procedures in the European Court of Human Rights:

> There are very few cases against Ireland and there are less oral hearings so you're all the time feeling ill at ease and strange you know and there's ... really no developed Bar there ... nobody is appearing all the time.

Appearances in these courts became more frequent as the century progressed and as the jurisprudence of the courts developed. In 1996 the *Bar Review* published some guidance for barristers practising in the European courts, provided by Justice Barrington.[130] One barrister described an experience in the European Court of Justice:

> It was easier to lose the case from something you said than that you would carry the day by your argument ... You could easily fall down a hole, a lot more difficult to actually make the decisive thing whereas if you have a couple of days in court here you're not at risk so you can have decisive moments in a case but you have a bit more time and a bit more time with the judge so it was completely different but you know fascinating all the same.[131]

There was undoubtedly an element of novelty to these kinds of court appearances, and one barrister recalled 'we all travelled out together'[132] to Strasbourg for a hearing.

Beyond the courtroom

How twentieth-century barristers spent their time depended on the nature of their practice and on the type of work with which they were involved at a given point in time. The popular perception may have been of days primarily spent

---

130 'The *Bar Review* talks to Judge Barrington', *B.R.* 1:1 (1996), 8.   131 B26.   132 B26.

arguing in the courtroom, but this is only part of the story. As one barrister described,

> Being in court is probably only 50% of the barrister's practice. It's all that paperwork.[133]

> For too many people, the dominant image of a barrister is that of someone prosecuting or defending in criminal cases or orating flamboyantly at tribunals. These are important but relatively small areas of legal activity.[134]

Another barrister, commenting in the 1920s, said:

> The great bulk of the business of the legal profession is not done in court. It is done in the office of the solicitor, in the study of the barrister, and in the Law Library.[135]

It was important to be well-prepared for a trial or an important hearing – one barrister described preparing at least ten drafts of their notes about a case, constantly refining until they were satisfied.[136] The challenge of paperwork was a recurring theme throughout the interviews.[137] However, Morison and Leith point out that the role involved more than paperwork and oratory:

> Rather than seeing the barrister as a reflective, scholarly individual dividing his or her time between a book-lined study and the rarefied, debating chamber atmosphere of the court ... We see the barrister more accurately portrayed as a fully social individual who must satisfy all sorts of competing demands, while at the same time carving out a living from a not particularly welcoming environment.[138]

Another important element of practice was the negotiation with opposing counsel and attempts to settle actions before they reached the court. Some judges actively encouraged barristers to settle cases. MacKenzie wrote in the early nineties that

> Anyone who has practised law will know that not until the parties are about to enter the door of the courtroom will they begin to negotiate seriously. Then you ask the judge's usher for about ten minutes to try and settle the case and at the end of that period you would hear kicking on the door giving access to court no. 1: [the judge] was becoming impatient. The usher was as terrified as everyone else.[139]

133 B12. 134 Adrian Hardiman, 'An innovative AG, Byrne will not be deficient in new skills needed in EU', *Irish Times*, 9 July 1999, p. 14. 135 Seanad Éireann deb., vol. 12, no. 6 (1 May 1929) (Samuel Lombard Brown). 136 B25. 137 See ch. 4. 138 John Morison and Philip Leith, *The barrister's world and the nature of law* (Berkshire, 1992), p. 18. 139 MacKenzie, *Lawful*

Based on his interviews with senior counsel practising in the area of personal injuries, McMahon pointed out in 1985 that '[e]xperienced senior counsel and insurance claims managers operate an unwritten tariff for certain injuries, e.g. £50,000 for loss of an eye, etc.'[140] He also pointed out that seniors and claims managers 'can with a good deal of accuracy "value" cases *between themselves* with a good measure of predictability'.[141] Some barristers greatly enjoyed negotiating and settling cases:

> I loved attempting to settle actions ... I think you sometimes even got greater satisfaction of settling a really difficult case.[142]

Sometimes clients insisted on proceeding with their case despite counsel's advice to settle. However, one barrister pointed out that if a judge hinted that they ought to settle, this could be more persuasive:

> You'd say to the client, 'you heard what the boss said' ... once the hint came from the judge, great chance of settling.[143]

This kind of work clearly necessitated having good working relationships with colleagues at the Bar, something discussed in chapters seven and twelve. One interviewee described the interpersonal aspect of the role:

> if you're working every day doing the sort of work that we do you become consumed. You can't do what we do without really ... knowing the brief, knowing the client, dealing with the difficulties of the solicitor, trying to get something past the judge. That is difficult, all of that is hugely stressful.[144]

Thus it is clear that functioning relationships between the barrister and the solicitor, the client and the judge could be crucial.

Working relationships

Several barristers emphasised how important it was to know the personalities and preferences of individual judges; for example, which ones were pro-defendant and which were 'a bit prosecution-minded'.[145] It was pointed out that on circuit, the judges got to know the individual barristers and solicitors quite well:

> The judge on your circuit, he gets to know you, gets to know the solicitor. Knows who he can trust, who can be a bit shaky or flaky ... the success of

occasions, p. 135. **140** Bryan McMahon, *Judge or jury? The jury trial for personal injury cases in Ireland* (Cork, 1985), p. 6. **141** Ibid. Emphasis in original. **142** B11. **143** B20. **144** B5. **145** B25.

most barristers would very much depend on the circuit judge … if a judge said to you 'well X, that's a very impressive argument but I just think I'm not with you on that,' the solicitor is saying 'wow, that guy made an impressive argument' – even if it could be bog stupid. But the judge said it and there'd be an element of 'oh the judge thinks highly of him you know, give him some papers for something else'.[146]

Some judges were known for their inefficiency, for example,

> The judge was incredibly slow. It was very hard to get work on … he was a decent fellow doing his best but he was slow and he was slow and wrong, you know, mostly.[147]

Many barristers who practised in the sixties and seventies experienced bullying or rudeness from judges. They were often described in very strong language by the barristers who had either appeared before them or who knew them by reputation. One judge, who was notoriously rude, was mentioned by several interviewees and described as 'a terrible tyrant … he was a savage and he was crude, he was an absolute beast of a man'.[148] Another was described as 'a real bastard' who 'would play intellectual games with you, just mess you around. Only for the purposes of his own enjoyment'.[149] Other terms employed to describe difficult judges – 'just horrific'[150] and 'as mean as the day was long'.[151]

> There were monstrous judges. [X] had a terrible reputation, [Y] was really difficult, pleasant but cold, like going into the freezer. And then there were others who just didn't have a clue what they were doing … and there were others who were waffly and intellectual and slow.[152]

One barrister noted that when he began practising in the forties,

> Judges were comparatively benign and on the whole there was no frighteningly nasty judges. There then came an age of some very rude judges. They are now far more civilised. It is unusual now for a judge to be unpleasant. I think the Bar would not take it anymore. They certainly would not put up with what we put up with at one stage in the sixties and seventies.[153]

Others gave examples of poor judicial conduct during this period, for example:

---

146 B20.   147 B18.   148 B9.   149 B7.   150 B3.   151 B7.   152 B4.   153 'Ralph Sutton, SC, called to the Bar, July 1948', *B.R.* 4:3 (1999), 152.

Back in the late seventies, eighties … judges were spoken of with a kind of horror: 'oh God, not your man, is he coming down on circuit?' … back then there were judges who were very dictatorial and bad mannered, rude and ignorant but there was such deference to the judiciary that you'd never say 'I'm sorry judge, I'm not taking that from you'. … I saw judges throw papers at barristers … in front of the public … there were a lot of bullies on the bench, really nasty members of the judiciary who terrified the hell out of most barristers appearing in front of them.[154]

The same barrister recalled feeling 'shell shocked' after seeing a judge shout at a fellow barrister and throw a heavy book at him in court. Another judge ordered Gardaí to arrest a barrister in court, because he did not want to hear his pleading about a sentence.[155] One barrister recalled of a particular judge,

There were barristers who refused to go to his court when they knew they had a case there; they'd hand the brief over pretending they had other commitments, just wouldn't go down there … he made life very difficult for all practitioners.[156]

Another barrister said of this judge's court, 'anything could happen there … he could be really awful … he would try and bully counsel'.[157] One barrister recalled a colleague who had been 'run off the circuit by the judge':

It was fairly clear the judge didn't think much of them, and solicitors obviously aren't going to brief someone if they feel it's a disadvantage to their client.[158]

Another similarly recalled a colleague who was 'told by the judge that he would run him off the circuit and he did by every kind of offence and cruelty.'[159] Other judges were described as having favourites:

He made life so difficult for the barrister who was running the case and I was for the defence. I got a relatively easy time in front of X, he knew my parents.

He might have people he particularly didn't like so he would just simply pick on them … So he would just basically make known his dislike.[160]

One barrister recalled entering the Bar room on a particular circuit and:

---

154 B20.   155 MacKenzie, *Lawful occasions*, p. 101. As a consequence, members of the Bar refused to appear in Trim Circuit Court until the judge apologised: ibid., pp 101–4.   156 B7.   157 B25. 158 B27.   159 MacKenzie, *Lawful occasions*, p. 49.   160 B25.

All the barristers in the room and there was dead silence ... a whole lot of people and they're all reading Circuit Court rules and it was X. They were all terrified of him. No jokes, no laughter, no nothing. 'Jesus, you know if I make one slip this kind of fellow is going to pounce on me in front of everybody', and I found that very bizarre.[161]

Writing about a different circuit, another barrister recalled the arrival of a new judge:

Life on the Eastern Circuit, from being cheerful and happy-go-lucky, changed into a situation of tension and anxiety. The solicitors were cowed as much as we were. There were no smiling faces outside the courtroom, no laughter or jokes in the Bar room.[162]

More than one barrister gave examples of 'barristers who were very colloquial, very nice, very lovely, very pleasant, going on the bench and becoming ... not very pleasant.'[163] The term 'judgitis' was used by some to describe this phenomenon:

It's a very prevalent phrase in the Law Library, judgitis. People get the bench and suddenly they're perfectly normal as barristers and within three months going, behaving like pigs, what the hell is wrong with them? I mean it's amazing how it happens. I have seen people appointed to the bench and you think, 'great appointment' and three or four months later you're saying, 'God, I was in front of X, what an absolute bollocks.'

X was a nightmare on the bench. Lovely man off it but an absolute nightmare on the bench.[164]

You're suddenly gone from 'hey Y' to 'morning judge, afternoon judge' ... you're suddenly deferring to someone who just happened to get a job.[165]

I remember Z going out playing golf with the Bar and coming on the first tee and saying, 'this is a golf tournament, we're all going to be casual. So just call me 'judge'.[166]

However, not all judges were seen as bullies, and several were singled out for their patience, particularly with junior barristers. For example, the following anecdote was recalled by a barrister reflecting on one of their earliest cases:

When my expert got into the box, I didn't seem to be able to ask him non-leading questions for some reason and [the opposing barrister] kept

161 B20.   162 MacKenzie, *Lawful occasions*, p. 50.   163 B7.   164 B7.   165 B20.   166 B20.

drumming his hands and saying 'objection', you see, and 'leading question' ... So this happened two or three times or maybe four times and [the judge] then very politely leaned forward and said '... it might help if you could, before you ask a question, if you would simply put the word what, when, where, why, how or who in front of the question and then [the opposing barrister] won't be able to object any more.' So this was the most beautiful put down you'd have received but it was a very helpful put down. You couldn't ever forget it for the rest of your life and you weren't destroyed by it, it was just nicely done.

One judge was described as being 'extraordinarily good to young people, even though one wasn't making much sense'.[167] Another was said to give 'such leeway that you were always very comfortable'.[168] One barrister reflected that during their time in practice, 'the quality of the judges improved hugely',[169] and several made the point that the rudeness of the past would no longer be accepted by counsel.[170] Some judges were known as being sticklers for etiquette and propriety; an anecdote regarding Chief Justice Kennedy records him as having been appalled when someone said 'OK' to him in court.[171]

It was also important for barristers to have a good working relationship with solicitors who briefed them:

> You have your client. You have your solicitor who in many ways is a much more important client ... the relations between the barristers and solicitors are absolutely key ... A good solicitor is as good as a good in-law because they're trustworthy, they pay you, if they get paid half the fee they will share it with you, they'll tell you if there's no money in this.[172]

Good communication and timeliness were emphasised as crucial to this:

> If you can do the work, solicitors will come back to you. 'Oh, he sent it back to me, it's done.' That's a great reassurance to a solicitor. So you're no good as a counsel if you're not talking to your solicitor or communicating with him or this is what to do with the case.[173]

> There had been the old tradition that paperwork was a burden and that you took your time at it and you did it at your leisure when you really had no other excuse and that, whereas [my master] always maintained that you should do your paperwork quickly and not allow it to build up so I adopted that approach and then I suspect solicitors when they get a reply you know

---

167 B25. 168 B20. 169 B4. 170 For a discussion of how barristers perceived appearing before an individual judge, see Frank Clarke, 'A view from the Bar', *B.R.* 3:3 (1998), 170. 171 Sheehy, *May it please the court*, p. 56. 172 B7. 173 B5.

in two weeks rather than in six months tend to come back to you that bit sooner.[174]

One barrister said that they always put 'huge amounts of work' into cases and this helped them to develop a strong reputation among the solicitors who briefed them.[175] Another pointed out:

> If you want to stay in the good cases, you have to then satisfy their demands and their requirements.[176]

Barristers and solicitors on circuit got to know one another quite well, as discussed in chapter ten.[177] Solicitors had considerable discretion over who to brief, and could occasionally exercise this with devastating consequences. One barrister recalled hearing of a case during the 1940s when local solicitors on a particular circuit were directed to 'withdraw work' from a barrister who took an affiliation suit on behalf of a young woman against a local priest. The solicitors were put under pressure by the local clergy 'to basically run him off the circuit'.[178]

As well as strong professional relationships with solicitors, some barristers also considered it important to have good interpersonal interactions with clients. One said it was very important to have

> Empathy with the client, forgetting about yourself and actually trying to put yourself into the client's shoes and how the client felt ... I could see myself in that person's shoes ... especially in the very serious cases they need to feel ... that the legal team that are representing them you know are really playing for them. You're putting on the shirt for that person and that you really will, you are a gladiator of course. You're getting into the ring too, you are, to slay the other fellow.[179]

A number of barristers described receiving

> An acknowledgement from the client that you have done a good job. Now once in a blue moon you might get somebody drop you a letter and say 'thanks very much for all your work'.[180]

> Really appreciative letters directly from clients after proceedings ... Gifts even sometimes.[181]

Some, however, said that this had been quite rare in their experience:

174 B12.   175 B24.   176 B23.   177 B23, B15.   178 B25.   179 B14.   180 B20.   181 B11.

I have a handful of thank you letters I would say. Only once in my life I had a call from a client thanking me.[182]

Another type of interpersonal interaction that could be crucial was the ability to communicate clearly with a jury, discussed further below.

Multiple counsel in civil actions

For much of the twentieth century, civil litigation could often involve six barristers in a single case, in addition to solicitors. The two-counsel rule meant that a senior counsel could not appear in a case without a junior counsel.[183] As early as the 1940s, Justice Gavan Duffy was critical of this. 'In England,' he wrote, 'except only in patent actions, two counsel and no more are allowed on taxation against a losing party.' He suggested that three counsel were allowed in Irish High Court actions because 'we can afford three because our fees are lower than the English'.[184] Solicitors feel that the client must have as one of his team of counsel Mr A or Mr B, the fashionable men of the day, though Mr A may be too busy to do more than open the case to the jury or Mr B to do more than cross-examine a witness, before departing to another Court: but Mr A and Mr B will get the very same fees as if they had attended the trial all the time.' Perhaps consider 'treating the employment of any senior counsel as a luxury, which a litigant should pay for in any event out of his own pocket.[185] He said that the use of senior counsel was 'becoming a fetish'.[186] Along with the two-counsel rule was a practice of having two seniors in civil actions, known as the 'two-senior rule'. This could of course generate very high fees for the losing party, who could be liable to pay the fees of all eight. In 1951 the president of the Incorporated Law Society criticised the two-senior practice, which he claimed had only recently emerged.[187] By 1969, the Bar Council was beginning to view the two-senior rule as a potentially restrictive practice.[188]

Gavan Duffy was very critical of the high costs that resulted, in his view, partly from the number of counsel, and partly from the way fees were calculated.

---

182 B8.　**183** From the nineteenth century, custom and etiquette meant that there was certain work reserved for junior counsel. This meant, according to Hogan, *The legal profession*, p. 80 that silks 'were not entitled to appear in court unless junior counsel had also been briefed in the matter.' Hogan also writes that these rules delineating which type of barrister could do certain types of work 'were in fact a variety of rules and codes often of a not very certain character.' The matter of the two-counsel rule was formalised by the Bar Council in 1912 when they approved rules relating to the privileges of the junior Bar: (1912) 46 *I.L.T.S.J.* 338 (28 Dec. 1912). In England and Wales, the two-counsel rule was evident up to the 1970s. It was considered contrary to etiquette for a senior to appear unless a junior was instructed to appear with them. In 1974 the director general of fair trading instructed the monopolies and mergers commission to examine this rule, and it was abolished in 1977.　**184** Memorandum dated 6 Nov. 1946, UCDA P152/38, p. 5.　**185** Ibid.　**186** Ibid.　**187** B.C.M., 7 Dec. 1951, and ch. 15.　**188** See ch. 16. In 1985, McMahon attributed the two-senior rule to the high cost of litigation in Ireland: McMahon, *Judge or jury*, p. 9.

In a 1946 letter to the Department of Justice marked 'private and confidential', he wrote:

> I am disturbed by the growing affliction imposed by our law costs upon the public ... There is an array of legal abuses today, bearing heavily on the innocent public, particularly on the losing litigant who has to pay another man's costs and is paying far too much.[189]

In his view, the bad practices were 'no part of the law of the land, but spring from bad legal practice or Bar regulations'.[190]

The Bar Council clashed with Minister Des O'Malley on these issues in the early seventies. During a Dáil debate on the Courts bill 1971, he said that members of the public tended to view the two-counsel rule as 'a bit of a racket'.[191] He said it would be 'a matter for the Bar and for solicitors and for insurance companies as to how many [counsel] they will employ'.[192] The mid-eighties saw further debate on the number of counsel in civil actions. In December 1987, the Bar Council adopted a new rule that not more than one senior and one junior should seek to recover fees on taxation in personal injuries actions in the superior courts. This took effect on the coming into force of the Courts Act 1988. Under this legislation, the minister for justice could specify by regulations the maximum number of counsel whose costs would be allowed by the taxing master.[193]

Jury Trials

One common aspect of criminal practice and, until 1988, civil practice was appearing before juries. Barristers had mixed views about juries;[194] some found them unpredictable:

> There is no accounting for what juries will do. No. You cannot guess, second guess, a jury. And that happened a lot ... I won cases I should never ever ever have won ... You also lose cases that you should win.[195]

Others had amusing anecdotes about juries; for example, one barrister recalled being harangued and called a 'fecking eejit' by a juror during his closing

---

189 Charles Gavan Duffy to S. Roche, sec. Dept. Justice, 25 Oct. 1946, UCDA P152/38. 190 Ibid. 191 Dáil Éireann deb., vol. 257, col. 5 (1 Dec. 1971). 192 See ch. 15. 193 Courts Act, 1998, s. 5. This particularly impacted personal injury actions in the High Court. 194 See generally R. O'Hanlon, 'The sacred cow of trial by jury', *Ir. Jur.* 25:1 (1990), 57. 195 B4.

statement.[196] One interviewee said that being able to handle juries was a particular skill:

You can either address a jury or you can't. And some people couldn't.[197]

Another recalled 'playing up' to the jury:

I have often been blamed for grovelling to judges and to the jury – I did. This was quite deliberate, because I believed it was in the best interests of my client.[198]

Another barrister described how it felt to receive a favourable jury verdict:

I think there's very little to beat the feeling when a jury come back in favour of your client ... particularly if it is an acquittal in a criminal trial or an award, or a big award in a civil jury trial ... the sense of elation that you feel when that happens is – I don't know any drug that could replicate it.[199]

As between jury trials and non-jury Special Criminal Court trials, one barrister expressed a distinct preference for the jury because 'at least you had some possibility of being acquitted'.[200]

The use of juries in civil actions decreased significantly in the twentieth century. The Courts Act 1971 abolished civil jury trial in the Circuit Court (where it was rarely availed of). The Committee on Court Practice and Procedure had advocated the retention of the right to trial by jury in the mid-sixties.[201] Writing in the early eighties, Casey noted that the civil jury

Remains available in the High Court where it is the norm, particularly in personal injuries and fatal accidents cases – much to the chagrin of insurers who blame juries for inflated damages awards and hence, higher premiums.[202]

Although the Prices Advisory Committee did not recommend the removal of juries from civil actions, it did suggest changes to the way juries assessed

196 B20. The barrister described his client in the case as adding, 'a complete gouger, I mean a really nasty piece of stuff.' 197 B20. 198 Patrick Lindsay, *Memories* (Dublin, 1992), p. 100. 199 B21. 200 B25. 201 Committee on Court Practice and Procedure, *Jury trial in civil actions. Jury challenges: third and fourth interim reports of the Committee on Court Practice and Procedure* (Dublin, 1966). 202 James Casey, 'Law and the legal system 1957–82' in Frank Litton (ed.), *Unequal achievement: the Irish experience, 1957–1982* (Dublin, 1982), p. 269.

damages in motor accident cases.[203] The removal of juries from civil actions was certainly under consideration by the time Casey was writing in the early eighties.[204] The impetus for this came from insurance companies, lobbying against what were deemed to be 'excessive' awards of damages by juries, which allegedly drove up insurance premiums.

The Bar Council and the profession generally opposed plans to limit or abolish civil juries. In a 1985 press conference, attended by 'a small number of press men and television representatives',[205] the Bar Council stressed that the administration of justice would not be strengthened by the abolition of civil juries.[206] It considered the arguments put forward in favour of restricting juries to have been 'misconceived'. It said that while these arguments were almost exclusively expressed in economic terms, there were 'compelling social and democratic reasons' for retaining civil juries.[207] In a letter to the minister for justice, the Bar Council accepted that some change was probably inevitable, but advised retaining civil juries for determining questions of liability; in all aspects of cases of assault taken against the Gardaí; for cases of professional negligence, and for defamation actions.[208] It also suggested that juries could receive assistance from judges when it came to damages. The chairman of the Bar also spoke on radio and television,[209] and there were articles in the press supporting the Bar's views.[210] The Bar Council was prepared to spend up to £5,000 on a public relations firm, and it set up a sub-committee to consider the issue.[211] A majority of High Court judges, and all of the judges of the Supreme Court were also opposed to any change,[212] and the cabinet was also apparently divided on the matter. The press conference referred to above was deemed to have been successful, as it led to widespread coverage of the issue in the press and on radio.[213] The Bar Council considered the issue to have been 'at least temporarily halted'.[214]

However, the matter did not rest there, and the next couple of years saw continued lobbying by the Bar Council to halt the removal of juries from civil actions.[215] In 1986, in a letter to all members of the Oireachtas, chairman of the

203 Prices Advisory Committee (Motor Insurance): *Report of enquiry into the cost and methods of providing motor insurance* (Dublin, 1982), p. 45. This committee was chaired by Nial MacLiam, and included barrister Kevin Lynch (called in 1949: Ferguson, *Barristers*, p. 232). See also Committee of Inquiry into the Insurance Industry, *Interim report on motor insurance* (Dublin, 1973). 204 E.g., Willy Clingan, 'Insurers call for end to juries in civil cases', *Irish Times*, 6 Apr. 1982, p. 13. 205 B.C.M., 22 June 1985. 206 'Bar Council defends jury system', *I.L.T.* 3 (1985), 149. 207 Ibid. 208 B.C.M., 22 June 1985. 209 B.C.M., 8 June 1985. 210 E.g., Bryan McMahon, 'The pros and cons of the jury system', *Irish Times*, 29 May 1985, p. 11 and Bryan McMahon, 'Dangers of tampering with jury system', *Irish Times*, 30 May 1985, p. 11. See, in response, an article by a claims manager at an insurance company: Dermot Ryan, 'Trial by jury does not necessarily mean justice', *Irish Times*, 20 June 1985, p. 13. 211 B.C.M., 8 June 1985. 212 Ibid. 213 E.g., Niall Kiely, 'Jury system to assess damages defended by Bar', *Irish Times*, 18 June 1985, p. 1. 214 B.C.M., 22 June 1985. In September 1985, Bryan McMahon's pamphlet, *Judge or jury*, was published by Cork University Press. This cogently dealt with the main arguments for and against retaining juries in civil actions. 215 E.g., B.C.M., 17 Feb., 12 May 1986.

Bar Council, Patrick McEntee, set out the profession's arguments against removing juries in civil actions,[216] including that it would 'remove from the public at large one of the very few opportunities they have to participate in the administration of justice.' He also argued that restricting civil jury trials would

> Transfer responsibility for setting standards of care in this country from the hands of a cross section of the community who, collectively, would probably have a wider experience of 'ordinary' living and a better appreciation of acceptable behaviour within the community into the hands of a judge.[217]

He added,

> The abolition of juries is the equivalent of buying a 'pig in a poke' and it does not make good sense to effect change for the sake of change.[218]

The Fine Gael–Labour coalition lost power in early 1987 and was replaced by a Fianna Fáil government. In May 1987, the Bar Council was advised that Fianna Fáil had changed its position, and now favoured the abolition of civil juries.[219] A delegation from the council met with minister for justice Gerry Collins, who confirmed the plan to reintroduce the Courts bill, which would also deal with the issue of the number of counsel allowed in an action.[220] Again in 1988 the Bar Council wrote to TDs, senators, trade unions and newspapers outlining its concerns about the proposed legislation.[221] In June 1988 the Courts Act 1988 was passed, essentially abolishing civil juries in personal injuries actions. This significantly changed the way such cases were litigated.

Work patterns

There was a culture at the Bar of working long hours, and all of those interviewed for this book recalled very long working days as a matter of course.[222] Sometimes the extended working day was a consequence of the challenging work environment in the busy Law Library, discussed in chapter eleven. Several described long working weeks of sixty[223] or eighty hours[224] as being fairly standard. The working day extended well beyond the hours of court sittings. Many barristers worked 'very long hours from early morning till very late at night.'[225]

216 The letter was read into the Dáil record by David Andrews: Dáil Éireann deb., vol. 368, no. 2 (18 June 1986). 217 Ibid. 218 Ibid. 219 B.C.M., 29 May 1987. 220 B.C.M., 2 Nov. 1987. 221 B.C.M., 23 Apr. 1988. 222 Carthy similarly identifies long working hours as an almost universal feature of the working lives of solicitors in the early twenty-first century. Suzanne Carthy, 'Inequality regimes and long hours a mixed methods study of gender inequality in the solicitors' profession in Ireland' (PhD, UCD, 2018), pp 170–220. 223 B12, B17. 224 B10. 225 B23.

One barrister referred to 'people calling meetings at eight o'clock in the morning or people having meetings at half past five at night',[226] while another described having consultations 'from seven o'clock in the morning until seven or eight o'clock at night'.[227] There was a general expectation of availability, and it was generally considered acceptable for solicitors or colleagues to contact barristers at late hours. For example, one recalled 'getting phone calls … even late into the evening,'[228] while another said 'you'd often get a call in the evening, oh frequently'.[229]

Barristers did not necessarily resent these long hours; one barrister spoke in very positive terms about the fact that 'there was no such thing as nine-to-five or nine-to-six or anything'.[230] One barrister described typically being at their desk by seven a.m. and 'I would never work beyond eight o'clock at night.'[231] These were long hours by most people's standards, but this barrister described themselves as efficient and disciplined, and did not consider such hours to be excessive. Another said they had 'never started work later than half five in the morning'.[232] Weekend work was also a norm; some worked 'at least one day a weekend'[233] while others worked 'every Saturday, every Sunday'.[234]

These work patterns were a standard part of working life for most barristers; the work became even more intense when deadlines loomed or when trials were running:

> Well, I work most nights until about eleven, but on the day before a case it could be two o'clock in the morning, get up at six to cover it again just to make sure.

> For some of the cases I was doing I was up until three and four in the morning and just coming into court pie-eyed.

The impact of these long working hours on stress levels is further considered in chapter seven.

* * *

Work at the Bar tended to be varied, lively, and filled with interpersonal interactions. Barristers routinely dealt with colleagues, clients, solicitors and judges, as well as witnesses, claims managers, court officials and Library staff. They drafted, negotiated, pleaded, strategised and somehow also tried to manage the day-to-day aspects of their individual practices. They often had little control over the nature of work that came their way, and for most of the century the typical practice was that of a generalist. A barrister's working life was

226 B24.　227 B12.　228 B13.　229 B1.　230 B11.　231 B1.　232 B5.　233 B13, B8. 234 B23.

characterised by periods of intense work and long hours, punctuated by quiet periods of waiting around. Most of those who were interviewed for this book said that they had, on balance, enjoyed their careers, despite the challenges:

> Maybe I was just one of the lucky ones, but I've loved every minute of it. Oh, I loved it, the challenge, I loved the whole court, the courtroom, the game of the courtroom. I loved it.[235]

This chapter has also examined some of the ways in which working at the Bar changed over time. As one barrister observed,

> I think over the late eighties and early nineties it started becoming a little bit more specialised, at that stage it became a little bit more technical.[236]

The nature of legal practice undoubtedly evolved over the course of the century. While the outward appearance of barristers, with their gowns, tabs and (eventually optional) wigs, changed little over the course of the century, there were ways in which their practices altered significantly. The introduction of state-funded legal aid, for example, had a significant impact on practice, as did the abolition of juries in personal injuries actions. Constitutional challenges, EU law, family law and judicial review were all novel developments at different points in time, while older kinds of litigation died out.

235 B16.   236 B7.

CHAPTER SEVEN

Stresses and supports

Introduction

For many barristers, the Bar was a challenging environment in which to work, and stress was unavoidable. This chapter examines some of the causes of stress for barristers, which included the pressures of high-value or high-stakes litigation, performance anxiety, and the unpredictability of the career. As well as a degree of uncertainty and unpredictability, barristers frequently experienced highs and lows. They developed different strategies for dealing with these, and support from colleagues was important. This chapter also includes reflections by barristers about the challenges and rewards of their careers at the Bar.

Causes of stress

Given the nature of the work, the long hours described in chapter six, the financial uncertainty described in chapter eight, the isolation and the sometimes inadequate infrastructure described in chapter eleven, it is unsurprising that many barristers spoke of the high levels of work-related stress and anxiety.

> It's a very intense job. It's very hard to work. I mean, there's no shortcuts in it really.[1]

> Look, I had some very, very good times at the Bar, I can't deny that. I had some pretty awful days of course but by and large … it was tough … It was always hard going.

Some found the very nature of litigation to be stressful; one said that 'all litigation is stressful, it doesn't matter what it was.'[2] Barristers described how the stress of appearing in court might affect them:

> Counsel for the state was babbling away. I hadn't a clue what he was talking about, not a clue and I thought, 'Christ, what am I even going to say? What am I going to do when I stand up? Don't know where I am'. And I just stood up and I started talking … talked about the date of arrest and from

1 B24.   2 B17.   3 B22.

there I went on, it just flowed out of me. Extraordinary ... And that's the way it was all the time. I'd rehearse what I was going to say and then you'd forget half of it and you couldn't remember the other bits and you'd copious notes and you'd look at them and say 'don't know what the hell that's about ...'

You go into a bit of a zone ... when you're in court.[3]

One said that anxiety was experienced by 'all barristers going into court', and that 'the only real way [nerves] can dissipate is if you've prepared properly.'[4]

To me it is an essential prerequisite that you read every single line because you can't cross examine unless you put the whole thing together like a jigsaw. Cross examination is like a jigsaw, if you miss a piece, you know a judge can say, 'well you never asked that' ... well how did I miss that? So there is a lot of that. So, you have to be on top of it all the time.[5]

Situations where cases were handed over at the last minute could mean that a barrister was ill-prepared for court,[6] and this exacerbated a stressful situation. Sheehy recalled some of the 'shocks' a barrister could be exposed to in the course of their work:

There comes, from time to time, a day when things go wrong. A brief, or some important document forming part thereof, is mislaid or lost ... or, worst of all, two or more cases in which he is briefed are all fixed for hearing on the same day, in different courts, and threaten to commence at the same precise moment.[7]

Barristers could be exposed to very serious criminal work, which included examining and cross-examining hostile, threatening or vulnerable witnesses and being exposed to potentially distressing documentary or photographic evidence. Those who were interviewed said little about the more traumatic aspects of criminal practice, and tended to gloss over details of this sort of work. One simply said,

I did murder trials. I did rape trials. I did everything. There was nothing I didn't do. Lots of drugs. Lots of sex. Lots of violence. Some terrible violence. Some horrible murder cases.

Some barristers described what it was like to represent high-profile criminals or gang members, as well as dealing with difficult and sometimes traumatising

4 B17.　5 B20.　6 B17.　7 Eugene Sheehy, *May it please the court* (Dublin, 1951), p. 66.

evidence. Counselling for or understanding of secondary or vicarious trauma was non-existent, and barristers developed their own ways of dealing with such experiences. One described a serious criminal trial as 'a truly exhausting experience'.[8]

Another source of stress for some was the performative aspect of legal practice. Litigation was spoken of as 'putting on a performance',[9] and some compared working at the Bar with working as an actor:[10]

> I always thought it was probably more like the acting profession than any other profession, you know. The insecurity of it, the putting on the front, the putting on the show, the fact that you're briefed from case to case, you're only as good as your last case, so much of it is about speaking, there is quite a bit of acting in court as well really.[11]

This could be a source of considerable anxiety. As one barrister put it, there was nowhere to hide if they were having a bad day: 'unlike, I think every other professional, you're on show literally every day you're in court.'[12] Another recalled an experienced colleague who used to be physically sick before appearing in court.[13]

Of course, not everyone found the performative elements of practice to be a source of stress; some relished this. One said, for example, 'the performance element of it is fantastic,'[14] while another said 'it was the sense of theatre about the courts which appealed to me'.[15] There were certainly a number of barristers whose colleagues described them as flamboyant.[16] One said that some 'just love the theatrical end of it', and viewed it as a theatrical production in which they played the leading role.[17] Some were critical of excessive theatricality in their colleagues, for example:

> There were people ... who were flamboyant and there were clients and solicitors who liked that but most barristers would have sort of seen beyond that and most judges would have seen beyond it very quickly.[18]

Another major source of anxiety for barristers was the volume of work. Some felt overwhelmed by too much work:

> There'd be times when I'd say, 'Jesus how am I going to deal with this?'

> I don't think I ever had a shortage of work .... My problem was doing it. What people euphemistically call 'work-life balance'.

8 T.F. O'Higgins, *A double life* (Dublin, 1996), p. 182.   9 B18.   10 Indeed, ch. 14 and 15 demonstrate that a number of Irish barristers also pursued theatrical interests on the stage or screen.   11 B4.   12 B23.   13 B7.   14 B22.   15 Patrick Lindsay, *Memories* (Dublin, 1992), p. 95. 16 E.g., B17.   17 B24.   18 B26.

In court absolutely every day … working early in the morning, working late, getting phone calls then even late into the evening, generally working at least one day a weekend you know just very high pressurised, huge amount of work. You know, being at everybody's beck and call all the time.

The pressure of disappointing people and … not being able to keep up with that and at the same time the more successful you got the more stuff came in.

MacKenzie recalled a colleague who had been bedridden with illness for a few weeks:

On his return I commiserated with him 'Not at all' said he, 'not at all. It was marvellous, I was able to lie in bed and do my work and now I have no solicitors pounding on my door. Everything is clear. The great thing is to get to the bottom of the bag'.[19]

Several cited the lack of security at the Bar as their main source of anxiety. Lee, in his memoir of practising in the mid-century, wrote that '[a] genuine insecurity was … often present because of the relative scarcity of work and the tragedy of the war'.[20] Almost everyone interviewed for this book commented on the fear that the flow of work might stop:

One of the things that's really stressful about being at the Bar is the uncertainty of work and the uncertainty of money and that's a constant … It's never totally irrational.

The unpredictability of it, the lack of control … it's an incredibly insecure profession.

You're always wondering 'where will the next case come from?'

Barristers live with the fear that no other profession has, I don't know any other profession where you feel your practice could disappear overnight … everybody always felt that somebody could come in and displace them.

The lack of security is the biggest threat or the biggest worry that you have as a barrister, the feeling that … you're going to be found out or that's all going to disappear.

Such worries were not exclusive to those in their early years of practice. When asked if their worries about not keeping an adequate practice going had ever abated, almost all of the barristers interviewed said that this worry never went

---

19 MacKenzie, *Lawful occasions*, p. 146.   **20** Lee, *A memoir*, p. 31.

away.[21] One barrister who had a busy practice said that even though the briefs kept coming in, 'it could all stop in the morning'. He talked about a 'sense of insecurity', and the risk that a solicitor or multiple solicitors might just stop briefing them.[22] Morison and Leith also identified this in their study, and observed that 'maintaining the correct level of work, and work of the right kind and at the right level of remuneration, remains a concern throughout a barrister's professional life'.[23]

> One of the big problems in the Bar is you're either going forward or back. There's no 'Goldilocks' moment.[24]

As well as personal uncertainty about one's own practice, barristers also worried about the future of the profession:

> That constant fear that what you're working towards is going to be changed by a force outside your control, that if you do personal injury, something like PIAB [Personal Injuries Assessment Board] down the line, there's, if you're doing criminal work, they'll change it to only have a tender system and only certain people will get work in it.[25]

There were always a handful of barristers prophesying the imminent demise of the profession. Discussions about solicitors' attendance rights, a fused profession, chambers and any proposed changes to practise[26] were underlain with genuine worry and anxiety.

Appearing before unpleasant or rude judges was also stressful:

> There were some very, very difficult judges in the High Court who were not pleasant ... and very demanding and quite rude and I think a lot of very junior practitioners ... felt them very difficult to deal with ... We would all come in green in the face because you'd just be feeling sick thinking someone was going to take you apart ... you were afraid, you know, if you had a fight with the judge that solicitor might never brief you again, that you would be blamed if something went wrong so you felt it could have an impact on your career ... so it was high anxiety.[27]

High-stakes cases included serious crimes in the Special or Central Criminal Court, constitutional challenges in the Supreme Court, or high-value commercial cases in the High Court. These brought with them another level of stress and hard work. For example:

21 B13, B14. 22 B6. 23 John Morison and Philip Leith, *The barrister's world and the nature of law* (Berkshire, 1992), p. 24. 24 B26. 25 B13. 26 See ch. 16. 27 B16.

There were times then when I was involved in some commercial cases which were probably which I was unaccustomed to dealing with and I found that dealing with big figures and big consequences and stuff like that would be quite stressful.[28]

Barristers would put in very long hours coming up to a deadline or a hearing date, and could be 'pretty consumed by it'.[29] Raymond Crotty, who instigated the challenge to the Single European Act in 1987,[30] later described his legal team working over Christmas 1986[31] to meet a series of deadlines.[32] The judgment was to be given after five p.m. on Christmas Eve, and the team had seven days in which to prepare a statement of claim. The growing legal team worked very hard over that period, and Crotty reflected: 'I had by now begun to realise why litigation is so infernally expensive.'[33]

Only a minority of those interviewed said they 'very seldom'[34] felt stressed by work at the Bar:

I never found it as stressful as some people did and I didn't do a huge amount of anything. I did a lot of different things ... I did bits of everything and I didn't find it that bad. I didn't find it that stressful.[35]

Another cause of work stress included the competitive aspect of working at the Bar as a self-employed individual.[36] At different points in the twentieth century, the Bar was perceived to be overcrowded, and people feared that there would not be enough work to go around. Even as early as in the 1930s, when there were only three hundred practising members of the Bar, commentators had the impression that there was overcrowding:

In Ireland to-day, there are at least 1,000 barristers, of whom scarcely more than 300 live by the law, and this figure includes court officials, district judges and judges. The young person who would become a barrister should ponder well before making a final decision. It is and always was, an over-crowded profession, and is now more overcrowded than ever.[37]

Low fees, or the non-payment of fees, was another stressful aspect of working at the Bar,[38] as were the cramped and noisy conditions of the Law Library.[39]

---

28 B15.   29 B4.   30 Reported as *Crotty v. An Taoiseach* [1987] IESC 4.   31 Raymond Crotty, *A radical's response* (Dublin, 1988), p. 111.   32 When the High Court sat on 23 December to hear the motion for an injunction, 'All were wigless and in mufti to assert that we were still on our Christmas holidays, but taking time off to deal with a matter that required immediate attention.' Ibid., p. 113. 33 Ibid., p. 120.   34 B19.   35 B21.   36 See pp 102–4.   37 William Joseph Maguire, *Guide to the professions: barristers-at-law and solicitors* (Dublin, 1931), p. 15.   38 See pp 151–4.   39 See pp 223–4.

Highs and lows

Many barristers described their work in terms of highs and lows, and in terms of emotional and hormonal swings. For example:

> The Bar is a stressful job. And it's particularly so because you have downtime at which there is great release of tension followed by a rapid increase in tension.[40]

This barrister described the build up of tension waiting for a case to go on, or the unexpected early finishing or settling of a case, which led to emotional highs and lows. One barrister described it as 'stop-start',[41] while another spoke in terms of adrenalin:

> You might have thought that for the next four days your nose was to the grindstone and you suddenly ... settled it and it is true that you could then go and take an afternoon after you know because you'd probably been up to three a.m. the night before, you weren't fit to do anything else and the adrenalin had been running ... keeping you going to do the case.[42]

Another described it in terms of energy:

> When I pass the door of the Supreme Court, I can feel the adrenalin coming out of it ... at eleven o'clock every day there is a gush of energy through the building you know that some people feel ... the schwizz of people around rushing and then the sort of intellectual energy that is electrifying the place.

Another barrister said that after being 'high' on a case, the aftermath was 'exhausting':

> You kind of think, 'oh God, I can't take another day of this' ... then you get a phone call ... and someone is asking you to do something else and you're off again.

Part of the highs and lows was the winning and losing of cases. This could of course be unpredictable:

> There were times when you went into court with a case where you were confident that you should win it and you lost it. And then there were cases

---

40 B18.   41 B10.   42 B11.   43 B4.

where you went in and you were certain you were going to lose it and you won it.[43]

Winning a case was described by one barrister as 'amazing ... one of the happiest days in your life'.[44] Barristers could also have a strong reaction to negative outcomes, which might leave 'a really sour taste.'[45] One recalled:

> It was the last day of term, and I could feel the perspiration dripping down and sure I lost, we lost, and they were looking for costs against us and it's ... it's hard.

They described sleepless nights and self-doubt. One recalled asking themselves, 'how could I have made such a mess? How could I have made such a mistake? How could I be so stupid? I am not fitted for this game.'

> If something that you thought was grand turns out to be a disaster, or if the case takes a completely different turn and you don't feel prepared ... 'could I have foreseen this? Could I have applied? Should we have done this? Should we have done that?' And the point is, so many things are unpredictable.

> There were moments of huge stress, huge frustration from time to time and you know when you lost the case you thought you should have won and then you wondered, God, what had you not said that you should have said? What could you have done?[46]

This sort of self-criticism and self-reflection could also take place on a bigger scale, for example if a barrister perceived a dip in their practice:

> If you're very busy particularly say one term and you're less busy the next year you're thinking 'I'm losing, something is happening, I'm not as busy as I was last term' and you begin to have thoughts about yourself and that maybe you're not doing something, you're not performing as well.[47]

Dealing with stress

Barristers developed different ways of dealing with the stress of work. Many cited the long (unpaid) vacations as essential recovery time, as well as something to look forward to during busy and stressful periods.

---

44 B25.   45 B25.   46 B11.   47 B14.

You live the life on the basis that you know that the vacations are coming up and you're going to have time to yourself.[48]

It's very hard work but it's great. It's great. Because you see we had loads of time off … That's the thing that keeps you going.[49]

The summer is a very long holiday and then there's three shorter ones, Christmas, Easter and Whitsun. Whitsun was lovely. It was always ten days; it was just lovely.[50]

You worked so hard during term time but … in those days, the vacations were much more real vacations than they are now.[51]

I'm available to everyone from the beginning of term right to the end of term, but when the term ends, I'm not available.[52]

One barrister said that the long vacations compensated for the eighty-hour work weeks during term-time.[53] Another barrister argued that the long vacations were 'misunderstood': 'people assume that you don't do any work at all during the vacation and that you're just paid so much money that it doesn't matter how you spend the two months in the summer.'[54] Others said that they used vacation time to catch up on paperwork:

> Most vacations I would have taken some time off and then try to do a bit of paperwork.[55]

> The whole of August off. I mean you'd usually work a bit in September, try and shovel the backlog. Paperwork was the killer, you know.[56]

The unpaid nature of the vacation was a consideration: 'in reality the more time you take off the worse it is for you … that's what being self-employed means'.[57]

The impact of stress

Several of the barristers who were interviewed for this book, when asked about 'work–life balance', indicated that they did not feel they had achieved such a balance, certainly during the busiest years of their practice.[58]

> It always felt as if I hadn't a minute. I always seemed to be working … looking back … I have loads of regrets that I didn't have more time with my kids when they were small, but I don't think there was an option.

---

48 B15.   49 B3.   50 B4.   51 B11.   52 B12.   53 B10.   54 B15.   55 B11.   56 B2.   57 B15.
58 E.g., B4, B24.

You have to give some time to the children, but you work every night, you come home, you have your dinner, and you work and then you might look at the news late at night or something like that, you know. And at the weekends, you work. I developed the habit of getting most of one of the days to the family and most of the other day to the work. So, I would usually work Sunday and do family stuff on Saturdays.

You would be tired. Driving home on a Friday evening ... that's strenuous because the family are there and they now need time, and you had to try to catch up with some work. So, at some stage over the weekend, you'd got to settle down and do some paperwork.

As noted in chapter eleven, many barristers tended to work partially from home and some had quite elaborate home offices, libraries and secretarial support. As well as providing a peaceful environment away from the busy Law Library, this was seen by some as a way to be present with their families. For example,

I had my office in my home so when I finished in court I came home, so the very fact that you're actually around, even if you're working, makes it much easier ... I was always at home for large parts of the day though I was working extremely long hours, ... I was fortunate to be around at all times when the kids were growing up.

I decided I had to have a library because ... my family wouldn't see me ... I could have a library because then at least I wouldn't be working in town.

I was able to do a huge amount of paperwork and meetings and consultations but I was able to do them to suit myself ... I did a lot of work at home.

Some barristers described being able to have evening meals with their families and then return to work.[59] They recalled returning to work after their children had gone to bed, and the tiredness that this caused.[60]

I used to ... be up early with them, do whatever you do before work, then you'd work your full working day, then I always made sure to be home by six or half six ... until nine I was completely theirs and I didn't scrimp on the bedtime stories or the bath, you know, we did the full routine and then when they went to bed I tramped back up the stairs into my little office and started again for another couple of hours so it was pretty gruelling.

Nobody enjoys going up to your study at nine o'clock at night when the children have gone to bed and you've eaten and going back up to work and being there til two in the morning and the butterflies in your stomach the next morning and going into court.

Despite efforts to juggle work and family life, there was often a strain on relationships. One interviewee suggested that marriage breakdown at the Bar was at a rate double the national average.[61] They pointed out that 'the life is desperate. It's so hard on a relationship'. Another said that it was 'extraordinarily difficult',[62] and another, that 'partners had to be understanding.'[63]

The Bar is a shocking place, very bad for interpersonal relations at home, because you are … consumed by your cases.

People found different ways to wind down or let off steam. Some mentioned hobbies such as painting, horses, golf or tennis. Other barristers relied on alcohol to deal with stress.

I would say it is very hard to switch off. Years ago people used to drink a lot. I'd say that's a part of the explanation. The judiciary were more impolite years ago and I'd say some people drank because they were afraid of the judges or you know, you know, they had problems with individual judges, etc., but the Bar is a very stressful place.[64]

This had been a feature of the Bar throughout the century; Charles Bewley, describing practising around 1915, recalled 'crowding into the bar for a drink after the labours of the day …'[65] One reflected that when they started in the sixties, 'the Bar was full of chronic alcoholics.'[66] This was part of an ingrained drinking culture:

We drank a lot on circuit, drank a lot of wine at dinner and then go out drinking after dinner.

I can recall silks being in there at half ten, eleven o'clock in the morning, cases settled and having gin … They'd be gone in an hour or two but they were there that early in the morning.[67]

When I started, the callover was at eleven and everybody just immediately decamped down to the bar … I went to Donegal for a short while but everyone on the circuit in Donegal was a roaring alcoholic … I think I was very lucky not to end up an alcoholic.

61 B14.   62 B24.   63 B18.   64 B5.   65 Charles Bewley, *Memoirs of a wild goose* (Dublin, 1989), p. 41.   66 B4.   67 B8.

We drank ourselves to oblivion at times ... There was a big drinking culture. Downstairs we had our own bar which is now gone and there was a back bar ... the barman ... was a friend to everybody to be fair ... he's an important person in our history because he knew everybody's secrets and he knew who the alcoholics were and he would try to give them watered down drink ... Just to try and keep them sort of sober.

One barrister who began practising in the eighties said that drinking was 'a big thing in the Bar'.[68] Another said that at that time some barristers drank before going into court:

There would have been the odd person having a sharpener in the morning, like ten o'clock.[69]

Several referred euphemistically to 'going out for lunch', or 'long lunches', which generally involved some alcohol.

If you had a good victory, you might go out to lunch and I think that used to be quite a big institution in the seventies and eighties and even into the nineties and I'd certainly do it a couple of times a year.[70]

In the old days, in the eighties, cases finished, people went off and celebrated then.[71]

Not everyone was able to deal with the stress of practising at the Bar. Several barristers interviewed talked about having considered leaving the Bar at some point, as a result of stress, either from overwork or underwork. A number also referred to former colleagues who had left, for various reasons. One described it as

Trading in the life of a happy go lucky sole practitioner, your own boss, nobody shoving you around the place, apart from a judge, you know, to the security of a job and knowing there was going to be a salary cheque at the end of the week or at the end of a month.[72]

One barrister attributed high numbers of people leaving the Bar to the rudeness of the judges: 'there was a high rate of attrition, people leaving during that period because I think some of the judges were very hard, very hard'.[73]

68 B7.   69 B25.   70 B25.   71 B23.   72 B14.   73 B16.

Collegial supports

In the absence of chambers, the support and camaraderie of fellow barristers was crucial. Members of the Bar were supposed to make themselves available to any colleague who requested help or advice:

> It was a tradition at the Bar ... that you could ask anybody any question and it was his or her obligation to stop what they were doing and to answer it if they could.[74]

> Mutual help in difficulty was a great tradition in the Law Library. No matter how large your practice, how many cases you had actively going, you were expected, by an unwritten law, to help and explain difficulties to the most inexperienced practitioner.[75]

> Each member is entitled as of right to seek counsel and advice from the other members of the Bar and call upon their accumulated wisdom and experience. All of them regard it as an unshakeable precept of their profession that a colleague who comes seeking advice, however inappropriate the time or the circumstances, must never be turned away.[76]

Mackey described this as 'an inflexible code of etiquette'.[77]

Paradoxically, those best placed to provide empathy and support were also, in a very real sense, one's competitors. Several interviewees commented on this 'strange dynamic',[78] and many used the imagery of soldiers in combat, or of 'kicking' or 'beating' one another.

> Nobody else understands except somebody else who does it, so there's that camaraderie of soldiers in the trenches. But on the other hand that's the person you're in competition with; so you're soldiers in the trenches together today but then you're going to have to shoot each other next week.[79]

> I would have a lot of many good friends and many of them we've worked together on cases on the same side, but the reality is if you're on the opposite side it's as if you never worked together ... vicious isn't the correct word but ... the determination to win the case for your client and to represent your client's interest outweighs any other consideration, and people make points against people who are friends that may be embarrassing for them that they have overlooked things or that they may have presented it wrong.[80]

74 B8.   75 MacKenzie, *Lawful occasions*, p. 19.   76 Ronan Keane, 'The future of the Irish Bar', *Studies* 54:216 (1965), 375, at 378.   77 Rex Mackey, *Windward of the law* (1965, and 2nd ed. 1991, Dublin), p. 21.   78 B24.   79 B24.   80 B23.

Even though you would be competing against them every day, I liked every one of them.[81]

Another barrister recalled a trial where he and the opposing counsel were 'beating each other up in court every day', then driving home from work together every evening because his colleague's car had broken down.[82] One barrister said that it was collegiate, but only

> To a point, because it then gets to a point where you are beginning to build up a practice and then you become a bit of a threat and people are less collegiate at that point … You then become the competition.[83]

> You're competing directly with other people all the time. If I'm a surgeon in the operating theatre I'm not doing that.[84]

> Underneath that camaraderie at the Bar … there's just naked competition … your opponent wants to kick your head off if they can … because that's their job … you're actually in a very visceral way competing for your colleagues work … there's whole layers of stuff built on it and nobody really necessarily wants to acknowledge that every day, but most barristers are very, very conscious of the fact that it is an extremely, a nakedly competitive environment and it works in a very ruthless way.[85]

Despite the competitive element, barristers still, on the whole, valued the support they received from colleagues:

> It's a very odd situation because people who are practising in the same area are essentially competitors to each other but yet they normally provide a very strong network.[86]

Allied to the sense of competition with colleagues was often a desire to appear successful and busy. Several barristers described people projecting success and confidence, even where such 'peacocking' did not have a strong grounding in reality. One barrister described 'the chill wind that blows around a barrister without a brief'.[87] Morison and Leith describe barristers being 'anxious to display that they were at least where they should be on the ladder'.[88] They wrote in the early nineties,

> There is perhaps a feeling that work gravitates towards the successful and that it is important to give signs that one is doing well. This is so perhaps especially in the Bar Library system, where without the brokerage services

81 B16.   82 Eilis Brennan, 'Moving on', *B.R.* 21:2 (2016), 56, at 57.   83 B10.   84 B23.   85 B26.
86 B11.   87 P.J. McEnery, 'Look back in love: conversations by an English fireside', UCDA P74/2,
p. 74.   88 Morison and Leith, *Barrister's world*, p. 35.

of a clerk, it is necessary to advertise oneself and one's success as widely as possible.[89]

Such displays of apparent success could take different forms. Several barristers interviewed described people wanting to give the impression of being very busy.

> At the more junior end of the profession, barristers greeting one another generally declared themselves to be 'very busy' or 'snowed under with work'.[90]

Healy also commented on barristers who cultivated an air of busyness:

> The hallucination that one is engaged in a huge practice is one that affects a surprising number of people. There was one poor man on the Munster Circuit, whom I can remember only once seeing in court; but if you met him on the way down to the Four Courts in the morning, and fell into step with him, he would always complain of the vast pile of work that was engaging his attention.[91]

Morison and Leith also observed that

> At the more senior levels, the displays of success take a more subtle form. Indeed, those who are most successful ... paradoxically adopt a more nonchalant and relaxed demeanour.[92]

This resonates with some comments from interviewees for this book, for example:

> The big thing was to give the appearance of not doing any work and yet being able to master everything.[93]

> In fact a lot of barristers who look very calm are good at appearing calm and relaxed when I don't think anybody thinks it isn't a stressful life.[94]

Aside from the desire to project success, the collegiate support could be limited by people's reluctance to acknowledge their fears and uncertainties to one another:

> I think that in the past it wasn't really talked about much. I think that people couldn't even admit their own pressures to another colleague in the Bar.[95]

---

89 Ibid. 90 Ibid. 91 Maurice Healy, *The old Munster Circuit: a book of memories and traditions* (Dublin, 1939), p. 260. 92 Morison and Leith, *Barrister's world*, p. 35. 93 B18. 94 B26. 95 B13.

Except maybe with your very, very good friends, we were all just scared in admitting any weakness at all you know … and also because [you're their] competitors as well … so how do you say well actually 'I'm too busy' to somebody who is going 'I don't have that much work'?

Much of the support at the Bar appears to have come in the form of the light relief provided by witty and humorous colleagues.

There's a lot of fun, you know, there's great craic, people can be very witty.[96]

If you are lucky enough to, to sit down and have coffee with X or Y … they're incredibly bright and you know you just have a laugh a minute … You can go in there and just laugh your day away.[97]

Another important support available at the Bar was financial support. The Benevolent Society of the Bar, established in 1895, operated on the basis of subscriptions from those members of the Library who could afford to donate,[98] as well as one-off donations and bequests. It provided temporary financial assistance to members who needed it – for example, due to illness or incapacitation. It also supported the dependants[99] of members of the Bar who had passed away suddenly, or without having made provision for them. One barrister who was interviewed pointed out that Ireland in the mid-twentieth century was not a wealthy country; there was no social welfare and barristers generally did not have pensions, so the benevolent fund had an important role to play.[100] It operated on a confidential basis, but published appeals for donations and summaries of its accounts,[101] as well as lists of donors.

* * *

Despite the stress and the worry, the strain on relationships, the overbearing relationships, unpaid fees and the burden of running a practice, most barristers were nevertheless very positive about their experiences at the twentieth-century Bar. Few of those interviewed regretted their choice of career. One interviewee commented, rather wistfully, 'I should have become a solicitor really, when you would make a bit of money',[102] while another said, 'I wouldn't go through it again'.[103]

The variation and social interaction was a big part of why many enjoyed the job so much. One described quite fondly 'interacting with country people and

---

96 B24.   97 B9.   98 E.g., in 1920 Hugh Kennedy subscribed two pounds and two shillings. UCDA P4/153.   99 As late as 1979 the annual appeal referred to the 'wives, widows and children of barristers'. (1979) 113 *I.L.T.S.J.* 39 (16 Feb. 1979).   100 B6.   101 E.g., (1969) 103 *I.L.T.S.J.* 45 (1 Feb. 1969); (1976) 110 *I.L.T.S.J.* 53 (28 Feb. 1976).   102 B18.   103 B24.

farmers' families and gas men and priceless fellows with gas lines'.[104] Some
appear to have been enamoured with almost all aspects of the work:

> I loved the advocacy ... I loved negotiations, I loved dealing, I loved
> attempting to settle actions and I enjoyed the interaction with solicitors
> instructing me and clients too and I loved, I think in a way I loved, the
> unpredictability and the variation both in terms of the type of work but
> also your working pattern.[105]

> I loved it. I just loved every minute of it.[106]

Several referred to the satisfaction they derived from helping clients:

> I think it's very satisfying ... to feel that a client has come in and you feel
> that they have been wronged and you've been part of putting that right, so
> I think that's very satisfying ... I suppose the counter to that is many times
> you're acting for the scurrilous party in the litigation and your objective
> there is to back them up which is perhaps not so attractive.[107]

> There is still something very appealing about doing a job where you know
> the research you do can fundamentally alter the outcome for someone
> because of your individual input. Absolutely ... it's a huge motivator.[108]

Others expressed the service ethic in terms of 'trying to get people into the
courts safely, get them home safely'.[109] Another said 'as a barrister you were only
doing public interest work really'.[110]

> If you are a solicitor and you become a partner the world is very insulated
> and controlled you know. The Bar was constantly changing, you're always
> being presented with new things, new people, new judges, new colleagues
> and it does keep you alert and it's you know interesting and then of course
> you have a ringside seat at a lot of really interesting things you know and
> that's the counterbalance to the stress.[111]

Morison and Leith described the working environment at the Bar as 'a complex,
often hostile one',[112] and the working life was punctuated with highs and lows.
The strong relationships between colleagues and the frequent opportunities to
socialise were important for both support and the relief of tension.

---

104 B3. 105 B11. 106 B16. 107 B16. 108 B22. 109 B5. 110 B18. 111 B26.
112 Morison and Leith, *Barrister's world*, p. 17.

CHAPTER EIGHT

Making a living at the Bar

Introduction

This chapter considers the financial side of practising at the Bar. Many barristers experienced lean years while they established their practices, and the sense of financial precarity often stayed with them throughout their careers. As independent self-employed individuals, there was no financial safety net for barristers unless they had independent means or family supports. They frequently had to 'chase' fees for all kinds of work. The introduction of free legal aid had a significant impact on barristers' earnings and career trajectories; it has been observed that there was no 'criminal Bar' until the introduction of criminal legal aid in the 1960s. However, both the civil and criminal legal aid schemes were fraught with difficulties when it came to both the processing of payments and the scales of fees, and on several occasions the profession clashed with the relevant government departments.

Making a living

The end of the twentieth century saw attention being focused on a relatively small number of very high-earning barristers, including those who were involved in tribunal work.[1] However, typical earnings for most of the twentieth century were more modest. Barristers' earnings often rose and fell with the economic health of the country. McEnery, who began practising in the twenties, wrote about barristers who had little work to do:

> I have known men in the Law Library who rarely if ever got a case but who remained there for years and seemed to enjoy the place and who put in their time by reading the law, taking reports of law cases for legal journals, living the social life of the place in the smoke room or the Bar restaurant.[2]

It is clear from reading first-hand accounts of those who were in practice in the thirties and forties, for example, that both the volume of work and the overall earnings at the Bar were quite modest. MacKenzie, for example, wrote that money was scarce and fees were low in the forties.[3] Writing in the early nineties,

---

1 See pp 323–5.   2 McEnery, 'Look back in love', UCDA P74/2, p. 70.   3 Patrick MacKenzie, *Lawful occasions: the old Eastern Circuit* (Cork, 1991), p. 8.

he mused that 'Nowadays, Round Hall people are supposed to have very high incomes, sometimes receiving several thousand pounds for a brief. In the 1940s, however, the recognised senior fee for a common law action with a jury was twelve guineas, or at the very most, fifteen.'[4] McEnery recalled the fee for his first brief on circuit as being three guineas.[5] Another barrister recalled:

> In the fifties and sixties, sure it was a sad business for the barristers. We were all getting so little.[6]

Another barrister in the sixties commented that 'in many respects the Bar is the worst paid profession in Ireland'.[7] The financial health of the Bar at different periods can be traced through the published accounts of the Bar Benevolent Society. For example, in 1931, it revealed 'the unhappy fact … that receipts were down but disbursements had increased.[8] Many annual subscribers had not paid their subscriptions.[9] The following year, it noted that there was 'a marked decrease in the number of new subscribers'.[10] When the number of barristers rapidly increased in the seventies, so too did the annual donations to the fund.[11]

Barristers' earnings also depended on their seniority; seniors and 'senior juniors' could command higher fees than those who had relatively little experience at the Bar. The following two statements about the earnings of juniors and seniors in the eighties provide an interesting contrast:

> When I went down in the eighties we were in the middle of a recession. There was very little work around and it was poorly paid, so you didn't really expect to make a living for about five years.[12]

> It was quite a prosperous time for the senior Bar in the seventies and eighties because of the personal injuries stuff. Because it was remarkably well paid, like, *really* well paid and really lots of cases settled and things like that.[13]

Different kinds of work attracted varying levels of fees. One barrister mentioned doing

> Difficult, hard conveyancing, trust stuff that probably nobody else wanted to do … a lot of it wouldn't have paid that much in terms of fees.

4 Ibid., p. 12.   5 McEnery, 'Look back', p. 71.   6 B15.   7 Ronan Keane, 'The future of the Irish Bar', *Studies* 54:216 (1965), 375, at 381.   8 (1932) 66 *I.L. T.S.J.* 3 (2 Jan. 1932). It had received £288, compared with £295 the previous year.   9 (1932) 66 *I.L. T.S.J.* 118 (14 May 1932). 10 (1933) 67 *I.L. T.S.J.* 130 (9 May 1933).   11 In 1976 the society reported that it had received over £4,700. Fifteen years previously, the annual figure was £650. Earnán P. de Blaghd (called in 1949: Ferguson, *Barristers*, p. 171), the honorary treasurer, was credited with achieving 'spectacular results' through his 'enthusiasm and industry.' (1976) 110 *I.L. T.S.J.* 53 (28 Feb. 1976). See also (1979) 113 *I.L. T.S.J.* 297 (8 Dec. 1979), where it was reported that expenditure for 1979 was double that of the previous year.   12 B10.   13 B25.

There were no mandatory scales of fees for barristers, and the rules of the superior courts did not specify counsel's fees. However, as early as the 1920s the Bar Council was engaged in examining and making recommendations in relation to fees at assizes.[14] Charging conventions were discussed between masters and devils, and between colleagues generally. The Bar Council also periodically published minimum fee scales.[15] An unofficial 'going rate' was generally accepted on the basis of the amount of an award in a civil action. In the late eighties, the maximum fee for counsel was generally one per cent of the damages recovered, subject to a minimum of 250 guineas.[16] The Bar Council also played a role in negotiating fees for legal aid work, as seen in chapter eight.

Fee relativity between senior and junior counsel meant that juniors generally charged a fee which was two-thirds that of the senior counsel. This convention was sometimes known as the 'two-thirds rule'. This was, according to Gavan Duffy, 'another amazing importation from England'. He was critical of the practise of junior counsel valuing themselves in relation to their seniors:

> In fact, in dozens of cases the junior is not worth one tenth of his senior, from inexperience, incapacity or indolence; and it is submitted that no shadow of justification exists for a grave abuse.[17]

Refresher fees for subsequent days in court were lower, usually amounting to half of the brief fee.[18] Clients who felt that the fees they were being charged were

14 E.g., in 1927 the Bar Council considered draft Circuit Court rules, which included counsel's fees. B.C.M., 2 May, 18 Nov. 1927. See also B.C.M., 15, 23 Jan., 5 Feb. 1920.   15 E.g., in 1954 at a general meeting of the Bar, a scale of minimum fees for Circuit Court work was agreed. These were published in (1954) 88 *I.L.T.S.J.* 136–8 (22 May 1954). See also correspondence relating to the scales, pointing out that fees should not be dependent on the outcome of the case. (1954) 88 *I.L.T.S.J.* 150 (5 June 1954). Revised minimum fees were drawn up by the Bar Council and approved by the Circuit Court rules committee in 1972 and 1977: (1972) 106 *I.L.T.S.J.* 197 (22 July 1972); (1977) 111 *I.L.T.S.J.* 205 (11 Sept. 1977). The Bar Council also issued tables of fees for High Court matters in the 1980s. E.g., in 1983 fees were set out for certain items: plenary proceedings, special summons, summary summons, motions for judgment, other motions, cases, advices, consultations and general. These were not related to the value of the case. No brief fees were mentioned, except for special summons and other motions, and these ranged from £13.65 for a summons in plenary proceedings to £69.30 for detailed advice on proofs before the master. See Fair Trade Commission, *Report of study into restrictive practices in the legal profession* (Dublin, 1990), para. 12.39. In 1988, revised scales included suggested brief fees for civil work in the Circuit Court. For tort and contract in the Circuit Court, where a case was valued between £2,500 and £5,000, the recommended brief fee was £157.50. For cases valued between £5,000 and £10,000, the recommended fee was £210.00, and for cases valued between £10,000 and £15,000, the recommended fee was £315.00.   16 F.T.C., para. 12.91. A guinea was traditionally one pound plus one shilling (21 shillings). After decimalisation in 1971, the term 'guinea' continued to be used in the context of legal fees. 250 guineas was the equivalent of £250 plus 5% so £262.50.   17 Gavan Duffy memorandum, p. 10. Some examples were given in submissions to the Fair Trade Commission in the 1980s; e.g., a murder trial in the Central Criminal Court in the late eighties could mean fees of £750 for the senior, £500 for the junior and £750 for the solicitor for the first day. F.T.C., para. 12.41.   18 Code of conduct, rule 10.9: 'The appropriate fee for junior counsel is

excessive could require their solicitor to submit them to the taxing master. There were two taxing masters attached to the High Court, appointed under statute.[19]

Several interviewees gave examples of the kinds of fees they earned. For example, in the sixties, a High Court motion was seven guineas, while a Circuit Court motion was three guineas.[20] Another said that in the sixties the fee to draft a civil bill would have been three guineas. One barrister said that by the late seventies, legal fees were beginning to rise, and that this was certainly the case by the time they were called in the early eighties.[21]

On the civil side, many barristers aspired to being placed on a 'panel' for an insurance company. A barrister called in the eighties said, 'at the time the big ambition for a lot of barristers was to be an insurance company panel ... that was guaranteed income'.[22] This meant that they were likely to be given well-paid cases for that company on a fairly long-term basis.

> By getting PMPA work I was suddenly seen by other insurance companies to be someone who an insurance company was using: 'let's use him'. Exposure is what mattered.[23]

With the rapidly increasing number of practising barristers in the nineties, those at the junior end of the profession increasingly felt the pressure of competition, and many found it difficult to establish themselves.

Criminal practice tended to be very poorly remunerated. O'Higgins, writing about practising in the forties and fifties, said 'crime did not pay',[24] and this was echoed in the interviews for this book.[25] A barrister who practised from the late forties onward commented that people 'did criminal work to oblige a solicitor who gave you other work'.[26] Mackenzie similarly noted that

> Legal aid was unknown in those times and, money being scarce, fees were very low. Very often criminal cases were done for practically nothing, though a nominal fee of some sort was expected.[27]

He said that in the fifties, '[t]he accused men, there being no legal aid in those days, usually produced £50, which was split between my solicitor and myself. No case lasted more than a day'.[28]

---

ordinarily two thirds of the fee paid to senior counsel.' **19** See rules of the superior courts 1986, order 99 and the Courts (Supplemental Provisions) Act 1961. The taxing master had to be a solicitor of at least 10 years standing. A series of cases in the 1970s considered the discretion of the taxing master in disallowing fees: *Dunne v. O'Neill* [1974] I.R. 180; *Kelly v. Breen* (unrep., H.C. 4 Apr. 1978, Hamilton J) and *State (Gallagher, Shatter) v. Toirleach de Valera* (unrep., S.C. 8 Feb. 1990). **20** B4. **21** B11. **22** B26. **23** B8. **24** T.F. O'Higgins, *A double life* (Dublin, 1996), p. 182. **25** E.g., B7. **26** 'Ralph Sutton, SC, called to the Bar, July 1948', *B.R.* 4:3 (1999), 152. **27** MacKenzie, *Lawful occasions*, p. 8. **28** Ibid., p. 108.

It often took several years before barristers were earning enough to live on. In the meantime, some were supported by family members or partners. As one barrister described it,

> To keep the wheels moving at the start requires industry, patience and optimism on the part of the young barrister. And to stay the course a few friendly solicitors, or an amenable bank manager, must provide the necessary fuel.[29]

It was hard to survive at the start of one's career when earnings were low or non-existent. Sometimes barristers did well in their devilling year, but their earnings dipped significantly after that. One recalled, 'I'd say I had a couple of lean years after my devilling year',[30] and another said that their third, fourth and fifth years were 'not busy at all'.[31] Another wrote that in his first year, he had earned

> The princely sum of one hundred and forty six guineas. In my second year, although I went religiously to every town, sat in the back of the court day in and day out, I only earned five guineas, and I was beginning to get very tired and fed up with the whole thing.[32]

Not everyone did well in their first year; one barrister, who was called in the late sixties, recounted earning just seven guineas in their entire first year. Many interviewees were able to recall with great clarity how much they had earned in their early years. For example, one barrister called in the late seventies, said:

> In my first year at the Bar I earned £1,260; the second year £2,600 ... my third year £3,400. I think I was in my fourth year before I passed £5,000.

For context, another barrister who began practising in the seventies compared their early-career earnings to those of solicitors:

> When I qualified ... the starting salary for a solicitor ... was about £1,200 or £1,500 ... I remember I earned £300 in my first year ... In the second year I earned £600, third year I earned £1,200. I doubled every year so that after about year three I was earning more than a starting solicitor ... So after 4 or 5 years I was earning a good lot more than my contemporaries who were solicitors.

It was estimated in the mid-eighties that half of all barristers were earning less than ten thousand pounds per annum, and that a substantial number of them

29 Eugene Sheehy, *May it please the court* (Dublin, 1951), p. 50.   30 B5.   31 B7.   32 MacKenzie, *Lawful occasions*, p. 47.

were earning less than five thousand. The Bar Council told the Fair Trade Commission that '[c]ollection of Law Library fees from many barristers was becoming extremely difficult.'[33] Several barristers mentioned milestones such as marriage or the purchase of a house that signalled to them that they had 'made it' and were earning enough.[34]

Morison and Leith point out that it was 'obviously easier to survive while earning little or no money if you come from a wealthy background'.[35] One barrister who was in receipt of family support said that 'after a few years on the circuit I found that I could pay my way and was really in practice as a barrister'.[36] Others explained how they were financially supported by their parents:

> Oh, my father supported me of course. That's what I expected ... I was probably two or three years getting established to the sense of being able to pay for myself ... At that stage I could do that, pay for the flat, I could accommodate myself here. No longer dependent on father.

> I remember telling my father that when I was starting off that the reality was that I was still going to look for support from him as if I was a student ... and that I would be looking from time to time for the use of the car and all of that and that that would go on for 3–5 years maybe.

Another barrister, whose father was a solicitor, said that this was helpful because

> I got a feed of work from him all the time and he also paid me, which other people didn't do.

Not everyone had this option, however. Lee recalled of the 1940s, 'few of us had a private income at a time when the old financial and social standards were being shattered and fewer still knew where to turn for professional preferment.'[37] Several barristers mentioned needing to take out loans or overdrafts in order to pay their way, and one pointed out the ease with which one could take out a mortgage even in the absence of a steady income.[38] Another barrister described getting into financial difficulties:

> I was broke. I had no money. I borrowed money from the bank and then couldn't pay it back ... I got more and more into difficulty with money, and then I got sued by two creditors.

However, this barrister's earnings soon improved, and

33 F.T.C., para. 7.99.   34 E.g., B7, B1.   35 John Morison and Philip Leith, *The barrister's world and the nature of law* (Berkshire, 1992), p. 25. See ch. 9, 3 and 12 on the importance of family connections.   36 O'Higgins, *Double life*, p. 88.   37 Lee, *A memoir*, p. 31.   38 B14.

1 The North-West Bar, July 1921. *Front row, l–r*: Anthony Babington, Marcus Begley, Robert A.E. Wood, Stewart Gaussen, John Leech, Thomas Henry Maxwell, James MacLoone, John Muldoon, Edward Sullivan Murphy. *Back row*: Robert Smylie, Edward Kelly, James Malachi Muldoon, Thomas Marnan, Martin Cyril Maguire, Thomas Jones Smyth, James Augustine Murnaghan, John Dougherty, James Geoghegan, Basil McGuckin, Joseph Flood, J.W. Johnston, P. Smith, W.F. McCoy, Thomas Aloysius Finlay, Daniel McMenamin. Reproduced by kind permission of the Bar of Ireland Digital Archive

2 Call to the Bar, Michaelmas 1922. (*l–r*): Joseph Kavenagh, Brian Magennis, Ralph Brereton Barry, Thomas Burke, Herbert Hamilton Hare, Donal O'Sullivan, Conor Alexander Maguire, James Joseph Walsh. William McFeely was called *in absentia*. Reproduced by kind permission of British Pathé

3 Portrait of Hugh Kennedy by Leo Whelan, 1926.
Reproduced by kind permission of The Honorable Society of King's Inns

4 Nora Durkan and Patrick Waldron: called to the Bar, Trinity 1948, later married 1961.
Reproduced by kind permission of the Bar of Ireland Digital Archive

5 Eric Hallinan received a knighthood in 1955, having worked in Nigeria, the Bahamas and Cyprus. Reproduced by kind permission of the National Portrait Gallery

6 Call to the Bar, Michaelmas 1961. In order of call: Kenneth Mills, Michael Eamonn O'Kennedy, Conal O'Toole, Hugh Joseph Hogan Magee, Aidan Browne, Linus Obonna, Ian Thomas, Patrick Raftery, Chukwunonyelu Joseph Metuh, David Andrews, Gerard Jombo Ufford, Fredrick Stanley Watson. Reproduced by kind permission from the Bar of Ireland Digital Archive

7 Marie Teresa Bourke (Mary Robinson) and Caroline Elizabeth Kenny, called to the Bar, Trinity 1967. Reproduced by kind permission of the Irish Photographic Archive

8 Barrister, Labour TD and former ceann comhairle of Dáil Éireann, Patrick (Paddy) Hogan, 1968. Reproduced by kind permission of RTÉ Archives

9 Call to the Bar, Michaelmas 1972. In order of call: Declan McGovern, Jane Flood, John O'Riordan, Edward McGarr, John Coughlan, Michael Forkin, Ciaran O'Loughlin, Thomas Bowman, John O'Toole, Aindrias Ó Cuiv, Bridget Mary Cotter, John Peart, Bernard Nono, Kieran Derham, John Bruton. Reproduced by kind permission of the Bar of Ireland Digital Archive

10 Cecil Barror playing the part of a judge in RTÉ drama 'The Dean', 1973.
Reproduced by kind permission of RTÉ Archives

11 Call to the Bar, Trinity 1973. In order of call: Mary Gormley, Peter Kelly, Justin Dillon, George Clarke, Fidelma Macken, Mary Geraldine Miller, Thomas Morgan, William Skelly, Peter Smyth, Seán McGrath, Michael McMahon, Thomas Heffernan, Raymond Groarke, Margaret Mary McStay, James Hamilton, Gerald Keys, Martin Conroy, Michael Campion, James McDonnell, Colm Allen. Reproduced by kind permission of the Bar of Ireland Digital Archive

12 Members of the Irish Bar called to the Bar of Northern Ireland, 1976. *Front row, l–r*: Eoin McGonigal, Paul Callan, Sean D. O'Hanrahan, John Cassidy, Eamonn Walsh. *Middle row*: Martin Kennedy, Vincent Landy, Dominic Lynch, Kenneth Mills, T.B. Hannon. *Back row*: Donal Barrington, John Blayney, Diarmuid O'Donovan, Mella Carroll, Ercus Stewart, Francis D. Murphy. Reproduced by kind permission of the Bar of Ireland Digital Archive

13 Catherine McGuinness on the RTÉ television quiz show 'Words Words Words' in 1979. Reproduced by kind permission of RTÉ Archives

14 Liam Devally presenting RTÉ's 'Cross Country Quiz' in 1979.
Reproduced by kind permission of RTÉ Archives.

15 Mella Carroll with Chief Justice Tom O'Higgins on her appointment to the bench of the High Court, 1980. Reproduced by kind permission of the Irish Photographic Archive

16 Colum Kenny at RTÉ, 1982. Reproduced by kind permission of RTÉ Archives

Eventually I remember a guy from the bank rang and he rang me and he said, 'what's happening? you're paying this back at a fierce rate' and I said 'well, I've just turned a corner, you know, so I'm delighted, I just want to get this off my back.' I wanted to get ... my creditors off my back, but anyway I did in a very short time, so I was very thrilled about that.

Other barristers took on additional work beyond the Bar in order to supplement their income:

You get alternative work you know; you work at night or you do other jobs, you go away and work for the summer.[39]

Several who were interviewed for this book recalled lecturing and tutoring in various universities and colleges.[40] One described this as 'a bit of a safety net ... income that was guaranteed every year'.[41]

Another stream of additional income was law reporting for the Council of Law Reporting for Ireland.[42] Describing how a barrister might get involved in law reporting, McEnery wrote:

When a man of mature years who perhaps has been in another profession changes to the Bar and joins the Law Library it would not be unusual for him in the first year or two when he is building up a practice to do some law reporting for the official reports which are issued every year by the Bar Council. In this way he is enabled while doing his own work to read generally in the law and also help the Council of Law Reporting in their task of selecting important cases for annual publication.[43]

Hall described law reporting as 'an art that requires intellectual and other gifts'.[44] One barrister reflected on their experience of writing law reports:

Now reporting a law case for inclusion in the *Irish Law Times Reports* is a much more complex task than merely reporting it for newspapers. ... A case which takes a day to hear can take a day to write up as an accurate report. The work is, of course, remunerative, but it is very exacting.[45]

---

39 B14.   40 E.g., B26, B27, B14.   41 B27.   42 The Council of Law Reporting for Ireland was established in 1866; see Eamonn G. Hall, *The superior courts of law: 'official' law reporting in Ireland, 1866–2006* (Dublin, 2007), ch. 3.   43 P.J. McEnery, 'Ireland, 1900–50. Glimpses in retrospect', UCDA P174/1, p. 157. He added, 'At any rate this is what George Gavan Duffy did for a time after he commenced practising as a barrister at the Irish Bar because it was in his capacity as one of the law reporters that I first was brought into personal contact with him.'   44 Hall, *The superior courts*, p. 12.   45 Bernard Shillman, 'Every journey has an end', NAI PRIV1367/11, pp 55–6.

Reporters for the *Irish Reports* had to be elected by members of the Council for Law Reporting.[46] The Council engaged reporters 'to report suitable cases ... on a salary basis' until the eighties.[47] After that, freelance reporters were used.[48] Salaried reporters in the early forties could earn between fifty and eighty pounds per annum.[49] By the end of that decade, a Supreme Court reporter could earn £120 and High Court reporters £75.[50] A decade later, new rates of payment meant that Supreme Court reporters could earn £450 while High Court reporters could receive £400 per annum.[51] There was another slight increase in the late sixties, but by the early seventies reporters complained to the Council that their salaries 'did not reflect the skills, responsibility and time involved in law reporting.'[52] They pointed out that the £500 paid to them was 'just over half the remuneration of the book boys in the Law Library who work part-time in unskilled occupations.'[53]

Other types of outside work would have been unusual. One barrister who began practice in the late eighties said, 'people didn't work in shops and there was a sort of attitude of "you don't do that".'[54] Working in the arts was more acceptable, though some barristers used pseudonyms for their work in the creative fields. Playwright and actor Denis Johnston, who was also a practising barrister for a time, used a pseudonym when acting. His biographer notes that '[f]or several years Denis remained technically *incognito* as E.W. Tocher, but almost everyone who went to plays knew who Tocher really was.'[55] John Kelly published his 1964 novel *Matters of honour* under the *nom de plume* John Boyle.

The written code of conduct in the late eighties provided that 'A practising barrister shall keep his practice as his primary occupation and he may not engage in any other occupation which is inconsistent with his practise at the Bar.'[56] It also stated that:

> An occupation shall be inconsistent with membership of the Bar if it takes up the greater part of the barrister's time or is involved with the instruction of solicitors or barristers or may adversely affect the barrister's reputation at the Bar or the standing of the Bar.[57]

On occasion, the Bar Council was asked to make a disciplinary ruling in relation to a member of the Bar working externally. For example, in 1971 a complaint was

---

46 In 1928 Marion Duggan was the first woman law reporter elected by the Council. She was appointed on probation, which was unusual, and was pressured to resign in 1934. Hall, *The superior courts*, p. 150.   47 Ibid., p. 12.   48 Ibid., pp 12–13.   49 Ibid., pp 166, 177.   50 Ibid., p. 184.   51 Ibid., p. 283.   52 Ibid., p. 325.   53 Ibid., p. 326, citing a memorandum on staff remuneration, 27 Oct. 1971, Archives of the Council of Law Reporting.   54 B26.   55 Bernard Adams, *Denis Johnston, a life* (Dublin, 2002), p. 93. In fact, in reporting on his play 'Storm song' in 1934, the *Irish Law Times* wrote that 'E.W. Tocher's "second self" is Mr Denis Johnston, Barrister-at-law.' It also added that Johnston's plays were 'violent departures from the conventional.' (1934) 68 *I.L.T.S.J.* 39 (10 Feb. 1934).   56 Code of conduct, rule 2.3.   57 Ibid., rule 2.4. Exceptions were listed for

made that a barrister was also the public relations officer for one of the political parties; the barrister refuted this and said he was merely a research officer. This was accepted by the council, but it nevertheless issued a ruling that working as a public relations officer was 'inconsistent with membership of the Law Library'.[58]

As well as earning fees, barristers had to consider their overheads, which included, at a minimum, the Law Library subscription. Hugh Kennedy kept detailed notes of his expenses, and as a busy senior counsel he appears to have had quite considerable expenses, including subscriptions to several law reports (amounting to over £28); fees for clerks and scriveners (£90); fees relating to the Law Library and its facilities (£25) and postage and stationery (£14). His total expenses in 1920 amounted to £322 13s. 1d., from a gross income of £1064 14s. 0d.[59]

Chasing payment

Marking a fee was one thing; actually receiving it could be a different matter. There could be inordinate delays in receiving payment – in one instance a barrister recalled a delay of seven years,[60] while another mentioned waiting nine years.[61] Some fees were never paid at all. A barrister who began practising in the early seventies said 'in my day there was an awful lot of non-payment, an awful lot'.[62] Some solicitors earned reputations for being serial defaulters.[63] Barristers ascribed different reasons for non-payment of fees:

> You wouldn't be paid at times and it could be a number of things. Occasionally it'd be a solicitor in trouble, some sort of personal trouble, gambling or alcohol or something like that.[64]

> They would say 'well, I haven't been paid' and you have no way of knowing if they have been paid or not.[65]

The reasons for non-payment were not always considered to be benign. Several barristers mentioned unscrupulous solicitors firms who took advantage of very junior barristers:

> There were solicitors who were unscrupulous and who would prey – and I'm using that word advisedly – who would prey on young barristers and their insecurities and knowing that they would do anything to get a brief and then not pay for it.[66]

> You were being used. Some solicitors, when you started off, they'd send you two High Court actions or someone would send you four actions and

'membership of the oireachtas, the European parliament or any local authority or any third level teaching post.' 58 B.C.M., 26 Mar. 1971. 59 UCDA P4/153. 60 B11. 61 B5. 62 B1. 63 B4, B11. 64 B2. 65 B22. 66 B14.

you'd think 'oh God, this is great, fantastic! I'm in with Paddy, I'm in with Joe.' You'd never get another brief from them ... They'd move onto the next fellow. And you never got paid by them either.[67]

There are solicitors who never intend paying, a lot of whom will instruct relatively junior juniors who are delighted to get the work and then you're too late or discover they're still doing this work and they haven't been paid for any of it.[68]

In your first few years ... there were certainly solicitors who would abuse you, who would ask you to do something and because you are so insecure and so desperate to be seen to be working you'd be going out working for half nothing.[69]

With seniority came greater security when it came to payment. One barrister pointed out that 'the dynamic does shift so they start to rely on you and ... if they want to use you again they'll have to pay you.'[70]

Barristers sometimes had to chase solicitors for their fees, and some accepted this as an inevitable part of their professional life:

I remember my master at one stage telling me that he fully expected not to be paid for 20–25% of the work he did as a junior on circuit. Just – solicitors wouldn't pay, clients wouldn't pay. You win a case you get your costs, the other side just actually never pay them.[71]

Barristers could not sue for their fees, and had very little recourse:

Your contact point is the solicitor and either the solicitor hasn't got paid – in which case he can't pay you – or the solicitor has got paid and has kept your money back. In which case, you know, you're kind of banging your head against a brick wall.[72]

People developed their own techniques for dealing with this, for example, one barrister wrote a letter to a defaulting solicitor, saying:

'If the reason for the non-payment of this is that you are in personal financial difficulty just let me know and I will not press the fee.' Now that would produce a lot of payments back because you don't want [a barrister] saying 'your man actually is close to going to the wall' ... That was a technique that worked.

---

67 B4. 68 B10. 69 B21. 70 B22. 71 B10. 72 B10.

Non-payment was less of an issue when it came to state work or legal aid work. By contrast,

> If you are a common law or circuit practitioner you're doing a 'mixum-gatherum' of cases. You'll only get paid for personal injury cases if you win them. You may not even get paid if there is a sort of all-in settlement, the solicitor may count you out of the deal. You will find it difficult to get paid for equity cases. You'll find it difficult to get paid for employment cases ... all these sort of cases, hard to get paid.[73]

Some barristers struggled to keep on top of their paperwork, and might forget to send out fee notes,[74] or were unable to keep track of what had been paid and what had not.[75] Some were too busy to pursue unpaid fees:

> Well of course there were people who didn't pay you ... I really hadn't time to pursue them and didn't do it.[76]

Others received payment but forgot to lodge their cheques:

> I was hopeless about fees ... I didn't care about them. I'd go around with uncashed cheques for months in my pocket.[77]

> If I'd been a solicitor, I would have gone to jail very rapidly for not managing client accounts properly. I was never good at that kind of thing.[78]

In the twentieth century, fees were often paid in cash; one barrister described 'a shuffle of pound notes into your pocket.'[79] Several barristers singled out Travellers as making prompt cash payments.[80]

Sometimes clients paid a nominal fee, which did not reflect the amount of work the barrister had put into the case. One recalled:

> I remember I did a family law case ... this fellow, very difficult husband, said to me, 'I'll look after you boss.' We had three appearances. He did very well in the custody for a child, came out on the third day, third sessions, and he said 'Jesus I'm very pleased with that result, that's great. I've got the custody of the young fellow.' I said, 'yeah lucky the judge gave you that.' 'Janey, you did a mighty job on it and of course I said I'd look after you' ... and he gave me a tenner! I was the laughing stock of the Bar. Three appearances in the Circuit Court and I got a tenner.

---

73 B10. 74 B29. 75 B18. 76 B19. 77 B8. 78 B29. 79 B20. 80 B17 described a Traveller client as 'incredibly polite.'

Conversely, a barrister might occasionally be surprised by a payment where none was expected. One told of a case which ran, against their advice, but at the client's request. The case ran for five days and was unsuccessful. They recounted their experience with the client afterwards:

> He said 'what do I owe you?' I said 'no, no.' 'Ah no, no, no,' he said, 'you gave me advice, I didn't accept it and I'm paying you.' 'Right – you don't have to.' He said, 'I'm a plumber, if someone says they want a pipe in I say "brilliant – they want it they pay me".' He says 'I'm paying you.' So I said: 'it's coming up to €3,500 for the whole thing.' He pulled out the cheque, didn't go see his solicitor at all, he said 'no, no you did the work, you told me. I didn't accept your advice.'[81]

As noted in chapter four, some barristers kept working beyond a normal retirement age, and this was partly due to financial insecurity. One barrister recalled:

> One colleague, whom I considered to be secure and mature, told me that at the Bar not only had one to keep going until one dropped but that his great fear was that he would die and leave his wife and children on the rates.[82]

As seen in chapter seven, financial insecurity was a source of anxiety for many barristers.

Criminal legal aid

In a paper delivered to the Statistical and Social Inquiry Society of Ireland in 1931, Thomas Moloney noted that there was no general right to free legal aid. State-funded criminal legal aid was essentially confined to murder cases in the first half of the century, and this was done on a voluntary, rather than a statutory basis.[83] O'Higgins complained that '[t]he fees payable on such assignments were miserably low and bore no relationship to the burden of work undertaken both by counsel and solicitor. Few murder cases were of short duration.'[84] People accused of other offences were also sometimes represented by the Bar for no fee; as Paddy McGilligan told the Dáil in 1934, 'there is a very big number of cases done gratis.'[85] Voluntary organisations which provided free legal advice or aid included the Society of St Vincent de Paul, the Irish Society for the Prevention of Cruelty to Children and the Irish Labour Defence League.[86] One commentator noted that:

81 B20. 82 Lee, *A memoir*, p. 44. 83 Thomas Molony, 'Legal aid for poor persons', *J. Soc. & Stat. Inq. Soc. Ir.* 15 (1930–37), 15. 84 T.F. O'Higgins, *A double life* (Dublin, 1996), p. 182. 85 Dáil Eireann deb., vol. 59, no. 5 (13 Nov. 1935); see also O'Higgins, *Double life*, p. 182. 86 E.g. 'Irish Labour Defence League', *Irish Times*, 2 Sept. 1929, p. 5; 'Several leaders: an application in

Both branches of the legal profession in this country have always regarded it as a duty to advise and assist poor persons without charge. In addition, various social, charitable and religious bodies have on occasion obtained the free services of solicitors and, where necessary, counsel to assist poor persons.[87]

An occasional parliamentary question was asked about the introduction of a more comprehensive system of legal aid, but the responses were negative or non-committal.[88] In 1946 the *Irish Law Times* welcomed the report of the Rushcliffe committee in England and approved of its recommendations for a more liberal scheme of legal aid.[89]

The criminal legal aid scheme was introduced by the Criminal Justice (Legal Aid) Act 1962.[90] The Bar had been involved in drafting the scheme from the outset. In June 1961 the chief justice sought the views of the Bar Council regarding the proposed new scheme.[91] The minister for justice then invited the council to submit suggestions for how such a scheme might operate. The Bar Council, accepting that the establishment of a free legal aid system was in the public interest, set up a sub-committee,[92] whose report was used to prepare a draft scheme for the minister. Under the scheme as enacted, assessment of eligibility for free legal aid was to be a matter of judicial discretion, based on the gravity of the charge and the means of the accused person. A legal aid certificate was granted automatically in cases of murder, and 'where essential in the interests of justice' in other cases. As O'Higgins observed, before the 1962 Act there was 'no recognised criminal Bar.'

> With the advent of criminal legal aid, and the almost simultaneous abolition of capital punishment ... A criminal Bar came into existence. No longer was it true, as it had been, that crime did not pay.[93]

court', *Irish Times*, 7 Mar. 1930, p. 7. See Claire Carney, 'The growth of legal aid in the Republic of Ireland – I', *Ir. Jur.* 14(1) (1979), 61, at 72. Later the Irish Council for Civil Liberties, Women's Aid and the Union of Students in Ireland provided supports. **87** Delany, *The administration of justice*, p. 85. **88** E.g., question raised by James Pattison, Dáil Éireann deb., vol. 61, no. 2 (25 Mar. 1936); question raised by Martin O'Sullivan, Dáil Éireann deb., vol. 93, no. 6 (30 Mar. 1944). **89** 'Legal aid to the poor' (1946) 80 *I.L.T.S.J.* 181 (20 July 1946). **90** 'Radical departure in scheme of free legal aid' *Irish Times*, 16 Feb. 1962. p. 5. The Bar Council later suggested that the Department of Justice had been 'more concerned to have on the statute book an Act which could be pointed to as a compliance with the European Convention than to establish a system of legal aid which was best calculated to fulfil the needs of those likely to be compelled to avail of it, or to facilitate legal practitioners charged with implementing the scheme for the protection of the needy charged with criminal offences.' 'Legal aid in criminal cases', memorandum submitted by the General Council of the Bar of Ireland to the minister for justice, 1975, 3, reproduced in Claire Carney, 'The growth of legal aid in the Republic of Ireland – II', *Ir. Jur.* 14:2 (1979), 211, at 215. **91** B.C.M., 31 June 1961. At that stage, the Bar Council had not yet approved of any scheme of free legal aid. **92** B.C.M., 20 Dec. 1961. **93** O'Higgins, *Double life*, p. 183. See also Patrick Gageby, 'Was there a criminal Bar and what happened to any such tradition?' in Daire Hogan and Colum Kenny (eds),

Although the Act was passed in 1962, the regulations for its implementation were not introduced until 1965. The background to this was that in July 1963 the minister sent a set of draft regulations to the Bar Council.[94] This included a scale of fees payable, something that had not formed part of the proposals submitted by the council to the minister in 1961.[95] In November 1963 a deputation from the Bar Council met with the minister to discuss the proposed regulations. Among other things, they informed the minister that the suggested fees were inadequate, but that the Council would be prepared to accept the proposal on an experimental basis, given the public importance of the scheme. The deputation from the Bar reported that the minister was warmly appreciative of this approach, and had assured them that the scheme would be reviewed after two years.[96]

The Criminal Justice (Legal Aid) Regulations 1965 came into effect, and the Bar Council 'strongly encouraged' members of the Bar to participate in the scheme.[97] In June 1966 another Bar Council sub-committee was established to review the operation of the scheme,[98] and it was mainly concerned with the scale of fees.[99] Its report was submitted to the minister for justice, but was rejected.[100] This was discussed at length by the Bar Council, which then wrote to the minister suggesting that the fees would in any case be re-examined at the end of the trial period.[101] In 1967 yet another Bar sub-committee conducted a review of the scheme.[102] It concluded that there was no justification for defence counsel being paid lower fees than prosecuting counsel. In December 1967 the Bar Council wrote to the minister asking that parity between counsel be adopted as the basis for criminal legal aid fees.[103] The chairman wrote to the minister on a number of occasions in 1968,[104] but these letters generally went unanswered. In October 1968 the Bar Council informed the minister that as a result of this failure to engage, the issue of withdrawing from the legal aid scheme would be discussed at a general meeting of the Bar.[105] This prompted a response from the minister,[106] who said he was also liaising with the Law Society about their proposals for fees. The issue was debated at the AGM on 17 December 1968, and the Bar voted not to withdraw from the scheme, and to continue to provide legal representation for those who could not afford it.[107]

In April 1969 the Bar Council requested the minister to accept a deputation from the Council,[108] but due to the minister's commitments, this did not take

Changes in practice and law (Dublin, 2013). 94 B.C.M., 31 July 1963. 95 'The annual general meeting of the Bar of Ireland' (1970) 104 *I.L.T.S.J.* 123 (21 Mar. 1970). 96 Ibid. 97 B.C.M., 5 Feb. 1965. 98 B.C.M., 8 June 1966. It was proposed to make joint submissions to the Department of Justice with the solicitors' profession. 99 B.C.M., 5 July 1966. 100 B.C.M., 20 Oct. 1966. 101 The Bar Council also pointed out some operational anomalies with the system, such as the fact that legal aid was being provided to 'wealthy farmers' sons, who technically had no property of their own but could nevertheless command significant means if they so wished.' B.C.M., 20 Oct. 1966. 102 B.C.M., 7 Apr., 1 Dec. 1967. 103 B.C.M., 12 Dec. 1967. 104 E.g., B.C.M., 20 Jan., 2, 26 Feb., 15 Mar. 1968. 105 B.C.M., 3 Oct. 1968. 106 B.C.M., 8 Oct. 1968. 107 B.C.M., 17 Dec. 1968. 108 B.C.M., 25 Apr. 1969.

place until 16 July.[109] This meeting was later described as 'futile'.[110] A 25% increase in fees was proposed, plus an additional consultative fee of three guineas in murder, manslaughter and dangerous driving causing death. This was unacceptable to the Bar Council, which pointed out that the figures had been arrived at without any consultation or negotiation. Again, the Bar Council sought parity between defence and prosecution counsel. They also highlighted other procedural and administrative defects in the scheme. It pointed out that the fees paid under comparable schemes in England, Wales, Scotland and Northern Ireland were higher than either the proposed 25% increase or the fees likely to be paid under a system of parity. The attorney general pursued the issue in the months following, but to no avail.[111]

The Bar Council recommended at the 1970 AGM that the Bar consider withdrawing from the scheme.[112] It was pointed out that although the costs for the entire criminal legal aid scheme were estimated at £20,00 per annum, only £9,000 was spent in 1968–9 and £16,000 in 1969–70.[113] After a spirited discussion, the Bar voted to withdraw from the criminal legal aid scheme. There went from being 154 to just 14 barristers listed for the scheme in 1970.[114] One barrister recalled,

> We organised a strike of all the legal aid barristers, we removed our names from the panels ... It had a bit of an impact. It did create a bit of a change and then speeded up the payment. I think there was another strike after that too ... That improved the payment and the frequency of payment, the scale and the frequency.[115]

In the Dáil, T.F. O'Higgins referred to it as a 'silly dispute'.[116] Following a series of meetings[117] between the minister for justice and representatives of the Bar, the minister was reluctant to accept parity of payment 'for political reasons.'[118] A revised scale was proposed, and rejected by the Bar Council,[119] but it was accepted by a majority at a general meeting of the Bar in October 1970.[120] One barrister commented that

> When I started off doing legal aid in the early 70s the fees were abysmal. Abysmal. And ... , so slow in getting paid.[121]

---

109 B.C.M., 1 July 1969. 110 B.C.M., 8 July 1969. 111 B.C.M., 24 Oct., 7, 28 Nov., 5 Dec. 1969. 112 B.C.M., 13 Feb. 1970, and 'The annual general meeting of the Bar of Ireland' (1970) 104 *I.L.T.S.J.* 123 (21 Mar. 1970). 113 These figures included the fees paid to solicitors. 114 Dáil Éireann deb., vol. 246, no. 11, 20 May 1970. 115 B4. 116 Ibid. 117 B.C.M., 23 Oct. 1970. 118 B.C.M., 5 Oct. 1970. 119 Ibid. 120 B.C.M., 23 Oct. 1970. One of the Bar's concerns was that if a system of civil legal aid were introduced, the criminal legal aid fees might be used as a benchmark; see further below. These fees were set out in the Criminal Justice (Legal Aid) (Amendment) Regulations, 1970 (S.I. 240/1970). 121 B4.

Another recalled that:

> If you got a legal aid case, in those days the fees for doing a legal aid trial
> was 35 guineas ... and the system for payment depended on solicitors
> filling forms and quite a lot of them weren't very good at that and then it
> might get stuck in one of the departments so you could end up doing a
> case and not being paid for a year or two.[122]

In February 1975 the Bar Council submitted 'an elaborate memorandum'[123]
to the minister for justice regarding the criminal scheme.[124] Among the
suggestions was a system of taxation of fees rather than a scale. It was also
pointed out that the assignment of legal representatives should be done at an
earlier stage of criminal proceedings. Minister Cooney was of the view that if the
revisions proposed by the Bar Council were implemented, this 'would require
substantial changes in existing legislation and would add significantly to the cost
of providing criminal legal aid.'[125]

In March 1975 the minister met with the Bar Council to discuss the
memorandum.[126] He did not expressly commit to accept their proposals.[127] The
minister suggested a fee increase for barristers, but the Bar Council was more
interested in a complete reorganisation of the system. Once again, the matter was
put to a general meeting of the Bar,[128] and barristers voted to withdraw from the
criminal legal scheme.[129] One interviewee remembered this strike:

> There was a legal aid strike and I hadn't a clue ... I was asked to do some
> criminal work in the District Court and I said 'yeah, why not?' ... we were
> ostracised because we broke the strike.

By July 1975 there were only four barristers' names on the legal aid panel,[130] and
the situation persisted for almost a year,[131] until a general meeting of the Bar
voted in July 1976 to resume working under the scheme. Barristers on the legal
aid panel only had to have been in practice for six months or more,[132] and
consequently many quite junior barristers were involved in this work.

122 B25.   123 B.C.M., 1 Nov. 1974.   124 See also B.C.M., 25 Nov. and 2, 9 Dec. 1974; 8 Jan.
1975.   125 Dáil Éireann deb., vol. 284, no. 5 (30 July 1975). He commented that 'criminal trials in
the Circuit Court, the Central Criminal Court and the Special Criminal Court have had to be
adjourned because of the withdrawal of barristers from the scheme.'   126 Its content had been
leaked to the press: B.C.M., 24 Feb. 1975.   127 Don Buckley, 'Cooney non-committal to Bar
Council', Irish Times, 7 Mar. 1975, p. 8.   128 B.C.M., 11 Apr. 1975. Don Buckley, 'Barristers may
withdraw services from state free legal aid scheme', Irish Times, 11 Apr. 1975, p. 4.   129 The
withdrawal took effect from 28 May 1975: B.C.M., May 1975. Solicitors withdrew in 1974 and
1975.   130 Dáil Éireann deb., vol. 284, no. 5 (30 July 1975).   131 B.C.M., 21 June 1976. Cooney
said that 'barristers have not been participating in the legal aid scheme since the recent withdrawal
of the Bar from that scheme'. He acknowledged that the backlog was causing some hardship.
132 B.C.M., 12 Feb. 1978, 12 Apr. 1986, 19 May 1987.

There were persistent problems with barristers getting paid under the criminal legal aid scheme, which one described as 'hopeless'.[133] An inefficient paper-based system (described as a 'six-stage process')[134] for processing payments led to lengthy delays, and many barristers were not being paid until eight months after they had completed their work. In late 1987 members of the Bar sought to propose new systems for payment, such as the introduction of a collection agency for state fees. The Bar Council sought upfront payments for barristers. In an editorial reflecting on an extraordinary meeting of the Bar in July 1988, the *Irish Law Times* reported:

> The inordinate delay in the payment of many fees due from the state has been a matter of great concern to the Bar for a considerable time. Yet, despite repeated representations by the Bar Council and, indeed, by many individual members of the Bar, there was no discernible improvement in the situation which became a cause of personal anguish – indeed many would argue severe hardship – to barristers who defend the less well-off sections of our society under the state's legal aid scheme.[135]

Barristers withdrew from the free legal aid scheme following the EGM.[136] However, the strike was suspended in September 1988. A new computerised payment system was promised, and barristers agreed to write off unpaid fees from the old scheme, where it was not possible to trace and process them.[137] In January 1989 there was another extraordinary general meeting of the Bar to discuss the ongoing problems with the criminal legal aid scheme, and once again there was a threat of withdrawal.[138]

More problems arose in 1993 because solicitors, who had to submit certification on behalf of barristers, were not doing this in a timely manner, leading to delays. The Bar Council then introduced a system of direct payment, with the council processing the claims. In 1995 there were further complaints from the Bar Council because of delayed payments for work carried out in the Dublin Circuit Court. Delays were experienced once more in 1996 due to under-staffing in the accounts department of the Department of Justice. Barristers threatened to withdraw from the scheme and the department agreed to rectify the understaffing problem. Arrears were paid, but the issue persisted. In 1997 the Bar Council threatened once again to withdraw from the scheme.[139] One cause

---

133 B29.   134 'Legal aid strike', *Irish Law Times* (ns) 6 (1988), 201.   135 Ibid. It added that '[u]nlike the vast majority of industrial actions this dispute is not concerned with the amount of money that should be paid for providing a valuable service; rather it's about the state's delay of eight months and, sometimes, longer in paying the barristers their fees.'   136 Ibid.   137 Carol Coulter, '3 Bar Council threats in 10 years to leave free legal aid scheme', *Irish Times*, 12 Aug. 1997, p. 4.   138 Maol Muire Tynan, 'Threat to free legal aid grows', *Irish Times*, 9 Jan. 1989, p. 6.   139 Coulter, '3 Bar Council threats'.

of delayed payments was the system of pay parity between prosecution and defence counsel. Fees for those working in the free legal aid scheme could not be specified until the fees for prosecuting counsel had been agreed.

Civil legal aid

The introduction of a statutory scheme of civil legal aid lagged behind the criminal scheme.[140] Describing how poorer litigants came to be represented in the fifties and sixties, O'Higgins wrote that 'it was rarely that a person who lacked means and who had a statable claim was denied access to the courts'.[141] This was done by engaging two seniors for the plaintiff, and they were only paid if the plaintiff won and was awarded costs. If they did not succeed, at least they only faced a loss relating to half a case each and it meant that in the meantime they could be getting on with other cases. The first Free Legal Advice Centre (FLAC) was set up in Mountjoy Square in Dublin in 1969 with the dual aims of providing free legal services, and campaigning for free civil legal aid.[142] This focus on campaigning distinguished FLAC from previous initiatives. Demand for the service grew, and O'Morain notes that 'by the time FLAC published its first report in 1972, it had handled 2,437 files.'[143] By the time of its second annual report, this had increased to 8,000 files. By 1979, there were 17 centres (15 in Dublin). Several barristers who were interviewed recalled their experiences volunteering, with one describing it as 'a really big eye opener for me'.[144] In the 1970s, FLAC threatened to close its centres unless a system of civil legal aid were introduced.[145] There was a limited form of civil legal aid available – for example, in 1973–4 there was a total of £45,000 available;[146] one group of law students estimated that two million pounds would be needed for a comprehensive scheme.[147]

By the mid-seventies, campaigning for the introduction of comprehensive civil legal aid was underway. A committee, chaired by Justice Pringle, was appointed by the minister for justice Patrick Cooney in 1974 to advise on the establishment of a free legal aid scheme for civil actions. Members of the Bar Council were initially divided over whether or not to support the development

---

140 Usually when public statements were made in the Dáil in favour of free legal aid, this did not include civil cases: e.g., Jack Lynch in 1948 said '[w]hile I do not advocate that legal aid should be given in all cases – civil cases, for instance – I would suggest that in most indictable criminal offences legal aid should be forthcoming for poor people who are unable to defend themselves.' Dáil Éireann deb., vol. 111, no. 12 (24 June 1948).   141 O'Higgins, *Double life*, p. 180.   142 Padraig O'Morain, *Access to justice for all: the history of the Free Legal Advice Centres 1969–2003* (Dublin, 2003), p. 7. In 1968 UCD undergraduate David Byrne discussed the idea of providing free legal advice to poorer members of the community with fellow students Denis McCullough, Vivan Lavan and Ian Candy.   143 Ibid., p. 9.   144 B25.   145 'Free legal aid panel set up: embracing civil actions', *Irish Times*, 11 May 1974, p. 15.   146 Ibid.   147 These were the 'socialist law group' – UCD law graduates, led by Colum Kenny, who were in their final years of professional training:

of a civil scheme, but nevertheless wrote to the minister for justice offering their assistance.[148] Addressing a meeting of the Law Society, Attorney General Declan Costello expressed the view that legal aid ought to be available to everyone as of right, and not as a matter of charity.[149]

In 1974 the Bar Council set up a sub-committee to prepare a report for the Pringle committee on civil legal aid.[150] It met with the committee in 1975.[151] The Bar also continued to engage with the minister for justice regarding the defects in the system of criminal legal aid.[152] The Pringle committee reported in 1977 and the report was published in 1978, recommending the introduction of a comprehensive state system of legal aid and advice. The report recommended that the new service be based on a choice-of-lawyer principle. It would operate through the services of solicitors and barristers in private practice, and solicitors employed full-time in community law centres. The entire service should be administered by a Legal Aid Board.

Carney notes that by 1979, '[t]he clamour for the introduction of state legal aid increased following publication of the Pringle report'.[153] FLAC threatened to withdraw its services if the Pringle recommendations were not implemented.[154] In February 1979 the case of *Airey v. Ireland*[155] was heard in Strasbourg, and in October the judgement of the court was delivered. The European Court of Human Rights was critical of Ireland's lack of a free legal aid scheme for family law matters, which was held to be a breach of the ECHR.

The chairman of the Bar Council met with the minister for justice to discuss the civil legal aid scheme on a number of occasions in 1979. Reporting on one such meeting, he said that 'When the Bar had been unable to agree to full-time salaried barristers appearing in court the minister had become very abrasive and had threatened the Bar with an attack in the newspapers'.[156] The council agreed that 'it was necessary to avoid confrontation with the minister as the Bar was vulnerable on its level of fees'. It was noted at a subsequent general meeting of the Bar that the principle of having full-time employed barristers in the proposed law centres was 'a threat to the independence of the profession and to the nature of the barrister as we understood it.'[157] A compromise suggested by the civil servants was that a barrister might contract his or her services to the Legal Aid Board for a period of two years, but the Bar Council considered this impractical. A different suggestion put forward by the council was the use of one-term retainers. Many members of the Bar were uneasy at the prospect of

---

'£2m free legal aid scheme proposed', *Irish Times*, 26 Feb. 1974, p. 13.   **148** B.C.M., 15 Feb., 1 Mar. 1974.   **149** 'Extension of free legal aid accepted by Costello', *Irish Times*, 13 May 1974, p. 15. **150** B.C.M., 28 June 1974. The following month, the Pringle committee asked the Bar Council for a submission. B.C.M., 3 July 1974. Progress was reported at B.C.M., 11 Nov. 1974.   **151** B.C.M., 3 Mar. 1975.   **152** B.C.M., 1 Nov. 1974.   **153** Carney, 'The growth of legal aid–II', p. 218.   **154** Niall Corr, 'Free legal aid' (letter), *Irish Times*, 8 Mar. 1979, p. 9. (Corr was the director of FLAC). **155** (1979) 2 E.H.R.R. 305. Josie Airey had been unable to obtain a judicial separation from her husband in the absence of civil legal aid.   **156** B.C.M., 2 July 1979.   **157** B.C.M., 16 July 1979.

salaried barristers. In November 1979, Department of Justice officials suggested an hourly rate for barristers retained by the legal aid board via a panel system.[158] The Bar Council agreed to this on an experimental basis, though expressing the view that the rates were lower than the normal 'going rate'. This payment structure was accepted by a general meeting of the Bar.[159] In January 1980, the Legal Aid Board came into being,[160] with Mella Carroll as the chair.[161] The Bar had issues with aspects of the scheme, such as the Board's insistence that all cases be brought at District Court level, and in 1983 a group of practitioners prepared a memorandum on this issue.[162] The Bar Council liaised frequently with the Board about fees, the distribution of cases by legal aid solicitors, and other matters.[163] By the late nineties, most of the Legal Aid Board's work related to family law.[164]

Because the civil legal aid scheme dealt with family law issues, FLAC changed its focus in the 1980s. Tribunal work, including employment law and welfare cases, was excluded from the official scheme, and FLAC began to fill this gap.[165] It established a series of welfare rights centres, and at a time of high unemployment, demand for these services was high. It also pursued test cases in the superior courts.[166] The Bar Council, as well as the Law Society and individual members of the legal professions, continued to provide financial support as well as legal expertise. FLAC remained 'sharply critical' of the limitations of the civil legal aid scheme,[167] which was finally given a legislative basis in the Civil Legal Aid Act 1995.

In other areas of civil practice, barristers continued to take on potentially unpaid work on a 'no win, no fee' basis, usually in personal injuries cases:

158 B.C.M., 5, 27 Nov., 3 Dec. 1979.   159 B.C.M., 19 Dec. 1979.   160 See Paul Murray, 'Government's civil law scheme set for New Year', *Irish Times*, 22 Dec. 1979, p. 8. Some reservations were expressed by various organisations, see e.g., Nigel Browne, '18 groups criticise new legal aid scheme', *Irish Times*, 9 Sept. 1980, p. 4. Understaffing and long waiting lists were frequent problems, see Padraig Yeates, 'The ins and outs of legal aid', *Irish Times*, 25 June 1990, p. 14. A commentator in 2000 noted that 'civil legal aid in Ireland is in perpetual chaos': Jenny Burley, 'Legal aid and family law in Ireland', *Alt. L. J.* 25:4 (2000), 169, at 169.   161 Part of the Board's role was to decide if applicants were entitled to legal aid, and what contributions should be made. Aid and advice would be provided via regional centres.   162 B.C.M., 13 May 1983.   163 B.C.M., 10 Nov. 1990; B.C.M., 13 Feb., 9 Oct. 1981; 16 July 1988.   164 Carol Coulter, 'Legal Aid Board plans a better service', *Irish Times*, 15 Nov. 1999, p. 4.   165 O Morain, *Access to justice*, p. 13.   166 E.g. *Cotter and McDermott v. the Minister for Social Welfare and the Attorney General* (1990) C.J.E.U. C–377/89. This secured welfare arrears for 70,000 married women following the state's failure to implement a 1979 EEC Directive. Counsel in the case were Mary Robinson and Gerard Durcan, against David Byrne and Aindrias O'Caoimh. Another example was *Hyland v. Minister for Social Welfare* [1989] I.R. 624. The Supreme Court deemed unconstitutional social welfare provisions which treated a married couple less favourably than an unmarried couple. Counsel for the plaintiffs were Mary Robinson, Eamon de Valera and Gerard Durcan, and representing the state were Peter Maguire, David Byrne and Brian Lenihan. See also *Foy v. an t-Ard Chláraitheoir, Ireland and the Attorney General* [2012] 2 I.R. 1. Counsel for the plaintiff were Bill Shipsey, Gerard Hogan and Siobhan Phelan. Counsel for the respondents were Diarmaid McGuinness and Bláthna Ruane, with Mary O'Toole and Nuala Egan for the notice parties.   167 See Free Legal Advice Centres, *The closed door: a report on civil legal aid services in Ireland* (Dublin, 1989).

In the old days people did take it on but it was more personal injuries because that is what a lot of the cases were. They might be over in a day or two. If you won you got your fee, if you didn't you invested a bit of your life but not a huge amount.[168]

Some barristers took on these cases because of a sense of social justice; one described 'being the mouthpiece for those who cannot speak for themselves in court'.[169]

This was a case I was asked to do. I met the parents. I liked the parents. I felt very sorry for them and I knew that I was never going to be paid and I was happy to do that. Most – if not all – of my colleagues will do that ... there is a responsibility that goes with that to do cases, hard cases, which will not be paid and that's very rewarding.[170]

Many barristers described similar motivations for taking on unpaid cases.

* * *

Reflecting on barristers who worked in the early part of the century, MacKenzie wrote,

Their incomes were low, the fees were miserably small, even taking into account the cost of living and inflation. What they were paid was in no way commensurate with the earnings of the Bar today. They laboured on without the benefits of modern machines, they worked day and night, there were no pension schemes, the life was precarious indeed.[171]

The common experience appears to have been one of low earnings in the early years. With seniority came greater security and predictability, but for many, low payment and non-payment were common hazards of the profession. At the other end of the scale were those who engaged in highly paid civil and commercial litigation, or who worked for tribunals at the end of the century, but these were very much the exception rather than the rule. One such barrister commented that working at the Bar

Gives you a standard of living you wouldn't have had. You pay a lot of taxes but everyone does, you get over that and you enjoy life.

As seen in chapter three, few admitted to financial motivations for joining the Bar, and it was rare for those interviewed to cite their 'financial success' as having been the most rewarding aspect of their years of practice. The reality of remuneration at the Bar was, for most people, a source of anxiety.[172]

168 B23.   169 B7.   170 B7.   171 MacKenzie, *Lawful occasions*, p. 151.   172 See ch. 7.

CHAPTER NINE

The gendered Bar

Introduction

As discussed in chapter two, the Sex Disqualification (Removal) Act 1919 removed the legal barrier to women entering the legal professions.[1] In November 1921 Frances Kyle and Averil Deverell were the first women to be called to the Irish Bar.[2] The experiences of these early women barristers have in recent years been documented and commemorated in exhibitions[3] and portraiture,[4] as well as through lectures,[5] conferences,[6] books,[7] periodicals,[8] poetry[9] and other events,[10] particularly in the context of the centenary of the 1919 Act and the entry of women into several legal professions.[11] These add to the growing body of

1 For a summary of the background to this legislation and the 'persons cases' which preceded it, see Hilary Sommerlad and Peter Sanderson, *Gender, choice and commitment: women solicitors in England and Wales and the struggle for equal status* (Aldershot, 1998), ch. 3.   2 The National Association of Women Lawyers in the US celebrated their call to the Bar, commenting 'Ireland has never been lacking in brawn; nor does it remain to be proven that the rapier-like wit of Irishmen is not possessed by Irish women as well.' 'Notes', *W.L.J.* 11:2 (1922), 13.   3 E.g., in April 2018 the King's Inns hosted an exhibition on Averil Deverell to mark the acquisition of the Deverell archive. The Bar of Ireland library services' 'Trailblazers' exhibition can be viewed at https://sway.office.com/fYhKtuDK7WTl5J68?ref=Link. See Vanessa Curley and Sarah Foley, 'Trailblazer', *B.R.* 26:5 (2021), 152.   4 E.g., portraits of Justice Mella Carroll now hang in both Dublin City University and the King's Inns; in 2017 a portrait of Justice Susan Denham was unveiled; in 2020, a portrait of Justice Mary Laffoy was added to the collection at the King's Inns; two portraits of Justice Catherine McGuinness were unveiled in 2022, one in the National Gallery and one in the University of Galway. The joint 'In Plain Sight' initiative between the Bar Council and the King's inns seeks to commission additional portraiture of women lawyers: www.lawlibrary.ie/inplainsight/. The first commissioned portraits are those of Kyle and Deverell, pictured on the cover of this book. At the time of writing, the next commissioned portrait will be of Frances Moran, by artist Vera Klute. As well as formal portraiture, the Bar of Ireland building on Dublin's Church St. was wrapped in a digital film depicting Deverell and Kyle.   5 E.g., the Irish Legal History Society's spring discourse in 2019 was delivered by Liz Goldthorpe on the topic of Deverell's legal career.   6 E.g., in 2021, one day of the annual Bar of Ireland chair's conference commemorated the centenary of the first women barristers. The podcast is available at www.lawlibrary.ie/podcast/.   7 E.g., Liz Goldthorpe, 'First woman to practise as a barrister in Ireland and the (then) United Kingdom, Averil Deverell, 1921, in Erika Rackley and Rosemary Auchmuty (eds), *Women's legal landmarks: celebrating the history of women and law in the UK and Ireland* (Oxford, 2019).   8 A special commemorative issue of the *Bar Review* was launched in November 2021: *B.R.* 26:5 (2021).   9 Poet Jane Clarke wrote 'In the Four Courts', a commissioned poem about Averil Deverell. It was published in the *Irish Times*, 1 Jan. 2022, p. 19, and the Bar Council's interview with the poet is available at www.lawlibrary.ie/podcast/.   10 These included a gala dinner at the King's Inns and a reception with President Michael D. Higgins at Áras an Uachtaráin in November 2021.   11 The first women solicitors, admitted in 1923, were Mary Dorothea Heron, Helena Mary Early and Dorothea Mary Browne. This centenary has been marked by the Law Society of Ireland in several ways, including articles in the *Law Society Gazette* and the publication of a booklet, The Law

literature examining the experiences of early women lawyers and judges in England[12] and other jurisdictions,[13] and critiques of the position of women in contemporary legal professions.[14]

Understandably, much recent focus has been on historic 'firsts' or 'trailblazers', but it is important not to let this obscure the broader story of how women experienced working in the legal professions. Indeed, this point was made twenty years ago by Bacik, Costello and Drew who observe, '[t]his phenomenon of the highly visible trailblazer woman should be understood not necessarily as an example of 'advances' made by women, but as a reminder of

Society of Ireland, *Celebrating a century of equal opportunities legislation: the first 100 women solicitors* (Dublin, 2019). See also Emma Hutchinson, 'First woman professor of law in Ireland, Frances Moran, 1925' in Rackley and Auchmuty (eds), *Women's legal landmarks*. See the First 100 years project: https://first100years.org.uk/, and its follow-on, 'Next 100 years': https://next100 years.org.uk/; Mary Redmond, 'the emergence of women in the solicitors' profession in Ireland' in Eamonn Hall and Daire Hogan (eds), *The Law Society of Ireland 1852–2002: portrait of a profession* (Dublin, 2002).   12 E.g., Patrick Polden, 'Portia's progress: women at the Bar in England, 1919– 1939', *Int. J. Leg. Prof.* 12 (2005), 293; Ron Pepitone, 'Gender, space, and ritual: women barristers, the inns of court, and the interwar press', *J.W.H.* 28:1 (2016), 60; Auchmuty and Rackley, 'The women's legal landmarks project: celebrating 100 years of women in the law in the UK and Ireland', *L.I.M.* 16 (2016), 30; Auchmuty and Rackley, *Women's legal landmarks*. Writing about women solicitors, Sommerlad pointed out that they 'experienced systemic subordination from the moment that they began to enter the profession in large numbers in the early 1980s. Hilary Sommerlad, '"A pit to put women in": professionalism, work intensification, sexualisation and work-life balance in the legal profession in England and Wales', *Int. J. Leg. Prof.* 23:1 (2016), 61.   13 E.g., Constance Backhouse, '"A revolution in numbers": Ontario feminist lawyers in the formative years 1970s to the 1990s' in Constance Backhouse and W. Wesley Pue (eds), *The promise and perils of law: lawyers in Canadian history* (Toronto, 2009); Constance Backhouse, 'What if? Career paths not taken: Claire L'Heureux-Dubé and politics', *Canadian J. L. & Soc. / Revue Canadienne Droit et Société* 29:2 (2014), 273; Kjell A. Modeer, 'From "rechtstaat" to "welfare-state": Swedish judicial culture in transition 1870–1970' in W. Wesley Pue and David Sugarman (eds), *Lawyers and vampires: cultural histories of legal professions* (Oregon, 2003); Joan Brockman and Dorothy E. Chunn, 'A new order of things: women's entry into the legal profession in British Columbia', *Advocate* 60 (2002), 385; Mary Jane Mossman, *The first women lawyers: a comparative study of gender, law and the legal professions* (Oxford, 2006). Rosemary Hunter, 'Discrimination against women barristers: evidence from a study of court appearances and briefing practices', *Int. J. Leg. Prof.* 12 (2005), 3; Virginia Drachman, *Sisters in law: women lawyers in modern American history* (Cambridge, MA, 1998). This examines women lawyers in the US from the 1860s to the 1930s, following their campaigns to be admitted to law schools and state Bars.   14 The late twentieth century also saw increased academic focus on the position of women lawyers in the wider common law world: e.g., Cynthia Fuchs Epstein, *Women in law* (New York, 1993); Carrie Menkel-Meadow, 'Portia in a different voice: speculation on a women's lawyering process', *Berkeley Women's Law Journal* 1 (1985) 39; Rosemary Hunter, 'Women in the legal profession: the Australian profile' in Ulrike Schultz and Gisela Shaw (eds), *Women in the world's legal professions* (Oxford, 2003); Georgina Murray, 'New Zealand women lawyers at the end of the twentieth century' in Schultz and Shaw (eds), *Women*; Clare McGlynn, *The woman lawyer: making the difference* (London, 1998); Hilary Sommerlad and Peter Sanderson, *Gender, choice and commitment: women solicitors in England and Wales and the struggle for equal status* (Aldershot, 1998); John Hagan and Fiona Kay, *Gender in practice: a study of lawyers' lives* (New York, 1995), focusing on women lawyers in Toronto; Margaret Thornton, *Dissonance and distrust: women in the legal profession* (Melbourne, 1996). Thornton, ch. 2, traces the experiences of early women lawyers in the Australian states. Albie Sachs and Joan Hoff Wilson, *Sexism and the law: a study of male beliefs and legal bias in Britain and the United States* (Oxford, 1978) include in their study of 'persons cases' the

continuing male domination.'[15] Glazer and Slater identify strategies employed by early women professionals: superperformance, separatism, subordination and innovation.[16] They add that while early women professionals did not consciously choose such strategies, 'it quickly became clear to them that entrance into the elite world of professionalism would require special strategies for women.'[17] 'Superperforming' women were pioneers, and often achieved historic 'firsts'. Bacik, Costello and Drew refer to this as the 'first woman to' phenomenon, and caution that this 'does not necessarily provide evidence of absence of discrimination, but rather often signals the continued and persistent exclusion of women – the exception that proves the rule.'[18]

While recognising the significance of the trailblazers and 'famous firsts', this chapter also seeks to go beyond commemoration, to consider the lived experiences of women at the Irish Bar in the twentieth century. It looks at the challenges they faced, the type of work they did, the strategies they adopted to succeed in a gendered environment, and the supports which were available to them.

The number of women joining

As demonstrated in chapter four, the number of women joining the Bar in the first decades after the Sex Disqualification (Removal) Act 1919 remained low. It was not the case that once the first women were called, there followed a rising wave of women eager to pursue careers at the Bar. In the first twenty years after Kyle and Deverell, there were never more than two women called in a year, and in many years there were none.[19] Similar patterns were evident in other jurisdictions; for example, Drachman notes that in the US in the 1930s, 'women had achieved modest professional success and recognised the limits of their progress, a pattern that barely changed until the mid-1970s.'[20] Thornton comments that in Australia, 'the participation of women in the legal profession remained at a token level until the 1970s.'[21] Bacik, Costello and Drew suggest

attempts by women to be admitted to medical degrees, to vote, to sit as councillors and to work as law agents.　15 Ivana Bacik, Cathryn Costello and Eileen Drew, *Gender injustice: feminising the legal professions?* (Dublin, 2003), p. 125.　16 Penina Migdal Glazer and Miriam Slater, *Unequal colleagues: the entrance of women into the professions 1890–1940* (New Brunswick, 1987), pp 211–22. They describe these strategies, p. 211, as 'pervasive'.　17 Glazer Slater, *Unequal colleagues*, p. 210. 18 Bacik, Costello and Drew, *Gender injustice*, p. 100. Innovation, another of Glazer and Slater's strategies, has meant in the legal sphere the adoption of new specialties by women entrants, something which is discussed further below.　19 Rackley and Auchmuty, reflecting on women in the legal professions of Ireland and the UK, note that 'progress has been astonishingly slow ... the arrival of women in the higher courts proved to take much longer than any of the campaigners of 1919 would have envisaged, as men's grip on the top levels of the judiciary held firm through their ability to decide who was chosen, and later through their ability to interpret "merit".' Erika Rackley and Rosemary Auchmuty, 'Women's legal landmarks: an introduction' in Rackley and Auchmuty (eds), *Women's legal landmarks*, p. 10.　20 Drachman, *Sisters in law*, p. 1.　21 Thornton, *Dissonance*, p. 64.

that 'the same impetus that had led to the legislative changes in the 1970s ... had also had an effect on women seeking to work at the Bar.'[22] These changes were referred to by some interviewees. One cited the removal of the public service marriage bar in 1973,[23] the Anti-Discrimination (Pay) Act 1974 and the Employment Equality Act 1977 as factors contributing to the increased numbers of women working outside the home.[24] As seen in chapter four, the number of women joining the Bar in the late seventies increased quite significantly. One woman barrister said that this 'improved matters greatly'.[25] Nevertheless, women remained a small minority: commenting on the late sixties and early seventies, one barrister recalled 'girls coming in ... gradually, only a trickle'.[26] Another, who began practising in the late seventies, said:

> It wasn't a diverse Bar. It certainly was male dominated in those days. You didn't have very many young ladies, you had some, but not very many young ladies.[27]

One woman said that by the late nineties there were 'enough that you didn't feel like you stood out'.[28]

Even when women began joining the Bar in significant numbers, the number of women progressing to senior counsel remained low. Frances Moran took silk in 1941, but the next woman, Mella Carroll, did not take silk until 1976 – over fifty years since women's first entry to the profession. By the late eighties there were still only 'a handful of women silks'.[29] It was considered newsworthy when, in 1997, three women took silk, raising the number of women seniors to eleven.[30] The appointment of women to judicial posts was equally gradual, if not more so; it was not until 1992 that women had been appointed as judges in courts at all levels.[31] Clearly the pace of change during the twentieth century had been slow. This was commented on by a barrister called in the early nineties, who said that

22 Bacik, Costello and Drew, *Gender injustice*, p. 73. 23 See Irene Mosca and Robert E. Wright, 'The long-term consequences of the Irish marriage bar', *Ec. & Soc. Rev.* 51:1 (2020), 1. 24 B11. 25 B1. 26 B8. 27 B23. 28 B24. 29 B28. 30 *Cork Examiner*, 4 Oct. 1997, p. 7. A similar pattern was evident at the Bar of England and Wales, where 5.3% of QCs were women in 1991–2: Hillary Sommerlad, 'The myth of feminism: women and cultural change in the legal profession', *Int. J. Leg. Prof.* 1 (1994), 31. In 1997–8, Hunter, 'Discrimination', at 4, found that only 5% of QCs at the Bar of Victoria were women. 31 The first woman to be appointed a District Court judge was Eileen Kennedy (formerly a solicitor) in 1964. Catherine McGuinness (called in 1977; Ferguson, *Barristers*, p. 367) was the first to be appointed to the Circuit Court in 1993; Mella Carroll (called in 1957: ibid., p. 153) was the first woman appointed to the High Court in 1980 and in 1992 Susan Denham (called in 1971: ibid., p. 363) was the first woman appointed to the Supreme Court bench. Women judges from other jurisdictions sometimes visited. E.g., at a gala dinner for members of the American Bar Association in the King's Inns in 1924, one of the guests was Judge Mary O'Toole, who had emigrated from Ireland at the age of 16 and became a court reporter, then an attorney, then a judge of the municipal court of the District of Columbia. She was a prominent member of the national association of women lawyers in the US. 'How we started: N.A.W.L. history chapter III', *Women Lawyers' Journal* 28:3&4 (1942), 23. I am grateful to Liz Goldthorpe for details about the 1924 King's inns dinner.

there were few female role models 'at the senior levels.'[32] This has been referred to as the 'trickle–up fallacy'[33] or 'pipeline fallacy'; that women are already achieving close to proportionate representation in almost all areas of the professions. Bacik, Costello and Drew describe as a 'powerful misperception' the idea that 'women's progress as lawyers is simply a matter of time, with increasing number of women studying law and entering the profession'.[34] In fact, they write, tracking the progression of women who entered the profession in the late twentieth century, 'women have failed to progress in the same manner or at the same pace as their male colleagues'.[35] As Rackley and Auchmuty observe,

> The trajectory of women's representation in the legal profession and the judiciary thus shows how landmarks for women are always partial and circumscribed, and almost always followed by a tightening of control by those whose power has been breached. The achievement of a landmark is rarely, if ever, the end of the story. Too often if signifies the start of another struggle; an even more bitter one since the impediments to justice and equality for women are no longer explicit but may be hidden, informal, and bolstered by practices not yet forbidden or even recognised, and always able to be denied by opponents protesting that 'women are equal now'.[36]

We turn now to examine the experiences of women who worked as barristers after 1921.

Experiencing gender discrimination at the Bar

The period covered by this book excludes the era when women were denied admission to the profession. Nevertheless, some discriminatory practices prevailed, even after the 1919 Act.[37] As Sachs and Hoff Wilson observe, 'It was hardly to be expected … that when the formal disabilities were removed, women would find a comfortable place for themselves in legal practice'.[38] Bacik et al. describe discrimination in this context as being 'the result of social structures and institutions, as much as individual conduct'.[39] It is worth observing that the prevalence of sexual discrimination at the Bar was a contested issue in interviews for this book.[40] Some male interviewees claimed never to have been aware of any discrimination or negative treatment on the basis of gender, for example:

32 B24.   33 Sommerlad, 'The myth of feminisation', 31.   34 Bacik, Costello and Drew, *Gender injustice*, p. 153.   35 Ibid.   36 Rackley and Auchmuty, 'Women's legal landmarks', pp 10–11. 37 Mossman, *The first women lawyers*, p. 2, wrote that in the early twenty-first century, that 'while individual women have achieved significant success in law, there is continuing evidence of systemic gender barriers.' As Fuchs Epstein, *Women in law*, points out, p. 81, '[t]he history of discriminatory practices by the legal profession is well documented', although she also notes that '[t]he dimensions of discrimination, its tonality, the consequences it has had for the patterning of women's experience in law and the ways it has changed and is changing are complex.'   38 Sachs and Hoff-Wilson, *Sexism and the law*, p. 178.   39 Bacik, Costello and Drew, *Gender injustice*, p. 156.   40 When asked

I've never seen in my experience, the late eighties and nineties and on, I've never seen any discrimination on gender grounds.

It wasn't that there was any overt discrimination or even covert – I mean, I wasn't conscious of that.

Some male interviewees also downplayed the extent of discrimination on circuit:

You never saw particular discrimination on circuit towards women, you know. All you might have seen was sometimes the solicitors might have been slower to give them work.

By and large the girls were well treated in the Law Library. A few old grudging people might, you know, be a bit nasty but that, that would be about all.

However, other men who were interviewed for this book were conscious that women barristers had faced additional challenges in the twentieth century:

I do think that women certainly had it harder, you know. ... they had to really work harder ... sometimes men get away with more.[41]

I think it was harder for young ladies in those days to get started.[42]

A woman barrister described 'the obvious blatant discrimination' as 'grim'.[43] Other men corroborated that there was discrimination against women:

Some people were either somewhat or quite hostile ... Some people were resistant to the idea of a woman at the Bar.[44]

It was male dominated and it was extremely difficult for women ... there was a lot of misogyny and she [a family member] would tell us about that ... she certainly experienced misogyny when she was in there in the seventies and the early eighties.[45]

if there was discrimination in the legal professions, the respondents in Bacik, Costello and Drew's study also responded differently depending on their gender. The researchers found that 'a significantly higher proportion of women than men had experienced disadvantage.' Bacik, Costello and Drew, *Gender injustice*, p. 276. The women surveyed for that study listed 'inappropriate comments', 'network exclusion', 'level of income/earnings', 'not getting certain work' and being given 'inappropriate tasks' as examples. In their interviews with women barristers in the 1990s, Connelly and Hilliard found that older male barristers were sexist towards more junior females. Alpha Connelly and Betty Hilliard, 'The legal profession' in Alpha Connelly (ed.), *Gender and the law in Ireland* (Dublin, 1993), pp 219–20. On 'inappropriate comments', Backhouse refers to 'underbreath comment[s]' made to early women lawyers in Canada; Constance Backhouse, '"To open the way for others of my sex": Clara Brett Martin's career as Canada's first woman lawyer' *Canadian J.W.L.* 1 (1985), 1, at 22. **41** B12. **42** B23. **43** B10. **44** B18. **45** B21, describing a

Some men were aware of their own bias or privileged viewpoint:

> X [a woman] complained bitterly of having had a terrible time on circuit
> ... But then I didn't see it that way and most of my colleagues and pals
> didn't see it that way but we would say that wouldn't we, do you know what
> I mean? We weren't looking at it from her point of view.[46]

Some women barristers gave specific examples of poor treatment of women
by male colleagues, for example:

> My bag was taken and flung out the window [by male colleagues].

> When I devilled my master had a solicitor who would physically close the
> door to prevent me going into consultations.

> I remember X [a man] commenting on my trouser suit ... I always
> remember him saying only women with long legs should wear trouser
> suits.

Others recalled sexism from judges. One barrister mentioned a judge who was

> Very misogynistic, had very traditional views about the role of women ...
> My master would get me to write down the value of the case before the
> judge gave the award ... I worked out that there was a 10/15% devaluation
> if the barrister presenting the case was a woman.

One gave an example of a judge referring to a woman barrister using her
husband's surname, so 'Mrs Z' when her name was in fact 'Ms X':

> He called her Mrs. Z throughout the whole case while she was presenting
> it in court, a name she never uses, which her client wouldn't have been
> introduced to her [as], her solicitor wouldn't have instructed her in that
> name, you know, that's where your client is saying 'does the judge not know
> who my barrister is?'[47]

Similarly, the participants in Bacik et al.'s study reported judges treating women
'with more derision than the males',[48] and with 'an air of scepticism'.[49]

By contrast, some women felt that they were treated equally at the Bar and
experienced no gender discrimination. One woman barrister who had a strong
family network at the Bar said:

family member's experiences at the Bar. **46** B18. **47** B10. **48** Quoted in Bacik, Costello and
Drew, *Gender injustice*, p. 284. **49** Ibid. Another recalled, p. 282, 'a friend who has had incredibly
personal remarks made to her at court.'

I didn't ever feel that I was treated badly and I certainly never felt it in terms of the way in which judges treated me.

Another said:

I don't think I ever had a bad experience by reason of being a woman.

These sentiments were very much in the minority however, and most of the women interviewed for this book recalled instances of overt or covert discrimination.

Whether or not the mid-century women barristers 'stuck out' or 'blended in' was also contested by the male interviewees. One man who began practising in the mid-sixties said that women barristers blended in and from what he could see they were treated the same as the men.[50] Similarly, another who joined the Bar around this time said:

They blended in with everybody. ... they blended in with everybody is my recollection, yes. They didn't actually stick out now, no they didn't, funnily enough.[51]

By contrast, a barrister who had joined in the early sixties said that the women 'definitely' stuck out:

Well, Averil, you saw her in the Library, she wore a hat all the time ... she sat on the right as you go into the Library ... You were aware of her. Fanny Moran swanned around in black ... and pretty intimidating, but I got on with her.[52]

There were sometimes subtle ways in which women were treated differently; for example, in 1955 the Bar Council wrote to Averil Deverell, Ethel Beatty[53] and Agnes Cassidy[54] to thank them for their assistance in hosting a sherry party for members of the Northern Bar.[55] Another way women were treated differently related to the way that barristers in the first half of the century addressed one another:

Everybody is obliged to address his fellows by their surnames or christian names as the case may be. No lords or sirs or misters are allowed. When the women arrived they were called Mrs or Miss as the case might be with their names but one would expect that where the ladies were concerned.[56]

50 B6. **51** B8. **52** B9. **53** Called in 1950; Ferguson, *Barristers*, p. 138. **54** Called in 1940; appointed as the first woman judge of the District Court in 1975. Cassidy also served as president of the Medico-Legal Association of Ireland and chair of the Adoption Board, and was appointed Reid professor of law at Trinity College. See ibid., p. 155. **55** B.C.M., 23 May 1955. **56** McEnery,

A lady called Miss Deverell, she was so old and so respected I never knew her Christian name.[57]

In his biography of Mella Caroll, Geoghean similarly recalls that she was referred to by her colleagues as 'Miss Carroll'.[58] In the listings of Bar Council membership, the *Irish Law Times* referred to 'Miss Carroll', while everyone else was simply listed by their first name (or initials) and last name.[59]

Facilities

For several decades after 1921, the facilities for women in the Law Library remained quite poor, and were consistently worse than those provided for men.[60] The refurbishment of the Four Courts following the damage inflicted during the Civil War provided an opportunity to incorporate facilities for women barristers – described by the *Irish Law Times* as 'special rooms ... designed for the use of lady members of the Bar'.[61] As discussed in chapter eleven, by 1949 there was a women's dressing room, variously referred to as the ladies' robing room or the women barristers' room.[62] Several times in 1950 and 1951 Averil Deverell wrote to the Bar Council complaining about its state of disrepair, and seeking improvements.[63] In 1953 it was pointed out that fuel for heating the women barristers' room was provided at their own expense, and that they were not supplied with an adequate number of towels.[64]

Between 1978 and 1979 the women's facilities were improved and expanded[65] in order to accommodate the growing number of women barristers.[66] However, continued expansion meant that by the mid-1980s this space, which included changing and shower facilities and a sitting area, had been outgrown and the need for proper facilities for women was once more on the Bar Council's agenda.[67] Further works were carried out and at the Bar's annual general meeting in 1987, the chairman acknowledged that women barristers had borne with and tolerated 'robing and rest room facilities which were wholly inadequate.'[68]

'Look back', p. 74. On the practice of calling people by their surnames, Mackenzie wrote: '"We were expected to call each other by our surnames no matter what the age difference was. Christian names were rarely used in those days except between friends. I couldn't bring myself to say "Fitzgibbon"' [to Frank Fitzgibbon]. Patrick MacKenzie, *Lawful occasions: the old Eastern Circuit* (Dublin, 1991), p. 5. 57 B8. 58 Hugh Geoghegan, 'Carroll, Mella Elizabeth Laurie', *D.I.B.* 59 E.g., 'General Council of the Bar of Ireland' (1968) 102 *I.L.T.S.J.* 56 (10 Feb. 1968). 60 This also appears to have been the case at the King's Inns. Máire Mac an tSaoi, *The same age as the state* (Dublin, 2003), comments, at p. 160: 'The benchers of King's Inns made no concessions to the existence of female students. That meant that there were absolutely no lavatory facilities for us in the building on Henrietta Street.' 61 'The Four Courts' (1930) 64 *I.L.T.S.J.* 293 (6 Dec. 1930). 62 B.C.M., 4 Mar. 1949. 63 B.C.M., 31 Mar. 1950; 27 July, 16 Nov., 14 Dec. 1951. 64 B.C.M., 23 Oct. 1953. 65 B.C.M., 6 Nov 1978; 22 Jan. 1979. The minutes note that '[t]he ladies would acquire a small refrigerator and an electric kettle for their room at their own expense.' See (1979) 113 *I.L.T.S J.* 75 (17 Mar. 1979). 66 See pp 74–5. 67 B.C.M., 20 Jan., 12 May 1986; 8 Oct., 9 Nov. 1987. 68 Bar of Ireland AGM, 19 Dec. 1987. Further refurbishment was carried out in the mid-nineties:

Sexual harassment

Some women at the Bar experienced sexual harassment.[69] Given the emphasis on socialising,[70] women barristers could find themselves attending evening events with colleagues where significant amounts of alcohol were consumed. Asked if they had ever witnessed anything inappropriate at these social events, one woman replied 'oh completely, absolutely, of course.'[71] Others gave examples:

> I did have to bat away some unwanted drunken attentions and stand up for myself a bit.[72]

> You had the usual people on social occasions and senior colleagues getting drunk and leering at you and hitting on you and saying inappropriate things, grossly inappropriate things at times ... if you couldn't put up with it then you weren't going to stay ... So people who stayed tended to be either thick skinned or quite good at batting off these situations. It was the 1980s.[73]

This was not limited to younger or more junior women; even at a more senior level, 'You still might get hit on by a judge at a benching.'[74] There were few institutional supports for women who experienced sexual harassment. One interviewee said, 'we got upset but there wasn't a lot you could do about it. You knew if you made a complaint the Bar Council weren't going to do anything'.[75] She recalled a particular instance:

> One colleague did make a complaint because she had been physically groped by a colleague and the Bar Council kind of banned him from the bars on the premises but it kind of became a big joke that so and so wasn't allowed downstairs.[76]

Following a couple of instances of harassment that were brought to the Bar Council's attention, in 1995 proposals were suggested to the Bar Council for procedures to deal with barristers who were having what were described as 'personal problems'.[77] It was suggested that a panel be created to support 'members who had a personal problem of one kind or another which was not a professional practice problem'.[78]

B.C.L.C., 12 May 1994.   **69** Bacik, Costello and Drew found that an 'alarmingly high figure' of 14 per cent of the women respondents in their study had experienced sexual harassment or bullying: *Gender injustice*, p. 285.   **70** See ch. 12.   **71** B10.   **72** B28.   **73** B10.   **74** The women barristers in Bacik, Costello and Drew's study similarly recounted instances of 'molestation', 'physical sexual harassment', 'sexual assault on one occasion by senior colleague', 'being "felt up" by a colleague', having to 'fend off sexual assault'. Bacik, Costello and Drew, *Gender injustice.*   **75** B10.   **76** B10. **77** B.C.M., 6 May, 13 Oct. 1995.   **78** Several members of the Council said that to proceed to have

Connections and networks

Attracting sufficient work in order to make a living could prove difficult for anyone joining the Bar, particularly those who were not well-connected. Some early women barristers, such as Avril Deverell,[79] Frances Moran[80] and Marion Duggan[81] supplemented their earnings,[82] though this does not appear to have been unusual among barristers at the time.[83]

The importance of connections and networks is explored in more depth in chapter twelve. These considerations affected all barristers, but could affect women barristers in specific ways also. It is certainly notable that many of the women who had successful careers at the Bar in the first decades after 1921 had personal or family connections and may have benefitted from their membership of and connection to relevant networks.[84] As Fuchs Epstein observes, while it was one thing to be a practising lawyer, it was quite another 'to be a true working partner in the camaraderie of the legal community.' She argues that the structure of the legal profession 'and the cultural views about the nature of men and women often prevent women from becoming fully integrated into the legal profession'.[85]

Male lawyers were more likely to have attended private or fee-paying schools,[86] and had strong ready-made networks on arrival at the Bar. The use of these and other networks for professional advancement was generally seen as a more male than female activity.[87]

a meeting with women members only would risk it being seen as a women-only problem. 79 Goldthorpe, 'First woman to practise as a barrister', p. 176. Deverell ran dog kennels from her home in Greystones, Co. Wicklow.   80 Moran was the first woman law professor in the UK and Ireland, and taught at both the King's Inns and Trinity College.   81 Duggan was also the first woman law reporter, from 1928 to 1934.   82 B1 and B3 similarly recounted working at secretarial and teaching jobs in the early years of their careers.   83 See ch. 5. Even in pursuing these extra jobs, women barristers sometimes faced barriers. Before appointing Frances Moran as professor at the King's Inns in 1932, a discussion was had among the benchers as to 'whether a lady was desirable as a professor.' K.I.B.M., 11 Apr. 1932. This comment in the minute book was struck out, (presumably retrospectively). Evidently there was some fear that having a female professor might prove disruptive; at the same meeting, the chief justice mentioned that 'it would be very desirable that either a bencher or the under treasurer should attend the lectures of the King's Inns professors to keep order and report.' K.I.B.M., 11 Apr. 1932. Order must have prevailed, and Frances Moran served as a respected professor at the King's Inns for a number of years. Both Mary Robinson and Agnes Cassidy were appointed Reid professor of law at Trinity College; see further ch. 10. 84 Deverell, for example, was related to several lawyers on her mother's side, and her father was clerk of the crown and peace for county Wicklow. She had an uncle who was a barrister in London and a cousin, Naomi Constance Wallace, who was one of the first women to be called to the English Bar in 1922. Goldthorpe, 'First woman to practise as a barrister', p. 176.   85 Fuchs Epstein, *Women in law*, p. 265.   86 Bacik, Costello and Drew, *Gender injustice*, p. 142. Hagan and Kay, *Gender in practice*, p. 70, made a similar finding.   87 The phrase 'boys' club' or 'old boys' network' cropped up continuously among the barristers surveyed for Bacik, Costello and Drew, *Gender injustice*, p. 233.

You wouldn't be in the loop. I mean it's just a lot of indirect stuff.[88]

One or two very, very good senior colleagues who brought me into very serious work, male colleagues ... they might have been a bit flirting ... but you just ignore that.[89]

A woman with children said that women didn't have 'the same networking as guys do and I'm not saying that they do it deliberately, it's just the pattern of their lives that allows them access to that.' By contrast, a woman who did not have children said that she found networking at the Bar very easy.

There was a high value placed on the solidarity of informal networks – some women were criticised for only using the Library for work and not for gossip or socialising.[90] Describing a woman barrister in the sixties, a male barrister said,

She was not collegiate. She wasn't ... she had no interest in Bar politics ... didn't seem to have any particular interest in the Bar per se.[91]

By contrast, some women were considered (or considered themselves) good networkers; for example,

She was quite gregarious and a nice person and all of that so she got on very well.[92]

Some women described the kind of social skills which were helpful:

I'm perfectly happy talking about sport, or whatever.

I clearly had the personality that could navigate it ... I could cut people down to size. I would have had that in common with a number of women in my generation who stuck at it and succeeded. ... Bit tough while also being a bit humorous you know. It didn't do to be strident though.

This demonstrates that women at the Bar sometimes needed to negotiate very specific social expectations.

Attire

Once the 1919 Act was passed and it became evident that women would be joining the Bar, some thought had to be given to what women barristers might wear in court. In Ireland, this did not cause major disquiet. The *Irish Law Times* reported in 1921 that Kyle and Deverell wore 'the usual wig and gown' at their call.[93] In

---

88 B22.   89 B3.   90 Connelly and Hilliard, 'The legal profession', p. 223.   91 B7.   92 B15.
93 (1921) 55 *I.L.T.S.J.* 274–5 (5 Nov. 1921). Similarly, the *Irish Times* reported that 'the ladies wore

January 1922, when reporting on the opening of the new law term, the same publication informed readers that Deverell 'wears the regulation wig and gown'.[94] In England, there were suggestions that women might wear a cap or biretta, instead of the wig. The *Irish Times* commented that while women preferred the wig,[95] English barristers 'were not enamoured of female competition', and there was a common view that the women ought to wear something different. As these matters were being debated by a committee of English judges and benchers, there was derision in the English press about the Irish women's wearing of horsehair wigs.[96] However, the *Irish Law Times* defended the Irish women barristers, stating that they looked 'far from ludicrous', and that the wig and gown were 'very becoming to the lady wearer'.[97] The *Irish Times* also observed that there was 'something comic in the spectacle of five learned judges giving serious thought to a matter of such a trivial kind'.[98] Ultimately, it was decided that women barristers in England should also wear the traditional wig, which should 'completely cover and conceal the hair.'[99]

The other aspect of professional attire was, of course, the clothing that women wore in the Law Library, and beneath their robes in court. In England in 1922, the *Daily News* suggested that 'coloured blouses and skirts, low necks and short sleeves' would be prohibited.'[100] Indeed, when the committee of English judges and benchers issued its guidelines later in 1922, it requested that women's dresses

> Should be plain, black or very dark; high to the neck, with long sleeves, and not shorter than the gown, with high, plain white collar and barristers' bands, or plain coats and skirts may be worn, black or very dark, not

the usual wig and gown, and well the garb became them'. 'First woman barristers: double record calls to the Irish Bar', *Irish Times* 2 Nov. 1921, p. 6. In an interview given to the *Belfast News Letter*, Kyle said that she did not like wearing the wig, and that she and Deverell had petitioned the lord chief justice against wearing it. She added that wigs for women had to be specially made so as to allow more space for their longer hair. *Belfast News Letter*, 21 Jan. 1922, p. 7. 94 (1922) 56 *I.L.T.S.J.* 11 (14 Jan. 1922). 95 'Wig or biretta', *Irish Times*, 14 Mar. 1922, p. 4. 96 'Portia's headdress. Judges deciding what women barristers must wear', *Daily News*, 14 Mar. 1922, p. 6. Articles in the *Justice of the Peace* and the *Daily News* were reproduced in the *Irish Law Times*: (1922) 56 *I.L.T.S.J.* 81 (1 Apr. 1922). The *Justice of the Peace* reported that Irish women had 'donned the horsehair wig with ludicrous effect. It is generally assumed that no such outrage will occur here ... The principle is clear. A woman in court as in church must have a head-covering, which technically a wig is not.' 97 (1922) 56 *I.L.T.S.J.* 81 (1 Apr. 1922). 98 'Wig or biretta', *Irish Times*, 14 Mar. 1922, p. 4. 99 Reported in 'Dress of women barristers', *Weekly Irish Times*, 8 Apr. 1922, p. 6. In March 1926, Mollie Dillon-Leetch appeared in court in Boyle, Co. Roscommon, wearing a hat and coat, and apologised to the judge for appearing wigless and gownless. This does not appear to have caused much difficulty; a male colleague, J.P. Burke, joked that he had offered to lend his wig, but that she was afraid of catching baldness, and Judge Roche joked that it did not matter, because 'the ladies are having less and less hair'. *Donegal News*, 13 March 1926, p. 6. It was also around this time that English newspapers published commentary about fitting wigs over women's hair becoming easier 'since the advent of bobbing'; e.g. 'Portia's problem', *Western Mail*, 3 Sept. 1928, p. 7. 100 'Portia's headdress. Judges deciding what women barristers must wear', *Daily News*, 14 Mar. 1922, p. 6.

shorter than the gown with plain white shirts and high collars and barristers' bands.[101]

While no such sartorial rules were specified in Ireland, women barristers tended to wear quite muted clothing under their gowns. For several decades there was an expectation that women barristers would wear skirts; one woman called in the late eighties recalled that 'nobody was allowed to wear trousers.'[102] Sometimes this was informally enforced by other barristers (male and female), and certain judges occasionally made their expectations very clear. One woman said that her master, also a woman, advised her in the mid-nineties not to wear trousers.[103]

> If you wore a trouser suit people would comment on it ... it was something that people noticed because it wasn't that common. Women wore skirts.

> I remember the person who first wore trousers in court ... There were all those issues around it. I mean it was very obviously male-dominated so it ran very much on that basis.

One woman said that negative comments about trousers only came from male colleagues,[104] while another said that sartorial issues were generally confined to the Law Library rather than the courtroom, because in court 'clothes weren't so much of an issue ... because you are wearing the gown'.[105]

Writing in the 1970s about the English Bar, Kennedy pointed out that '[t]o be the very model of a perfect lady barrister means looking as indistinguishable as possible from one's male colleague.'[106] This contrasts with the experiences of Irish women who were expected to dress in a feminine way, in skirts. On the other hand, even in the realm of skirts, women were expected to conform to male notions of acceptability; one interviewee recalled a complaint being made to the Bar Council about a woman barrister in the 1960s who wore miniskirts.[107] Aside from the expectation of skirt-wearing, one woman barrister was thankful that there was no expectation of high-heeled shoes:

> You'd have to have something fairly flat and you're literally running up and down stairs ... you were literally carrying a lot of boxes ... so it's just not practical to be going around with high heels and then you'd see these very elegant high-heeled female solicitors coming in from the shiny big firms and ... certainly at the criminal Bar that would not have been the look.

---

101 Reported in 'Dress of women barristers', *Weekly Irish Times*, 8 Apr. 1922, p. 6.   102 B13.
103 Bacik, Costello and Drew also noted that 'Until the early-1990s, women tended not to wear trouser-suits, although this was not prohibited by any rule and appears to have changed through practice': *Gender injustice*, p. 70.   104 B24.   105 B24.   106 Kennedy, 'Women at the Bar,' p. 159.
107 B19.

In their 1993 study, Connelly and Hilliard described the dress regime at the Bar as 'emblematic of an atmosphere in which there is great pressure to conform and censure of those who do not',[108] and this is certainly borne out in the interviews for this book. The wearing of wigs also has an important, often unstated, gender dimension:[109]

> Some women barristers have expressed the view that wearing a wig may be helpful in order to mask their relative youth and indeed gender. This view is based on the underlying premise that gender bias is operational in the court system, and that women somehow need manly gravitas (conferred ostensibly by the wig) in order to be taken seriously.[110]

There were evidently competing requirements that women both blend in at the male-dominated Bar, while also presenting in an acceptably feminine way.

Attrition

Although the first women barristers were called in 1921, it took many decades for women to constitute a significant proportion of the profession. By the 1960s they represented 10% of those being called to the Bar, and by the 1990s half of all persons called to the Bar were women.[111] The number of women called to the Bar did not necessarily translate into representation within the profession however. There was a higher attrition rate for women than for men, and many women had broken career paths.[112] A number of female interviewees reflected on this:

> It's a bit like the pyramid ... you've got a load at the bottom ... but as you move up through the ranks sure there's a huge falloff in the middle. I mean it's so hard to get the work, then when you get the work, it's hard to do the work, you do the work, it's so hard to get paid. Then if you want to have children or a house, you know there's no paid maternity leave, there's no holiday leave, there's no sick pay. There's nothing like that. So you would have to ask after a while, 'what are the attractions of this job?'

> The attrition rate for women was much higher than for men because factored into everything else you then had people getting married and having kids and the cost of maintaining a practice when you're not actually working ... if you were earning £30,000 a year, was it worth, you know, keeping your Law Library subscription and your overheads and paying a childminder? And what actually would you be earning after all of that?

108 Connelly and Hilliard, 'The legal profession', p. 219. 109 Bacik, Costello and Drew, *Gender injustice*, p. 70. 110 Ibid. 111 Connelly and Hilliard, 'The legal profession', p. 214. 112 Ibid.,

There were quite a few women but there was a very high rate of attrition, you know maybe 40% women came in. A small group, say about thirty, but quite a few left you know within the first couple of years. But those who stayed did very well.

Rackley and Auchmuty, focusing primarily, but not exclusively, on England and Wales, observe that in the early decades, '[w]omen who went down the barrister's route found themselves excluded, unsupported, criticised and harassed, and struggled to succeed at the Bar for decades thereafter'.[113] Of the small number of women joining the profession in Ireland in the early twentieth century an even smaller number remained in full-time practice for more than a few years. Some were called to the Bar but never practised, for various reasons. For example, Onora Ní Shúilleabháin, called in 1972, received the John Brooke Scholarship for the highest overall marks in her exams at the King's Inns,[114] but was advised against going into practice in the male-dominated Law Library. She therefore remained working in the civil service, until required to leave her position due to the marriage bar. Following the individual stories of the early women barristers, one can see that some did not practise at all, while others practised only briefly. For example, the third woman called to the Bar, Mary (Mollie) Dillon-Leetch, left the Bar upon marriage.[115] This was repeated by some women barristers throughout the century:

They would have been very bright women, you know, but all the men were looking for wives and a lot of them just married and started a family and never came in ... Gave up their careers in the first or second year at the Bar.[116]

A male barrister who had begun practising in the 1920s reflected in later years on one of his classmates, Antonia MacDonnell,[117] who had practised for a number of years.

Had she continued she would in my opinion have done quite well but as usually happened at that time where women were concerned, marriage swallowed up the profession and a woman whom one knew very well and deserved to do well in her professional life was heard of no more except in terms of family life. This is what happened in her case.[118]

p. 220.   113 Rackley and Auchmuty, 'Women's legal landmarks', p. 9.   114 Ferguson, *Barristers*, p. 364.   115 Dillon-Leetch was called in 1923; Ferguson, *Barristers*, p. 175. This was also seen in other jurisdictions; for example, Thornton notes that in Australia, 'many of the early women law graduates devoted themselves entirely to marriage and children, and hence dropped out of the public eye.' Thornton, *Dissonance*, p. 66.   116 B3; also B8.   117 Called in 1925: Ferguson, *Barristers*, p. 239.   118 P.J. McEnery, 'Look back in love: conversations by an English fireside', UCDA P74/2, p. 205. After her marriage to an army officer, McEnery was godfather to her

Even when the number of women joining the Bar began to increase significantly in the 1970s, a proportion continued to seek disbarment in order to pursue careers as solicitors. From the late 1960s to the late 1970s, approximately one woman per year sought disbarment.[119] Between 1977 and 1980 approximately two women per year sought disbarment,[120] and for the remainder of the 1980s it was an average of one a year or less.[121] Women who left to pursue other types of careers did not have to be officially disbarred, so these figures represent just one group who sought another type of legal career.[122] It is therefore 'impossible to obtain reliable figures on drop out rates of barristers by gender.'[123] However, it is possible to consider overall attrition rates for some periods. For example, Bacik, Costello and Drew present the following statistics:[124]

Figure 9.1. Women leaving the Bar

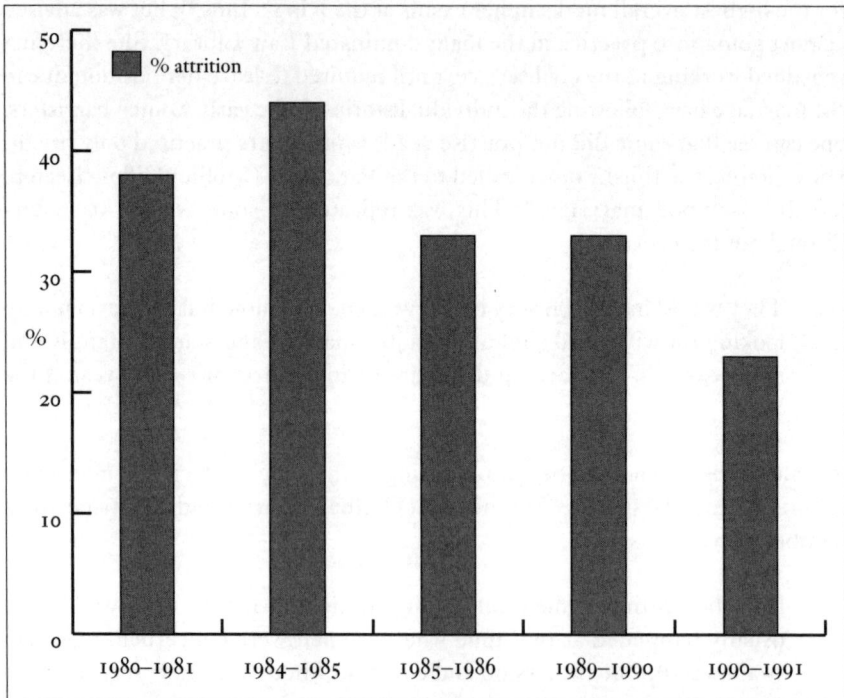

daughter, Antonia Blaise. Professor Agnes O'Farrelly of UCD was the godmother. 119 K.I.B.M., 24 Oct. 1968; 31 Oct. 1969; 11 Jan. 1971; 29 Jan. 1974; 19 July 1974; 6 Feb. 1975. 120 K.I.B.M., 1 Mar. 1977; 20 July 1977; 24 May 1978; 14 Sept. 1978; 5 Feb. 1979; 4 July 1980. 121 K.I.B.M., 12 Feb 1982; 6 Oct. 1986; 12 Jan 1987; 24 May 1989; 18 July 1989. 122 The number of women who sought to be called to the English Bar was quite low, and few who sought this second call actually intended to relocate to the UK. NAI 2009/74/742. 123 Bacik, Costello and Drew, *Gender injustice*, p. 74. 124 Figures from ibid.

As well as leaving to work as solicitors, women left the Bar in order to pursue careers in 'different jobs within the legal profession',[125] such as roles in different parts of the civil service,[126] including the Department of Foreign Affairs,[127] or in-house counsel in the private sector.[128] The benefits of such careers included 'a better structure for your life … in terms of maternity pay, in terms of career progression'.[129] Some went on to play significant roles in Irish public life, as chairs of public commissions[130] and politicians,[131] while others had enriching careers in diverse fields as broadcasters,[132] authors,[133] poets[134] and librarians.[135]

Gendered practice areas

Women who remained at the Bar and had successful careers often found themselves working in one of a small number of practice areas. In *Gender injustice*, it was pointed out that '[w]omen may find it easier to establish niches in new fields, thereby avoiding institutional barriers that may surround established lucrative areas.'[136] At the Irish Bar, many women specialised in family law;[137] one barrister commented that in the 1980s, women were 'dominating family law'.[138] Connelly and Hilliard estimated in 1993 that between 75 and 80 per cent of barristers in this area were women.[139] Bacik, Costello and Drew point out that

---

125 B16.   126 See further ch. 14; e.g. Gretta Flood (called in 1926): Ferguson, *Barristers*, p. 189, worked in the housing department of Dublin corporation. Ita Heslin (called in 1951: ibid., p. 206) worked in the High Court office, and as assistant examiner, registrar of wards of court, and registrar of the Supreme Court. Ann Callery (called in 1955 as Mary Callery: ibid., p. 150) later worked in the Revenue Department. Onora Ní Shúilleabháin (called in 1972: ibid., p. 364) worked in the central office of the Four Courts and in the probate office; Mary Murphy (called in 1972: ibid., p. 364) also worked in the civil service. See trailblazers exhibition.   127 E.g., Máire Mac an tSaoi (called in 1944: ibid., p. 240); Jane Flood Liddy (called in 1972: ibid., p. 364) and Emer Kilcullen (called in 1972: ibid.). See further, ch. 14 and trailblazers exhibition.   128 E.g., B12 said that both of the women on his circuit left for in-house legal advisor jobs, one in the public sector and one in the private sector.   129 B10. However, it is worth pointing out that salary scales for women may not have equalled those for men. E.g., an advertisement in the *Irish Law Times* in 1957 for a legal advisor in the Land Commission sought barristers or solicitors with at least twelve months' experience. The top of the salary scale was advertised as £1,109 for men and £895 for women: (1957) 91 *I.L.T.S.J.* (12 Jan. 1957).   130 E.g. Miriam Hederman O'Brien chaired a number of commissions in the seventies and eighties, and was the first woman to be appointed to the board of an Irish publicly listed company in 1985. See further ch. 10; 'Dr Miriam Hederman O'Brien obituary: trailblazer for women', *Irish Times*, 19 Mar. 2022, p. 12 and Ferguson, *Barristers*, p. 204.   131 Mary Robinson went on to become president of Ireland and UN high commissioner.   132 Una McAuliffe Linehan (called in 1944) had a successful career at Radio Éireann and later RTÉ: see Ferguson, *Barristers*, p. 229 and trailblazers exhibition.   133 E.g., Barbara Keating (called in 1972: ibid., p. 264) co-authored a series of novels with her sister, Stephanie Keating, including *Blood sisters* (Penguin, 2005).   134 E.g., Máire Mac an tSaoi was a poet and critic.   135 E.g. Brigit Walsh (called in 1945) was assistant librarian (1938–44) and then librarian of King's Inns from 1944–69. See further ch. 14 and Ferguson, *Barristers*, p. 314. Mary Neylon (called in 1949) took over as librarian from Bridget Walsh in 1970, remaining in post until 1984. See further ch. 10 and Ferguson, *Barristers*, p. 264.   136 Bacik, Costello and Drew, *Gender injustice*, p. 10.   137 Connelly and Hilliard, 'The legal profession', p. 217.   138 B7.   139 Bacik, Costello and Drew, *Gender injustice*, p. 217.

This had come about partly for historical reasons, since at the same time that legislative changes introducing legal separation and other family law remedies in the 1970s and 1980s began to generate a great deal of litigation in this area, the numbers of women entering legal practice began to increase significantly.[140]

While this is certainly part of the story, it is interesting to note that there was 'a global tendency for family law practice to be dominated by women.'[141] Many women chose family law 'because they felt that that was an area that they would get work.'[142] Women were often perceived as being better at this and some clients were biased in their favour.[143] However, there were downsides to specialising in this area. For example, family law cases were held *in camera*, and

> People don't go into the family law courts to watch the barristers, the way they might have gone in to watch X or Y in a PI or a big criminal case, so it didn't do anything to raise a lawyer's profile.[144]

Conveyancing was another area which was open to women; one barrister said it was seen as 'a woman's job',[145] while another described it as 'respectable'[146] for women. Conveyancing was considered to be tricky, technical and difficult,[147] and it involved mainly paperwork rather than court appearances.[148] As with family law, it would not lead to much exposure for somebody quite junior in their career.[149] This lack of exposure could affect women's likelihood of taking silk; McGlynn makes the point that in England and Wales, an essential part of being deemed suitable to take silk was to have 'good standing', which meant being 'known'.[150] Having less courtroom experience would have been unhelpful for many women in this regard.[151]

---

140 Ibid., p. 263.   141 Ibid. This tendency for women to practise in family law was also found in Victoria: Hunter, 'Discrimination', at 21–3. This study found that 'women are often thought, by clients, solicitors, clerks and male colleagues, to have an inherent empathetic quality which makes them suited to this area of law', at p. 22. The development of male and female practice areas was mirrored in England and Wales: J. Rogers, 'Representing the Bar: how the barristers' profession sells itself to prospective members', *Leg. Stud.* 32:2 (2012), 202, at 220. Women barristers in England and Wales were more likely to specialise in family law rather than commercial or corporate law. Bar Council, *Barristers' working lives: a second biennial survey of the Bar* (London, 2013). Bar Council, *Snapshot: the experience of self-employed women at the Bar* (London, 2015).   142 B11.   143 For similar reasons, B3 said she got a lot of 'cases of women who have women problems ... very serious cases where women have had private problems ... because the men don't want to discuss it so I'm brought into the consultation ... women have very serious back problems, they can't have sex ... they have to discuss that with them and of course the men aren't going to do that.'   144 B10.   145 B18.   146 Quoted in Bacik, Costello and Drew, *Gender injustice*, p. 264.   147 B10.   148 Quoted in Bacik, Costello and Drew, *Gender injustice*, p. 264.   149 B10.   150 McGlynn, *The woman lawyer*, p. 157.   151 While women barristers may have lacked some visibility in the Irish courts, their existence was certainly acknowledged abroad. For example, in 1945 the International Federation of Women Lawyers extended to Irish women lawyers an invitation to attend their fifth international congress in Los Angeles. Rosalind G. Bates (president IFWL) to Sean Nunan (Irish

They were all doing advisory work, conveyancing. Nobody was doing a court practice.[152]

Another said that women were 'regarded as suitable for things like conveyancing, tax; opinion work as opposed to court work.'[153]

Neither family law nor conveyancing would have been considered high profile or attractive work. Some work in the criminal field was carried out by women, but not necessarily the most high-profile or prestigious work. Connelly and Hilliard found in 1993 that there were 'few women defence counsel, and only a few more acting for the prosecution'.[154] An interviewee reflected that

On the defence side … I didn't think they were very ready and willing to brief women in the big trials which are the murder trials … I think while they were quite happy to have women up to a certain level doing their defence cases they weren't so happy having women in the big cases.[155]

In the late eighties, the 'sexy' work, according to one barrister, was personal injuries work and serious crime.[156] Another said:

There was no question of [women] being permitted to touch any of the big stuff … they wouldn't have been trusted with things like big commercial cases or jury actions or big personal injury cases.[157]

One interviewee said there was 'absolutely no doubt'[158] that commercial law was also seen as being very gendered.

---

ambassador), 24 Dec. 1948, NAI DFA/6/408/222 I. However, the invitation was sent to the Department of External Affairs; thence to the Department of Justice and then it was forwarded to both the Bar Council and the Incorporated Law Society. It took so long to reach the women lawyers (over three months) that it was too late to send a delegate. Malcolm McEllis (Bar Council) to sec. Dept. External Affairs, 28 June 1950, NAI DFA/6/408/222 I. However, a solicitor, Adeline Butler, was subsequently appointed as vice-president for Ireland. An invitation to the sixth congress, in Rome, was received the following year, but again the notice was too short, and no member of the Bar (or the solicitors' profession) could attend. Cecilia Hurley (solicitor) to sec. Dept. External Affairs, 14 May 1949, NAI DFA/6/408/222 I. Founded in Mexico City in 1944, the Federation drew its members from legal professions around the world, and in the 1950s passed resolutions relating to a range of issues such as adultery, property law, drug addiction, divorce, illegitimate children, inheritance, adoption, taking husband's name or wife's name, death penalty, juvenile courts, support for United Nations, women judges, prisoners of war (aftermath WW2), the legal status of women and legal education. A few years later, a delegation from the ABA welcomed at a reception in the Four Courts included several women lawyers. Vincent P. McDevitt (ABA) to John L. MacSweeney (Bord Fáilte), 29 Apr. 1957, NAI DFA/6/434/479. This was treated as a significant state occasion (see ch. 13) and there was a great deal of thought given to the dress code for the occasion. The Law Society was advised to specify 'black tie' on the invitations, with the representative for the ABA noting that '[t]he women will wear evening dresses, some of which will be long, others short. Of course, that would depend upon the personal taste of each woman.' McDevitt to Eric A. Plunkett (Law Society), 5 June 1957, NAI DFA/6/434/479. **152** B16. **153** B21. **154** Connelly and Hilliard, 'The legal profession', p. 218. **155** B24. **156** B10. **157** B21. **158** B22.

The Office of the Director of Public Prosecutions (DPP) was established in 1974 following the passing of the Prosecution of Offences Act 1974.[159] It assumed some of the prosecutorial powers previously held by the Office of the Attorney General. Towards the end of the century, more women began to be briefed by the state in criminal cases. One reflected:

> I personally think the state deserves credit for addressing these things at that particular time ... the attorney general ... over the years started to brief women so ... the state is a massive employer of barristers so in circumstances where all that work was opening up that was a great bonus for women.[160]

The Bar Council was at times proactive in this regard. It noted in 1986 that there were only three women prosecutors in the state,[161] and it wrote to the DPP about it.[162] By 2003, the DPP retained 150 barristers on various panels, thirty-four of whom were women. Eight out of thirty-two county prosecutors were women.[163]

Sources of work

Several barristers referred to the difficulty some women encountered with the briefing practices of individual solicitors or solicitors' firms. Solicitors were at times reluctant to brief women, not just in the specific 'male' areas identified above but as a general principle.

> I think solicitors hadn't got used to briefing lady barristers, and there was probably a sense that if they briefed them they mightn't do as well in court, and certainly the older solicitors might be a bit like that and clients mightn't have been as open to that or solicitors might have felt that clients weren't open to it, so I think that was where the difficulty was. I think it was just much more difficult for young ladies to start off.[164]

> Some solicitors felt their clients wouldn't feel properly represented by a woman and I think that probably continued a bit into the eighties in terms of criminal work, some circuit work and throughout the circuits ... There are some women who unfortunately felt that they weren't getting instructions from solicitors because they were women and there was undoubtedly ... a prejudice against instructing women.[165]

---

159 The first DPP was Eamonn Barnes, called in 1957, who served 1974–99: Ferguson, *King's inns barristers*, p. 134. 160 B13. 161 B.C.M., 29 Oct. 1986. 162 B.C.M., 12 Dec. 1986. 163 Bacik, Costello and Drew, *Gender injustice*, p. 270. 164 B23. 165 B11.

I remember one solicitor telling me that he would never brief a woman because he said the clients wouldn't accept it ... But I never had a client say I don't want a woman. To be honest I'm not sure that they really thought about it one way or the other.[166]

Again, the briefing practices of state bodies in the late twentieth century went some way to alleviating this. One barrister said that when the public sector 'started paying attention to gender representation', the offices of the attorney general and chief state solicitor 'realised that they would have to send thirty per cent of the work that they sent out to women, so it was just another example of how certain areas of law suddenly became available to women where they hadn't been available in the past.'[167]

Another source of work was 'handovers'. If a busy barrister found him or herself double booked they would pass on some of their work to a colleague. There was often a gendered dimension to this; men would tend to handover almost exclusively to other men.[168] One woman described this as a 'vicious circle':

Solicitors would give these briefs to men; men would pass them onto other men and those men would get a reputation for being good in court or good at the PIs or good at the crime and it became harder and harder for women to break into that.

She said that women in general didn't get cases handed to them from other barristers.[169] They tended to get their work from solicitors whereas men would get quite a lot of their work from other barristers. Another woman was conscious of the impression of gendered handovers, but said that in the High Court, one would always have had to check with the solicitor before handing over, and that barristers did not have complete discretion in this regard.[170]

Managing personal and family life

Choosing not to marry seems to have been a factor in the success of a number of early women barristers.[171] It would have been unusual in early and mid-twentieth-century Ireland for a married woman to have a professional career, and

166 B28.   167 B10.   168 A small number of women barristers in Bacik, Costello and Drew's study mentioned receiving work from women colleagues, and one said that 'Female friends recommended me for briefs when over-loaded': *Gender injustice*, p. 288.   169 She also recounted an anecdote about Mary Robinson referring to men handing over briefs to one another in the bathroom during an election speech.   170 B11.   171 E.g., Averil Deverell. The first woman eligible to be called to the Bar in Ireland, Madeline Collins, did not pursue her career because she got married: see Hutchinson, 'First woman professor', p. 204. Thornton, *Dissonance*, p. 66, notes that many early women graduates in Australia 'did not marry at all, a characteristic of early women graduates generally.' Glazer and Slater, examining early women professionals in the United States,

most women barristers who married then left the profession. By contrast, by the later twentieth century some successful women barristers emphasised the importance of having fully supportive spouses or partners. Some of those who joined the profession in the later decades of the century also had childcare responsibilities and found it difficult to manage both their careers and their family commitments. One simply said 'there was no balance', while another described this period of their lives as 'just a mess'. These pressures manifested in several ways, with regard to pregnancy, maternity leave, childminding and family life.[172]

Navigating pregnancy at the Bar could be challenging. Many women were cautioned to conceal their pregnancies for as long as possible:[173]

> I was advised not to tell people … No, no, no, no. Absolutely not.

> I was so worried … I just didn't know what to do and I couldn't tell anyone to discuss it because everyone had told me 'don't tell anyone'. So, I was kind of fretting and fretting and fretting … The lore at the Bar was savage at the time. It was 'don't tell anyone until the very last possible minute' and 'stay out for the least possible time' … pretend it isn't happening … nobody knew I was pregnant until right before the end … I basically concealed it for as long as I could and nobody knew so I just got on with it and it was really difficult, it was really difficult.

Some women reported receiving negative comments or looks from colleagues during their pregnancy.[174] However, not everybody felt that they were negatively treated during their pregnancies. One recalled that during her pregnancy, a more senior colleague was concerned, and when she was absent from the Law Library he enquired 'is the little lady alright?'

Having concealed their pregnancy until a very late stage, and sometimes working right up to or beyond their due date, women barristers then felt pressure to return to work very quickly. Paid maternity leave was not available, and there was no culture of taking extended time at home:

> In those days … there was no such thing as, say, people taking time off to have babies … I always thought if I was a solicitor that is what I would expect of my barrister and I wouldn't tolerate and I wouldn't expect a client to tolerate the fact that somebody wasn't available for a month.

point out that '[v]ery few of the women who reached the highest places married.' Glazer and Slater, *Unequal colleagues*, p. 212.   **172** These issues were also identified by Connelly and Hilliard, 'Gender and the legal professions', pp 223–4.   **173** In her study of the solicitors' profession in the twenty-first century, Carthy also found that 'concealment of pregnancy, and delayed and strategic disclosure of pregnancy was a recurring theme.' Suzanne Carthy, 'Inequality regimes and long hours: a mixed methods study of gender inequality in the solicitors' profession in Ireland' (PhD, UCD, 2018), p. 90.   **174** E.g., B3.

> In my day you didn't even write to your regular solicitors saying, 'I'm
> expecting a baby … and I'm going to take three months maternity leave'.

Some women tried to plan their pregnancies to coincide with court vacations,
and managed to take a month or two of leave.[175] Others returned to work within
a very short time:

> I was back at work within three weeks because I would have lost everything
> if I hadn't.

> I took a week out when each of my children were born.[176]

The return to work meant putting in place adequate childcare arrangements.[177]
It was observed in relation to the English Bar in the 1990s that there was a
seldom-voiced view that women who have children necessarily demonstrated
'reduced commitment to the workplace'.[178] Irish women barristers also seem to
have been conscious of this view, and some sought to maintain the same levels of
availability and apparent commitment to work as they had previously. One
woman described having two nannies who worked in shifts.[179] Another was
advised by colleagues who had children '"just make sure you get a full-time
childminder, 24/7, and get back in the harness as fast as you can" and "if you're
not back in you're going to lose your practice."' Many felt the need to continue
working just as hard as before

> If you wanted to keep your practice you had to show that you were available
> 24/7 just like the men were … looking back, I mean, I have loads of
> regrets that I didn't have more time with my kids when they were small but
> I don't think there was an option.[180]

Those who did not continue to make themselves available '24/7' found that they
missed out on work:

> You're a sole practitioner and the litigation must go on and therefore I
> think it is inevitable that some work has to be handed over to colleagues if

175 E.g., an interviewee quoted in Bacik, Costello and Drew, *Gender injustice*, p. 208, reported
hearing from colleagues that 'careful planning is necessary to have babies at the start of vacations.'
176 An interviewee quoted in Bacik, Costello and Drew, *Gender injustice*, p. 247 similarly said 'due
to the fact that I was self-employed I worked until the day my daughter was born and returned to
work 3 days later.' This was not exclusively a Law Library phenomenon: Carthy, *Inequality regimes*,
p. 153, found a small number of women who had taken just one week (or even less) as maternity
leave. 177 One woman said that on her return to work, male colleagues would frequently ask her,
'who's minding that child now?', which she felt was an insinuation that she ought to be at home
taking care of the baby. 178 McGlynn, *The woman lawyer*, p. 150. 179 B12. 180 In a similar
vein, Carthy, 'Inequality regimes', p. 201, found examples of women solicitors pretending that they

you decide to take a period out ... I knew at the time that there were other
male colleagues working in the same area ... who were regarded as more
freely available and would have been instructed in things where I might
well have been instructed if I hadn't been known to have the young family
... Obviously you lose a bit of work when you have a child at the Bar and
you're out for a while.

This barrister recalled feeling 'furious' when a solicitor withdrew work from her
after her baby was born.

Some women were financially supported by their partners, and could afford
to 'take the hit' if their practice suffered.

I was lucky enough you know that my husband had enough money.

I was being supported by my husband and, therefore, we were very lucky
we weren't dependent on my income.

Having already established a strong practice was also an important factor. As one
woman observed,

If you come down and you're having a baby before you've an established
practice you can forget it, you can throw in the towel.[181]

Women on circuit

Mary Dillon-Leetch was the first woman to practise on a circuit.[182] In the early-
to-mid-twentieth century, the number of women practising on circuit tended to
be very low.[183] For example, one interviewee said there were only two women on
his circuit for several years, and both had left by the time a third joined.[184]
Another said that there was only one woman on his circuit who 'had a substantial
and reasonable practice'.[185] Reflecting on her early years in practice, former Chief
Justice Susan Denham said she was the only woman on the Midlands Circuit.[186]

Several barriers might discourage women from joining a circuit or prevent
them from having a successful circuit practice. These could include the attitude
of the Circuit Court judge towards women;[187] the briefing preferences of country

did not have children.   181 B22.   182 She practised on the Western Circuit until her marriage in
1926. Kathleen Phelan (called in 1927: Ferguson, *Barristers*, p. 281) practised on the Southern
Circuit, as well as in Dublin.   183 Helena Kennedy, 'Women at the Bar' in Robert Hazell (ed.),
The Bar on trial (London, 1978), p. 156, notes that, depending on the circuit, women could attend
only some dinners, or no dinners, or no meetings. See further Brian Abel-Smith and Robert
Stevens, *Lawyers and the courts: a sociological study of the English legal system 1750–1965* (London,
1967), pp 431–2.   184 B12.   185 B15, talking about 4–6 years post-call. In Bacik, Costello and
Drew, *Gender injustice*, p. 279, one male focus group participant, while denying that discrimination
existed, commented that in the past, very few women barristers would go on circuit, while most
male barristers started there.   186 'Remarks of the Hon. Ms Justice Susan Denham', *Hibernian
Law Journal* 17 (2018), 144 at 145.   187 E.g., B10.

solicitors;[188] the difficulties of juggling family commitments while travelling away from home;[189] and the male-dominated networking.[190] Experiences were not negative on every circuit however, and some judges made a point of publicly welcoming newly arrived women barristers on their first appearance.[191]

It is interesting to note that the published memoirs of circuit life[192] rarely mention the existence of women barristers, and one could be forgiven on reading them for assuming that there were no women practising on circuit. They apparently did not participate in the social side of the circuit. Lee writes about circuit dinners as a scene where 'younger men enjoyed the company of their colleagues'.[193] Several of these memoirs were published in the 1990s, by which stage women made up almost half of those being called to the Bar.

A presumption of maleness

The language used to describe barristers and their work was often gendered, with a presumption of maleness. Representations of barristers in twentieth-century literature and popular culture[194] were predominantly male. The leaders of the Bar Council were, with the exception of Mella Caroll (1979–80), men, and these were generally the spokespersons and representatives of the profession in society.

The Bar Council minutes sometimes make reference to the 'wives' of visiting delegates from other Bars; the presumption being that the delegates themselves would be men. For example, writing about a joint meeting of the benchers, the Bar and the Law Society, the president of the High Court referred to 'members and their wives'.[195] Similarly, at a dinner given jointly by the Bar Council and the Law Society in 1975, the minutes recorded that 'For reasons of space it would only be possible to have the delegates, the Bar Council, the Law Society council, and their wives, and a few guests'.[196] It was also reported that a 'ladies committee' had 'arranged a programme for the visiting wives.'[197] The othering of women barristers was also evident from general statements about barristers that focused on maleness. For example, an Irish representative at the CCBE in Paris in 1974, remarked that the other Bars had 'sent their top men'.[198] An article defending the

---

188 E.g., B11, B23.   189 E.g., B11 said she stopped practising on circuit after having a baby.
190 See Bacik, Costello and Drew, *Gender injustice*, p. 279.   191 E.g., Siobhan Ite Nic Churtain (called in 1937) made her first appearance at Cork Circuit Court in January 1938 and, as the *Irish Law Times* reported, 'she was warmly welcomed by Judge T. O'Donnell, who wished her a long and prosperous career at the Bar' (1938) 72 *I.L.T.S.J.* 46 (5 Feb. 1938).   192 E.g., Gerard A. Lee, *A memoir of the South-Western Circuit* (Dublin, 1990); Patrick MacKenzie, *Lawful occasions: the old Eastern Circuit* (Dublin, 1991); Patrick Lindsay, *Memories* (Dublin, 1992); T.F. O'Higgins, *A double life* (Dublin 1996); Rex Mackey, *Windward of the law* (Dublin, 1991).   193 Lee, *A memoir*, p. ix.
194 See ch. 15.   195 Davitt to Costello, 27 Feb. 1957, NAI TSCH/3/S16108 A.   196 B.C.M., 16 Oct. 1975.   197 It was later decided that 'members of the Bar Council should each pay the cost of their own and their wives' dinner.' B.C.M., 24 Oct. 1975.   198 B.C.M., 25 Mar. 1974.

continued existence of the Bar as a separate profession called it 'a body of highly skilled professional men'.[199]

Sachs and Hoff Wilson, writing about the exclusion of women from the professions, argue that

> The professions, like clubs and elite schools, were not simply institutions from which women happened to be absent. Their maleness became part of their character, so that the admission of women was seen as not merely adding to their number or introducing some novelty, but as threatening the very identity of the institutions themselves.[200]

Thus, some of the skills and attributes of the typical 'good' barrister were quite gendered. Although writing about the late nineteenth-century Paris Bar, Savage's observations could also be applied to the mid-twentieth-century Irish Bar:

> The masculine virtues of the advocate were most apparent in his singular talent and exclusive function, public speech ... The masculinity of the advocate had to do with the physicality of public speaking, having a booming voice to fill a courtroom and hold the attention of a rapt audience for hours on end. Great oratory also relied on the supposedly male characteristics of reason, logic and clarity, as opposed to subtlety, intrigue or prevarication: its directness, its very publicity made it masculine.[201]

This type of loud or booming oratory was mentioned by a number of male interviewees as being part of their professional approach. For example:

> I wasn't afraid of people and I would shout at judges, at the witnesses and be rude to the judges and that was the qualification to build up a practice.

> Someone told me 'at the Bar you just stand and shout at people'. That'll suit me. A couple of drinks and waffle away.

Some women were of the view that solicitors and clients valued this type of lawyering:

> They want some sort of ... big strong man to do the case ... a deep voice, a big boomer, a shaper.[202]

Women who did not conform to these stereotypes sometimes struggled. An example was given by one of the male interviewees:

---

199 Ronan Keane, 'The future of the Irish Bar', *Studies* 54:216 (1965), 375, at 376. The article refers to barristers as men throughout.   200 Sachs and Hoff-Wilson, *Sexism and the law*, p. 170.
201 John Savage, 'The problems of wealth and virtue: the Paris Bar and the generation of the fin-de-siecle' in Pue and Sugarman (eds), *Lawyers and vampires*, p. 199.   202 B22.

One of the girls was so shy that when she'd speak in court … you'd barely hear her, and I do think that one of the things that a judge wants is to hear the barrister. And I think that even the client likes to know what the barrister might be saying for or on his or her behalf, so I think a loud voice can sometimes help.[203]

On the other hand, women who were able to conform to male norms could do very well. One male interviewee described a female colleague as having been 'very forceful', and progressing to senior counsel.[204] Connelly and Hilliard found in their study in the early nineties that 'advocacy skills and a flair for debating' were viewed as significant skills for barristers, and that '[m]en were perceived as being socialised into these qualities in a way that women were not'.[205] As noted above, the memoirs published by Irish barristers from the sixties onward would have done little to dispel common public perceptions of the Bar as a male-dominated profession.

Menkel-Meadow asked in 1985 whether the presence of women lawyers might lead to different ways of lawyering.[206] Several interviewees expressed the opinion that women were more likely to be better prepared, and did well in complex areas:

I found that most women put in better work than men …they weren't going to get caught out. Men might be a little bit, you know, lackadaisical, chancers, yeah, chancers, is probably the word but a little more lackadaisical. Most women had their work really well done.[207]

This echoed the findings of both Bacik, Costello and Drew in 2003[208] and Connelly and Hilliard in 1993,[209] suggesting that there were indeed different ways of 'being' a barrister.

* * *

Mossman commented in 2006 that 'gender remains deeply embedded within traditional legal norms and professional cultures'.[210] Acker's theory of gendered organisations can be useful for conceptualising some of the experiences of women at the Bar.[211] She sets out a framework of five interacting processes that

---

203 B12. 204 B7. 205 Connolly and Hilliard, 'The legal profession', p. 220. 206 Carrie Menkel-Meadow, 'Portia in a different voice: speculation on a women's lawyering process', *Berkeley Women's Law Journal* 1 (1985) 39. 207 B12. 208 An interviewee quoted in Bacik, Costello and Drew, *Gender injustice*, p. 264, observed that '[t]here's not a lot of law in PI. Women tended to do well at areas involving a bit of law, maybe they are more hesitant about engaging in 'hustling'. 209 Women barristers were described by Connelly and Hilliard, 'The legal profession', pp 220–1 as 'more conscientious, and very diligent.' They also found, p. 221, that women were perceived as 'less adversarial, more open to negotiation, and less interested in winning on points.' 210 Mossman, *The first women lawyers*, p. 5. 211 Joan Acker, 'Hierarchies, jobs, bodies: a theory

show how gender can operate at work. The first relates to gender divisions.[212] Acker argues that the gender of those performing different kinds of work becomes a shorthand for those people's attributes and suitability. She argues that organisations are divided along gender lines, and that different types of work are associated with the different genders. This was evident in the tendency of women barristers to specialise in conveyancing and family law,[213] and the male domination of high-profile civil and criminal litigation. Acker also refers to gender symbolism; the idea that organisational gender divisions can be expressed and reinforced through images and symbols of masculinity and femininity.[214] This might include the proliferation masculine artistic depictions of the Bar and of male portraiture.[215]

Third, Acker discusses gendered interaction, arguing that gender differences are evident through interpersonal interactions.[216] An example of this is the convention that women barristers were called 'miss', while men called each other by their first names. Male barristers also frequently referred to women as 'girls' and in one instance, 'little lady'. Sachs and Hoff-Wilson refer to this as 'archaic courtesy'.[217] Acker also argues that gender is enacted through things like dress, deportment and presentation;[218] so, for example, the expectation that women barristers would wear skirts. Finally, Acker refers to gendered norms.[219] The structures and norms of an organisation can be constructed in a way that is based on a male experience as the norm. Examples here would be the disparity between the facilities for men and women in the Law Library; the frequent use of words like 'men' as collective nouns for barristers, and a culture of working hours which presumed no caring responsibilities.

Change at the Bar was incremental. Women went from being a tiny minority in the twenties to arriving in increasing numbers in the seventies.[220] The difference in visibility and representation of women in the courts over twenty or thirty years is illustrated by comparing the following two anecdotes; the first from the early seventies and the second from the late nineties:

> To get a divorce *a mensa et thoro* she had to go to the High Court where it was heard by a jury of 12 men. So, the only woman in court was the

of gendered organisations', *Gender & Soc.* 4:2 (1990), 139. Her theory of gendered organisations has been developed and refined over time; in Joan Acker, 'Inequality regimes gender, class, and race in organisations', *Gender & Soc.* 20:4 (2006), 21 she developed a framework of inequality regimes. **212** Acker, 'Hierarchies', at 146.   **213** Connelly and Hilliard, 'The legal profession', p. 217. **214** Acker, 'Hierarchies', at 146.   **215** Nikki Godden-Rasul, 'Portraits of women of the law: re-envisioning gender, law and the legal professions in law schools', *Leg. Stud.* 39:3 (2019), 1: 'One of the ways that women's roles in shaping law and society have been overlooked and obscured is by the visual over-representation of men in public spaces. Men from all time periods who are to be honoured and revered are constructed in statues, named in roads, boats and buildings, and depicted in portraits in stately homes, universities and other social institutions', at 2.   **216** Acker, 'Hierarchies', at 146–7.   **217** Sachs and Hoff Wilson, *Sexism and the law*, p. 179.   **218** Acker, 'Hierarchies', at 147.   **219** Ibid.   **220** By the 1990s there were increasing numbers of women

plaintiff ... I can't say I was outraged by the injustice of this. I mean when I think about it, I *am* outraged when I think back on it ... This was truly appalling. The language, the questions, the whole attitude, the approach, the judge's attitude, the jury ... A jury action to decide the most intimate affairs.[221]

I remember ... it would have been in the timeframe we're talking about, one of my devils saying to me 'do you notice anything unusual about that case?' I said 'no you mean about the people in it, the witnesses'? 'No the practitioners, barristers, solicitors'. I said 'no'. 'You were the only man.' The judge was a woman, the registrar was a woman, my solicitor was, everybody, I was the only man. And I didn't notice.[222]

Women continued to experience different forms of discrimination, and gender-specific challenges, and one woman reflected on the mutual supports which helped with this:

There were very few of us ... we stuck together ... the collegiality was very, very good ... we were very close you know because we were all in the same boat.[223]

This is yet another example of the collegiality and solidarity discussed in chapters ten and twelve.

elected to the Bar Council.   221 B18.   222 B9.   223 B3.

CHAPTER TEN

Working on circuit

Introduction

Working life on the circuits was different from Dublin-based practice.[1] One barrister, called to the Bar in 1938, described going on circuit as 'joining a group of barristers who left Dublin each week to follow a particular judge as he sat in different towns on his circuit.'[2] Many barristers in the twentieth century lauded the 'camaraderie'[3] and 'communal life'[4] of the circuits. Others described the relationship between circuit barristers as familial,[5] and said that there was 'a fierce sense of belonging'.[6] Circuit life also had its challenges, however, including expense, transportation issues, poor accommodation and the difficulty of establishing oneself on a circuit.

Following the partition of Ireland, the Free State was divided into eight circuits by section 37 of the Courts of Justice Act 1924: the Dublin, Cork, Northern, Western, Midland, Eastern, South-Western and Southern Circuits.[7] The number of circuits fluctuated over time and the divisions were redrawn on several occasions; in 1937[8] the number of circuits was increased to nine,[9] and in 1960 it was reduced to eight once more.[10] The Courts Act 1964 allowed for the

---

1 Polden notes that in England, most barristers intending to pursue a common law practice joined a circuit. Patrick Polden, 'Portia's progress: women at the Bar in England, 1919–1939', *Int. J. Leg. Prof.* 12 (2005), 293, at 310.   2 T.F. O'Higgins, *A double life* (Dublin, 1996), p. 75.   3 Patrick Lindsay, *Memories* (Cork, 1992), p. 124.   4 Gerard A. Lee, *A memoir of the South-Western Circuit* (Dublin, 1990), p. ix.   5 Rex Mackey, *Windward of the law* (2nd ed., Dublin, 1991), p. 160. 6 Hugh Geoghegan, 'The changing face of the circuits during the past twenty-five years' in Daire Hogan and Colum Kenny (eds), *Changes in practice and law* (Dublin, 2013), p. 39.   7 In the early nineteenth century there were six circuits: the North-East (Louth, Monaghan, Armagh, Down, Antrim), the North-West (Derry, Donegal, Tyrone, Fermanagh, Cavan, Longford), the Connaught (Leitrim, Sligo, Roscommon, Mayo, Galway), the Munster (Clare, Limerick, Kerry, Cork), the Leinster (Kilkenny, Tipperary, Waterford, Wexford, Wicklow) and the Home Circuit (Meath, Westmeath, Kildare, Carlow, King's County and Queen's County). Section 62 of the Supreme Court of Judicature Ireland Act 1877 provided that the lord lieutenant could by order in council, 're-arrange the circuits or reduce their number.' The Home Circuit was abolished in 1885 and its counties were redistributed. See (1885) 19 *I.L.T.S.J.* 121 (7 Mar. 1885). One barrister commented that the circuits 'had little regard for geography when they included two Munster counties, Tipperary and Waterford, in the so-called 'Leinster Circuit': Eugene Sheehy, *May it please the court* (Dublin, 1951), p. 62.   8 Circuit Court (New Circuits) Order 1937 (S.I. 309/1937), under the Courts of Justice Act 1936, s. 13.   9 The Dublin, Cork, North-Eastern, North-Western, Western, Midland, Eastern, South-Eastern and South-Western Circuits.   10 Circuit Court (New Circuits) Order, 1960 (S.I. 70/1960), under the Courts of Justice Act 1953, s. 16. These were the Dublin, Cork, Northern, Midland, Eastern, South-Western, South-Eastern and Western Circuits.

renaming or reorganisation of circuits as needed, and several counties were transferred from one circuit to another during the twentieth century.[11]

The circuit system established in 1924[12] was in some respects a continuation of the nineteenth-century assizes, which had dealt with the vast majority of indictable crime and civil cases.[13] These had been a significant aspect not only of barristers' practices but also of life outside of Dublin. While it was a new court with different jurisdiction,[14] many aspects of the circuit experience for barristers remained unchanged.[15] Some circuits were still referred to by their pre-1924 names well into the twentieth century. For example, a barrister applying to take silk in 1947 described himself as having practised on the Munster Circuit since 1928.[16] Another barrister commented that in the seventies and eighties, the South-Eastern Circuit was still referred to as the Leinster Bar.[17]

Choosing a circuit

Barristers who chose to practice on circuit expressed different motivations for doing so. One interviewee decided to try circuit practice because their father, brother and spouse had all done so.[18] Others had less specific reasons and were drawn to the sense of camaraderie:

> I had a sort of a romance with ... going on circuit. I had some notion that I'd love to be on circuit down in, you know, Kilkenny and places like that ... stuff that I'd read gave me a sense of how wonderful Circuit could be.[19]

A barrister might choose a particular circuit for his or her own reasons; perhaps family or political connections tied them to a particular county, or perhaps they felt that work would be easier to come by in one region rather than another. Some devils joined a circuit because their master practised there.[20] In the early twentieth century it would have been unusual for a barrister to switch from one circuit to another.[21]

11 E.g., several changes were made under the Courts Act 1964, s. 3: Sligo was moved from the Northern to the Midland Circuit and Laois was moved from the Midland to the South-Eastern Circuit by the Circuit Court (Alteration of Circuits) Order 1964 (S.I. 206/1964). Five years later, Wexford was transferred from the Eastern to the South-Eastern Circuit: Circuit Court (Alteration of Circuits) Order 1969 (S.I. 201/1969). 1978 saw Laois transferred from the South-Eastern Circuit to the Midland Circuit: Circuit Court (Alteration of Circuits) Order 1978 (S.I. 327/1978). In 1999, Sligo was transferred from the Midland to the Northern Circuit: Circuit Court (Alteration of Circuits) Order 1999 (S.I. 387/1999). 12 Courts of Justice Act 1924, pt. 2. 13 See N. Howlin, 'The Irish courts system and the court houses' in Colum O'Riordan, Paul Burns and Ciaran O'Connor (eds), Ireland's court houses (Dublin, 2019) and Ronan Keane, 'The voice of the Gael: Chief Justice Kennedy and the emergence of the new Irish court system', Ir. Jur. 31 (1996), 204. 14 It had jurisdiction in all but the most serious criminal cases, as well as in areas of civil law: Courts of Justice Act 1924, ss. 48 and 49. 15 Geoghegan, 'The changing face', p. 37. 16 Letter to C. Ó Dálaigh, 23 Nov. 1947, NAI 2003/4/7. 17 B18. 18 B11. 19 B5. 20 B7. 21 It was also unusual in the nineteenth century: Hogan, The legal profession in Ireland, p. 43.

It was sometimes necessary to pay a small fee to join a particular circuit.[22] One barrister described, in the 1980s: 'writing a letter seeking to be accepted onto the circuit and the members of the circuit voted as to whether or not I could be accepted as being a member of the circuit'.[23] In some places a new barrister was welcomed to the circuit by the presiding judge. For example, in 1932 Judge William Gleeson welcomed Violet Kempton to the Midland Circuit,[24] and in 1938 three new barristers were given 'a hearty welcome' by Judge Moonan in Letterkenny.[25] However, Patrick Lindsay, who joined the Western Circuit in the 1940s, said that 'there was no welcoming of anyone to the Bar in those days; you just came, appeared and the county registrar probably told the judge who you were'.[26]

Local Bar associations

Generally, a barrister practising on a particular circuit was a member of the local Bar association. These regional Bar associations were voluntary societies which pre-dated the 1924 circuits.[27] Some were based on the geographic boundaries of the older circuits, such as the Leinster and Munster Bars, while others operated at county level, such as the Wexford Bar association[28] and the Cork Bar.[29] It was not always necessary to be a member of the local Bar in order to practise on that circuit.[30] One interviewee pointed out that one could be 'a member of the Connaught Bar but not the actual Western Circuit'.[31]

Bar associations had their own rules and regulations,[32] and played both a regulatory and representative role for their members. In terms of representation, the local associations communicated with the Bar Council with regard to changes which might affect their members' working lives. For example, when in 1956 it was proposed to change the dates on which the High Court travelled on circuit, the Bar Council received representations from the Northern Circuit, the Midland Circuit, the Connaught Bar, the Munster Bar, the Leinster Bar and the

---

22 A.R. Hart, *A history of the Bar and inn of court of Northern Ireland* (Belfast, 2013), p. 66, notes that a small fee had to be paid in order to join one of the Northern Circuits. MacKenzie wrote of a similar fee for the Eastern Circuit: Patrick MacKenzie, *Lawful occasions: the old Eastern Circuit* (Dublin, 1991), p. 22. Maurice Healy, *The old Munster Circuit. A book of memories and traditions* (London, 1939), p. 89, also described an entrance fee for joining the Munster Circuit.   23 B7. 24 *Irish Times*, 20 Jan. 1932, p. 5. The same judge also welcomed Oliver D. Gogarty on his first appearance at Longford Circuit Court: (1932) 66 *I.L.T.S.J.* 60 (23 Jan. 1932).   25 (1938) 72 *I.L.T.S.J.* 55 (30 Jan. 1928). The barristers were H.A. McDevitt, Edward Fahy and C. Cole. 26 Lindsay, *Memories*, p. 99.   27 Hart notes that '[w]hen these societies were formed cannot now be established because of the loss and destruction of early records, but that such societies with their own rules were in existence in the eighteenth century at least seems highly probable.' Hart, *History of the Bar*, p. 65.   28 B.C.M., 6 Mar. 1971.   29 E.g., B.C.M., 26 Mar. 1971; 12 July 1976. There was also a north and east Cork Bar association: B.C.M., 9 Nov. 1981.   30 Hogan, *The legal profession*, p. 43, notes that this was also the case in the nineteenth century.   31 B12.   32 In 1964 a Dublin Bar association was established, and it was thought that the rules drawn up by the Munster and Leinster bars might be of use. B.C.M., 18 Dec. 1964.

South-Western Bar.[33] Sometimes there might be meetings of the circuits before general meetings of the Bar, so that local issues could be raised.[34] In terms of regulation, sometimes the local Bar associations wrote to the Bar Council seeking guidance or adjudication on disciplinary matters which arose. In 1959, for example, the Munster Bar informed the Bar Council about a barrister who was carrying out other business.[35] In 1976 the Cork Bar wrote to the Bar Council asking 'whether some means of having it represented on the Bar Council could be achieved, so that they might be better informed of what was going on'.[36]

Transportation and expenses

Having decided to practise on circuit, there were a number of practical matters which loomed large for a barrister. First, there were considerable expenses to take into consideration. The sitting in each town usually lasted for one week, or occasionally for two weeks. Except in those circuits closest to Dublin, it was usual was for barristers to remain in the town for the duration. The combination of travel costs, accommodation and meals meant 'the biblical casting of bread upon the waters'[37] for new barristers. The meticulous notes kept by Hugh Kennedy in the 1920s give an indication of the type of expenditure a circuit practice necessitated. He recorded the following for spring 1920 at Ennis:[38]

	$£$	s	d
1. Fares, rail and road	3	10	6
2. Bar cess	1	10	0
3. Bar circuit steward's fee	1	0	0
4. Hotel	3	1	0
5. Sundries		13	0
6. Judge's man		2	6
Total	9	17	0

McEnery, who began travelling on circuit in 1927, later recalled that 'the best hotel one could find in a country town charging 7s., 6d. for bed and breakfast, 2d. for lunch and 5d. for dinner and return fare to Dublin about 17d.'[39]

---

33 B.C.M., 19 Oct. 1956. The following year, when further changes were proposed for the Circuit Court circuits, the secretary of the Leinster Bar wrote to the Bar Council expressing concern: B.C.M., 29 July 1957. In 1964, the Midland Bar communicated their concerns about the clashing of the Leinster and Midland Circuits, which was having an effect on their practice: B.C.M., 30 Nov. 1964. 34 E.g., in 1981 there were meetings of the Midland, Dublin, Western and Cork Circuits. A joint meeting of the Bars of Limerick, Clare and Kerry was held, as well as a joint meeting of the Leinster, Wicklow and Kildare Bars: B.C.M., 11 May 1981. 35 B.C.M., 26 June 1959. 36 B.C.M., 12 July 1976. 37 O'Higgins, *Double life*, p. 75. 38 'Circuit expenses 1920: Ennis. Spring', UCDA P4/153. He also recorded a £2 annual subscription fee for the Munster Circuit. 39 McEnery, *Look back*, p. 72.

Towns on the circuit could be distinguished as either 'principal towns' or 'day towns',[40] the latter being smaller and less busy. In the principal towns, a week might be spent on criminal business and a week on civil business.[41] One barrister said that they found the expense of circuit life off-putting, and thus did not pursue it.[42] Another recalled that 'although I had very little money, I decided to take my chance on circuit. What money I had, I prayed, would cover me for about a year, and by then I hoped I would have earned enough to carry on.'[43]

For much of the twentieth century, most barristers who worked on circuit lived in Dublin and travelled down weekly:

> The tradition would have been that you were a barrister, you were Dublin-based unless you were in the reaches of Kerry in which instance you might have based yourself down in Kerry or based yourself in Galway or perhaps in Donegal. But most others were really focused in Dublin and then went down from the Monday evening to the Friday, down to circuit.[44]

> Of my contemporaries who went on circuit, certainly more than half of them were based in Dublin and travelled to wherever the circuit was on.[45]

In the 1920s, some travelled to the circuit by car, and those with cars often gave lifts to their colleagues.[46] Travelling to the circuits during the Emergency years could be laborious due to fuel rationing. Lee describes travelling to Limerick on the slow, turf-fuelled, wooden trains, which ran only twice per week during the war.[47] At that time, the journey lasted many hours and barristers brought their own food and refreshments, because often nothing else would be available.[48] Similarly, MacKenzie describes taking almost two hours to travel to Wicklow on a train fuelled by 'damp turf and a few sticks'.[49] The situation worsened as the war progressed:

> People practising in Wexford commenced using the bus, which departed from the quays in Dublin and did not stop until it came to Bray. A journey of seventy miles or so took about five hours.'[50]

By contrast, in the years after the war, when more efficient steam trains were introduced, 'a degree of prosperity was commencing for barristers and we often travelled first class with meals served in the carriage. This was luxury indeed compared with war-time travel'.[51] One barrister who was called in the 1960s

---

40 B15.   41 In the nineteenth century, the towns on each circuit were generally visited in a particular order: Hogan, *The legal profession*, p. 42.   42 B25.   43 O'Higgins, *Double life*, p. 76.   44 B12.   45 B27.   46 McEnery, *Look back,* p. 82, describes driving down to circuit with Gardner Budd (called in 1927; Ferguson, *Barristers*, p. 147) in 1927. He added, p. 88, '[w]e had many journeys together in his little car all round the circuit for the next twelve years.'   47 Lee, *Memoir*, p. 2.   48 Ibid., p. 18.   49 MacKenzie, *Lawful occasions*, p. 5.   50 Ibid., p. 22.   51 Lee, *Memoir*,

recalled travelling frequently by train from Dublin to Cork.[52] By the late twentieth century, it was more usual for barristers to travel by car, either alone or with colleagues,[53] or by hitchhiking.[54] The driving could be quite gruelling, for example.

> I remember one week I drove about 8,000 kilometres … Different town every night. I mean, that's not worth it.[55]

> In the 1980s … driving from Dublin to Ennis took five hours. The roads were appalling and, you know, you'd hit Limerick and then you were only halfway there.[56]

Another barrister estimated that they covered 'an average of 30,000–40,000 miles a year'.[57]

The tradition of travelling down from Dublin continued well into the twentieth century, with one interviewee recalling that in the 1970s, there was 'a strict rule … that you weren't allowed to live on circuit.'[58] The rationale for this was said to be an assumption 'that you would never go to a circuit town before the court was on because you weren't going to be trying to curry favour with friends or solicitors'.[59]

Accommodation on circuit

Barristers on circuit tended to stay in hotels. Generally one particular hotel in the principal town was designated the 'Bar hotel', and this was where the barristers stayed and dined together. According to one barrister, 'the tradition was you stayed in whatever hotel the judge didn't stay in'.[60]

In the 1930s and during the war years, accommodation was inexpensive, making it easier for new barristers to join a circuit and cover their expenses until their practice took off. Lee recalls a daily rate of one shilling for a hotel in Limerick, which covered a bed, three meals and use of the Bar room.[61] In Wexford in the 1940s, the Bar hotel cost ten pounds per week.[62] While relatively inexpensive, the accommodation in regional towns could be quite basic. According to Lindsay, however,

> The circuit-going barristers owe a great debt to what were known as the 'Bar hotels' where we stayed. They were kind, they were not particular whether you paid your bill after a bad circuit or not, but we always finished up not owing them anything.[63]

pp 3–4.   52 B4.   53 E.g., B2, B15.   54 E.g., B12.   55 B2.   56 B7.   57 B12.   58 B15.   59 B15.
60 B12.   61 Lee, *Memoir*, p. 3. Sometimes solicitors called for barristers at the hotel; e.g., McEnery, *Look back*, p. 83, recalled being woken in his hotel room by a colleague one morning who told him 'there's a solicitor down below with a brief for you.' He went downstairs and found the solicitor in the hotel's dining room.   62 MacKenzie, *Lawful occasions*, p. 23.   63 Lindsay, *Memories*, p. 133.

One barrister recounted hearing tales of the poor state of circuit hotels from the mid-twentieth century, saying that they were 'so awful' that barristers 'slept in their clothes'.[64] Another pointed out that the hotels were 'moderate ... we didn't have the money because the earnings weren't very high'.[65] Catering standards could also be of dubious quality; MacKenzie, recalling his first day on the Eastern Circuit in Wicklow, describes going for lunch in a dingy establishment across the street from the courthouse, where all that was on offer was boiled eggs and tea.[66] Another barrister described going to 'the single hotel ... giving out the boiled dinner in the middle of the day.'[67]

Accommodation was not always in hotels. One barrister described formally joining a particular circuit in the 1980s because 'I got to know some people down there and I was able to stay in their houses'.[68] Another barrister said that '[a]nybody who had relatives might stay with their relatives'.[69] Towards the end of the century, 'the idea of the barristers all staying in one hotel ... was beginning to peter out because you had some people who lived on circuit and went back to their homes.'[70]

Socialising on circuit

Life on circuit necessarily involved very close contact with other members of the profession, especially in the first half of the twentieth century. Writing about the nineteenth century, Hogan observes that '[r]ules of circuit life, both social and professional devcloped'.[71] This was no less true in the twentieth century, with traditions and conventions as regards travel, accommodation and dining continuing and evolving.

Members of the circuit dined together in the evenings, generally with a certain amount of formality in the early part of the century.[72] MacKenzie recalled that on the Leinster Circuit, '[a] strict code was observed. Attendance at dinner was compulsory and punctual.'[73] By contrast, there was 'nothing like this in the Eastern counties of Dundalk [sic], Meath, Kildare, Wexford, Wicklow'.[74] As late as the 1970s, the Leinster Circuit was distinguished as being more formal than others. McEnery, called in the 1920s, recalled that when he attended his first circuit session in Kilkenny, the most senior member of the Bar present in the town

> Told me that he would have to make a speech at the dinner and I would also have to make a speech as the most junior member. That was the rule. The most senior and the most junior member made speeches on

---

64 B9.   65 B20.   66 MacKenzie, *Lawful occasions*, p. 10.   67 B2.   68 B7.   69 B15.   70 B23.
71 Hogan, *The legal profession*, p. 44.   72 Hart, *History of the Bar*, describes the twentieth-century dining practices on the Northern Circuit, pp 262–3.   73 MacKenzie, *Lawful occasions*, p. 22.
74 Ibid.

behalf of the Bar. The dinner was a grand affair with the wines and champagne flowing etc.[75]

Towns on the circuit where barristers dined together were known as 'mess towns', and there would be several on each circuit designated as such. Some barristers considered dining in mess towns to be an obligation of circuit practice.[76]

A Bar dinner was generally presided over by the most senior member of the circuit, referred to as the 'father'.[77] One barrister remarked 'if you went on circuit there was the father of the Bar and he presided and you didn't miss dinner'.[78] Formal circuit dinners might take place once or twice a year.[79] Many barristers found these dinners to be both entertaining and educational. One barrister on the South-Western Circuit recalls having lengthy discussions on 'legal, social and historical topics' during these dinners.[80] Another barrister described 'over dinner or drinks or whatever there would often be conversation about law, legal topics, that was a fantastic apprenticeship'.[81] Others recalled the more gregarious side of circuit dinners; for example, 'a lot of wine would be consumed, a lot of singing out of tune'.[82]

Bar dinners were generally the exclusive domain of the members of the Bar – solicitors, for example, generally did not attend.[83] However, barristers on circuit might also be entertained by local solicitors. Jasper Wolfe, for example, a Skibbereen-based solicitor, TD and president of the Law Society, was known for his hospitality to barristers, solicitors and officials while on circuit.[84] He would often reserve a private room in his favourite public house, as well as serving a buffet lunch in his own home.[85] In the late sixties and seventies, a barrister described 'sing songs with solicitors at two o'clock in the morning paralytic with drink'.[86] Another said that in the seventies and eighties, 'the solicitors would maybe take a table of ten people out for a night or whatever and it was great craic ... It was very good fun and it wasn't wild but it was always good craic.'[87] One barrister described occasionally being joined by the judge in the evening: 'the judge might condescend to dine with you once a week, once a fortnight ... but that was a different dinner to the dinner you had with your colleagues'.[88] Circuit Bars usually had their own supplies of wine, and they might receive donations of wine from, for example, recently appointed judges or senior counsel.[89] On the

---

75 McEnery, *Look back in love*, p. 73.   **76** E.g., B11.   **77** E.g., O'Higgins, *Double life*, p. 85 and Geoghegan, 'The changing face', p. 39. When the numbers in the profession were smaller, the father would have known all members of the circuit, but as the numbers increased this level of familiarity was not possible, e.g., B8. Presumably by late in the century there were also 'Mothers' of local bars but I have not found reference to any examples in the secondary literature or in the interviews.   **78** B9. Others referred to 'the father of the circuit', e.g., B7.   **79** B2.   **80** Lee, *Memoir*, p. 31.   **81** B18.   **82** B20.   **83** Geoghegan, 'The changing face', p. 39.   **84** Jasper Ungoed-Thomas, *Jasper Wolfe of Skibbereen* (Cork, 2008), p. 247.   **85** Ibid.   **86** B20.   **87** B15.   **88** B12.   **89** Hart, *A history of the Bar*.

Leinster Circuit, absence from Bar dinners merited a fine, which was usually extracted in the form of a 'presentation of wine for the cellar.'[90] This also contributed towards each circuit's wine supplies, generally stored in the cellar of the circuit hotel in the first half of the century.

The Bar of each circuit had a regulatory and disciplinary role which predated the Bar Council.[91] These were not very formal proceedings, but gentle rebukes and teasing which were deemed sufficient to remind circuit members about points of etiquette, tradition or codes of conduct.[92] Hogan considers the regulatory role of the circuit Bars to be 'one of the more obscure subjects in the history of the profession'.[93]

Although Geoghegan views the differences between the circuits as insignificant,[94] several barristers interviewed for this book remarked on the 'enormous difference'[95] between the various circuits. Sometimes this was attributable to differences in judicial personalities and preferences, and in other places the differences were entrenched in custom. There were certainly reputational differences between circuits. The Eastern Circuit, for example, was said to be 'unfashionable' in the 1940s:

> Because it was near Dublin, its denigrators said that it was full of trespassers who came in for a day and were not real circuiteers. Many of the towns were close to Dublin and, with proper transport, there was no need to spend a week in a hotel. There was therefore no mess, no circuit wine cellar and no silver.[96]

By contrast, the Midland Circuit was described as 'a hard living, hard drinking establishment'[97] and the Western as 'colourful',[98] suggesting that both had strong drinking cultures.[99] Many characterised the Leinster Circuit as formal; one said it was for 'posh people',[100] another that 'it conformed to much more traditional ideas'.[101] It had its own set of silver for formal dining right into the seventies and eighties.[102] The level of formality on the Leinster Circuit was such that a new member was considered a 'probationer' for their first year or so, and had to dine a certain number of times in the late sixties.

---

90 MacKenzie, *Lawful occasions*, p. 22.   91 Geoghegan, 'The changing face', p. 38.   92 See further ch. 16.   93 Hogan, *The legal profession*, p. 46. Written rules were published in the nineteenth century in relation to at least one circuit Bar. The rules of the home Bar, published in 1820, are discussed in detail by Hogan, *The legal profession*, pp 46–9. It is unclear whether the written rules of the nineteenth century reflected the realities of circuit practice.   94 Geoghegan, 'The changing face', p. 39. One interviewee also downplayed any significant differences between the Midland and Western Circuits. (B12)   95 B20.   96 MacKenzie, *Lawful occasions*, p. 22.   97 Ibid., p. 75.   98 Ibid., p. 112.   99 See the discussion of drinking culture at pp 136–7.   100 MacKenzie, *Lawful occasions*, p. 22.   101 B4.   102 B6.

Relationships on circuit

An overriding theme of both the interviews conducted for this book, and the published memoirs of twentieth-century barristers, is the close relationships developed on circuit. Several described the 'very strong social networks':[103]

> On a circuit there were ten or twelve people living with each other for effectively five days of the week because you went down on circuit on a Monday evening, you came back Friday so you had a very very close relationship ... You probably ate breakfast together, you probably had lunch together if you bothered with lunch and you certainly dined together most evenings.[104]

> Being introduced to a new group of people with whom I become very close over the years and so my colleagues on circuit meant a huge amount to me at the time and continued throughout my time at the Bar.[105]

One aspect of the close relationships on circuit was the self-regulation this brought about. According to one barrister, 'you were known to all of your colleagues and you had to behave ... you had to behave because if you didn't behave everyone else would know about it immediately'.[106] Another was that support might be extended to a barrister who fell on hard times. A story recounted in the *Irish Law Times* in the 1960s told of an older barrister, the father of the North-East Circuit, who ran into financial difficulty. His circuit colleagues wished to support him discreetly, and concocted a complicated fictitious case on which the barrister might advise, and advanced funds to a local solicitor so that the barrister could be well paid.[107] The relative closeness between members of the Bar was also sometimes reflected in their relationship with the Circuit Court judge:

> The benefit of being on a circuit is that you're familiar and [judges] know you and they trust you. So if ... the local judge knows you, they're going to believe you but I suppose equally if you pull the wool they'll never trust you again.[108]

A corollary of the close-knit network on circuit was that outsiders might find it difficult to work there. A Dublin-based barrister who found him or herself attending a circuit would not always be made to feel welcome: 'a stranger, even a "big name" stranger can find the going tough enough'.[109] One barrister described a sense that an outsider was taking work that should rightfully have been dealt

103 B11. 104 B12. 105 B18. 106 B8. 107 'A Law Library story' (1962) 96 *I.L. T.S.J.* 257 (29 Sept. 1962). This story was also recounted by McEnery, *Look back in love*, pp 116–18. 108 B22. See pp 113–16 for further discussion of the relationship between barristers and judges. 109 Lindsay,

with by a circuit regular.[110] Other interviewees specifically referred to the experiences of women who joined circuits. Several remarked on the low number of women on particular circuits,[111] and one said that the nature of court-based circuit work could make it more challenging for women to establish circuit practices.[112]

Circuit hierarchies

Hierarchies on circuit could be very important. Junior barristers who had recently joined a circuit could expect to be supported by their more established circuit colleagues.[113] This sometimes extended beyond moral support and professional advice, to include financial support. For example, one interviewee who began practicing in the early seventies remarked that:

> People were very generous. There was no question of the very junior guy paying for a drink or anything of that kind. Oh yeah, the other guys insisted on that and were very generous.[114]

According to O'Higgins,

> An old tradition was always honoured by a congenial circuit Bar. In whatever way it was achieved – whether by nod or wink, between the established barristers on circuit and the local solicitors – somehow the new man on the circuit always earned, as a minimum, just enough to cover his hotel and travelling expenses. And that generally continued until he found his feet or decided to give up.[115]

In addition, sometimes solicitors might also look out for recently called barristers, supplying them with straightforward work: 'the more generous-spirited solicitors would ensure that … they'd get whoever … was the most junior … to do work which would have been relatively simple work'.[116]

The professional lives of those on the circuit were interwoven to the extent that a decision by one member to take silk or join the bench impacted upon the careers of others.[117] There was a finite amount of work available,[118] and one barrister's move, for example, to the bench, meant that there might be more work available for other colleagues. As discussed in chapter four, some people applied

---

Memories, p. 124.   110 B1.   111 B15; B12. See pp 188–9.   112 B11.   113 B15.   114 B18. 115 O'Higgins, *Double life*, p. 75.   116 B15.   117 See further pp 54–5.   118 Sometimes much of the work on a particular circuit was concentrated in a few very successful and busy barristers. On one occasion, the Donegal solicitors association complained to the Incorporated Law Society about delays on the circuit. The circuit barristers pointed out that the delays were a result of most work being sent to one or two practitioners, who became overwhelmed. B.C.M., 20 Oct. 1966.

for silk when a member of their circuit was elevated to the bench, because it meant there was a vacancy on the circuit.[119] There was a perceived order in which barristers on circuit should progress their careers; a barrister who was called in the 1960s commented that as a new barrister, 'you have to wait for people to move on before you get a breakthrough'.[120] Up to at least the late 1960s there was a practice of consulting members of one's circuit before deciding to take silk, partly because they might be affected by the move.[121]

For much of the twentieth century, the Circuit Court judge associated with a particular circuit could have a significant influence on the working lives of circuit barristers. The importance of the judge-barrister relationship has already been alluded to in earlier chapters; on circuit, this relationship could take on another dimension. As one barrister who began practising in the sixties put it, 'the success of most barristers would very much depend on the circuit judge'.[122] One talked about becoming 'attuned' to different judges' 'methods and idiosyncrasies.'[123] Barristers who were called in the seventies made similar remarks about the circuit judge's control:

> You were under the control … of the sitting Circuit Court judge who would very much have had his stamp on the circuit.[124]

> With most circuits … in those days, only having one judge … your career on the circuit was fairly dependent on at least getting a fair crack of the whip from that judge.[125]

The impact of an individual judge was not always positive. In 1976, a member of the Bar Council pointed out that 'a circuit judge could make … life and a living impossible to a person they did not like'.[126] Some circuit judges were known to be patient with new barristers, for example:

> His modus operandi was that he was kind to the juniors who came for the first 6 months and then he came down like a ton of bricks … In other words he'd let you find your feet a bit but then he would give you no quarter.

Other judges were known to forego a 'settling in' period for new barristers; one particular judge's approach was described as 'a baptism of fire'.[127] Another, recounting their experiences on a particular circuit, said that the judge 'terrified everybody and masses of barristers left the circuit'.[128]

---

119 For example, on the elevation of Brian Walsh to the bench in 1959, one of his circuit colleagues sought to take silk: letter to sec. govt., 25 Nov. 1959, NAI 2003/4/7.　120 B4.　121 B.C.M., 27 Oct. 1967.　122 B20.　123 McEnery, 'Look back', p. 89.　124 B15.　125 B27.　126 B.C.M., 7 Jan. 1979.　127 B22.　128 B20.

Some circuit judges were known to sit for very long hours; one was said to 'pack cases in and you'd be doing a criminal case, even starting a jury at maybe nine o'clock at night'.[129] By contrast, others took a more relaxed approach; one judge in the sixties

> Used to rise for afternoon tea at 3 o'clock, no matter what was on ... You know you could be addressing a jury and suddenly out of the blue: 'I think we'll have tea now' ... And he would sit there, tea and cake, and the jury would be sitting there outside going 'jaysus, where's the team gone?'[130]

Similarly, a barrister who worked on circuit in the seventies recalled:

> The chances in those days of the judge hearing more than two cases a day was nil ... he wasn't interested in sitting too late and he would rise at four and if the case wasn't finished and we were leaving the town the next day he'd say 'I'll adjourn that ... to the next sittings back here' ... So you could have a break of a couple of months in between the beginning and the end of a case ...[31]

Some circuits were busier than others. In 1947 Judge Gleeson in Roscommon expressed his dissatisfaction at how busy his court was, and said he was doing the work of three judges.[132] The *Irish Law Times* observed that it was 'an extraordinary state of affairs to have one Circuit Court judge overworked while a number of other Circuit Court judges are idle for half the year. In 1963, a question was raised in the Dáil about the number of days of Circuit Court sittings. Charles Haughey, minister for justice, published details of exactly how many days each Circuit Court judge had sat in open court over the previous three years. Evidently some judges had sat for twice the number of days that others had.[133]

Circuit work

Establishing oneself on circuit could take some time; several barristers recalled spending time attending court sessions as spectators rather than participants.[134] Perseverance was essential for a new barrister on a circuit. One barrister notes that '[t]here was a saying, which was accepted as true by all newcomers on a circuit, that if you were not seen in each town, and seen again and again, you might as well stay at home.'[135] One barrister described it as 'a very long apprenticeship',[136] and O'Higgins reflected on 'how hard it was to be in town

---

129 B17.   130 B20.   131 B15.   132 (1947) 81 *I.L.T.S.J.* 34 (8 Feb. 1947).   133 Dáil Éireann deb., vol. 206, no. 4 (3 Dec. 1963).   134 See also ch. 3.   135 O'Higgins, *Double life*, p. 75.   136 B25.

after town without work'.[137] Another, called in the 1990s, said the circuit they joined 'was absolutely dominated by two or three people. A bit of an old duopoly.' Others saw this in a more positive light:

> You sat in court and you watched all the cases so you learnt an awful lot from that and seeing how people examined and cross examined and how they reacted to, interrelated to the judge.[138]

Beginning one's career on circuit had the advantage of providing the junior barrister with a broader experience than he or she would expect in Dublin. This was true on both the civil and the criminal side, and was commented upon by a number of interviewees. Those on circuit generally 'did a vast range of work'[139] and were exposed at a junior level to criminal work that they probably would not have gotten in Dublin.[140] It was also easier to network with solicitors and establish reputations with them on circuit:

> You had the advantage that you would get work on circuit, advocacy work perhaps easier than in Dublin. Some of the solicitors would get to know you fairly quickly down there and they would give you cases so you'd get up on your feet and that gave you a lot of experience, and you'd do all sorts of cases.[141]

> Solicitors on circuit who were acting for plaintiffs would be willing to give you that sort of work at an early stage and perhaps easier to get than it was in Dublin where there would have been more people and perhaps more difficult to get to know solicitors if you didn't have connections. So it was easier to get started undoubtedly on circuit and if you were prepared to work, solicitors were prepared to give you work so that was a good experience.[142]

Generally speaking, the facilities for barristers on circuit were minimal. At different times, the various circuit and Bar associations made representations on behalf of their members in relation to the facilities available to them.[143] County courthouses would often have a room of some sort in which barristers could change their clothes for court, store papers, and perhaps read over briefs. In the

---

137 O'Higgins, *Double life*, p. 86.   138 B18.   139 B1.   140 B17.   141 B23.   142 B22.   143 E.g., in 1933 the Dublin Circuit and District Courts' Bar Association complained to the Department of Justice about delays in the Dublin Circuit and District Courts. (1933) 67 *I.L.T.S.J.* 8 (7 Jan. 1933). In 1928 the Bar Council discussed setting up a circuits association to look after the interests of members of the Bar practising on circuits outside of Dublin: B.C.M., 20 Jan 1928. However, nothing came of this discussion. In 1984, the minister for justice (Michael Noonan) addressed the Limerick Bar in relation to a number of areas of concern, including delays and complaints against solicitors. 'Minister addresses Limerick Bar Association', *Irish Law Times* (ns) 2 (1984), 97.

early twentieth century, some of these were repurposed grand jury rooms.[144] Writing about joining the Leinster Circuit in the 1920s, McEnery said the 'barristers room' in Waterford was 'off the court and there was usually a good fire there and fellows sitting around chatting.'[145]

In the first half of the century, barristers staying at Bar hotels on circuit were usually given the use of a communal room out of which to work; O'Higgins describes having 'a sitting-room reserved each evening for writing or studying.'[146] Lee similarly mentions the provision of a 'Bar-room' in each hotel in the South-Western Circuit, 'where cases were prepared and legal knowledge was shared'. He describes it as providing 'valuable training for young barristers in the practise of their craft'.[147] The extent to which use was made of hotel Bar rooms could vary between towns. For example, it was observed that in the 1940s, '[t]he camaraderie on the Clare Circuit was never as clearly apparent as in Limerick or Kerry. While a Bar-room was provided [in the hotel] it was never as popular a *rendezvous* as its counterpart in the other counties.'[148] Speaking about the 1970s in Waterford, one barrister described the Bar room simply as a robing room, rather than a place in which to focus on paperwork or hold consultations:

> We had a Bar room which was the front room of the hotel across the road from the court but that was simply a room for changing into your wig and gown and walking across the street, sometimes through the cattle that were marching through.[149]

McEnery, writing about Dungarvan in the 1920s, similarly describes the hotel as being directly opposite the courthouse, so

> We had to go to and from the court and hotel across the road in wigs and gowns to the admiration of the multitude. It was quite a usual sight when the court sittings clashed with a fair day to see the bobbing heads of four or five barristers in wigs and gowns making their way carefully from one place to the other through a seething mass of bullocks and heifers, swishing their tails and lowing, and the prospective buyers and sellers engaged in vociferous bargaining on a roadway liberally bespattered with fresh cow dung.[150]

Solicitors may not have been excluded from Bar rooms as thoroughly as they were from the Law Library in Dublin; O'Higgins, for example, recalled that on the Midlands Circuit in the thirties, '[f]rom time to time a solicitor would come, hurrying into the Bar room, calling out for some barrister and handing him a

---

144 E.g., in Limerick: see Lee, *Memoir*, p. 5.   145 McEnery, 'Look back, p. 70.   146 O'Higgins, *Double life*, p. 85.   147 Lee, *Memoir*, p. ix.   148 Ibid., p. 47.   149 B18.   150 McEnery, 'Look back', p. 87.

brief for later in the week or later that day, or, if the barrister they needed was one of those already consulting outside, leaving the brief on the Bar room table.'[151] In other places, the room was a shared space accommodating both branches of the profession.

* * *

As with other aspects of life at the Bar, the circuits were not immune from changes over the course of the century. Practices relating to travel, accommodation and dining evolved. Writing about the South-Western Circuit, Lee reflects on the impact of tourism and price increases:

> During the war years and for a considerable time later this communal life remained intact and hotel expenses remained reasonable. With the coming of tourists, improved transport and high inflation, cracks began to appear on this monastic edifice. Bar-rooms were no longer provided in hotels and expenses for accommodation and meals greatly increased.[152]

The advent of personal motor cars and better road systems also contributed towards the decline of some circuit traditions.[153] Mackey noted in the 1990s that while the circuits and the camaraderie continued, 'the motor car has greatly invaded the close association between the circuiteers who can now return each day to Dublin from towns where in former times they would live together for a week'.[154] Geoghegan also notes the increasing tendency for barristers to live on circuit and return home each evening.[155]

Another change to circuit practice identified by interviewees was the change in practice areas:

> Landlord and tenant has gone, criminal injury, malicious damage, criminal injury has gone, rights of way unheard of anymore, squatters title … unheard of, all resolved apparently.[156]

The increased number of barristers on circuit was also remarked upon by interviewees.[157] The decline of the drinking culture on circuit was also discussed. As one put it, 'I think the drinking stopped, well it didn't stop, it reduced considerably over time.'[158]

The circuits were re-drawn several times during the twentieth century,[159] and the number of circuit towns decreased. For example, on the Cork Circuit in the

---

151 O'Higgins, *Double life*, p. 87.   152 Lee, *Memoir*, p. ix.   153 E.g., Geoghegan, 'The changing face', p. 40.   154 Mackey, *Windward*, p. 160.   155 Geoghegan, 'The changing face', p. 40.   156 B8.   157 B8.   158 B4.   159 See, e.g., the Circuit Court (New Circuits) Order 1937 (S.I. 309/1937), under the Courts of Justice Act 1936, s. 13; the Circuit Court (New Circuits) Order

1970s it was 'commonplace for all of us to go to eleven towns in Co. Cork, now there are seven left I think'.[160] In December 1994 the Circuit Court review working group[161] published a report which proposed to have smaller circuits with single judges sitting in the larger towns. Both the Bar Council and the Law Society identified what they considered to be deficiencies in these proposals. The Bar Council suggested that the proposal to retain larger circuits 'will lead to a greater spread of work among the Bar and allow a greater number of younger counsel, on whom the future of the profession of advocates depends, to get experience and establish themselves with solicitors on circuit.'[162] The Law Society pointed out that representatives from neither branch of the legal profession sat upon the review group.

Even as practices on circuit evolved, barristers were conscious of past traditions. One barrister remarked that by the late seventies and early eighties,

> You didn't have the circuit dinners you had on *The old Munster Circuit* where every night they're all staying in the same hotel, but you would have had a few barristers staying in the one hotel and they would go. But it would be a very informal dinner and it would be more business-like, in the sense people would go to eat because they had to eat and they'd go back and work. So, you didn't have the sort of collegiate dinners that you had as described in Healy and the other books, it was different.[163]

Reflecting in the early twenty-first century on the changes to the circuit system, Geoghegan notes that the inevitable change was 'a natural consequence of more modern and efficient ways of providing legal services.'[164]

1960 (S.I. 70/1960), under the Courts of Justice Act 1953; the Circuit Court (Alteration of Circuits) Order 1964 (S.I. 206/1964) and the Circuit Court (Alteration of Circuits) Order 1969 (S.I. 201/1969), under the Courts Act 1964. **160** B8. **161** Established by Minister for Justice Máire Geoghegan-Quinn in March 1994 and chaired by the president of the Circuit Court, Judge Frank Spain. The committee was to review the circuits of the Circuit Court to determine the optimum size and number of circuits and the number of venues with a view to ensuring the efficient working of the Circuit Court in all areas. **162** 'Bar Council's response to the Circuit Court review working group', *Irish Law Times* (ns) 13 (1995), 98, at 99. **163** B23. **164** Geoghegan, 'The changing face', p. 39.

CHAPTER ELEVEN

The Law Library

Introduction

Unlike in England and Wales, where barristers worked out of chambers or residential inns of court, the Irish Bar was characterised by its communal Law Library, 'a vast office or chamber for barristers.'[1] Morison and Leith wrote in the 1990s that the library system 'radically' affected how work was allocated compared to chambers system: 'briefs may be passed on from colleagues in a Bar Library ... because they are overcommitted or because the fee is simply not worthwhile to them.'[2] A barrister interviewed for this book commented that in the library system, 'your fate wasn't dependent on getting into chambers.'[3] Although this has been described as 'a uniquely Irish institution',[4] barristers in Northern Ireland and Scotland also worked out of libraries.[5] Nevertheless, the library system was certainly in the minority in the common law world. The centrality of the Law Library to the Irish profession was later enshrined in the Bar Council's code of conduct, which stated: '[t]he Law Library is the central and primary place of practice for the Bar of Ireland.'[6]

Throughout the twentieth century, the Dublin Law Library operated on a subscription basis, requiring all practising barristers to be members and to pay an annual fee.[7] Subscription rates were periodically reviewed, and lower rates[8] applied to juniors and to members who did not live in Dublin and were thus

1 Patrick MacKenzie, *Lawful occasions: the old Eastern Circuit* (Dublin, 1991), p. 15. Similarly, A.M. Sullivan, 'The last forty years of the Irish Bar', *The Cambridge Law Journal* 3:3 (1929), 365, described it, at 367, as 'an immense chamber'.   2 John Morison and Philip Leith, *The barrister's world and the nature of law* (Berkshire, 1992), p. 27.   3 B26. B10 said: in London ... if you can't get into chambers, that's it. You're never going to have a serious practice as a barrister. We have a very high ... dropout rate but it's a dropout rate, you know, when you've had the chance to give it a go and to cut your teeth and see how it actually works, not a dropout rate because you can't get in the door in the first place.' For a clerk's view of London chambers in the twentieth century, see A.E. Bowker, *A lifetime with the law* (London, 1961).   4 MacKenzie, *Lawful occasions*, p. 15.   5 On the Northern Ireland Law Library, see A. Hart, *A history of the Bar and inn of court of Northern Ireland* (Belfast, 2013), pp 113, 119. Hart describes the plans for building the Law Library in 1921. It was modelled on the Dublin Law Library and the work patterns which had been established there. The advocates' library in Scotland was both a workplace for barristers and the national law library for Scotland: see Andrea Longson, 'The advocates' library', *Legal Information Management* 9 (2009), 35.   6 *Code of conduct for the Bar of Ireland*, adopted by the Bar – 30th July 1985, rule 8.1. Rule 8.2 stated: 'It is desirable that all practising barristers should be members of the Law Library.'   7 In the early twentieth century there was a separate subscription for the dressing room: B.C.M., 12 Dec. 1923; Maurice Healy, *The old Munster Circuit: a book of memories and traditions* (London, 1939), p. 43.   8 As an example of the differing rates, in 1948 Dublin-based seniors paid £7, 7s. while country seniors paid £4, 4s.: B.C.M., 2 July 1948. In 1971, senior counsel paid £115; junior

unlikely to use the Library very frequently.[9] The Library subscription gave barristers access to a repository of legal sources and a workspace. The Library was staffed,[10] and as the century progressed barristers had access to facilities such as phones, copiers and computers, as well as books, law reports and legislation. The Bar Council in the 1980s considered the Library to be the 'best system for the profession and for the public'.[11]

> It maintained the profession as a very open one, where people could set themselves up as members of the profession at minimal cost. It also exposed them to daily contact with all of their colleagues from the lowest to the highest in terms of experience. It encouraged a continuing process of being kept up to date and being made aware of the law.[12]

A number of twentieth-century barristers described the Law Library as a 'club',[13] while others characterised it as a sanctuary.[14] Many emphasised the collegiality, friendships and supports generated by this working arrangement, which engendered much gossip and humour.[15] One described it as 'a friendly place in which you were encouraged.'[16] In 1923, William Magennis described the Library as:

> A scene where history more than legal history was made; where men, he added amidst laughter, discussed not only law but scandal, and retailed not only the latest legal decision, but also the latest social reports.[17]

Cork had its own facilities, including a Bar room where meetings of the Cork Bar took place.[18]

As will be seen, while the Law Library as a concept was something which had existed since the previous century, the physical entity underwent many changes in the twentieth century.

---

counsel £75 and country members £20: general meeting of the Bar, 21 June 1971.   **9** This inevitably led to tensions if country members were seen to be spending a lot of time in the Library: Bar Council Library Committee (B.C.L.C.), 9 Dec. 1993; 20 Jan. 1994. A 'Cork rate' was also available from 1950: B.C.M., 20 July 1950. In 1994 it was pointed out that there was 'quite an irregularity between the Dublin rate, country rate and Cork rate'; B.C.L.C., 24 Mar. 1994. Two Limerick-based members were refused the reduced rate in 1977: B.C.M., 22 July 1977, and a barrister who lived in Dublin but spent a lot of time in Galway on circuit was refused the country rate in 1986: B.C.L.C., 23 Oct. 1986. In 1995 the library committee said that the 'country rate' was available to members whose principal place of business was 100 miles from Dublin.' B.C.L.C., 14 Dec. 1995.   **10** See further below.   **11** Fair Trade Commission: *Report of study into restrictive practices in the legal profession* (Dublin, 1990), para. 11.14.   **12** Ibid.   **13** Sheehy described it as 'one of the best clubs in the world'. Eugene Sheehy, *May it please the court* (Dublin, 1951), p. 50. Shillman similarly described it as a club in his unpublished memoir: Bernard Shillman, 'Every journey has an end', NAI PRIV 1367/11, p. 13.   **14** Rex Mackey, *Windward of the law* (2nd ed., Dublin, 1991), p. 21.   **15** E.g., M. McDonnell Bodkin, *Recollections of an Irish judge: press, Bar and parliament* (London, 1914), p. 86.   **16** B26.   **17** Dáil Éireann deb., vol. 5, no. 7 (12 Oct. 1923).   **18** E.g., B.C.M., 25 Feb.

The Law Library, 1921–2

In 1921, barristers worked out of the two-storey Law Library, designed by Thomas Drew, in the east wing of the Four Courts.[19] This was widely praised as a significant improvement on the previous Library, which had been converted into robing rooms.[20] As described in chapter two, in 1922, barristers and the courts decamped to the King's Inns,[21] where they operated in cramped, albeit adequate, conditions.[22] After the destruction of the Law Library in July 1922, the courts and the Bar remained in situ, with the commissioners of public works recording that

> The business of the courts had been carried on under great difficulties in the King's Inns. This building, which was made available by the public spirit of the benchers, is stately and beautiful in appearance, but totally inadequate in the space it affords for the needs of the courts and the court offices.[23]

A plan soon emerged to house the courts and Bar in the 'secure and spacious'[24] state apartments in Dublin Castle.

Dublin Castle

The commissioners wrote to Lord Chief Justice Molony in January 1923, hopeful that new premises at Dublin Castle would be operational the following month.[25] Having operated out of the King's Inns for over a year, members of the

---

1952. In the 1940s, a Limerick-based barrister sought to pay a reduced Library subscription, but was informed by the Bar Council that he would be treated in the same manner as the members of the Cork Circuit, which meant abandoning his individual seat in the Law Library: B.C.M., 4 Feb. 1949. **19** Griffin, 'Post Gandon', p. 242, describes it as having 'a gallery 122 feet long and 38 feet wide. The book stacks divided by Corinthian columns were arranged in bays as in the King's Inns. The room ended with a venetian window decorated in stained glass.' The Four Courts Library Act 1894 (57 & 58 Vict., c. 4) had provided £115,000 from the suitors' fund. The Library was formally opened on 15 April 1897. A memorandum on the Law Library, in 1923, stated that 'The new Library consisted of (a) the library proper equipped to seat about 270, bookcases being ranged in recesses around the room and a gallery running along three sides of it; (b) a solicitors' room, 37 ft. long by 20 ft. wide; (c) a room of the same size over used as a private reading room for barristers; (d) a bar; (e) cellars beneath the library used as robing rooms.' NAI FIN/1/665. **20** Griffin, 'Post Gandon', p. 237. **21** 'King's Inn's library', (1922) 56 *I.L.T.S.J.* 104 (22 Apr. 1922). The *Irish Law Times* advised that '[s]olicitors and their clerks should "call" barristers there in the usual way.' **22** Lord Chief Justice Molony had proposed at a meeting of the benchers in April that 'the King's Inns premises be placed at the disposal of the government for carrying on the administration of justice.' K.I.B.M., 20 Apr. 1922. Details of how and where the courts were to operate were published in (1922) 56 *I.L.T.S.J.* 108 (29 Apr. 1922). In August, following the destruction of the Library, the King's Inns Library remained open on days when judges of the High Court were sitting, so as to facilitate barristers: K.I.B.M., 31 Aug. 1922. **23** Commissioners of public works in Ireland, *Ninety-first annual report* (Dublin, 1924), p. 7. **24** Kenneth Ferguson, *King's Inns barristers 1868–2004* (Dublin, 2005), p. 100. **25** K.I.B.M., 11 Jan. 1923.

Bar were eager to move,[26] but progress was slow.[27] Two members visited the castle and reported back that,

> Although St Patrick's hall has been allocated as a library for the Bar, no shelves had been as yet provided for law books, and that no rooms had been allocated as dressing rooms or lavatory accommodation.[28]

The move took place in March 1923.[29] Although there had been some delay in opening the new premises, and not everything was completed, it was quite a speedy move, all things considered.[30] By 1924, the commissioners of public works reported that:

> St Patrick's hall has been fitted up as a law library (furnishing not yet completed) and a suite of rooms near it has been prepared for the use of the Bar in lieu of the rooms and furniture which they lost at the destruction of the Four Courts.[31]

They also reported that 'the provision of Bar robing rooms and lavatory accommodation was practically completed'.[32] By early 1925, the Bar's accommodation was fully completed.[33] As well as the library in St Patrick's hall, there was a conference room and a number of consultation rooms.[34]

Contemporary reports describe the space as having 'undergone in a very brief space of time a remarkable transformation'.[35] The new Library was considered a 'very fine Law Library',[36] and on the whole, members of the profession seem to have been pleased with the temporary accommodation.[37] One newspaper opined that the central location of the new premises made it an improvement on the Four Courts.[38] When it opened in April 1923, it was 'quite crowded with busy barristers at an early hour' on the first day.[39]

---

26 Alfred Dickie KC strongly objected to suggestions that the Bar might remain at the King's Inns, pointing out that Dublin Castle had been refurbished 'at great expense' whereas Henrietta Street had 'no accommodation for the Bar whatever.' (1924) 58 *I.L.T.S.J.* 117 (13 May 1924).   27 B.C.M., 24 Jan. 1923.   28 Ibid.   29 (1923) 57 *I.L.T.S.J.* 82 (31 Mar. 1923).   30 Details of the move are documented in the Kennedy papers, UCDA P4/1049–1052. Further improvements were made during the 1923 long vacation.   31 Commissioners of public works in Ireland, *Ninety-second annual report* (Dublin, 1924), p. 6.   32 Ibid., p. 13.   33 Commissioners of public works in Ireland, *Ninety-third annual report* (Dublin, 1925), p. 5.   34 (1923) 57 *I.L.T.S.J.* 89–90 (7 Apr. 1923). There was also a luncheon room for the exclusive use of members of the Bar. The *Irish Law Times* described the availability of 'a very good, if limited, variety of seasonable, palatable and nourishing food.' (1930) 64 *I.L.T.S.J.* 119–20 (17 May 1930).   35 *Irish Independent*, 24 Jan. 1923, p. 4. See also *Irish Independent*, 25 Jan. 1923, p. 3 and 8 Mar. 1923, p. 4.   36 *Freeman's Journal*, 11 Apr. 1923, p. 7. 37 E.g., (1923) 57 *I.L.T.S.J.* 89–90 (7 Apr. 1923). The Bar Council held its first meeting in Dublin Castle on 26 April 1923.   38 *Strabane Chronicle*, 7 Oct. 1922, p. 3.   39 *Evening Herald*, 11 Apr. 1923, p. 1. Members of the public also appear to have been satisfied with the relocation of the courts, with one enthusiastically surmising that '[t]he premises will be more eminently suited for courts of law than even in the Four Courts before its destruction. They are for one thing far more central.' *Strabane Chronicle*, 7 Oct. 1922, p. 3.

Stocking the shelves

It has been observed that 'books were of prime importance to the Bar and as a result the law library was at the heart of their profession'.[40] Aside from losing their place of work, one of the first challenges facing the profession in 1922 was the loss of the library's collections of books and reports. An estimated 40,000 volumes had been destroyed, 'many of them irreplaceable first editions.'[41] It was essential that the library be restocked as soon as possible, so as to facilitate an expeditious return to the normal functioning of the Bar. In July 1922, the Bar sought £20,000 in compensation 'for the contents of the law library and the various rooms adjacent thereto' and £10,000 'for the contents of the dressing rooms belonging to the members of the Bar.'[42]

In October 1922, Law Officer Hugh Kennedy assured the Bar Council that the government would fund the restocking of the law library shelves.[43] This was based on his reliance on a meeting with Department of Finance official Con Gregg,[44] although the two men's accounts differed as to what precisely was agreed at that meeting. The money was not forthcoming, and between October 1922 and January 1924, Kennedy and Gregg exchanged increasingly testy letters.[45] The understaffed Department of Finance was under considerable strain dealing with the consequences of the Treaty settlement as well as the cost of the destructive Civil War.[46] By early 1923 both the benchers[47] and the Bar Council[48] were made aware of various private book collections that were available for purchase. Kennedy shared the Bar Council's concern that these private collections would likely be snapped up by buyers in England unless steps were taken. Relying on Kennedy's assurances, the Bar Council authorised two members to purchase books on behalf of the Bar, to the value of £1,000.[49]

---

40 Clancy, 'The Four Courts building', p. 89.   41 *Cork Examiner*, 3 July 1922, p. 6. A memorandum in 1923 pointed out that while the board of works had paid for various aspects of the Law Library, there was no record of the board ever having paid for books, which were presumed to be the property of the General Council of the Bar of Ireland. Memorandum on the Law Library, Four Courts, NAI FIN/1/665.   42 Matheson Ormsby Prentice to sec. provisional govt., 12 July 1922, NAI FIN/1/665; B.C.M., 11 July 1922.   43 He said, 'the provisional government would probably be willing to pay for any law libraries at present on the market which might be bought by the Bar', B.C.M., 9 Oct. 1922.   44 Pauric J. Dempsey and Shaun Boylan, 'Gregg, Sir Cornelius Joseph ('Con')', *D.I.B.*, describe Gregg as 'the chief architect of the new Irish civil service ... Widely regarded as the ablest civil servant in Ireland.' He later returned to the British civil service where he played senior roles in the board of Inland Revenue in the thirties and forties.   45 Kennedy to Gregg, 20 Oct. 1922; Kennedy to Gregg, 23 Feb. 1923; Kennedy to Gregg, 15 Mar. 1923; Kennedy to Gregg, 29 Nov. 1923; Gregg to Kennedy, 6 Dec. 1923; Kennedy to Gregg, 31 Dec. 1923; Gregg to Kennedy, 9 Jan. 1924, NAI FIN/1/665.   46 Ronan Fanning, *The Irish Department of Finance 1922–58* (Dublin, 1978).   47 Justice Dodd stated his willingness 'to give his library and shelving for the new library to be formed at the Castle at such remuneration as might hereafter be decided: K.I.B.M., 11 Jan. 1923.   48 The library of the late Serjeant Matheson was offered at £300: B.C.M., 24 Jan. 1923.   49 B.C.M., 7 Feb. 1923. At subsequent meetings, small sums of money were approved for purchases of book collections. In Mar. 1923, the *Irish Independent* reported that members of the Bar had 'subscribed £1,000 towards providing books' for the new library. *Irish Independent*, 9 Mar. 1923,

Kennedy explained to Gregg that this had put the Bar library committee 'in a very awkward position', as it had to borrow from a number of members of the Bar[50] in order to pay for the books it had bought.[51]

Following further correspondence, Alfred Dickie[52] met with James John McElligott[53] in the Department of Finance. Following this meeting, it was agreed that that £2,500 would be a reasonable sum for replacing the books (although they would potentially be valued at £10,000)[54] and £1,000 was paid to Dickie and Samuel Brown[55] as trustees.[56]

Despite the confusion and the dispute over the responsibility to purchase books, by the time the Dublin Castle Law Library had re-opened in April 1923, a 'considerable number' of law books had been secured. Some were purchased by members of the Bar with the approval of the Bar Council, as noted above,[57] and others were donated. The English Bar, for example, gifted three sets of English law reports.[58] The *Cork Examiner* reported that there were '[n]early 5,000' law books in the library, but that 'a great many' would be needed 'to bring it to the standard of the Four Courts library'.[59] By October 1923 it was reported that 'a large number of additional volumes' had been received. Librarian Fred Price continued the process of restocking the library shelves throughout the sojourn in Dublin Castle. Aston notes that he went on 'an extended buying tour' in Ireland and the United Kingdom, and by 1931 the library contained 'about 10,000 volumes.'[60]

As well as compensation for the books on the library shelves, compensation was also sought by individual members of the Bar for personally owned books and other items.[61] For example, William Cotter Stubbs[62] £278, 15s. for the

p. 4.   50 Mr Samuel Lombard Browne KC 'and other members of the Bar' contributed. 51 Kennedy to Gregg, 29 Nov. 1923, NAI FIN/1/665.   52 Dickie (called 1893: Ferguson, *Barristers*, p. 173) had been appointed to the Bar Council in recognition of 'all the trouble he had taken with regard to the proper housing of the Bar in Dublin Castle': B.C.M., 11 May 1923.   53 McElligott helped to set up the new Department of Finance in 1923 and was appointed secretary of the department in 1927. Sean Cromien, 'McElligott, James John ('Jimmy')', *D.I.B.* writes that McElligott's 'strong emphasis on austerity was a useful corrective to the unreasonable expectations of the young and inexperienced politicians who took over from the British administration in 1922 and the equally inexperienced politicians who took office after the first change of government in 1932.' 54 McElligott to Michael Corrigan, chief state solicitor, 23 Jan. 1924, NAI FIN/1/665. Some months previously, Dickie had said that it had been agreed that if suitable accommodation were provided by the state, the Bar would only pursue a claim for the books which had been destroyed, valued at around £5,000. (1924) 58 *I.L.T.S.J.* 117 (13 May 1923).   55 Called in 1881 and granted silk in 1899, Brown was one of the senior members of the Bar. Ferguson, *Barristers*, p. 145.   56 McElligot to Dickie, 19 Feb. 1924, NAI FIN/1/665.   57 There were also gratuitous donations, including a gift of 'valuable book cases' from Lord Justice O'Connor on his retirement: *Donegal News*, 19 Jan. 1924, p. 6.   58 *Irish Independent*, 9 Mar. 1923, p. 4.   59 *Cork Examiner*, 12 Apr. 1923, p. 6.   60 Jennefer Aston, 'From Law Library Society to Law Library: the first 180 years, 1816–1996', *L.I.M.* 11 (2011), 168, at 170. 61 Solicitors Matheson Ormsby Prentice on behalf of the trustees of the Council of the Bar of Ireland submitted a claim for compensation to cover '[b]ooks, papers, manuscripts, furniture and other articles being the contents of the law library and wigs, gowns, furniture and fittings and other articles deposited in and attached to the Bar robing or dressing room at the Four Courts'. Matheson Ormsby Prentice to sec. provisional govt., 12 July 1922, NAI FIN/1/665.   62 Stubbs (called in 1882: see

destruction of his property.[63] As well as specific books[64] and documents, a suit of clothes and a bowler hat, his claim included quite a number of household items.[65] Malachi Muldoon[66] was reported to have claimed £40 compensation for the manuscript of a play entitled 'The playwright', which had been left in his Law Library locker.[67]

Return to the Four Courts

The 1926 report of the commissioners of public works included a drawing of the planned new layout of the Four Courts complex. This included the new law library, a smoke room, a tea room, and consultation rooms. The commissioners predicted that '[t]he court offices and other accessory rooms will be greatly improved in spaciousness and simplicity of arrangement'.[68] Construction work commenced in that year, and the *Irish Law Times* reported that the plans, designed by T.J. Byrne,[69] were 'highly satisfactory',[70] and continued to publish periodic updates on the project's progress.[71] Similarly, the Office of Public Works also reported annually on progress with the refurbishment and rebuilding.[72] The Bar was allowed to have some input into the design, and in 1928, Alfred Dickie said that 'everything that the Bar had suggested for their convenience had been carried out'.[73] In 1929 the *Evening Herald* reported that the location of the new Law Library, on the site of the old dining room, would be 'one of its greatest assets. It will be so placed as to render it easily accessible from all parts of the building'.[74]

In their 1934 report, the commissioners of public works included a detailed description of the new accommodations for the Bar, and included floorplans of both the pre-1922 Four Courts complex and the new layout. There were robing rooms, offices and a refreshment room in the western part of the north block.

Ferguson, *Barristers*, p. 303) served as crown prosecutor for Louth and Monaghan. He served as assistant legal commissioner, a fellow and an active member of the Royal Society of Antiquaries, and the compiler of various digests of law reports. He was also the examiner of title in the Irish Land Commission. **63** William Cotter Stubbs, barrister-at-law, 16 Hatch Street, Dublin, NAI FIN/COMP/2/28/476. **64** He claimed for forty-two books in total, mostly relating to property law topics, including *Coote on mortgages*, Carson's *Real property statutes*, Snell's *Equity*, Carleton's *County courts*, several on conveyancing and landlord and tenant, and volumes of the Royal Society of Antiquaries. **65** These included a nail brush (sixpence), a clothes brush, a hair brush, and everything needed to make eggs, tea and toast. **66** Muldoon was called in 1913; see Ferguson, *Barristers*, p. 260. **67** *Freeman's Journal*, 26 July 1922, p. 2. Muldoon was the author of several plays; see ch. 15. **68** Commissioners of public works for Ireland, *Ninety-fourth report* (Dublin, 1926), p. 7. **69** Byrne was the principal architect in the office of public works. See Helen Andrews, 'Byrne, Thomas Joseph', *D.I.B.* **70** (1926) 60 *I.L.T.S.J.* 134 (29 May 1926). **71** E.g., (1930) 64 *I.L.T.S.J.* 219 (30 Sept. 1930); 'The Four Courts', (1930) 64 *I.L.T.S.J.* 293 (6 Dec. 1930); (1931) 65 *I.L.T.S.J.* 111 (9 May 1931). **72** Commissioners of public works for Ireland, *Ninety-sixth report* (Dublin, 1929); *Ninety-seventh report* (Dublin, 1930); *Ninety-eighth report* (Dublin, 1931); *Ninety-ninth report* (Dublin, 1933). **73** 'The reconstructed Four Courts', (1928) 62 *I.L.T.S.J.* 85 (7 Apr. 1928). **74** *Evening Herald*, 19 Jan. 1929, p. 1.

The Law Library, formerly on the first floor of the east wing, has been placed on the main axis of the buildings at ground floor level and communicates by spacious lobbies with the Supreme and High Courts, located in the front block.[75]

The new, spacious Library was completed in August 1931, and so began the 'onerous work'[76] of relocating once more. As recorded by the *Cork Examiner*,

Today, the stripping of the Law Library at Dublin Castle began. The books were placed in baskets and conveyed by lorry across the river to their new home in the reconstructed Four Courts ... Thousands of volumes have to be removed. With them go the lawyers' desks, which are handsome bits of furniture, and will be utilised in the new Library. The bookshelves, which were erected in St Patrick's Hall in the Castle when it was being converted into a library, are of the flimsiest and most inexpensive description, and the removal of them will be easy. They were so fixed as not to damage the walls of the fine apartment.[77]

Half of the library staff were deployed in packing up the estimated 10,000 books at Dublin Castle,[78] while the other half unpacked and reshelved the books in the new library. Chief Justice Kennedy lingered at the Castle, observing the packing, which was carried out under the supervision of librarian Frederick Price and John Campion, the crier.[79] A few days later, the robing and consultation rooms were dismantled and transferred.[80] The fittings for the Law Library in Dublin Castle had been 'of a temporary character,'[81] so that when the time came to move the Library back to the Four Courts, the apartments were quite easily restored to their former state.[82]

As the new Four Courts complex neared completion, there were security concerns. In August 1931 the minister for justice was told that there was 'a serious danger of an attempt being made to destroy the Four Courts before those buildings are occupied'. The building and grounds were patrolled by armed Gardaí but by mid-August the Gardaí themselves sought military intervention.[83]

---

75 Commissioners of public works for Ireland, *One hundredth report* (Dublin, 1934), p. 7. It was also noted, at p. 8, that by arrangement between the benchers and the Law Society, an exchange of interests in parts of the former buildings was made to enable the north block to be replaced to allow a new axial and ground floor position for the Law Library. The benchers now had a chamber and offices in the west wing of the front block.   76 (1931) 65 *I.L.T.S.J.* 111 (9 May 1931). 77 *Examiner*, 11 Aug. 1931, p. 8.   78 (1931) 65 *I.L.T.S.J.* 202 (22 Aug. 1931).   79 Ibid.   80 Ibid. 81 *Examiner*, 12 Apr. 1923, p. 6.   82 See, e.g., *Examiner*, 14 Aug. 1929, p. 7, where it was reported that '[t][he removal of bookshelves and desks can be accomplished without damage to the fine apartment, for in fitting it to its present use care was taken that the structure should not be interfered with.'   83 Dept. Justice to each member of the exec. council, 26 Aug. 1931, NAI TSCH/3/S4290.

The cabinet agreed that military backup should be made available if needed.[84] Ultimately these fears were not realised.

Chief Justice Kennedy wrote to James Fitzgerald Kenney, the minister for justice, in July 1931 proposing that there be 'a ceremonial reopening of the Four Courts'.[85] He proposed that the ceremonial inauguration and symbolic handing over of keys in the round hall should be preceded by a procession of the judges.[86] He also suggested the playing of the national anthem and the mounting of the flag over the building, as well as unofficial religious ceremonies to mark the occasion.[87] While the occasion of the return to the Four Courts complex was one to be marked, the executive council, concerned about security issues and financial constraints, decided that there should be no official opening of the courts.[88] In a letter to the chief justice, the minister for justice explained:

> We are taking all possible precautions to see that the Four Courts are not blown up or otherwise destroyed ... a formal opening would be a direct incentive to the making of an attempt to wreck the building and if there be a formal opening an attempt of this nature will inevitably be made.[89]

Hogan suggests that the decision to dispense with a formal opening was the right one given the continued potency of the threat posed by paramilitary organisations.[90] The new building was duly opened on 12 October 1931 without formal ceremony,[91] although 'the occasion did not go altogether unrecognised', and the chief justice gave a short address in the Supreme Court expressing his appreciation for 'the magnificent work of reconstruction and restoration which had been accomplished through the office of public works'.[92]

The new Law Library at the Four Courts met with mixed reviews.[93] Clancy points out that while the changes to the exterior architecture were relatively minor, 'the internal changes were far more radical for the Bar'.[94] Contemporary

---

84 Sec. exec. council, Diarmuid Ó hÉigceartuigh, to sec. Dept. Justice, 26 Aug. 1931, NAI TSCH/3/S4290. Ó hÉigceartuigh was 'Dermot O'Hegarty, the "civil servant of the revolution", the man perpetually behind the scenes'; Frank Pakenham, *Peace by ordeal: the negotiation of the Anglo-Irish Treaty, 1921* (London, 1935), at p. 121 Among other things, he was secretary of the executive council of the Free State (1922–1932); commissioner of public works (1932–49) and then chairman of the commission. 85 Kennedy to Fitzgerald-Kenney, 8 July 1931, UCDA P4/1058 (33). 86 Kennedy to Fitzgerald-Kenney, 15 Aug. 1931, UCDA P4/1058 (22). 87 There were Catholic, Church of Ireland and Jewish religious ceremonies: (1931) 65 *I.L.T.S.J.* 249 (17 Oct. 1931). 88 Kennedy was engaged in extensive correspondence about the reopening: UCDA P4/1058. 89 Fitzgerald-Kenney to Kennedy, UCDA P4/1058 (3), (4). 90 Gerard Hogan, 'Kennedy, the Childers habeas corpus application and the return to the Four Courts' in Costello (ed.), *The Four Courts*, p. 217. 91 As the new court offices began to function and judges began sitting in the new courtrooms, workmen were completing the finishing touches to the building: (1931) 65 *I.L.T.S.J.* 249 (17 Oct. 1931). 92 Ibid. 93 One barrister later wrote 'I very much enjoyed my years at the castle and felt half sorry when we moved to the restored Four Courts.' McEnery, 'Look back in love', UCDA P74/2, p. 62. However, he also noted, p. 113, that the Library in the Four Courts had 'a lot more room than in St Patrick's hall'. 94 Clancy, 'The Four Courts building', p. 95.

news reports described the new Library as 'easily approached from all quarters'[95] and 'sufficiently commodious ... planned in every way to satisfy the lawyers' needs.'[96] The *Irish Law Times* was also very positive in its descriptions of the refurbishment of the complex:[97]

> The Law Library, standing in a central and prominent position, is the largest single apartment in the group. The ceiling is of coved panelling and is fitted with an ingenious and effective lighting system. There are two annexes and a lofty gallery to the Library. There are substantial quarters in the building for a care-taking staff, a well fitted kitchen and two restaurants are provided – one for lawyers and one for the public. There are excellent accommodations for judges, barristers and solicitors, and special rooms have been designed for the use of lady members of the Bar.[98]

Not everyone was convinced. One barrister, who started practising in the 1940s, wryly observed that '[t]he rebuilding of the Law Library at the rear of the Four Courts was designed by somebody whose speciality must have been hay sheds.'[99] As will be seen, once the initial enthusiasm had subsided, for most of the twentieth century there were complaints about the physical space provided for barristers. One described it as 'a chamber without any beauty and without the excuse of being even functional'.[100]

The restoration of the 90,000 square metres of the Four Courts had been 'a mammoth task',[101] taking nine years and involving hundreds of people.[102] Its completion was 'a signal achievement for the new state, since it has a return to political stability and normality following the devastation caused by the Civil War.'[103] The emphasis on functionality over embellishment was understandable given the scale of reconstruction in the first decade of the Free State.

The departure of the Law Society

Following the reconstruction of the Four Courts, the Incorporated Law Society was housed in a part of the complex known as the solicitors' buildings, situated close to where the original solicitors' building had been built in 1841.[104] The Law Society had held their original property under a lease from the King's Inns

95 *Evening Herald*, 26 Aug. 1930, p. 4.   96 *Examiner*, 16 Apr. 1930, p. 8.   97 'The new Four Courts', (1931) 65 *I.L.T.S.J.* 214–5 (5 Sept. 1931).   98 'The Four Courts', (1930) 64 *I.L.T.S.J.* 293 (6 Dec. 1930). See p. 172 for further discussion of the accommodation for women.   99 MacKenzie, *Lawful occasions*, p. 12.   100 Ibid.   101 Hogan, 'Kennedy, the Childers habeas corpus application', p. 207.   102 Commissioners of public works for Ireland, *One hundredth report* (Dublin, 1934). 103 Hogan, 'Kennedy, the Childers habeas corpus application', p. 207.   104 Daire Hogan, 'The Society from independence to 1960' in Eamonn G. Hall and Daire Hogan (eds), *The Law Society of Ireland 1852–2002: portrait of a profession* (Dublin, 2002), pp 73–97, 80. Hogan notes at p. 73 that after the destruction of the Four Courts, the Law Society was housed at 45 Kildare Street. See K.I.B.M., 2 Nov 1925. They joined with the King's Inns benchers to employ an architect 'to

benchers, subject to a nominal rent.[105] The arrangement for the new building was that the benchers would convey the fee simple of their property at the Four Courts site (which included the site of the former solicitors' building) to the Law Society. The Law Society would then lease the property to the commissioners of public works for 99 years at a nominal rent.[106] The commissioners would lease the new solicitors' building to the Law Society under similar terms. The negotiations were protracted and the various conveyances had not been completed by the time the new complex was completed and the society entered into possession in 1931.[107] The lease to the Law Society was agreed in 1954.[108]

By the 1960s, the Law Society was considering moving to a new premises. Like barristers, solicitors were also feeling the effects of increasing numbers joining their profession.[109] Given the perennial overcrowding in the Law Library, the Bar Council were interested in taking over the space when it was vacated, and made enquiries as early as 1968.[110] By 1976 negotiations were still ongoing.[111] The Law Society wished to lease the premises to the Bar Council, but the Bar Council did not relish the prospect of rent reviews. The deal fell through later that year due to problems with the Law Society's new premises at Blackhall Place.[112] Hall notes that '[p]rotracted negotiations in relation to the sale of the solicitors' buildings in the Four Courts to the Bar ended in 1977.'[113] Their new premises opened in 1978, but they retained an office and consultation rooms in the former solicitors' building.[114] A special committee of the Bar Council was appointed in 1978 to consider how best to use the additional space acquired from the Law Society.[115] It had been envisaged that part of the former Law Society premises would be leased out by the Bar Council to the board of works as a temporary courtroom, but in 1978 it was felt that there was an immediate need for the space.[116]

---

prepare plans of their destroyed buildings and make an estimate of the cost of reconstruction.' Hogan, 'The Society from independence', p. 80. See also K.I.B.M., 25 Oct. 1924. **105** The lease was for 999 years at one shilling per annum: Griffin, p. 241. Following the destruction of the Four Courts, the commissioner of public works had written to the Department of Finance that 'the Four Courts buildings were not altogether government property,' and enclosed a map attempting to demonstrate who owned what. J.J. Healy, secretary, commissioners of public works to William O'Brien, sec. Ministry of Finance, 27 July 1922, NAI TSCH/3/S4290. **106** K.I.B.M., 1 Nov 1926. The benchers were of the view that the government should provide accommodation for them in the Four Courts, and that these should be at least as good as their former premises, because they would be losing that under the new agreement. On the background to the title for the solicitors' premises, see Daire Hogan, 'Solicitors and the Four Courts' in C. Costello (ed.), *The Four Courts.* **107** Eric A. Plunkett, 'Attorneys and solicitors in Ireland' in Incorporated Law Society, *Record of the centenary of the charter of the Incorporated Law Society of Ireland, 1852–1952* (Dublin, 1952). **108** Hogan, 'The Society from independence', pp 73–97, 82. **109** Eamonn G. Hall, 'The modern era: Blackhall Place, rights of audience and court dress, delays and reforms in the legal system' in Hall and Hogan (eds), *The Law Society of Ireland*, pp 121–39, 123. **110** B.C.M., 3 Oct. 1968. **111** Ibid., 31 May 1976. **112** Ibid., 8 Sept. 1976. **113** Hall, 'The modern era', pp 121–39, 125. **114** Hogan, 'The Society from independence', pp 73–97, 83. **115** Interim report of the sub-committee of the Council of the Bar of Ireland, 1982. **116** B.C.M., 6 Mar., 3 Apr. 1978. See below

Using the library

As noted, the library had amassed a considerable collection of books and reports by the time of its return to the Four Courts. The collections could be accessed via the 'book boys':[117]

> They were old and they would climb up and get the particular volume and the volumes that were valuable were kept in a press and the press contained the entirety of the valuable books and documents, about the size of a fridge ... There were no Irish books at the time.[118]

Physical copies of case reports were an important part of the library's collection. They were supposed to be consulted in the library:

> You could make do ... there was always books ... if you wanted to read a copy of the *Irish Reports* you always could. It's just that, you wouldn't be able to bring it home. You'd have to photocopy it when photocopies were introduced.[119]

Sometimes books went missing and by the late 1990s, the Bar Council's library committee was of the view that the Law Library 'appeared to be in a state of chaos and untidiness'. Proposals were made to overhaul some of the library services such as book retrieval and collection.[120]

Some barristers used the Library as a meeting-place[121] where they could consult with their colleagues about legal matters, as well as engaging in social interactions. Others made use of the book collections and case reports, or processed paperwork.

> I would have been waiting for a case, I'd be sitting there reading the papers or doing something or answering the phone ... I would be doing some legal business or chatting to colleagues ... about some legal matter as well as some casual stuff but most people would have been around the Library.[122]

> It should be remembered that the work of a barrister is not limited to court work. There is a considerable volume of chamber work such as writing counsel's opinions, replying to cases to advise clients, settling deeds and court documents etc. and for such work the Law Library is the barrister's workshop.[123]

for more discussion about later expansion of the Library, and ch. 13 for further discussion of the relationship with the solicitors' profession. 117 See further below. 118 B25, who began practising in the mid-seventies. 119 B17. 120 B.C.M., 25 Oct. 1995; 30 Nov. 1995. 121 T.F. O'Higgins, *A double life* (Dublin, 1996), p. 71. 122 B18. 123 Shillman, 'Every journey', pp 14–15.

Solicitors could leave messages or deliver briefs for barristers at the Library. The names of barristers who were wanted by solicitors were continually announced either by a staff member's 'booming'[124] voice, or later by a PA system. One barrister wrote that:

> This bellowing went on unceasingly all day from ten until four but after a little while the noise of the bellowing and the shouting of barristers to the book boys to get them books and the general noise hubbub had no effect on you and you never heard anything but the sound of your own name being called out.[125]

This all meant that the Law Library was generally a busy, bustling place. A barrister called to the Bar in the 1940s commented that '[t]he word "library" suggests a room hushed and scholarly, but that in the Four Courts was like the tower of Babel.'[126] He described it as a 'forum of great animation, a hive of activity, of legal, political, literary and humorous conversation'.[127] Another writer, recalling the early twentieth century, wrote that there was 'invariably a buzz of activity and a continuous background noise of voices engaged in discussing cases, the law in general and indeed almost everything else under the sun.'[128] O'Higgins also observed that barristers soon became used to 'the continual calling of names', although one immediately became alert and aware if one's own name or something similar to it was called'.[129] Some barristers suggested that the crier called each name at a specific pitch, so as to better allow them to identify their own name.[130] One barrister commented that

> The criers were very good, and the criers were capable of making or destroying you ... Because they would say 'oh, I never heard of that gentleman', I'd say, if you were shirty with them.[131]

Many barristers found that the noise and overcrowding made it a 'difficult' place in which to engage with intricate or complicated paperwork:[132]

> You couldn't work effectively in a very busy situation where names were being called out; if somebody, a solicitor, comes to the door of the Law Library your name was called out over a tannoy and then you would have this name calling all day long, phones all day long, you couldn't get any concentrated work done at your desk.[133]

---

124 O'Higgins, *Double life*, p. 72. See further, p. 234.   125 McEnery, *Look back*, p. 114.
126 MacKenzie, *Lawful occasions*, p. 16.   127 Ibid., p. 13.   128 James Comyn, *Their friends at court* (London, 1973), p. 124.   129 Ibid.   130 See further, p. 234.   131 B9.   132 B4, B17.   133 B16.

This drove many barristers to spend some of their time working from home, away from the noise and bustle.

Working from home

Working from home was seen by many busy barristers as they only way to complete their paperwork:

> It was too noisy … you couldn't have the concentration and you couldn't have the papers so I worked from home throughout the seventies and the eighties … Anyone with a titter of wit, if I may put it that way, would just be there when they are in court or to look up something they didn't have at home.

> If you had a couple of opinions, proofs to write and you had two or three hours, you know waiting for your case to get on, you couldn't get it done. And people would come up and say 'do you want a coffee?' and you couldn't say 'no, I don't want a coffee'. And then you're going home to do that three hours' work that you had during the day, but you couldn't use.[134]

Some barristers had quite sophisticated home work environments, with private libraries, and, later, fax machines[135] and computers. For example:

> I started building up my own library at an early stage of the Bar. I invested a lot of money in books, and in those days it was reports because you didn't have all of the databases.[136]

One barrister described receiving papers at home which were faxed from solicitors, and laboriously piecing them together into something coherent:

> Reams and reams and reams and reams and reams … of glossy toilet paper … I would try and cut them up … in my kitchen … and putting them all together and getting the brief and then dictating the defence … and faxing it back to the solicitor.[137]

Many barristers developed a pattern of dividing the working day into time spent in the courts and Library, and time spent at home. Working from home was not always limited to solitary paperwork. Comyn comments that in the early twentieth century, consultations were sometimes held 'in the evenings, at counsel's home'.[138] A barrister who was called in the 1950s similarly recalled

---

134 B16.   135 B7.   136 B23.   137 B7.   138 Comyn, *Their friends at court*, p. 57.

cycling out to his master's house in the evenings, to 'go through various things for a couple of hours'.[139]

Particularly for those with busy practices, this could mean that the working day was elongated, with early starts and late finishes, as discussed in chapter six. In the first half of the twentieth century, 'hybrid working' was facilitated by the 'legal express',[140] a specialised daily courier system for members of the Bar.[141] The Library's opening hours were quite limited, and at the end of each working day, briefs and papers would be placed into bags and collected by the staff of the legal express. The papers would be delivered to the homes of the barristers, and they would be collected early the following morning. Another advantage of this system was that it enabled barristers to walk to and from the Library each day, without the burden of carrying papers and briefs.[142] Comyn described this as 'a splendid service',[143] and recalled his excitement of the nightly arrival of the legal express when he was a child.[144] MacKenzie gave a colourful description:

> As the air in the Library became more foul, the day's work came to an end. Briefs and paper were put into black cloth bags and tied with red silk rope. At five o'clock the 'legal express' arrived. A horse with a canvass-covered cart, managed by a husband and wife, named O'Connor, stopped at the nearest doorway. They collected all the bags, dumped them into the cart and drove around the inner suburbs of Dublin delivering the brief bags. They finished the round at about seven o'clock, and early next morning they collected the bags and brought them back placing them on each subscriber's desk in the Library.[145]

There were geographical limits to this service. Reflecting on moving house from Killiney to Rathmines, for example, McEnery considered one of the advantages to be that he would no longer have to carry heavy briefs, but could instead avail of the legal express service.[146]

---

139 B19. Healy also describes many late evenings working on briefs, as well as sitting down at nine o'clock to discuss a case at the house of the 'leader'. Healy, *The old Munster Circuit*, p. 49.   140 Ibid.
141 Before the legal express this service was carried out by 'bagwomen', described by Carson's biographer as 'a wretched-looking class who carried the heavy bags of briefs, and sometimes books as well, on their backs, or wheeled them in makeshift perambulators.' Edward Marjoribanks, *The life of Lord Carson* (London, 1932), vol. 1, p. 21. Ross described them as 'a strange class of messengers, some old men, some old women and some girls.' Ross, *The years of my pilgrimage*, p. 24.
142 In 1969 it was noted that the delivery of the bags in the morning was frequently hampered by the Library doors not being opened on time at 9.30: B.C.M., 28 Nov. 1969. Over the years, different operators took over the service; for example, retired bus driver Thomas Carty took it on in 1968. B.C.M., 2 Feb. 1968. In 1948 the owner of the legal express purchased a van: B.C.M., 13 Feb. 1948. The providers of the legal express were affected by petrol rationing in the 1950s: see B.C.M., 19 Dec. 1956.   143 Comyn, *Their friends at court*, p. 57.   144 Ibid., p. 125.   145 MacKenzie, *Lawful occasions*, p. 19.   146 McEnery, *Look back*, p. 168.

Robing, smoking and refreshment

The Law Library's footprint continuously changed throughout the twentieth century.[147] Rooms and spaces changed their functions in accordance with the needs of the profession, the arrival of new technology and the expansion in the number of members of the profession. For example, as noted above, when the Four Courts was remodelled in the late 1920s and early 1930s,[148] the impact of the Sex Disqualification (Removal) Act 1919 was factored into the design, with facilities for both women jurors and women barristers.[149] There was a 'ladies' robing room, sometimes referred to as the 'lady barristers' room', and a sitting room for women.[150] Complaints were frequently made about this accommodation over the years[151] and it was refurbished and expanded in the late 1970s as more women joined the profession.[152] By 1985 the women's sitting room was described as 'an unjustified luxury' given the overcrowding in parts of the building.[153] Within a couple of years there was further refurbishment of these facilities.[154] Robing rooms were of course also available for the male members of the Bar. Healy recalled paying one guinea per year to the robing room, in exchange for which 'your wig and gown were minded and, when necessary, mended for you; clean bands were laid out every morning'.[155] Limited laundry services were provided, with fresh tabs or bands and towels available, although in practice the towels were sometimes wet[156] and the bands were sometimes dirty.[157]

Catering facilities for members of the Bar were provided in the form of a space variously referred to as a luncheon room,[158] refreshment room,[159] coffee room,[160] or tea room.[161] This gave barristers a private space in which to eat and drink, and, perhaps equally important, to socialise, gossip and let off steam:

> Everybody was around the place together and you were in the Law Library and you went to the coffee room … and you'd sit down at any table.[162]

---

147 In 1987, following some substantial refurbishment, it was pointed out that 'the geography of the Library has changed quite dramatically.' Bar of Ireland AGM, 19 Dec. 1987.   148 See above.   149 See further, ch. 9.   150 They paid for fuel to heat this room at their own expense, and later paid for electrical appliances: B.C.M., 23 Oct. 1953; B.C.M., 22 Jan. 1979.   151 For example, B.C.M., 31 Mar. 1950; 27 July 1951; 16 Nov. 1951; 14 Dec. 1951; 12 Nov. 1981.   152 B.C.M., 6 Nov. 1978; 22 Jan. 1979.   153 B.C.M., 13 June 1985.   154 B.C.M., 12 May 1986; 8 Oct., 9 Nov. 1987, Bar of Ireland AGM, 19 Dec. 1987.   155 Healy, *The old Munster Circuit*, p. 45. Lindsay recalled paying two guineas; Patrick Lindsay, *Memories* (Dublin, 1992), p. 100.   156 B.C.M., 18 Jan. 1929.   157 B.C.M., 24 Mar. 1988. Barristers laundered their own collars: B.C.M., 20 Jan. 1981.   158 B.C.M., 21 Jan. 1949.   159 B.C.M., 17 Apr. 1951.   160 B.C.M., 15 June 1951.   161 B.C.M., 13 Oct. 1994. The refurbishment of this space in the early 1950s necessitated the involvement of the Board of Works, the Department of Finance, the Department of Justice, the Bar Council and a catering company; B.C.M., 15 June 1951; 19 Oct. 1951; 18 Jan. 1952. There was also a public restaurant in the Four Courts complex, but the Bar Council declined to get involved with plans for its refurbishment when approached by the Dublin Solicitors' Bar Association. B.C.M., 1 May 1958.   162 B11.

You know the last thing anybody really goes there for is coffee or tea. It's for a bitch or exchange of views … what scandal is going on and who's doing things they shouldn't be doing, with whom they should not be doing them … there would an awful lot of that type of conversation.[163]

Such was the strength of feeling about the need for a coffee shop that when one catering company left it was suggested that the Bar Council should write to the taoiseach 'drawing attention to the public necessity for catering facilities.'[164] There was, at various times, dissatisfaction with the standard of catering.[165]

In 1960 the board of works agreed to construct a licensed bar in the Four Courts for the use of members of the Bar.[166] As seen in chapter twelve, networking and socialising was an important aspect of life at the communal Bar. In chapters six and seven, it was seen that there was a strong drinking culture at the Bar in the twentieth century. The spouse of one barrister wrote to the Bar Council to complain about the existence of the bar – an indication, perhaps, of its effect on the marriage.[167] Another barrister recalled

There was a bar in the Four Courts and then when they built the building in Church Street in 1994/1995 they put in a club and bar in it so there was always a group of people who stayed in the workplace drinking.[168]

For a long time there was a tradition of smoking in the Law Library. When the Library was housed in Dublin Castle, it was common for members to begin smoking at four o'clock in the afternoon, to the extent that the Bar Council had to issue a prohibitive resolution.[169] The refurbished Library at the Four Courts included a smoke room where, apparently, 'chaft and "leg pull" [were] the order of the day.'[170] MacKenzie recalled that in the forties and fifties,

The predominant smell in the Library was of tobacco, of cigars used by those attempting to give up smoking, of pipe tobacco and of brands of cigarettes which gave several of the members lung cancer. I regularly brought my robes home to give them an airing outside to try and rid them of the small before sending them to the cleaners.[171]

The provision of a space in which to smoke did not always prevent members of the Bar from smoking in non-designated areas. This frequently arose as a source of irritation. In 1968 it was pointed out that while most barristers observed the rules with regard to smoking in the Library, there were 'about a

163 B7.   164 B.C.M., 18 May 1951.   165 In 1945 'a large number' of barristers signed a petition complaining about the standards in both the public and the Bar restaurant: B.C.M., 23 Apr. 1945. See also B.C.M., 19 Jan. 1951; 31 Mar. 1990; 7 Mar. 1992.   166 B.C.M., 15 Jan. 1960. 167 B.C.M., 17 July 1981.   168 B10.   169 B.C.M., 11 Feb. 1927.   170 Sheehy, May it please the court, p. 50.   171 MacKenzie, Lawful occasions, p. 13.

dozen regular defaulters'.[172] In the early 1970s, the Bar Council wished to convert the smoke room into a secure storage area for books considered likely to be stolen.[173] Users of the smoke room 'would be accommodated elsewhere'.[174] However, a vote was taken against this at a general meeting of the Bar. In 1989 the library committee proposed that the prohibition of smoking in the library should be enforced. The potential damage to books and equipment, the fire risk and the health hazard for non-smokers were all cited as reasons, but some members of the Bar Council were opposed to such a measure. One pointed out that 'over half the library was already a no smoking area, therefore, those who smoked should not cause a problem for those who do not'.[175] Nevertheless, it was decided to enforce the rule and instead to allow members to smoke in the adjoining blue room.[176] Three years later, complaints about barristers smoking in the library came before the Bar Council once more, and it was pointed out that some members of the council were among the frequent transgressors.[177] The availability of a place in which to smoke continued until a general smoking ban was introduced by legislation in the twenty-first century.[178]

Maintaining the Four Courts

Unsurprisingly for an older building with many additions and alterations, problems frequently arose in relation to the physical space and material condition of the Law Library. Even when it was newly renovated there were problems; in 1932, the *Irish Law Times* reported that

> The Law Library is very cold on Mondays and exceedingly 'stuffy' for the remainder of the week. In the lavatory there is a copious supply of hot water in the morning when it is not needed so much, but in the afternoon, when hot water is needed, none is available.[179]

Responsibility for much of the day-to-day maintenance and upkeep of the Law Library (such as lighting and ventilation) fell to the board of works, also known as the commissioners of public works or the OPW.[180] Already by 1935 the OPW reported having had to improve the ventilation in the Law Library.[181] Issues arose at various stages in relation to the ventilation,[182] lighting,[183] clocks,[184]

---

172 B.C.M., 3 Oct. 1968.   173 B.C.M., 23 June 1972.   174 Ibid.   175 B.C.M., 25 Nov. 1989. 176 Ibid.   177 B.C.M., 9 Nov. 1991.   178 The Public Health (Tobacco) (Amendment) Act 2004. 179 (1932) 66 *I.L.T.S.J.* 60 (23 Jan. 1932). It soon afterwards reported that a sub-committee had been appointed to consider the ventilation problems in the Law Library. (1932) 66 *I.L.T.S.J.* 120 (14 May 1932). Improvements were reported in 1934: (1934) 68 *I.L.T.S.J.* 11 (13 Jan. 1934), although the chief justice later complained about ventilation in the Supreme Court: (1934) 68 *I.L.T.S.J.* 301 (3 Nov. 1934).   180 E.g., B.C.M., 15 Oct. 1948; 7 Nov. 1969.   181 Commissioners of Public Works for Ireland, *One hundred and third report* (Dublin, 1935).   182 E.g., B.C.M., 15 Oct. 1948; 19 Jan. 1951.   183 E.g., B.C.M., 1 Dec. 1967; 7 Nov. 1969. B.C.L.C., 18 May 1995.   184 'Clocks in the

bathrooms,[185] telephones[186] robing rooms,[187] catering[188] and smoking in the library.[189] The Bar Council at times found the board slow and difficult to deal with, and one can sense the exasperation in the council's minutes. For example, in 1969 it was recorded that '[i]t now appeared that at long last the board of works were really going to install new lighting in the library'.[190] This was after the attorney general had submitted to the parliamentary secretary a detailed account of the correspondence between the profession and the board to date, and it very much reads like a point near the end of a lengthy saga.

From the seventies on, one of the main complaints in relation to the library was overcrowding, which is discussed further below.

Technology in the Library

Between 1921 and 1999 the technical and communication facilities at the Law Library changed dramatically. This was a result of the Bar Council's continual revision of the facilities throughout the period. As early as the construction of the second Law Library in the 1890s, there were plans to have it 'in telephonic communication with the various courts'.[191] In the late 1920s, a sub-committee of the Bar Council was formed to consider the provision of a phone service in the Library at Dublin Castle.[192] In the 1940s, the phone system in the Four Courts library was apparently chaotic. There were three coin boxes outside the Library, usually staffed by a boy of about sixteen years of age.[193] Another phone and a soundproof booth were added in 1948.[194] Five new telephone extensions were installed in 1973,[195] and more coin-operated phones were installed in 1976.[196] One barrister recalled:

> Four phones. For everybody. So you would be called by the receptionist and there were little boxes, you had a little pigeonhole, and if anybody had phoned for you there was a little note in there so you could check your box every now and again and you would see if somebody phoned you and then you would have to dial up.[197]

In the 1980s a new system was installed, but it was dogged by problems with charging for calls.[198] By the mid-eighties there was one phone between every four members, and by 1987 there was one between two.[199] The same year also saw the

---

Four Courts' (1950) 84 *I.L.T.S.J.* 53 (4 Mar. 1950).   185 B.C.M., 12 May 1986 (women's bathroom); 18 Jan. 1929.   186 B.C.M., 26 Oct. 1984; 9 Feb. 1985.   187 E.g., B.C.M., 31 Mar. 1950; 14 Dec. 1951; 12 Nov. 1981; Bar of Ireland AGM, 19 Dec. 1987 (women's robing room). 188 E.g., B.C.M., 19 Jan. 1951.   189 E.g., B.C.M., 11 Feb. 1927; 3 Oct. 1968.   190 B.C.M., 7 Nov. 1969.   191 *Dublin Evening Telegraph*, 10 Aug. 1895, p. 8.   192 B.C.M., 19 Dec. 1929. 193 MacKenzie, *Lawful occasions*, p. 19.   194 B.C.M., 6 Feb., 24 Mar., 30 Apr. 1948.   195 B.C.M., 9 Mar. 1973.   196 B.C.M., 18 Oct. 1976.   197 B14, describing the late seventies and early eighties. 198 B.C.M., 11 June 1983; 26 Oct 1984; 13 Dec. 1984; 9 Feb. 1985.   199 Bar of Ireland AGM,

introduction of an optional voice mail service for those members who wished to pay for it.[200] The phone system was upgraded again in the 1990s.[201]

Other technologies introduced at different stages in the twentieth century were telex[202] and Xerox machines,[203] photocopiers,[204] dictating machines,[205] fax machines,[206] a video message screen[207] and printers for use with personal laptops.[208] For over twenty-five years there was a single typist in the Library. In 1966 the desirability of a typing pool was raised at an annual general meeting of the Bar.[209] It was estimated that one typist would be needed for every eight members using the service,[210] and the space required to accommodate ten to fifteen new typists proved to be a problem.[211] By 1969 there still was not enough space to establish a full typing pool,[212] and by the late 1970s the limited typing pool was under strain and may not have been accessible to all.[213] The typists were paid directly by those who engaged their services: one barrister recalled that in the mid-eighties 'there was a pool of typists you could pay by the sheet in the Four Courts'.[214] In 1982 one typist left because of the impossibility of collecting payments owed to her.[215] By this stage, some barristers were doing their own typing on manual typewriters in the eighties,[216] and later electronic typewriters.[217]

Around this time, some also began to use personal dictation machines when drafting paperwork, and delivered tape recordings to typists or secretaries on a daily basis. This system in the 1980s was described as follows:

> Barristers would drive around the city of an evening dropping off tapes to widowed ladies who would do the typing.[218]

> Most people had a dictation machine and you dictated onto these mini tapes … I had a share of a secretary … and I would drive to her house and I would drop in two or three tapes maybe of a Monday and then I'd call on a Wednesday to pick that up and I'd drop a couple more tapes and I'd do the same on the Friday and that's the way we all worked. We all had someone who was typing letters for us or documents for us somewhere.[219]

---

19 Dec. 1987.   **200** Ibid.   **201** B.C.M., 1 May 1993; B.C.L.C., 25 Oct. 1995.   **202** B.C.M., 21 Mar., 2 May 1977.   **203** Ibid.   **204** B.C.M., 19 Dec. 1987.   **205** B.C.M., 7 Mar., 11 July 1969. These were the subject of complaints by some Library users.   **206** Bar of Ireland AGM, 19 Dec. 1987.   **207** Ibid.   **208** B.C.L.C., 25 Oct. 1995.   **209** Bar of Ireland AGM, 18 Nov. 1966. **210** B.C.M., 13 Jan. 1967.   **211** Ibid.   **212** B.C.M., 7 Feb. 1969. In the mid-seventies some typists were moved into what had formerly been a space for telephones. B.C.M., 7 Mar., 31 May 1976. **213** Interim report of the sub-committee of the General Council of the Bar of Ireland, 1982. **214** B10. The pool was still very limited in numbers: the sub-committee proposed that the number of typists be raised to six.   **215** B.C.M., 4 Feb. 1982.   **216** B10.   **217** E.g., B.C.M., 8 Apr. 1981. B3 recalled borrowing money to learn how to 'touch type' and carrying out typing jobs to support their income at the Bar in their early years.   **218** B7.   **219** B16.

Others employed their own secretaries to carry out typing and other administrative tasks.[220] These secretaries did not have workspaces in the Law Library but operated from their own homes, from the homes of barristers or from private rented offices:[221]

> Really top barristers like X had a string of secretaries who came into the house.[222]

> People like Y had his own secretary in his house and as I got busy I ended up with my own secretary in my home.[223]

The use of dictaphones lasted beyond the introduction of compact, lightweight personal laptops in the twenty-first century; one interviewee pointed out that 'above a certain age everyone uses the dictaphone'.[224]

The technological advances at the Bar were not limited to telephone systems and dictaphones. As early as 1968, a member of the Bar suggested investigating the feasibility of setting up a computer system for legal work.[225] The Bar Council was of the view that 'these were early days for such studies', but it wrote to the English Bar Council to enquire about developments there.[226] In 1979, the Bar became a subscribing member of the Society for Computers and the Law,[227] and the library committee commenced conducting research into the ways in which barristers might use computers in the course of their work.[228]

In 1980 there were plans to install a computer terminal as a pilot project in conjunction with UCD and the National Board for Science and Technology. It would be set up as a database for Irish constitutional law.[229] However, the funding for the proposed project fell through,[230] the software was deemed 'not very good',[231] and ultimately a Swedish system was preferred. The terminal was installed in 1982 in the Bar Council's room, as it had to be accessible to persons who were not members of the Law Library.[232] A few years later, the librarian feared that members of the Bar might damage it if allowed to operate it,[233] and sought to restrict its used to Library staff. It was hoped to purchase additional machines, to be operated by Library staff. By 1987, a decision was made to install a computerised book issue system.[234]

---

220 B1, B7, B23. 221 They were later accommodated in office facilities in the Law Library's satellite buildings. 222 B7. 223 B16. 224 B24. 225 B.C.M., 3 Oct. 1968. 226 See pp 267–76 for further discussion of relationships with other Bars. 227 In 1970 the Law Society of England and Wales set up a committee to look at the possible uses of computers in solicitors' offices. The Society was then established in 1973 to promote the use and understanding of information technology in the context of the law. See further 'A brief history of SCL – tech law for everyone', www.scl.org/about/history. 228 B.C.L.C., 11 July 1979. 229 B.C.L.C., 30 June 1980. This subject was deemed most suitable because of John Kelly's up-to-date research. 230 B.C.L.C., 29 July, 17 Oct. 1980. 231 B.C.L.C., 14 Oct. 1981. 232 B.C.L.C., 14 Dec. 1981; B.C.M., 1 June 1982. Members of the Bar Council were given a demonstration on how to use it. 233 B.C.L.C., 23 Oct. 1986. 234 Bar of Ireland AGM, 19 Dec. 1987. See further Jennefer Aston, 'From Law Library Society to Law Library: the first 180 years, 1816–1996', *L.I.M.* 11 (2011), 168, at 171.

From the late 1980s, new electronic information systems were developed for the dissemination of case reports, legislation, digests and academic works.[235] 1987 saw the creation of the Bar's first in-house database, the 'judgment information for the Law Library,' known as 'JILL'.[236] The Bar realised that computer databases would have a significant impact on legal research, and one member pointed out that if solicitors had access to databases such as Lexis, barristers would need similar access.[237] Aston points out that '[t]he Library was one of the first Irish libraries to apply new technology to solve the age-old problem of finding information'.[238]

An advisory group was established to advise and support barristers who wished to purchase their own machines,[239] and in 1991, a daily laptop loan service was established.[240] These proved to be very popular, and by 1995 there was considerable pressure on the limited stock.[241] In the same year, formal training on computer-based legal research was introduced for devils.[242] From the mid-1990s, articles in the *Bar Review* and the *Irish Law Times* examined, analysed and explained new technologies for barristers seeking to use personal computers, email and electronic databases.[243] A member of the Library staff described purchasing a computer as 'very much like starting a diet, it's one of those things you can always do tomorrow but you know it will eventually have to be done.'[244] One barrister who purchased their own laptop in the late 1990s described it as a 'huge, big, heavy … lump of a laptop.'[245]

It was around this time that Susskind published his book predicting the impact that information technology would have on the practise of law,[246] and

235 The JILL database contained synopses of all reported and unreported Irish written judgments since 1983. The LEXIS database had full-text versions of various series of law reports. Cian Ferriter, 'On-line: an introduction to electronic legal research', *B.R.* 2:1 (1997), 32, at 33. In 1987 it was noted that 'the JILL system and LEXIS have contributed greatly in areas of information retrieval and research': Bar of Ireland AGM, 19 Dec. 1987. Academics writing in 1994 noted that '[i]nformation technology in the legal services sector is as yet mainly confined to information retrieval and the automation of existing processes and procedures'. This would also appear to have been the case in Ireland. Jeff Watkins and Lynn Drury, 'The pressures on professional life in the 1990s', *Int. J. Leg. Prof.* 1 (1994), 369, at 383. 236 Aston, 'From Law Library Society', at 171. 237 This was at a special meeting of the Bar Council in White's Hotel, Wexford, to which a member of the English Bar, John Toulmin QC, had been invited. B.C.M., 3 May 1986. 238 Aston, 'From Law Library Society', at 171. 239 B.C.M., 13 Oct. 1986. 240 General meeting of the Bar, 31 Oct. 1991. 241 B.C.L.C., 25 Oct. 1995. 242 General meeting of the Bar, 31 Oct. 1991. 243 For example: Cian Ferriter, 'The virtual Law Library', *B.R.* 1:1 (1996), 6; Ferriter, 'On-line'; Jennefer Aston, 'Electronic publishing', *B.R.* 2:6 (1997), 255. There was also a growing number of articles in the *Irish Law Times*, e.g. Darius Whelan, 'Lawyers and the internet', *I.L.T.* (ns) 14 (1996), 212; Dermot Hennessy, 'How to use the internet effectively for legal research', *I.L.T.* (ns) 15 (1997), 214; Barry Phillips, 'Getting the most from the internet', *I.L.T.* (ns) 16 (1998), 150. See ch. 5 for a discussion of the changes in legal practice around this time. 244 Greg Kennedy, 'Buying a computer and other traumatic experiences', *B.R.* 1:2 (1996), 10. 245 B24. 246 Richard E. Susskind, *The future of law: facing the challenges of information technology* (Oxford, 1998). Susskind's main argument, at p. 292, was that 'legal practice and the administration of justice will no longer be dominated by print and paper in tomorrow's legal paradigm. Instead, legal systems of the information society will evolve rapidly under the considerable influence of ever more powerful

members of the Bar engaged with both the challenges and opportunities presented.[247] The Law Library launched its own webpage in 1995,[248] and in its first edition in 1996, the *Bar Review* informed members of the Law Library that email would be available on the Library's networks by the end of the year:

> Documents prepared on a word processor can be sent electronically without the need for printing and faxing/posting, by using electronic mail. Documents in paper form can be converted into electronic format using scanners (similar to those in use at supermarket checkouts) and then stored or sent electronically.[249]

That year, the Law Library 'embarked on a programme of computerisation and training,' beginning with a pilot project in the Church Street building which allowed barristers to access legal databases from their desktop computers. Another pilot involved a dial-in system to allow barristers on circuit to access the Library's databases remotely using a modem.[250] An article in 1997 explained how electronic legal research worked:

> The database may be stored on a CD-ROM (a compact disk similar to a music CD), a 'floppy' disk (a small square disk inserted into the computer) or on a hard disk of a computer (the internal storage space of the machine). If the database is held on a machine away from your office machine or network, you can access it 'on-line' i.e. by requesting and transmitting information down a telephone line connected to the 'remote' machine which stores the material you wish to access.[251]

In the same year, a new computer room was established in the basement of the Law Library, with eight computer terminals, initially only available for word processing.[252] As Ferriter pointed out, these new technologies could impact upon barristers' work patterns:

> Why do your research in a cramped Library when you could do it at home? Why come in to the Library on Friday afternoon to get materials for the weekend when you can access the materials at seven o'clock on Sunday night?[253]

This says much about barristers' work patterns, discussed earlier in chapter five.

---

information technologies. **247** E.g., Cian Ferriter, 'The future of law', *B.R.* 2:5 (1997), 201, who considered that Susskind saw in information technology 'the solution for problems that really lie elsewhere.' **248** Ferriter, 'The virtual Law Library', at 6. **249** Ibid. **250** Ibid. **251** Ferriter, 'On-line', at 32. **252** Aston, 'Electronic publishing', at 256. **253** Ferriter, 'The virtual Law Library', at 7.

Library staff

Integral to the smooth functioning of the Library were its librarians[254] and other staff. As noted above, access to the Library was restricted to barristers. It was the job of one individual sitting near the entrance to ensure that no solicitor or other person gained entry, and to call out the names of barristers who were requested by visitors. Until the mid-twentieth century, the names were called out without the benefit of any sort of public address system, so the person who held this position needed to have a strong voice. Indeed, one holder of this office, John Campion, was described as having a 'clear, far-reaching and well-modulated' voice.[255] The crier sat at a desk on a dais near the entrance and only barristers could pass his desk into the Library. While some barristers described being in fear or in awe of Mr Campion,[256] he was generally described as being very protective of barristers, particularly against irate solicitors.[257] Another crier, Tommy Whelan, was remembered in the following terms by a barrister called in the late sixties:

> There was a fella called Tommy in the Law Library ... and if a solicitor wanted you, you'd to go to Tommy first and he'd say 'Mr. A., jaysus he's out the door.' ... I remember barristers who wouldn't go for coffee without saying to Tommy, 'oh Tommy if someone is looking for me, I'll be in the Bar restaurant'. Just in case a solicitor arrived, called out your name and you weren't answering.

Other barristers recall the staff members known as 'book boys', who were known for their expertise.[258] They would fetch books for barristers and would sometimes also make recommendations. Lindsay describes them as having 'extraordinary' knowledge: '[i]f you asked them for a book dealing with any particular kind of problem, they would immediately find the correct text book.'[259] In a world before computerised legal databases, such knowledge was extremely valuable. MacKenzie notes that the book boys

---

254 Aston, 'From Law Library Society', at 168–71, provides an overview of the individuals who held the office of librarian.   255 O'Higgins, *Double life*, p. 72. McDonnell Bodkin, called in the 1870s, describes 'a big man with a big voice.' McDonnell Bodkin, *Recollections of an Irish judge*, p. 85. See obit., *Irish Times*, 31 Dec. 1948, p. 3. Mr Campion was followed by Joe Kelly, Pat Redmond, Tommy Whelan and Paddy Nulty, several of whom feature in memoirs focusing on the period from the 1930s. See, e.g., Lindsay, *Memories*, p. 100; O'Higgins, *Double life*, p. 72; Noreen Mackey, *The secret ladder* (London, 2005), p. 85 and MacKenzie, *Lawful occasions*, p. 16.   256 Ibid.   257 O'Higgins, *Double life*, p. 72; Comyn, *Their friends at court*, p. 124; Healy, *The old Munster Circuit*, p. 47.   258 Aston, 'From Law Library Society', at 171, notes that they 'had an encyclopaedic knowledge of the stock and were able to locate anything that a member might require.'   259 Lindsay, *Memories*, p. 100.

Were all called by their Christian names. Knowing quite a deal of law, they could find you precedents, that is reported cases, on practically any topic. They knew the year of each Act, they could turn up important sections, and knew the names of the best textbook for each aspect of law.[260]

Lindsay emphasised the book boys' 'efficiency, helpfulness and courtesy'.[261] Another staff member who was admired was Frederick Price, appointed in 1922:[262]

> In the 1940s the whole administration lay upon the shoulders of Mr Fred Price, a tall man in a dark grey suit, whose office was a roll top desk in the right hand corner of the Library. He bought the law reports, collected subscriptions, banked the money, paid the wages and knew the situation of every textbook in the Library. He had no secretary, no typewriter, he did everything by hand, and the place was superbly run.[263]

In one corner of the Library was a cupboard known as 'the shop', which originally sold stationery, stamps, forms and documents[264] and later books, phone tokens, court bands, and collars.[265]

The early telephone systems required operating staff, and a succession of teenage boys were employed as 'phone boys' in the forties, fifties and sixties.[266] By 1969 a telephonist was employed to operate the switchboard,[267] with a second telephonist added four years later.[268] Before the advent of personal computers there were typists, one of whom was unfortunately described as 'not affable and not approachable' and 'intimidating to the younger people'.[269] Other staff members included robing room attendants,[270] whose duties included:

> 1) Robing of new barristers on call. 2) Robing new silks. 3) Purchase of wigs. 4) Purchase of gowns. 5) Distribution of bands daily.[271]

There was no attendant stationed in the ladies' robing room;[272] the women presumably had to make do without this kind of help. By 1980 the robing

---

260 MacKenzie, *Lawful occasions*, p. 17.   261 Lindsay, *Memories*, p. 100.   262 Aston, 'From Law Library Society', at 169.   263 MacKenzie, *Lawful occasions*, p. 15.   264 Ibid., p. 14.   265 Aston, 'From Law Library Society', at 171. It was reported as making a loss in 1980: B.C.M., 12 Dec. 1980. By 1981, 'daily stock checking and cash checking' remedied these losses. B.C.M., 8 Apr. 1981. The shop was broken into in 1985: B.C.M., 9, 20 Feb. 1985. An embargo on recruitment into the civil service meant that no night security staff could be employed. In 1987, it was proposed that credit in the shop should be discontinued. B.C.L.C., 12 Feb. 1987.   266 See, for example, B.C.M., 28 Oct. 1949; 27 Oct. 1950; 2 Feb. 1951; 9 Apr. 1956; 3 May 1963; 26 June 1964.   267 B.C.M., 2 Feb. 1968; 7 Mar. 1969.   268 B.C.M., 5 June 1972.   269 B.C.M., 7 Feb. 1969.   270 Sam Kelly and Vincent Cleary were two such attendants: B.C.M., 9 Apr. 1956.   271 B.C.M., 20 Jan. 1981.   272 Ibid. See ch. 9.

attendant was considered 'a luxury',[273] and it was suggested in 1980 that when long-serving robing room attendant Sam Kelly retired, he should not be replaced.[274]

Longevity of service was common among those who worked in the Law Library. Campion, for example, worked in the Library for fifty years.[275] In 1976, Sam Kelly and Fred Stevens were presented with gold watches to mark their fifty years of service.[276] Pat MacDonald worked in the Library for forty-seven years from 1956.[277] Paddy Nulty worked in the Library for forty-two years.[278] Family connections also seem to have been a feature. For example, Pat MacDonald's grandfather, Pat Geraghty, had worked in the Library for sixty-two years, from 1894,[279] and his twin brother, Albert, also worked in the Library as a book boy.[280] Book boy Pat Redmond's brother, Terry Redmond, operated the legal express from 1964.[281]

As crier, McDonald provided assistance to barristers beyond the Library: 'often I would help out in the barristers homes at weekends or during the vacation with gardening or whatever needed doing'.[282] In some cases, it is clear that individual barristers developed close or affectionate relationships with members of staff. This can probably be traced to a number of factors: the usefulness of the services they provided, their protectiveness of barristers, their provision of service in the domestic sphere, their longevity and thus their familiarity.

A crowded workplace

As discussed in chapter four, the number of persons being called to the Bar was relatively stable from the 1920s up to the late 1960s. Until 1967, an average of twenty-four persons per year were called, and not all of these became members of the Law Library. From about 1968 the numbers began to climb, and there was a three-fold increase in the number of people being called. The Fair Trade Commission in its 1990 report also remarked upon the 'considerable increase' in numbers in the profession, pointing out that the total number of barristers increased by 235% between 1968 and 1990.[283] It is also possible to trace the Library occupancy levels through comments made by interviewed barristers. One, who was called in the mid-sixties, recalled having their own desk right next to their master when called.[284] Another, called in the late sixties, said:

273 B.C.M., 12 Dec. 1980. 274 Ibid. Mr Kelly died soon after this discussion, before his retirement: B.C.M., 20 Jan. 1981. The work was subsequently offered to Pat MacDonald. The staff administrator said it was 'merely a valeting job, there was no work, skilled or otherwise in it'. B.C.M., 22 Jan. 1981. There were complaints from other staff members when they were later expected to cover some of the duties of a 'toilet attendant': B.C.M., 17 Feb. 1982. 275 Sheehy, *May it please the court*, p. 50. 276 B.C.M., 26 Jan. 1976. 277 'A lifetime in the law', *B.R.* 1:2 (1996), 16. He worked as deputy crier, crier, junior dressing room attendant and supervisor. B.C.M., 7 Mar. 1969; 27 May 1982. 278 B.C.M., 7 Feb 1969. 279 'A lifetime in the law', at 16. 280 B.C.M., 2 Feb. 1968. 281 B.C.M., 13 Jan. 1964. 282 'A lifetime in the law'. 283 F.T.C., para 7.28. 284 B6, called in the mid-sixties.

My first seat was at the back wall, and I didn't like where I was sitting and somebody was smoking a pipe beside me and I thought: 'no'. I moved. I think at the time you could just move. There were spare seats, you could actually just get up and move.

In later years there were not enough seats for everyone. Describing the early nineties, one barrister said, 'the place was stuffed and you were lucky to find anywhere to sit'.[285] Descriptions from the seventies and eighties reflected similar realities:

There was a time when I was in the Law Library when it was so crowded that … they almost paid you to share your seat.[286]

By 1990 there would have been 1,000 members … So, there was a real issue about accommodation … if you had a seat, you were definitely sharing it with somebody else or you were squatting on somebody else's seat or whatever. So getting a seat was a big issue.[287]

In 1980 it was pointed out that there was seating in the Library for 268 persons, but a requirement to accommodate 362. The Bar Council estimated that within a year, there would be a need for a further 45–65 seats.[288] The need to expand and improve the facilities was pressing, and the Bar Council considered its mandate as

To invest members' subscriptions in providing space for barristers and in providing a comfortable and quiet environment in which to work with an adequate supply of books and services and with better communications.[289]

In 1984, members of the Bar Council met with the minister for justice to discuss the accommodation problems in the Law Library.[290] Short-term solutions included converting spaces in the library complex into seating areas. For example, there was an expansion into the basement of the Four Courts in the 1980s.[291] However, it was evident that such measures were not sufficient to cater for the increasing numbers of barristers joining the Library each year. In its submission to the Fair Trade Commission, the Bar Council noted that '[t]he

---

285 B22, called in the early nineties. 286 B3. 287 B7. 288 Interim report of the sub-committee of the General Council of the Bar of Ireland, 1982. 289 Ibid. 290 B.C.M., 3 Dec. 1984. This was in the context of the redevelopment of the Four Courts Hotel site, which later became Áras Uí Dhálaigh; see further below. There was speculation that, for example, the public restaurant might be relocated to the new building, thus freeing up space; B.C.M., 3 Dec. 1984. 291 B.C.M., 27 Jan. 1986. This was purchased from the board of works: B.C.M., 17 Sept. 1986. Dressing rooms and bathrooms were relocated there, and the existing robing rooms were converted to additional desk space. B6, B7 and general meeting of the Bar, 21 Nov. 1986. There was some debate over the type of desk space to be installed, as this would affect whether there were 117 or 147 new seats: B.C.M.,

physical fabric of the Library had been put under the greatest of strain'.[292] The Library was becoming an increasingly difficult and uncomfortable place in which to work.[293]

The possibility of small groups of barristers renting private offices outside the Law Library was raised as early as the 1970s. On 14 July 1975 the Bar Council ruled that

> It was inconsistent with membership of the Law Library for two or more barristers to conduct their practice from chambers or offices in association with each other without the consent of the Bar Council.[294]

This meant that applications occasionally came before the council from barristers who wished to take rooms elsewhere. In response to one such query in 1976, the Council resolved that 'ultimately there could be no valid objection to a single barrister having an office in Dublin',[295] although it would be undesirable to share a building where other tenants were 'solicitors, insurance companies, or the like'.[296]

It was the idea of shared facilities that caused the most concern. In 1977, for example, a group of seven senior members of the Bar formed a limited company in order to become a tenant in Dollard house, on Wellington Quay. They planned to share secretarial and other services, share their libraries, and use the space for consultations.[297] The proposal was considered by the Bar Council, several of whom had to excuse themselves from the discussion as they were either part of the group or had been invited to join and had declined. It was generally felt that,

> If this example were followed the cream of talent would be taken from the Library and those remaining would be regarded as second rate. This was contrary to the whole history of the Library where the whole talent of the Bar had been available to any barrister who had a problem; these places would be in competition with the Library.[298]

Six members of the Bar unilaterally took offices at nearby Arran Square in 1991, without having sought advance approval from the Bar Council.[299] One barrister who was involved in this move described feeling

> Just really frustrated at how our lives were being dominated by the fact that we had nowhere to work during the day. You were in the Law Library

10 Apr. 1987. **292** F.T.C., para 7.98. **293** This cannot have been helped by the practice by some members of eating 'full lunches' and drinking coffee at their desks: B.C.M., 29 June 1994; B.C.L.C., 12 May 1994. **294** B.C.M., 16 Feb. 1976. **295** B.C.M., 15 Mar. 1976. **296** Ibid. The consent of the Bar Council should also be obtained before accepting work from another tenant. **297** B.C.M., 4 July 1977. **298** B.C.M., 4 July 1977. A special meeting was called on 10 July 1977 to discuss this. **299** B.C.M., 12 Oct. 1991.

getting nothing done, you've masses of work to do and you're working at home all night because you got nothing done during the day ... There was a lot of fear about at the time. I think people in general were afraid that these would turn into chambers where work would be shared and that the people who were in the Law Library really wouldn't have a chance to compete and I think everyone was afraid it was going to set up a two-tier Bar, the successful people and then the also-rans.

One interviewee was invited to make this move but declined because 'one of the biggest diseases barristers suffer from is inertia'. There was some disgruntlement among members of the Bar who were concerned that this might lead to a chambers-style system:

There was a real concern that that was going to bring out then the concept of chambers. And chambers would see the death knell of the library system.

Other members of the Bar expressed anger about this exodus:

We had one or two general meetings of the Bar ... and there were a lot of angry things said you know, that ... people were out for their own vested self interests ... fear makes people say lots of things that they later regret.

Another described how the move was viewed by some as a 'betrayal of the great traditions of the Irish Bar'.[300] However, the Arran Square occupants agreed to abide by the code of conduct and the professional practices committee accepted this.[301]

It was not only the Dublin-based barristers who were suffering from overcrowding in the 1980s. The Cork Library was under similar pressure, though on a smaller scale. A scheme to purchase new premises was proposed in 1985 but involved considerable expenditure,[302] and was later dubbed 'over-ambitious and not financially viable'.[303] In early 1986 a 'scaled-down scheme' was proposed, which would provide offices for those who wished to pay for them, and open-plan desks for others. The plan was based on having fifty subscribing members, and although at that time there were only thirty-five in Cork, it was projected that this number would grow.[304] As with the Dublin Bar, opinion in Cork was divided as to the desirability of any change.[305] The costs appear to have been underestimated and the demand from Cork members overestimated.[306] After some vacillation,[307] this scheme too was abandoned.[308]

300 B26.   301 B.C.M., 9, 30 Nov. 1991.   302 B.C.M., 26 July 1985.   303 B.C.M., 27 Jan. 1986.
304 B.C.M., 11, 27 Jan. 1986.   305 B.C.M., 12 Apr. 1986.   306 B.C.M., 30 July 1986.
307 B.C.M., 2, 10, 17 Sept.; 6, 21 Oct. 1986.   308 B.C.M., 17, 28 Nov. 1986.

New premises for the Law Library

Aside from internal expansion and the creation of new desk spaces, from time to time suggestions had been made over the years regarding the expansion of the Library into other premises. For example, one barrister wrote that he had 'often expressed the view that when the Henrietta Street buildings were for sale the benchers should have tried to purchase them and convert them into chambers. It would have been quite convenient to Green Street and the Four Courts'.[309] In the late 1970s, the Four Courts Hotel was for sale.[310] It was too expensive for the Bar to purchase and renovate,[311] and was bought by the State[312] and developed as Áras Uí Dhálaigh. One barrister expressed regret that '[w]e didn't buy the damn thing'.

By the late 1980s concerted efforts began to be made to expand beyond the confines of the Four Courts complex. The Land Registry building on Inns Quay was mooted in the 1980s[313] and again in 1990.[314] Other nearby premises which were considered included the Ormond Hotel,[315] Beresford Place,[316] River House,[317] Dollard House on Wellington Quay[318] and Inns Court on Winetavern St.[319] Proposals to purchase property and expand the Law Library to satellite buildings received mixed reactions from members of the Bar, and any move in this direction was mired in internal controversy. Concerns were frequently expressed about the evolution of a 'two-tier Bar',[320] and there were fears about the collapse of the library system:

> Proposals which allowed people to operate from offices outside the Library would mean that the people concerned would be lost to the Library completely and thereby undermine one of its principal strengths.[321]

Others wondered about a possible 'cartel aspect'.[322] There was also the issue of cost. Members of the Bar would ultimately have to pay for any changes, and therefore needed to be convinced that it would be worthwhile.[323] Opinion was

---

309 Lindsay, *Memories*, p. 101. The potential purchase of property on Henrietta Street was discussed by the Bar Council in 1983: B.C.M., 11 Mar. 1983.   310 B.C.M., 4 July 1977. 311 B.C.M., 22 Sept. 1975.   312 B.C.M., 5 Apr. 1976.   313 B.C.M., 27 Jan. 1986. It was noted that both the taoiseach and the chief justice had been sympathetic to the idea of the Bar obtaining accommodation in the Public Record Office or the Land Registry, but, as the Bar Council pointed out 'since there was now no money the move of these premises would be put on the long finger. 314 Bar of Ireland AGM, 17 Dec. 1990.   315 B.C.M., 20, 22, 27 Jan. 1986. An offer of £5,000 had been made for an option on the Ormond building.   316 B.C.M., 20 Jan. 1986.   317 B.C.M., 27 July, 12 Oct., 30 Nov. 1991.   318 This was rejected and was later described as 'a full London-style chambers proposal.' B.C.M., 12 Dec. 1988.   319 B.C.M., 8, 12 Dec. 1988.   320 B.C.M., 12 Dec. 1988.   321 Ibid.   322 Ibid.   323 At a general meeting of the Bar on 27 Nov. 1986, for example, concern had similarly been expressed about the increase in library subscriptions, the cost of the recent extension to the basement, and the potential cost of purchasing a new premises.

also divided over whether any new premises should supplement or replace the existing Law Library.[324]

By 1990 the Bar Council recognised that the existing space was 'the absolute minimum that could be tolerated'.[325] As one barrister recalled,

> Much as there was fun in the Library and there was a nice sense of 'this is the way it's always been', it couldn't work with the numbers, it couldn't work with the work that was being required to be done.[326]

It was unanimously agreed at the 1990 AGM that the Bar Council should investigate the possibility of acquiring further space within the Four Courts complex,[327] and a sub-committee was established to look at acquiring new premises for expansion.[328] At a general meeting of the Bar in July 1991, it was indicated that two premises were being considered by the sub-committee,[329] and members were warned that subscriptions might rise by 50%.[330] While members of the Bar and Bar Council waited to hear what proposals would be put forward by the premises committee, there was some fear that in the interim more barristers would continue to move unilaterally to new premises.[331] There was also some urgency on a financial side, because of specific taxation incentives that would lapse in 1993.

In May 1992 the committee proposed the establishment of a 'single-tier Law Library to be located at Arran Square', with differing levels of financial contribution from barristers at different stages in their careers.[332] One barrister later described the plan as

> A bigger Law Library if you like, more space ... but it still would have everyone doing the same kind of thing so instead of having a very narrow desk you'd have had ... a big space.[333]

Although the report was adopted in principle by the Bar Council, it was met with mixed opinions. One member pointed out that one of the disadvantages of a 'single tier' system was that it might not stop the 'top flight barristers' from moving out of the Library and into private offices.[334] Other members agreed that some barristers would wish to provide a higher level of service to clients, and that

---

324 B.C.M., 20 Jan. 1986. 325 Bar of Ireland AGM, 17 Dec. 1990. 326 B26. 327 Bar of Ireland AGM, 17 Dec. 1990. 328 B.C.M., 10 Jan. 1991. 329 General meeting of the Bar, 20 July 1991. 330 One premises under consideration was River House on Chancery Street: B.C.M., 27 July 1991. Within six months, a decision had been taken to 'shelve' this plan. B.C.M., 30 Nov. 1991. Arran Square was also under consideration: B.C.M., 12 Oct. 1991. Given the significance of any potential expenditure, it was decided that the Bar as a whole ought to be consulted. The committee circulated a questionnaire to members seeking views on whether to raise subscriptions significantly in order to purchase new premises, but the response rate was low and opinion was evenly divided. 331 B.C.M., 7 Mar. 1992. 332 B.C.M., 2 May 1992. 333 B27. 334 Ibid.

'imposing uniformity' would partially defeat the purpose of the move. It was suggested that it would hold back barristers at the top end, while imposing a burden on those with more modest practices. It was also pointed out that the proposal did not consider the position of 'country members'.[335]

The plans were debated at length and revised during 1992,[336] and it was agreed to put a range of proposals before a general meeting of the Bar in July 1992. Several interviewees recalled that junior members of the Bar 'voted it down because they thought all the leaders of the Bar were going to jump ship and go into this other place'. Another said, 'junior people didn't have the money and it wasn't particularly well sold to us'. By contrast, some senior members of the Bar would have preferred 'to pay even more again to get something bigger'. Although the Bar rejected the proposals for Arran Square, it was agreed that there should be 'a sort of round robin or a survey on the attitudes of the Bar to sharing facilities'.[337] Members of the Bar were then surveyed over the 1992 long vacation, and those who responded[338] were generally found not to favour a move to Arran Square. However, it was clear by this stage that there an impetus for change. As one member of the Bar reflected, '[i]t was unrealistic ... They didn't change but the world changed and then they had to change with it.'[339]

While the debate about Arran Square was floundering, negotiations were afoot in relation to some property on nearby Church Street. One barrister recalled 'there was a big group of us trying to get the Bar to buy up a lot of the vacant property to set up a really new big modern Law Library ... but there was huge resistance to that at the time.' Those who were determined to pursue this project were divided on whether to formally bring their proposal before the Bar Council. Two adjoining sites on Church Street were purchased by a member of the Bar in 1992. He was given authorization by the chairman of the Bar Council, although the treasurer of the council was not fully informed about the project.

A document relating to the site was circulated to the Bar Council in October, and the chairman explained that the Bar would have an option either to develop the site or hold it as a land bank.[340] This proposal was discussed at length and a range of opinions were expressed as to its desirability and viability.[341] A barrister who was privy to the discussions at the time observed that '[t]here was a rump in the Bar Council, they didn't want anything to happen'. Unlike the Arran Square plan, which had envisaged everyone having access to the same resources, the Church Street plan was different. One interviewee summed it up as follows:

> When you started into practice, you would have had a desk and you would only pay a small amount for your desk but maybe when you were in five

335 Ibid.   336 B.C.M., 3 June, 5, 20 July 1992.   337 B5.   338 The response rate was about 50%.
339 B17.   340 B.C.M., 17 Oct. 1992. He suggested that members of the Bar who did not wish to purchase premises such as those proposed for Arran Square could have a rental option in any potential development at Church St.   341 B.C.M., 17 Oct., 13 Nov. 1992.

years you could share maybe an office with two others, and you would have one secretarial space between two. And then as you went on as you wanted to have a suite with meeting rooms you could pay more for that. So that we would have kept the whole Bar together but would have been able to keep young people there at a lesser price than the very successful people who were paying much, much more for a much enhanced facility.[342]

Fear about evolving into chambers-style arrangements partially drove the move to new premises. As one barrister observed, 'providing the buildings in Church Street was deliberately done by the Bar Council to avoid the Bar breaking into chambers'.[343]

Planning permission was sought and granted within six months,[344] and plans for developing the site proceeded quite quickly in order to avail of tax incentives.[345] The Church Street building opened in 1994. For the first time, the Bar provided its own facilities rather than relying on those provided by the state. There was double tax relief available which made renting an office relatively affordable.[346] One barrister who had been involved in the developments recalled that the Church Street building 'was so successful there was a waiting list.'

> The Church Street building … was great because barristers then could have a room and you could have two or three rooms in a set. The barristers worked independently but they could share some facilities like a secretary if they wanted to, maybe fax facilities and things like that in those days.[347]

Some thought that the move 'should have happened years before',[348] and others expressed regret that plans to transform the site of the state-owned Jameson Distillery into a 'legal quarter'[349] were never realised.

The Church Street building was followed a couple of years later by the development of another site on the same street, which became known as the Distillery building. This development was described as 'a much bigger operation'[350] and 'an awfully big enterprise'.[351] The success of the Church Street project meant that financing this second, bigger premises was much more straight-forward, and one barrister who was involved at the time recalled an 'aggressive bidding war' between financial institutions. The site was purchased by the Bar in the spring of 1995 and the building was soon ready for occupation. In a 1997 editorial, the *Bar Review* noted that the completion of the work at the Distillery site represented 'a watershed in the development of the Bar.'[352] It continued:

---

342 B16. 343 B10. 344 B.C.M., 16 Jan., 20 Mar., 1 May, 19 June, 26 July 1993. 345 B.C.M., 12 Mar. 1994. 346 B7, B27, B11. 347 B23. 348 B18. 349 B5. 350 B23. 351 B7. 352 Editorial, 'Developing the Law Library', *B.R.* 2:7 (1997), 265 at 265.

For the first time since the founding of the Law Library there will be a general seating and library space for members at a remove from the Four Courts; for the first time all the membership of the Bar will, regardless of physical location, be able to access the same suite of electronic services through the 'virtual Law Library'.[353]

The new, modern workspaces were described as bringing about 'a revolution in the concept of the Law Library'.[354] Those who availed of the new spaces were pleased with them:

> On days that I wasn't in court it meant that I could do much more effective work in my office in the Distillery building, whereas before that it was very hard, it had got very hard to work in the Law Library.

> It was somewhere to put your books, somewhere to do work.

> As soon as I moved into my own office ... I was able to have people in for meetings ... the work could be done overnight, the stuff was going back, you're suddenly being able to do stuff by email. Everything was suddenly much more efficient, and I had a much better quality of life.

The move to new premises was described by some as a 'substantial achievement',[355] and 'very much part of the move to modernity'.[356]

* * *

The Law Library as a workplace was continually evolving in the twentieth century. The first major changes were necessitated by the 1922 destruction, and later changes were precipitated by advances in technology and increasing numbers of barristers. The major developments impacted on the way barristers carried out their work. They also impacted upon the social aspects of the Bar, including whether devils could sit near their masters, or whether people completed paperwork at home or in the Library.

Complaints about the Law Library were a constant feature of life at the Bar from the 1920s, though the exact nature of complaints varied. Members advocated for better, cleaner, brighter, more efficient and more technologically advanced workspace; they argued for facilities for robing, reading, storage and socialising. Incrementally, the Law Library evolved from a few cramped and temporary rooms in the King's Inns in the early twenties to a multi-site, technology-enabled complex of buildings by the end of the century.

353 Ibid.   354 Ibid. By Nov. 1998, almost all of the new workspaces had been rented: 'Distillery reception', *B.R.* 3:3 (1998), 117.   355 B26.   356 B7.

CHAPTER TWELVE

Networks at the Bar

Introduction

As self-employed individuals, it was important for barristers to find ways to connect with colleagues. Working at the Bar was, to some degree, dominated by both formal and informal networks. Barristers dined together, drank together, played sports together. Many developed strong and long-lasting friendships, and some had sexual or romantic relationships with their colleagues. Later in the century, increasing diversity and professionalism changed the nature of socialising and networking at the Bar. While the social side of the Bar was undoubtedly good fun for many, it also served an important purpose in the development of professional identity and the transmission of norms and values.[1] As one of the interviewees for this book commented, 'within the fun there is also a lot of learning as to how things are done and what's the norm.'[2] Flood observes that professional knowledge 'is not merely absorbed through individual study but must be augmented by social interaction with those who will show the correct deportment and responses in the professional community.'[3] This can also be viewed in terms of Bourdieu's theory of social capital; the idea that individual social capital derives from social status, and empowers individuals to exert control over resources. Bourdieu also stressed the importance of securing social capital through the generation of good will.[4] Put another way, Morison and Leith note,

> Given the lack of independence, barristers must be ever careful to succeed in interpersonal relationships: failure to do so could result in lost work, and could mitigate against future advancement.[5]

As will be seen, these interpersonal networks took many forms.

---

1 See further, ch. 16. 2 B24. 3 John Flood, 'Traditions, symbols, and the challenges of researching the legal profession: the case of the cab rank rule and the Bar's responses', *Int. J. Leg. Prof.* 29:1 (2022), 3, at 22. 4 Pierre Bourdieu, *Distinction: a social critique of the judgement of taste* (London, 1986) and Pierre Bourdieu 'The forms of capital' in John G. Richardson (ed.), *A handbook of theory and research for the sociology of education* (New York, 1986), pp 241–58. See Ben Fine, *Theories of social capital: researchers behaving badly* (London, 2010). 5 John Morison and Philip Leith, *The barrister's world and the nature of law* (Basingstoke, 1992), p. 18.

Family and social networks

Reflecting on his experiences as a King's Inns student in the early seventies, Colum Kenny wrote that 'family and political connections seemed to provide special advantages when it came to professional advancement'.[6] Such connections could certainly be extremely useful in establishing oneself at the Bar, and the importance of having a network at the early career stages was discussed in chapter three. As well as family connections, either within the two branches of the legal profession or in relevant fields such as insurance, other useful networks may have been developed through school,[7] university, church,[8] sports[9] or time spent working in other fields before joining the Bar. Friendships formed while studying at the King's Inns were considered important and were maintained by many barristers throughout their careers.[10] A barrister who was called in the late eighties said:

> There were different ways of getting on. You were either connected to people in insurance or banking or to solicitors' firms or you were connected to politics and you were going to get on in that way or indeed you were connected to your own chums from school and you were going to get on.[11]

There was certainly a perception that having 'good contacts' was important for a successful career at the Bar; for example, speaking in the Dáil in 1995, Derek McDowell said

> It is essential … that to become a good barrister, one must have decent contacts. This, in turn, implies or suggests that one must have contacts in the legal profession, in business or with people who are prepared to push business, directly or indirectly.[12]

Not everyone had networks in the legal professions which they could tap into. Sometimes would-be barristers were warned of the risks for those who were unconnected. For example, in his biography of John A. Costello, called in 1914, McCullough writes: '[w]ith no connections in the legal profession, Costello was warned he was mad to try to make a career in law.'[13] Another barrister, called in the forties, recalled:

---

6 Colum Kenny, *Tristram Kennedy and the revival of Irish legal training, 1835–1885* (Dublin, 1996), p. x.   7 B13 commented: 'some of these private schools … will meet at the beginning of the year and invite the new boys … out for a pint, you know, and the old boys from the schools.'   8 See pp 76–8, where it was suggested that some Protestant solicitors preferred to brief Protestant barristers. 9 See further, pp 254–6.   10 B6, B11.   11 B13.   12 Dáil Éireann select committee on legislation and security (5 Dec. 1995).   13 David McCullagh, *The reluctant taoiseach: a biography of John A. Costello* (Dublin, 2011), p. 25. His first year as a barrister seemed to bear out those warnings, as he

I knew that it was not going to be easy and that there was a long arduous road ahead of me, with no tradition in my family of law, something which was regarded as very important at that time.[14]

Bacik et al. found in their survey of practising barristers at the turn of the century that a 'surprisingly high number of respondents' reported that they had 'no previous links with the legal profession'.[15] Those without family connections were often acutely aware of the perceived advantages enjoyed by others, and were at times resentful of what they considered unwarranted success. For example, interviewees commented:

I've seen colleagues going in who weren't a wet day there, and given loads of work because they've families and everything. And my goodness … the neck of them.

It certainly makes your life easier … I saw good fellows come to the Bar with me and fail and I saw poor enough fellows succeed because they had family connections.

Some barristers were conscious of their own advantage in this regard, for example:

Because my mother had been at the Bar some people knew her – so that helped, and because my master was who he was – that helped.

Others who had strong family connections did not consider these to be relevant factors in their success, and ascribed their career progression to talent, good luck, or a combination of both.[16]

Political connections

It is clear from chapters four and ten that many barristers were politically active and politically connected. One barrister commented:

earned 'a grand total of 5 guineas.' However, within five years he had established a successful practice. Patrick Lindsay, *Memories* (Dublin, 1992), p. 95, wrote that by the forties, Costello was 'the busiest man in the Library, but never too busy to offer a helping hand to even the most junior member.'   **14** Lindsay, *Memories*, p. 95.   **15** Bacik, Costello and Drew, *Gender injustice*, p. 221. They also found that women were slightly less likely to have family connections.   **16** E.g., O'Higgins, *Double life*, p. 73, described the Bar as 'a profession in which success will depend on his personal knowledge, skill and experience.' Family connections or networks are not mentioned as relevant factors. O'Higgins was called to the Bar by his great-uncle, Chief Justice O'Sullivan. On his very first day in the Law Library, he received a brief from Niall McLoughlin of Arthur Cox, who was the master to Tom's brother Michael. His uncle, the chief justice, called him to his office on the same day and gave him a cheque for £50. He also mentions how straightforward it was for him to choose a circuit on which to practise; his father was TD for Laois-Offaly, so he went for the Midland

There was also a lot of politics which was fun. A lot of barristers were involved in politics. I was involved in politics. There was a huge number of colleagues who you know were seriously involved in politics and I got to know a lot of people.[17]

Some were conscious that political connections could help their career progression. For example:

My father had said to me – without knowing much about anything – he did say 'if you join one of the cumanns out in UCD you'll do much better at law'.

Political patronage was certainly a factor in some barristers' success, and was seen as essential for securing much-coveted state work.[18] One barrister, describing his practice in the thirties and forties, wrote:

The criminals I prosected were nil. Employment as a prosecuting counsel is the reward which the political party in power gives to practising barristers whose nationalism consists in helping to keep that party in office. In that respect, I am not such a nationalist.[19]

Another barrister who joined the Bar in the late forties similarly commented,

To be politically identified then was not a hindrance to practice, but it was a complete obstacle to getting state work if you were on the wrong side. This was accepted at the Bar. No one questioned that when there was a change of government that the state work went to different barristers.[20]

A barrister who was called in the fifties similarly said of state work,

You didn't qualify for that unless you went with a prevailing power … unless you prostrated yourself … before them you didn't get any work.[21]

The converse of this was, of course, the risk of losing state work when there was a change in government. McEnery wrote:

A whole crowd of barristers from the attorney general down who had been appearing as state counsel would now feel the draught of unemployment

---

Circuit. 'Already I knew from my father of several solicitors who, on my call to the Bar, had expressed interest in me, with the implied, if not actually articulated, promise of some work', p. 76. He frequently did work for a solicitor who was also his father's election agent and legal advisor when it came to constituency matters, p. 77. **17** B10. **18** See ch. 3 and 6. **19** Bernard Shillman, 'Every journey has an end', NAI PRIV1367/11, p. 41. **20** 'Ralph Sutton, SC, called to the Bar, July 1948', *B.R.* 4:3 (1999), 152. **21** B15.

from that direction, and would be supplanted by a crowd of new barristers who were known to be or supposed to be supporters of the party of the new government.[22]

Sometimes people wrote to government ministers to lobby for state work based on political affiliations. When a Fianna Fáil supporter wrote to Taoiseach Jack Lynch in the 1960s seeking support for the appointment of one of his colleagues as prosecutor for county Mayo, Lynch replied:

> There is no specific appointment as public prosecutor. I take it that what Mr X is interested in is being briefed by the attorney general in criminal prosecution. This is a matter for the attorney general and you can be assured that the Fianna Fáil national executive has no say in it. I will however pass on your representations on behalf of Mr X to the attorney general.[23]

In subsequent correspondence, it transpired that the individual in question had already been appointed by the attorney general;[24] perhaps more than one person had been lobbying on his behalf.

Timing could be important, and if a vacancy arose it was sometimes necessary to move quickly to secure an appointment. In 1970, Minister for Lands Sean Flanagan[25] wrote to Minister for Justice Des O'Malley, stating: 'I understand there is a vacancy for prosecuting counsel in County Donegal ...'[26] before recommending a specific individual who he described as 'a very capable man'. This recommendation was passed on to the attorney general, but as it turned out, a different appointment had already been made.[27] In another example of a government minister recommending a potential prosecutor to the minister for justice, Brian Lenihan, minister for transport, wrote of one individual 'I know him personally and can recommend him with confidence'.[28] The barrister in question was twenty-four years of age and had been called to the Bar just two years previously, but was added to the panel of state prosecutors on the basis of this recommendation.[29]

Later in the 1970s, Fine Gael barrister and TD John M. Kelly commented that when he was at the Bar, and Fianna Fáil was in power,

---

22 McEnery, 'Look back', p. 152.　23 Jack Lynch to Patrick J. Berrins, 16 Oct. 1970, NAI 2003/4/127. Aindrias Ó Caoimh was the attorney general.　24 Att. Gen. to sec., Dept. Taoiseach, 30 Oct. 1970, NAI 2003/4/127.　25 Flanagan was a qualified solicitor and had studied at UCD: Diarmaid Ferriter, 'Flanagan, Seán', *D.I.B.*　26 Sean Flanagan to Des O'Malley, 31 Dec. 1970, NAI 2003/4/127.　27 O'Malley to Flanagan, 5 Jan. 1971 and Colm Condon to Flanagan, 7 Feb. 1971, NAI 2003/4/127.　28 Brian Lenihan to Colm Condon, 26 June 1972, NAI 2003/4/127. See also Lenihan to Condon, 30 Aug. 1972, NAI 2003/4/127.　29 Condon to Lenihan, 21 Aug. 1972,

There was a total exclusion of anybody who did not belong to the Soldiers of Destiny, who bore the stain of original sin of membership of Fine Gael or the Labour Party. There was total exclusion of people who had no politics and who could not bring themselves to go through the motions of pretending that they had and this was most unjust of all.[30]

It was generally accepted that political connections were also a route to judicial appointments.[31] One interviewee commented, for example:

I never minded people being members of Fianna Fail, Fine Gael or their being made judges, well they'd put their time into the party good luck to them was my view of that ... I didn't think it was unfair ... I didn't see anything wrong with it. I was free to do the same thing if I wanted to. I didn't. That was my choice.[32]

Political networks also manifested themselves in other ways at the Bar. In a letter to Jack Lynch TD in 1972, one barrister referred to a circular letter Lynch had sent, requesting funds for Fianna Fail's EEC campaign. The barrister wrote:

I wholeheartedly endorse the views of the Fianna Fáil and Fine Gael parties regarding entry into the EEC. Financial circumstances at the Bar can be affected to a great extent by the allocation of state work. The lack of state work can be very detrimental, both in financial and experience terms to any young barrister. Perhaps in different circumstances I would have found it financially possible to support your campaign.[33]

The clear implication was that this individual would not support the political campaign because he had not received any state work. One barrister who was also an elected TD recalled that when he voted against the Taoiseach, he was removed from the panel of one of the leading insurance companies. He had essentially put all his eggs into this basket, so the withdrawal of this strand of work was a significant blow to his practice.[34]

Eating and drinking

A graduate of the King's Inns must have attended the prescribed number of formal dinners before being awarded the Barrister-at-Law degree. This was a long-established custom, although the dinners were temporarily suspended

NAI 2003/4/127.   30 Dáil Éireann deb., vol. 298, no. 8 (20 Apr. 1977).   31 See generally Paul C. Bartholomew, *The Irish judiciary* (Dublin, 1971) and Jennifer Carroll MacNeill, *The politics of judicial selection in Ireland* (Dublin, 2016).   32 B8.   33 Letter to Jack Lynch, 25 Apr. 1972, NAI 2003/4/127.   34 David Andrews, *Kingstown republican* (Dublin, 2007), p. 96.

during times of turmoil, such as during the Civil War[35] and the Second World War.[36] The dinners were intended to be collegiate occasions at which aspiring barristers might learn from established practitioners. Writing in the 1960s, Mackey observed that

> The requirement of eating dinners is a relic of the days, which indeed lasted into modern times, when there was no set course of legal study and the embryo barrister was expected to befit himself for his avocation by tasting the Attic salt of the disputations of his elders, and garnering the learned crumbs which dropped from their prandial discourse.[37]

In the 1980s, representatives from the university law schools expressed criticism of the 'dubious educational value'[38] of the custom of dining.

Reminiscences about the culinary standards of these occasions were, with some notable exceptions,[39] less than effusive. The wine served was usually praised, for quantity if not always for quality. Barristers who were interviewed for this book had mostly positive experiences of dining at King's Inns. One commented that they enjoyed the formality,[40] but others questioned its utility:

> If you had dinner with the benchers at the King's Inns as a student, if you wanted to go to the toilet, you'd ask permission of the benchers ... A message would be sent to Mr. Justice X, you know. What the hell was that for?[41]

Some students appreciated the novelty of dining and the camaraderie:

> The dinners ... were eccentric, they were new to us. The idea of a formal dinner that you had to go to as part of your studies when there was beer and wine available ... that was just fairly magical really.[42]

Others enjoyed the drinking culture that was an integral part of the experience:

> Good God almighty, how we drank ... you get free wine, free beer, free wine and then of course you'd stumble down to the King's Inns pub down at the end and you get to know people ... It's great fun.

This tradition of formal dining did not necessarily end when one was called to the Bar. The culture of communal dining on circuit was examined in chapter

35 McEnery, *Look back*, p. 50.   36 Rex Mackey, *Windward of the law* (2nd ed., Dublin, 1991), p. 98.
37 Ibid., pp 22–3.   38 Fair Trade Commission, *Report of study into restrictive practices in the legal profession* (Dublin, 1990), para. 7.51.   39 MacKenzie, for one, described the food as 'excellent'. Patrick MacKenzie, *Lawful occasions: the old Eastern Circuit* (Cork, 1991), p. 53.   40 B6.   41 B20.
42 B18.

seven, and barristers also continued to attend dinners at the King's Inns throughout their careers, either as part of the scheduled dining for students, or to mark certain occasions, such as benchings, or visits by members of other Bars and benches.[43]

In addition to the more formal dining occasions, the importance of informal socialising was highlighted by a number of interviewees, for example:

> Friendships are forged and that's very important in a high stress environment, that people actually get to let their hair down and get to know each other in a different environment and learn a bit about each other personally ... You'd hear so many stories about things that happened in court.[44]

As Morison and Leith observe, barristers were not office-bound, and had 'many opportunities to meet with colleagues in a collegiate atmosphere and discuss the various happenings in the courts and such like'.[45]

Many barristers mention going out to lunch or dinner with colleagues to celebrate winning or settling a case. This might involve casual drinks in the Four Courts bar or a local pub, or it could be something more elaborate such as dinner in a city-centre hotel or restaurant. One barrister recalled:

> If a trial came to an end, a long trial or for example if something unexpectedly settled and people had money in their pocket they'd say, 'right, we'll bring you out for lunch' ... I can't remember what the case was, but we had been scheduled to do something and then it came to an end and those were the days when people didn't have mounds of paperwork to get back to or the next trial starting the next day so they would go for a good old lunch and have great fun.[46]

There was also a tradition of regular Friday night drinks for some members of the Bar:

> There was a big social side, I think. They used to go down to the bar ... and you would have a good number on the weekends, the Friday nights, go down there and then they'd go off, somewhere.[47]

---

43 B3. Barristers interviewed for this book mentioned special occasions such as 'people taking silk and people taking benches.' See ch. 13 for examples of dining with visiting Bars.   44 B24. Although most interviewees mentioned lunches, dinners and drinks, B22 said that sometimes barristers also met for breakfast or brunch: 'They might come in the morning and do a bit of work and then ... there was quite a few of them who would go off for breakfast together you know and have their nice full Irish breakfast before they went into court.'   45 Morison and Leith, *Barrister's world*, p. 13.   46 B24.   47 B23.

> Maybe we'd go for a drink on a Friday evening … or very frequently we'd go to lunch on Friday … It was great fun.[48]

> People who were within the same area of practice who might have had occasionally reason … to go out to lunch on a Friday and if you settled a case, you know, you might go off with the people, both sides very often.[49]

Several barristers interviewed for this book mentioned the prevalence of the drinking culture at the Bar, something explored in chapter five. There were perceived to have been regional differences when it came to the drinking culture. Describing the social scene at the Cork Bar around the early seventies, one barrister recalled:

> Circuit dinners twice a year where everyone would have a good lash at it. When the High Court would come to Cork there'd be dinner or the seniors who were all away from home might ask you out to dinner in a restaurant in Cork and you'd go and there'd be a bit of drinking there and that might be a bit conspicuous.

Another who was called around the same period said, 'I think Cork didn't have a drinking tradition. Dublin had more of it … It didn't have a drinking tradition and largely because most of us were busy, there wasn't time to do it. The idea of a drink at lunch time was out, just didn't exist.'

There were performative aspects to the drinking and dining culture at the Bar, and the subtle power imbalances manifested themselves in different ways.[50] For example, junior members of the Bar often found that their drinks and meals were paid for by more established colleagues:

> If you went out with older people who were doing it, they would always pay … They would always pick up the tab for dinner … and that was nice.[51]

This could be a combination of generous collegiality and conspicuous consumption, and it was particularly evident from the 1980s onward, with some individuals wishing to be perceived as generous, which implied wealth, success and status.[52] In their study of barristers in the early nineties, Morison and Leith observed that when they went to pubs where barristers drank, they found it impossible to buy a round of drinks: '[t]he competition among barristers to treat an ever-increasing circle was intense'.[53] One interviewee recalled being taken to lunch by a more established colleague:

---

48 B1. 49 B11. 50 For further discussion of the performative side of the Bar, see p. 128. 51 B22. 52 See ch. 7. 53 Morison and Leith, *Barrister's world*, p. 35.

He was very, very good to me and I remember he would always take myself
out, myself and another junior counsel out for lunch ... there was an awful
lot of people who would just say 'take young so-and-so along to the lunch'
... and so there was multi-generation friendships.[54]

As discussed in chapter three, for many people the master-devil relationship
did not end when the formal period of pupillage ended. Many engaged in the
tradition of having dinner or lunch together to mark the end of each legal year:

The lunch was great, the barristers' lunch, the devils' lunch, the end of
term lunch. Fantastic networking event. Information gathering event.
You'd meet so many other barristers. It was only barristers, it wasn't
solicitors. So it's not networking in that sense but you'd get to know
colleagues, older and younger, so you'd be exposed to a lot of people with
a lot of experience.[55]

The tradition was that the master would host and therefore pay for dinner for as
many of their former devils as were able to attend.[56]

The gendered aspects of drinking and dining with Bar colleagues were
highlighted by several interviewees:

Even the Friday night going to the pub was gendered ... women can join
in but it was always seen as a male thing.

There was quite a bit [of socialising], I think, I think there was one or two
of us because we were young and we were okay looking so we were invited
around ... every Friday, we went to the Chancery Inn.

Women sometimes experienced inappropriate or uncomfortable interactions on
these nights out, as discussed in chapter nine.

Sports

There were a small number of sporting societies at the Bar. The most popular,
for much of the twentieth century, was the Bar golf society. It was active
throughout the war years, despite the challenges of transportation faced by
members. It frequently hosted other Bar golf societies, and members travelled
to play matches.[57] Barristers also mentioned informal groups for soccer, Gaelic
games and rugby.[58] One interviewee talked about the strength of these groups
who travelled and socialised together.[59] They described how their involvement
with the sports groups helped them:

---

54 B7.   55 B24.   56 B11, B7.   57 See further, ch. 13.   58 E.g., in 1982 the Bar Council
subvented a home match between the Bar rugby club and the Liverpool Bar rugby club, B.C.M., 2
Apr. 1982.   59 B13.

If you engaged yourself in the sports, that, I suppose, gave you a familiarity or made you at least known to some of the others so that helped.[60]

I was a little bit lucky I suppose because I was playing a bit of rugby ... I'd say that was a bit of an introduction for me.

There was a rugby club and I played in that and there was a soccer club and I played in that.

Others mentioned membership of the Bar cricket club, which in 1982 hosted members of the Australian Bar cricket club at the King's Inns.[61] A 1952 article in the *Irish Law Times* also said that 'table-tennis, bowls and croquet have their devotees' among the legal profession. Barristers who played tennis were often members of the Fitzwilliam Tennis Club, and on several occasions lawn tennis teams representing the Irish Bar played against the English Bar.[62] Horse racing was also popular among barristers. MacKenzie, who began practising in the forties, recalled that many of his colleague were 'extremely interested in racing'.[63]

Each March and June in the Law Library sweeps were held on the grand national and derby. These events were organised by the youngest juniors, presumably because they had time to do this. Invariably, to everyone's annoyance, the sweeps were won by those with the greatest practice.[64]

He said that before he came to the Bar, there had been 'an unwritten rule', that 'no cases would go on during the Punchestown meeting. Everything had to be disposed of or settled before 12.30 to allow the judges and everyone away'.[65]

Much of this networking and socialising around sport was gendered, and the Bar sporting societies were male-dominated.[66] At its 1927 AGM in Dublin Castle, the Bar golf society changed its rules so that only male members of the Bar and judiciary could be members.[67] This ruling was not overturned until the 1970s. Even after the ban on women members was lifted, women found it difficult to engage fully with the golf society. For example, one said that she did not play golf because she had young children. Another said that she was unable to engage in informal networking due to the demands on her time with young children. One woman recalled attending a meeting of the golf society where a male colleague proposed a motion that women should not be admitted. Recounting the incident, she said, '[h]e did it for fun. I burst into tears.' An

60 B21. 61 B.C.M., 28 June, 16 July 1982. 62 E.g., in 1969 a team of four men travelled to London: (1969) 103 *I.L.T.S.J.* 259. 63 MacKenzie, *Lawful occasions*, p. 120. 64 Ibid. 65 Ibid., p. 121. 66 However, one woman who was interviewed mentioned taking part in football five-a-sides, which was 'great because you got to know people'. 67 Joseph Healy proposed the rule change at the AGM, presided over by Justice Fitzgibbon. Up to this point, Averil Deverell had been a prize-winning member of the society. Information provided by Liz Goldthorpe based on her research into the archives of the Bar golf society.

anecdote described by several interviewees as 'a stain',[68] and 'awful'[69] related to a North-South golf outing at a golf club in Northern Ireland that did not allow women members. The woman member of the Bar golf society was not allowed to use the facilities at the golf club and this caused some controversy among members of the Bar. Even as late as 1989, there were references to the golf society's 'players and wives'.[70]

Not everyone wished to get involved with these formal social or sporting groups at the Bar. Several interviewees described the cliquey nature of some of these social networks. One barrister, for example, described the Bar golf society as 'forbidding'.[71] Others felt excluded because of their ability:

> I didn't have any great ability at sports, so I didn't get involved in those. I did play soccer with people from the Bar but not as any part of the organised thing. There'd be non-Bar people there as well. So I wasn't involved in the sporting societies.

It could be quite difficult for women to fully engage in these networking opportunities, sometimes because they felt excluded by the 'suffocatingly male'[72] atmosphere. Bacik, Costello and Drew point out that while '[m]ale camaraderie, sports talk (and some occasional action), and after hours socialisation' may have seemed harmless, they were nevertheless 'crucial to progress in legal careers' and there were 'career costs for non-conformity.'[73]

Other ways to network

Some barristers were members of private members clubs including the St Stephen's Green Club, the Hibernian Irish Services Club, and the Kildare Street and University Club (and its predecessors). One commented,

> I liked the club side of life, you know. It is nice, it's something that barristers do ... There is a sort of legal fraternity there.[74]

Some barristers were also members of groups such as the Freemasons,[75] the Knights of Malta[76] and the Knights of Columbanus.[77] The Fitzwilliam Tennis Club was also popular, and many barristers were members of external golf clubs, either in Dublin or around the country. The Bar itself was described by some as

---

68 B7.   69 B11.   70 James Comyn, 'Notebook', *I.L.T.* (ns) 7 (1989), 109.   71 B21.   72 B5.
73 Bacik, Costello and Drew, *Gender injustice*, p. 149. They add that '[w]omen often put faith in their academic and workplace achievements as guarantors of success.'   74 B17.   75 E.g., Alexander Blood: obit., *Irish Times*, 14 June 1933, p. 8.   76 E.g., Charles Lysaght, 'O'Mahony, Eoin Seosamh', *D.I.B.* and Noel Peart, who was president of the Irish association of the Sovereign Military Order of Malta. Ferguson, *King's inns barristers*, p. 231 and Anthony (Tony) Behan, interviewed Jan. 2000, National Folklore collection, UCD.   77 E.g., Vincent Grogan: Diarmaid Ferriter, 'Grogan,

a club;[78] one said it was 'the best club in Ireland',[79] and others referred to 'clubbiness'[80] or a sort of 'clubable-ness'[81] at the Bar.

Bar groups with a more professional focus began to emerge from the late 1980s.[82] These included the Association of Employed Barristers,[83] the Criminal Law Practitioners Association,[84] the Criminal Bar Committee[85] and the Young Barristers Society.[86] These essentially brought together members of the profession who had common interests. When Ireland joined the EEC, the Society for the Study and Practice of European Law was formed, with membership drawn from barristers, solicitors, judges, and academic lawyers. A member of the Bar was nominated as the first vice president.[87] This is evidence of the increasing professionalisation of the Bar, which will be explored further in chapter sixteen. There was an increasingly outward focus and engagement with foreign Bars and international issues of concern to advocates.

Friendship groups

It was noted in chapter five that supportive colleagues and friends were important for people at the Bar. A barrister reflecting on their long career observed:

> The Bar is the best place possible for friendships. I think it is no place for enemies. You can't afford enemies and that is the great thing about the Bar. It is not quarrelsome. You can't keep yourself to yourself. You've got to be friendly. Apart from that compulsion, you have every opportunity to be friends with people. You have such enormously wide choice and such very easy access to people. This friendship is in the interest of the public. It is because we get on so well and have such good relations with each other, that we can do people's business.[88]

Most of the barristers interviewed for this book indicated that they had made and kept very close friends at the Bar during their years in practice. One explained:

> You spend so much time together and it's not just working time you spend, there's an awful lot of downtime in the Library where you're sitting around having coffee and, you know, waiting for the next case or waiting for the jury to come back or waiting while your case is waiting to be called, there's

Vincent Benedict', *D.I.B.* 78 B6. 79 B9. 80 B5. 81 B18. 82 Some pre-dated this, such as the Medico–Legal Society of Ireland, established in 1956, whose membership included barristers, solicitors, judges, doctors and coroners. 83 E.g., B.C.M., 8 Feb. 1992, 1 May 1993. 84 Ibid., 27 Feb., 26 Mar. 1988. 85 E.g., ibid., 30 Nov. 1991. 86 E.g., ibid., 9 Nov. 1991. 87 Ibid., 9 Nov. 1973. 88 'Ralph Sutton, SC'.

an awful lot of waiting around, sitting around and it's occupying that time and you spend that with people you have an affinity with.[89]

There was tradition in the barristers' tea rooms that colleagues were free to join any table where there was space:

There were perhaps one or two tables of very well established groups that you mightn't join but apart from that, you'd sit down with everybody so you got to know people quite quickly.[90]

Some of the friendships that were developed at the Bar extended to personal and family lives with people holidaying together and inviting one another to family events. One interviewee described this: 'your entire social family, recreational and business life is the Law Library'.[91] Another commented:

You get to know some of them and [their] wives and children, bit of that as well. But I'd say no more than a normal workplace with a little bit extra added because of these dinners and things like that.[92]

Romantic or sexual relationships between members of the Bar were also relatively common, and marriages between barristers were not unusual. Several interviewees mentioned having sexual or romantic relationships with other barristers. Relationships between barristers and solicitors were also fairly common:

So you're hanging around and … there's a good looking woman solicitor there and you'd go and talk to her you know, preferable to the musty auld fellow who was a friend of my Da … I would say women solicitors were a focus for male barristers … they're … women you're most likely to meet.

Some barristers commented on the insular nature of the Irish Bar:

Once you become part of this, it's a very incestuous institution and it's very easy to get sucked in.[93]

To avoid this, not everyone fully embraced the social side of the Bar. Some mentioned the importance of maintaining friends outside the Bar,[94] in order to have some escape from the 'all embracing and limiting … vocation' of the law.[95] Others expressed a dislike for networking:

89 B21. 90 B11. 91 B14. 92 B2. 93 B14. 94 E.g., B14, B17, B27. 95 B19.

It was important but I wasn't good at it ... I would have gone to Bar dinners which I really didn't want to go to.

There were also those who did not socialise much with members of the profession due to their commitments elsewhere. These included both family and farming responsibilities, for example:

I married within a year of going to the Bar so I didn't socialise down in the bar with the other young unmarried people or go out.

I had a home to go to. I didn't go drinking at night-time with the boys.

I got married and I had a child and you completely lose interest in hanging around with your colleagues if what they're basically doing is drinking.

My social life would be limited probably ... I had too many obligations. When I came back [to the farm] there'd be responsibilities, things to be looked after.

The nature of social cohesion at the Bar differed between Dublin and the circuits. One barrister said that the social network in Dublin 'wasn't so strong'.[96] Barristers who lived outside of Dublin sometimes felt isolated and cut off from the Bar social scene, and one commented that when they returned to their home county, they felt that they were missing out on the Dublin 'intellectual milieu'.[97]

* * *

Personal networks were crucially important and people leaned on their pre-established connections, as well as forging new ones at the Bar. There seems to have been a general belief that knowing the right people was an important aspect of getting started at the Bar, and there are many examples of individuals getting their first case or their first big case as a result of knowing the right person. That is not to say that being well-connected was the only way to succeed; many people without 'connections' did very well at the Bar. As Morison and Leith put it, '[t]hose without contacts must shift for themselves'.[98]

Many barristers characterised their colleagues as supportive, and used words like 'camaraderie' and 'fun' when discussing their networks and relationships. As Gavin Duffy observed, in the Four Courts there was 'a certain "esprit de corps", which is a great help to the Bar'.[99] Similarly, McEnery, who was called in the 1920s, wrote:

---

96 B11. **97** B19. **98** Morison and Leith, *Barrister's world*, p. 28. **99** 'Memorandum in favour of the amalgamation of barristers and solicitors, June 1946', Gavan Duffy to taoiseach, 4 June 1946.

If one was not blest with many briefs one was never bored. There was always the social life of the place, the books, the legal conversations and the various courts where the cases were being heard. There was always something interesting going on.[100]

Many of the barristers interviewed for this book cited the friendship and camaraderie at the Bar as being the most enjoyable aspects of their careers. The other side of this camaraderie was, however, the competition between barristers, discussed in chapter five.

It is possible to identify a number of changes at the Irish Bar when it came to social networks. As previously noted, one barrister pointed out, for example, how long leisurely lunches following a win became a thing of the past. Some of these changes reflect the increasing diversity of the Bar, while others are probably products of the increased professionalisation since the turn of the twenty-first century.

NAI TSCH/3/S13867.   100 McEnery, 'Look back in love: conversations by an English fireside', UCDA P74/2, p. 74.

CHAPTER THIRTEEN

The Bar's external relations

Introduction

The Irish Bar in the 1920s was not entirely cut off from international Bar associations, and many barristers in the Free State were keen to establish Ireland's place among the professional Bar associations of the common law world. International networks do not appear to have been particularly strong during the early decades if the Irish Free State, but by the mid-century, the Bar was establishing and maintaining relations with other Bar societies and with international associations of lawyers or advocates.

By necessity, at an institutional level, the Irish Bar maintained relations with a number of external bodies, including neighbouring Bars, the Incorporated Law Society of Ireland, the Council of Law Reporting and the university law schools. Notably, its relationship with the Bar of Northern Ireland, which soured in the 1920s, had improved significantly by the turn of the century. As the century progressed, the Bar was increasingly cognisant of the significance of European and international laws.

The relationship with the Bar of Northern Ireland

The deteriorating relationship between the Bars of Ireland and Northern Ireland in the 1920s was examined in chapter two. As the two states drifted further apart, both in politics and in law, the split became entrenched. Both Bars were small, with the Northern Bar even more so. There were no reciprocal arrangements between the two Bars for many years. Barristers from one jurisdiction did not have an automatic right of audience in courts in the other jurisdiction; nor was it a straightforward matter to be called to the other Bar. In 1944, the under treasurer of the King's Inns, Theodore Tobias, received a letter from Lord McDermott relating to reciprocity in admission and call.[1] On searching his office, Tobias found a letter received from Newton Anderson, the secretary to the Courts of Justice in Northern Ireland, dated 1926. This letter had enclosed a provisional rule for the calling of Free State barristers to the Bar of Northern Ireland. A draft reply was found with it, asking for further particulars.[2] Following this discovery, Tobias wrote to Anderson for clarification, stating that he had responded to the request for information in June 1927, but had received no reply.[3]

---

1 K.I.B.M., 11 Jan. 1944. 2 K.I.B.M., 18 Jan. 1944. 3 Newton Anderson to Theodore Tobias,

Accordingly, when the rules of our Inn were revised and reprinted in 1935, the benchers concluded that the benchers of the King's Inns did not wish to pursue the matter further, and decided that the provisional rule should be revoked and expunged. The position, accordingly, is that there neither is, nor has there been at any time reciprocity between the two Inns in the matter of call.[4]

The benchers appear to have been somewhat embarrassed at this turn of events, and wrote that it was 'by inadventure' that the letter had remained unanswered, and suggested that the issue might be reconsidered.[5] Ultimately, however, the benchers of Northern Ireland unanimously resolved that the matter of reciprocity should not be reopened.[6] Thus, there remained a situation where there was no reciprocity between the two Bars.

Despite strained relations at an institutional level, there were interpersonal relationships which traversed the border, particularly where there were shared mutual interests such as golf. The Bar golf society was a vehicle to encourage friendly relations between the two Bars. In 1951 the Northern Ireland Bar golfing society was founded,[7] and in 1952 a match was played between the two societies at Newcastle, Co. Down.[8] Later that year, it was proposed to entertain the Northern Ireland Bar golfing society on the occasion of another match between the two golfing societies.[9] This took place at Portmarnock in April 1953.[10] The King's Inns benchers allowed the use of the Inns for a 'sherry and cocktail party' and made a grant of £50 towards the expenses.[11] Another sherry party was held in 1955,[12] and in 1956 it was noted in the *Irish Law Times* that the annual golf match between the two Bars was 'the most noteworthy feature of the year'. It described these events as 'outstandingly successful'.[13]

In 1965 Chief Justice Ó Dálaigh, along with President of the High Court Cahir Davitt, Attorney General Colm Condon and King's Inns Treasurer Justice Murnaghan were hosted at a reception at the Northern Ireland inn of court, along with members of the English legal professions.[14] In 1967 the benchers sponsored a reception for members for the Northern Ireland Bar who were

28 Jan. 1944, in K.I.B.M., 17 Apr. 1944. 4 Ibid. 5 K.I.B.M., 1 June 1944. 6 Newton Anderson to Theodore Tobias, 1 June 1944, in K.I.B.M., 8 June 1944. N.I.B.M., 1 June 1944, cited in A.R. Hart, *A history of the Bar and inn of court of Northern Ireland* (Belfast, 2013) p. 318. 7 See ibid., p. 253, citing minutes of the Northern Ireland Bar golfing society. 8 Ibid. 9 B.C.M., 12 Dec. 1952. The Bar Council appointed a sub-committee to consider the best form of hospitality – dinner or a sherry party. B.C.M., 30 Jan. 1953. 10 (1953) 87 *I.L.T.S.J.* 142 (16 May 1935). 11 K.I.B.M., 20 Jan. 1953. 12 B.C.M., 27 Jan. 1955. 13 (1956) 90 *I.L.T.S.J.* 301 (22 Dec. 1956). A 1957 proposal for a party for visiting members of the Northern Ireland Circuit failed. Instead, it was decided to support the Bar golf society in giving a party for the Northern barristers, but that council funds should not be used for this. B.C.M., 8 Apr. and 7 May 1957. Averil Deverell, who was not eligible to be a member of the Bar golf society, nevertheless assisted at the sherry reception, along with Ethel Beatty and Agnes Cassidy: B.C.M., 23 May 1955. 14 'Chief Justice for Belfast reception', *Irish Times*, 6 Oct. 1965, p. 7.

visiting for the annual golf match.[15] The question of where to hold the event was discussed by the Bar Council at length, and it was decided to allow the Bar golf society to choose between either the King's Inns or the Dublin Zoo.[16] The two golfing societies continued to meet and entertain one another,[17] and one barrister observed that

> In the golf there was quite a good relationship ... but even then ... occasionally late at night there might be a slight bit of friction or people squaring up to each other a little bit.[18]

After the Bar golfing societies began to hold annual matches, the matter of reciprocity was briefly reopened in 1958 when, according to Hart, Justice Murnaghan wrote to Lord Chief Justice MacDermott. The matter was considered by the benchers of Northern Ireland, but ultimately the proposal did not come to fruition.[19]

In 1964, the King's Inns benchers amended the rules of the Inns so that members of the Northern Irish Bar of three years' standing could be called to the Irish Bar, subject to the production of a certificate of call and a certificate that the applicant was a 'proper person' to be called to the Irish Bar.[20] An Irish-language requirement was not imposed.[21] This was the same arrangement as was in place for members of the English Bar, as discussed further below. However, this amendment was not replicated for Irish barristers who wished to be called to the Northern Bar. A Dublin-qualified barrister whose work might potentially require appearance in court in both jurisdictions generally had to first be called to the English Bar. This required certification from the attorney general that the barrister was a fit and proper person to be called.[22] Such was the position for a Louth-based barrister who wrote in 1972:

> Living here in this border county, I would very much like to get called to the Northern Ireland Bar, but found that, although we allow Northern barristers to be called here, that they do not reciprocate, and you have to be a practising member of the English Bar for three years before being

15 K.I.B.M., 3 Apr. 1967. This was expressly to enable the Bar, not the Bar golf society, to entertain the Northern Bar. 16 B.C.M., 5 May 1967. 17 E.g., B.C.M., 16 May 1969; 3 Apr. 1978 (a 'tournament instituted by Lord Justice Scarman following upon Sunningdale', involving the Bars of Ireland, Northern Ireland and Great Britain). 18 B26. 19 Hart, *History of the Bar*, p. 318, citing a memorandum prepared by J.A.L. McLean, under-treasurer of the inn of court for Northern Ireland on 24 Mar. 1975. 20 Hart, *History of the Bar*, p. 319. 21 The Legal Practitioners (Qualification) Act 1929, s. 3 provided: 'nothing in this section contained shall prevent the chief justice from admitting to practise as a barrister-at-law in the courts of Saorstát Eireann any member of three years' standing at any other Bar who has been admitted to the degree of barrister-at-law by the benchers of the Honorable Society of King's Inns, Dublin, pursuant to a reciprocal arrangement whereby members of the Bar of Saorstát Eireann may be admitted to practise at such other Bar.' 22 See the letters regarding certification at NAI 2009/74/742.

admitted to the Northern Bar. I have therefore decided to get called to the English Bar and take it on from there.[23]

The same barrister mentioned that two of his colleagues in Northern Ireland, judges Turlough O'Donnell and Ambrose McGonigal,[24] were trying to have him called to the Northern Irish Bar without having to first be called in England, but he was doubtful as to whether that would work.

By the mid-seventies, it was clear that there was a growing momentum towards reciprocity and better relations between the two Bars. This was partly facilitated by the accession of the UK and Ireland to the EEC;[25] the Bars now had more common cause. Both were members of the newly established UK-Ireland Bars liaison committee,[26] which facilitated the exchange of information and the maintenance of relations between the Bars.[27] When changes in fees structure were under consideration in the early 1970s, comparative analysis with fees at the English and Northern Ireland Bars was carried out.[28] This required the exchange of letters with both Bars, indicating at least a level of formal civility in north-south relations. Cooperation on other minor matters continued through the 1970s and 80s.[29]

During the Troubles, the Irish Bar on several occasions expressed its support for members of the bench and Bar in Northern Ireland who came under attack. In the aftermath of the Bloody Sunday attacks in Derry in 1972, a general meeting of the Bar was called at the request of more than one hundred members to discuss a resolution condemning the attack, and calling on members of the Bars of England and Northern Ireland to join their demand 'that all appropriate steps be taken at national and international level to ensure that those responsible be brought to justice'.[30] Lord Chief Justice Lowry[31] is said to have played a

23 Letter to Att. Gen. Colm Condon, 12 May 1972. NAI 2009/74/742. Hart notes that 'the requirement of three years' practise was a requirement of the English Bar for applicants from the Irish Bar who wished to be exempted from the regulations concerning pupillage and restricted practise.' The King's Inns no longer required three years' practise from English barristers and would not require it of Northern barristers. Hart, *History of the Bar*, pp 319–20. 24 Both O'Donnell and McGonigal played an active part in trying to establish reciprocity and good relations between the two Bars. See Hart, *History of the Bar*, pp 317–20. 25 Hart, *History of the Bar*, p. 321, notes that members of the Irish Bar who appeared in Northern Ireland usually did so under the reciprocal arrangements rather than under the EEC directive. 26 B.C.M., 14 Apr. 1972. A Bar Council representative planned to attend the 1972 meeting in Edinburgh, and to learn about the English Bar's arrangements for operating within the common market. See also B.C.M., 28 Sept. 1984. 27 E.g., B.C.M., 7 May 1979. In the early 1980s, copies of the rulings of the Bar Council were sent to the Bar Council of Northern Ireland: B.C.M., 5 Jan. 1981. 28 E.g., B.C.M., 2 Feb., 16 Feb., 15 Mar. 1976. 29 E.g., when membership of the International Bar Association was being considered, it was suggested that the Irish Bar seek joint membership with the Bar of Northern Ireland, so that the costs could be shared. B.C.M., 10 June 1983. 30 B.C.M., 7 Feb 1972. This motion was considered to be out of order however, because of the unwritten rule that the only matters which could be the subject of a general meeting of the Bar were those which touched the Bar in its professional capacity. At the aborted meeting, Donal Barrington pointed out that the interests of the Bar 'extended beyond mere money', and said that in 1799 the Bar had passed a political resolution not to pass the Act of Union. 31 Lowry was called to the Bar of Northern

significant part in re-establishing connections between the Bars of the north and south during the 1970s and 80s.[32] An attempt was made on his life in 1982, and in response the Bar Council issued a press statement expressing:

> Its condemnation of the attempted murder of Lord Lowry, lord chief justice of Northern Ireland, who has made so great a contribution towards the reconciliation of all communities in Northern Ireland and in defence and expansion of the rule of law.[33]

When other members of the Northern judiciary were the subjects of terror attacks, the Bar Council publicly stated its sympathy for the bereaved and support for those who were attacked.[34]

The matter of reciprocal arrangements between the two Bars was raised in Dublin on several occasions in the early seventies.[35] In 1975 Justice O'Donnell in Northern Ireland prepared a memorandum for his fellow benchers suggesting that the time had come to reconsider the issue of reciprocity, particularly in light of the accession of both the United Kingdom and Ireland to the EEC.[36] Finally, in February 1976, the Northern Ireland benchers adopted a new rule allowing for members of the Irish Bar of three years' standing to be called to the Bar of Northern Ireland.[37] Following this, groups of Northern Ireland barristers were called to the Irish Bar.[38] From time to time there were also 'special calls', especially for Northern Ireland barristers.[39] Such calls were essentially symbolic gestures of goodwill rather than indications of a serious intention to practise in the other jurisdiction. One barrister who was called to the Bar of Northern Ireland said that this did not mean that doing work in the other jurisdiction was feasible:

> All law is local ... and being an advocate in our system, a significant amount of that involves knowing the system, the rules, the practice and the judges, not in a friendly sense but having some sense of how this judge is going to behave ... That's not as easily translated. I was briefed in one thing in the North ... it's actually very hard. You don't feel that comfortable. There's a whole hinterland of information and procedure and

Ireland in 1947, and was appointed lord chief justice in 1971. See Robert Carswell, 'Lowry, Robert Lynd Erskine', *D.I.B.*   32 Hart, *History of the Bar*, p. 319.   33 B.C.M., 5 Mar. 1982. In 1987, the Bar Council wrote to Lord Lowry offering sympathies on the death of his wife. B.C.M., 10 July 1987.   34 E.g., following the murder of Judge William Doyle in Belfast in 1983, the Bar Council issued a statement of sympathy to the family, B.C.M., 17 Jan. 1983.   35 B.C.M., 14 Dec. 1973; B.C.M., 18 Jan. 1974. Reciprocity with the English Bar was also under discussion.   36 He pointed out that the Irish language requirement set out in the Legal Practitioners (Qualification) Act 1929 would not apply to members of the Northern Ireland Bar: Hart, *History of the Bar*, p. 318.   37 In the same month, the Bar Council reported that discussions were to take place with the Bar of Northern Ireland regarding membership and subscriptions to each other's libraries. B.C.M., 21 June 1976.   38 See, e.g., Ferguson, *Barristers*, pp 366–8.   39 E.g., in Apr. 1986, June 1989, Nov. 1993, Feb. 1996. See ibid., pp 373, 379, 386, 388.

law that you would have to learn … I think Paddy McEntee went up to do one or two trials. I think some people, some Northern barristers, came down, but it was still very unusual.[40]

The position of barristers from both jurisdictions came to be considered a number of times in the context of membership of the EEC.[41] In 1979, the standing committee of the Bar Council had to consider the position of a QC from Northern Ireland appearing in an Irish court under EEC rules.[42] Matters of etiquette concerned the Bar Council, such as who would be the leader in such a case.[43] It envisaged that such issues were likely to arise more frequently in the future.[44] Indeed these matters arose again in 1980 when a Northern Ireland QC was due to appear in a criminal case in Dublin, leading a Northern junior.[45] The Northern QC, who had previously been called to the Irish Bar, asked to be given silk so that he could appear at the inner Bar in Dublin, but the attorney general was of the view that only practising members of the Irish Bar could take silk. The Bar Council agreed, pointing out that 'silk was the mark of professional eminence'.[46] The standing of Northern Ireland barristers who wished to appear in Irish courts was raised again in 1986.[47]

By 1984, it was reported that the Northern Ireland Bar was 'anxious to re-establish contact with the King's Inns' and it was proposed that a number of them would attend special dining at the King's Inns.[48] The Northern barristers wished to pay for their own meals, but in an exercise of diplomacy, the Bar Council resolved to pay, on this first occasion. Individual Irish barristers hosting the tables would pay for the wine.[49] This event took some planning, and was scheduled to take place in April 1985.[50] In 1985 it was also suggested that the dates of the traditional long vacation might be altered so as to align better with the vacation in Northern Ireland, which began in mid-July.[51]

The thaw in the relationship which was evident from the 1970s[52] resulted from a number of factors, including membership of the EEC, and the personal

40 B26.   41 In particular, Directive 77/249/EEC of 22 March 1977 (facilitating the effective exercise by lawyers of freedom to provide services); Directive 89/48/EEC (on the recognition of higher education diplomas awarded on the completion of three years of professional education and training of at least three years' duration); and Directive 98/5/EC of the European Parliament and of the Council of 16 February 1998 (facilitating lawyers practising on a permanent basis in a member state other than that in which the qualification was obtained).   42 B.C.M., 26 Mar. 1979. 43 Where a Northern Ireland barrister had also been called to the Bar of Ireland, the issues of precedence did not arise, and it was decided to keep a list of all those Northern barristers called to the Irish Bar 'who might still be alive'.   44 This was an issue affecting the status of lawyers from EEC member states generally. See also B.C.M., 7 May 1979.   45 B.C.M., 23 Jan. 1980. 46 B.C.M., 23 Jan., 14 Mar. 1980.   47 B.C.M., 7 Nov. 1986.   48 B.C.M., 26 Oct. 1984. 49 B.C.M., 28 Sept. 1984.   50 B.C.M., 10 Jan., 9 Feb. 1985.   51 B.C.M., 23 Feb. 1985.   52 E.g., in 1971, the Bar Council wrote to Lord MacDermott, recently retired as lord chief justice of Northern Ireland, to mark the fiftieth anniversary of his call to the Bar: B.C.M., 16 July 1971. In November of the same year, he was elected an honorary bencher of the King's Inns. K.I.B.M., 11 Nov. 1971. He was to be informed of his election at a dinner at the Inns the following evening. In

relationships and friendships forged through the various sporting organisations. The role of golf has been mentioned, and in the 1980s, rugby[53] and cricket[54] also provided a basis for social contact between the two Bars, and these were joined in the 1990s by soccer.[55] The passage of time was also important; as Hart observes, by the mid-seventies 'those individuals now in positions of leadership represented a new generation less influenced by the experiences of the past'.[56] However, the lack of cross-border mobility meant that contact outside of sporting engagements was limited:

> I would say a lot of people at the Northern Bar went through their lives without ever meeting barristers from Dublin and vice versa ... If you took out the people who didn't play golf and who didn't play rugby, very little other contact.[57]

The same barrister mused that 'in one sense the relationship between the Bar north and south was probably a bit better than the general relationship between people north and south ... in the sense there was contact and a degree of sympathy or fellow feeling'.[58]

Relationship with other Bars

From time to time members of the legal professions in other countries visited Ireland and they were generally welcomed and entertained by the Irish Bar. These were often relatively low-key visits by small groups of practitioners from North America.[59] The financial burden of hosting and entertaining these groups was sometimes keenly felt by the Bar Council.[60] A planned visit by the Australian

1978 Dick Ferguson of the Northern Ireland Bar suggested that there be an annual gathering of the members of the two Bars. B.C.M., 3 Apr. 1978. While the Bar Council was open to this, the proposal ultimately went nowhere. B.C.M., 26 Feb. 1979. **53** B.C.M., 11 Apr. 1987. **54** B.C.M., 22 July 1989. **55** B.C.M., 1 May 1993. **56** Hart, *History of the Bar*, p. 319. **57** B26. **58** B26. **59** These included the Washington DC Bar Association, B.C.M., 31 Jan. 1977; the Illinois State Bar Association, B.C.M., 8 Feb., 7 Mar. 1992; the Toronto Advocates Society, B.C.M., 30 Jan. 1970; the Montana Bar Association and a group of Massachusetts trial lawyers, B.C.M., 8 Feb. 1992. **60** E.g., anticipating a visit by members of one Bar association in 1976, the Bar Council hoped that the entertainment for this group could be relatively modest, as a larger delegation from the Australian Bar Association was also planned for later that year. B.C.M., 5 Apr., 21 June 1976. On another occasion, funding was obtained from Bord Fáilte to subsidise a dinner at the King's Inns for one hundred members of the Toronto Advocates Society. B.C.M., 30 Jan. 1970. The visit also included two dinners at the Gresham Hotel (each Bar hosting the other in turn), and during the day there were 'discussions on legal topics between the Canadians and Irish.' B.C.M., 19 Mar. 1970. The visit was later deemed 'a great success', B.C.M., 8 May 1970. The following year a member of the Irish Bar Council travelled to Toronto to speak at a commemoration dinner, B.C.M., 26 May 1971. In 1956, when planning a visit by the American Bar Association (see below), the taoiseach was concerned that 'it might be thought that we intended to pay their travelling and hotel expenses, and this, of course, would be quite impracticable.' John A. Costello to John J. Hearne, 13 Nov. 1956, NAI TSCH/3/S16108 A. On another occasion, the Bar Council took the view that 'they could not

Bar Association in 1987[61] grew so that there were more visitors than anticipated, and the Bar Council minutes record, perhaps somewhat trepidatiously, 'up to 180 Australians may now come to the dinner'.[62]

Members of other Bars were also frequently hosted via the Bar golf society. The *Irish Law Times* noted that matches with the English Bar were discontinued after the Second World War.[63] However, the tradition was revived some years later. In 1962 the Bar golf society hosted the English Bar golfing society at Portmarnock, and the following year they travelled to London.[64] In 1989 James Comyn wrote about annual matches between the English and Irish Bar golf societies, adding some colourful detail about the meals afterwards, which were 'not teetotal'.[65] In 1990 members of the Australian Bar were entertained by the Bar golf society.[66]

Relations between the English and Irish Bars were generally cordial. Aside from social and sporting events, the Irish Bar was also in touch with the English Bar regarding other matters from time to time. For example, the English Bar donated copies of law reports after the Dublin Law Library was destroyed in 1922,[67] and in 1981 the English Bar sent copies of its updated code of conduct to the Bar Council.[68]

In 1922 a rule was passed by the English inns of court governing the admission of Irish barristers to the English Bar.[69] An Irish-qualified barrister had to have practised for three years before they were eligible for call to the English Bar, and a similar rule applied for English barristers.[70] Irish-qualified barristers wrote to the attorney general for certification that they had been called.[71] Some had qualified in Ireland and then joined the colonial legal service, and did not intend to return to practise in Ireland. Others made it clear that they had no intention to practise at the English Bar; they simply wished to be able to say that they had been called.[72] The Irish barristers seeking such certification seem to have greatly outnumbered the English-qualified barristers being called to the Irish Bar. In the late eighties, the English inns of court expressed some concerns about this in a memorandum presented to the chairman of the Bar Council via the UK-Ireland Bars liaison committee. Three problems were identified; first, that reciprocal call arrangements should be bona fides; the inns of court wished to put a stop to 'the practice whereby Irish barristers with the minimum three years practice sought to be called to the English Bar without any intention of

---

undertake to act as hosts to every group of lawyers who might choose to visit the country', but in the context of one particular planned visit, 'since the Council would not be involved in either the financing or organisation of the function' it would seek the approval of the benchers for a dinner. B.C.M., 31 Jan. 1977.　61 B.C.M., 24 Jan. 1987.　62 Ibid.　63 (1956) 90 *I.L.T.S.J.* 301 (22 Dec. 1956).　64 (1963) 97 *I.L.T.S.J.* 176 (22 June 1963).　65 James Comyn, 'Notebook' *Irish Law Times* (ns) 7 (1989), 109.　66 B.C.M., 14 July 1990. The Bar Council provided a subvention towards the entertainment costs.　67 See p. 216.　68 B.C.M., 13 Feb. 1981.　69 K.I.B.M., 31 Aug. 1922. 70 K.I.B.M., 2 June 1926.　71 See the letters at NAI 2009/74/742.　72 E.g., one barrister seeking certification wrote, 'I am not thinking of forsaking the Irish Bar.' Letter to Att. Gen. Kevin Dixon,

practising but merely to add a further qualification to their curriculum vitae'.[73] The inns of court did not wish the call to the English Bar to be a purely social affair; nor did they want Irish-qualified barristers to use the call to the English Bar as a 'stepping-stone' to other Bars. The Bar Council liaised with the King's Inns education committee, suggesting a system of certification limited to bona fide applicants.[74] This matter was resolved within a few months, and the proposals outlined by the Bar Council were accepted.[75] From the 1970s, the UK-Ireland Bars liaison committee met regularly to discuss matters affecting members of the various Bars.[76]

The position in relation to other common law jurisdictions was less straightforward. In 1963 Gerard O'Reilly, in Auckland, New Zealand, wrote to Eamon de Valera to report 'a dishonour that is being shown to the Irish Bar by the New Zealand Law Society.'[77] He had been called to the Irish Bar in 1949 and moved to New Zealand six years later. The New Zealand Law Society required Irish-qualified barristers to pass an exam before they could join the Bar there. On the basis that there was no such requirement for English-qualified barristers, O'Reilly, who worked in the public service, refused to take the exam and was not admitted to the New Zealand Bar. It was suggested that the requirement would be waived if there were a similar arrangement for New Zealand-qualified barristers who wished to be called to the Irish Bar. Soon afterwards, Roger Hayes[78] in the Department of Justice wrote to Dermot Waldron[79] in the Department of External Affairs asking for a summary of the recognition of calls to the Bar in commonwealth countries.[80] The Department considered the rules relating to the Bars of Malaya, East Pakistan, West Pakistan, Uganda, Rhodesia, Ceylon, Nyasaland, Trinidad and Tobago, South Africa and Sierra Leone. Different rules applied in the various jurisdictions. For example in Malaya, those who were called to the Irish Bar pre-1922 could practise, while in Ceylon and Uganda, it was necessary to pass an exam.[81] In 1990, a former member of the Irish Bar, called in 1981 and originally from Zambia, wished to be called to the Bar of Zambia, and required the Bar Council to write to the president of Zambia on his behalf.[82] Australian-qualified barristers could be called to the Irish Bar

---

7 Nov. 1945, NAI 2009/74/742. Another wrote 'I don't intend to practise in England, but I should like to have the qualification.' Letter to Ó Dálaigh, 14 July 1946, NAI 2009/74/742. 73 B.C.M., 9 Nov. 1989. 74 Ibid. 75 B.C.M., 25 Nov. 1989; 13 Jan. 1990. 76 E.g., B.C.M., 9 Oct. 1980. Meeting of the heads of the UK and Irish Bars, mentioned in the B.C.M., 13 Oct. 1990. The Fair Trade Commission noted in its report that there were no equivalent reciprocal arrangements for English-qualified solicitors. Fair Trade Commission, *Report of study into restrictive practices in the legal profession* (Dublin, 1990), para. 7.156. 77 Gerard O'Reilly to Eamon de Valera, 8 Apr. 1963, NAI JUS/90/113/4. 78 Called in 1940: Ferguson, *Barristers*, p. 202. 79 Called in 1948: ibid., p. 312. Waldron served as both legal advisor and ambassador. 80 Roger Hayes to Dermot Waldron, 4 May 1963, NAI JUS/90/113/4. 81 'Foreign lawyers practising in Eire [Ireland], NAI JUS/90/113/4. 82 B.C.M., 12 May 1990. The chief justice of Zambia, in response to a query from the Bar Council, wrote that the barrister had an action pending against the Zambian authorities on the question of his call for the Bar, and refused to comment further. The Bar Council

without much difficulty if they had been practising for three years. The late eighties and early nineties saw small groups of Australian barristers being called; for example, in 1987, 1988 and 1989.[83] In July 1991 a group of fifty-five Australians were called,[84] and in October twelve more were called.[85] In 1993 Akbar Ali Malik, a member of the Pakistani Bar, was called.

Whatever about reciprocity with other commonwealth jurisdictions, suggestions of admitting American-qualified lawyers to the Irish Bar were never entertained. In the early years of the Free State, lawyers from the United States occasionally considered practising in Ireland. They usually wrote to a government minister seeking information or permission to do so. For example, in 1934 Patrick McSweeney from Newport, US, wrote to the minister for education asking for the syllabi of Irish colleges, and also asking 'the requirements and conditions to be met to enable an American lawyer to have the privilege of also practising law in Ireland'.[86] However, American qualifications were 'not recognised in the Saorstát courts and an American lawyer who wishes to practise here would require to pass the necessary examinations and to be admitted as a solicitor or be called to the Bar as the case may be.'[87] Patrick Barrett, from Cleveland, Ohio, who was visiting Achill island in 1939, wrote to the minister for justice saying that he had often been asked about requirements for American lawyers in Ireland because of his Irish birth and Irish education.[88] He received a rather terse reply that 'American legal qualifications are not recognised in this country.' In 1936 the King's Inns benchers recorded that an American-qualified lawyer who was originally from Ireland had recently returned from San Francisco and wished to be called to the Irish Bar. This was refused, on the grounds that there was no reciprocity agreement with Bars other than the English Bar.[89] The lawyer then enrolled in the King's Inns, and sought to have an exemption granted after he had completed his first year, but this too was refused.[90] He was called to the Bar in 1942, having been awarded the Barrister-at-Law degree.[91] In 1986 it was pointed out to the Bar Council that Irish barristers of five years' standing could be called to the Bar of New York without having to undertake any examinations. This was in the context of the King's Inns refusing to admit an American lawyer to the Irish Bar, on the basis that only lawyers from jurisdictions with divided professions could be admitted.[92]

let the matter rest. B.C.M., 13 Oct. 1990.   83 See Ferguson, *Barristers*, pp 376–80.   84 Ibid., p. 382.   85 Ibid., p. 383.   86 Patrick McSweeney to T. Derrig, min. education, Nov. 1934, NAI JUS/90/113/4.   87 J. O'Conor, private sec., min. justice to private sec., min. for education, Nov. 1934, NAI JUS/90/113/4.   88 Barrett to P.J. Ruttledge, min. justice, 9 Feb. 1939, NAI JUS/90/113/4.   89 K.I.B.M., 21 Oct. 1936.   90 K.I.B.M., 11 Oct. 1937.   91 Nicholas Barron, called in 1942; Ferguson, *Barristers*, p. 135.   92 B.C.M., 19 Oct. 1986.

Hosting the ABA

The American Bar Association (ABA) visited on a number of occasions.[93] The first of these was in 1924, and was an opportunity for the Irish legal community to showcase the state's new legal order to an international audience. The ABA was planning a special meeting in London in the summer of 1924,[94] and were pleased to receive an invitation from Lord Chief Justice Molony to visit Dublin and attend a dinner at the King's Inns.[95] Around 200 American and Canadian lawyers accepted the invitation.[96] They travelled by special train service from London to Holyhead, where they boarded a ferry to Ireland.[97] After a garden party at the viceregal lodge[98] and a dinner at the King's Inns, there was a special train to Killarney for 'three days of festivities', which included garden parties, a gala ball, a golf tournament, a regatta, and a concert featuring the army band and John McCormack.[99] The visit was deemed a success by the ABA members.[100]

Another visit was planned by the ABA as part of their annual conference taking place in London in 1957.[101] This became a very formal state occasion, necessitating cooperation between the Bar Council, the benchers, the Law Society and government departments.[102] One aspect of the visit was the negotiation and lobbying over the conferring of honorary degrees and honorary benchings for visiting lawyers. Six months after the original proposal of the ABA visit, John J. Hearne,[103] the Irish ambassador to the US, pointed out that Chief Justice Warren would be at the London meeting, as well as other notable American and Irish-American lawyers. One in particular was Michael Francis Doyle[104] from

---

93 E.g., B.C.M., 12 July 1985. The ABA criminal lawyer division visited in 1989 and the Bar Council planned both a mock trial and a reception. B.C.M., 28 Jan., 25 Feb. 1989.   **94** 'Special London meeting', *A.B.A.J.* 10:5 (1924), 326. The letter of invitation was reproduced at *A.B.A.J.* 10:4 (1924), 257.   **95** Invitations had also been received from the French and Scottish legal professions: 'Special London meeting', *A.B.A.J.* 10(5) (1924), 326.   **96** 'The visit to Ireland', *A.B.A.J.* 10:9 (1924), 664. Functions were planned by both the French and Irish Bar associations, with clashing dates, and many delegates chose the Irish visit. *American Bar Association visit to England, Scotland and Ireland 1924, memorial volume* (New York, 1926), p. 75.   **97** *American Bar Association visit*, p. 75.   **98** The names of attendees were listed in the *Freeman's Journal*, 31 July 1924.   **99** *American Bar Association visit*, p. 76. Mr Howard S. Harrington, of Dunloe Castle, Killarney and formerly of the New York Bar, 'took charge of all the arrangements commencing in London and ending only at the conclusion of the various entertainments.' *American Bar Association visit*, p. 76.   **100** John M. Tierney, justice of the Supreme Court of the state of New York, wrote, '[t]he hospitality of our hosts was unbounded. They opened their homes and their hearts to their visitors.' *American Bar Association visit*, p. 76. It was reported in the *A.B.A.J.* that the visitors 'returned with a high appreciation of the hospitality of the Irish Bar': 'The visit to Ireland', *A.B.A.J.* 10:9 (1924), 664.   **101** For an account of the London visit, see Charles S. Rhyne, 'President's page', *A.B.A.J.* 43(9) (1957), 771; Jonathan Stone, 'Our London meeting: an Englishman's impression', *A.B.A.J.* 43(9) (1957), 818 and a number of items in the October and November 1957 issues. **102** See, e.g., B.C.M., 1, 20 Feb. 1957.   **103** Called in 1919, Hearne had previously served as parliamentary draughtsman, legal advisor to the Department of External Affairs and high commissioner to Canada, and had been heavily involved in drafting the 1937 constitution. See ch. 14 and Ferguson, *Barristers*, p. 204.   **104** Doyle communicated with the Irish ambassador on behalf of the president of the ABA. Ambassador John J. Hearne to John A. Belton, assistant secretary, dept.

Philadelphia, who had been immortalised in Lavery's painting of the trial of Roger Casement and who said he had defended Casement 'at his own expense'. Hearne suggested to Taoiseach John A. Costello that 'it would be a gracious act on the part of the Bar of Ireland if, as a tribute to the defender of Casement, he was called to the Irish Bar'.[105] He later wrote that Doyle's 'great ambition in life' was to be made an honorary member of the Irish Bar.[106] The fact that the Irish ambassador to the United States, the taoiseach and the assistant secretary in the Department of External Affairs had all been called to the Bar was undoubtedly helpful in ensuring high-profile honours were bestowed on these visiting lawyers. The taoiseach also raised the possibility of the National University of Ireland conferring honorary degrees on both Doyle and Warren,[107] though it appears that this suggestion may have first come from Doyle himself.[108] Costello felt that the decision about honorary benching disposed of the proposal for conferring honorary degrees.[109]

When de Valera was appointed taoiseach he recommended to the senate of the National University of Ireland that Chief Justice Warren should receive an honorary LLD. Upon hearing about this, Doyle wrote directly to de Valera asking that his name might also be considered for an honorary degree. He set out his résumé, which listed acting '[a]s counsel for Sir Roger Casement in his trial in London' as one 'the outstanding services which I have rendered in the cause of Irish freedom'.[110] However, as noted in a memo in the Department of An Taoiseach, '[t]he precise *locus standi* of Mr Michael Francis Doyle at the trial of Roger Casement in 1916 is far from clear'. He was characterised as 'a distinguished American lawyer' who 'was present in an advisory capacity'.[111] In

external affairs, 17 Jan. 1957, NAI DFA/6/434/479. (Belton was called to the Bar in 1927 and later served as ambassador. Ferguson, *Barristers*, p. 137.)   105 Hearne to Costello, 3 Oct. 1956, NAI TSCH/3/S16108 A.   106 Hearne to Sean Murphy, sec. Dept. External Affairs, 4 Dec. 1956, NAI TSCH/3/S16108 A.   107 Costello to Hearne, 13 Nov. 1956, NAI TSCH/3/S16108 A. 108 Hearne to Murphy, 4 Dec. 1956, NAI DFA/6/434/479. Hearne wrote that Doyle had suggested the conferring of an honorary degree on Chief Justice Warren.   109 N.S. Ó Nualláin, sec. Dept. Taoiseach to Murphy, 15 Mar. 1957, NAI DFA/6/434/479.   110 He also mentioned acting 'as counsel for the leaders of the Irish cause in this country; as counsel for Dr McCartan, General Liam Mellowes, Mrs Terence McSwiney, Donald O'Callaghan, Lord Mayor of Cork, as well as many Irishmen in this country charged with breaches of Espionage and the War Acts; and also as one of the first organisers of the bond drive and recipient of the first bond issued, and in addition thereto I presented the resolutions of recognition to the United States Senate, and also accompanied the first Irish delegation to the League of Nations in Geneva.' Doyle to de Valera, 10 May 1957, NAI TSCH/3/S16108 A. He also enclosed a copy of the citation which accompanied an award conferred by the Assumption Fathers, in Rome. Doyle also alluded to one thing 'yet to be finished. It is to clear the scandal which the British sought to smear the name of Roger Casement. Several times have I sought to have his hallowed dust removed from the Pentonville prison yard to his beloved Ireland and thus far without success, because of the refusal of the British government.' He promised to send a copy of Alfred Noyes' book, *The accusing ghost*, to de Valera. Copies of the correspondence between Doyle and Noyes are available in NAI DFA/6/434/479. Hearne wrote that Doyle had 'for forty years been a staunch advocate in the United States of the integrity of Casement's life.' Hearne to Belton, 17 Jan. 1957, NAI DFA/6/434/479.   111 Note, Ó Nualláin, 13 May 1957, NAI TSCH/3/S16108 A. The note cited the 'Sinn Fein rebellion handbook 1917',

a letter to Alfred Noyes[112] in December 1956, Doyle described himself as 'the American counsel for Sir Roger Casement during his trial for treason'.[113] Although he described himself as 'counsel' for Casement, he was not, in fact, a member of the English Bar.[114] In a second memo, the Department of An Taoiseach concluded that '[a]ll the available evidence regarding Mr Doyle's role at Casement's trial indicated that one would be unsafe in going any further than saying that Mr Doyle was present at the trial, and assisted the defence of, Roger Casement.'[115]

In May 1957 Doyle once more pressed his case for an honorary degree:

> If you are about to communicate to de Valera concerning the suggestion of honorary degrees for Chief Justice Warren and others visiting Dublin, I would deeply appreciate it if you would kindly include my name with your recommendation. Such honour from an Irish university would be treasured beyond expression ... Kindly regard this, however, as a suggestion with no sense of obligation on your part.[116]

His lobbying seems to have worked, and his name was considered among other proposals for honorary degrees by the senate of the NUI in July 1957.[117]

compiled by the *Weekly Irish Times*, p. 138; Herbert O. Mackey, *The life and times of Roger Casement* 1954, p. 127, and Birkenhead's *Famous trials of history*, p. 253.   112 Noyes was the author of *The accusing ghost: or justice for Roger Casement* (London, 1967), which suggested that the 'black diaries' attributed to Casement were forgeries.   113 Michael Francis Doyle to Alfred Noyes, 12 Dec. 1956, NAI DFA/6/434/479.   114 A.M. Sullivan, Artemus Jones and Professor J.H. Morgan were counsel at the trial, instructed by George Gavan Duffy. It appeared that Casement's sister had requested permission, via the American embassy, for Doyle to appear for Casement.   115 Note, Ó Nualláin, 22 May 1957, NAI TSCH/3/S16108 A. This memo referred to an extract from Wm. J. Moloney, 'The forged Casement diaries', Dublin 1936 – which quoted the *San Francisco Examiner*. 116 Doyle to Hearne, 8 May 1957, NAI DFA/6/434/479. Hearne forwarded this request to the Department of External Affairs, noting that Doyle wished for the honorary degree in addition to the honorary benching. Hearne to Murphy, 13 May 1957, NAI DFA/6/434/479.   117 NUI extraordinary meeting of senate, 19 June 1957, NAI DFA/6/434/479. Also considered were Herbert Brownell, Vernon Francis Gallagher (university president), Alfred Whitney Griswold (university president), David F. Maxwell (lawyer), Charles Munch (conductor), Earl Warren (chief justice). Professor Patrick McGilligan, who would read the addresses for the conferring, sought more information about the legal careers of Doyle and Warren and the cases with which they had been involved: Belton to Hearne, 10 July 1957, NAI DFA/6/434/479. The case suggested by Warren included *Brown v. Board of Education* (1954) 347 U.S. 483; *Bolling v. Sharpe* (1954) 347 U.S. 497 (school segregation); *Hernandez v. Texas* (1954) 347 U.S. 475 (representative jury); *Quinn v. USA* (1955) 349 U.S. 155 (contempt of congress, fifth amendment, refusal to answer); *Emspak v. USA* (1955) 349 U.S. 190 (similar); *Bart v. USA* (1955) 349 U.S. 219 (similar, refusing to answer questions by sub committee of Un-American Activities Committee); *Peters v. Hobby* (1955) 349 U.S. 376 (fired from professorship for membership of communist party); *Pennsylvania v. Nelson* (1956) 350 U.S. 497 (relationship between state and federal criminal laws); *Fikes v. Alabama* (1957) 372 U.S. 191 (death sentence, due process for black man); *Watkins v. USA* (1957) 354 U.S. 178 (refusal to testify to Un-American Committee); *Sweezy v. New Hampshire* (1957) 354 U.S. 234 (constitutional limits of legislative inquiry). Hearne to Belton, 18 July 1957, NAI DFA/6/434/479. Doyle wrote back that he had been the US member of the court of arbitration in the Hague for

The question of the honorary call to the Bar or honorary benching received considerable attention in early 1957. John Belton, on behalf of Liam Cosgrave, the minister for external affairs, wrote to McGilligan, now attorney general, explaining that there were only a small number of honorary benchers, all of whom were 'distinguished Irish lawyers'.[118] He asked McGilligan whether, in his capacity as a bencher, he thought there was any possibility of Doyle being accepted as an honorary bencher.[119] A few weeks later, Cahir Davitt, president of the High Court, told Costello that it would be proposed at the next meeting of benchers that Warren would be made an honorary bencher and Doyle admitted as a member of the Bar.[120] He sought more information about Doyle, 'his standing in his profession and generally. At present we know nothing apart from the Casement business.'[121]

The benchers determined that both Doyle and Warren should become honorary benchers. Costello pointed out that although Doyle had wished for an honorary call to the Bar, this would be 'the greater honour for him'.[122] In April 1957 it was discovered that the US attorney general, Herbert Brownell, would also be travelling to Ireland,[123] and he too was made an honorary bencher.[124] The honorary benchings were done by the benchers at their meetings in April and May 1957,[125] and were deemed to be confirmed once accepted by Warren, Brownell and Doyle, without any formal ceremony. Writing to Brownell, Hearne pointed out that an honorary benching was 'the highest distinction in the benchers power to bestow'.[126] When Chief Justice Warren was informed of his honorary benching he was 'deeply grateful'[127] and accepted immediately. By the end of May, Doyle's formal acceptance of the benching had still not been received.[128]

Around 5,000 members of the ABA attended the conference in London. Their representative, Boris Kostelanetz, had expressed the hope that they might 'visit Ireland and have a status of something more than tourists'.[129] He suggested

twelve years. Belton to Seamus Wilmot, registrar of the NUI, 26 July 1957, NAI DFA/6/434/479. 118 He listed President Sean T. O'Kelly, James Murnaghan, W.E. Wylie, William Black and Serjeant A.M. Sullivan, QC. Belton to Patrick McGilligan, att. gen., 5 Feb. 1957, NAI DFA/6/434/479. However, Sullivan had resigned from his position as honorary bencher in 1956 following a controversy related to the Casement trial. See 'Serjeant Sullivan leaves honorary post in King's Inns', *Irish Times*, 6 Aug. 1956, p. 7. 119 Belton to McGilligan, 5 Feb. 1957, NAI DFA/6/434/479. 120 Davitt to Costello, 27 Feb. 1957, NAI TSCH/3/S16108. 121 Ibid. In March, however, McGilligan said that he had forwarded the proposal to the chief justice 'but found it so unenthusiastically received' that he did not press it. He suggested that the benchers be approached directly, but had 'little hope' that the honorary benching would proceed. Secretary, attorney general's office to Belton, 19 Mar. 1957, NAI DFA/6/434/479. 122 Costello to Hearne, 8 Apr. 1957, NAI DFA/6/434/479. 123 Hearne to Costello, 12 Apr. 1957, NAI DFA/6/434/479. 124 Davitt to Murphy, dept. external affairs, 10 May 1957, NAI DFA/6/434/479; K.I.B.M., 10 May 1957. 125 K.I.B.M., 2 Apr. 1957; 10 May 1957. 126 Hearne to Brownell, 1 May 1957, NAI DFA/6/434/479. 127 Chief Justice Earl Warren to Hearne, 10 May 1957, NAI DFA/6/434/479. 128 Belton to Hearne, 20 May 1957, NAI DFA/6/434/479. 129 Boris Kostelanetz to John A. Costello, 2 Apr. 1956, NAI TSCH/3/S16108 A. A 'Catholic lawyer tour of Europe' was also

'a single reception together with a tour of the courts, important landmarks, etc.', and was sure that this would 'thrill' the American lawyers. The Irish legal professions were determined to put on a good show for the visiting Americans.[130] After a joint meeting of the benchers, the Bar and the Law Society,[131] it was estimated that 'counting members and their wives, some 200 persons will have to be entertained'. In addition, there would be 200 representatives of the Bar and 200 from the solicitors' profession 'including wives'.[132] A reception took place at the Four Courts on 31 July.[133] A black-tie reception also took place at Dublin Castle on 2 August, with about 500 high-profile guests including judges, lawyers, court officers, politicians, senior public servants, academics, university registrars, newspaper editors, clergy, representatives of religious groups and sporting bodies, and anti-partition lawyers from Northern Ireland.[134] Combined with the honours bestowed on Warren, Brownell and Doyle, the visit was a great – if expensive – success.

The connection with the ABA was continued, albeit intermittently, after the successful 1957 visit. For example, the ABA and the Bar Council occasionally corresponded on matters of interest,[135] and representatives of the Irish Bar attended the ABA meetings in San Francisco in 1982;[136] in Atlanta in 1983;[137] and in Chicago in 1984.[138] The ABA visited Ireland in 1985[139] and again in 1989.[140]

Aside from the ABA, the Irish Bar also communicated with other international lawyers' bodies, such as the International Academy of Trial

promoted as part of this trip, visiting 'the historical and religious shrines of Dublin, Paris, Milan, Venice, Bologna, Florence and Rome.' Advertisement, *A.B.A.J.* 43:4 (1957), 301. **130** Justice Davitt, the president of the High Court, suggested a jointly-hosted evening reception in Iveagh House, and wondered if the president of Ireland would also consider a garden party. Davitt to Costello, 22 Oct. 1956, NAI TSCH/3/S16108 A. **131** B.C.M., 20 Feb. 1957; K.I.B.M., 22 Feb. 1957. **132** Iveagh House was deemed too small for such numbers, K.I.B.M., 22 Feb. 1957. **133** Davitt to Costello, 27 Feb. 1957, NAI TSCH/3/S16108 A. The cost would be about £30 a head. The benchers, Law Society and Bar would each contribute £200, and the balance made up from the benchers, barristers and solicitors who attended. K.I.B.M., 22 Feb. 1957; B.C.M., 20 Feb. 1957; 7 May 1957. The reception was to be similar to that given by the Law Society in their centenary year: K.I.B.M., 22 Feb. 1957. **134** Several lists of invitees and potential invitees in NAI TSCH/3/S16108 A. The lord chief justice of Northern Ireland, Lord MacDermott, Judge Black, the senior bencher in Belfast, and the secretary of the Northern Ireland Law Society were all invited. Belton to Murphy, 28 June 1957, NAI DFA/6/434/479. Such was the high-profile nature of the event that RTÉ wanted to broadcast a 30-minute lecture by Chief Justice Warren on the US Supreme Court's recent cases on desegregation: Maurice Gorham, Director of RTÉ, to Belton, asst. sec., Dept. External Affairs, 8 Mar. 1957, NAI DFA/6/434/479. They proposed 'a serious approach to the subject on the lines of our series of Thomas Davis Lectures.' They also wished to record Michael Francis Doyle reminiscing about his role in the Roger Casement trial. However, Warren and Doyle's schedules were to be so busy that Belton suggested that 'only tape recordings would be feasible.' Belton to Gorham, 17 June 1957, NAI DFA/6/434/479. It was later decided to have only interviews on news programmes: Gorham to Belton, 22 June 1957, NAI DFA/6/434/479. **135** E.g., B.C.M., 22 Oct. 1971. **136** Ibid., 17 May 1982. **137** Ibid., 10 June 1983. **138** Ibid., 12 Apr. 1984. Following the 1984 meeting, the chairman remarked that he was 'keenly aware of the need to discourage American lawyers from practising in Europe.' **139** Ibid., 12, 26 July 1985. See 'American Bar Association in Dublin', *I.L.T.* (ns) 3 (1985), 180. **140** Ibid., 23 Apr. 1988; 28 Jan., 25 Feb. 1989.

Lawyers. When the academy sought the attendance of 'ten top barristers' at a seminar in Dublin in July 1971, a notice inviting applications was posted in the Law Library.[141] The American Trial Lawyers Academy visited in 1979 and were given a tour of the Four Courts and invited to dine at the King's Inns.[142] In 1980, the Bar Council joined the Irish National Committee of the International Chamber of Commerce.[143] This would allow members of the Bar to be nominated as arbitrators in international arbitration tribunals.[144]

Irish barristers abroad

In addition to hosting visitors from abroad, sometimes members of the Irish Bar travelled overseas to participate in international conferences and congresses,[145] including meetings of the ABA.[146] In 1948, the Bar Council sought to send a delegation to the second conference of the International Bar Association at the Hague.[147] The Bar's involvement in such events was patchy, and in the early decades of the century the expense involved was usually seen as prohibitive. However, by the 1960s Irish society and the profession was beginning to think in more international terms. In 1967, the chairman of the Bar Council reported that Justice Brian Walsh was concerned about the 'the inadequate representation' of the Irish Bar at the meetings of the International Bar Association, pointing out that the solicitors' profession were well represented and attended regularly.[148] Membership was inexpensive, at £30 per annum, and the Bar Council decided that 'in principle it was desirable that the Bar Council should be a member'.[149] They wrote to the IBA and were surprised to discover that the Incorporated Law Society would be hosting the IBA's biennial conference in Dublin in 1968.[150] The Bar Council's minutes record that:

> It would cost the society around £10,000, and that if we were to join we could hardly avoid subscribing less than £1,000. It was agreed

141 Ibid., 21 Mar. 1971.   142 Ibid., 5 Mar. 1979.   143 Ibid., 13 June 1980.   144 Ibid., 9 Nov. 1981.   145 Members of the judiciary were also invited to address Bar associations overseas. E.g., in 1928, Hugh Kennedy addressed the ABA in Seattle during its semi-centennial celebrations. This was published as: 'The character and sources of constitution of the Irish Free State', *A.B.A.J.* 14:8 (1928), 437. In 1936 Justice Hanna delivered a paper to the ABA in Boston: 'The bench and Bar of Ireland in the nineteenth century', *A.B.A.J.* 22:11 (1936), 761.   146 In 1930 the American Bar Association invited members of the Irish Bar to attend their annual meeting in Chicago, B.C.M., 21 Feb. 1930.   147 B.C.M., 11 June 1948. A notice was placed in the Law Library inviting interested members to apply, and support was sought from the minister for external affairs. The first meeting of the IBA had taken place in New York in 1947, with delegations from 22 nations. Ireland was represented by an observer at the inaugural meeting. 'International Bar Association is organised', *W.L.J.* 32:4 (1947), 61. A brief history of the IBA was published in (1961) 95 *I.L.T.S.J.* 204 (2 Sept. 1961).   148 B.C.M., 27 Apr. 1966.   149 B.C.M., 6 May 1966.   150 This was publicised in the *American Bar Association Journal*: 'International Bar Association meets in Switzerland', *A.B.A.J.* 52:12 (1966), 1148. The Law Society had long been involved in the IBA; e.g., it was represented at the seventh biennial congress in Cologne in 1959 (1959) 93 *I.L.T.S.J.* 67 (14 Mar. 1959), and at the

17 Pádraig Augustine Ó Síocháin wearing one of his Aran knits, 1985.
Image from the public domain (wikimedia commons)

18 *Johnston and Others v. Ireland*, 1986. Representing the State at the European Court of Human Rights. *L–r*: James O'Reilly, P. Smyth, Department of Foreign Affairs, Dermot Gleeson, Jane Liddy (Deputy Legal Adviser, Department of Foreign Affairs). Reproduced by kind permission of the Bar of Ireland Digital Archive

19 *Johnston and Others v. Ireland*, 1986. Representing the Applicant at the European Court of Human Rights. *L–r*: M. O'Leary (Solicitor), Mary Robinson, William Duncan. Reproduced by kind permission of the Bar of Ireland Digital Archive

20 Visit by members of the Bar to Cuba, 1987. *L–r*: Martin O'Kennedy, David Nolan, James Connolly, Brian Lenihan (Jr), Henry Downing, Jane Murphy, Patricia Ryan, Barbara Connolly, Fidel Castro, Mrs O'Kennedy, Stephen Lanigan O'Keeffe, Maureen Clarke, Michael Feehan, David Kennedy, Michael O'Shea. Reproduced by kind permission of the Bar of Ireland Digital Archive

21 Following his legal career, Conor Maguire presented 500 episodes of 'In the Mood', a popular big band and swing music programme on RTÉ. Reproduced by kind permission of the RTÉ Archives

22 Bar football team, 1994. *Sitting*: Kevin Feeney, Des O'Neill, Kevin O'Higgins, Paul Gilligan, Fergus O'Hagan. *Standing*: Francis D. Murphy, Hugo Hynes, Denis McCullough, Diarmuid O'Donovan, Henry Murphy, Joe Finnegan, James Connolly, James Nugent, Peter Shanley, Tom Teehan. Reproduced by kind permission of the Bar of Ireland Digital Archive

23 Group of Attorneys General. *Front row, l–r*: Patrick Connolly, Anthony Hederman, David Byrne, Michael McDowell. *Middle row, l–r*: Eoghan Fitzsimons, Harold Whelehan, John Murray, Peter Sutherland. *Back row, l–r*: Dermot Gleeson, John Rogers. Reproduced by kind permission of the Bar of Ireland Digital Archive

24 Main floor of the Law Library located in the east wing of the Four Courts, pre-1922. Reproduced by kind permission of the Irish Architectural Archive, Curran Collection

25 View of the ruined Law Library (*left-hand side*) from the Four Courts dome. Reproduced by kind permission of the Irish Architectural Archive

26 Stained glass window in the pre-22 Law Library. Reproduced by kind permission of the Irish Architectural Archive

27 Plan for the new Law Library, 1927. Reproduced by kind permission of the Irish Architectural Archive, Honorable Society of King's Inns Collection

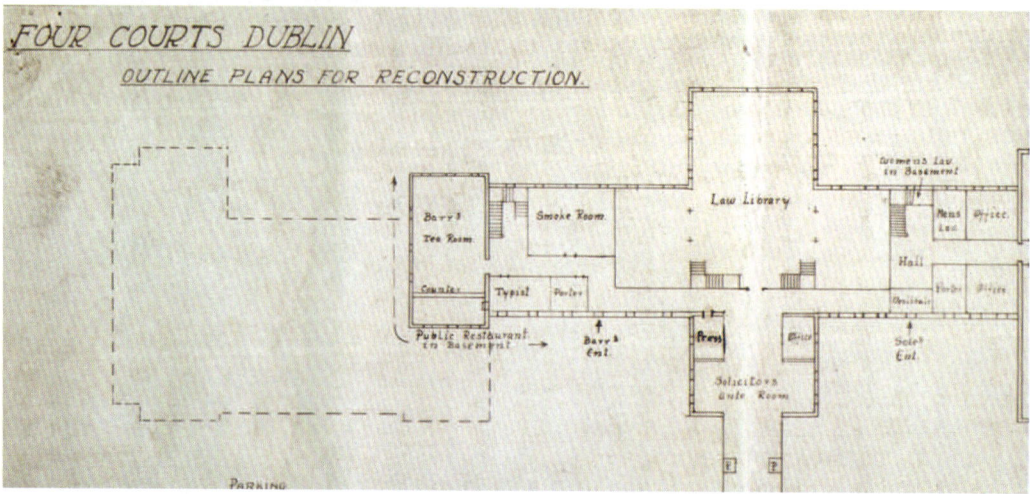

FOUR COURTS DUBLIN
OUTLINE PLANS FOR RECONSTRUCTION.

THE · FOUR · COURTS · DUBLIN ·   BENCH · END · COURT Nº 5

28 Court No. 5 in the refurbished Four Courts.
Reproduced by kind permission of the Irish Architectural Archive

29 St Michan's Church, Church Street, 1951.
Reproduced by kind permission of the Irish Architectural Archive

30 Washington Street Courthouse, Cork City, 1978.
Reproduced by kind permission of Irish Architectural Archive

31 Four Courts Bar, 1983. Reproduced by kind permission of the Irish Photographic Archive

32 Main floor of the Law Library in the 1970s; includes James Salafia, Mark de Blacam and Ronan Keane. Reproduced by kind permission of the Bar of Ireland Digital Archive

33 The sites of the Church Street and Distillery buildings.
Reproduced by kind permission of the Bar of Ireland Digital Archive

34 151 Church Street before the development of the Distillery building. Reproduced by kind permission of the Irish Architectural Archive

35 May Lane view of 151 Church Street, before the development of the Distillery building. Reproduced by kind permission of the Irish Architectural Archive

Church Street

A prestigious new office development

This development is arranged for members of the Irish Bar by the Bar Council of Ireland. It is situated adjacent to the Four Courts Dublin.

36 Development of the Church Street Offices.
Reproduced by kind permission of the Bar of Ireland Digital Archive

unanimously that the council should not join the International Bar Association.[151]

In advance of the planned conference, members of the Bar Council met with the Law Society to discuss the planned itinerary, which included a number of dinners and functions in the King's inns, the Four Courts and other locations. The Law Society 'made clear that the participation of the Bar was wholeheartedly welcome', but because the preparations were at an advanced stage and could not be altered, this 'created a problem of Bar participation.' The Bar Council proposed being named as joint hosts for some of the receptions, depending on the level of subvention required (it hoped to contribute £250).[152] It was pointed out that '[t]he Bars of Great Britain and Northern Ireland were all members of the IBA and would be participating at the conference, and it would appear strange for us to be absent',[153] and so the Bar Council finally joined.[154] However, appointing a regular representative to the European committee of the IBA was deemed to involve 'prohibitive expense'.[155]

By 1979, the Bar was in arrears of three years on its IBA subscription.[156] In 1978, a money-saving suggestion was made at a meeting of the joint UK and Irish Bars committee in London. It was proposed that in order to save expense, perhaps one person could represent all the Bars at certain international meetings, but the proposal was rejected.[157] A similar proposal was made in 1983, that the Bar of Ireland should be joint members with the Bar of Northern Ireland, 'to share costs'.[158] The chairman, who had attended a recent meeting of the IBA in Rome,[159] described it as '[l]argely an American, English-speaking organisation, and aimed largely at the commercial side of the law'. He was of the view that the Irish Bar should continue membership and attend the occasional meeting when this could be afforded.[160]

Financial barriers were not the only things that impeded Irish participation in international networks. Sometimes the effort required was simply deemed too much. The year after the IBA conference had been hosted in Dublin, the IBA sought to appoint a Dublin correspondent to facilitate 'a possible interchange of lawyers'.[161] A number of memoranda on aspects of Irish legal practice were prepared for the IBA, but a member of the Bar who had been asked to complete one of these complained that it involved too much work, and could not complete it.[162] When the IBA wrote that it was planning to set up a section on business law,

eighth congress in Salzburg in 1961: (1961) 95 *I.L.T.S.J.* 204 (2 Sept. 1961).   **151** B.C.M., 4 Nov. 1966.   **152** B.C.M., 12 Dec. 1967. Further discussion in B.C.M., 19 Dec. 1967.   **153** B.C.M., 10 Nov. 1967.   **154** The courts did not sit on the first two days of the conference of the International Bar Association. B.C.M., 2 Feb. 1968.   **155** B.C.M., 10 May 1968.   **156** B.C.M., 10 Jan. 1979. **157** B.C.M., 20 Nov. 1978.   **158** B.C.M., 10 June 1983. By 1988 it was reported that there were 114 Irish members of the IBA, out of a total membership of 11,263. *I.L.T.* (ns) 6 (1988), 150. **159** B.C.M., 13 May 1983.   **160** B.C.M., 10 June 1983.   **161** B.C.M., 28 Nov. 1969.   **162** Ibid.,

it was feared that this would involve too much work from those involved and 'it was decided that the council would not participate in this scheme'.[163]

As early as the 1960s, some members of the Irish Bar were beginning to be cognizant of the nascent European jurisprudence.[164] European integration also nudged the Irish Bar towards further developing relations with other Bars.[165] From 1972 on, the Bar was also associated with the Council of Bars and Law Societies of Europe, or CCBE.[166] It was pointed out at the outset that 'it was probable that we in Ireland would not be able to afford the expense of sending our full delegation on all occasions.'[167] It was proposed to cooperate with the Scottish Advocates Society 'to avoid domination by London'.[168] A new sub-committee of the Bar Council, known as the EEC committee, undertook to study 'what would be the equivalent of a barrister on the continent' and 'arrangements with King's Inns for the registration of foreign lawyers.'[169] A member of the Bar Council described the CCBE as seeing itself as 'the Bar Council of Europe'.[170] On another occasion, it was pointed out that 'the other countries were more concerned that big American firms would buy up firms in Europe and from them send their staff all over the community.'[171] Irish representation on the CCBE was more regular and reliable than its participation in the IBA[172] because the financial strain was not too severe. The subscription fee was split with the

5 Dec. 1969.   163 Ibid., 27 Feb. 1970. By 1971 the Bar Council was in a position to vote to approve the membership of other national Bar associations in the IBA, and voted in favour of the Law Society of Hong Kong; the Law Society of Kenya; the Nigeria Bar Association and the Law Society of Rhodesia, B.C.M., 21 Mar. 1971.   164 E.g., in 1962 Sean MacBride wrote to Chief Justice Ó Dálaigh, 'With the advent and extension of the EEC, the European Court, with its own defined jurisdiction, is now a reality. Whether we become full or associate members of the EEC, the jurisdiction and procedures of this court will be of some considerable importance to Irish lawyers. Even apart from cases involving Irish interests, it will open a new forum in which Irish lawyers could practise.' MacBride to Ó Dálaigh, 30 Apr. 1962, UCDA P51/1 (42). He offered to teach a series of lectures on European law, which would be available free of charge to lawyers, law students and civil servants. His offer was made because 'I am probably more in touch with these new developments than most lawyers and that a lot of the relevant documentation is published only in French.'   165 In October 1970 an international legal conference on the expansion of the EC, sponsored by the British Institute of International and Comparative Law, took place in Dublin. 170 lawyers, mainly from Scandinavia, the UK and Ireland, participated. (1969) 103 I.L.T.S.J. 494; (1970) 104 I.L.T.S.J. 469.   166 The CCBE was established in 1960 and had its genesis 'during a boat trip on the Rhine for a congress of the Union Internationale des Avocats (UIA) in Basel, Switzerland', www.ccbe.eu/about/history/. It was established in response to the perceived threat to the independence of European lawyers posed by the EEC.   167 B.C.M., 23 June 1972. 168 The UK, like all other member states, was entitled to send 3 delegates to the CCBE, but needed to represent the Bar of England and Wales; the Advocates Society; the Bar of Northern Ireland; the Law Society of England; the Writers to the Signet; the Scots Law Society and the Law Society of Northern Ireland. The Scottish advocates were not among those directly represented in the UK's delegation.   169 B.C.M., 23 June 1972.   170 B.C.M., 13 May 1983. In 1986 the president of the CCBE represented the Irish Bar at the IBA annual meeting in New York. B.C.M., 30 July 1986. 171 B.C.M., 2 Jan. 1973. The Irish representative at the 1974 meeting commented on how seriously the other Bars viewed the CCBE: B.C.M., 25 Mar. 1974.   172 Ibid., 7 Dec. 1981.

Law Society,[173] and in the 1980s the Irish Bar's representative paid for their own expenses in travelling to meetings.[174]

By the 1980s the Bar was developing stronger links with international associations,[175] including the ABA, as discussed above. In 1988, the Bar Council approved the nomination of a member of the Irish Bar for the director generalship of the International Bar Association.[176] The Bar Council also engaged with the Union Internationale des Advocats,[177] which was described as 'more European and more like a Bar organisation'.[178]

The 1990s saw even more international networking.[179] The Irish Bar continued to send a representative to IBA meetings,[180] including in New York,[181] and Venice.[182] It was also represented at meetings of the Union Internationale des Advocats.[183] Invitations from young Bar associations were forwarded to the Young Barristers Society.[184] In 1990 the Bar participated in a project run by the Youth Employment Board which involved a working visit by a number of Irish lawyers to the Soviet Union for two weeks, followed by a reciprocal visit by Soviet lawyers to Ireland.[185] Members of the Bar occasionally sought financial assistance from the Bar Council in order to allow them to travel for these events.[186]

Relationship with the Incorporated Law Society

At an individual level, barristers worked with solicitors and maintained good professional relationships. As Morison and Leith note,

---

173 Ibid., 12 Jan. 1973; 13 July 1973.   174 E.g., ibid., 9 Oct. 1980; 7 Dec. 1981. It was pointed out in 1986 that the Bar Council's representative on the CCBE 'Should be fluent in French and should also be of some substance so that the leadership of the delegation should be in the hands of the Bar.' Ibid., 27 Jan. 1986.   175 In 1981 the chairman of the Bar Council visited several foreign Bars and was 'congratulated on his stamina.' Ibid., 9 Nov. 1981. When the CCBE secured new accommodation in the mid-eighties, the Bar Council contributed £250 toward 'a suitable gift from Ireland', ibid., 13 Dec. 1984.   176 Ibid., 27 Feb. 1988. The member was unsuccessful: ibid., 16 July 1988. A meeting of the IBA council took place in Dublin in May 1986. 'Report on the third conference of the section on general practice of the International Bar Association', W.L.J. 31:4 (1985), 20.   177 The IUA was established in Belgium in 1927. According to its institutional history, 'After the First World War, a group of Luxembourgish, Belgian and French lawyers gave birth to the idea that it became essential to help certain Bars to modernise and to maintain international contacts.' In 1950, the secretary general of L'Union Internationale Des Avocats invited the Irish Bar to send a delegate to its next congress in Luxembourg. B.C.M., 14 Jan. 1950. The Council appreciated the invitation but indicated that it could not promise to send a delegate, as the congress was to take place during the legal term.   178 B.C.M., 13 May 1983.   179 Although sometimes invitations issued by international bodies to the Bar Council were not always dealt with in a timely manner, and sometimes no Irish representative therefore travelled to the event. In June 1985, for example, it was reported that documentation relating to a Council of Europe colloquy at Bordeaux had only been received by the Bar a few days before the closing date for applications. The delay appears to have arisen in the Department of Foreign Affairs. B.C.M., 8 June 1985.   180 B.C.M., 21 Jan. 1995.   181 Ibid., 23 July 1990.   182 Ibid., 12 May 1990.   183 Ibid., 8 June 1991. 184 Ibid., 9 Nov. 1991. These included the Young Bar of Ypres and the Business Brussels Young Bar. 185 Ibid., 31 Mar. 1990.   186 E.g., in 1993, several members received support to attend an international conference in Australia on family law and childrens' rights, ibid., 1 May 1993.

At every stage, barristers are dependent on solicitors in private practice, business or government, not only to give them work of the right kind and on the correct scale but to pay them promptly. The advocate is always dependent on those others involved in the preparation and presentation of his or her case.'[187]

At an institutional level, there were generally very cordial relations between the Bar Council and the Incorporated Law Society. As noted in chapter eleven, until the late sixties the Law Society's premises were located within the Four Courts complex, and this often required close cooperation on practical matters.[188] The two professions often worked together on issues of mutual interest. One example is the proposals in the 1923 report of the judiciary committee.[189] In 1928, the Bar Council invited the Law Society to form a joint committee to consider making a joint recommendation to the executive council regarding various procedural issues relating to oral evidence, the jurisdiction of the Circuit Court and the right to trial by jury.[190] From the 1970s, the Bar Council and the Law Society worked collaboratively with regard to membership of the CCBE,[191] and jointly hosted meetings in Dublin.[192] In 1933, a joint committee of the Bar Council and the Law Society was established to consider the lack of availability of Irish legal textbooks.[193]

From time to time, ad hoc meetings took place between representatives of the two legal professions.[194] A joint consultative committee was proposed by the Law Society in 1952,[195] with members nominated by both the Law Society and the Bar Council.[196] It considered matters of mutual interest, such as the Courts of Justice Act 1953,[197] which dealt with judicial remuneration and appointments. The joint committee was concerned about 'the undesirability of four judges sitting as the Supreme Court,'[198] and the sittings of the master of the High Court.[199] It also dealt with complaints. For example, the Law Society complained about the practice of barristers having consultations with insurance officials in the absence of solicitors. The Bar Council issued a ruling that barristers ought not to meet with clients or their representatives in the absence of the client's solicitor.[200]

---

187 Morison and Leith, *Barrister's world*, p. 18.   188 E.g., B.C.M., 6 Feb. 1948 (re phones). 189 *Report of judiciary committee* (Dublin, 1923).   190 B.C.M., 16 Mar. 1928. A joint meeting was held; ibid., 22 Mar. 1928, and the Law Society subsequently told the Bar Council that they had written to the minister for justice about the Courts of Justice Act 1926, ibid., 15 June 1928. 191 E.g., ibid., 1 Mar. 1974.   192 Ibid., 3 Feb. 1975; 7 Dec. 1981; 11 May 1983. For the 1975 visit, there was a dinner at the King's Inns, jointly hosted by the Bar and the Law Society, an address by the president of Ireland, and a reception provided by the attorney general. Ibid., 11 Mar. 1983. For the 1975 meeting, '[t]he only difficulty had been the apportionment of expenses between the Bar and the Law Society.' Ibid., 3 Feb., 3 Mar. 1975.   193 Eamonn G. Hall, *The superior courts of law: 'official' law reporting in Ireland, 1866–2006* (Dublin, 2007), p. 157.   194 E.g., B.C.M., 18 Apr. 1966 (re universal liability).   195 Ibid., Aug. 1952, referring to a letter of 6 May 1952.   196 Ibid., 13 Oct., 8 Dec. 1952.   197 Ibid., 1 Dec. 1952. At a general meeting of the Bar in 1952, the Bar's 'grave' concerns relating to the 1952 Act were discussed. Ibid., 12 Dec. 1952.   198 Ibid., 21 Dec. 1954.   199 Ibid., 1 Apr. 1954.   200 Ibid., Aug. 1953.

A similar liaison committee was established in the 1960s, with the intention that this would meet regularly.[201] It discussed matters of mutual interest, as well as addressing issues raised by the Law Society, such as barristers' fees. In 1969, when both branches of the legal profession were contemplating the potential impact of joining the EEC, the liaison committee considered the proposed directive on the freedom of lawyers to practise in other states.[202] The Bar Council was concerned by developments in the early seventies, particularly the implications of the *Rayners v. Belgium* case,[203] and it resolved to have 'close and continuing consultations with the Law Society on all these matters'.[204] The professions also worked together on matters relating to the free legal aid system;[205] for example, when considering withdrawing from the scheme in 1975, the Law Society informed the Bar Council that it would be 'unlikely to recommend a formal withdrawal from the legal aid scheme unless the Bar did so first, but would probably do so if the Bar so moved.'[206]

The committee was dormant for some years, and became active again in the early eighties[207] and nineties.[208] The two professions engaged constructively on matters such as barristers listing their areas of speciality in the law directory,[209] and dealt with minor complaints. For example, in 1985 the Law Society pointed out that it was sometimes difficult for solicitors to contact barristers at the Law Library. The Bar Council pointed out that there were more courts sitting than there had been in the past and that 'counsel were much more apt to be out in different parts of the building and not easily contacted'. It was also pointed out that sometimes it took a considerable time for barristers to come from the upstairs library to the door to meet with solicitors, and then 'solicitors were inclined to leave before counsel arrived.' The chairman of the Bar Council also made the point that

> The Bar was the only profession where a solicitor or any other person could come casually to the Law Library and ask to see a barrister without having made a prior appointment. It could not be automatically guaranteed that a barrister would be there when called.[210]

201 Ibid., 24 May 1966 (reporting on second meeting). It was noted that all of the Bar Council reps but only one of the Law Society reps was present, until near the end of the meeting. By 1967 it was reported that there had been three satisfactory meetings held. Ibid., 13 Jan. 1967. 202 Ibid., 28 Nov. 1969. In 1970 the Bar received a report from the Economist Intelligence Unit of Ireland on the implications of the directive regarding the freedom of barristers to plead in all member states. 203 In 1974 the council wrote to the minister for justice regarding its concern regarding the case of *Rayners v. Belgium* (1974) C.J.E.U. Case 2/74, in which the plaintiff claimed the right to freedom of establishment as a lawyer under the terms of the Treaty of Rome. B.C.M., 29 Apr. 1974. The minister replied that the Irish members of the working party on the draft directive had taken a similar view. The case was discussed further at B.C.M., 11 Oct. 1974. 204 B.C.M., 11 Oct. 1974. See also ibid., 28 Apr. 1975. 205 E.g., ibid., 28 Apr. 1975. 206 Ibid., 20 Mar. 1975. 207 Ibid., 17 May 1982; 13 May 1983. 208 E.g., ibid., 13 Jan. 1990. 209 Ibid., 12 July 1985. 210 Ibid.

There were always certain issues where tension existed between the two professions. Any hint that the solicitors' profession was attempting to encroach upon the Bar's territory was generally met with resistance, whether this related to minor issues[211] or more significant matters. One of the hallmarks of the barristers' profession was, historically, the exclusive right to address the courts. According to Boon and Flood:

> The barristers' monopoly of advocacy, and with it domination of the bench and profession, evolved over 700 years ... In the early nineteenth century, the Bar consolidated its role as a specialist consultancy and advocacy profession acting only on referral from solicitors. Solicitors accepted this inferior role but secured a lucrative and secure monopoly over conveyancing, the transfer of land.[212]

Solicitors had some rights of audience in the twentieth century, but this tended to be concentrated in the lower courts. Before the introduction of legal aid, the rules of the superior courts allowed representation at the Central Criminal Court by a solicitor, where a person did not have the means to pay for counsel. The solicitors' right of audience cropped up in the Bar Council minutes from time to time. For example, in 1927, attention was drawn to the fact that 'some solicitors had lately been in the habit of moving motions in court'.[213] The issue arose again in 1928, particularly in relation to the rights of solicitors' clerks. A solicitor's clerk had applied to have a consent made a rule of court and Justice Hanna had refused to hear him, stating it was not an application to be moved by a solicitor in the High Court.[214] McEnery, writing about practising in the early 1930s, wrote about solicitors who,

> Scornful of the advocacy of young barristers ... and keen on local publicity, insisted on doing their cases without briefing a barrister. There were a few of those types of solicitors in every town and very unpopular they were with the young barristers. We felt they were taking the bread out of our mouths for their own selfish ends but I suppose we were selfish too.[215]

In 1951, it was reported in the press that the president of the Law Society commented adversely on the practice of engaging two senior counsel in certain

---

211 For example, in 1982 the Bar cricket club hosted members of the Australian Bar cricket club at the King's Inns. A complaint was later made to the Bar Council because one of the Irish members had invited a solicitor to attend. The latter had arrived in evening clothes with his wife and had thereupon been told 'publicly and in forceful language' by a member of the Bar 'to go away'. The Bar Council felt that the incident reflected badly on the profession, and the chairman wrote a letter of apology to the solicitor. B.C.M., 28 June, 16 July 1982. 212 Andy Boon and John Flood, 'Trials of strength: the reconfiguration of litigation as a contested terrain', *L. & Soc. Rev.* 33:3 (1999), 595, at 595. 213 B.C.M., 11 Feb. 1927. 214 B.C.M., 27 Jan. 1928. 215 McEnery, *Look back*, p. 133.

cases, stating that this practice had only recently developed.[216] Members of the Bar Council suggested writing to the Law Society to point out that 'if the Society had complaints regarding the conduct of cases that they should first have approached the Council rather than making their complaints the subject of a pronouncement.'[217] A carefully worded letter was drafted and sent to the Law Society a few weeks later.[218]

In 1952, the president of the High Court wrote to the Bar Council because a solicitor sought permission to appear in the Central Criminal Court to defend a client. A member of council had also received a press inquiry about this case. Different views were expressed by members of council, including that 'the High Court should not be deprived of the services of the Bar' and that 'persons unable to afford the services of both counsel and solicitor should not be deprived of legal assistance.' It was also pointed out that the solicitors' profession 'showed a tendency to encroach on counsel's privilege'.[219]

The majority view of the Committee on Court Practice and Procedure in 1971 was that solicitors should have a right of audience in all courts.[220] Two senior counsel on the committee[221] disagreed with this, setting out their reasons in an extensive minority report. This considered the specialised nature of advocacy and the relatively high number of solicitors compared with barristers.[222] They considered potential cost savings to be unlikely, and argued that the solicitor's close relationship with the client was a 'drawback'.[223] Despite the minority views expressed, section 17 of the Courts Act 1971 conferred a right of audience on solicitors for all courts. A barrister who was in practice before 1971 lamented the change:

> I don't think we are respected by solicitors to the same extent that we were 50 years ago or 40 years ago. One of the reasons for that is I think that they gave solicitors a right of audience in the High Court and the Supreme Court I think, consciously or unconsciously, probably unconsciously the idea filtered out that we were all the same. We're not. But again, that's me going back to the sixties and seventies at a time when we certainly were not the same.[224]

When debating the 1971 Act, Minister O'Malley expressed a hope that solicitors would exercise their rights,[225] but by the late 1980s, however, it was reported that

---

216 B.C.M., 7 Dec. 1951. See 'The law', *Irish Times*, 27 Nov. 1951, p. 5. 217 Ibid. 218 B.C.M., 14 Dec. 1951. 219 Ibid., 14 Nov. 1952. A sub-committee was appointed to consider the matter, and a written report was sent to the president of the High Court, B.C.M., 21 Nov. 1952. 220 Committee on Court Practice and Procedure, *Thirteenth interim report. The solicitor's right of audience* (Dublin, 1971), p. 10. 221 These were Edward Micks and James McMahon. 222 *Thirteenth interim report*, pp 14–15. 223 Ibid., p. 16. 224 B8. 225 Dáil Éireann deb., vol. 257, col. 5 (1 Dec. 1971).

with 'very few exceptions', the exercise of this right by solicitors was 'minimal',[226] even in the Circuit Court. They appeared fairly regularly in the master's court, and the Bar Council noted that while it was uncommon for solicitors to conduct trials, they did make various interlocutory applications.[227] Boon and Flood examined the similar phenomenon of solicitors being reluctant to appear in the higher courts in England and Wales, even after they had been granted this right in the early nineties.[228] Reflecting on the relationship between the two branches of the legal profession, Boon and Flood observe that '[a]s relationships change over time, differences are recast and redrawn, creating more uncertainty over what was once settled turf.'[229]

Both the Bar Council and the Law Society made representations to the Fair Trade Commission in the eighties.[230] The commission examined, among other things, issues which affected both branches of the legal profession, including solicitors' right of audience in the superior courts, the need to access barristers via solicitors,[231] and the very fact of having a divided profession.[232] After hearing from various witnesses, the commission concluded that 'the fact that the legal profession is divided into two branches is not the primary cause of the problems of restrictive practices, though it may facilitate their continuance. It does not believe that fusion of the profession would eliminate these problems'.[233] It was, however, in favour of the introduction of a 'common vocational course' for the training of solicitors and barristers.[234] When the commission's report was published, the two bodies sought to present 'a united front'.[235]

The tradition of having separate legal professions was questioned at different stages during the twentieth century, and proposals for a fused legal profession were often expressed in terms of the potential cheapness and convenience for clients. In his 1946 memorandum, for example, Justice Gavan Duffy, argued in favour of the amalgamation of barristers and solicitors.[236] He provided some

---

226 One notable exception was Alan Shatter, who appeared in both the High Court and the Supreme Court. The Fair Trade Commission later reported that he had 'also been involved in some disputes with the taxing master regarding the appropriate fees for the exercise of this right.' F.T.C., para. 8.3.   227 Before 1971, High Court judges had sometimes permitted solicitors a right of audience for an adjournment or an interlocutory order.   228 Boon and Flood, 'Trials of strength'. They note, at 596, that in England and Wales, '[f]aced with the market-oriented 1980s and 1990s, the Bar's hegemony began to dissolve. As a part of this process, the battle over rights of audience in the higher courts brought to a head the historic tension between branches of the profession.' 229 Boon and Flood, 'Trials of strength', at 600.   230 See pp 346–51.   231 The Law Society was not in favour of any change to this. F.T.C., para. 9.11, although the commission itself held that '[c]lients, including professional clients, should be able to approach barristers directly', F.T.C., para. 9.33.   232 Ibid. See further, ch. 16.   233 F.T.C., para. 6.45.   234 Ibid., para. 7.142. The proposed institute of legal education would have been similar to the Institute of Professional Legal Studies in Northern Ireland.   235 B.C.M., 3 Mar. 1990.   236 'Memorandum in favour of the amalgamation of barristers and solicitors, June 1946', Gavan Duffy to taoiseach, 4 June 1946, NAI TSCH/ 3/S13867. See also the memoranda and correspondence at George Gavan Duffy papers, UCDA P152/38. Around this time, Gavan Duffy was also involved in advising the taoiseach about the establishment and composition of a law reform committee 'to inquire into matters of law reform and furnish reports and recommendations thereon to the government.' Gavan Duffy to taoiseach,

historical context for the development of the legal professions and argued that the division was 'due to the accidents of history; there is no inherent necessity for that expensive fissure, artificially created, and it seems hard to justify on any logical grounds'.[237] He also criticised '[t]he shocking rule (from England) that generally the client cannot consult the barrister directly, but must go through a solicitor, which prevented the client in many instances from going for advice straight to the man who can give it and requires him to pay an intermediary whose services he may not need at all'.[238] He noted that vested interests in both professions would oppose any proposed reform, and pointed out that fusion of professions would also mean fusion of the authorities – the benchers, Bar Council and the 'more efficient' Law Society, as well as blending the law libraries.[239]

> Solicitors have offices, clerks and stenographers, typewriters, safes and filing systems, while barristers work at home with such help from time to time as they can afford, in the evening and sometimes late at night. Amalgamation would put law work on a business-like basis and would go far to facilitate its proper conduct. Solicitors are expected to keep proper records of all their work, but barristers need keep none and at most they generally keep only some kind of note of the fees due to them by solicitors.[240]

In 1983 the Law Society invited the Bar Council to share its AGM. The Council was wary of this, fearing it might be 'a step on the way to amalgamation.'[241] This invitation was discussed at length, with the Bar Council wary of giving offence to the solicitors' profession, but at the same time, its view was that

> It was evident that the Law Society was attempting to give the impression, both at home and abroad, that it was the dominant part of the legal profession. This scheme would reinforce that impression; would blur the distinction between the two branches; and might assist them in their schemes for amalgamation.[242]

The Bar Council continued to resist any suggestion of amalgamating the two professions.

Other external relations

The Bar was also in frequent communication with the Incorporated Council for Law Reporting, and members of the Bar both served on the council and worked

13 Mar. 1945, UCDA P152/35.　237 Ibid., p. 1.　238 Gavan Duffy memorandum, p. 8. 239 Ibid., p. 9.　240 Ibid., p. 10.　241 B.C.M., 13 May 1983.　242 Ibid., 10 June 1983.

as law reporters.[243] The relationship between the Bar Council and the Law Reporting Council was generally cordial. For example, when the Law Reporting Council wanted to use the old grand jury room in the Four Courts for storage in 1921, the Bar Council had no objection.[244] Delay in the reporting of judgements was a constant problem in the first half of the century,[245] and attempts were made by both bodies to work together to resolve this.[246] The two bodies also worked together (along with the Law Society) on the publication of Irish legal textbooks and treatises. In the mid-eighties, the Council of Law Reporting engaged in 'significant canvassing of all members of the Law Library who did not at that time subscribe to the reports. It offered special rates for members of the Bar, and discounts for juniors in their first five years.[247] In the early nineties, the council's precarious finances were bolstered by 'the negotiation of a "bulk" supply agreement' with the Bar Council.[248] Hall writes that Michael McDowell SC 'led the campaign for the Council'. Members of the Bar were very dissatisfied when it transpired that the Bar Council entered into this deal without consulting members. The deal meant that members of the junior Bar would pay £16 per quarter for access to the Irish Reports, while seniors would pay £24 per quarter. The matter was discussed at a general meeting of the Bar in November 1990, at which over three hundred people were present.[249] The Bar Council was accused of poor communication and failing to consult with members, but ultimately the deal, which Hall characterises as mutually beneficial, stood.[250]

The legal professions and the university law schools liaised with one another over issues such as the establishment of a consultative committee on law reform in the sixties. This involved cooperation between the Bar Council, the benchers, the Law Society and the university law schools.[251] In 1973 there was a proposal to establish a single European law centre in Dublin.[252] Osborough writes that 'meetings of law librarians, academic lawyers and representatives of the two branches of the profession were held over a three-year period' to discuss the possibility of a joint Law Library, but he suggests that 'every Law Library of any standing in the state wished to go its own way'.[253] The Reid professorship at Trinity College also involved collaboration between the Bar and the third level sector, and sometimes lengthy correspondence.[254]

The Bar also maintained a relationship with the university law schools. There were two major reviews of Irish legal education in the twentieth century: the Fair Trade Commission, which is considered further below, and the 1967 Commission

243 See pp 149–50. 244 B.C.M., 20 Dec. 1921. 245 Hall, *The superior courts*, pp 132–41. Hall notes, pp 237–322, that this reached a critical point in the sixties, and, p. 374, a committee on delay was established in 1989. 246 E.g., in 1959 a memorandum was signed by members of the Bar regarding the difficulty in obtaining copies of unreported judgments, seeking the cooperation of the Incorporated Council. B.C.M., 20 Feb., 6 Dec. 1959 and 5 Jan. 1960. 247 Hall, *The superior courts*, p. 369. 248 Ibid., p. 375. 249 B.C.M., 10 Nov. 1990. 250 Hall, *The superior courts*, pp 375–6. 251 B.C.M., 24 May 1966. 252 W.N. Osborough, *The law school of University College Dublin* (Dublin, 2014), p. 212. 253 Ibid. 254 E.g., B.C.M., 19 Feb., 7 May 1973; 27 Jan. 1975; 9 July, 15

on Higher Education.[255] The 1967 commission, chaired by Cearbhaill Ó Dálaigh, emphasised the role of university law schools in providing legal education, and recommended that a university degree be an essential part of legal education.[256]

Both UCD and Trinity students were allowed exemptions from King's Inns examinations, and were expected to cooperate with the King's Inns education committee regarding the content and assessment of law courses.[257] This worked well for much of the century, though not always. Delany observed in the mid-sixties that 'there is no other profession which expresses any hesitation concerning the teaching of its subject at a university. It is only the professional lawyers who seem to be doubtful whether their subject can properly be taught within academic halls'.[258] Pressures such as the increased number of King's Inns students in the seventies placed a strain on the relationship.[259] In its 1990 report, the Fair Trade Commission observed that

> The past decade had witnessed a dramatic, and profoundly disquieting, cleavage between the university law schools and the legal professions in relation to the fundamentals of legal education.[260]

Representatives from the university law schools claimed that

> There were adverse pressures being applied by the professional bodies to reduce the intake of students into the university law schools, to revise the content of certain courses in a way which was detrimental to the intrinsic academic value of those courses, and to alter the syllabus along lines that did not take account of legitimate expectations of those students who did not intend to pursue a professional career.[261]

The commission recommended the establishment of an advisory committee on legal education. Following the publication of its report, a series of meetings took place between the Bar Council, the Law Society and the university law schools, and this led to the establishment of the joint advisory committee on legal education and training,[262] chaired by Justice Ronan Keane.

Other than clashes over issues such as student numbers and pathways to professional qualification, the Bar and the universities tended to be mutually supportive. For most of the twentieth century, there were many barristers who combined their work at the Bar with teaching in the academic law schools.[263]

Aug. 1979; 4 July 1980. **255** See Osborough, *The law school*, pp 169–70. **256** Tom O'Malley, 'Legal education and training in Europe: Ireland, *Int. J. Leg. Prof.* 2 (1995), 63, at 73. **257** Ibid., p. 27; R.B. McDowell and D.A. Webb, *Trinity College Dublin, 1592–1952: an academic history* (Cambridge, 1982), pp 193 and 330–1. The law schools at Cork and Galway did not enjoy the same exemptions: Osborough, p. 27. **258** V.T.H. Delany, *The administration of justice in Ireland* (2nd ed., Dublin, 1965), p. 83. **259** See ch. 5. **260** F.T.C., para. 7.39. **261** Ibid. **262** See Dáil Éireann deb., vol. 440, no. 3 (10 Mar. 1994). **263** Osborough, *The law school*, pp 189–91.

O'Malley notes that in the 1980s, each of the law schools had 'a solid core of full time teaching staff'.[264] The Bar Council occasionally subvented student endeavours and courses in the universities.[265]

* * *

Knowing how much interaction the Irish Bar had with legal professions elsewhere gives us a better sense of the profession's awareness of legal and professional developments overseas. Despite some of the visits and links described in this chapter, it would appear that in the first half the century, the Bar had a primarily local or national focus. This was reflective of Irish society more generally during these decades. The relationship with the Bar of Northern Ireland was particularly poor for much of this period. Part of this local focus included frequent liaising with organisations such as the Law Society, the university law schools, the Board of Works,[266] and the Council of Law Reporting. For the legal system to function effectively, it was necessary for such bodies to maintain strong professional links and to work collaboratively where necessary.

Internationally, there were some efforts to foster and maintain links and networks, even in the 1920s, though this often depended on the willingness and enthusiasm (and sometimes the finances) of individual barristers. Things that were done on an institutional level were often as a result of internal or external pressure being exerted, or strong-minded individuals. The pressure might come from the judiciary, as in the case of Justice Walsh, or from the Bar's own fears about how non-participation in certain events or networks might be perceived. The development of international human rights law and Ireland's accession to the EEC led to greater international collaboration, including with the Bar of Northern Ireland. The 1990s witnessed a transformation in the Irish economy, and an increasingly international focus, which was reflected at the Bar.

264 O'Malley, 'Legal education', at 64.   265 E.g., B.C.M., 16 Jan. 1976; 18 Jan. 1992; 18 Oct. 1968.
266 See pp 215–29.

CHAPTER FOURTEEN

Barristers' contribution to public life

Introduction

This chapter considers barristers' contribution to public life both in Ireland and further afield. Not everyone who qualified as a barrister practised at the Bar; some went on to careers in commerce or finance, or served the state as elected representatives or public servants. A number of barristers had success in broadcasting, sport and the arts. For some, working at the Bar was combined with activities in these other spheres. The point was made in chapters three and five that many of those who were called to the Bar had qualifications in diverse fields. In 1992, Hugh O'Flaherty observed that this was a very positive dimension to the Library:

> I was struck by the sheer versatility of members of the Bar. I refer, in particular, to the many members of the Bar who had qualified in other disciplines; in fact, it is fair to say, I think, that nearly every occupation and profession was represented, and continues to be represented, in the Law Library ... I have often wondered what alchemy the idea of practising law possesses to lure so many highly qualified people from other occupations to the role of the advocate.[1]

The international contribution made by Irish barristers is also worthy of note; as will be demonstrated in this chapter, they worked in legal systems throughout the commonwealth in the early part of the century, and later chaired major international and European bodies.

Contribution to Irish public life

The foundation of the state

There was a long tradition of barristers playing significant roles in Irish public life, and from the very foundation of the state in the 1920s, the presence and influence of barristers was evident. This continued throughout the century. Members of the Bar were involved in the drafting of the 1922 and 1937 constitutions and the designing of the new courts system. They were the civil

---

1 Hugh O'Flaherty, 'The independent Bar and the defence of human rights' in James O'Reilly (ed.), *Human rights and constitutional law: essays in honour of Brian Walsh* (Dublin, 1992), pp 169–

servants, public commentators, judges, elected representatives and government ministers of the new state. They were consulted on many aspects of public life, sitting on state boards and departmental working groups; and of course, through their primary activity, litigation, they helped to define and refine personal and political rights.

The contribution of barristers to the drafting of the 1922 constitution was already discussed in chapter two. Four out of the ten committee members were barristers,[2] as well as two members of the secretariat.[3] Having such a preponderance of barristers on the committee brought a number of advantages. First, they were able to digest and synthesise a large volume of legal materials, including foreign constitutions, and quite quickly come up with concrete proposals.[4] Second, they were undoubtedly alive to the need for precision in the drafting language; third, as members of the relatively diverse Law Library they were used to working alongside colleagues from different faiths and political backgrounds, and this helped things to run relatively smoothly; and finally, the presence of so many lawyers added to the perceived legitimacy of the committee and its work.

Considerable work on the drafting of the 1922 constitution has been carried out by Mohr,[5] Cahillane[6] and Farrell.[7] The final text was completed in time for elections in June 1922, and the constitution came into force on 6 December 1922.[8] Darrell Figgis later wrote that a constitution 'contains the fundamental law of a state.'[9] The constitution is a statement of the values and ethos of the new state and its system of government. It is also a legal document requiring careful drafting. As Brunet points out, '[l]awyers could understand the constitution and the making of laws'.[10] Who better to draw up a blueprint for a new state than a group of lawyers?

---

70.   2 Hugh Kennedy, John O'Byrne, Kevin O'Shiel and James Murnaghan. See ch. 2.   3 Edward (or 'Ned') Millington Stephens and Patrick Albert O'Toole. A fifth lawyer on the committee was Clemens J. France, a US labour lawyer. See p. 23.   4 Swift McNeill wrote, p. ix, that '[t]he drafters took as their model, like the framers of the American constitution, the British constitution of their own times and endeavoured to improve on that model.' In his view, p. xiii, the constitution was 'a moment of brilliant constructive statesmanship and of profound political genius'.   5 See, e.g., Thomas Mohr, 'British involvement in the creation of the constitution of the Irish Free State', *D.U.L.J.* 30 (2008), 166; Thomas Mohr, 'Law and the foundation of the Irish state on 6 December 1922', *Ir. Jur.* 59 (2018), 31; Thomas Mohr, 'The influence of Chief Justice Hugh Kennedy on Irish legal scholarship and publishing', *Ir. Jur.* 64 (2020), 97.   6 Laura Cahillane, *Drafting the Irish Free State constitution* (Manchester, 2016).   7 Brian Farrell, 'The drafting of the Irish Free State constitution I', *Ir. Jur.* 5 (1970), 115; Brian Farrell, 'The drafting of the Irish Free State constitution II', *Ir. Jur.* 5 (1970), 343. See also D.H. Akenson and I.F. Fallin, 'The Irish Civil War and the drafting of the Free State constitution: the drafting process', *Éire-Ireland* 5:2 (1970), 10; Bill Kissane, *New beginnings: constitutionalism and democracy in modern Ireland* (Dublin, 2011); Darragh Gannon and Fearghal McGarry, 'Remembering 1922' in Darragh Gannon and Fearghal McGarry (eds), *Ireland 1922: independence, partition, civil war* (Dublin, 2022) and Colum Kenny, *Midnight in London: the Anglo-Irish Treaty crisis* (Dublin, 2022).   8 See Mohr, 'Law and the foundation of the Irish state'.   9 Darrell Figgis, *The Irish constitution: explained by Darrell Figgis* (Dublin, 1922), p. 16.   10 Mélanie Brunet, '"Good government, without him, is well-nigh impossible": training

Chapter two also mentioned barristers' contribution to the judiciary committee in 1923. This was established to draft a new courts system for the new state.[11] Again, there was a preponderance of members of the Bar: John O'Byrne, Hugh Kennedy, Timothy Sullivan,[12] William J. Johnston,[13] James Creed Meredith[14] and Cahir Davitt sat on the committee alongside six others.[15] The committee focused not only on reconstructing the judiciary but also on reforms to improve efficiency of the machinery of justice. Cosgrave had advised the commission to consider such issues as the centralisation or decentralisation of the courts, the number of judges needed and the necessary qualifications for appointment. In 1923 the committee published its relatively concise report.[16] Keane describes the changes proposed by the commission as 'relatively far-reaching',[17] although, as he points out, there were several potential reforms, such as the fusion of the two legal professions or the abolition of the adversarial system, which received little or no attention. However, Keane notes,

> The reluctance of the committee as a body to be adventurous in this area was understandable, given that only one of its members was a layman. While proposals such as the end of the adversarial system and the fusion of the professions may not seem particularly revolutionary to us to-day, they had a distinctly radical flavour in the nineteen twenties.[18]

Some of the proposed reforms proved controversial, and were discussed at length in the Dáil and at meetings of the Bar.[19] One matter which concerned

future (male) lawyers for politics in Ontario, Quebec, and Nova Scotia, 1920–1960' in Constance Backhouse and W. Wesley Pue (eds), *The promise and perils of law: lawyers in Canadian history* (Toronto, 2009), p. 55. 11 The establishment of the committee, its terms of reference and final report were reported on in the press; e.g., 'Legal system inquiry: judiciary committee and terms of reference', *Irish Times*, 31 Jan. 1923, p. 7; 'Judiciary committee: preliminary meeting', *Irish Times*, 3 Feb. 1923, p. 8. 12 O'Sullivan was called in 1895 and took silk in 1918. He practised on the Munster Circuit and was appointed the first president of the High Court in 1924, and chief justice in 1936. See Ferguson, *Barristers*, p. 305 and Lawrence William White, 'Sullivan, Timothy', *D.I.B.* 13 Called in 1892, Johnston had a busy practice on the North-East Circuit and took silk in 1911 when he was appointed a county court judge. He edited both the *New Irish Jurist and Local Government Review* and the *Irish Law Times and Solicitors' Journal*, and authored a number of treatises and scholarly articles. He was appointed to the High Court in 1924, and was one of the only new appointees with judicial experience. See Ferguson, *Barristers*, p. 214 and Patrick Gageby, 'Johnston, William John', *D.I.B.* 14 He was called to the Bar in 1901, practised on the North-East Circuit, and took silk in 1918. A Protestant nationalist, he was president of the Dáil Supreme Court from 1920–2. See Tadhg Foley, 'Meredith, James Creed', *D.I.B.* and Ferguson, *Barristers*, p. 253. 15 Sir Charles O'Connor, former master of the rolls, was also a member, as was Louis Walsh (Luaigh Breathnach), a solicitor and district justice; Henry Murphy, former crown solicitor for Monaghan; William Hewat, president of the Dublin Chamber of Commerce; Patrick Brady, former president of the Incorporated Law Society. Sir James Campbell (Lord Glenavy) chaired the commission. Barrister Michael Smidic acted as secretary. Smidic was called in 1908 as Michael Smithwick; see Ferguson, *Barristers*, p. 300. 16 *Report of judiciary committee.* 17 Ronan Keane, 'The voice of the Gael: Chief Justice Kennedy and the emergence of the new Irish court system', *Ir. Jur.* 31 (1996), 204, at 215. 18 Ibid. 19 E.g., B.C.M., 7 Nov. 1923; 'The judiciary bill', *Irish Times*

members of the legal profession was the dates for the long vacation.[20] The jurisdiction of the new Circuit Court raised what Kotsonouris describes as 'a storm of protest'[21] in the Dáil, which lasted for several days. An advantage, from a litigant's perspective, was that they would not have to travel to Dublin for cases valued under £300. The Bar Council met with the Law Society to discuss these and other proposed measures. Fifty barristers had signed a letter asking the council to consider the 'general scope of various provisions of the judiciary bill as they believed that the same would seriously affect the future of the profession without conferring any advantages to taxpayers or litigants'.[22] In the Dáil, members of the Bar, led by William Redmond[23] and William Magennis,[24] vehemently opposed the measure and introduced a proposal on behalf of the Bar Council. In Kotsonouris' words,

> The house was constantly warned of the legal Armageddon that would follow from circuit judges forever traversing the country, sans books, sans the latest reports, and above all, sans the collective wisdom of the Law Library in its physical manifestation ... It is hard to exaggerate the unflagging opposition to a proposal whose purpose was to effect increased efficiency and a considerable reduction in costs.[25]

Another proposal which proved controversial related to the rule-making committees for each court.[26] The bill diverged from the commission's recommendations and vested this power in the minister for home affairs. This was considered by many to be an unwarranted invasion of the judiciary's domain. It would have allowed, for example, the minister to prescribe the dress to be worn by both judges and advocates in court.[27] Kennedy's proposals for a mode of address to judges also failed, and 'my lord' was retained.[28]

Constitutional development

Fifteen years after the drafting of the 1922 constitution, barristers were also intimately involved in the drafting of its successor. As Coffey points out, the 1937 constitution 'came into being in a period of intense historical significance, when the liberal democratic regimes of Europe were crumbling.'[29] Barrister John Hearne was the person most closely associated with the drafting of the new

---

12 Oct. 1923, p. 7.   **20** See, for example, a letter to the *Irish Times,* signed 'Attorney at Law': *Irish Times,* 3 May 1923, p. 3. The committee sought the views of the Bar on issues such as the length of the long vacation. B.C.M., 11 May 1923.   **21** Mary Kotsonouris, *Retreat from revolution: the Dáil Courts, 1920–24* (Dublin, 1994), p. 115.   **22** B.C.M., 26 Oct. 1923.   **23** Redmond was called in 1910. See Marie Coleman, 'Redmond, William Archer', *D.I.B.* and Ferguson, *Barristers,* p. 287. **24** See Marie Coleman, 'Magennis, William' *D.I.B.*   **25** Kotsonouris, *Retreat from revolution,* p. 115.   **26** See Keane, 'The voice of the Gael', at 221.   **27** See pp 96–7.   **28** See pp 352–4. **29** Donal Coffey, *Drafting the Irish constitution, 1935–37; transnational influences in interwar Europe*

constitution,[30] which he said promised 'a great new national fulfilment'.[31] Based on diary entries for de Valera's private secretary, Coffey demonstrates the 'singular importance of Hearne on the drafting process'.[32] The other members of the drafting committee which was set up in 1936 were civil servants Maurice Moynihan, Michael McDunphy and Philip O'Donoghue,[33] but most of the substantive drafting was in the hands of Hearne and de Valera.[34] Despite not being practising barristers, O'Donoghue and Hearne were called to the inner Bar in 1939 in recognition of their work on the 1937 constitution.[35]

In August 1966 an informal committee of elected representatives was established 'to review the constitutional, legislative, and institutional bases of government'.[36] The Constitution Review Group was established in 1995 to review the constitution and 'establish those areas where constitutional change may be desirable or necessary'.[37] This was the first major, systematic analysis of the 1937 constitution since its initial drafting, and the fifteen-person committee, chaired by Dr T.K. Whitaker, included three senior counsel,[38] four junior counsel[39] and one barrister-civil servant.[40] Briefing material was provided by three additional barristers.[41]

(London, 2018), p. xi.   **30** Called in 1919, Hearne was appointed assistant parliamentary draughtsman in 1923 and was legal advisor to the Department of External Affairs in 1929. In his own words, 'It happened that when I was of three years standing at the Bar, an event took place which changed the course of the lives of many Irish lawyers and gave to the legal profession itself a new place, and a new influence in the country – I mean the establishment of the Irish Free State in the year 1922. For my own part I was invited to work with the first attorney general and spent five years in that department of the new government. When our Foreign Office was set up I became its first legal adviser, a post which I occupied for over ten years.' Address at the annual meeting of the State Bar of California, delivered at the Ambassador Hotel, Los Angeles, 17 Sept. 1956. UCDA P291/26, p. 3. See Eugene Broderick, *John Hearne: architect of the 1937 constitution of Ireland* (Dublin, 2017); Dermot Keogh, *The Vatican, the bishops and Irish politics, 1919–1939* (Cambridge, 1986); Brian Kennedy, 'John Hearne and the Irish constitution', *Eire-Ireland* 24:2 (1989), 121; Ferguson, *Barristers*, p. 204.   **31** John Hearne, 'Constitution and the national life', UCDA P291/4, p. 1. He described the 1922 constitution, p. 6, as 'not, as we all know, entirely of our own making.'   **32** Coffey, *Drafting the Irish constitution*, pp 11, 148–52. He notes, p. 151, that 'Hearne was not a secular drafter.'   **33** Called in 1919 and appointed to the Circuit Court in 1924. From 1929–59 he served as legal assistant to the attorney general. Daire Hogan, 'O'Donoghue (Patrick) Philip', *D.I.B.*   **34** Coffey, *Drafting the Irish constitution*, pp 45–51, also points out that the cabinet also had considerable input, and notes the contributions of the Jesuits and such individuals as Bishop John Charles McQuaid, George Gavan Duffy, and parliamentary draughtsman Arthur Matheson.   **35** Ferguson, *Barristers*, p. 408.   **36** The members were TDs David Andrews, Don Davern, Seán Dunne, Denis Jones, Robert Molloy, T.F. O'Higgins, Gerard Sweetman and James Tully; and senators Eoin Ryan, Michael O'Kennedy and James Dooge. George Colley was the chair, and in Nov. 1966, Seán Lemass replaced Don Davern. A number of matters were referred to the attorney general; see *Report of the committee on the constitution* (Dublin, 1967), pp 141–4. It also relied on some recent legal scholarship by barristers including Rory O'Hanlon, Ralph Sutton, Vincent Grogan and Donal Barrington.   **37** *Report of the Constitution Review Group* (Dublin, 1996), p. iii.   **38** David Byrne, Mary Finlay Geoghegan and Dermot Gleeson.   **39** James Hamilton, Gerard Hogan, Diarmaid McGuinness and Bláthna Ruane.   **40** Francis Mahon Hayes; see further below. For analysis of the committee's work, see Andrew Butler and Rory O'Connell, 'A critical analysis of Ireland's Constitutional Review Group report', *Ir. Jur.* 33:1 (1998), 237.   **41** Eileen Barrington, Barry Doherty and Michael Conlon.

A number of barristers interviewed for this book discussed their involvement in drafting proposed constitutional amendments at various points in the eighties and nineties. They also contributed to the national debate on these major constitutional and social issues; for example, the views of many barristers were evident during the abortion debates of the early 1980s. Much of the drafting of the eighth amendment was done by members of the profession, and the pro-choice anti-amendment campaign included a number of high-profile barristers. MacCormaic points out that

> In February 1983, when the campaign was at its height, ninety-eight barristers – almost a quarter of all the barristers practising in the country at the time – made a statement from the Four Courts in which they denounced the proposed amendment.[42]

One of the interviewees commented on political activism at the Bar:

> In the eighties there was the abortion referendum ... there was the divorce referendum and there was certainly a lot of activism within the Bar, a lot of political activism within the Bar and there would have been large numbers of people in the Bar who would have supported the move for divorce. There were also large numbers against it.[43]

Barristers also informed political parties' stances on these issues; for example, a barrister interviewed for this book recalled drafting a position paper on divorce for one of the political parties in the nineties.

As well as revising the constitution, barristers were of course actively involved in constitutional litigation. As Mac Cormaic points out, '[l]awyers practising in the early years of the state ... were not taking cases that pushed at the boundaries of judges' powers and the Constitution. Whether they were nationalist or unionist, they tended to be quite conservative in this regard'.[44] Elgie et al. write that until the sixties, 'the judges adhered to English constitutional theory of parliamentary supremacy'.[45] They note that the appointments of Cearbhall Ó Dálaigh and Brian Walsh to the Supreme Court signalled the beginning of a period of 'judicial activism', particularly because both were 'influenced by the judicial activism of the Warren United States Supreme Court.'[46] The legal profession realised that the door was open to creativity.[47] This judicial activism did not operate in a vacuum. Advocates such as Donal Barrington played a significant role in taking on cases of public importance, crafting novel arguments,

---

42 Ruadhán Mac Cormaic, *The Supreme Court* (Dublin, 2016), p. 280.   43 B21.   44 Mac Cormaic, *The Supreme Court*, p. 46.   45 Robert Elgie Adam McAuley and Eoin O'Malley, 'The (not-so-surprising) non-partisanship of the Irish Supreme Court', *Ir. Pol. Stud.* 33:1 (2018), 88, at 92. 46 Elgie et al., 'The (not-so-surprising) non-partisanship', at 93. See also Ronan Keane, 'Judges as lawmakers: the Irish experience', *Radharc* 4 (2003), 81.   47 Mac Cormaic, *The Supreme Court*, p. 114.

carrying out research and presenting the court with well-reasoned advocacy. Writing in the early nineties, Hugh O'Flaherty pointed out that '[t]he citizens of this country have been well served by the part that a free and independent Bar has played in the defence of liberty and the development of the constitution.'[48] The development of a rights-based jurisprudence would not have been possible without the work of barristers, some of whom took on cases on a *pro bono* basis.[49] As well as those who represented plaintiffs, it is important to note that members of the independent Bar also put forward novel arguments in representing the state.

> You know, things were changing in the seventies ... the *Magee* case happened ... that was huge ... *Byrne* had happened about three or four years beforehand. There were these decisions which you began to sort of realise were formative. *Byrne v. Ireland* was huge. I don't think enough really has been thought or considered about the pre-Ó Dálaigh-Walsh Supreme Court ... there were judges who were injecting ... radicalism into the Supreme Court before Walsh and Ó Dálaigh arrived. But when they arrived ... this really broke out as a dynamic thing. You could feel it.[50]

Several of those who were interviewed for this book were involved in major constitutional litigation and spoke of their enjoyment and sense of satisfaction doing this kind of work.

As elected representatives

Aside from contributing to the constitutional frameworks of the state, many barristers were elected to public office, representing different parts of the political spectrum.[51] Three Irish presidents have been barristers: Cearbhall Ó Dálaigh;[52] Mary Robinson[53] and Mary McAleese.[54] For almost half of the period

48 O'Flaherty, 'The independent Bar', p. 174.   49 See pp 160–3 for a discussion of barristers' activism with FLAC.   50 B5.   51 Some barristers who pursued political careers did so in other jurisdictions. For example, Lancelot Ernest Curran, called in 1923, served as a unionist MP for the Stormont constituency of Carrick in the forties and fifties. See David Murphy, 'Curran, Sir Lancelot Ernest', *D.I.B.* and Ferguson, *Barristers,* p. 168. He also served as attorney general for Northern Ireland from 1947 to 1949 and was later appointed to the Northern Ireland bench. 52 See Ferguson, *Barristers,* p. 271 Ó Dálaigh was called (as Carroll O'Daly) in 1934 and served as attorney general, 1946–8, and 1951–3. He was a judge of the Supreme Court, 1953–61, and chief justice, 1961–73. He joined the European Court of Justice in 1973 and served as president of Ireland from 1974–6. See further Aidan Carl Matthew (ed.), *Immediate man: cuimhní ar Cearbhall Ó Dálaigh* (Dublin, 1983); Ronan Keane, 'Ó Dálaigh, Cearbhall', *D.I.B.* and the Ó Dálaigh papers, UCDA P51.   53 Robinson was a prominent member of the Irish Bar in the seventies and eighties. Called to the Bar as Marie Teresa Bourke in 1967, she practised initially on the Western Circuit. Robinson was Reid professor of law at Trinity College Dublin, 1969–75, and worked part-time at the Bar. See (1969) 103 *I.L.T.S.J.* 430 (8 Nov. 1969). She took silk in 1980; was president, 1990–7, and UN high commissioner for human rights, 1997–2002. See Ferguson, *Barristers,* p. 142, Mary Robinson, *Everybody matters: a memoir* (London, 2013).   54 McAleese was called to the Bar of

covered by this book, the office of taoiseach was held by someone who was a qualified barrister: John A. Costello,[55] Jack Lynch,[56] Liam Cosgrave,[57] Charles Haughey,[58] Garrett FitzGerald[59] and John Bruton.[60] Several people who served as tánaiste in the twentieth century were also called to the Bar, including Michael O'Leary,[61] Dick Spring[62] and Brian Lenihan (snr).[63] As MacKenzie observed,

> Tánaistí and ministers and parliamentary secretaries abounded, falling-over themselves in the Library with joy when their party came into power, and trooping back when they were kicked out. Their political friends seldom let them down and they usually ran into good business.[64]

Kevin O'Higgins,[65] James FitzGerald-Kenney;[66] James Geoghegan[67] and Brian Lenihan (snr) were all called to the Bar and served as ministers for justice. Other high-profile barrister-politicians, typically associated with either Fianna Fáil or

---

Northern Ireland, where she practised briefly. She was called to the Irish Bar in 1978. She was Reid professor of law at Trinity College Dublin and was elected president in 1997. See Ferguson, *Barristers*, p. 368.   **55** Called in 1914, Costello served as attorney general, 1926–31; was elected a TD in 1933 and served as taoiseach, 1948–51, and 1954–7. See ibid., p. 164; Charles Lysaght, 'Costello, John Aloysius', *D.I.B.*; David Harkness, 'Costello, John Aloysius (1891–1976)', *D.N.B.*; David McCullagh, *The reluctant taoiseach*, and the John A. Costello papers, UCDA P190. **56** Lynch combined his studies at the King's Inns with work in the civil service and his involvement in the GAA. He was called in 1945 and left the civil service in order to pursue his practice in Cork. He was elected a TD for Fianna Fáil in 1948. He had intended to maintain his legal practice, but his work for Fianna Fáil absorbed most of his time. He held a number of ministerial posts, including education, finance, industry and commerce, and served as taoiseach, 1966–73, and 1977–9. Commenting on his approach as taoiseach, a private secretary in the Department of Education said 'He liked to mull things over. He liked to consider every bit of evidence – a product of his legal training – and he was good on legislation'; James Dukes, cited in Bruce Arnold, *Jack Lynch: hero in crisis* (2001), p. 42. See Ferguson, *Barristers*, p. 232; Ronan Fanning, 'Lynch, John Mary ('Jack')', *D.I.B.* and Dermot Keogh, *Jack Lynch: a biography* (Dublin, 2008).   **57** See Ferguson, *Barristers*, p. 163. Cosgrave was called in 1943 and joined the inner Bar in 1958. He served as taoiseach, 1973–7.   **58** See ibid., p. 202. Haughey was called in 1949 but did not practise at the Bar. He served as taoiseach, 1979–81, in 1982 and 1987–92.   **59** FitzGerald was called in 1947 but did not practise. See ibid., p. 186. He served as taoiseach, 1981–2 and 1982–7.   **60** Bruton was called to the Bar in 1972: ibid., p. 364. He served as taoiseach, 1994–7.   **61** O'Leary began his career in the 1950s as a trade union official. He served as a TD, 1965–87 and was called to the Bar in 1981, while still a sitting TD. He was leader of the Labour party and tánaiste, 1982–2. In 1987 he retired from the Dáil and practised as a barrister until his appointment as a district judge in 1992. See Patrick Maume, 'O'Leary, Michael', *D.I.B.* and Ferguson, *Barristers*, p. 371.   **62** Spring was called in 1975 and was elected a TD for Labour in 1981. He became the leader of the Labour party the following year, and served as minister for the environment, energy and minister for foreign affairs. See Ferguson, *Barristers*, p. 366.   **63** Lenihan was called in 1952 and practised on the Midland Circuit. He served as both a senator and a TD for Fianna Fáil, and held several ministries, including foreign affairs in 1973 and 1979–81. See Ferguson, *Barristers*, p. 229 and Lawrence William White, 'Lenihan, Brian Joseph', *D.I.B.*   **64** Patrick MacKenzie, *Lawful occasions: the old Eastern Circuit* (Dublin, 1991), p. 12.   **65** Called in 1899, Ferguson, *Barristers*, p. 274. He was minister for home affairs, 1924–7. **66** See ibid., p. 187. He was minister, 1927–32.   **67** Geoghegan was called in 1915 having already qualified and practised as a solicitor. He was elected as a TD for Fianna Fail in 1930. He served as minister for justice 1932–3. He served briefly as attorney general before being appointed to the

Fine Gael, included Fionán Lynch (Ó Loingsigh),[68] John Maurice Kelly,[69] Tom O'Higgins,[70] James Dillon,[71] John Lymbrick Esmonde,[72] Sean MacBride,[73] Declan Costello,[74] Theodore Conyngham Kingsmill Moore,[75] Patrick Lindsay,[76] Seán O'Leary,[77] Brian Lenihan (junior),[78] Eoin Ryan,[79] Michael McDowell[80] and David Andrews.[81] The relative dearth of women in the Oireachtas during this period is reflected in this list of barrister-politicians, as is the twentieth-century dominance of the Fianna Fáil and Fine Gael parties. As one TD (a former solicitor) said,

Supreme Court. See ibid., p. 192 and Pauric J. Dempsey, 'Geoghegan, James', *D.I.B.*   **68** Lynch was one of the Anglo-Irish Treaty negotiators in 1921, and held several ministerial posts in the twenties and early thirties. He was called to the Bar in 1931 and practised on the Midland Circuit. He was leas-cheann comhairle of Dáil Éireann, 1938–9, and was later appointed a judge of the Circuit Court. See Ferguson, *Barristers*, p. 275.   **69** Called in 1957, he was a Fine Gael TD, 1973–89, a professor of law at UCD and the author of several influential legal textbooks. He practised on the Leinster and Eastern Circuits in the late fifties. See Ferguson, *Barristers*, p. 218; Obituary, *The Times*, 26 Jan. 1991; Ronan Keane, 'Kelly, John Maurice', *D.I.B.*   **70** Called in 1938, O'Higgins was a TD, 1948–73, served as minister for health and was later appointed to the bench. See Ferguson, *Barristers*, p. 274 and T.F. O'Higgins, *A double life* (Dublin, 1996).   **71** Dillon was called in 1931 and was TD from 1932 to 1969, serving also as minister for agriculture. He was the leader of Fine Gael in the early sixties. See Ferguson, *Barristers*, p. 174.   **72** Esmonde was called to the Bar in 1921: ibid., p. 182. He became a senior counsel in 1942. He served as MP for Tipperary North, 1915–18, and later as a Fine Gael TD, 1937–44 and 1948–51. See Lawrence William White, 'Esmonde, Sir John Lymbrick', *D.I.B.*   **73** MacBride served as minister for external affairs and received the Nobel peace prize in 1974. He was called in 1937 and took silk in 1943. See ibid., p. 234.   **74** Son of John A. Costello, he was called in 1948, and took silk in 1965. He served as attorney general, 1973–77, a TD, 1951–69, and a judge of the High Court, 1977–98: see ibid., p. 163.   **75** Kingsmill Moore was called in 1918: ibid., p. 257. He served as a senator in the 1940s before being appointed to the High Court, and was also the author of a popular book on fly-fishing: T.C. Kingsmill-Moore, *A man may fish* (London, 1960).   **76** Lindsay was called in 1946, he was appointed master of the High Court in 1975 and elected to the Dáil on his 6th attempt. See Ferguson, *Barristers*, p. 229 and Patrick Lindsay, *Memories* (Dublin, 1992).   **77** O'Leary was called in 1980, practised as both a barrister and an accountant and served as Lord Mayor of Cork and later as a senator. He was a director of elections for Fine Gael in the 1980s, and was appointed to the Circuit Court in 1995. See Ferguson, *Barristers*, p. 370 and 'Former FG activist who was elevated to the High Court', *Irish Times*, 6 Jan. 2007, p. 12.   **78** He was called to the Bar in 1984 and was elected to the Dáil in 1996. See Ferguson, *Barristers*, p. 372 and Patrick Maume, 'Lenihan, Brian', *D.I.B.* Lenihan later held several ministerial briefs.   **79** Ryan was called to the Bar (as Ó Riain) in 1945 and was a Fianna Fáil senator for many years while practicing at the Bar. He was involved in modernising the party in the 1950s, and was later appointed leader of the party in the Seanad. He was a director of various companies, and was chair of the New Ireland Assurance Company for many years. See Pádraig Conway, 'Ryan, Eoin', *D.I.B.* and Ferguson, *Barristers*, p. 277.   **80** McDowell was called in 1974 (ibid., p. 365) and was first elected as a Progressive Democrat TD in 1987. He was appointed attorney general in 1999, and later served as minister for justice and a member of Seanad Éireann.   **81** Andrews was called in 1961: ibid., p. 131. In his own words, '[k]nowing it would be a good while before I could hope for any income from law I took a job with the *Irish Press*.' David Andrews, *Kingstown republican* (Dublin, 2007). Reflecting on his juggling of two careers, Andrews described his colleagues at the Bar as being very supportive, particularly as he went in and out of politics. By way of example, he recalled, p. 80, the occasion when he lost his ministerial salary and was sent to the back benches when there was a change in Fianna Fáil leadership: 'it seems to have become known that I was broke. Colm Condon was concerned for me. He got me a brief'. Andrews served as a TD, 1965–2002, and held several ministerial positions, including foreign affairs, defence and marine, and took silk in 1992. See Maureen Cairnuff, *Who's*

I believe that the Bar is one of, if not the most, conservative collection of workers in the country ... It is no accident that the main conservative parties in the country are heavily supported by barristers and they are to be seen to the fore in each of those parties.[82]

High-profile barristers involved with the Labour party included Patrick Hogan[83] and of course Mary Robinson.[84] The Bar Council was entitled to nominate barristers for the cultural and educational panel, one of the five vocational panels for the Seanad.[85]

Such a preponderance of lawyers in parliament was common to other common law countries in the twentieth century. A writer on the Canadian legal profession, Brunet, notes that 'between 1920 and 1960, discourses and activities in law schools clearly promoted this link between the legal profession and politics ... As a profession of service, legal practice was thought naturally to lead to public office'.[86] She also observes that '[p]ublic office often went hand in hand with nation-building, especially in the earlier decades of the twentieth century'.[87] It was not only in common law countries that lawyers formed a large part of the political elite; the same was evident in places such as Finland. For example, Konntinen writes that after Finnish independence in 1917,

So many of the presidents of the republic have been lawyers by education. A legal education was for a long time one of the most important qualifications for higher posts in political life.[88]

This was also the case in other common law jurisdictions such as Australia, New Zealand and the United States.[89]

As public servants

In the first decades of the new state, as well as holding public office, members of the Bar served the state in other ways. They were court officials,[90]

who in Ireland: the influential 1,000 (Dublin, 1984), p. 2.   82 Dáil Éireann deb., vol. 414, no. 1 (4 Dec. 1991) (Patrick McCartan).   83 Called in 1936; Ferguson, *Barristers*, p. 208. He practised for some years on the South-West Circuit. Hogan served as ceann comhairle for sixteen years and leas ceann comhairle for ten years: obit., 'Mr. Patrick Hogan dies after distinguished career', *Irish Times*, 25 Jan. 1969, p. 15.   84 See above.   85 See the Seanad Electoral (Panel Members) Act 1947.   86 Brunet, '"Good government"', p. 50.   87 Ibid.   88 Esa Konntinen, '"Finland's route" of professionalisation and lawyer–officials' in W. Wesley Pue and David Sugarman (eds), *Lawyers and vampires: cultural histories of legal professions* (Oregon, 2003), p. 109.   89 See, e.g., Mark C. Miller, *The high priests of American politics: the role of lawyers in American political institutions* (Tennessee, 1995).   90 Marion Duggan was the fifth woman called to the Bar, in 1925, and had been a Dáil Court official as well as an activist and suffragist. See Mary Kotsonouris, *Retreat from revolution* (Dublin, 1994), p. 132. See Ferguson, *Barristers*, p. 179 and trailblazers exhibition: www.law library.ie/about/history/trailblazers–1919–2019–100-years-of-women-at-the-bar/. Patrick Crump (called in 1928: ibid., p. 167) had also worked as an official in the Dáil Courts, and then later worked in the High Court office. Another example is Con Curran, registrar of the High Court and the

superintendents of An Garda Síochána,[91] members of state bodies,[92] civil servants[93] and, of course, members of the judiciary. Miriam Hederman O'Brien,[94] for example, had a long career in public life following her call to the Bar in 1954. Among other contributions, she chaired the Commission on Taxation (1980–5), the expert group on the Blood Transfusion Service Board, the Commission on Funding of the Irish Health Services (1989) and the Broadcasting Complaints Commission (1977–80).[95]

Vincent Grogan was called to the Bar in 1937 and practised until 1943, when he joined the office of the parliamentary draughtsman. He was later the director

Supreme Court. Ita Heslin, called in 1951 (ibid., p. 206), worked in the High Court office, and later as assistant examiner, registrar of wards of court, and registrar of the Supreme Court. 91 Turlough MacNeill (son of Eoin McNeill), called in 1927 (ibid., p. 246), and Michael Leahy, also called in 1927 (ibid., p. 226). Henry Windle, called in 1934 (ibid., p. 319), was a superintendent and Eamonn 'Ned' Coogan, called in 1941 (ibid., p. 162), was an assistant commissioner. He was later an elected representative for Fine Gael; see Pauric J. Dempsey, 'Coogan, Edward (Eamonn, 'Ned')', D.I.B. 92 E.g., James Meenan (called in 1935: ibid., p. 252) practised for a number of years and later became a prominent political economist. He served on several government commissions on such issues as emigration, decimal coinage and income taxation. Among other things, he was a director of the Central Bank from 1949–58 and a member of the court of governors of the Bank of Ireland from 1958–78. He also served as both chairman and president of the Royal Dublin Society. See James Meenan papers, UCDA LA/56 and Finola Kennedy, 'Meenan, James Francis', D.I.B. Mella Carroll, called in 1957 (Ferguson, Barristers, p. 153), later chaired the Commission on Nursing, the Legal Aid Board and the second Commission on the Status of Women. See trailblazers exhibition. Denham, called in 1971 (ibid., p. 363), chaired the working group on a courts commission from 1995 to 1998. Vincent Landy, called in 1947 (ibid., p. 255), chaired the Broadcasting Complaints Commission and the Legal Aid Board. See Fand, 'Lawyer's opinions highly valued', Irish Times, 29 Jan. 2000, p. 16. 93 John Belton, called in 1927, worked in the Department of External Affairs and was ambassador to Sweden and Canada. Michael Andrew Lysaght Rynne, called in 1924, also had a distinguished career in this department as, inter alia, legal advisor, assistant secretary and ambassador to Spain. See Ferguson, Barristers, p. 293. Diarmuid, or Jeremiah, Fawsitt had been a senior civil servant before being called to the Bar in 1928. As a diplomat, he served with the Irish delegation that negotiated the Treaty in 1921. He was appointed to the bench in the 1940s. Patrick Long, 'Fawsitt, Diarmuid (Jeremiah)', D.I.B. and Ferguson, Barristers, p. 184. Gretta Flood was called to the Bar in 1926 while employed in the housing department of Dublin corporation; see Ferguson, Barristers, p. 189. Ann Callery, called in 1955 as Mary Callery, later worked in the revenue department (ibid., p. 150). Onora Ní Shúillcabháin, called in 1972 (ibid., p. 364), worked in the central office of the Four Courts and in the probate office while studying at the King's Inns, and remained in the civil service after qualifying. Mary Murphy, called in the same year, also continued her career in the civil service. See trailblazers exhibition. William Maguire, called in 1916 (ibid., p. 248), worked in the Revenue Commissioners for 45 years; obit., Irish Times, 26 July 1956, p. 7. He was also the author of Guide to the professions: barristers-at-law and solicitors (Dublin, 1931). P. Declan Quigley, called in 1947, practised on the Western Circuit before joining the civil service in 1956. He worked in the departments of local government, health and social welfare before joining the Office of the Attorney General, where he was appointed senior legal assistant in 1971. The Irish Law Times noted in 1984 that he had been 'legal advisor to the Irish side at the Sunningdale conference in 1973, and he was head of the Irish delegation at many international conferences on air law and sea law.' 'Retirement of chief advisor', I.L.T. 2:10 (1984), 186. See Ferguson, Barristers, p. 285. 94 Ibid., p. 204 and 'Dr Miriam Hederman O'Brien obituary: trailblazer for women' Irish Times, 19 Mar. 2022, p. 12. 95 She was the first woman to be appointed to the board of an Irish publicly listed company (Allied Irish Bank) in 1985, and was appointed chancellor of the University of Limerick in 1998. See Dónal de Búitléir and Frances Ruane (eds), Governance and policy in Ireland: essays in honour of Miriam Hederman O'Brien

of the Statute Law Reform and Consolidation Office.[96] Grogan worked closely with Roger Hayes, who had been called to the Bar in 1940. Hayes was assistant secretary in the Department of Justice and served as a law reform commissioner from 1977 to 1984.[97] Thomas Joseph Coyne, called to the Bar in 1922, worked as a senior civil servant in the Department of Home Affairs, and later in the Department of Justice, where he served as principal officer, assistant secretary and secretary.[98] Patricia O'Brien, called to the Bar in 1979,[99] practiced until 1988 and later worked as senior legal adviser to the attorney general, legal counsellor at the Irish permanent representation to the EU and legal adviser to the Department of Foreign Affairs.

As broadcasters, journalists and commentators

Some members of the Bar had multifaceted careers in public life as broadcasters, journalists and commentators. Eoin Seosamh O'Mahony, for example, known as 'the Pope', is described as 'a barrister, genealogist, journalist, and broadcaster'[100] and was called to the Bar in 1930. Lysaght writes that O'Mahony, working as a prosecutor in Cork, 'sometimes disconcerted the court by pleading for leniency for those he was retained to prosecute'.[101] He later found regular legal practice to be restrictive and 'preferred to concentrate on causes that engaged his own enthusiasm'.[102] He was an active member of the Irish Georgian Society, and frequently delivered lectures to local historical societies. He published book reviews and obituaries in the newspapers, and had a weekly column in the *Sunday Review*. He also hosted a genealogical programme on RTÉ radio called 'Meet the clans'.[103] In addition to these various activities, he ran for election to public office on a number of occasions.[104]

Cecil Barror was an 'actor, singer, broadcaster, sportsman and raconteur'[105] who was called to the Bar in 1954.[106] Liam Devally was a radio and television host

---

(Dublin, 2003). **96** While director of the Statute Law Reform and Consolidation Office, Grogan revised and republished V.T.H. Delany, *The administration of justice in Ireland* (2nd ed., Dublin, 1965). In 1961 he delivered a paper to the Medico-Legal Society of Ireland on 'Law and custom in Ghana' (1961) 95 *I.L.T.S.J.* 294, having been invited by Ghana's military government to draft their constitution. **97** Hayes was called in 1940; see Ferguson, *Barristers*, p. 202. **98** Ibid., p. 165. Philip O'Donoghue, who was involved in drafting the 1937 constitution, was legal assistant to the attorney general, 1929–59: Daire Hogan, 'O'Donoghue (Patrick) Philip', *D.I.B.* Brigid Cotter was a chemist in the state laboratory and the Department of Agriculture, who later was called to the Irish Bar in 1972. She funded three student prizes for law students at the University of London. Linde Lunney and Rob Bohan, 'Cotter, Bridget Mary', *D.I.B.* and Ferguson, *Barristers*, p. 364. **99** Ferguson, *Barristers*, p. 369. **100** Ibid., p. 275 and Charles Lysaght, 'O'Mahony, Eoin Seosamh', *D.I.B.* **101** Lysaght, 'O'Mahony, Eoin Seosamh', *D.I.B.* **102** He was one of the supporters of poet Patrick Kavanagh during his libel action in the fifties: see ch. 15. **103** Charles Lysaght described the Sunday-lunchtime programme: 'O'Mahony interviewed the famous or well-born of a chosen surname, adding his own sometimes idiosyncratic observations in a mellifluous Cork voice.' Charles Lysaght, 'An Irishman's diary', *Irish Times*, 12 Sept. 2018, p. 13. See RTÉ Radio talk scripts in English, UCDA P261. **104** Hubert Butler, 'Eoin O'Mahony, the man who tried to change the quality of life', *Irish Times*, 21 Feb. 1970, p. 12. **105** Obituary: 'Barrister, actor, singer and broadcaster', *Irish Times*, 30 Oct. 1999, p. 18. **106** He worked in the law offices of the

and singer, who later practised at the Bar after being called in 1974, and was appointed a Circuit Court judge in 1991.[107] Playwright Denis Johnston worked as a BBC war correspondent during the Second World War, and went on to hold senior positions in the organisation.[108] Una McAuliffe Linehan, called in 1944, had a successful career at Radio Éireann and later RTÉ.[109] Other public commentators who had qualified for the Bar included journalists Stephen Barrett,[110] David Andrews, Colum Kenny[111] and Vincent Browne.[112] In his retirement, Justice Conor Maguire hosted a music programme on RTÉ radio called 'In the mood', which focused on music from the big band era – Patrick Lindsay commented 'I'm told it's quite a good programme'.[113]

Literary and artistic contributions

There have long been links between members of the Bar and the arts in Ireland, and the Bar has included poets,[114] actors,[115] critics,[116] novelists[117] and playwrights,[118] as well as individuals who have promoted Irish language,[119]

ESB. See Ferguson, *Barristers*, p. 135. **107** Obituary, 'Quick-thinking compere and Irish-speaking barrister', *Irish Times*, 12 May 2018, p. 12. And Ferguson, *Barristers*, p. 365. His *Irish Times* obituary described him as 'a household name in Ireland in the 1960s and 1970s', who was 'as successful in his legal career as he had been in his broadcasting one.' **108** Patrick Maume, 'Johnston (William) Denis', *D.I.B.* In 1945 he was awarded an OBE for his services to broadcasting. See further below. **109** See Ferguson, *Barristers*, p. 229 and trailblazers exhibition. **110** Barrett worked in increasingly senior roles in the *Cork Examiner* in the 1930s, and practised on the Munster Circuit from 1946 until his appointment to the Circuit Court in 1973. He was also active in politics, representing Fine Gael both locally in Cork and in the Dáil. Pauric J. Dempsey, 'Barrett, Stephen Declan', *D.I.B.* and 'Judge Stephen Barrett dies', *Irish Times*, 9 Sept. 1976, p. 13, Ferguson, *Barristers*, p. 134. **111** Called in 1974: ibid., p. 365. Kenny has published numerous books and articles, cited in this volume, on the history of the Irish Bar. **112** Browne was called in 1997 and practised briefly. See ibid., p. 390. **113** Lindsay, *Memories*, p. 115. **114** E.g., Donagh MacDonagh, see further below, and Máire Mac an tSaoi, called in 1944: see Ferguson, *Barristers*, p. 240. In her memoir, *The same age as the state* (Dublin, 2003), she comments, p. 161, that while she never practised, 'the qualification came in handy when I applied to join external (now foreign) affairs. **115** E.g., Ralph Brereton Barry was an actor before joining the Bar in 1922, and continued to be an active member of the Dublin arts scene throughout his career at the Bar. Pauric J. Dempsey, 'Barry, Ralph Brereton', *D.I.B.* See Abbey Theatre archive, www.abbeytheatre.ie/ archives/person_detail/ 10316/. Early in his career he visited the USA with a delegation from the Irish, English, and Scottish Bars led by Sir John Simon. He died in 1943 in Dublin as a result of typhoid fever, contracted on circuit in Letterkenny. See obit., (1943) 77 *I.L.T.S.J.* 308 (18 Dec. 1943); Ferguson, *Barristers*, p. 135. **116** E.g., Anthony Cronin, who was called to the Bar in 1948 but did not practise, was a poet and critic, and served as cultural and artistic adviser to the government in the 1980s. He was described by Colm Toibín as 'for more than half a century, Ireland's most prominent man of letters'; Colm Toibín, 'Anthony Cronin obituary', *The Guardian*, 24 Jan. 2017, p. 35. See also Ferguson, *Barristers*, p. 166 and Cairnduff, *Who's who*, p. 36. **117** E.g., Barbara Keating, called in 1972, later co-authored novels with her sister, Stephanie Keating, including *Blood sisters* (London, 2005). Ferguson, *Barristers*, p. 264. **118** E.g. Denis Johnston (called in 1925: ibid., p. 214) was a prolific playwright and director; see pp 326–7. **119** E.g., Pádraig Augustine Ó Síocháin was called to the Bar in 1936. He was the author of several law books in both English and Irish: P.A. Ó Síocháin, *The criminal law of Ireland* (Dublin, 1940) ran to eight editions and was translated into Irish; P.A. Ó Síocháin, *Dlí coiriúil na h-Éireann* (Dublin, 1964). He specialised in trade union law. An Irish language activist, in 1948 he changed his surname from Sheehan to Ó Síocháin and he

culture[120] and genealogy.[121] The contribution of these barristers, and others, to the shaping of public perceptions of the Bar is explored further in chapter fifteen.

Academic, business and sporting life

As well as the Bar's involvement in the arts, many barristers went on to posts which impacted on the commercial and economic life of the country.[122] Some went on to take holy orders,[123] some were military lawyers[124] and others were

founded the national language revival movement. He was also a journalist, aviation enthusiast, filmmaker and rally driver. In 1952 he owned a company which sold traditional Aran knits in the United States and Canada. See Linde Lunney and Maurice Cronin, 'Ó Síocháin (Sheehan), Pádraig Augustine', *D.I.B.*, and Ferguson, *Barristers*, p. 297. His non-legal publications included P.A. Ó Síocháin, *Aran Islands of legend* (Dublin, 1962), P.A. Ó Síocháin, *Ireland: a journey into lost time* (Dublin, 1983), and P.A. Ó Síocháin, *Ireland: journey to freedom* (Kells, 1990). Dubhglas Mac Fhionnlaoich was active in the Gaelic League and was the son of Peadar Toner Mac Fhionnlaoich (Peadar McGinley), known as Cú Uladh, 'the hound of Ulster': Vincent Morley, 'Mac Fhionnlaoich, Peadar Toner (McGinley, Peter Toner; "Cú Uladh")', *D.I.B.* **120** Liam Price, called in 1919, was one of the first district justices appointed in 1924. He served as vice-president of the Royal Irish Academy and president of the Royal Society of Antiquaries of Ireland, and was a founding member of both the National Monuments Advisory Council and the Irish Folklore Commission, and was a published authority on Irish place-names. Andrew O'Brien and Linde Lunney, 'Price, Liam', *D.I.B.* and Ferguson, *Barristers*, p. 284. Constantine Curran, called in 1910, was well known for his promotion of the literary works of his friend James Joyce. He never practised as a barrister, but took silk in 1938. He served as registrar of the High Court and the Supreme Court, 1921–2, but was better-known for his 'other career as a writer on art, architecture, and drama … However, the area where he had most expertise and achieved most renown was in architecture'; Bridget Hourican and Pauric J. Dempsey, 'Curran, Constantine Peter ("Con")', *D.I.B.* and Ferguson, *Barristers*, p. 168. **121** Thomas Ulick Sadleir, called in 1906 (ibid., p. 294), practised on the Leinster Circuit until 1916. He was a genealogist who worked in the Office of Arms and later the genealogical office. He published extensively on Irish family histories, architecture, and social history, with over 300 articles in books, pamphlets, and historical journals. He later worked as assistant librarian at the King's Inns. Ibid., p. 294; Susan Hood, 'Sadleir, Thomas Ulick ("Tom")', *D.I.B.* and Ferguson, and obit., *Irish Times*, 3 Dec. 1957, p. 8. **122** E.g., Joe McGough enlisted in the defence forces in 1940 and was called to the Bar in 1951, and in 1960 he retired from the defence forces to practise at the Bar. He later worked on the board of the state agency An Bord Bainne, and helped to launch Kerrygold butter in 1962. After a number of high-profile years with Bord Bainne, he returned to the Bar in 1978 where he combined his practice with various company directorships. Terry Clavin, 'McGough, Joseph Christopher (Joe)', *D.I.B.* and Ferguson, *Barristers*, p. 242. One of his roles was as judge advocate on the staff of the adjutant general. John O.P. Bourke was called in 1958 and later served as managing director and chief financial officer in the Bank of Ireland in the seventies and eighties. Ibid., p. 142 and Cairnduff, *Who's who*, p. 11. Peter Sutherland was chairman of Allied Irish Bank, 1989–93. **123** E.g., Brendan Leahy, called to the Bar in 1983, was ordained a priest in 1986, later becoming bishop of Limerick, See Ferguson, *Barristers*, p. 371. Aideen Kinlen, called in 1959, later joined the Sacred Heart Order: ibid., p. 223. Ruth Mary Sheehy had joined the Sacred Heart Order some years before being called in 1960: see ibid., p. 29. **124** E.g., Christopher Alexander Preston, called in 1937, served as judge advocate general of the defence forces; see ibid., p. 284 and Declan Costello, 'Christopher Preston', *Irish Law Times* (ns) 2(4) (1984), 74. Preston also contributed to the drafting of the Statute Law Revision Act 1983. William Brian Moran, called in 1932, practised until 1939 before serving in the First World War. He was a judge advocate, 1939–60, and was then appointed deputy judge advocate general. Ferguson, *Barristers*, p. 258 and Moran to Condon, 26 July 1966, NAI 2009/74/742.

known for their sporting successes, for example in cycling,[125] rugby[126] and Gaelic games.[127]

A number of barristers combined their work at the Bar with academic careers. High-profile examples include Frances Moran, who was appointed Reid professor in Trinity College Dublin in 1925.[128] Agnes Cassidy was appointed to the same chair in 1950,[129] as were Mary Robinson and Mary McAleese in later years.[130] John Kelly[131] was professor of Roman law and jurisprudence at UCD. There were also many others who taught part-time in various institutions.[132] Librarians in the Law Library[133] and in the King's Inns[134] were also qualified barristers.

Philanthropic and public interest contributions.

The first chair of the Free Legal Advice Centres (FLAC) was barrister and future attorney general, David Byrne. Hardiman described the establishment of FLAC as 'a striking initiative' and a response to 'the near total lack of legal

125 E.g., Colm Christle, a cyclist who won the first Rás Tailteann in 1953, was called to the Bar in 1960: Ferguson, *Barristers*, p. 156.   126 E.g., Charles Vesey Boyle (called in 1937: ibid., p. 143) played rugby for Ireland in the 1930s: (1938) 72 *I.L.T.S.J.* 83 (12 Mar. 1938) and see further below; and Dick Spring, who played for Munster, London Irish and Ireland. See 'How rugby put Spring in step', *Irish Times*, 27 Feb. 2008, p. 4.   127 E.g., Éamonn (Edward) Mongey, called to the Bar in 1955, was a well-known Mayo Gaelic footballer in the 1940s and 50s, and wrote a Gaelic football column in *The Sunday Press* for many years. He was later appointed registrar of the Supreme Court. Sean Rice, 'Mayo mourns passing of legend', *Mayo News*, 25 Sept. 2007 and Ferguson, *Barristers*, p. 256. He was remembered by one of the interviewees for this book as a 'great Gaelic player' and the Irish examiner for the King's Inns. Jack Lynch was also a successful GAA player. Marcus de Búrca (called in 1949, ibid., p. 171) practised at the Bar in the fifties and joined the Attorney General's Office in 1960, working as a parliamentary draughtsman. He published *The GAA: a history* (Dublin, 1980). His other publications included *Murder at Marlhill* (Dublin, 1993), about the wrongly convicted Harry Gleeson. 'Obituary, Barrister and author of first major GAA history', *Irish Times*, 13 Mar. 2010, p. 12.   128 This was the first appointment of a woman to a Dublin University chair in any subject. She was also professor of property law at King's Inns, 1932–68, and later regius professor of laws at Trinity College from 1944–63. Moran had been called in 1924 and in 1941 she became the first woman to take silk, though she never practised at the inner Bar. See Ferguson, *Barristers*, p. 257.   129 Ferguson, *Barristers*, p. 155. Moran also attended the Nuremberg trials in Germany and in 1947 toured Canada speaking of the experience. See R.B. McDowell and D.A. Webb, *Trinity College Dublin 1592–1952: an academic history* (Cambridge, 1982), pp 453, 481, 547.   130 Kader Abdul Asmal, an English barrister, who was called to the Irish Bar in 1975 (ibid., p. 366) was a senior lecturer in law at TCD and Dean of the Faculty of Arts. Cairnduff, *Who's who*, p. 4.   131 Called in 1957, Kelly practised for a few years before being appointed professor at UCD in 1965. He also served as a Fine Gael TD, a government minister, and briefly as attorney general. See Ronan Keane, 'Kelly, John Maurice', *D.I.B.* and Ferguson, *Barristers*, p. 218.   132 See p. 150.   133 These included Frederick Price (called 1895); Ferguson, *Barristers*, p. 284. Price was librarian, 1922–50; Reginald Harrison (called in 1929: ibid., p. 201). Harrison was librarian, 1950–68; William Hurley (called in 1956: ibid., p. 211) was librarian, 1968–79, though he retained the title on retirement).   134 These included Joseph Carton (called 1891: ibid., p. 153 and see (1931) 65 *I.L.T.S.J.* 263 (31 Oct. 1931)); Joseph Carton (called 1891; Ferguson, *Barristers*, p. 153 and see (1931) 65 *I.L.T.S.J.* 263 (31 Oct. 1931)). Bridget Walsh, called in 1945, was assistant librarian, 1938–44, and then librarian of Kings Inns, 1944–69. See Ferguson, *Barristers*, p. 314. Mary Neylon was called in 1949 and took over as librarian from Bridget Walsh in 1970, remaining in post until

services for the disadvantaged ... Apart from the individual clients served, the existence of the centres did much to bring about statutory provision for law centres staffed by professional lawyers.'[135] FLAC also received financial support from the profession; for example, in 1987 when it needed funds for administrative support, the Bar Council proposed to levy members of the Bar (those who were aged under 65 years and had practised for ten years or more).[136] By 1994, some £45,000 had been raised for FLAC by members of the Bar.[137] Aside from FLAC, many barristers were involved in charities for various causes, and a number of those interviewed discussed their work with these organisations.[138] Fundraisers and appeals were quite common at the Bar; for example, the barristers' conference of the Society of St Vincent de Paul was active in fundraising in the 1940s.[139]

International contributions

Imperial contributions

The contribution of Irish barristers to the British empire and later to the commonwealth was, until recently, relatively under-examined.[140] Silvestri argues that 'Ireland's engagement with the British empire took a variety of forms ... and the multifaceted Irish imperial experience cannot be reduced to simply "Irish anti-imperialism".'[141] O'Shea, for example, traces the earliest Irish members of the Kenyan legal professions, in the years before 1920.[142] She writes that around

1984. Ferguson, *Barristers*, p. 264. **135** Adrian Hardiman, 'An innovative AG, Byrne will not be deficient in new skills needed in EU', *Irish Times*, 9 July 1999, p. 14. See pp 160–2. **136** B.C.M., 5 Dec. 1987. **137** £15,000 donated to FLAC', *Irish Law Times* 12 (1994), 100. **138** E.g., B14. Vincent Grogan, for example, helped to establish the charity Concern, as well as participating in the Society of Saint Vincent de Paul's free legal aid service. Diarmaid Ferriter, 'Grogan, Vincent Benedict', *D.I.B.* **139** (1943) 77 *I.L.T.S.J.* 61 (6 Mar. 1943); (1944) 78 *I.L.T.S.J.* 34 (5 Feb. 1944); (1945) 79 *I.L.T.S.J.* 59 (10 Mar. 1945); (1947) 81 *I.L.T.S.J.* 278 (29 Nov. 1947). **140** Examples of scholarship include Ronayne's tracing of the contribution of Irish lawyers to the states of Australia in the nineteenth century. This practice continued in the early decades of the twentieth century. Jarlath Ronayne, *First fleet to federation: Irish supremacy in colonial Australia* (Dublin, 2002). See also Peter Moore, 'Irish lawyers and judges in South Australia, 1836–1914' in Susan Arthure et al. (eds), *Irish South Australia: new histories and insights* (Adelaide, 2019). **141** Michael Silvestri, 'British imperial intelligence and anticolonial revolutionaries during and after the Great War' in Patrick Mannion and Fearghal McGarry (eds), *The Irish Revolution: a global history* (New York, 2022), p. 239. **142** O'Shea, 'Irish legal geographies in the era of emergency: independent Ireland, colonial Kenya, and the British colonial legal service', *Éire-Ireland* 51:1&2 (2016) 243, at 249–50, writes that '[o]utside of these high legal ranks, throughout the 1920s Irish settlers, attracted by the "unprecedented opportunities for acquiring land" promised in *Irish Times* advertisements, grew steadily in numbers. By 1922 the East Africa Irish society was up and running in Nairobi with the objective a "brotherhood" in East Africa for residents who were Irish born or of Irish parentage': 'Life in the colonies: Irishman in Africa: a Kenya society', *Irish Times*, 1 Jan. 1936, p. 48. In 1934 the *Irish Law Times* reported on social events held by the society: (1934) 68 *I.L.T.S.J.* 145 (2 June 1934). By 1936 the society had branches in Nairobi, Kakamega (Goldfields), Eldoret, and Mombasa, and around a hundred members, including several barristers.

1920, law graduates in Ireland considered their opportunities at home to be limited. O'Shea also writes that newly qualified barristers in particular felt 'frustrated with the overcrowding of the legal profession at home and beset by a sense of impeded social mobility'.[143] Others in such situations moved to England; for example Henry W. Farrell, who was called in 1918 but delayed commencing practice because of the First World War. He later wrote that he 'attended courts regularly for over two years' but found it 'impossible to make a living in those troubled times at the Bar'. Instead he joined the civil service in England.[144]

In 1920, Sir Hamar Greenwood, the last chief secretary for Ireland, asked Lord Milner, secretary of state for the colonies, when making appointments to the colonial legal service to 'consider especially members of the Irish Bar'. He wrote:

> The gentlemen of that Bar have had a hard time and will have a worse time owing to the cessation of much of the work of the courts in Ireland. They have logically refused to touch the Sinn Féin courts and they suffer for it. There are excellent men among them who would do credit to your service and be most useful servants of the crown. I beg you to consider them.[145]

This followed a tradition which had been evident since the nineteenth century, when 'Irish barristers regularly took up colonial appointments.'[146] O'Shea writes that by 1930, Trinity College Dublin was the sixth-biggest recruiting university for the British colonial service.[147]

In the early years of the Free State there was a steady flow of Irish barristers to far-flung parts of the empire. This appears to have been driven partly as a consequence of advertising by the colonial office[148] and partly by a perceived lack of opportunity at home. For example, the son of one barrister who served in the commonwealth said that for many barristers in the 1920s 'things were very bad

---

143 O'Shea, 'Irish legal geographies', at 253.   144 Farell to O'Byrne, 11 Oct. 1925, NAI 2009/74/742.   145 Greenwood to Milner, 24 Aug. 1920, TNA CO 877/1, cited in O'Shea, 'Irish legal geographies', at 249.   146 Ferguson, *Barristers*, p. 119.   147 O'Shea, *Ireland and the end of the British empire*, p. 160. In a lecture delivered at the London School of Economics in 1948, Sir Sidney Abrahams remarked that a career in the service 'may lead to a considerable experience of the world, its peoples, and its laws.' Sidney Abrahams, 'The colonial legal service and the administration of justice in colonial dependencies', *Journal of Comparative Legislation and International Law* 30:3–4 (1948), 1, at 1.   148 Ellen Feingold, *Colonial justice and decolonization in the High Court of Tanzania, 1920–1971* (Cambridge, 2018), p. 33. E.g., see an article by Grattan Bushe, legal advisor to the Colonial Office and to the dominions, reproduced in the *Irish Law Times* from the English *Law Journal*: 'The colonial legal service', (1936) 70 *I.L.T.S.J.* 231 (12 Sept. 1936), which noted that '[m]any barristers are probably unaware of certain opportunities which are offered to them for practising their profession abroad – not in private practice, but in the government service.' The requirements were four years of practice at the Bar, and being under the age of forty. It also noted that 'their prospects of promotion at any given time are not restricted to the comparatively few opportunities in the particular colony in which they happen to be serving, but extend to the whole colonial empire. There is, in consequence, a good deal of movement from colony to colony within the legal service.' Feingold notes that the colonial office also targeted

... there was no work in Ireland'.[149] He also said that in England, 'practically all the judges were Irish because they could not get work.' His father, Eric Hallinan from Cork, was called in 1924. He practised at the Irish Bar for five years before embarking on a forty-year career in the various colonial legal administrations. He served as an attorney general, a puisne judge, a justice of appeal and a chief justice in Nigeria, the Bahamas, Trinidad, Cyprus, the West Indies and Bermuda.[150] Frederick William Johnston, called in 1925, joined the colonial service and served as puisne judge of Nigeria and a member of the West African Court of Appeal.[151] Similarly, Patrick Branigan was called in 1928 but left the Bar after two years. He came from a family of modest means, and '[a]fter two years of practice, he decided that his responsibilities to his family required a steadier income and he entered the colonial service in 1931'.[152] He held a number of posts in the colonial service, including as administrative officer in Kenya in 1931 and crown counsel in Tanganyika in 1933. He was appointed solicitor general of Rhodesia in 1938. He was minister for justice and attorney general of the Gold Coast from 1948–54.[153] Paget John Bourke was also called in 1928, joined the colonial legal service and served in the Seychelles, Palestine and Kenya. He was chief justice of Sierra Leone and Cyprus in the fifties.[154] Writing to Attorney General Maguire in 1939 just after he had accepted his position in the Seychelles, he said he would not return for three years, but that it was 'an excellent climate and I am quite looking forward to it'.[155]

This pattern continued in the early thirties. For example, Geoffrey Rudd was called in 1932 and practised in Dublin until 1936, when he was appointed a resident magistrate in Kenya. He was chief justice and legal adviser to the government of Aden, 1944–5, and a judge of the Supreme Court of Aden, 1944–51.[156] From 1951 to 1963 he was a puisne judge in Kenya.[157] Brian A. Doyle was called in 1932 and practised in Dublin and on the South-Western Circuit before joining the colonial legal service in 1937. He served as attorney general in Fiji.[158] Theodore David Wallace was called in 1931 and practised on the Munster

Scottish lawyers. **149** Irish Life and Lore, 'Edward G. Hallinan (b. 1937)', track 1, www.irishlife andlore.com/product/edward-g-hallinan-b-1937/. **150** Ferguson, *Barristers*, p. 198. O'Shea, *Ireland and the end of the British empire*, discusses some of the cases over which he presided, pp 162–7. **151** Ferguson, *Barristers*, p. 213 and call certificate dated 29 Aug. 1950, NAI 2009/74/742. **152** 'Obituary of Sir Patrick Branigan, colonial service lawyer in East Africa who went on to draft independence constitutions for Malta and Ghana', *Daily Telegraph*, 18 Nov. 2000, p. 27. **153** See (1961) 95 *I.L.T.S.J.* 61 (11 Mar. 1961) and Ferguson, *Barristers*, p. 144. **154** See ibid., p. 143. Another who left in the twenties was Henry Ambrose Webb, who took silk in 1920 and was a member of the Bar Council, 1916–21. He joined the District Court in Palestine in 1921, where he remained until 1933. He then served in Kenya, Sierra Leone and Tanganyika throughout the thirties and forties: ibid., p. 315; obit., 'Sir Henry Webb', *Irish Times*, 22 May 1964, p. 13 and Feingold, *Colonial justice and decolonization*, who notes, p. 45, that three of the ten legal and judicial officers in 1936 were members of the Irish Bar. **155** Paget Bourke to Maguire, 18 Feb. 1939, NAI 2009/74/742. **156** See Ferguson, *Barristers*, p. 292 and www.europeansineastafrica.co.uk. **157** See *Official Gazette for the Colony and Protectorate of Kenya* 53(59), 27 Nov. 1951. **158** Call certificate dated 11 Oct. 1950, NAI 2009/74/742 and Ferguson, *Barristers*, p. 178.

Circuit before being appointed as crown counsel in Kenya in 1934,[159] and was appointed crown counsel in Kuala Lumpur in 1939. He was appointed attorney general of Borneo in 1947, and Tanganyika in 1951.[160] Also called in 1931 was Ian Rawdon Greene, who practised on the Munster Circuit for some years. His cousin, Richard Cherry, later wrote that he 'worked up a fair practice. He was not satisfied, however, with his prospects, and decided to apply for a post in the colonial service.' He went to Tanganyika as crown counsel in 1936, and was soon promoted to circuit judge in Zanzibar. By 1939 he was said to be 'doing very well.'[161] John Sydney Richard Cole, called in 1935,[162] served as attorney general of Nigeria, the Bahamas, Somaliland and Tanganyika, and as minister for legal affairs in Tanganyika, before returning to Ireland and pursuing an academic career.[163]

Over the next few decades, members of the Irish Bar continued to follow similar career paths into the colonial legal service. They served as attorneys general and crown counsel, for example, in the Gold Coast,[164] Hong Kong[165] and Malaya.[166] They sat as senior members of the judiciaries of the Bahamas,[167] Gibraltar[168] Somaliland,[169] Hong Kong,[170]

159 He also served for a time as acting solicitor general in Kenya: *Official Gazette of the Colony and Protectorate of Kenya* 40:7, 1 Feb. 1938.   160 Ferguson, *Barristers*, p. 313 and obit.: Mr Theodore David Wallace, *Irish Times*, 2 Jan. 1952, p. 5. During the Japanese occupation of Singapore, he was interred in Changi Jail, where he suffered 'great privations' which affected his health.   161 Richard T. Cherry to Patrick Lynch, 18 May 1939, NAI 2009/74/742.   162 Ferguson, *Barristers*, p. 158 and Helen Andrews, 'Cole, John Sydney Richard', *D.I.B.*   163 In 1965 he was appointed as Reid professor at Trinity College Dublin. He co-authored, with W.N. Denison, *Tanganyika: the development of its laws and constitution* (London, 1964), and later published J.S.R. Cole, *Irish cases on evidence* (Dublin, 1972) and *Cases on criminal law* (Dublin, 1975). See 'J.S.R. Cole, an appreciation', *Irish Times*, 7 Feb. 1990, p. 13.   164 Henry William Butler Blackall (called in 1912) practised for three years before serving in the First World War. He was appointed crown counsel in Kenya in 1919, and was the attorney general of the Gold Coast, 1932–43, and president of the West African court of appeal, 1948–51. (1943) 77 *I.L.T.S.J.* 45 (13 Feb. 1943) and (1943) 77 *I.L.T.S.J.* 63 (6 Mar. 1943). See Ferguson, *Barristers*, p. 140. Victor Elyan (called in 1949) was a resident magistrate in Accra, Gold Coast: ibid., p. 181 and certification of call, 4 Oct. 1952, NAI 2009/74/742.   165 Desmond Mayne (called in 1943) decided in 1961 to retire as principal crown counsel in Hong Kong: Mayne to Ó Caoimh, 17 Feb. 1961, NAI 2009/74/742. Dermot Neil Egerton Rea (called in 1951) was senior crown counsel and a district judge in Hong Kong. Ferguson, *Barristers*, p. 286 and Egerton Rea to Colm Condon, 29 Mar. 1965, NAI 2009/74/742.   166 Michael Hogan (called in 1936); Ferguson, *Barristers*, p. 207. Frederick G. Cooke (called in 1944) was legal advisor to the states of Kedah and Perlis in Malaya. certification for English Bar, 21 Apr. 1952, NAI 2009/74/742 and Ferguson, *Barristers*, p. 162.   167 Oscar Bedford Daly (called in 1904) practised initially on the North-East Circuit and later practised in Kenya after serving in the First World War. He was chief justice of the Bahamas from 1939–45. Daly also served in Kenya and was president of the East Africa Irish Society in 1929. See www.europeansineastafrica.co.uk, Ferguson, *Barristers*, p. 169 and obit., *Irish Times*, 30 June 1953, p. 5.   168 Maurice Cherry Greene (called in 1919: Ferguson, *Barristers*, p. 196) was chief justice of Gibraltar from 1941–2.   169 Ian Rawdon Greene (called in 1931: ibid., p. 196) was a judge of the High Court of Somaliland.   170 E.g., Michael Hogan (called in 1936: ibid., p. 207) was appointed chief justice of Hong Kong in 1955. Arthur McMullin (called in 1945: ibid., p. 245) practised as a crown counsel and then senior crown counsel in Uganda in the 1950s and early 60s. He joined the Hong Kong judiciary in 1961 and served as a magistrate, in the District Court, as a puisne judge, in the High Court, and as a justice of appeal from the 1960s–80s. He later served as a non-permanent justice of the Court of

Brunei,[171] Cyprus,[172] the Seychelles,[173] Tanganyika,[174] Kenya,[175] the Leeward Islands,[176] Jamaica,[177] Trinidad and Tobago,[178] and Uganda.[179] Irish barristers were also represented in more junior judicial appointments in such places as Tanganyika,[180] Rhodesia,[181] the Gold Coast,[182] Malaya,[183] and Cyprus.[184] Some of

Final Appeal. See www.hkcfa.hk/en/about/who/judges/ former/index_id_27.html. William Silke (was called in 1955: ibid., p. 299) served as a judge in Borneo in the 1960s before joining the Hong Kong judiciary in 1969, serving until 1994: www.hkcfa.hk/en/about/who/judges/former/ index_id_29.html. Timothy Creedon (called in 1943: ibid., p. 166) served as a judge in Kowloon: see certification for English Bar, 16 June 1958, NAI 2009/74/742. **171** Michael Hogan was chief justice of Brunei, 1964–70: ibid., p. 207. **172** Herbert Stronge (called in 1900: ibid., p. 303) was chief justice of Cyprus, 1931–8. Charles Vesey Boyle was appointed in 1958. See O'Shea, *Ireland and the end of the British empire*, p. 91. O'Shea, pp 24–5, also traces the Irish legal presence in Cyprus from 1898, including Maurice Cherry Greene (see above); Patrick Walsh (called 1898: Ferguson, *Barristers*, p. 314); Henry Blackall (see above); Lancelot Lloyd Blood (called in 1920: ibid., p. 141); Bernard Crean (called in 1912: ibid., p. 165). **173** E.g., Dr Patrick Stanislaus Walsh, called in 1898, was appointed chief justice of the Seychelles in 1931, having previously been president of the District Court in Cyprus. The *Irish Law Times* called him 'an Irishman well known in Dublin': (1931) 65 *I.L.T.S.J.* 251 (17 Oct. 1931). **174** Ambrose Henry Webb (called in 1909) was chief justice of Tanganyika, 1940–5. Ferguson, *Barristers*, p. 315. Francis Xavier Rooney (called in 1948; Ferguson, *Barristers*, p. 291) practised in Tanganyika and wrote 'I find Dar-es-Salam an attractive place to live in, and if betimes it is a little too hot, I console myself with memories of the bitter cold of an Irish winter. I find that the tropics have an enchantment which delights and Tanganyika must be one of the most interesting countries in the world.' Rooney to Ó Dálaigh, 8 Mar. 1952, NAI 2009/74/742. **175** E.g., Ambrose Henry Webb was a puisne judge of the Supreme Court of Kenya, 1933–7: Ferguson, *Barristers*, p. 315. Joseph Alfred Sheridan (called in 1907) served as a puisne judge, 1920–8 and as acting chief justice of Kenya, 1928–9, and chief justice of Kenya, 1934–46: ibid., p. 298. John P. Murphy (called in 1946) was a judge in Mombasa. Certification for English Bar, 10 July 1962, NAI 2009/74/742 and Ferguson, *Barristers*, p. 262. O'Shea, 'Irish legal geographies', at 244 demonstrates that Irish-born judges in Kenya 'rarely challenged or contested the position of the colonial establishment', and were 'remarkably conservative' compared with their English and Scottish counterparts. **176** Charles James Griffin (called in 1898) was appointed chief justice of the Leeward Islands in 1919. 'Chief justice of the Leeward Islands', *Irish Times*, 17 Jan. 1919, p. 2 and Ferguson, *Barristers*, p. 196. Herbert Stronge practised on the North-East Circuit and was chief justice of the Leeward Islands from 1925 to 1931. **177** David Sherlock (called in 1904) practised on the Munster Circuit and later served as a judge on the Jamaican Court of Appeal: (1938) 72 *I.L.T.S.J.* 83 (12 Mar. 1938) and 77 (1943) *I.L.T.S.J.* 242 (2 Oct. 1943) and Ferguson, *Barristers*, p. 298. **178** Henry William Butler Blackall was appointed chief justice of Trinidad and Tobego in 1943: (1943) 77 *I.L.T.S.J.* 63 (6 Mar. 1943) and 'New chief justice of Trinidad', *Irish Times*, 5 Feb. 1943, p. 3. **179** Charles James Griffin was chief justice of the Uganda Protectorate, 1921–32. **180** John Joseph Webb (called in 1928: Ferguson, *Barristers*, p. 315) was a resident magistrate in Tanganyika. **181** James Ryan (called in 1939: ibid., p. 292) was a resident magistrate in Northern Rhodesia in 1958. James Menary (called in 1949: ibid., p. 253) also practised in Rhodesia and was legal draughtsman for the Northern Rhodesia government. See T.C. Tobias to Ó Dálaigh, 16 Sept. 1952 and certification for English Bar, 12 May 1964, NAI 2009/74/742. Brendan Peter O'Byrne (called in 1954: ibid., p. 267) was crown counsel in the Attorney General's Department in Lusaka, Northern Rhodesia. See certification for English Bar, 30 July 1955, NAI 2009/74/742. **182** Thomas Andrews Dennison (called in 1936: ibid., p. 173) was a district magistrate (1948) and then a puisne judge (1950) in the Gold Coast. See 'Belfast man new Gold Coast puisne judge', *Irish Times*, 16 June 1950, p. 1. **183** Donal Good (called in 1935: ibid., p. 194) was appointed a legal advisor in Malaya in 1952 and was later puisne judge in the federation of Malaya: See 'Social and personal', *Irish Times*, 23 May 1952, p. 7. **184** E.g., Maurice Cherry Greene was appointed president of the District Court in Cyprus in 1928. From 1960 to 1963, Barra O'Briain, formerly president of the Circuit Court in Ireland, was

those who were called to the Irish Bar then joined the civil service in places such as Ceylon[185] and India,[186] and there were also Irish barristers in the colonial legal service in Palestine.[187]

During what Allott describes as Africa's 'late colonial scene', 'colonial legal servants who hailed from Ireland constituted a striking proportion of the membership of the colonial legal service, whether as crown counsel, law officers, or members of the professional judiciary.'[188] Despite this, O'Shea points out that

> Historical writing aimed at investigating Irish judicial traffic to and from imperial trouble spots during the endgame of empire has been notably absent. This omission is partly symptomatic of the habitual divorcing of independent Ireland's contributions to empire from the hegemonic nationalist narrative.[189]

From the 1950s the colonial service was no longer seen as a 'lucrative and exotic path',[190] or even a safe option, as independence movements emerged in Palestine, Ceylon and Burma, and 'emergencies' developed in Kenya and Malaya. However, O'Shea points out that Irish judges and lawyers were still willing to take up posts in places like Cyprus during its 'emergency' years. She makes the point that the administration of 'British justice' during these years 'lay in the hands of several Irish judges', and that Cypriot confidence in the judiciary remained quite strong.[191] Allot similarly noted that in 1950s Africa, 'colonial legal civil servants who hailed from Ireland ... constituted a striking proportion of the membership of the colonial legal service, whether as crown counsel, law officers or members of the professional judiciary.'[192]

The Irish barristers who joined the colonial legal service came from both Catholic[193] and Church of Ireland[194] backgrounds. O'Shea argues that 'class, not

---

seconded to the United Nations and served as chief justice of Cyprus.   **185** David Miller Steen, called in 1898: ibid., p. 302.   **186** James Augustine Sweeney, called in 1927: ibid., p. 306. **187** Michael Hogan served in the colonial legal service in Palestine (ibid., p. 207); Maurice Cherry Greene was appointed a puisne judge in Palestine in 1937: ibid., p. 196. William Fitzgerald (called in 1923: ibid., p. 187) was attorney general of Palestine, 1937–43, and chief justice of Palestine, 1944–8: 'Former Palestine chief justice dies', *Irish Times*, 10 July 1989, p. 10.   **188** Anthony Allott, 'The *Journal of African Law*, 1957–96: then and now,' *J. African L.* 40:2 (1996), 143 at 145. **189** Helen O'Shea, 'Irish legal geographies in the era of emergency: independent Ireland, colonial Kenya, and the British colonial legal service', *Éire-Ireland* 51:1&2 (2016), 243 at 244.   **190** O'Shea, *Ireland and the end of the British empire*, p. 161.   **191** Ibid., p. 162. Akenson suggests that Irish men who emigrated to South Africa tended to have elite and professional status, despite only accounting for 3–5% of the white population. Donald Harman Akenson, 'The Irish, ethnic studies and the historiography of South Africa' in Donald Harman Akenson, *Occasional papers on the Irish in South Africa* (Grahamstown, SA, 1991), pp 79–81.   **192** Allott, 'The *Journal of African Law*', at 145. **193** E.g. Geoffrey Rudd, Eric Hallinan, Paget John Bourke, Henry Blackall and Joseph Sheridan. Another example was James Patrick Trainor (called in 1954), who joined the colonial service in 1954, and was appointed legal officer in Malaya; (1954) 88 *I.L.T.S.J.* 236 (18 Sept. 1954). He worked in Singapore and Cyprus, see Ferguson, *Barristers*, p. 310.   **194** E.g., Charles Vesey Boyle served in the Royal Artillery and Royal Air Force during the Second World War. He joined the colonial legal

religious background, was the determining factor for a colonial legal service career in the 1950s.'[195] The majority in the twenties and thirties were Trinity-educated.[196] Several of them were knighted for their services to the empire and the commonwealth, including Eric Hallinan, Patrick Branigan, Joseph Sheridan, Wilfrid Hugh Hurley, Henry Blackall, Oscar Bedford Daly, Charles James Griffin and Paget John Bourke.

Decolonisation

When the British empire began to fracture, particularly after the Second World War, members of the Irish Bar also contributed to decolonisation.[197] An example of one such barrister was James Skinner. He was called to the Bar in 1946, and worked on the Leinster Circuit. He left the Law Library in 1950[198] and took up a post in Northern Rhodesia when faced with 'bleak career opportunities in a moribund Irish economy'.[199] He was later called to the Rhodesian Bar and represented African nationalist defendants, with whom he identified. He got involved in politics, and the training of public servants, and helped to draft the new constitution for Zambia.[200] He served as chief justice, attorney general and minister for legal affairs. He resigned as chief justice in 1969, and in the same year was appointed chief justice of Malawi, where he remained for sixteen years.[201]

Skinner was not the only Irish barrister who contributed to the drafting of new constitutions in emerging postcolonial states. Patrick Branigan, who served as both attorney general and chief justice of the Gold Coast, helped to draft the independence constitutions for both Malta in 1947 and Ghana in 1948.[202] Vincent Grogan, with his legislative drafting experience, acted as a consultant constitutional and legislative drafter for the governments of Ghana, Swaziland and Botswana. In 1969 he was invited by Ghana's military government to redraft their original constitution.[203] Arthur Wheeler had a long career in the legal system of post-independence Nigeria.[204] Wilfrid Hugh Hurley, called in 1935,

---

service in 1946 and served in Malaya, Kenya and Cyprus.   **195** O'Shea, *Ireland and the end of the British empire*, p. 189.   **196** O'Shea, 'Irish legal geographies', notes, at 255, that Denis Coffey, resident magistrate in Kenya, 1939–48, was 'one of the few Irish lawyers in the colonial legal service at that time to have studied at UCD'.   **197** See generally Rachel L. Ellett, 'Courts and the emergence of statehood in post-colonial Africa', *N.I.L.Q.* 63:3 (2020), 343.   **198** B.C.M., 30 Jan. 1970.   **199** Turlough O'Riordan, 'Skinner, James John', *D.I.B.*   **200** O'Riordan, 'Skinner' and Ferguson, *Barristers*, p. 299. See 'Skinner resigns Zambian judiciary', *Irish Times*, 24 Sept. 1969, p. 1 and obit., *The Times*, 6 Nov. 2008, p. 73.   **201** He applied to re-join the Law Library in 1970, as did James O'Grady (called in 1957), who had left in 1960 and worked as crown counsel in Zambia: B.C.M., 30 Jan. 1970.   **202** 'Obituary of Sir Patrick Branigan, colonial service lawyer in East Africa who went on to draft independence constitutions for Malta and Ghana', *Daily Telegraph*, 18 Nov. 2000, p. 27.   **203** Diarmaid Ferriter, 'Grogan, Vincent Benedict', *D.I.B.*   **204** Arthur William Edge Wheeler (called in 1953: Ferguson, *Kings Inns barristers*, p. 316) served as crown counsel in Nigeria, and later as a crown counsel in the new Federation of Nigeria. Post-independence, he served in the Northern province as deputy solicitor general, director of public prosecutions, a judge of the High Court and chief justice from 1975 until 1980. See obit.: 'Dublin-born barrister among

was chief justice of the High Court of Nigeria, 1960–7.[205] Barra O'Briain was first president of the post-independence Cypriot High Court in 1960,[206] and O'Shea suggests that this was indicative of 'the good reputation of his Irish predecessors in Cyprus'.[207]

James Aiden Quinn was called in 1957 and was appointed assistant attorney general in West Cameroon in 1964, and procurator general in 1966.[208] He was attorney general of the Seychelles (1972–6) and later chief justice of the Seychelles (1976–7), the Gilbert Islands (1977–81) and Botswana (1981–7).[209] He served as a judge in the Solomon Islands (1977–9), was special prosecutor in the Falkland Islands (1981), drafted proposed revisions to the constitution of Dominica[210] and worked on the immigration appeals tribunal in the UK (1990–2004). Henry Graham, called in 1963, practised on the North-East Circuit until 1967, when he was appointed then state counsel to the government of Kenya.[211]

The United Nations and the European project

There was some limited involvement by the Irish Bar in international affairs in the first decades after independence. For example, in 1930 a delegation including John Hearne and Kathleen Phelan represented the Irish Free State at the international conference on the codification of international law at the Hague.[212] However, it was not until the late fifties that Irish barristers began making an international impact beyond the colonial and post-colonial activities described above. Ireland took its seat on the United Nations in 1955. This marked a turning point in international relations following several decades of relative isolation.[213] As O'Sullivan points out, 'Irish support for decolonisation played a central role in constructing the state's identity at the United Nations.'[214] Several

last links with British rule in Africa', *Irish Times*, 14 Dec. 2013, p. 14. After his retirement, Wheeler chaired the Foreign Compensation Commission (FCC) until 1995. Established in the aftermath of the Second World War, the FCC calculated the amount of compensation British claimants were entitled to under international and British law for losses suffered abroad. See S.W. Magnus, 'The Foreign Compensation Commission', *Int. & Comp. L. Q.* 37:4 (1988), 975. **205** Ferguson, *Barristers*, p. 211. **206** O'Shea, *Ireland and the end of the British empire*, p. 153. **207** Ibid., p. 154. She observes that 'the judges may not have been easily identifiable as Irish. In accent and manner, they were more akin to English public schooled 'gentlemen' than any reductive Irish stereotype – one Athens Radio commentator, present at a trial presided over by [Eric] Hallinan, merely described him as "British".' **208** Quinn to Condon, 28 Feb. 1967, NAI 2009/74/742, and Ferguson, *Barristers*, p. 286. He had also served as crown counsel in Nyasalad in 1960. See Nyo' Wakai, *Under the broken scale of justice: the law and my times* (Cameroon, 2009) and Carlson Emmanuel Wunde, Anyangwe, 'The administration of justice in a bi-jural country: the United Republic of Cameroon' (PhD, University of London, 1979). **209** Republic of Botswana, *Government Gazette* 19:35, 24 July 1981. **210** Roger Bingham, 'Overseas aid goes legal?', *New Law Journal* 142:6568 (1992), 1268. **211** Certification for English Bar, 25 Apr. 1968, NAI 2009/74/742. **212** 'For the Hague: a Free State delegation', *Irish Times*, 12 Mar. 1930, p. 7, and 'Status of women: legal profession', *Irish Times*, 21 Jan. 1932, p. 97. **213** Ireland was one of several states in the UN, referred to as 'fire brigade' states, which demonstrated a strong commitment to the principles of international law. **214** Kevin O'Sullivan, *Ireland, Africa and the end of empire: small state identity in the Cold War, 1955–75* (Manchester, 2013), p. 1.

barristers, both within Ireland and abroad, played significant roles in this. For example, the minister for external affairs when Ireland joined the UN was Liam Cosgrave (a qualified barrister), who identified Ireland as a post-colonial state and supported decolonisation in Africa.[215] Seán MacBride was later appointed UN commissioner for Namibia, and was awarded the Nobel Peace Prize in 1974 before his return to the Bar in 1977.[216] Francis Mahon Hayes served as Ireland's permanent representative to the UN in New York from 1989–95,[217] and Mary Robinson was appointed UN high commissioner for human rights in 1997.[218] As part of the general tendency for members of the Bar to enter the civil service, there were a number of qualified barristers who contributed to the workings of the Department of External or Foreign Affairs. They also played significant, though less-high profile roles in Ireland's international relations. They included Thomas Joseph Coyne in the twenties and thirties,[219] Máire Mac an tSaoi in the forties,[220] Mahon Hayes in the sixties and seventies[221] and Jane Flood Liddy[222] and Emer Kilcullen[223] in the seventies.

From the mid-century onward, Irish involvement in European affairs was evident, and several members of the Bar contributed in different ways to what can broadly be termed 'the European project'.[224] They sat on various bodies, including the Organisation for European Economic Cooperation[225] and the Council of Europe.[226] A number were involved in the drafting of the European Convention on Human Rights and Fundamental Freedoms,[227] and sat on the European Commission on Human Rights.[228] Irish judges on the European Court of Human Rights were Philip O'Donoghue,[229] Brian Walsh,[230] Conor Alexander

215 See O'Sullivan, *Ireland, Africa and the end of empire*, ch. 1. 216 Ronan Keane, 'MacBride, Seán', *D.I.B.* and Ferguson, *Barristers*, p. 234. See further Anthony J. Jordan, *Seán MacBride: a biography* (Dublin, 1993). 217 Called in 1952, he practised on the Southern Circuit before joining the civil service: Turlough O'Riordan, 'Hayes (Francis) Mahon (Joseph)', *D.I.B.* and Ferguson, *Barristers*, p. 202. 218 In 2008 Patricia O'Brien was appointed the under-secretary-general for legal affairs and UN legal counsel. 219 Called in 1922, he was seconded to the Department of External Affairs, serving the Vatican and the League of Nations, 1929–34: ibid., p. 165. 220 Called in 1944: ibid., p. 240. 221 He served as a legal advisor, counsellor and assistant secretary in the Department of External Affairs in the sixties and seventies. Turlough O'Riordan, 'Hayes (Francis) Mahon (Joseph)', *D.I.B.* and Ferguson, *Barristers*, p. 202. 222 Called in 1972, she worked as legal adviser in the Department of Foreign Affairs: ibid., p. 364, and trailblazers exhibition. 223 Also called in 1972 and a legal adviser in the Department of Foreign Affairs: ibid., p. 364, and trailblazers exhibition. 224 Miriam Hederman O'Brien received the European Order of Merit for her contribution towards European understanding and integration in 1984: *Irish Times*, 5 Feb. 1998. Peter Sutherland was instrumental in the creation of the Erasmus programme to facilitate student mobility within the EU. 225 E.g., Seán MacBride (called in 1937: Ferguson, *Barristers*, p. 234). He had a largely Dublin-based criminal practice, took silk in 1943, and three years later founded the political party Clann na Poblachta. He was elected to the Dáil in 1947 and sat on various European bodies in his capacity as minister for foreign affairs. His fluency in French was undoubtedly an asset. Ronan Keane, 'MacBride, Seán', *D.I.B.* 226 E.g., Emer Kilcullen sat on a steering committee for human rights on the Council of Europe. 227 Seán MacBride and attorney general Cecil Lavery: called in 1915: Ferguson, *Barristers*, p. 225, and T.A. Finlay, 'Lavery, Cecil Patrick Linton', *D.I.B.* 228 E.g., Philip O'Donoghue sat on the commission in 1965, and Jane Liddy did so from 1987–99. She was appointed president of its first chamber. See trailblazers exhibition. 229 Served on the ECtHR 1971–80. 230 Called in 1941 (Ferguson, *Barristers*, p. 313), Walsh practised for a time on

Maguire,[231] Richard McGonigal[232] and John Hedigan.[233] Irish barristers were of course also involved in litigation before the court of human rights, notably in the cases of *Ireland v. the UK*,[234] *Open Door and Dublin Well Woman v. Ireland*,[235] *Airey v. Ireland*,[236] *Johnston v. Ireland*[237] and *Norris v. Ireland*.[238]

Barristers were involved in promoting[239] and negotiating[240] Ireland's accession to the European Economic Community in 1973. Internally, the benchers and the Bar Council actively sought to engage with the new legal system.[241] Irish judges sat on the European courts.[242] Four of Ireland's seven European commissioners in the twentieth century were barristers: Richard Burke,[243] Peter Sutherland,[244] Michael O'Kennedy[245] and David Byrne.[246] Irish judges in the European Court

the North-East Circuit. Aged 43 he was appointed to the Supreme Court, and served on the ECtHR, 1980–98. He was the first president of the Law Reform Commission, 1975–85. Charles Lysaght, 'Walsh, Brian Cathal Patrick', *D.I.B.*   **231** Called in 1922 (Ferguson, *Barristers*, p. 248) and practised on the Western Circuit, having previously been on the roll of solicitors. He served as attorney general, 1932–6, and was appointed chief justice in 1946. He sat on the ECtHR, 1965–71. Marie Coleman, 'Maguire, Conor Alexander', *D.I.B.*   **232** Called in 1925, McGonigal sat on the ECtHR, 1959–64. Ferguson, *Barristers*, p. 241 and A.R. Hart, 'McGonigal, Richard', *D.I.B.* **233** Called in 1976 (Ferguson, *Barristers*, p. 367) and appointed to the ECtHR in 1997.   **234** (1977) ECtHR, 5310/71. This case challenged the implementation of internment without trial in Northern Ireland in August 1971. It centred on the use of 'interrogation methods known as "the five techniques" on individuals detained without trial by British security forces during the conflict in Northern Ireland in the 1970s. The commission unanimously found that the five techniques amounted to torture under Article 3 ECHR, but the ECtHR overturned this decision and found that the five techniques amounted to inhuman and degrading treatment only. The Irish legal team included Francis Mahon Hayes and Jane Liddy from the Department of Foreign Affairs, along with the attorney general, four senior counsel and one junior counsel. O'Donoghue was the Irish judge on the court. The judgment was revised in 2018: *Ireland v. United Kingdom*, 2018 ECtHR 5310/71. **235** (1988) ECtHR 14234/88. The Irish lawyers included Emer Kilcullen, Dermot Gleeson (called in 1970; Ferguson, *Barristers*, p. 363), James O'Reilly (called in 1977: ibid., p. 367) Frank Clarke (called in 1973: ibid., p. 364), Adrian Hardiman (called in 1974: ibid., p. 365) and Brian Murray (called in 1989: ibid., p. 379).   **236** (1979) 2 E.H.R.R. 305. The Irish lawyers included John Cooke (called in 1966: ibid., p. 162), Mary Robinson, Jane Liddy and Niall McCarthy (called in 1946: ibid., p. 236) and Adrian Hardiman, 'McCarthy, Niall St John', *D.I.B.*).   **237** (1982) ECtHR 9697/82. The Irish lawyers included Dermot Gleeson, James O'Reilly, Mary Robinson, William Duncan and Jane Liddy from the Department of Foreign Affairs.   **238** 1983 ECtHR 10581/83. The Irish lawyers included Mary Robinson, Dermot Gleeson, James O'Reilly and Edward Comyn. **239** E.g., David Byrne.   **240** E.g., Mahon Hayes. Jack Lynch had accompanied Sean Lemass on his tour of the EEC capitals, canvassing support for the Irish application.   **241** E.g., K.I.B.M., 30 Apr., 6 June, 20 June, 1 Oct. 1973.   **242** E.g., John Cooke sat on the Court of First Instance. **243** Called in 1973; Ferguson, *Barristers*, p. 365. He had been elected to the Dáil in 1969 and was appointed minister for education in 1973. Burke appointed to the commission twice, serving 1977–81 and 1982–5. See obit., 'Politician twice posted to EEC Commission', *Irish Times*, 19 Mar. 2016, p. 14.   **244** Called in 1968, he sat on the commission, 1985–9. He also served as director general of the General Agreement on Tariffs and Trade, 1993–5, and was then the first director general of its successor, the World Trade Organisation. He also chaired the European Institute for Public Administration, 1991–6. He was a non-executive chairman of Goldman Sachs International and British Petroleum in the late 1990s. See Ferguson, *Barristers*, p. 306. Obituary, 'Father of globalisation championed free trade, migration and the EU', *Irish Times*, 8 Jan. 2018, p. 7 and 'Peter Sutherland: 25 April 1946–7 January 2018', www.ucd.ie/newsandopinion/news/2018/january/07/petersutherland25april1946 7january2018/.   **245** Called in 1961 (Ferguson, *Barristers*, p. 275), O'Kennedy served as a Fianna Fáil senator, TD and minister for foreign affairs and finance.   **246** Called in 1970 (ibid., p. 363), Byrne also served as attorney general, 1997–9. He was also heavily

of Justice were Thomas O'Higgins,[247] Cearbhaill O'Dálaigh,[248] Nial Fennelly[249] John Murray[250] and Fidelma Macken.[251]

* * *

Although Curran described the Bar as 'a formal and conservative profession',[252] many people at the Bar were at the forefront of the foundation of the state, and displayed both innovation and resourcefulness. While it is impossible to capture all of the activities of barristers beyond the Law Library, this chapter has established that barristers were prominent figures in Irish public life in the twentieth century. Arguably no other group was as actively involved in the architecture of the state. Pue's observation that '[l]awyers, like novelists, journalists, poets, comedians, or scholars, are word spinners'[253] rings true when considering the involvement of the Irish Bar in the artistic, cultural and literary history of twentieth-century Ireland. Later, barristers often took a lead on key political and social issues.

In the twenties and thirties in particular, they spread out around the common law world and worked in other jurisdictions as advocates, judges and legal advisers. Barristers also made significant contributions to international legal and political cooperation through the United Nations, the European Court of Human Rights and the EEC.

involved in the development of international commercial arbitration procedures, and was the founding chairman of FLAC, the free legal advice centres. Hardiman, 'An innovative AG'. **247** Called in 1938, O'Higgins was also chief justice, 1974–84, before sitting as a judge in the European Court of Justice, 1985–91. Ferguson, *Barristers*, p. 274. **248** See above; called in 1934, Ó Dálaigh sat in the ECJ, 1975–85. **249** Called (as Michael Patrick Fennelly) in 1964 (ibid., p. 184), Fennelly was also chair of the Legal Aid Board from 1983–90, and sat on the ECJ, 1995–2000. **250** Called in 1967 (ibid., p. 263), Murray also served as attorney general (1982, 1987–91) and later as chief justice. He sat on the ECJ, 1991–9. **251** Called in 1973: ibid., p. 364. In 1999 she was appointed as the first woman judge from any EU country on the ECJ. **252** C.P. Curran, *Under the receding wave* (Dublin, 1970), p. 122. **253** Pue, *Lawyers' empire*, p. 5.

CHAPTER FIFTEEN

Perceptions of the profession

Introduction

This chapter considers the different ways that the Bar was perceived externally during the twentieth century. It looks at how barristers perceived themselves and their collective image, as well as considering the relationship between the Bar and the Irish media. Writing in the 1990s, Marron noted that there was in Ireland 'a negative attitude toward the press among politicians, members of the judiciary, and the public at large,'[1] and this also appears to have been true in relation to the legal profession. This chapter also examines representation of the barristers' profession in the media and in political discourse. In addition, it considers how the Irish Bar was portrayed in literature, and how barristers themselves contributed to this cultural representation. As noted in chapter fourteen, many members of the Bar were actors, authors, playwrights and public representatives, and were in a position to shape public perceptions of their profession.

The Bar's relationship with the media

Pue writes about the importance of 'professional myth', and argues that '[c]ollective stories define identities'.[2] It was often considered important to shape these 'myths' or narratives. In the twentieth century the Bar Council sought to control the profession's exposure in the media, and were wary of members giving interviews for newspapers, radio or television. Ireland's national broadcaster, RTÉ, began regular television broadcasts in 1961,[3] and in the same year the Bar Council was asked by the Incorporated Law Society what its views were on counsel appearing on television.[4] It is evident therefore, that from the very outset, the legal professions grappled with the new media. By way of example, a barrister wrote to the Bar Council in early 1965, enclosing a letter from Telefís Éireann. This barrister asked for a ruling as to whether it would be proper for them to appear on television in a programme known as 'Cover story'. The

---

1 Maria B. Marron, 'Levels of professionalism and professional efficacy among journalists in Ireland', *Gazette* 56(1) (1996), 37, at 38. 2 W. Wesley Pue, *Lawyers' empire: legal professions and cultural authority, 1780–1950* (Vancouver, 2016), p. 4. 3 President Eamon de Valera's first address on Irish national television can be viewed on the RTÉ archives: www.rte.ie/archives/exhibitions/681-history-of-rte/704-rte–1960s/139351-opening-night-presidents-address/. His expression of fear at the possibilities that television might bring may well have been shared by both the Bar Council and the Law Society. 4 B.C.M., 12 May 1961. This prompted the establishment of a

Council considered the matter and decided that it would be acceptable, providing no reference was made to the practice of their profession.[5]

From the 1970s the Bar Council was increasingly having to deal with appearances by barristers in newspapers and on television and radio. Its concerns, as will be seen below, ranged from the propriety of barristers penning newspaper columns, to the giving of interviews about current controversies, social issues or cases. The Bar's code of conduct prohibited barristers from advertising themselves as such, or touting for business,[6] and this partly accounts for the Bar Council's wariness. While the restrictive approach favoured by the Bar Council might seem unduly suspicious of the media, its primary motivation was often to ensure that members continued to operate within the code. Some barristers undoubtedly walked a fine line, and the Bar Council sought to control this sort of media engagement. It may also have feared sensationalist, tabloid-style reporting, although as Boyle and McGonigle noted, 'Irish newspapers compared, for example, with the British tabloid press, must appear to an objective observer to be quite restrained in their approach and style.'[7]

In 1970, a series of articles appeared in the *Irish Times* penned by a barrister whose name was accompanied by the title 'our legal correspondent'.[8] This matter was discussed by the Bar Council, which had instructed the barrister to publish 'either under his own name simply, or under the title 'legal correspondent, but not both together.'[9] Three years later, a retired judge wrote to the Bar Council enquiring about the propriety of writing articles in a daily newspaper under his own name. He was informed that he might publish under his own name, 'but he should not permit his legal qualifications, or the fact that he was a former judge, to appear'.[10] In 1972, it was reported that an announcement of a call to the Bar had appeared in the 'social & personal' columns of the press. This was deemed undesirable, 'and while it was probably not the young man's fault', the Bar Council wrote him 'a polite letter' to highlight the impropriety.[11] Again, the concern in relation to the code of conduct is evident.

The Bar Council also frowned upon barristers discussing their cases in media interviews. In 1973 the Council discussed a recent article in a Sunday newspaper which stated that a certain member of the Bar was willing to offer his services

subcommittee to consider the Bar's position.   5 B.C.M., 19 Feb. 1965.   6 This prohibition was clearly stated in 1987: code of conduct, rule 6.1: 'A barrister may not do or cause to be done on his behalf anything for the purpose of touting, whether directly or indirectly or which is likely to lead to the reasonable inference that it was done for such purpose.'   7 Kevin Boyle and Marie McGonagle, *A report on press freedom and libel* (Dublin, 1988), p. 4.   8 For example: David Goldberg, 'Springboks – legal or illegal?', *Irish Times*, 7 Jan. 1970, p. 11; David Goldberg, 'Trinity and the Gardaí', *Irish Times*, 13 Mar. 1970, p. 12; David Goldberg, 'The price of malice', *Irish Times*, 24 Mar. 1970, p. 9; David Goldberg, 'Contraception and the law', *Irish Times*, 9 Apr. 1970, p. 11.   9 B.C.M., 10 Apr. 1970. After this the author appears to have written under his name, without the title of 'our legal correspondent'; for example, David Goldberg, 'Our inadequate penal system', *Irish Times*, 21 May 1970, p. 12 and David Goldberg, 'Human rights in court', *Irish Times*, 2 July 1970, p. 11.   10 B.C.M., 28 Sept. 1973.   11 Ibid., 28 July 1972.

free in the conduct of a possible impending case.[12] In the same year, a barrister appeared on television and gave statements made to newspapers concerning one of his cases, and the chairman phoned him 'and advised him of the impropriety'.[13]

In 1982, a complaint that a barrister had appeared on a television programme in her capacity as a barrister was referred to the professional practices committee.[14] A separate complaint was referred in relation to a different barrister speaking regularly on a consumer affairs radio programme.[15] However, when complaints were made about a third member of the Bar giving press interviews without permission in 1989, he threatened to sue the Bar Council if they took action against him for alleged breaches of the code of conduct.[16] This approach appears to have had the desired effect.

The Bar Council was also concerned about the publication of photographs of barristers.[17] In 1966, for example, a photo and article about a woman barrister appeared in a national newspaper. Following complaints, she wrote to the Bar Council to defend herself, saying that she had given no interview to the paper and had no photograph taken on the occasion. The material had been obtained on a former occasion. She regretted the matter very much, apologised, and trusted that 'no further cause of offence might arise.'[18] She was backed up by her master and the matter rested. In early 1972 a number of photographs of counsel appeared in national newspapers and the Bar Council wrote to the individuals requesting an explanation for this.[19] The following year, there was some controversy over photos of a number of counsel taken in connection with a trial at Green St. The barristers in question replied that they did not know that such photographs breached any rule of etiquette.[20] The Bar Council accepted this, but passed a formal ruling in relation to these kinds of photos:

> Save on the occasion of his call to the Bar, or to the inner Bar, or upon becoming a Judge, a barrister ought not to authorise or permit a photograph of himself to be taken in the context of his membership of the Bar. Studio portraits in robes on the aforementioned occasions are permitted, as are portraits for use at an exhibition of portraits.[21]

In 1974, however, it was unanimously agreed that on the occasion of the sixtieth anniversary of his call to the Bar, John A. Costello might allow photographs of himself to be taken, and give newspaper and television interviews.[22]

When, in 1987, the code of conduct was given formal written expression for the first time, rule 6.10 governed media appearances by barristers. It covered the

12 Ibid., 7 May 1973. 13 Ibid., 28 Sept. 1973. 14 Ibid., 5 Mar. 1982. 15 Ibid., 2 Apr. 1982. 16 Ibid., 10 Jan. 1989. 17 Rule 6.15 of the code of conduct published in 1987 only permitted barristers to be photographed as barristers on specific occasions: being called to the Bar or the inner Bar, or being appointed a judge. 18 B.C.M., 20 Dec. 1966. 19 Ibid., 11 Feb., 2 June, 15 Dec. 1972. 20 Ibid., 25 Feb. 1972. 21 Ibid. This ruling was posted in the Law Library. 22 Ibid., 1

wide range of situations which had been considered by the Bar Council in the preceding years.[23]

There was sometimes tension evident in the relationship between the Bar and the press. In 1965, an article in the *Irish Press* claimed to have received information from the minister for justice, Brian Lenihan regarding plans to reduce litigation costs by allowing solicitors and barristers to undertake work that was traditionally within the remit of the other profession.[24] When there was on official denial or confirmation of these claims, the chairman of the Bar Council published a letter in the *Irish Law Times* outlining the important role of the Bar in an adversarial system, the role of the Law Library as a site of training and advice, the need to maintain the distinction between the two professions and the importance of the two-senior rule in ensuring representation for clients who could not afford fees.[25] When the Bar Council clashed rather publicly with minister for justice Des O'Malley in the early seventies over comments he made in the Dáil about the two-counsel rule, this gave rise to a number of public statements and newspaper articles.[26] In 1975 the Bar Council stated that it was 'the only authorised body to communicate with the press, radio and television concerning the affairs of the Bar'.[27] This followed leaks from a general meeting of the Bar to the newspapers – the *Irish Times* had reported that a meeting in June 1975 'ended in disorder'.[28] In December of that year, the *Irish Times* reported on another general meeting of the Bar, where legal fees were discussed, and noted that members of the Bar had been critical of the Bar Council. The paper reported that members of the Bar were planning to increase the fees they charged.[29] In January 1976, presumably in an attempt to better control the narrative, the chairman wrote to the *Irish Times* to provide accurate excerpts from the general meeting. This resulted in another article being written, this time appearing on the front page, which included quotes from the chairman's

---

Nov. 1974.   **23** It stated that a barrister: 'a. May broadcast in his own name on a non legal subject but may not disclose that he is a barrister; b. May appear as an actor if it is not disclosed that he is a barrister; c. May speak on a legal or quasi legal subject only with the consent of the Bar Council and subject to such conditions as the Council may impose; d. In general should not broadcast more than once in six months; e. May not appear in robes or act the part of a barrister; f. May not broadcast on any matters in which he has been engaged as Counsel; g. May not broadcast about his practice at the Bar.'   **24** 'Changing court system', *Irish Press*, 1 Nov. 1965, p. 5. The Bar Council met to consider these rumours: B.C.M., 3, 5 Nov. 1965. It was of the view that the rumours amounted to kite-flying by officials in the Department of Justice.   **25** 'Bar Council rejects merger proposal', *Irish Times*, 29 Nov. 1965, p. 11. See (1965) 99 I.L.T.S.J. 394 (18 Dec. 1965) and B.C.M., 24 Nov. 1965.   **26** 'Barristers hit back at O'Malley', *Cork Examiner*, 8 Dec. 1971, p. 1; 'O'Malley tells Bar Council: check facts', *Irish Press*, 10 Dec. 1971, p. 3.   **27** B.C.M., 8 Jan. 1975.   **28** For example, Don Buckley, 'Decision to aid Cooney angers barristers', *Irish Times*, 7 June 1975, p. 8. This controversy related to the withdrawal by barristers of their services to the criminal legal aid scheme in May 1975. The newspaper reports stated that members of the Bar had arranged a general meeting on foot of concerns about members of the Bar Council communicating with the minister for justice without consulting with them. The Bar Council had been in contact with the minister regarding the composition of a committee to examine the workings of the criminal legal aid scheme.   **29** Don Buckley, 'Barristers raise fees by 66%', *Irish Times*, 18 Dec. 1975, p. 7.

letter.[30] Further correspondence led to additional reporting the following day, when the newspaper noted that the letter from the chairman had stated that the reports of the general meeting of the Bar were 'unauthorised' – but also pointed out that an 'official spokesman for the Bar said in an RTÉ radio interview that the reports were "roughly accurate".'[31] This controversy and the associated negative publicity trundled on through early 1976.[32] In February, an article in the *Sunday Independent* alleged:

> The Bar library, once a fruitful source of news for reporters, has been closed tight to the press of late because of some embarrassing leaks. A member of the Bar committee was revealing sensitive information to a reporter and his colleagues were infuriated. A trap was set for the informant, through the rather obvious ploy of sending each member of the committee different agendas.[33]

The chairman was of the view that this raised the possibility of a libel action, and legal advice was sought.[34] The columnist subsequently reported on the potential libel action, commenting that the Bar 'did not like my reference to their "leakage" problem'.[35] A few years later, the incoming chair of the Bar Council was sought for interview by several newspapers and was encouraged by the council to grant these interviews 'and do the best for the profession'.[36] This seems to have represented a move away from the earlier position.

By the early 1980s, the Bar Council sought to reset its relationship with the media. A dinner at King's Inns was planned at which newspaper editors would meet and establish relations with the Bar Council.[37] Before the dinner there was some discussion of protocol by the Council:

> On the question of statements on matters of public interest it seemed that Bar Council should not pronounce on matters of general politics such as divorce, contraception, etc., but that perhaps it should speak if it were a matter of say the laws of evidence.[38]

Afterwards, the chairman reported that it had been made clear that the Bar Council could not speak on moral or political issues and could not comment on particular cases other than their legal aspects. The press for its part wanted the

---

30 Don Buckley, 'Bar rejects criticism', *Irish Times*, 13 Jan. 1976, pp 1, 7.   31 Don Buckley, 'Barristers issue fees row letters', *Irish Times*, 14 Jan. 1976, p. 6.   32 Don Buckley, 'Bar moves to forestall fees row', *Irish Times*, 17 Jan. 1976, p. 7; Don Buckley, 'Barristers' retreat from fees confrontation indicated', *Irish Times*, 30 Jan. 1976, p. 8. Editorial, 'Barristers' decision on fees today', *Irish Times*, 31 Mar. 1976, p. 7; Don Buckley, 'Bar calls in accountants for fees report', *Irish Times*, 24 May 1976, p. 1.   33 'Wigmore', 'Secret doings at the Bar!', *Sunday Independent*, 8 Feb. 1976, p. 26: '[h]owever, the plan had failed.'   34 B.C.M., 9, 16 Feb. 1976.   35 'Wigmore', 'Privy to yours truly', *Sunday Independent*, 22 Feb. 1976, p. 30.   36 B.C.M., 3 Oct. 1979.   37 Ibid., 5 Mar. 1982.   38 Ibid.

Bar to have a person or persons ready to speak on particular problems or cases as they arose. It was agreed that a small panel would be established to deal with queries and make statements.[39]

Unfortunately, this does not appear to have been effective in the longer term. In 1986 it was pointed out that there was a significant amount of adverse criticism of the Bar in the press. One senior counsel complained that 'there was an enormous amount of ignorance about the Bar among journalists and they received all the criticism from outside bodies but got nothing from the Bar in return.'[40] With echoes of the King's Inns dinner in 1982, it was suggested that 'it would be desirable to get in the journalists and brief them fully on the way the Bar operated'.[41] The Council also discussed whether it might not be wiser to relax its rules on publicity and permit barristers to appear on the radio and television and write in the press on current matters affecting the law without inhibition.

Three things were discussed by members of the Bar Council as contributing to the poor reporting on the profession. First, there was a perception that a number of recent cases had given bad publicity to the profession, 'simply because the public did not understand the issues involved'.[42] Second, it was pointed out that 'the Dublin newspapers no longer had professional shorthand takers of notes of cases and the reports of them were extremely condensed and often absolutely garbled, whereas in the provincial papers a full detailed account of all the hearing was given and was much more comprehensive.' Third, members of the Council admitted that some of the Bar's own practices gave rise to criticism – for example, the two-counsel rule, which had as one consequence quite high fees.[43]

In 1981 a permanent public relations committee was established by the Bar Council.[44] The following year, it was agreed to engage a public relations firm and 'call on their services from time to time and when needed'.[45] However, this did not work out as planned, as the fees charged by the firm were considered to be wildly excessive.[46] In 1988 the Bar Council engaged a public relations consultant.[47] On a number of occasions thereafter in the eighties and nineties, the Bar had the benefit of professional PR advice.[48]

Other public engagement

Aside from the 'official' public engagement by the Bar Council, there were other ways in which members of the Bar engaged with society and the public

39 Ibid., 2 Apr. 1982.   40 Ibid., 23 Sept. 1986.   41 Ibid.   42 See pp 324–5.   43 B.C.M., 23 Sept. 1986.   44 Ibid., 13 Feb. 1981.   45 Ibid., 12 Feb. 1982.   46 Ibid., 5 Mar., 17 May, 11 June 1982. 47 Ibid., 26 Mar. 1988. The making of such an appointment had been suggested by a member of the Bar twenty years previously, in 1965, but the Bar Council considered this 'rather farcical in view of the fact that they have not even got a secretary yet'; B.C.M., 16 July 1965. In 1970, the Bar Council received an unsolicited approach from a PR company which represented the English Bar, but they did not enter into any agreement: B.C.M., 3 July 1970.   48 E.g., B.C.M., 11 Nov. 1995.

imagination. A number of volumes of memoirs were published by former members of the Bar around the 1990s, including Lee's writings about the South-Western Circuit,[49] Patrick MacKenzie on the Eastern Circuit,[50] and memoirs by Patrick Lindsay,[51] Charles Bewley,[52] Thomas O'Higgins[53] and James Comyn.[54] A second edition of Rex Mackey's book was also published around this time.[55] It is interesting to note that when the Bar Council published the code of conduct in written form for the first time in 1987, it included the following:

> A barrister who has retired from practice may write memoirs of his experience at the Bar using due discretion in regard to cases in which he has been engaged, the feelings of persons concerned and strictly observing the rules of this code with regard to professional confidence.[56]

Perhaps this mention of the writing of memoirs inspired or encouraged some of the autobiographical writers in the subsequent few years. There must have been a perceived public appetite for such autobiographical works in the nineties, with publishers clearly taking the view that there was a potential readership for books about the working lives of barristers. No doubt the entertaining style in which they were written engaged readers both within and outside the legal professions. They perpetuate the positive image of the Bar as a place of laughter, teasing, camaraderie and fun.

Some of these books were first-person accounts of experiences of the Bar,[57] and can be considered alongside unpublished memoirs, for example those of McEnery[58] and Shillman.[59] They all follow a similar narrative structure: the early years of struggling to establish a practice, followed by success as a result of perseverance and/or some good luck. They also tend, like the earlier memoirs from the nineteenth and early twentieth centuries, to focus on amusing or

---

49 Gerard A. Lee, *A memoir of the South-Western Circuit* (Dublin, 1990). **50** Patrick MacKenzie, *Lawful occasions: the old Eastern Circuit* (Dublin, 1991). **51** Patrick Lindsay, *Memories* (Dublin, 1992). **52** Charles Bewley, *Memoirs of a wild goose* (Dublin, 1989). **53** T.F. O'Higgins, *A double life* (Dublin, 1996). **54** James Comyn, *Their friends at court* (Chichester 1973); James Comyn, *Lost causes* (London, 1982) James Comyn, *Irish at law: a selection of famous and unusual cases* (London, 1983); James Comyn, *Summing it up: memoirs of an Irishman at law in England* (Dublin, 1991); James Comyn, *Watching brief: further memoirs of an Irishman at law in England* (Dublin, 1993); James Comyn, *Leave to appeal: further legal memoirs* (Dublin, 1994) and James Comyn, *If your lordship pleases: legal recollections* (Dublin, 1996). **55** Rex Mackey, *Windward of the law* (2nd ed., Dublin, 1991). **56** Code of conduct, rule 6.4. **57** Reviewing A.M. Sullivan's *Old Ireland* in 1927, the *Irish Law Times* noted that many of the stories therein were 'the frequent anecdotage of the Bar library, and in that atmosphere they are quite allowable and highly appreciated, but they are not, we think, for other audiences.' (1927) 61 *I.L.T.S.J.* 297 (10 Dec. 1927). George Egerton points out that there is a difference between memoir and autobiography. Memoir is oriented towards external events and other people while an autobiography is focused 'primarily inward.' George Egerton, 'The anatomy of political memoir: findings and conclusions' in George Egerton (ed.), *Political memoir: essays on the politics of memory* (London, 1994), p. 346. See also Liam Harte (ed.), *A history of Irish autobiography* (Cambridge, 2018). **58** P.J. McEnery, *Look back in love: conversations by an English fireside*, UCDA P74/2, written in 1982. **59** Bernard Shillman, *Every journey has an end*, NAI

entertaining anecdotes and to gloss over the struggles and the more personal aspects of working at the Bar.

Portrayal of the Bar in public discourse

The many barristers who held high-profile public positions[60] could make public statements about aspects of the profession which reached a wide audience. Thus elected representatives speaking about the Bar or the Law Library in the Dáil did much to shape the public perception of the profession. For example, in 1977 John Kelly projected what he considered to be a dominant public opinion:

> The Bar is a very easy target of fun. Barristers are conventionally vulgarly regarded as grasping, venal, anxious to pile up bags of fees and it does not matter what happens to the client; it may take twelve years to get his case done and he may be ruined by it. All these are legends about the legal profession ... There are minds inside and outside the media, the public service and everywhere else that are offended at the sight of barristers in wigs and gowns scuttling around with dusty documents.[61]

One former accountant who joined the Bar commented in the mid-eighties that the remuneration was quite similar to earnings in other professions:

> Since I changed my profession and became a lawyer I find that the level of earnings which my colleagues have is not out of line with what one earns in other professions. The traditions and standard of professionalism which I have seen among both the solicitors and barristers compares very favourably with what I saw in my previous profession.[62]

Depictions of barristers in public discourse often conformed to one of a few dominant narratives, and some of these were quite negative. Several commentators highlighted the perceived elitism of the Bar, and claimed that this was intimidating to the public:

> Many of our people not familiar with courts are definitely unnerved when they enter a court of justice for the first time, particularly the High Court, and look upon these people in wigs and gowns.[63]

> Wigs and gowns are worn to cow and frighten the humble country plaintiff or defendant, and to add importance to the profession.[64]

> It is easy to get a cheap thrill by mocking the wearing of wigs and gowns.[65]

PRIV1367/11, written in the early sixties.　**60** See ch. 14.　**61** Dáil Éireann deb., vol. 298, no. 8 (20 Apr. 1977) (J.M. Kelly).　**62** Dáil Éireann deb., vol. 111, no. 5 (12 Feb. 1986) (O'Leary). **63** Dáil Éireann deb., vol. 159, no. 5 (11 July 1956) (Murphy).　**64** Dáil Éireann deb., vol. 243, no. 1 (2 Dec. 1969) (O.J. Flanagan).　**65** Dáil Éireann deb., vol. 111, no. 5 (12 Feb. 1986)

Another TD said that people were 'afraid of barristers. They think it is bad enough to have to go to a solicitor and are deadly afraid of judges'.[66] One interviewee said that the public perception of barristers was:

> Upper class fellows, you know, tweedy voices, tweedy accents, hunting, fishing and shooting, too much wine, too much bullshit, overpaid.[67]

Specific events and issues were sometimes damaging to the Bar's reputation. For example, in the 1980s the Macarthur affair involved the discovery of murderer Malcolm Macarthur at the home of the attorney general in the midst of a national manhunt.[68] This led to the resignation of the attorney general. One of the controversies surrounding the case was that Macarthur was tried for only one of two murders to which he had confessed, which led to speculation about conspiracies and cover ups.[69] The Father Niall Molloy case in 1985 involved the death of a priest in suspicious circumstances, and the controversial acquittal of the prime suspect.[70] The case attracted a lot of criticism of the legal professions, and conspiracy theories abounded for some years after.[71] In the Kerry babies case, Joanne Hayes was accused of giving birth to and murdering twin babies apparently conceived with different fathers.[72] Incriminating statements were obtained from her and her family members, under what they claimed was coercive and intimidating interrogation. The DPP ordered that the charges against her be struck out, but the public interest in the conduct of the Gardaí

(Michael O'Leary). **66** Dáil Éireann deb., vol. 298, no. 8 (20 Apr. 1977) (Thomas Meany). **67** B2. **68** See Conor Lally, 'Then and now: Malcolm Macarthur', Irish Times, 28 June 2011, and Mark O'Connell, A thread of violence (London, 2023). **69** See, e.g., Mary McAleese, 'Trial of Macarthur shows legal loopholes', Irish Times, 24 Jan. 1983, p. 13; Peter Murtagh, 'Coverage of Macarthur case to be investigated', Irish Times, 21 Aug. 1982, p. 1; 'Taoiseach may face action over TV remark', Irish Times, 20 Aug. 1982, p. 1; Peter Murtagh, 'Court refuses contempt order against Haughey', Irish Times, 2 Sep. 1982, p. 1; 'Willy Clingan, '300 to testify in murder trial', Irish Times, 10 Sept. 1982, p. 1; Macarthur charge dropped', Irish Times, 19 July 1983, p. 1. **70** Fr Mulloy was found dead in the bedroom of Richard and Theresa Flynn. Richard Flynn was prosecuted for manslaughter and he claimed he had hit the priest in self-defence, whereupon Mulloy fell down and died. The state pathologist testified that the blows received by Mulloy were the cause of death, and was asked whether damage to the heart might have contributed to his death. He could not rule out the possibility that the victim's heart failed in the course of his death. There was evidence of six blows to the head, and counsel for the defence suggested, in the absence of the jury, that only the first three blows had been delivered by his client, and the last three were as a result of falling and hitting his head on the bedpost, the bed and the floor. He suggested that the case was unsafe to put to the jury, and the judge instructed the jury that the state pathologist had said there was a possibility that Mulloy had died of a heart attack. At a subsequent inquest, evidence undermined this theory of the victim banging his head three times. It later transpired that the judge in the case was an acquaintance of the parties involved, through a shared interest in horseracing. **71** E.g., Sean Flynn, 'New Molloy case inquiry likely to await civil action', Irish Times, 29 Apr. 1988, p. 6; Sean Flynn, 'Circumstances of priest's death still not fully explained', Irish Times, 28 July 1986, p. 8; Harry McGee, 'Truth about Fr Molloy's death still unclear', Irish Times, 2 Apr. 2015, p. 3; Peter Murtagh, 'Shatter to ask senior barrister to review Fr Molloy case', Irish Times, 6 Nov. 2013, p. 4. **72** Tom Inglis, Truth, power and lies: Irish society and the case of the Kerry babies (Dublin, 2003).

was such that a tribunal of inquiry was established in 1984.[73] The tribunal, which sat in Tralee and was conducted by Justice Kevin Lynch, generated significant public interest and media reporting, with public demonstrations of support for Joanne Hayes.[74] Together with a number of other incidents in the 1980s,[75] this affair damaged public confidence in the legal system and the Garda Siochána. It is striking that these controversies continue to unfold in 2023.

From the 1990s, a number of high-profile tribunals of inquiry were established under the Tribunals of Inquiry (Evidence) Act 1921.[76] Tribunals had been established on a number of occasions since the foundation of the state, but few of them attracted much attention to the legal profession until the tribunal of inquiry into the beef processing industry (the beef tribunal), chaired by Justice Liam Hamilton.[77] This ran from 1991 to 1994, examining illegal practices and malpractice in the Irish beef processing industry. Also in the 1990s were the Finlay and Lindsay tribunals that looked into hepatitis C and HIV infections from tainted blood transmissions; the McCracken and Moriarity tribunals that examined corrupt payments to politicians Michael Lowry and Charles Haughey; and the Mahon tribunal that examined corruption in the planning process.

Between them, these tribunals were extraordinarily expensive, and some, such as the beef, Moriarity and Mahon tribunals ran for several years.[78] The expenses

---

73 *Report of the tribunal of inquiry into the Kerry babies case* (Dublin, 1985). Inglis, *Truth, power and lies*, p. 6, describes this as 'one arm of the state, the judiciary, producing the truth about another arm, the executive – in this case the police.'   74 Inglis, *Truth, power and lies*, pp 201–2. In 1985, *Magill* published Gene Kerrigan, 'The Kerry babies case: an analysis of Mr Justice Lynch's report', *Magill*, Nov. 1985, p. 16. It was strongly critical of the judge and his findings: Gene Kerrigan, 'The Kerry babies scandal: scapegoats', *Magill*, 14 Nov. 1985, p. 36, at 40. In response, Justice Lynch wrote a detailed response in the same magazine in March 1986, criticising Kerrigan, Gay Byrne and the 'Late Late Show': Kevin Lynch, letter, *Magill*, March 1986, p. 21. He wrote, at 22: 'I have had to endure totally unwarranted and snide attacks not only on the report but on myself also.' In preparing my report, I overlooked none of the evidence. I spent the whole of the long vacation in the summer of 1985 combing through the transcripts of the evidence to make absolutely sure that I overlooked no piece of evidence.' He claimed, at 27, that much of what had been written and implied about him was 'grossly untrue and clearly defamatory'. The *Magill* saga continued, with Kerrigan publishing a response in the next issue: Gene Kerrigan, 'We still say the judge got it wrong', *Magill*, April 1986, p. 35.   75 Other issues in the 1980s negatively impacted public confidence in the legal system more broadly. For example, the first tribunal of inquiry into the fatal Stardust fire, chaired by Justice Ronan Keane, was controversial, as it concluded that the cause of the fire was arson, thus absolving the nightclub owners from responsibility: *Report of the tribunal of inquiry on the fire at the Stardust, Artane, Dublin on the 14th February, 1981* (Dublin, 1982). See newspaper reports: 'Stardust fire tribunal is holding first meeting today', *Irish Times*, 2 Mar. 1981, p. 7. Dick Hogan, 'Stardust tribunal "waste of time"', *Irish Times*, 20 May 1983, p. 7. The imposition of fully suspended sentences on those responsible for the murder of Declan Flynn in Fairview Park in 1982 also attracted much negative commentary, though this was directed more at the judiciary than the Bar.   76 Section 1(1) allowed for inquiries into 'definite matters of urgent public importance'.   77 See Liam Hamilton, *Report of the tribunal of inquiry into the beef processing industry* (Dublin, 1994).   78 The Law Reform Commission in 2005 noted the '[d]isenchantment with the cost and length of tribunals of inquiry.' Law Reform Commission, *Report on public inquiries including tribunals of inquiry* (LRC 73–2005), para 1.11.

involved included both the fees for the tribunal's own legal team, and the fees paid to the legal teams representing those appearing before the tribunals. The Law Reform Commission later estimated that 'approximately 70% of the cost of the beef tribunal and 80% of the cost of the McCracken tribunal were attributable to third-party legal fees'.[79] Very high fees were paid to some barristers for their work on these tribunals, and this attracted significant commentary in the media and in public discourse generally.[80] Several barristers interviewed for this book were of the opinion that this had a negative effect on the public's overall perception of their profession:

> Back in the nineties when I started, the beef tribunal was on and that did a lot of damage to the Bar. A lot of damage to the Bar.[81]

> I think [the public perception] has changed a bit alright with tribunals and things like that.[82]

> I think the tribunals did a lot of harm to the Bar because you got ... millionaire tribunal barristers, shouldn't have happened, did happen. That was the State's fault. Wasn't the Bar's fault. You ask someone, 'do you want some money?', they say 'of course, give me some money!' You know, that's always going to happen.[83]

The negative association with the tribunals of inquiry is also evident from newspaper reporting on the profession. The *Irish Times*, for example, in 1997, commented that '[s]ince the beef tribunal, the image of "fat-cat lawyers" is one barristers have found difficult to shake off'.[84] MacCormaic notes that by the turn of the century, 'the public standing of the legal profession had been severely undermined by the inflated fees lawyers had been paid for their work in a series of public tribunals into suspected planning and political corruption whose value and usefulness were still contested.'[85]

On the other hand, not all public perceptions were so negative. Morison and Leith point out that one of the popular images of the barrister was:

---

79 Ibid., para. 7.43.　80 See Frank Barry and John O'Dowd, 'The age of tribunals', *Studies* 90:357 (2001), 58, noting the adversarial nature of tribunals of inquiry. Barry and O'Dowd also reproduce some of the headline figures for legal fees paid to counsel, and compare these with the fees paid to solicitors, barristers in criminal cases, and the American lawyers in the trial of O.J. Simpson. Newspapers at this time also reported on challenges for junior barristers trying to earn a living. These difficulties were reported in the media, for example: Anthea McTiernan, 'The price of justice', *Irish Times*, 7 Dec. 1993, p. EL4; Uinsionn Mac Dubhghaill, 'Young barristers face years of hardship', *Irish Times*, 15 Feb. 1991, p. A2; Anne Byrne, 'Long route to big money in bottom-heavy professions', *Irish Times*, 19 Sept. 1995, p. A14.　81 B10.　82 B19.　83 B17.　84 Carol Coulter, 'Bar Council to expand services', *Irish Times*, 2 Sept. 1997, p. 7.　85 Mac Cormaic, *The Supreme Court*, p. 330.

Someone very learned in the texts of law: someone in a wig and gown who spends time immersed in ancient books searching for arcane points of law emerging only to triumph in the courtroom by outwitting the opposition. The printed word, according to this view, is the very life source of the barrister, whether in the form of legislation, reported court decisions, or in the briefs (tied with pink ribbon) which follow the barrister from library or chambers to court and back.[86]

Even newspaper accounts of the profession were not always entirely negative. The *Irish Times* noted in the late 90s that 'the success of the hepatitis C tribunal and the Dunnes payments tribunal has gone some way towards justifying the profession in the public eye.'[87] The introduction of a formalised *pro bono* scheme in 1997 also attracted positive media attention.[88]

Literary and folk representations

In chapter fourteen it was noted that several Irish barristers wrote poetry, plays and fiction. Sometimes these depicted the world of the Law Library, the courts and trials. One of the most famous playwrights who practised at the Irish Bar was Denis Johnston. Called in 1925,[89] he then spent a couple of years shuttling between chambers in London and the theatre scene in Dublin.[90] Adams points out that although his father, High Court judge William Johnston, wanted a legal career for him, Denis was already feeling the lure of theatrical life.[91] In 1927 he started practising at the Irish Bar – according to Adams he simply 'turned up at the Law Library in Dublin Castle and started to practise as a barrister. He avoided "devilling" and worked just for himself.'[92] He continued to perform on stage under the name E.W. Tocher, and 'did not let his work at the Bar interfere with his dramatic activity'.[93] For several years he combined both careers successfully.[94] He had his supporters at the Bar, and, for example, in 1934 the *Irish Law Times* reported on several of his plays which were being performed that year.[95] He also filmed a silent version of Frank O'Connor's short story *Guests of the nation*.[96] His play *Strange occurrence on Ireland's Eye* was inspired by the nineteenth-century conviction of William Kirwin for the murder of his wife,

86 John Morison and Philip Leith, *The barrister's world and the nature of law* (Basingstoke, 1992), p. 17.   87 Coulter, 'Bar Council to expand services'.   88 Ibid.   89 Ferguson, *Barristers*, p. 214.
90 Bernard Adams, *Denis Johnston, a life* (Dublin, 2002), p. 75.   91 Ibid., p. 74.   92 Ibid., p. 92. He worked on circuit in Monaghan and Louth, and 'liked chancery work and appeals best – where he could speak to a judge directly. Juries tended to put him off'. He had an average of two cases a month 'which provided him well enough to live on, and he was still subsidised by his father.'
93 Ibid.   94 See Patrick Maume, 'Johnston (William) Denis', *D.I.B.*   95 E.g., (1934) 68 *I.L.T.S.J.* 44 (17 Feb. 1934); (1934) 68 *I.L.T.S.J.* 283 (13 Oct. 1934); (1934) 68 *I.L.T.S.J.* 328 (1 Dec. 1934).
96 Frank O'Connor, *Guests of the nation* (Dublin, 1931). The film was released in 1935, and was one of Ireland's first silent movies: see www.imdb.com/title/tt1937174/.

Maria Kirwin. It was set in Dublin Castle and the Central Criminal Court in 1937.[97] *Blind man's buff*[98] was set in the Law Library, the Central Criminal Court and the State Solicitor's Office.[99] *Murder hath no tongue* (originally *Death at Newtownstewart*) was written for television in 1948[100] and was based on the conviction and hanging of police constable Thomas Montgomery for the murder of William Glass.

While Johnston is probably the most well-known barrister-playwright from this period,[101] he was far from the only one. Marion Duggan, for example, wrote a play in 1934 entitled *The murder at Mrs Clancy's*. The *Irish Law Times* was encouraging, anticipating a 'large attendance of Miss Duggan's friends and colleagues at the Bar ... Miss Duggan is devoting the proceeds to charity.'[102] Joseph Malachi Muldoon[103] wrote several plays, including *A Trinity student*[104] and *The West's awake*.[105] Richard Johnson's play *The evidence I shall give* featured the fictional Justice McHenry presiding over a courthouse in Barrabeg.[106] Bernard Duffy, called in 1907, was another barrister whose plays were staged in the Abbey Theatre.[107] Donagh MacDonagh, who was called in 1936 and appointed to the District Court in 1941, published several volumes of poetry, and two of his plays were performed in the Abbey, including *Happy as Larry*, which was critically-acclaimed and was later staged in London's West End and on Broadway.[108] His play *Step-in-the-hollow*[109] was a comic courtroom drama

---

97 First performed in the Abbey Theatre in 1962: www.abbeytheatre.ie/archives/production_detail/3819/. **98** First performed in the Abbey Theatre in 1936: www.abbeytheatre.ie/archives/production_detail/2338/. **99** Fellow barrister Cecil Barror starred in the original production at the Abbey Theatre. Some of Barror's other roles were also in plays dealing with legal themes. For example, 'In the train', based on the short story by Frank O'Connor, in which a group of people return from Dublin in the aftermath of a murder trial. It was first performed in the Abbey Theatre in 1937. **100** *Radio Times*, 29 Jan. 1939, issue 800, p. 17. **101** A notable example from earlier in the century was Pádraig Pearse. **102** (1934) 68 *I.L.T.S.J.* 152 (9 June 1934). The play was described as 'an Irish detective thriller.' **103** Called in 1913: Ferguson, *Barristers*, p. 260. He was Sinn Féin's director of elections in the early twenties and was arrested in 1923: Eoin O'Caoimh, 'Arrest of Mr Malachi Muldoon: Sinn Fein's protest', *Irish Times*, 6 Sept. 1923, p. 7. He was arrested again and charged in relation to an alleged stolen money order in 1927: 'An alleged stolen money order: charge against a barrister', *Irish Times*, 21 May 1927, p. 1. He later successfully sued Patrick Hogan for defamation: 'Solicitor sues minister: £3,000 damages claimed', *Weekly Irish Times*, 12 May 1928, p. 13 and William Murphy, 'Hogan, Patrick J. ('Paddy')', *D.I.B.* It will be recalled that Muldoon sought compensation when one of his manuscripts was destroyed in 1922: ch. 11. **104** J. Malachi Muldoon, *A Trinity student: a comedy in four acts* (Dublin, 1913). **105** J. Malachi Muldoon, *The West's awake; or the dawn of freedom. A national play in three acts. Founded on a collection of historical facts* (Dublin, 1921). It was performed in the Queen's Theatre in 1920: 'Platform and stage', *Irish Times*, 13 Mar. 1920, p. 8. His other plays included J. Malachi Muldoon, *The red redeeming dawn: a national drama in three acts; being a sequel to 'The West's awake'* (Dublin, 1920); J. Malachi Muldoon, *Children of the lost province: a play in three acts* (Dublin, 1930). **106** It was performed at the Abbey Theatre in January 1961: www.abbeytheatre.ie/archives/production_detail/3768/. **107** *The coiner*, for example, had multiple runs between 1916 and 1934: Abbey Theatre Archives, www.abbeytheatre.ie/archives/person_detail/14689/. See Nicholas Allen, 'Duffy, Bernard Joseph', *D.I.B.*, Ferguson, *Barristers*, p. 173 and obit., 'Mr B.J. Duffy', *Irish Times*, 2 Apr. 1952, p. 5. He left the Bar in 1915, and continued his involvement in the theatre. **108** See www.abbeytheatre.ie/archives/person_detail/11466/. For more details of his plays, poetry and broadcasting, see Niall MacDonagh's blog https://donagh.macdonagh.net/. **109** First performed

starring Hilton Edwards as fictional judge Redmond O'Hanlon.[110] Rex Mackey[111] wrote a number of radio plays as well as a weekly series for RTÉ television in 1969 called *Justice at large*.[112] It was set around the District Court of fictional Ballyslattery. Kenneth Deale, called in 1935, was appointed to the Circuit Court bench in 1951. Throughout the forties, fifties and early sixties, he was a prolific playwright, writing under the pseudonym 'Paul Martin'.[113] He wrote about 150 scripts for Radio Éireann, as well as several crime dramas for BBC radio, and a play, *The conspiracy*, which ran for a number of weeks in the Abbey Theatre in 1966.[114] As Roche-Tiengo observes, 'it is apparent that the theatre and the law in Ireland have always lived in each other's shadows.'[115]

Members of the Bar also expressed their creativity by writing fiction. Bernard Duffy, mentioned above, also wrote two novels, *Oriel*,[116] and *The rocky road*.[117] In John M. Kelly's posthumously published novel, *The polling of the dead*,[118] the protagonist was a practising barrister and political advisor. Reflecting Kelly's own experiences of combining a career at the Bar with a political career, the protagonist tells us that 'politics and law don't really mix very well as both of them turn into full-time occupations'.[119] The book is rich with detail about the minutiae of Bar practice, for example:

> I began going through the statement of claim with a thick red pencil, underlining the bits that would need emphasis, and making marginal notes.[120]

> The lobby outside the Law Library was congested with solicitors and insurance company claim managers, with counsel, litigants and witnesses. The whole place smelled of unclean lino, stale cigarette smoke, and old, shiny suits.[121]

> The telephone boy called me over just as I was putting my bag on my desk in the Library … here, I thought, was some bastard solicitor from Twomileborris or Cloonfad who wanted free advice over the phone, or was too lazy to write a letter, or both.[122]

at the Gate Theatre in March 1957. **110** Bridget Hourican, 'MacDonagh, Donagh', *D.I.B.* **111** Called in 1938 as Arthur Mackey: see Ferguson, *Barristers*, p. 244. See 'Witty barrister with a gift for writing. Rex Mackey SC', *Irish Times*, 20 Nov. 1999, p. 18 and T.A. Finlay, 'Mackey, Rex', *D.I.B.* Author of *Windward of the law* (1965, and 2nd ed. 1991, Dublin). **112** Depictions of barristers and courtrooms on English television shows could also have been viewed by Irish audiences. These included, for example, *Rumpole of the Bailey* (ITV, 1978–94), *Boyd Q.C.* (ITV, 1956–64), and *Kavanagh Q.C.* (ITV, 1996–2000). **113** Pauric J. Dempsey, 'Deale, Kenneth Edwin Lee', *D.I.B.* and Ferguson, *Barristers*, p. 172. Deale authored, among other things, *Beyond any reasonable doubt? A book of murder trials* (Dublin, 1971). **114** See www.abbeytheatre.ie/archives/play_detail/10344/. **115** Virginie Roche-Tiengo, 'The judge and the human Hansard in Brian Friel's theatre' in Adam Hanna and Eugene McNulty (eds), *Law and literature: the Irish case* (Liverpool, 2022), p. 233. **116** Bernard Duffy, *Oriel* (London, 1918). **117** Bernard Duffy, *The rocky road* (Dublin, 1929). **118** John Kelly, *The polling of the dead* (Dublin, 1993). **119** Ibid., p. 1. **120** Ibid., p. 2. **121** Ibid., p. 7. **122** Ibid.

The legal world was also represented in twentieth-century Irish literature by non-lawyers, some of whom drew on their own courtroom experiences. For example, the work of Colm Tóibín is said to have been 'shaped by his encounters with Ireland's court systems.'[123] Justice Eamon Redmond, Tóibín's High Court judge in *The heather blazing*,[124] represents one of the better-known fictional depictions of life at the Bar and on the bench.[125] McNulty describes the book as revealing 'the complex dialogues – between the competing claims of natural law, legalism, originalism, and the doctrine of unenumerated rights – that are at play in the progress of Irish constitutional law at the end of the twentieth century.'[126] Looking at legal processes from a different perspective is Edna O'Brien's *Down by the river*,[127] a literary retelling of the infamous *X case*.[128] Barr writes that her 'third-person narrative lambastes the hypocrisies of a metropolitan judiciary as well as the emotional privations of the rural West where the crime is committed.'[129] O'Brien evocatively calls up

> Corporeal figures of knowledge and gravity, the white of their wigs changing colour as they pass under the rotunda of livid light, ribs of yellow hair, smarting, becoming phosphorescent, powerful men, men with a swagger ... briefs and ledgers, the whole paraphernalia of the law in motion.[130]

Several of Brian Friel's plays include judicial figures or legal processes. *The freedom of the city*[131] depicts a judicial tribunal of inquiry following violent suppression of a civil rights meeting, reminiscent of the events of Bloody Sunday. *Aristocrats*[132] features the fictional District Justice O'Donnell. In *The doubtful paradise*,[133] the protagonist's barrister son is suspended from the Bar. Roche-Tiengo suggests that '[t]he spectators in Brien Friel's plays are often

123 Adam Hanna and Eugene McNulty, 'Introduction. Law and literature: the Irish case' in Hanna and McNulty (eds), *Law and literature*, p. 9. They were referring to *The heather blazing* as well as journalistic pieces 'Inside the Supreme Court' (1985) and 'A brush with the law' (2007). 124 *The heather blazing* (London, 1993). 125 Tóibín was interviewed by Justice Gearty in 2022 about the depiction of judges and lawyers in his work, and about his interactions with barristers: 'In conversation with Colm Tóibín, and The Hon. Justice Ms Mary Rose Gearty', available via www.lawlibrary.ie/podcast/. 126 Eugene McNulty, 'Original intent: the limits of legal imagination in Colm Tóibín's *The heather blazing*', *Law and Literature* 32:3 (2019), 399, at 400. See also Liam Harte, 'History, text, and society in Colm Tóibín's *The heather blazing*', *New Hibernia Review / Iris Éireannach Nua* 6:4 (2002), 55. 127 Edna O'Brien, *Down by the river* (London, 1996). 128 *Attorney General v. X* [1992] IESC 1. 129 Rebecca Anne Barr, 'Rape narratives, women's testimony and Irish law in Louise O'Neil's *Asking for it* and Winnie Li's *Dark chapter*' in Hanna and McNulty (eds), *Law and literature*, p. 200. See also Jane Elizabeth Dougherty, 'From invisible child to abject maternal body: crises of knowledge in Edna O'Brien's *Down by the river*', *Critique: Studies in Contemporary Fiction* 43(4) (2012), 393. 130 O'Brien, *Down by the river*, p. 5. 131 First performed in the Abbey in Feb. 1973: www.abbeytheatre.ie/archives/production_detail/ 4579/. 132 First performed in the Abbey in 1979: www.abbeytheatre.ie/archives/production_ detail/797/. 133 First performed in Belfast in 1960. 134 Roche-Tiengo, 'The judge and the

given the authority bestowed on the jurors in a courtroom.'[134] Themes of justice and revenge, played out in the legal system, frequently feature in Irish plays and fiction. Eamon Jordan has written about ideas of justice in the works of Martin McDonagh,[135] revealing 'the important role played by performative popular culture in processing jurisprudential abstraction'.[136]

When well-known literary or artistic figures were involved in legal proceedings, this tended to capture the public interest. For example, Patrick Kavanagh's 1954 libel action[137] was said to be 'one of the most sensational Irish court cases of the decade'.[138] Quinn writes that the case 'received extensive newspaper coverage and was treated as a major social event, with photographs of the many distinguished figures in attendance'.[139] The jury found that he had not been libelled. In a subsequent late-night revue at the Pike theatre, T.P. McKenna included a sketch that was 'a comic send-up of Costello's cross-examination' at the trial.[140] Eoin 'the Pope' O'Mahony encouraged Kavanagh's supporters to contribute to a fund for his appeal.[141] The appeal in the Supreme Court also attracted public attention, though not to the same extent as the original trial.[142] The appeal was allowed with costs, and a majority in the Supreme Court ruled that there should be a new trial.[143] The case was ultimately settled.[144]

Hanna and McNulty observe that '[t]here are particular cultural and historic reasons in Ireland why writers are so consistently granted a serious hearing concerning public life, in particular concerning issues of justice'.[145] They describe the relationship between law and literature as 'a dialectical hall of mirrors that is perhaps as old as law and literature themselves'.[146] These various depictions of the working lives of barristers, judges and litigants contributed towards the public's understanding of the profession. The connections between law and literature in Ireland did not stop there, and there were many overlaps between the legal and literary scenes. For example, playwright Brian Friel was

human', p. 241. **135** Eamon Jordan, *Justice in the plays and films of Martin McDonagh* (Cham, 2019). **136** Adam Hanna and Eugene McNulty, 'Introduction. Law and literature: the Irish case' in Hanna and McNulty (eds), *Law and literature*, pp 9–10. **137** This followed a 'profile' of Kavanagh in the weekly *Leader*, a literary and political magazine, which had been interpreted by Kavanagh's supporters as 'an unmitigatedly hostile attack'. Antoinette Quinn, *Patrick Kavanagh: a biography* (Dublin, 2001), p. 315. **138** Quinn, *Patrick Kavanagh*, p. 326. Kavanagh was represented by John Esmonde, Thomas Connolly, Thomas A. Doyle and Niall McCarthy. They faced John A. Costello, James McMahon, W. O'B. Fitzgerald, Brian Walsh, Fergus Flood and W.D. Finlay, representing *The Argus* and *The Leader*. See further, the Kavanagh archive, IE/ UCD/SC/KAV. Anthony Behan, interviewed in 2000, recalled Costello's cross examination of Kavanagh, saying he was 'at him for days'. Anthony (Tony) Behan, interviewed Jan. 2000, Oral history project 2000, National Folklore collection, UCD. **139** Ibid. **140** Quinn, *Patrick Kavanagh*, p. 329. **141** Contributors included John Betjemen, T.S. Eliot and Jack B. Yeats: Quinn, *Patrick Kavanagh*, p. 330. **142** Quinn, *Patrick Kavanagh*, pp 337–8. **143** Ibid., p. 342. **144** Ibid., p. 345. **145** Hanna and McNulty, 'Introduction', p. 11. They point to a lecture delivered by poet Seamus Heaney to the Irish Human Rights Commission in 2009, entitled 'Writer and Righter'. Heaney spoke about the relevance of poetry in times of societal upheaval and unrest. See Seamus Heaney, *Writer and righter: fourth IHRC annual human rights lecture, 9 December 2009* (Dublin, 2010). **146** Hanna and McNulty, 'Introduction. Law and literature: the Irish case', p. 1.

appointed to the Seanad in 1987, and W.B. Yeats before him. Many members of the Bar were involved in the cultural life of the country; for example, Ralph Brereton Barry had been an actor before joining the Bar in 1922, and continued to be an active member of the Dublin arts scene throughout his career at the Bar.[147]

Many of the Irish folk representations of lawyers focus on their apparent greed, venality and cleverness.[148] Such depictions generally did not distinguish between branches of the profession.[149] However, the Irish Folklore Commission includes in its collections a small number of twentieth-century interviews with people who had knowledge of the courts and the legal system. These incorporate vignettes of members of the Bar. For example, one interviewee, Anthony Behan, had worked as a legal clerk for solicitor Michael Noyk and had interacted with many members of the Bar, delivering briefs and so on. He described one barrister as 'rather a disaster as a barrister, in my opinion.'[150] He added that, to succeed at the Bar,

> You have to be a man for all seasons and you have to be able to handle clients … and you certainly have to be able to read the judge.

He recalled many aspects of legal practice in the twentieth century, including trends in litigation. He recalled people who joined the Bar from the civil service and were 'extraordinarily successful'. He also remembered discussing a case with a very senior member of the Bar, who hoped the case would settle, because he said, 'I've had a terrible run of luck recently.' Behan found it 'extraordinary that a leading light of the Bar was shaken by a run of bad cases'.[151]

John Kelly, a retired court clerk, was interviewed by the Folklore Commission two years after Behan.[152] His observations on members of the Bar included that one 'had a magnificent voice', and that 'there were a few others whose voices were noticeable'. He said that many early career barristers took jobs as radio announcers and news readers to supplement their incomes in the days before television. He was unsure whether barristers ever trained their voices, but recalled that 'some of them were impressive, whether it was just natural ability or what it was.' He singled out John A. Costello as having

---

147 Pauric J. Dempsey, 'Barry, Ralph Brereton', *D.I.B.* See Abbey Theatre archive, www.abbey theatre.ie/archives/person_detail/10316/. Early in his career he visited the USA with a delegation from the Irish, English, and Scottish Bars led by Sir John Simon. He died in 1943 in Dublin as a result of typhoid fever, contracted on circuit in Letterkenny. See obit. (1943) 77 *I.L.T.S.J.* 308 (18 Dec. 1943); Ferguson, *Barristers*, p. 135.   148 See, for example, the folk depictions in Eanna Hickey, *Irish law and lawyers in modern folk tradition* (Dublin, 1999).   149 Most of the stories captured by the Irish Folklore Commission appear to pre-date the period covered by this book. However others would appear to be from the twentieth century, e.g., a story told by William Rourke, Co. Roscommon, in the late sixties relating to the state solicitor for Roscommon acting opposite his son in court; he described 'the father and son scouldin' one another.' National Folklore Commission, 1839 (41–3).   150 Behan interview, Folklore Collection.   151 Ibid.   152 Interview with John Kelly, 2002. National Folklore Collection, UCD.

A loud voice. When he'd be addressing a jury, if you were outside in the round hall in the afternoon when things would be a bit quiet, you'd hear his voice inside.

However, not all barristers, in Kelly's view, had impressive voices – in relation to some, he said it was 'dreadful to be listening to them'.[153]

Barristers' impressions of the public's perception

Barristers' own views of how they were viewed by the public varied. Some thought that the public viewed them in a largely positive light, while others reflected on what they perceived as generally negative depictions. A number made the point that the public view of the profession tended to be quite negative until an individual had cause to engage the services of a barrister. One interviewee felt it was essential to try 'to convince the public of the importance of having an independent Bar.'[154]

As an example of members of the profession believing that the public held the Bar in high esteem, Hugh O'Flaherty wrote in 1992: '[t]he practice of law in this country has not attracted the type of opprobrium that it has elsewhere'.[155] Barristers who were interviewed for this book expressed some similar views.[156] One who was called in the 1950s recalled that:

> People highly respected them I would think ... famous barristers like Cecil Lavery and Richard McGonagle ... there were undoubtedly ... very highly professional people ... and they were always prepared to present their case and have it prepared. They were highly respected and I think that flowed over to the public.[157]

Two barristers who were called in the 1980s also reflected on the positivity associated with the profession:

> I think by and large people had a good perception of barristers in those periods.[158]

> I think it was regarded highly during my time ... And I think all of us at that time had a sense of 'this is an important professional with standing and with stature in society', and that in itself is an achievement.[159]

---

153 Kelly also provided colourful descriptions of a number of judges. 154 B23. 155 Hugh O'Flaherty, 'The independent Bar and the defence of human rights' in James O'Reilly (ed.), *Human rights and constitutional law: essays in honour of Brian Walsh* (Dublin, 1992), p. 170. 156 See also Ann-Marie Hardiman, 'Father of the Bar', *B.R.* 27:5 (2022), 127. In an interview, retiring barrister Ronnie Robins commented, 129, that in the sixties there was 'huge deference to a barrister', which in his view was unjustified. 157 B19. 158 B11. 159 B7.

Others were of the view that the most positive impression of barristers was generated by their work with individual clients:

> I think significant numbers of people had good experiences of barristers acting for them at what is usually a very stressful and difficult time of their lives when they're involved in court proceedings.[160]

> Certainly in the country and in the country towns clients were very delighted to have barristers. I think they felt it added something and the relationship would probably be more casual and easy and more informal.[161]

By contrast, one barrister suggested in 1965 that the average client might not perceive the value of having a barrister:

> His exasperation at what he considers a waste of his money may be aggravated by the fact that he probably will not see the barrister until the day his case is on; and if no litigation is involved, he may not see him at all. The barrister for him is a remote and unreal figure; and, if he actually goes to court, he may well be irritated by the appearance for the first time of a wigged and stranger who proceeds before the case to ask him a great many questions which his solicitor has already put to him and which he is tired of answering.[162]

Several reflected on having received thoughtful letters, cards or gifts from appreciative clients, 'after some difficult things, you know. Where they felt that you'd really kind of helped them'.[163] By contrast, Rex Mackey wrote amusingly,

> One of the many misconceptions the layman has about a barrister's life is that he is constantly the recipient of the humble thanks of grateful clients. Nothing could be further from the truth, and the barrister who does not obtain his fee in a criminal case before he goes to court is due for a rude awakening. On this topic the advice of one of the best and most experienced defender of prisoners at the Bar was, 'Always get it when the tears are in his eye'.[164]

Aside from positive views held by the wider public, some barristers noted that their parents and families held the Bar in high esteem, and were proud of their sons and daughters who joined the profession:

> I remember when I was called to the Bar ... my mother and father said 'we're so proud of you, you've achieved something', and I don't think if I'd

160 B11.   161 B23.   162 Ronan Keane, 'The future of the Irish Bar', *Studies* 54:216 (1965), 375.
163 B11.   164 Mackey, *Windward*, p. 159.

said 'well I'm a structural engineer' … I mean they would have been proud of me of course but the fact I was a barrister. There was an element of 'oh – really isn't that great! You must be proud.'[165]

By contrast, another barrister recalled their parents' concern at their decision to pursue a career at the Bar: '[m]y poor father thought that there was no chance I'd ever make a living … he was certainly concerned'. This barrister said they were always quite pleased if details of their earnings were stated in the Oireachtas, because their parents would be reassured: 'I was always delighted because I was never quite sure that he actually thought I was making a living'.

Most of the barristers interviewed were also conscious of negative portrayals of their profession in the media and among the general public. A few common themes emerged. First, that barristers were overpaid:

> I know what most people think of barristers, that they're fat cats, that they're overpaid and they do no work … I think they think we're spoiled.[166]

Another member of the Bar, in 1965, made a similar point:

> The layman sometimes thinks of the courtroom barrister as a languid silk earning gigantic fees for a few hours spent in conducting Hollywood–style cross–examination.[167]

Also commonly raised was the elite nature of the Bar.[168] The aloofness[169] or mystique[170] of barristers was alluded to in the Dáil on a number of occasions. Several interviewees recalled stereotypes about the profession from their early years; for example, one said that there was a perception outside of the profession that a barrister needed to be 'forceful and pushy and vibrant and extrovert'.[171] The same barrister added that 'I probably had the same stereotype in my own mind which is why I hadn't planned to go to the Bar … I had never met a barrister until I went to the Law Library so I probably had the same stereotype.' Several others addressed what they considered to be misconceptions about the profession:

> I think like every profession there are cases where they might let the side down a bit you know but then … how can the public judge the performance of a barrister?[172]

> I think the perception is totally wrong in relation to the amount of work that is done and the amount of service that is given to the state. There is an awful lot of work done, an awful lot of service given to the state.[173]

---

165 B7. See ch. 6.   166 B16.   167 Keane, 'The future of the Irish Bar', 375, at 380.   168 See ch. 5.   169 B9.   170 B22.   171 B24.   172 B19.   173 B1.

It is seen as a very elitist profession. It's very very hard to get in there. It's only people who went to Gonzaga or Belvedere or Blackrock who are there. It's not like that at all. The journalists feed on that I think. Politicians feed on it to an extent too.[174]

One barrister was of the view that barristers in the past were treated with more respect: 'I don't think we're paid the same respect or our opinions are as valued as they would have been forty years ago.'[175] This barrister said that when they were in their early years of practice, the public perception was 'unquestionably better' than in the early twenty-first century.

* * *

A barrister noted at a general meeting of the Bar in 1991 that 'the Bar has had a bad press since biblical times and would continue to do so because barristers are independent both individually and collectively'.[176] This rather pessimistic view was probably not entirely true of the twentieth-century Bar, as individual practitioners were generally respected for their work and expertise, both at the Bar and elsewhere. However, the view of the profession by the end of the century, and depictions of the Bar in media and literature, generally adhered to the stereotype of the clever, loud, male, middle-class, aloof and expensively educated barrister in a wig and gown.

Public perceptions of the profession changed over time, and during certain periods, such as in the 1980s, the Bar attracted negative attention. Public attitudes were influenced by whichever controversy dominated the headlines, so it was important for the Bar to maintain good relations with the media. The Bar traditionally had strong political connections and it usually had friends in relevant government departments. By the end of the century, it is evident that the Bar Council was increasingly aware of the value of good public relations.

174 B17.   175 B8.   176 B.C.M., 20 July 1991.

CHAPTER SIXTEEN

Regulating the profession

Introduction

Earlier chapters considered the camaraderie, networking and social supports at the Bar. We have seen what it meant to be a sole practitioner and also examined the way this isolation was tempered by strong networks and solidarity. The profession was more than simply a collection of individual practitioners. Freidson wrote in the 1980s that the term 'profession' was 'a socially valued label, with the possibility of social, economic, political or at the very least symbolic rewards accruing to those so labelled'.[1] Being part of a profession entailed both exclusivity and discipline; all professions traditionally required some degree of regulation. This meant that entry was controlled, and that standards and norms were enforced. As a self-regulating profession, the Bar carried out this regulation in exchange for exclusivity over the provision of services.[2] This chapter explores how the King's Inns and the Bar Council each played a role in this, as did the individual barristers who constituted the group.

As will be seen, attempted incursions on the regulatory role of these bodies were strongly resisted. In the 1990s, Pue surveyed a variety of publications, position papers and other documents produced by lawyers' professional organisations across Canada. A broad study of these documents threw up some general assertions or principles: that it is important that lawyers' bodies be self-governing; that freedom, democracy and 'the rule of law' depend on lawyers' being independent of state control; that constitutional governance requires the existence of a self-governing legal profession; that there can be no independent judiciary without an independent Bar; that legal professions have developed their own ethical codes; that the governing bodies act to protect the public

---

1 Eliot Freidson, 'The theory of professions: state of the art' in Robert Dingwall and Philip Lewis (eds), *The sociology of the professions: lawyers, doctors and others* (London, 1983), p. 26. He also wrote, p. 25, that professions 'gain their distinction and position in the marketplace ... from their training and identity as particular, corporately-organised occupations to which specialised knowledge, ethicality and importance to society are imputed, and for which privilege is claimed.' In the 1960s a sociologist came up with a composite definition for professions based on a meta-study of 22 scholars: skill based on theoretical knowledge; training and education; demonstration of competence by passing a test; integrity maintained by adherence to a code of conduct; a professional organisation and service for the public good.' Geoffrey Millerson, *The qualifying associations: a study in professionalisation* (London, 1964; 1998 ed.), p. 3. 2 Ivana Bacik, Cathryn Costello and Eileen Drew, *Gender injustice: feminising the legal professions?* (Dublin, 2003), p. 157. 3 W. Wesley Pue, *Lawyers' empire: legal professions and cultural authority, 1780–1950* (Vancouver, 2016), pp 17–18.

interest.[3] Many of these principles are common to legal professions in other common law jurisdictions, and were certainly in evidence for much of the twentieth century in Ireland.

The roles of the King's Inns benchers and the Bar Council

In the twentieth century, the regulation and control of the barristers' profession was split between the King's Inns benchers and the Bar Council. Bartholomew characterised the role of the benchers in the early seventies as follows:

> [They] control entry into the profession, determine the educational syllabus, conduct the final examination, admit to the degree of Barrister-at-Law, and have power to disbar a barrister guilty of unprofessional conduct. In a word, the primary concerns of the benchers are to educate students for the Bar and then to maintain the traditions of the profession.[4]

He described the benchers as 'self-perpetuating, in effect filling vacancies in their own ranks'.[5] The constitution of King's Inns was revised in 1979 to give ordinary barristers a greater say in its government. The council of King's Inns, established in 1980, was made up of benchers, judges, members of the practising and the non-practising Bar.[6] However, as Bacik, Costello and Drew point out,

> The benchers retained the function of admitting candidates to the degree of Barrister-at-Law, and of disbarring of barristers. The benchers thus play an important role in the education and call to the Bar of aspiring barristers.[7]

The benchers' minutes contain examples of complaints being made about barristers. In one instance in 1929, a member of the Bar was temporarily suspended from practice.[8] In the 1950s, following controversial revelations[9] and a rather public row conducted in a large part through the letters pages of the *Irish Times*,[10] thirty-four barristers presented a memorial to the benchers

---

4 Paul C. Bartholomew, *The Irish judiciary* (Dublin, 1971) p. 23.   **5** Ibid.   **6** Senator Eoin Ryan described the new council as having 'brought many changes and reforms, modernised the education system as far as members of the Bar are concerned and very much improved the quality of the education available.' Seanad Éireann deb., vol. 101, no. 2 (22 June 1983).   **7** Bacik, Costello and Drew, *Gender injustice*, p. 77.   **8** For example, K.I.B.M., 5 June, 10, 25 Oct., 1 Nov. 1929.   **9** The controversy arose because Sullivan, who had represented Roger Casement at his treason trial, later disclosed Casement's homosexuality in an interview with René MacColl. This was subsequently revealed in René MacColl, *Roger Casement: a new judgment* (London, 1956). In his 1952 memoir, Sullivan had also written, 'Casement was not completely normal and one of the abnormalities of his type is addiction to lamentable practices. He also had the further affliction of the craving to record erotica, and this horrible document was in the hands of the crown.' A.M. Sullivan, *The last serjeant* (London, 1952), p. 271.   **10** The correspondence filled the letters page in April, May and June

complaining about the conduct of Serjeant A.M. Sullivan.[11] He was accused of having 'disclosed matters of a confidential nature purporting to have been obtained by him as counsel from his client'.[12] They requested that his name be struck from the roll of honorary benchers, whereupon Sullivan himself requested that his name be removed.[13] In the early 1970s, the conduct of a barrister accused of stealing wigs[14] was considered by the benchers,[15] the Bar Council and the chief justice. The benchers opened an enquiry to consider the case, and the barrister in question was invited to attend or be represented. A sub-committee of judicial benchers (rather than barrister benchers) was appointed to hear the case, because it concerned 'investigating a conflict of testimony between a member of the Bar and a servant of the Bar of many years standing.'[16] In another instance, in the 1980s, a number of benchers received confidential correspondence with a complaint against a barrister.[17]

Members of the general council of the Bar, generally referred to as the Bar Council, were 'democratically elected by secret ballot'[18] at annual elections. People expressed different reasons for seeking election. One said they were 'just interested in trying to look at ways of making the profession more professional',[19] while another was concerned with 'the welfare of barristers, what you would do to improve the services the barristers were giving'.[20] A constitution for the Bar Council was adopted in the early twentieth century[21] and periodically reviewed.[22] The Council comprised several sub-committees, some of which changed over the years. Generally speaking, the most significant committee was the Bar library committee, which was 'responsible for running the Library'.[23] Its importance is also evident from the records of the Bar Council. A perennial problem for the library committee was barristers' failure to pay their Llibrary subscriptions on time, and it frequently had to pursue members for arrears.[24]

1956, despite the editor declaring, on 30 April, that correspondence on the issue 'is now terminated.' *Irish Times*, 30 Apr. 1956, p. 5. 11 This is reproduced in Ferguson, *Barristers*, p. 305. 12 K.I.B.M., 13 Apr. 1956. 13 'Serjeant Sullivan leaves honorary post in King's Inns', *Irish Times*, 6 Aug. 1956, p. 7. 14 See pp 95–6. 15 K.I.B.M., 3 Dec. 1971; 9, 18 Feb., 24 Mar. 1972; 30 Apr. 1973. See also B.C.M., 29 Jan., 26 Feb., 27 Mar., 30 Apr. 1971. 16 K.I.B.M., 9, 18 Feb. 1972; 23 Mar. 1972. The names of the judicial benchers were drawn from a hat. 17 K.I.B.M., 11 May 1987. 18 Bartholomew, *The Irish judiciary*, p. 23. 19 B16. 20 B23. 21 B.C.M., 16 Jan., 20 Feb. 1914. 22 E.g., ibid., 14 July, 4, 6 Nov. 1922 (changes to the circuits); ibid., 7 Dec. 1925 (voting and membership of the council). When the Bar Council sought, in the early 1970s, to convert the Law Library smoke room into a storage area for books, a vote was taken against this at a general meeting of the Bar. This led to a debate over whether the constitution of the Bar should be amended to allow a decision of the Bar Council to be overruled by a vote at the general meeting of the Bar. The Bar Council capitulated on the issue of the smoke room in order to avoid such an amendment. Ibid., 23 June, 28 July 1972. 23 B15. 24 E.g., in 1921 a barrister was threatened with exclusion from the library and the dressing room if their arrears were not paid. B.C.M., 25 Oct. 1921. There were a 'considerable number' of subscribers in arrears in the late twenties. Ibid., 15 Feb. 1929. Eight members of the Bar were recorded as being in arrears the following year: ibid., 21 Feb. 1930. The chair of the committee said in the mid-seventies that such was the level of arrears that '92 letters to defaulters' had been sent out during the whit vacation.' All defaulters had been contacted at least twice, and the Bar Council recommended that the names of defaulters should be posted in the

Other sub-committees came and went, considering issues such as criminal legal aid;[25] television;[26] education and devilling[27] and the EEC.[28] One barrister recalled serving on a sub-committee which 'basically had to do with our liaison with politicians ... because I knew politicians'.[29] Liaison committees and consultative committees also communicated externally with the Law Society, the judiciary and with other Bars.[30]

While the King's Inns controlled entry to the profession via the Barrister-at-Law degree, and could disbar barristers, the Bar Council was generally concerned with the day-to-day operation of the Law Library, the provision of services to barristers, and the imposition of discipline in less serious cases. Instances of misconduct could be reported to the Bar Council, which could be asked to give rulings on specific matters.[31] These might then be communicated to members of the Bar by posting notices on a board in the Library.[32] For example, in 1972 a barrister requested a ruling because

> He had frequently been asked by solicitors to recommend barristers who did particular types of work. He considered that he should not do this, yet he had felt churlish at not doing so. Might a barrister recommend a colleague to a solicitor as being suitable or competent to undertake a particular type of case?[33]

The Bar Council agreed that in such a case it was customary to give the names of all, or most of those who did that work, and that therefore it might be said that it was permissible to inform the solicitor of the persons competent in that field.

Barristers often liked to celebrate milestones such as taking silk, but sometimes the Bar Council was of the view that this went too far. For example, in 1971, a dinner was planned to celebrate someone taking silk, and invitations were sent to 'every solicitor in the three counties of Kerry, Limerick and Clare, as well as to other people'.[34] The invitations came in the names of three solicitors, rather than from the barrister. The Bar Council was unsure whether the barrister was aware of the dinner being organised, or had any role in the planning of it, but it ruled that he ought not to attend and that it amounted to advertising. The

---

Library: ibid., 21 June 1976. A decade later, it was reported that there was 'a hard core' of barristers 'who were regularly on the list of arrears and appeared to be able to pay.' There were also others 'who were getting more and more into arrears and it appeared to be unrealistic to expect that they would ever be able to pay': ibid., 3 Feb. 1986. **25** See pp 154–60. **26** See pp 315–20. **27** B.C.M., 13 Jan. 1967. By this time the sub-committee 'appeared to be moribund.' **28** See ch. 13. **29** B10. **30** See pp 267–70. **31** E.g., in 1954 a member of the Bar sought a ruling on the propriety of delivering a lecture on a legal topic: B.C.M., 9 July 1954. In 1967 a junior member sought a ruling in relation to fee relativity where the senior in his case had marked a special fee. B.C.M., 17 Feb. 1967. **32** E.g., in 1956 a notice was displayed regarding a ruling against a barrister who had removed books from the library without signing, and that a fine had been imposed on him: B.C.M., 4 May 1956. Relevant correspondence and information were also displayed on a notice board, e.g., B.C.M., 30 July 1956; 10 Jan. 1976. **33** B.C.M., 15 Dec. 1972. **34** Ibid., 4 Mar. 1971.

Bar Council was also concerned that the event preceded the actual call to the inner Bar. Following some slightly acrimonious correspondence, it was pointed out that there was no imputation of the barrister's conduct – simply that 'they should not attend a function which had already been arranged by others'.[35]

Sometimes the council wrote to a member of the Bar, on foot of a complaint, directing them either to take action or to cease engaging in particular conduct. The barrister usually gave an undertaking as requested; for example, in 1955 a barrister agreed not to hold himself out as a practising barrister while working in 'front of house' in a Dublin theatre.[36] Sometimes a barrister found guilty of misconduct might be temporarily excluded from the Library.[37] Barristers against whom a disciplinary decision was made could appeal to the King's Inns benchers and then to the courts. The Bar Council's professional practices committee was established in 1975 'to save time at council meetings by considering, reporting on and making recommendations on specific complaints before council meetings.'[38] It also had 'a general function of regulating desirable and undesirable practices at the Bar not related to specific incidents.'[39] From 1988 onward, the professional practices committee included a layperson.

Up to the 1980s, the Bar's disciplinary procedures 'hadn't really developed',[40] according to one barrister. Some members were not even aware of the framework for disciplinary procedures:

> I had no awareness. I know there was a professional practices committee. It all did seem a bit shrouded in secrecy you know. I suppose everything was quiet and I suppose if you were on an inside track, you might hear what might be coming out of it.[41]

Another said that they were aware that disciplinary procedures existed, 'but that is about it.'[42] Another barrister commented that:

> It was kind of *ad hoc* and all very loose and anybody who wanted to challenge those disciplinary proceedings could usually do so and they would, usually, and the Bar Council usually backed off.[43]

Another said, 'I don't recall such things being in printed form in the sixties and seventies.'[44]

By the mid-eighties, however, the existing system of regulation at the Bar was coming under pressure. With increasing external scrutiny[45] and a growth in numbers at the Bar, it was decided to produce a written code of conduct.[46] The

---

35 Ibid., 26 Mar. 1971. See also ibid., 30 Apr. 1971.   36 Ibid., 3 Mar. 1955.   37 E.g., in 1956, a barrister was excluded from the library and dressing rooms from 30 Oct. until the first day of Hilary term the following Jan.: B.C.M., 27 Oct. 1956.   38 B.C.M., 7 July 1975.   39 Ibid.   40 B1.
41 B22.   42 B24.   43 B21.   44 B8.   45 See pp 346–51.   46 Ralph Sutton SC was heavily

draft code was submitted to the chief justice, the president of the High Court and the council of King's Inns for approval,[47] and there were several meetings held in order to obtain comments and feedback from members of the Bar.[48] After much detailed consideration by the Bar Council,[49] the written code was adopted in 1985[50] and published in 1987. The code referred to 'hitherto unwritten rules and practices of the Bar'.[51] It included provisions on barristers' relationship with solicitors, other barristers, the Law Library, the Bar Council, the court and the public at large. It set out general principles for practising barristers; the duties of barristers in criminal cases; rules for overseas practice; and rules relating to fees and senior counsel. Some of these were adapted from the English Bar's code of conduct.[52]

In the late eighties, the Bar Council estimated that it dealt with between 20 and 36 complaints per annum.[53] Complaints about barristers might come from fellow barristers,[54] clients,[55] or solicitors.[56] Complaints were also made by barristers regarding judges[57] or politicians.[58] Complaints could arise between barristers where there was 'serious tension between colleagues'.[59] One barrister recalled being reported to the Council by a barrister who

> Was incredibly successful and very able … I did a case that he just wouldn't attend to. The solicitor came to me the night before and said 'look, would you ever have a go at this for me? I can't get anything out of [X]'. I did it. [X] reported me for taking a case of his.[60]

---

involved in the drafting: see obit., 'Exemplar of courtly behaviour at the Bar', *Irish Times*, 4 Dec. 1999, p. 8. Some members of the Bar Council objected to the very idea of a written code of conduct claiming that solicitors and accused persons would use it 'to make life difficult for the Bar'; that it would be a 'sneaks' charter' and that it would give too much power to the Bar Council. B.C.M., 11 Mar. 1985.   **47** B.C.M., 10 Jan. 1984. It was also later proposed to send drafts to the army legal service, the Law Society, the director of public prosecutions and the attorney general: B.C.M., 2 May 1985.   **48** B.C.M., 3 Dec. 1984. It was reported that the main difficulties which arose related to 'the rules for dress'. The Bar Council later resolved to present the draft code to the Bar 'without the rules relating to dress in order that frivolity of discussion should be avoided and proper attention be paid to the main issues'. B.C.M., 2 May 1985.   **49** B.C.M., 9, 23 Feb., 11 Mar., 2 May 1985.   **50** In July 1986 a notice was posted in the Law Library stating that the code was now in force: B.C.M., 7 July 1986.   **51** Bar Council, *Code of conduct for the Bar of Ireland, adopted by the Bar 30th July 1985*, p. 1. In 1989 a general meeting of the Bar agreed to adopt a code of conduct for lawyers in the EEC as an annex to the general code. B.C.M., 10 June 1989, 22 July 1989.   **52** B.C.M., 5 July 1984.   **53** Fair Trade Commission, *Report of study into restrictive practices in the legal profession* (Dublin, 1990), para. 16.7.   **54** E.g., B.C.M., 27 Oct. 1956.   **55** E.g., ibid., 19 Mar. 1957.   **56** E.g., in 1926 a solicitor accused a barrister of touting: B.C.M., 23 June 1926. However, the solicitor was unable to substantiate this claim, so it went no further: B.C.M., 15 July 1926. Sometimes complaints were made by solicitors about private matters, such as personal debts owed by barristers, in which the Bar Council had no role: e.g. B.C.M., 10 June 1949.   **57** E.g., in 1953 a barrister complained of having been excluded from court by a District Court judge: B.C.M., 27 Oct. 1953. See also B.C.M., 17 July 1970, where several barristers complained about a District Court judge who refused to certify for counsel in the District Court.   **58** E.g., B.C.M., 31 Jan. 1969.   **59** B4.   **60** B9.

Another barrister recalled a complaint relating to charging cards that could be used to pay for printing and catering:

> All the devils were downstairs having their drinks on a Friday, getting their cigarettes and everything on this card and they weren't paying their bills. And this amounted up to nearly a million over a couple of years. You can imagine – all their meals, everything![61]

This barrister wrote to the Bar Council to complain but found the Council to be ineffective, and in denial that there was any problem. However, a year or so later the card system was changed to one in which money had to be pre-loaded.

More serious than complaints to the Bar Council or the benchers was the prospect of being sued for professional negligence. In the 1960s, Lord Denning described barristers' traditional immunity from suit:

> Beyond doubt the barrister was treated differently from other professional men. He could not sue for his fees. He could not even make a contract for them with his client. Nor with the solicitor who represented the client. The obligation to pay him was an obligation which was binding in honour, not in law. Such was the position of the advocate in the Roman law. Such was the position of the barrister in our English law.[62]

This also reflected the position in Irish law. In *Rondel v. Worsley*, the English Court of Appeal had affirmed barristers' immunity from negligence actions taken against them regarding their work as lawyers.[63] In 1967 Keane surmised that this was likely to be followed in the Irish courts.[64] However, the Bar Council was nevertheless concerned about what the potential removal of the immunity might mean for members of the Irish Bar. It began to explore the possibility of introducing insurance against professional negligence.[65] It grappled with the possibility that appearing to take practical steps in relation to professional negligence, such as taking out insurance, 'would weaken the Bar's stand against the principle of liability'.[66] There was also the issue of whether to make such professional indemnity insurance compulsory for all members. This would add to the expense of Library subscriptions.

Hearing the appeal in *Rondel v. Worsley*, the House of Lords unanimously confirmed the continuing existence of barristers' immunity, based on public

---

61 B3.   62 *Rondel v. Worsley* [1966] EWCA Civ J1020–2, para. 12.   63 Ibid. This followed some uncertainty arising from the decision of the court of appeal in *Hedley Byrne and Co. v. Heller and partners* [1964] AC 465. See David Capper, 'The demise of the advocate's immunity', *NILQ* 57 (2006), 391.   64 Ronan Keane, 'Negligence of barristers', *Ir. Jur.* 2:1 (1967), 102.   65 B.C.M., 1 Dec. 1967. In early 1968 the Bar Council wrote to the English Bar Council and the Scottish Faculty of Advocates seeking information about how such insurance operated in those jurisdictions. It also considered collaborating with the Incorporated Law Society. B.C.M., 8 Jan. 1968.   66 B.C.M., 12

policy.[67] Barristers' independence had to be ensured so that they could fulfil their duties to the court. In 1968 the minister for justice referred the issue of professional liability to the Committee on Court Practice and Procedure.[68] In its fourteenth interim report in 1971, the committee pointed out that there was considerable uncertainty and a lack of public interest in this issue.[69] No action was taken. The matter seems to have rested for some time, and Capper points out that in the wider common law world, 'advocates' immunity expanded in the decade immediately after this decision.'[70]

By the late 1980s, the right of dissatisfied clients in other common law jurisdictions to sue barristers for negligence[71] was a cause for concern at the Irish Bar. In 1989 members voted overwhelmingly to introduce a mandatory scheme of professional indemnity insurance.[72] This would ensure that barristers were covered in the event that they were sued. A member of the Bar Council said that

> It was in the public interest and in the interests of the profession that it should be able to assure clients of the profession that in the event of such negligence, albeit a rare occurrence, there would be the proper means of recourse available to an injured party.[73]

Recalling the debate at the time, one interviewee said that while some colleagues were 'dead set against the move', others felt it was 'absolutely necessary'.[74]

Informal regulation

The collegiality of the Bar was partly supposed to ensure that professional norms and etiquette were communicated to and learned by all members.[75] New

---

July 1968. **67** *Rondel v. Worsley* [1967] 3 W.L.R. 1666. **68** B.C.M., 20 Jan. 1968. A member of the Bar Council also sat on this committee, and sought the council's suggestions as to how to proceed if the issue was pursued. **69** Committee on Court Practice and Procedure, *Fourteenth interim report. Liability of barristers and solicitors for professional negligence* (Dublin, 1971), p. 13. **70** Capper, 'The demise of the advocate's immunity', p. 395. See, e.g., the New Zealand decision of *Rees v. Sinclair* [1974] 1 N.Z.L.R. 180. In Ireland, Costello P in *HMW v. Ireland* [1997] 2 I.R. 142 stated, obiter, that '[b]ecause the barrister is required to put his public duty before the apparent interest of his client the public interest requires that on the grounds of public policy the barristers' immunity from suit be maintained.' **71** E.g., *Saif Ali v. Sydney Mitchell* [1980] A.C. 198, where a 3:2 majority in the House of Lords disapproved of *Rondel* in relation to legal pleadings. At the start of the twenty-first century, the House of Lords in *Hall v. Simons* [2002] 1 A.C. 615 ruled that advocates' immunity should not be retained for civil cases, or criminal cases where a conviction had already been quashed. Capper suggests, at 404, that 'two decades of gradual attrition sufficiently weakened the immunity that it was ripe for plucking by the time *Hall v. Simons* came to be decided.' See also Stephen O'Halloran, 'Peek-a-boo I can sue you: barristers' immunity in the twenty-first century – part I', *I.L.T.* 26 (2008), 278; Stephen O'Halloran, 'Peek-a-boo I can sue you: barristers' immunity in the twenty-first century – part II', *I.L.T.* 26 (2008), 304 and Ray Ryan and Des Ryan, 'A Bar to recovery? Barristers, public policy, and immunity from suit', *B.R.* 10:6 (2005), 209. **72** B.C.M., 22 July 1989. Similar mandatory insurance schemes had already been introduced for Bars in the UK. **73** Extraordinary general meeting of the Bar, B.C.M., 22 July 1989. **74** B16. **75** See

barristers learned what was acceptable and what was not from their masters, and from other colleagues.[76] One barrister summed up the basis for many of the professional conduct rules at the Bar as: 'everything is done in accordance with seniority.'[77] The same barrister emphasised that an additional layer of regulation existed on circuit:[78]

> When you're on circuit ... there's a code of conduct, an unwritten code of conduct. We have the Bar code of conduct, which is the one that applies to all barristers, but on the circuit, it is an even more defined code of conduct.[79]

The intimacy of the Bar, at least until the late twentieth century, was often a check on barristers' conduct. One barrister who was in practice from the late 1950s commented that this sort of 'self-regulation' was quite effective because of the small number of barristers at that time:

> If somebody misbehaved everyone knew about it immediately and we were all conscious of that.[80]

They said that the absence of a written code of conduct until the expansion of the Bar in the eighties was evidence that it had not been needed up to that point. Another barrister echoed this point that the tight-knit nature of the Bar for much of the twentieth century meant that poor practices or misconduct were usually quite obvious:

> The whole concept of the Bar was built on collegiately and correct conduct. Ethics. Honesty. Fairness. Integrity ... You will always have somebody who will take a shortcut and you know those types of people tend to get fairly well identified fairly quickly ... it is a small community.[81]

Gavan Duffy similarly wrote in the 1940s that 'the Bar through the close contact of its members in the Four Courts maintains a high standard of conduct'.[82] There were unwritten conventions with which one needed to comply. For example, the tradition of offering help or advice to more junior members:

> Mutual help in difficulty was a great tradition in the Law Library. No matter how large your practice, how many cases you had actively going, you were expected, by an unwritten law, to help and explain difficulties to the most inexperienced practitioner.[83]

---

ch. 12. **76** See pp 38–44. **77** B12. **78** See pp 203–4. **79** B12. **80** B8. **81** B12.
82 'Memorandum in favour of the amalgamation of barristers and solicitors, June 1946', p. 13.
Gavan Duffy to taoiseach, 4 June 1946, NAI TSCH/3/S13867. **83** Patrick MacKenzie, *Lawful*

Another convention at the Bar was what was known as the 'cab rank rule'; the idea that barristers did not distinguish between desirable and undesirable clients, and would accept any brief they were offered (unless there was a clear conflict of interest).[84]

Most minor breaches of discipline or etiquette were often dealt with informally or through peer pressure, rather than through formal mechanisms. This sort of quiet enforcement of the code of conduct and etiquette was usually considered preferable to having entirely formal proceedings. One said that the father of the Bar:

> Would come over and just say, 'listen just a little point that came to my notice, I don't want to really make anything of it but what you did wasn't absolutely hunky dory, do take a look at that you know and try and ensure it doesn't happen again', and if that advice is taken, that's the end of it.[85]

> If somebody stepped out of line, or what the Bar would consider stepping out of line in court, someone would pull you aside ... and say 'you can't behave like that' ... either 'that's not the way we do things around here' or 'that's not ethical' ... and they weren't sort of saying 'I will report' but ... they'd mark their card.[86]

> If ever I had a query with the professional practice committee, I would always approach someone on that. I would say 'who's on the committee?' and they'd give me their names and I'd approach somebody like that ... I never made a complaint against a barrister but if I was ever obliged to, that's what I would do ... it's not a good idea to have a sort of confrontation in hearing and a ruling on that.[87]

This point was made by a member of the Bar Council in the early eighties:

> By far the most important element was professional discipline which was achieved with hardly any reference to the Bar Council by what might be termed peer pressure. In this we were the envy of all other systems and it was vital to maintain it. The English Bar felt that it was losing control of discipline.[88]

---

occasions: the old Eastern Circuit (Dublin, 1991), p. 19.   **84** In England in the late nineties, Boon and Flood pointed out that the cab rank rule was a fairly recent development: Andy Boon and John Flood, 'Trials of strength: the reconfiguration of litigation as a contested terrain', *Law & Society Review* 33:3 (1999), 595. In making this point they cited Eric Hobsbawm and T. Ranger (eds), *The invention of tradition* (Cambridge, 1992) and Paul DiMaggio and Walter Powell, 'The iron cage revisited: institutional isomorphism and collective rationality in organisational fields', in Paul DiMaggio & Walter Powell (eds), *The new institutionalism in organizational analysis* (Chicago, 1991). **85** B12.   **86** B24.   **87** B17.   **88** B.C.M., 7 Sept. 1982.

It is evident that by this stage, the scene was set for changes in the way the Bar was regulated. It is also worth noting that there were a number of practices at the Bar which were frequently the subject of both internal discussion and external comment. These included rules and conventions relating to fees, as well as the two-counsel rule and issues relating to solicitors' right of audience in the superior courts; the potential fusion of the two legal professions and the idea of introducing a system of chambers.

The profession under scrutiny

The most thorough external examination of the profession in the twentieth century was carried out by the Fair Trade Commission.[89] Following sporadic contacts between the commission and the Bar in the seventies,[90] in April 1984, the minister for industry, Des O'Malley, asked the commission to investigate restrictive practices in the Irish legal profession.[91] The commission was to examine practises that led to increased legal costs to consumers and which reduced or limited employment opportunities in the legal profession. This would include restrictions on advertising and direct access, as well as issues such as legal education and fee fixing. The commission received over eighty submissions from interested parties, which included the Bar Council, individual barristers, non-practicing barristers and university law teachers.[92] There then followed forty days of meeting with stakeholders, six-and-a-half of which involved the Bar Council.[93] The topics considered by the commission were wide-ranging.[94]

The commission's report was anticipated as something which would undoubtedly have an impact on the profession, and many barristers awaited the report with some dread. A view developed that some changes to the profession would be inevitable. One barrister, for example, told the Bar Council that:

89 This was established by the Restrictive Trade Practices Act 1953, s. 2. The Restrictive Practices Act 1972 provided that 'the Fair Trade Commission shall continue in being but shall, from the passing of this act, be known as the restrictive practices commission.' Its remit was extended to cover the provision of services, as well as the supply of goods. Despite the name change, many predecessors continued to refer to the 'Fair Trade Commission', and the report into the legal professions in 1990 was published under the name of the original commission. 90 E.g., the commission queried the role of the Bar Council in setting fees. B.C.M., 2 Feb. 1976. The Bar Council wrote back that the purpose of minimum fee scales was 'to protect the beginners from exploitation, and to preserve standards.' If the committee objected to fee scales, the Bar Council was prepared to abandon them. 91 This was done under s. 12 of the Restrictive Practices Act 1972. As early as 1969, the Bar had begun to consider the need for reform in relation to restrictive practices: B.C.M., 16 May 1969. One member of the council pointed out that 'quite apart from anything that might come from the Fair Trade Commission, the Bar should make changes if it was to escape criticism from the public.' 92 F.T.C., para. 1.8. The names of those who made submissions and met with the commission were kept anonymous. 93 Ibid., para. 1.9. 94 These were: limitations on the provision of legal services; division of the profession; education and admission; solicitor's right of audience; access to barrister; number of legal representatives; organisation of legal practice and insurance; fees; advertising; legal personnel; paralegals and legal executives; disciplinary

There would be very considerable changes over the next few years in the way which legal and quasi legal services were provided. Once the Fair Trade Commission reports ... the position would be changed dramatically ... the key to the survival of the Bar Council was in its role as providing disciplinary jurisdiction for the Bar.[95]

Some members of the Bar Council made the point that a combination of the Fair Trade Commission report and pending reform legislation 'made it imperative that the Bar say at the earliest possible date that it had no restrictive practices.[96]

The matter took up much of the Bar Council's attention in the late eighties. Over the summer and autumn of 1989 its public affairs committee engaged in 'a programme of briefing and lobbying' with 'the press and politicians in anticipation of the commission's report'.[97] The council sought different ways to engage with colleagues at the Bar 'to determine the kind of response the Bar should make to such proposals'.[98] In December, the Bar Council decided that it would be prudent to contact solicitors on the circuits about their likely response to the commission's report.[99] Some months later the president of the Law Society contacted the chairman of the Bar Council suggesting that they present a united front in relation to the commission's report.[100]

The views of the commission and the arguments put forward by the Bar Council are worth considering in some detail. The commission identified some criticisms of the divided profession, which included inefficiency, duplication, excessive fees; the fact that barristers were often unnecessarily retained; the fact that some clients never spoke to their barristers; the fact that clients could not negotiate fees with barristers, and the fact that barristers could not be sued for negligence.[101] The Bar Council disputed claims that the division of the profession caused inefficiency, was more costly, or lacked public confidence.[102] It put forward several arguments against a fused profession, including that it would give large solicitors' firms a huge advantage over smaller, rural firms, and that it would dilute the specialist knowledge available at the Bar. It also argued that fusion would result in court proceedings becoming more protracted and less well ordered.[103] The commission agreed with this analysis.

The commission believed that the distinction between junior and senior counsel[104] was unnecessary:

If certain barristers wish to limit the type of work which they do, and to set their own high fees, they should be free to do so, and to make this

procedures; and miscellaneous matters.   95 B.C.M., 12 Dec. 1988.   96 B.C.M., 14 May 1988. 97 B.C.M., 14 Oct. 1989.   98 B.C.M., 28 Jan. 1989. E.g., a committee of leaders of circuits was suggested, as was a special meeting of the Bar and a seminar for all members. It was agreed to have the circuits nominate one or two representatives to discuss the anticipated proposals.   99 B.C.M., 9 Dec. 1989.   100 B.C.M., 3 Mar. 1990.   101 F.T.C., para. 6.5.   102 Ibid., para. 6.23.   103 Ibid., ch. 6.   104 See ch. 3 and 4.

information directly known to their clients, without the need for artificial differentiation by title. Leading barristers should become known by their ability and reputation, as in other professions, rather than being identified in some mysterious fashion by the government. The legal system could function perfectly satisfactorily without the titular honour of senior counsel.[105]

It considered that the title of senior counsel, if retained, should be conferred by the profession itself 'as a mark of honour only', and not by the government.[106]

The fact that clients could not directly engage counsel, but could only do so through a solicitor,[107] was criticised. The commission concluded that this was 'unfair and contrary to the common good',[108] and suggested that barristers favoured the practice 'because it increased their isolation, mystique and status.'[109] However, the Bar Council was 'prepared to contemplate the possibility, in the case of advisory and paper work, of direct access from experts other than patent agents and trade mark agents.'[110] The issue of having a high number of counsel in individual cases was also considered by the commission. The Bar Council explained that the number of lawyers retained depended on a number of factors, including the complexity of the facts, whether there were difficult issues of law involved, the length of the case, and the 'impecuniosity of the client':

> Where a client is impecunious he is more likely, somewhat paradoxically, to be represented by more rather than fewer lawyers. This is because his lawyers are likely to be unpaid unless costs are recovered from the other side. By retaining more than one lawyers the risk of his legal representatives being unpaid is spread more widely. This practice, which is in the public interest, is one which is accepted by solicitors, barristers and clients as a method of ensuring access to, and representation in, the courts by all citizens no matter what their means.[111]

The commission did not see much merit in the argument about spreading the risk of not being paid, and briefing two seniors:[112]

> Senior counsel usually take on cases for impecunious clients only where they consider that there is some prospect of winning and obtaining fees from the other party, and there is no evidence to suggest that fees are not received in a significant number of cases, which might justify the practice. In the vast majority of cases, as well, settlement is reached out of court, with acceptance of counsel's fees after some negotiation.[113]

---

105 F.T.C., para. 1.157.   106 Ibid., para. 1.157.   107 The Law Society was of the view that access to a barrister should only be through a solicitor: ibid., para. 9.11.   108 Ibid., para. 9.32.   109 Ibid., para. 9.6.   110 Ibid., para. 9.20.   111 Ibid., para. 10.17. See ch. 8.   112 Ibid., para. 10.39.   113 Ibid.

The system of listing cases in the superior courts was also discussed as a factor in these practices.[114] The related issue of legal fees was also considered by the commission. Various parties had complained about high fees, 'which was said to be due both to excessive rates and the number of counsel involved'.[115] There were complaints that 'legal fees often depended on the value of the case, rather than upon the complexity of the case'.[116] The Bar Council defended their fees scales on the basis that they were useful to new barristers and taxing masters;[117] that minimum fees helped to maintain professional standards; that they helped solicitors to estimate how much the case would cost,[118] and that the recommended fees did not represent price-fixing. The commission was of the view that fees should be set by the respective rules committees of the courts, rather than by the profession itself,[119] and pointed out that this would also get rid of the two-thirds rule and the practice of refreshers being half of the brief fee.[120] It also recommended that fees be agreed in advance, not based on the value of the award.[121]

In submissions to the commission, there were some suggestions that barristers should be able to operate as limited companies, and that they ought to be able to form partnerships with other barristers and establish chambers.[122] The system of requiring them all to be self-employed[123] was described as wasteful.[124] The commission's view was that the sole practitioner was in a very vulnerable position. It expressed support for barrister-solicitor partnerships, or perhaps mixed practices with, for example, estate agents or accountants.[125] The Bar Council pointed out that barristers were independent, and were paid by honoraria not fees, so they had 'no business, in the legal sense, which they could carry on with another person with a view to profit'.[126] The commission argued that some advantages would accrue to barristers if they were permitted to form partnerships:

> Barristers in partnership would be able to process work more efficiently; they would be able to secure a regular salary from the onset of their professional careers; they would be able to have an income while incapacitated from work; they would be able to evade personal responsibility for negligence claims and fix the partnership with that responsibility.

---

114 Hearing dates could not always be predicted with accuracy. To ensure the case would in fact be heard, more than one counsel would be briefed. The Law Society agreed that because of the listing system (with 25 jury cases listed per day in the High Court), operating 'on a single-counsel basis was totally impracticable'. Ibid. 115 Ibid., para. 12.60. 116 Ibid., para. 12.61. 117 Ibid., para. 12.89. 118 Ibid., para. 12.90. 119 Ibid., para. 12.143. 120 Ibid., para. 12.144. 121 Ibid., para. 12.146. 122 F.T.C., para. 11.4. See ch. 11. 123 See ch. 6. 124 F.T.C., para. 11.4. 125 Ibid., para. 11.5. 126 Ibid., para. 11.12. See ch. 6. The Law Society had no strong views on the

However, the Bar Council argued that none of this was necessarily to the public's advantage.[127]

The commission was highly critical of the restrictions on barristers advertising, and concluded that barristers should be allowed to advertise their services in the same way that solicitors could.[128] It said that restrictions on cold calling and direct mailing should be lifted, and that barristers should be allowed to advertise fees for specific services and hourly rates.[129] The Bar Council was adamant that it 'totally and absolutely' rejected advertising by barristers, arguing that 'the harm would be that a barrister might project himself into a practice that he had not earned on merit.'[130]

Employed or in-house counsel should, in the commission's view, be allowed to appear in court on behalf of their employer,[131] something which the Bar Council 'very strongly opposed'.[132] Finally, the commission was extremely critical of the processes and procedures for dealing with complaints about barristers. It considered that disbarment should be a matter for the courts, not the Inns.[133] It also expressed surprise at the involvement of the judiciary with the barristers' profession through the King's Inns, around half of whose benchers were judicial benchers. It argued that the bench and Bar were separate professions, and that there was '[n]o sound reason for any aspect of the profession of barrister to be influenced by the direct participation of the judiciary'.[134] It recommended the creation of a legal ombudsman to deal with complaints about barristers.[135]

The wide-ranging final report of the Fair Trade Commission on the legal profession was published in July 1990. Its recommendations were, as predicted, critical of many aspects of the barristers' profession. The chairman had already anticipated a 'most formidable workload'[136] in dealing with the report. The council had begun to formulate opinions and positions in relation to the various issues raised in the report. It noted the proposal that the granting of silk should not involve the government, and suggested that 'the chief justice, the attorney general and the chairman of the Bar Council might act in this matter in the future'.[137] It was prepared to put the issue of fee relativity to the profession, and it said it would continue to defend the mandatory junior on the basis of service to the client and continuity of the profession. In light of the proposed concession on fee relativity, the amount paid to the junior would be a reflection of his or her contribution to the case.[138] On the issue of fees, the council favoured free

organisation of barristers' practices: ibid., para. 11.9.   127 Ibid., para. 11.12. It listed potential disadvantages, which included that members of the same partnership could not represent conflicting interests. It argued strongly that partnerships would limit clients' choices, especially outside Dublin and Cork, and would 'sap the independence of the barrister'. Ibid., para. 11.13. 128 Ibid., para. 13.57.   129 Ibid., para. 13.60.   130 Ibid., para. 13.29.   131 Ibid., para. 14.46. 132 Ibid., para. 14.8.   133 Ibid., para. 16.49.   134 Ibid., para. 16.50.   135 Ibid., para. 16.52. 136 B.C.M., Jan. 1990. The other major issues on the agenda were the criminal Bar and the reform of the Bar's constitution and code of conduct.   137 B.C.M., 7 Sept. 1990.   138 Ibid.

negotiation on fees, and it would agree not to issue scales of fees and would withdraw existing recommended fee scales. During discussions on the report, the chairman of the council pointed out that the Bar's constitution made no reference to a disciplinary committee, and he expressed 'grave misgivings about the current disciplinary procedures of the Bar Council were they to be the subject of challenge.'[139] The council agreed to indicate to the minister that it proposed to establish a committee to formalise its disciplinary procedure. Extraordinary general meetings of the Bar were convened in 1990 and 1991.[140] In May 1991, Minister for Justice Ray Burke discussed the various recommendations with Bar Council representatives and reported that they were 'actively considering proposals for change'.[141]

Although some barristers were highly critical of the report,[142] by the mid-nineties several issues raised by the commission had been addressed, albeit there remained some matters in relation to which no change was apparent. This included advertising, partnerships, the divided professions,[143] and direct lay access.[144] Also under scrutiny around this time was barristers' court attire. Legislative changes to the wearing of wigs and gowns were effected with the Criminal Evidence Act 1992 and Courts and Court Officers Act 1995.[145]

Looking back on the late eighties and nineties, one barrister said that politicians 'were gunning for the Bar at the time',[146] while another recalled feeling 'under siege':

> I think people were worried because obviously they felt that it would impinge on their own careers but I think in fairness at a larger level people were [concerned] that it would damage the institution of the Bar and would make inroads on its independence.[147]

Barristers remained self-regulating despite the recommendations by the Fair Trade Commission. One barrister who was very much against the idea of external regulation pointed out that 'We were left to our own devices, and it seemed to work'.[148] Nevertheless, there was an impetus towards reform and modernisation evident for the rest of the nineties. This was apparent in relation to such matters as the expansion in numbers[149] and the need for new physical infrastructure.[150] Internal sub-committees and reports[151] scrutinised practises and recommended reforms.

---

139 Ibid.   140 B.C.M., 21 July 1990.   141 Dáil Éireann deb., vol. 408, no. 1 (8 May 1991). See also B.C.M., 13 Apr. 1991.   142 E.g., one derided it as 'a model of ineptitude'. Rex Mackey, *Windward of the law* (2nd ed., Dublin, 1991), p. 194.   143 Dáil Éireann deb., vol. 404, no. 1 (4 Dec. 1991).   144 Dáil Éireann deb., vol. 438, no. 4 (8 Feb. 1994).   145 See p. 97.   146 B14.   147 B21.   148 B8.   149 See pp 69–71.   150 See pp 240–4.   151 E.g., the Gallagher report in 1995.

The Bar Council's representative role

The Bar Council had a representative as well as a disciplinary role. Aside from ensuring that subscriptions were paid, the Bar Council liaised externally with such bodies as the Law Society, the judiciary, relevant government departments, such as the Department of Justice, and bodies such as the Board of Works, which controlled the physical infrastructure of the Law Library.[152] In chapter thirteen, we saw that the Bar Council played a representative role with the press, though not always with success. In chapter eight, we saw the Bar Council frequently liaising with the Department of Justice over the legal aid schemes.

The issue of modes of address for judges in the superior courts illustrates how the Bar Council could be galvanised into action. Since the foundation of the state, the standard mode of address was 'my lord'. Indeed, an American judge visiting Ireland in 1924 commented on this:

> The form of address to the presiding justice is 'my lord' or 'your lordship'. This seems somewhat incongruous in the Irish Free State but in a state of transition the Bar evinces its usual conservatism by continuing to use the forms to which they have been accustomed until they find a better.[153]

An attempt was made in 1936 to introduce 'A Bhreithimh' and 'A Phríomh-Bhreithimh',[154] but this was unsuccessful and members of the Bar continued with 'my lord'. Section 45 of the Courts (supplementary provisions) bill 1959 proposed a similar change. The chief justice was to be addressed as 'A Phríomh Breithimh' and all other judges were to be addressed as 'A Bhreithimh'. Where more than one judge sat together they were to be referred to as 'A Bhreithiúna'. Up to this point, modes of address had been determined by the superior courts rules committees, and not by legislation.

These proposals proved controversial and were discussed at length by the Bar Council.[155] Objections rested on several grounds; chiefly that the proposed new modes of address would 'unnecessarily interfere with the traditional mode of address in court and inevitably tend to confusion and loss of dignity'; and they would 'impose an embarrassment on the professions and the public involving loss of dignity to the courts and do a disservice to the advancement of the Irish language and in any event would not be capable of enforcement'.[156] Some also opposed the change on constitutional grounds, claiming inconsistency with articles 8(2) and 34 of the constitution.[157] A memorandum was circulated to the

---

152 See ch. 11 and 13.   153 Justice John M. Tierney of the New York Supreme Court, writing in *American Bar Association visit to England, Scotland and Ireland 1924, memorial volume* (New York, 1926), p. 76.   154 The proposal on that occasion had originated with Chief Justice Kennedy: Memorandum to exec. council from Dept. Justice, 1 Feb. 1936. 'Wearing of wigs by judges and members of the Bar and mode of address to judges', NAI TSCH/3/S8613.   155 B.C.M., 20 Mar., 30 June 1961.   156 Ibid., 20 Mar. 1961.   157 Ibid.

taoiseach, chief justice, presidents of the High and Circuit Courts, the attorney general and the president of the Law Society.[158] The following month, a deputation from the Bar Council met with the minister for justice 'and had an exhaustive discussion with him.'[159] The High Court rules committee also engaged with the minister's parliamentary secretary on the matter.[160] Barrister and senator Brian Lenihan[161] described the whole affair as 'much ado about nothing'.[162]

Patrick McGilligan TD, also a barrister,[163] similarly described it as 'a trivial matter and one that might have been left entirely to the judgment of members of the profession'.[164] Noting that the Bar Council had reacted 'very strongly', he argued for leaving the power to determine modes of address with the rules committee.[165] Charles Haughey may have been quite astute in his comment that 'the basic objection was to the fact that this was being taken from the rules committee and done by legislation.'[166] Self-regulation had been one of the hallmarks of professional identity up to this point. The chief justice wrote to the chairman regarding the proposals, and in June 1961 a special meeting of the Bar Council was convened to further consider the matter. The Bar Council 'strongly' opposed any change to the mode of address and it objected to anything other than 'my lord' in the English language.[167] Following this furore, the Courts (Supplemental Provisions) Act 1961 was passed without the provision altering judicial modes of address.

However, the matter was still not fully resolved by 1962. Justice Barra O'Briain, on his return from acting as president of the High Court of Cyprus,[168] informed Chief Justice Ó Dálaigh and the president of the High Court that he no longer wished to be addressed as 'my lord' in court. This was communicated by the chief justice to the Bar Council and was the subject of discussion between the chairman and the chief justice in chambers, as well as at meetings of the Bar Council.[169] Various modes of address were considered by the Bar Council and

158 Ibid., 30 June 1961. 159 Ibid., 17 Apr. 1961. 160 Ibid., 15 June 1961. Senator Michael Hayes described the proposed provisions as 'a result of confused thought and of an endeavour to use the Irish language, not as it should be used as a living vigorous tongue, but as a kind of political weapon to prove that you want to do something about it when, in fact, you do not want to and, if you did, you would not know how to do it.' Seanad Éireann deb., vol. 54, no. 19 (9 Aug. 1961). 161 Called in 1952: Ferguson, *Barristers*, p. 227. 162 Seanad Éireann deb., vol. 54, no. 19 (9 Aug. 1961), adding: 'I see no great burden on the intelligence of myself or any other member of the legal profession in addressing the court in the terms: "may it please the court" or "if the court pleases" instead of the mode of address used heretofore "may it please your lordship" or "if your lordship pleases."' 163 Called in 1921: Ferguson, *Barristers*, p. 241. 164 Dáil Éireann deb., vol. 187, no. 8 (22 Mar. 1961). 165 Ibid., adding: 'I would have thought that more objection would be taken to the clothes, the robes, that have to be worn by members of the Bar. Some people are very fond of them. Some people dislike them very much. But, seeing that they are, in fact, an old court dress I would have thought there would have been more hostility directed to the robes than to the method of address. The vocative that we use to anybody is not a very important matter.' 166 Seanad Éireann deb., vol. 54, no. 19 (9 Aug. 1961). 167 B.C.M., 30 June 1961. 168 See ch. 14. 169 B.C.M., 23 Nov. 1962; Edward Micks, chair of the Bar Council, to Ó Dálaigh, 2 Feb. 1962,

they concluded that 'the title which judges of the superior court possess is the traditional title of 'my lord' and that order 105, rule 1 does not exclude the use of "my lord" as a method of address.'[170] The chairman of the Bar Council informed the chief justice that if the superior judges did not agree with this mode of address, the Council would be happy to send a deputation to discuss it further.[171] There the matter appears to have rested.

This incident demonstrates how effective the Bar Council could be when it felt that its interests or the interests of members was under threat. It was able to lobby effectively to maintain the status quo, and having so many qualified or practising barristers in senior positions in the state[172] certainly helped. It also demonstrates the territoriality felt by some members of the profession; the Bar did not welcome external interference in legal practice. This territoriality would be seen again when proposals were made to legislate for the abolition of wigs and gowns in the 1990s.

The relationship between Bar Council and the profession

Some barristers did not view the Bar Council as representing their views or their interests. This disjoint between the council and members of the Bar was evident in some of the comments made by interviewees for this book. Asked how the Bar Council was perceived, one barrister said 'I was never conscious of them ... I didn't get in their way and they didn't get in my way. I recall no complaints made about me'. Others were sceptical of the council's organisation and management, and one barrister who practised from the thirties until the sixties described the Bar Council 'not so much a disciplinary body as it is a committee of management of a club'.[173] Sometimes the misalignment of the Bar Council leadership with views of members of the profession became public. For example, in a rather public row with the Bar Council in the seventies,[174] Minister Des O'Malley said that members of the profession, who were not members of the Bar Council, welcomed his proposals. He criticised the 'tone and content' of the Bar Council's response to him, which he considered unrepresentative of the Bar's views.[175]

In the spring of 1986, members of the Bar Council spent a weekend in Wexford discussing what might be done to alleviate some of the problems caused by the huge expansion of the profession.[176] They agreed that the administration of the Bar needed radical overhaul. Consequently, they engaged a management consultant, who recommended the appointment of a director general of the Bar. A job specification was drawn up, candidates were shortlisted and interviewed, and the Bar Council selected the person they considered most suitable for the position. When the matter was discussed at a general meeting of the Bar in

UCDA P51/12. **170** B.C.M., 30 Nov. 1962. **171** Micks to Ó Dálaigh, 2 Feb. 1962, UCDA P51/12. **172** See pp 295–300. **173** Bernard Shillman, 'Every journey has an end', NAI PRIV1367/11, p. 14. **174** See p. 120. **175** 'O'Malley tells Bar Council: check facts', *Irish Press*, 10 Dec. 1971, p. 3. **176** See ch. 5 and 11.

November 1986,[177] members of the Bar were irked that they had not been consulted about these developments.

The chairman argued that '[t]he profession could not any longer be administered by part-time and overworked administrators', which, given the increase in numbers[178] and the various pressures facing the profession in the eighties, appeared to be an entirely valid position for the council to take. However, the fraught meeting highlighted the fact that the Bar Council seemed to be operating more-or-less independently of the membership. The chairman said that they had been meeting twice a month on the matter, for fifteen months, and indicated that the profession should trust them to make the right decisions. A communication deficit was identified: '[t]raditionally, communication had been by word of mouth'.[179] Efforts had been made to provide relevant updates via a newsletter, but this had not been entirely successful.

* * *

Despite perceptions of the legal profession as being steeped in tradition, it has been observed elsewhere that many of the 'hallmarks' of modern legal professionalism are relatively recent developments.[180] Proposals to externally regulate aspects of legal professions are often 'said to contravene historically derived principles'.[181] To take the Irish Bar, the publication of a code of conduct, the disciplinary powers and structures of the Bar Council, the education and training of barristers and an understanding of the parameters of the profession were all in a state of flux in the twentieth century.

Self-regulation was highly valued by the profession, and Mungham and Thomas' observations about the English legal professions applied equally to Ireland:

> Given the specialised nature of law, it is argued that only the professionals themselves are properly qualified for the task. The service nature of the profession means that self-control becomes the order of the day.[182]

The push for external regulation and oversight continued into the twenty-first century,[183] and these encroachments were usually resisted by the Bar. Sachs and Hoff-Wilson point out that a feature of the barristers' profession is that

---

177 General meeting of the Bar, B.C.M., 27 Nov. 1986.   178 See ch. 5.   179 General meeting of the Bar, B.C.M., 27 Nov. 1986.   180 Wesley Pue, *Lawyers' empire*, p. 24.   181 Ibid., p. 19. 182 Geoff Mungham and Philip A. Thomas, 'Solicitors and clients: altruism or self-interest?' in Dingwall and Lewis (eds), *The sociology of the professions*, p. 135.   183 E.g., Competition Authority, *Competition in professional services: solicitors & barristers* (Dublin, 2006). In Nov. 2010, the government signed a memorandum of understanding with the EU/IMF which included a commitment to establish an independent regulator and implement the outstanding recommend-ations of the competition authority. In Oct. 2011, Minister for Justice Alan Shatter published the

It involves the grouping together of people who compete fiercely with each other for income and prestige, but stand firmly united against encroachment on their territory from the outside world. It is this dualism that produces the combative camaraderie so characteristic of lawyers.[184]

This defence of territory by the Bar was evident throughout the twentieth-century. The late twentieth-century Irish Bar was characterised by resisting attempts at state interference, whether through legislation, adverse comment in the Dáil, or investigation by statutory commissions. This coincided with the significant changes in legal practice,[185] an explosion in numbers at the Bar,[186] an increase in technical, specialised and highly-paid legal work, and pressure on Bar infrastructure,[187] and required the profession to reflect on both its current position and its future trajectory.

Legal Services Regulation bill.   184 Albie Sachs & Joan Hoff Wilson, *Sexism and the law: a study of male beliefs and legal bias in Britain and the United States* (Oxford, 1978), pp 180–1.   185 See ch. 6.   186 See pp 69–70.   187 See pp 240–4.

CHAPTER SEVENTEEN

Conclusion

This has been a book of striking contrasts. It has examined the barristers' profession from different angles. The everyday experiences of individual barristers are presented alongside the major national and international issues which impacted upon the profession. We have seen the Irish Bar's influence on the world stage, as well as the traditions and challenges of practising in Ireland's country towns. Individual barristers' struggles with financial security clash with external perceptions of their being overpaid. Other contrasts have also presented themselves; the need to appear confident and successful while dealing with the anxiety and insecurity of being self-employed; the social nature of the Bar, which contrasted with the individualism of the sole practitioner; the Bar's acceptance of some kinds of differences, but not others. It was a place where individualism came up against collectivity on a daily basis. The inexperienced devil might literally rub shoulders with the leading advocates of the day. The gravity and seriousness of the practice of law contrasted with barristers' literary and artistic contributions and their appearance on radio, stage and screen. It was a traditionally elite profession, but with a nod to egalitarianism that contrasted with legal professions based on chambers systems elsewhere. An Irish barrister's practice could take them from battling through a pungent fair day in an Irish country town, to appearing before an international court in Luxembourg or Strasbourg. They could go from representing someone in the District Court for brawling, to crusading on behalf of someone wronged by the state in a constitutional challenge. They might represent some clients, knowing that they would never be paid, or earn substantial fees for prolonged tribunal work. They could go from socialising and enjoying pub banter with a friendly group of colleagues, to battling sleepless nights and crippling anxiety about the future of their practice.

Among all of these contrasting perspectives, some common themes are evident. First, it is evident that the Bar was both nationally and internationally outward-looking. The Bar's international focus was both individual and collective. Individually, barristers joined the colonial legal service or worked as advocates or judges in other common law jurisdictions. Some published articles in international law journals.[1] Later, they took advantage of opportunities presented by Ireland's membership of the EEC.[2] Some maintained individual

---

[1] E.g., Alfred Denis Pringle (called in 1925: Ferguson, *Barristers*, p. 284) frequently contributed to the *Journal of Comparative Legislation and International Law*. E.g., A.D. Pringle, 'British Isles: Eire', *J. Comp. Leg. & Int'l L.* 32:1 (1950), 29.   [2] Ch. 14.

memberships of such organisations as the International Academy of Comparative Law.[3] Collectively, the Bar Council engaged with international bodies such as the ABA,[4] the IBA and the CCBE.[5] Visiting Bars were hosted, while Irish barristers visited other jurisdictions, sometimes as part of major international congresses. Members of the Bar also contributed to the development of the United Nations, the European Convention on Human Rights, and the jurisprudence of both the European Court of Justice and the European Court of Human Rights.[6] Closer to home, the Bar maintained a working relationship with the Incorporated Law Society, and its relationship with the Bar of Northern Ireland began to improve from the 1970s.[7]

The Bar was well-connected with politicians and policy-makers. As seen in chapter fourteen, in common with other jurisdictions many qualified barristers found themselves in positions of power beyond the Bar. Barristers were to be found working in government departments and in private industry, as well as serving as elected representatives. At different times throughout the period, the Bar could count as its own presidents,[8] taoisigh,[9] tánaistí,[10] members of the Oireachtas,[11] government ministers,[12] senior civil servants,[13] ambassadors,[14] chairs of financial institutions,[15] university professors,[16] journalists[17] and business leaders.[18]

A consequence of being so well-connected was that the Bar could wield considerable social and political influence. When members of the Bar lent their support to particular movements or ideas, they often brought with them a sense of legitimacy. Many barristers were politically active, involved either in party politics or social activism. In chapters thirteen, fourteen and sixteen there were several examples of the Bar Council liaising with government ministers and other decision-makers over issues which were of concern to the Bar. Members

3 E.g., Henry Hanna. See letter to the editor, *Irish Times*, 4 Mar. 1938, p. 6, where Hanna sought to encourage other members of the legal profession to join in the establishment of an Irish branch of the academy. The purpose was 'to foster the study of comparative law'.   4 In 1928, Hugh Kennedy delivered a paper to the ABA in Seattle, published as: 'The character and sources of the constitution of the Irish Free State', *A.B.A.J.* 14:8 (1928), 437. In 1936, Henry Hanna was one of a group of representatives of the Irish Bar to tour several North American cities on the invitation of the ABA. His lecture on the history of the common law in Ireland was said to have been very well received at Harvard: 'Death of Mr. H. Hanna, K.C.', *Irish Times*, 22 Mar. 1946, p. 2. The paper was published as Henry Hanna, 'The bench and Bar of Ireland in the nineteenth century', *A.B.A.J.* 22:11 (1936), 761.   5 Ch. 13.   6 Ch. 14.   7 Ch. 13.   8 Both Cearbhall Ó Dálaigh and Mary Robinson practised at the Irish Bar.   9 E.g., John A. Costello, Jack Lynch and Liam Cosgrave.   10 E.g. Michael O'Leary, Dick Spring and Brian Lenihan (snr).   11 E.g., Fionán Lynch (Ó Loingsigh), John Maurice Kelly, Tom O'Higgins, James Dillon, John Lymbrick Esmonde, Sean MacBride, Declan Costello, Theodore Conyngham Kingsmill Moore, Patrick Lindsay, Seán O'Leary, Mary Robinson, Brian Lenihan (jnr), Eoin Ryan, Patrick Hogan and David Andrews.   12 E.g., James FitzGerald-Kenney, James Geoghegan.   13 E.g., John Belton, Thomas Joseph Coyne, Jane Flood Liddy.   14 E.g., John J. Hearne, Michael Andrew Lysaght Rynne, P. Declan Quigley, Vincent Grogan.   15 E.g., Miriam Hederman O'Brien, Peter Sutherland.   16 E.g., Frances Moran, Patrick McGilligan, J.M. Kelly.   17 E.g., Stephen Barrett, David Andrews, Colum Kenny.   18 E.g., Joe McGough, Michael Wymes.

were also involved in areas not directly related to legal practice, including developing Ireland's foreign policy from the sixties onward. It is doubtful whether any other professional group has had as much influence over shaping Ireland's legal, political and international policies. Barristers also contributed to the cultural life of the state as language activists,[19] playwrights,[20] poets,[21] authors,[22] actors[23] and broadcasters.[24]

There were always those at the Bar who 'just wanted the world to stop at the Judicature Act'.[25] In the words of Curran,

> When we were disentangling from the British connection, the legal profession as a whole were above all things anxious to preserve all that was possible of old forms and precedents. True to the motto on the King's Inns dining plate – *nolumus mutari* – our elders still hoped to carry on with the minimum change. The 'old gang' ... had, behind their own obsolescent and honourable loyalties, much timidity and an ingrained professional conservatism.[26]

There are many examples of members of the Bar strongly opposing change.[27] In 1962, Sean MacBride commented that '[l]awyers are traditionally slow to adjust themselves to changing circumstances, and on this score often incur criticism for being uncooperative'.[28] At a stormy general meeting of the Bar in 1990 one member of the Bar pointed out:

> The decisions of the Bar Council to install a new switchboard, to purchase the solicitors' building, to arrange life assurance, to subvent King's Inns, each and all of which many members had reasons for arguing against at the time.[29]

However, as this quote indicates, despite opposition in some quarters, the Bar pressed on and continually adapted to a changing world. As the century progressed, it was impacted by changes in geopolitics, technology, economics and social policy. The physical workplace is one area where the evolution of the profession is clearly evident.[30] One barrister said that the physical redevelopment

---

19 E.g., Dubhglas Mac Fhionnlaoich, Pádraig Ó Síocháin.   20 E.g., Denis Johnston, Malachi Muldoon, Richard Johnson, Kenneth Deale.   21 E.g., Donagh MacDonagh, Anthony Cronin. 22 E.g., Barbara Keating, Bernard Duffy, John M. Kelly.   23 E.g., Cecil Barror, Ralph Brereton Barry.   24 E.g., Rex Mackey, Conor A. Maguire.   25 B26.   26 C.P. Curran, *Under the receding wave* (Dublin, 1970), pp 122–3.   27 E.g., many resisted the proposed expansion of the Law Library in the 1990s.   28 MacBride to Ó Dálaigh, 30 Apr. 1962, UCDA P51/1 (42).   29 B.C.M., 21 Nov. 1990. The issue at this meeting was the Bar Council's negotiated contract with the Incorporated Council for Law Reporting. One effect would be to increase subscription levels.   30 Although the opening of the Courts of Criminal Justice complex at Parkgate Street was outside the time period for this book, a number of interviewees mentioned this as having 'led to a little of a fracturing of the Bar (e.g. B12). B15 said that before this change, 'you always had a cross pollinisation between the

of the Library was 'probably the biggest change' they had experienced.[31] While most were positive about the new developments,[32] others regretted the impact on the original Library complex; one lamented that said 'the Law Library is just a different place altogether.'[33]

A slower pace of work in the early decades of the century became unsustainable as legal practice became increasingly complex. As seen in chapter six, new areas of practice developed, while others fell away.[34] One barrister reflected on some of the changes he had perceived over a fifty-year career:

> When I was devilling and for years after that, the kind of practice we did was very different. Personal injuries actions were always jury actions. On the non jury side, a lot of cases involved the construction of documents and construction of Wills. The sort of commercial work that exists now, did not exist then on anything like the same scale. Discovery had not been discovered, which meant that cases were much shorter. A brief was always just what you could put under your arm. It was a brief. Now a brief needs a wheelbarrow to carry it round.[35]

Technological advances altered barristers' work practices. Several barristers associated new technologies with increased speed and a greater volume of written work. In the earlier decades of the century, briefs were slim, written pleadings were not expected and the volume of discovery documents was manageable. The advent of email altered dramatically the ways in which barristers and solicitors communicated, and the availability of digitised and electronic reports had an equalising effect. At the same time, this necessitated the development of new skills. A barrister who had been called in the early seventies observed that 'research through technology was an enormous change'. Asked if they welcomed the technological changes of the 1990s, this barrister replied '[w]elcome is the wrong word, I suppose. I just had to do it'.[36] Evidently the Law Library was quick to embrace new technologies and was ahead of other libraries in this regard. The Bar Council became more active towards the end of the century, and began hiring professional staff to serve the needs of the expanding Bar.

It was demonstrated in chapter four that the number of barristers increased as the century progressed. One consequence of this was that the social ties that bound members of the Bar were not as strong by the end of the century. It was no longer necessarily the case that all barristers knew one another. Several interviewees pointed out that this trend continued into the twenty-first century:

criminal practitioners and the civil practitioners.' 31 B27. 32 See p. 244. 33 B3. 34 E.g., in the early eighties, Casey observed that '[t]he outstanding development in constitutional law ... is the burgeoning of judicial review.' James Casey, 'Law and the legal system 1957–82' in Frank Litton (ed.), *Unequal achievement: the Irish experience 1957–1982* (Dublin, 1982), p. 271. See ch. 6. 35 'Ralph Sutton, SC, called to the Bar, July 1948', *B.R.* 4:3 (1999), 152. 36 B2.

> People don't know people anymore … when I came to the Bar you found all the busiest of people and the best known names at their desks in the Law Library and you clearly don't do that anymore.[37]

One barrister recalled that in the sixties and seventies, the most senior members of the profession were much more approachable for junior members, due to the small size of the Bar.[38] While the tradition that all members of the Bar had to provide advice to colleagues on request continued, as time went on, junior members were less likely to be familiar with the leaders at the Bar.

From the 1950s there was 'a steady increase in the use of specialised tribunals outside the regular court system'.[39] Several major tribunals of inquiry were established in the 1990s. The introduction of state-funded legal aid in the sixties had a major impact upon criminal practice.[40] This was cited by a number of barristers as one of the main changes in practices that they had witnessed. Circuit practice changed significantly over the century, with less emphasis on communal dining and staying together in hotels as a homogenous group.[41] The arrival of women barristers in 1921 and their gradually increasing presence and visibility over the next eighty years[42] was another area of significant change, as were the changes to professional regulation which resulted from external pressures in the eighties and nineties.[43] The Bar in the late 1990s was certainly a good deal more diverse than the Bar of the early twenties.

Thus the Irish Bar in the twentieth century can be characterised as outward-looking, connected, influential and evolving. Despite its frequent perception as 'ancient and venerable', or as old and stuffy, it has been constantly evolving. The Bar of 1999 looked very different from the Bar of 1921, and the past quarter of a century has witnessed further significant changes. One interviewee posed the question,

> So, are lawyers conservative? You bet they are. So, if you are looking for change, you'll find twenty good reasons why they won't.[44]

This reflects the fact that there were always those at the Bar who feared for the future of the profession, and it would appear that this tradition has endured into the twenty-first century. Discussions about solicitors' attendance rights, a fused profession, chambers and any proposed changes to practice were infused with worry and anxiety. However, despite feelings of being under siege since the 1980s, the Bar has continued to evolve and endure. Many of its traditions have altered to suit a twenty-first-century profession in a changing world, while others have remained intact.

---

37 B10.   38 B6.   39 Casey, 'Law and the legal system', p. 268. Examples included An Bord Pleanála, the Labour Court, the Employment Appeals Tribunal and the Criminal Injuries Compensation Tribunal.   40 Ch. 8.   41 Ch. 10.   42 Ch. 9.   43 Ch. 16.   44 B2.

In chapter two, we set the scene for this this book by describing what it was like to be a practicing barrister in the early 1920s in Ireland. The major upheavals (and minor adjustments) described in subsequent chapters rendered the Bar quite different eighty years later. By the 1990s, the number of barristers had grown and members no longer necessarily knew their colleagues well. The overcrowding in the Law Library was being alleviated by the development of new Library spaces in the neighbourhood. This facilitated barristers who found themselves dealing with increasingly complex cases and voluminous paperwork. Trials had lengthened, written pleadings were becoming the norm and some barristers were engaging in lengthy tribunals. Technology was making an impact – barristers were beginning to grapple with digital law reports, laptops and word processing, and email was starting to creep in. There were significantly more women at the Bar, working in a greater range of areas, and the number of women seniors was slowly starting to increase. The *Bar Review* was established in 1996 as the Bar's own periodical, and from 1995 the Law Library had its own webpage. The Bar Council became increasingly professionalised, more actively involved in regulating and representing the profession and providing new services to members. All of these developments in the 1990s reflected the wider social and economic changes taking place in the context of the nascent 'Celtic tiger' boom.

The barristers' profession was unique among Irish professions in many ways; the public nature of much of the work, the financial insecurity, the cementing of social bonds through traditions and rituals. Keane described it in the sixties as 'the Cinderella of the professions'.[45] It also differed from many overseas legal professions, with its communal workspace in the Law Library. One barrister who was interviewed for this book commented on what they thought made the barristers' profession unique:

> We have a huge responsibility and our huge responsibility is to the public and to our client … you're there for the whole country.[46]

Several interviewees expressed a similar public service ethic.

This book has considered the highs and lows of practice at the Bar, and has taken a multifaceted and interdisciplinary approach to constructing a history of the profession. In chapter one, it was pointed out that the gap between 'historical research and professional rhetoric'[47] must be bridged in order to understand the history of the Bar and its role in society.[48] By exploring first-person narratives of working at the Bar, along with primary source materials for the twentieth century, it is hoped that this book has gone some way towards bridging that gap.

---

45 Keane, 'The future of the Irish Bar', 381.   46 B3.   47 W. Wesley Pue, 'The use of history in the development of lawyers' mythologies' in Pue, *Lawyers' empire*, p. 26.   48 Ch. 1.

Bibliography

ARCHIVAL SOURCES

National Archives of Ireland:
Department of Foreign Affairs: NAI DFA/6/434/479; NAI DFA/1/GR/1100; NAI DFA/5/316/1/47; NAI DFA/6/408/222 I
Department of Finance: NAI FIN/1/665; NAI FIN/1/3873; NAI FIN/COMP/2/28/476
Department of Justice: NAI JUS/90/113/4; NAI 2008/117/607
Department of An Taoiseach: NAI TSCH/3/S16108 A; NAI TSCH/3/S13867; NAI TSCH/3/S6694 B/62; NAI TSCH/3/S4290; NAI TSCH/3/S8613
Office of the Attorney General: NAI AGO/2002/16/475; NAI 2003/4/7; NAI 2005/159/8; NAI 2009/74/742; NAI 2011/17/871
Private Papers: NAI PRIV1367/11

UCD Archives:
UCDA LA/56 (James Meenan)
UCDA P4 (Hugh Kennedy)
UCDA P51 (Cearbhall Ó Dálaigh)
UCDA P74 (P.J. McEnery)
UCDA P190 (John A. Costello)
UCDA P152 (George Gavan Duffy)
UCDA P237 (Declan Costello)
UCDA P261 (RTÉ radio scripts)
UCDA P291 (John Hearne)

King's Inns Benchers' minutes
King's Inns papers
Transcripts from interview recordings
Minutes of the Bar Council
Minutes of the Bar Council Library Committee

OFFICIAL PUBLICATIONS

Commissioners of Public Works for Ireland, *Reports* (1924–34)
Committee on Court Practice and Procedure, *Fourteenth interim report. Liability of barristers and solicitors for professional negligence* (Dublin, 1971)
Committee on Court Practice and Procedure, *Jury trial in civil actions. Jury challenges: third and fourth interim reports of the Committee on Court Practice and Procedure* (Dublin, 1966)

Committee on Court Practice and Procedure, *Thirteenth interim report. The solicitor's right of audience* (Dublin, 1971)
Dáil Éireann debates
Dáil Éireann, *Miontuairisc an chead Dála, 1919–1921: Minutes of proceedings of the first parliament of the Republic of Ireland, 1919–1921* (Dublin, 1922)
Department of Justice, *Liosta de tharmaí dlíthiúla a bhaineas le dlí conradh, maraon lena n-iontamhail sa Ghaeilge* (Dublin, 1950)
Department of Justice, *Téarmaí dlí; Béarla-Gaeilge, Gaeilge-Béarla* (Dublin, 1959)
Fair Trade Commission, *Report of study into restrictive practices in the legal profession* (Dublin, 1990)
Law Reform Commission, *Report on public inquiries including tribunals of inquiry* (LRC 73–2005)
Office of the Attorney General, *Annual report 1996–7* (Dublin, 1997)
Official Gazette of the Colony and Protectorate of Kenya
Report of the committee on the constitution (Dublin, 1967)
Report of the judiciary committee (Dublin, 1923)
Report of the tribunal of inquiry into the Kerry babies case (Dublin, 1985)
Report of the tribunal of inquiry on the fire at the Stardust, Artane, Dublin on the 14th February, 1981 (Dublin, 1982)
Republic of Botswana Government Gazette
Seanad Éireann debates

LEGAL SOURCES

Constitutions and Legislation:
Constitution of the Irish Free State (1922)
Bunreacht na hÉireann (1937)
Supreme Court of Judicature Ireland Act 1877
Four Courts Library Act 1894
Sex Disqualification (Removal) Act 1919
Government of Ireland Act 1920
Restoration of Order in Ireland Act 1920
Courts of Justice Act 1924
Courts of Justice Act 1926
Legal Practitioners (Qualification) Act 1929
Workmen's Compensation Act 1934
Courts of Justice Act 1936
Seanad Electoral (Panel Members) Act 1947
Restrictive Trade Practices Act 1953
Courts of Justice Act 1953
Courts (Supplemental Provisions) Act 1961
Courts Act 1964
Restrictive Practices Act 1972
Statute Law Revision Act 1983

Criminal Evidence Act 1992
Courts and Court Officers Act 1995
Employment Equality Act 1998
Courts Act 1998
Public Health (Tobacco) (Amendment) Act 2004

Statutory Instruments:
Rules of the Superior Courts 1926
Circuit Court (New Circuits) Order 1937
Circuit Court (New Circuits) Order 1960
Circuit Court (Alteration of Circuits) Order 1964
Circuit Court (Alteration of Circuits) Order 1969
Circuit Court (Alteration of Circuits) Order 1978
Rules of the Superior Courts 1986
Circuit Court (Alteration of Circuits) Order 1999

Case law:
Airey v. Ireland (1973) ECtHR 6289/73
Attorney General v. X [1992] IESC 1
Bart v. USA (1955) 349 U.S. 219
Bolling v. Sharpe (1954) 347 U.S. 497
Brown v. Board of Education (1954) 347 U.S. 483
Cotter and McDermott v. the Minister for Social Welfare and the Attorney General (1990)
     C.J.E.U C-377/89
Crotty v. An Taoiseach [1987] IESC 4
D.P.P. v. Barnes [2006] IECCA 165
Dunne v. O'Neill [1974] I.R. 180
Emspak v. USA (1955) 349 U.S. 190
Fikes v. Alabama (1957) 372 U.S. 191
Foy v. an t-Ard Chlaraitheoir, Ireland and the Attorney General [2012] 2 I.R. 1
Hall v. Simons [2002] 1 A.C. 615
Hernandez v. Texas (1954) 347 U.S. 475
HMW v. Ireland [1997] 2 I.R. 142
Hedley Byrne and Co. v. Heller and partners [1964] A.C. 465
Hyland v. Minister for Social Welfare [1989] I.R. 624
Ireland v. The United Kingdom (1977), (2018) ECtHR 5310/71
Kelly v. Breen (unrep., H.C. 4 Apr. 1978, Hamilton J)
Norris v. Ireland (1983) ECtHR 10581/83
O'Crowley v. The Minister for Justice and the Minister for Finance [1935] I.R. 536
Open Door and Well Woman v. Ireland (1988) ECtHR 14234/88
Pennsylvania v. Nelson (1956) 350 U.S. 497
Peters v. Hobby (1955) 349 U.S. 376
Quinn v. USA (1955) 349 U.S 155
Rees v. Sinclair [1974] 1 N.Z.L.R.
Rayners v. Belgium (1974) C.J.E.U. Case 2/74

Rondel v. Worsley [1966] EWCA Civ J1020-2; [1967] 3 W.L.R. 1666
Saif Ali v. Sydney Mitchell [1980] A.C. 198
State (Gallagher, Shatter) v. Toirleach de Valera (unrep., S.C. 8 Feb. 1990)
Sweezy v. New Hampshire (1957) 354 U.S. 234
The King (Little and Ó hUadhaigh) v. Cooper 1924) 58 I.L.T.S.J. 316
Watkins v. USA (1957) 354 U.S. 178

NEWSPAPERS AND PERIODICALS

Belfast News Letter
Cork Examiner
Daily News
Daily Telegraph
Donegal Democrat
Donegal News
Drogheda Independent
Dublin Evening Telegraph
Evening Herald
Examiner
Fermanagh Herald
Freeman's Journal
Hibernian Law Journal
Irish Examiner
Irish Independent
Irish Law Times and Solicitors' Journal
Irish Law Times (new series)

Irish Press
Irish Times
Leader
Magill
Mayo News
Meath Chronicle
Skibbereen Eagle
Strabane Chronicle
Sunday Independent
Sunday Press
The Argus
The Guardian
The Leader
The Times
Weekly Irish Times
Western Mail
Women Lawyers' Journal

SECONDARY WORKS

Abel, Richard, 'Lawyer self-regulation and the public interest: a reflection', *Legal Ethics* 20:1 (2017)

Abel, Richard L., *English lawyers between market and state* (Oxford, 2003)

Abel-Smith, Brian and Robert Stevens, *Lawyers and the courts: a sociological study of the English legal system, 1750–1965* (London, 1967)

Abrahams, Sidney, 'The colonial legal service and the administration of justice in colonial dependencies', *Journal of Comparative Legislation and International Law* 30:3–4 (1948)

Acker, Joan, 'Hierarchies, jobs, bodies: a theory of gendered organisations', *Gender & Society* 4:2 (1990)

Acker, Joan, 'Inequality regimes gender, class, and race in organisations', *Gender & Society* 20:4 (2006)

Acland, Lucinda and Kate Broomfield, *First: 100 years of women in law* (London, 2019)

Adams, Bernard, *Denis Johnston, a life* (Dublin, 2002)

Aiken, Síobhra, *Spiritual wounds: trauma, testimony and the Irish Civil War* (Newbridge, 2022)

Akenson, D.H. and I.F. Fallin, 'The Irish Civil War and the drafting of the Free State constitution: the drafting process', *Éire-Ireland* 5:2 (1970)

Albisetti, James, 'Portia ante Portas: women and the legal profession in Europe, ca. 1870–1925', *Journal of Social History* 33:4 (2000)

Allott, Anthony N., 'The *Journal of African Law*, 1957–96: then and now,' *Journal of African Law* 40:2 (1996)

American Bar Association, *Visit to England, Scotland and Ireland 1924, memorial volume* (New York, 1926)

Andrews, David, *Kingstown republican* (Dublin, 2007)

Anyangwe, Carlson Emmanuel Wunde, 'The administration of justice in a bi-jural country: the United Republic of Cameroon' (PhD, University of London, 1979)

Arnold, Bruce, *Jack Lynch: hero in crisis* (Dublin, 2001)

Ashley, Louise, 'Making a difference? The use (and abuse) of diversity management at the UK's elite law firms', *Work, Employment and Society* 24:4 (2010)

Aston, Jennefer, 'Electronic publishing', *Bar Review* 2:6 (1997)

Aston, Jennefer, 'From Law Library Society to law library: the first 180 years, 1816–1996', *Legal Information Management* 11 (Cambridge, 2011)

Auchmuty, Rosemary and Erika Rackley, 'The women's legal landmarks project: celebrating 100 years of women in the law in the UK and Ireland', *Legal Information Management* 16 (2016)

Bacik, Ivana, 'Averil Deverell', Trinity Monday Memorial Discourse, 25 Apr. 2022

Bacik, Ivana, Cathryn Costello and Eileen Drew, *Gender injustice: feminising the legal professions?* (Dublin, 2003)

Backhouse, Constance and W. Wesley Pue (eds), *The promise and perils of law: lawyers in Canadian history* (Toronto, 2009)

Backhouse, Constance, '"A revolution in numbers": Ontario feminist lawyers in the formative years 1970s to the 1990s' in Backhouse and Pue (eds), *The promise and perils of law* (Toronto, 2009)

Backhouse, Constance, '"To open the way for others of my sex": Clara Brett Martin's career as Canada's first woman lawyer', *Canadian Journal of Women and the Law* 1 (1985)

Backhouse, Constance, 'What if? career paths not taken: Claire L'Heureux-Dubé and politics', *Canadian Journal of Law & Society / Revue Canadienne Droit et Société* 29:2 (2014)

Baker, George Blaine and Jim Phillips (eds), *Essays in the history of Canadian law: in honour of R.C.B. Risk* (Toronto, 1999)

Baker, John, *The legal profession and the common law: historical essays* (London, 1986)

Baker, J.H., *The common law tradition: lawyers, books and the law* (London, 2000)

Bakkalbasioglu, Esra, 'How to access elites when textbook methods fail: challenges of purposive sampling and advantages of using interviewees as "fixers"', *The Qualitative Report* 25:3 (2020)

Bar Council [UK], *Barristers' working lives: a second biennial survey of the Bar* (London, 2013)

Bar Council, *Code of conduct for the Bar of Ireland, adopted by the Bar – 30th July 1985*

Bar Council [UK], *Snapshot: the experience of self-employed women at the Bar* (London, 2015)

Barker, David, *A history of Australian legal education* (Australia, 2017)

Barmes, Lizzie and Kate Malleson, 'The legal profession as gatekeeper to the judiciary: design faults in measures to enhance diversity', *Modern Law Review* 74:2 (2011)

Barr, Rebecca Anne, 'Rape narratives, women's testimony and Irish law in Louise O'Neil's *Asking for it* and Winnie Li's *Dark chapter*' in Hanna and McNulty (eds), *Law and literature: the Irish case* (Liverpool, 2022)

Barry, Frank and John O'Dowd, 'The age of tribunals', *Studies* 90:357 (2001)

Bartholomew, Paul C., *The Irish judiciary* (Dublin, 1971)

Bewley, Charles, *Memoirs of a wild goose* (Dublin, 1989)

Bingham, Roger, 'Overseas aid goes legal?', *New Law Journal* 142:6568 (1992)

Birkenhead *Famous trials of history* (New York, 1926)

Blackwell, M., 'Taking silk: an empirical study of the award of queen's counsel status, 1981–2015', *Modern Law Review* 78 (2015)

Boon, Andy and John Flood, 'Trials of strength: the reconfiguration of litigation as a contested terrain', *Law & Society Review* 33:3 (1999)

Bourdieu, Pierre, 'The forms of capital' in John G. Richardson (ed.), *A handbook of therory and research for the sociology of education* (New York, 1986)

Bourdieu, Pierre, *Distinction: a social critique of the judgement of taste* (London, 1986)

Bourke, Mary, 'The education of the Irish barrister', *Justice – Irish Student Law Review* (1966)

Bourne, J., and M. Mossman, *Helena Normanton and the opening of the Bar to women* (Hampshire, 2016)

Bowen-Rowlands, Ernest, *Seventy-two years at the Bar: a memoir* (London, 1924)

Bowker, A.E., *A lifetime with the law* (London, 1961)

Boyle, Kevin and Marie McGonagle, *A report on press freedom and libel* (Dublin, 1988)

Brand, Paul, 'The birth and early development of a colonial judiciary: the judges of the lordship of Ireland, 1210–1377' in W.N. Osborough (ed.), *Explorations in law and history* (Dublin, 1995)

Brand, Paul, 'The early history of the legal profession of the lordship of Ireland, 1250–1350' in Daire Hogan and W.N. Osborough (eds), *Brehons, serjeants and attorneys* (Dublin, 1990)

Brand, Paul, *The origins of the English legal profession* (Oxford, 1992)

Brayden, W.H., *Republican courts in Ireland* (Chicago, 1920) (reprint of W.H. Brayden, 'Sinn Féin courts in operation', *American Bar Association Journal* 6:4 (1920))

Brennan, Eilis, 'Moving on', *Bar Review* 21:2 (2016)

Brett, C.E.B., 'Two eighteenth-century provincial attorneys: Matthew Brett and Jack Brett' in Hogan and Osborough (eds), *Brehons, serjeants and attorneys* (Dublin, 1990)

Brockman, Joan and Dorothy E. Chunn, 'A new order of things: women's entry into the legal profession in British Columbia', *The Advocate* 60:3 (2002)

Broderick, Eugene, *John Hearne: architect of the 1937 constitution of Ireland* (Dublin, 2017)

Brooks, Christopher, *Lawyers, litigation and English society since 1450* (London, 1998)

Brundage, James A., *The medieval origins of the legal profession: canonists, civilians, and courts* (Chicago, 2008)

Brunet, Mélanie, "'Good government, without him, is well-nigh impossible": training future (male) lawyers for politics in Ontario, Quebec and Nova Scotia, 1920–1960' in Backhouse and Pue (eds), *The promise and perils of law* (Toronto, 2009)

Bryan, Audrey, '(In)equality of opportunity and educational reform in Ireland in the sixties' in James Kelly and Susan Hegarty (eds), *Schools and schooling, 1650–2000: new perspectives on the history of education – the eighth Seamus Heaney lectures* (Dublin, 2017)

Burley, Jenny, 'Legal aid and family law in Ireland', *Alternative Law Journal* 25:4 (2000)

Bush, J.A. and A. Wijffels (eds), *Learning the law: teaching and the transmission of law in England, 1150–1900* (London, 1999)

Butler, Andrew and Rory O'Connell, 'A critical analysis of Ireland's Constitutional Review Group report', *Irish Jurist* 33:1 (1998)

Cahillane, Laura and Donal Coffey (eds), *The centenary of the Irish Free State constitution: constituting a polity?* (London, 2023)

Cahillane, Laura, *Drafting the Irish Free State constitution* (Manchester, 2016)

Cairnduff, Maureen, *Who's who in Ireland: the influential 1000* (Dublin, 1984)

Cairns, John, *Law, lawyers, and humanism: selected essays on the history of Scots law*, volume 1 (Edinburgh, 2015)

Capper, David, 'The demise of the advocate's immunity', *Northern Ireland Legal Quarterly* 57 (2006)

Carney, Claire, 'The growth of legal aid in the Republic of Ireland – II', *Irish Jurist* 14:2 (1979)

Carroll MacNeill, Jennifer, *The politics of judicial selection in Ireland* (Dublin, 2016)

Carswell, Robert, 'Founding a legal system: the early judiciary of Northern Ireland' in Larkin and Dawson (eds), *Lawyers, the law and history* (Dublin, 2013)

Carswell, Robert, '*Eheu fugaces*: fifty years in the Northern Ireland courts' in Hogan and Kenny (eds), *Changes in practice and law* (Dublin, 2013)

Carthy, Suzanne, 'Inequality regimes and long hours a mixed methods study of gender inequality in the solicitors' profession in Ireland' (PhD, UCD, 2018)

Casey, James, 'Law and the legal system 1957–82' in Frank Litton (ed.), *Unequal achievement: the Irish experience 1957–1982* (Dublin, 1982)

Casey, James, 'Republican courts in Ireland 1919–1922', *Irish Jurist* 5:2 (1970)

Casey, James, 'The genesis of the Dáil Courts', *Irish Jurist* 9:2 (1974)

Casey, James, *The Irish law officers* (Dublin, 1996)

Chan, Elizabeth, 'Women trailblazers in the law: the New Zealand women judges oral histories project', *Victoria University of Wellington Law Review* 45 (2014)

Chaserant, Camille and Sophie Harnay, 'Self-regulation of the legal profession and quality in the market for legal services: an economic analysis of lawyers' reputation', *European Journal of Law and Economics* 39:2 (2015)

Clancy, Tomás, 'The Four Courts buildings and the development of an independent Bar of Ireland' in C. Costello (ed.), *The Four Courts* (Dublin, 1996)

Clancy, P., *College entry in focus: a fourth national survey of access to higher education* (Dublin, 2001)

Clarke, Frank, 'A view from the Bar', *Bar Review* 3:3 (1998)

Clarke, Gemma, 'Violence against women in the Irish Civil War, 1922–3: gender-based harm in global perspective', *Irish Historical Studies* 44:165 (2020)

Cochrane, A., 'Illusions of power: interviewing local elites', *Environment and Planning A* 30:12 (1998)

Cocks, Raymond, *Foundations of the modern Bar* (London, 1983)

Coen, Mark, '"Radical reforming legislation" or "the politics of illusion"?: enacting the Criminal Evidence Act 1992', *Dublin University Law Journal* 43:1 (2022)

Coen, Mark, Niamh Howlin, Colette Barry and John Lynch, *Judges and juries in Ireland: an empirical study* (Dublin, 2020)

Coffey, Donal, 'The judiciary of the Irish Free State', *Dublin University Law Journal* 33:1 (2011)

Coffey, Donal, *Drafting the Irish constitution, 1935–37: transnational influences in interwar Europe* (London, 2018)

Cole, J.S.R. and W.N. Denison, *Tanganyika: the development of its laws and constitution* (London, 1964),

Cole, J.S.R., *Cases on criminal law* (Dublin, 1975)

Cole, J.S.R., *Irish cases on evidence* (Dublin, 1972)

Competition Authority, *Competition in professional services: solicitors & barristers* (Dublin, 2006)

Comyn, James, 'Notebook', *Irish Law Times* (ns) 7 (1989)

Comyn, James, *If your lordship pleases: legal recollections* (Dublin, 1996)

Comyn, James, *Irish at law: a selection of famous and unusual cases* (London, 1983)

Comyn, James, *Leave to appeal: further legal memoirs* (Dublin, 1994)

Comyn, James, *Lost causes* (London, 1982)

Comyn, James, *Summing it up: memoirs of an Irishman at law in England* (Dublin, 1991)

Comyn, James, *Their friends at court* (Chichester 1973)

Comyn, James, *Watching brief: further memoirs of an Irishman at law in England* (Dublin, 1993)

Conley, John M., 'Tales of diversity: lawyers' narratives of racial equity in private firms', *Law & Social Inquiry* 31:4 (2006)

Connell, Peter, *Eamonn Duggan counsel to the revolution* (Meath, 2021)

Connolly, Alpha and Betty Hilliard, 'The legal profession' in Alpha Connolly (ed.), *Gender and the law in Ireland* (Dublin, 1993)

Conroy, Pauline, 'Employment policy' in Suzanne Quin and Bairbre Redmond (eds), *Disability and social policy in Ireland* (Dublin, 2003)

Coolahan, John, 'The impact and aftermath of the free education policy initiative,' in J. Harford (ed.), *Education for all?* (Oxford, 2018)

Corfield, P.J., *Power and the professions in Britain, 1700–1850* (London, 2000)

Costello, Caroline (ed.), *The Four Courts: 200 years* (Dublin, 1996)

Costello, Declan, 'Christopher Preston', *Irish Law Times* 2:4 (1984)

Cox, Steven and William Canby, 'Consumer information and the pricing of legal services', *Journal of Industrial Economics* 30 (1982)

Crotty, Raymond, *A radical's response* (Dublin, 1988)

Cukwurah, A.O., *The settlement of boundary disputes in international law* (Manchester, 1965)

Curley, Vanessa and Sarah Foley, 'Celebrating a century of women in the law: using historical exhibitions to enhance user engagement and promote a library service', *Legal Information Management* 21:1 (2021)

Curran, C.P., *Under the receding wave* (Dublin, 1970)

Curran, John Adye, *Reminiscences of John Adye Curran KC, late county court judge and chairman of quarter sessions* (London, 1915)

Daly, Tom, 'Hugh Kennedy: Ireland's (quietly) towering nation-maker' in Rehan Abeyratne and Iddo Porat (eds), *Towering judges: a comparative study of constitutional judges* (Cambridge, 2021)

Davitt, Cahir, 'The civil jurisdiction of the courts of justice in the Irish republic 1920–1922', *Irish Jurist* 3:1 (1968)

Dawson, N.M., 'The rank of queen's counsel: judicial perspectives', *King's Law Journal* 24 (2013)

de Búitléir, Dónal and Frances Ruane (eds), *Governance and policy in Ireland: essays in honour of Miriam Hederman* (Dublin, 2003)

de Búrca, Maurice, *Murder at Marlhill* (Dublin, 1993)

de Búrca, Maurice, *The GAA: a history* (Dublin, 1980)

De Vere White, Terence *The road of excess, a life of Isaac Butt* (Dublin, 1946)

De Vere White, Terence, *Kevin O'Higgins* (Tralee, 1966)

De Vere White, Terence, *A fretful midge* (London, 1957)

Deale, Kenneth, *Beyond any reasonable doubt? A book of murder trials* (Dublin, 1971)

Deech, R., 'How the Legal Services Act 2007 has affected regulation of the Bar', *Legal Information Management* 11 (2011)

Delany, V.T.H., *Christopher Palles, lord chief baron of her majesty's court of exchequer in Ireland, 1874–1916* (Dublin, 1960)

Delany, V.T.H., *The administration of justice in Ireland* (2nd ed., Dublin, 1965)

Delany, V.T.H., *The administration of justice in Ireland* (4th ed., Dublin, 1975)

Delany, V.T.H., 'Law and custom in Ghana', (1961) 95 *I.L.T.S.J.* 294

Denny, Kevin, 'What did abolishing university fees in Ireland do?' UCD Geary Institute discussion paper series, May 2010: www.ucd.ie/geary/static/publications/working papers/gearywp201026.pdf.

Desmond, Margaret, 'Methodological challenges posed in studying an elite in the field', *Area* 36:3 (2004)

Devereaux, Simon, 'Arts of public performance: barristers and actors in Georgian England' in David Lemmings (ed.), *Crime, courtrooms and the public sphere in Britain, 1700–1850* (London, 2012)

Devlin, Richard F., 'Regulating lawyers: north American perspectives and problematics', *The International Lawyer* 50:3 (2017)

Dickson, Brice, *The Irish Supreme Court* (Oxford, 2019)

DiMaggio, Paul and Walter Powell, 'The iron cage revisited: institutional isomorphism and collective rationality in organisational fields' in Paul DiMaggio & Walter Powell (eds), *The new institutionalism in organizational analysis* (Chicago, 1991)

Dougherty, Jane Elizabeth, 'From invisible child to abject maternal body: crises of knowledge in Edna O'Brien's *Down by the river*', *Critique: Studies in Contemporary Fiction* 43(4) (2012)

Dowling, John, 'Why you should consider your pension requirements now', *Bar Review* 2:2 (1997)

Drachman, Virginia, *Sisters in law: women lawyers in modern American history* (Cambridge, MA, 1998)

Duffy, Bernard, *The rocky road* (Dublin, 1929)

Duffy, Bernard, *Oriel* (London, 1918)

Duman, Daniel, 'The English Bar in the Georgian era' in Wilfrid Prest (ed.), *Lawyers in early modern Europe and America* (London, 1981)

Duman, Daniel, *The English and colonial Bars in the nineteenth century* (London, 1983)

Earls FitzGerald, Thomas, *Combatants and civilians in revolutionary Ireland, 1918–1923* (London, 2021)

Edge, Peter W., 'Lawyers' empires: the anglicisation of Manx Bar and judiciary', *International Journal of the Legal Profession* 19 (1994–5)

Egerton, George, 'The anatomy of political memoir: findings and conclusions' in George Egerton (ed.), *Political memoir: essays on the politics of memory* (London, 1994)

Elgie, Robert, Adam McAuley and Eoin O'Malley, 'The (not-so-surprising) non-partisanship of the Irish Supreme Court', *Irish Political Studies* 33:1 (2018)

Eliott, Marianne, *Theobald Wolfe Tone* (2nd ed., Liverpool, 2012)

Ellett, Rachel L., 'Courts and the emergence of statehood in post-colonial Africa', *Northern Ireland Legal Quarterly* 63:3 (2020)

Enright, Seán, *After the rising: soldiers, lawyers, and trials of the Irish Revolution* (Dublin, 2015)

Enright, Seán, *Easter Rising 1916: the trials* (Dublin, 2014)

Epstein, Cynthia Fuchs, *Women in law* (New York, 1993)

Fallon, Aengus, 'The foundational legislation of the Garda Síochána (1922–1926)', *Irish Jurist* 62 (2019)

Fallon, Aengus, 'Statute law and the foundations of the Irish Free State (1922–1926)' (PhD, UCD, 2019)

Fanning, Ronan, *The Irish Department of Finance, 1922–58* (Dublin, 1978)

Faris, Neil, 'The Bar in Northern Ireland and the royal commission on legal services', *Northern Ireland Legal Quarterly* 39:3 (1988)

Farrell, Brian, 'The drafting of the Irish Free State constitution I', *Irish Jurist* 5 (1970)

Farrell, Brian, 'The legislation of a "revolutionary" assembly: Dáil decrees, 1919–1922', *Irish Jurist* 10:1 (1975)

Feingold, Ellen, *Colonial justice and decolonization in the High Court of Tanzania, 1920–1971* (Cambridge, 2018)

Ferguson, Kenneth (ed.), *King's Inns barristers, 1868–2004* (Dublin, 2005)

Ferriter, Cian, 'On-line: an introduction to electronic legal research', *Bar Review* 2:1 (1997)

Ferriter, Cian, 'The future of law', *Bar Review* 2:5 (1997)

Ferriter, Cian, 'The virtual Law Library', *Bar Review* 1:1 (1996)

Ferriter, Diarmaid and Susannah Riordan (eds), *Years of turbulence: the Irish Revolution and its aftermath* (Dublin, 2015)

Ferriter, Diarmaid, *A nation and not a rabble: the Irish Revolution 1913–1923* (London, 2015)

Ferriter, Diarmaid, *Between two hells: the Irish Civil War* (London, 2021)

Fewer, Michael, *The battle of the Four Courts: the first three days of the Irish Civil War* (London, 2018)

Figgis, Darrell, *The Irish constitution. Explained by Darrell Figgis* (Dublin, 1922)

Fine, Ben, *Theories of social capital: researchers behaving badly* (London, 2010)

Fitzpatrick, Peter, *The mythology of modern law* (London, 1992)

Flanagan, J.R., *The Munster Circuit: tales, trials and traditions* (London, 1880)

Flood, John, 'Traditions, symbols, and the challenges of researching the legal profession: the case of the cab rank rule and the Bar's responses', *International Journal of the Legal Profession* 29:1 (2022)

Flood, John and Avis Whyte, 'Straight there, no detours: direct access to barristers', *International Journal of the Legal Profession* 16:3 (2009)

Flood, John and M. Hviid, *The cab rank rule: its meaning and purpose in the new legal services market* (London, 2013)

Foster, Gavin, *The Irish Civil War and society: politics, class, and conflict* (Basingstoke, 2015)

Foucault, Michel, 'Intellectuals and power' in D.F. Bouchard (ed.), *Language, counter-memory, practice: selected essays and interviews by Michel Foucault* (Oxford, 1977)

Foxton, David, *Revolutionary lawyers: Sinn Féin and crown courts in Ireland and Britain, 1916–23* (Dublin, 2008)

Free Legal Advice Centres, *The closed door: a report on civil legal aid services in Ireland* (Dublin, 1989)

Freidson, Eliot, 'The theory of professions: state of the art' in Robert Dingwall and Philip Lewis (eds), *The sociology of the professions: lawyers, doctors and others* (London, 1983)

Freidson, Eliot, *Profession of medicine: a study of the sociology of applied knowledge* (Chicago, 1988)

Friedman, M., *Capitalism and freedom* (Chicago, 1962)

Friedmann, Gretchen, *The Treaty: the gripping story of the negotiations that brought about Irish independence and led to the Civil War* (Dublin, 2021)

Gageby, Patrick, 'Was there a criminal Bar and what happened to any such tradition?' in Daire Hogan and Colum Kenny (eds), *Changes in practice and law* (Dublin, 2013)

Gamble, Charles, *Solicitors in Ireland: 1607–1921: the Incorporated Law Society's work* (Dublin, 1921)

Gannon, Darragh and Fearghal McGarry, 'Remembering 1922' in Darragh Gannon and Fearghal McGarry (eds), *Ireland, 1922: independence, partition, civil war* (Dublin, 2022)

Gannon, Darragh and Fearghal McGarry, *Ireland, 1922: independence, partition, civil war* (Dublin, 2022)

Garahy, John, 'A Trinity of women: the first women solicitors in Ireland', First 100 years project: https://first100years.org.uk/a-trinity-of-women-the-first-women-solicitors-in-ireland/

Garvin, Tom, *1922: The birth of Irish democracy* (Dublin, 1996)

Geoghegan, Hugh, 'The changing face of the circuits during the past twenty-five years' in Daire Hogan and Colum Kenny (eds), *Changes in practice and law* (Dublin, 2013)

Geoghegan, Hugh, 'The relationship of the attorney general to Bar and bench' in Bláthna Ruane, Jim O'Callaghan, David Banville and John L. Murray (eds), *Law and government: a tribute to Rory Brady* (Dublin, 2014)

Geoghegan, Hugh, 'Three judges of the Supreme Court of the Irish Free State: their backgrounds, personalities and mindsets' in Larkin and Dawson (eds), *Lawyers, the law and history* (Dublin, 2013)

Geoghegan, Mary Finlay, 'The Honorable Society of King's Inns: developments in legal education, 1988–2013' in Daire Hogan and Colum Kenny (eds), *Changes in practice and law* (Dublin, 2013)

Geoghegan, Patrick, *1798 and the Irish Bar* (Dublin, 1998)

Geoghegan, Patrick, 'Daniel O'Connell and the law' in Felix M. Larkin and N.M. Dawson (eds), *Lawyers, the law and history* (Dublin, 2013)

Geoghegan, Patrick, 'Daniel O'Connell and the Magee trials, 1813' in M. Brown and S.P. Donlan (eds), *The laws and other legalities of Ireland, 1689–1850* (Farnham, 2011)

Gibney, John and Kate O'Malley, *The handover: Dublin Castle and the British withdrawal from Ireland, 1922* (Dublin, 2022)

Gibney, John and Zoë Reid, *The Treaty: records from the archives* (Dublin, 2021)

Gilb, C.L., *Hidden hierarchies: the professions and government* (New York, 1966)

Gill, Garrett Edward, 'A half-century in the Law Library', *Irish Law Times* 10 (1992)

Gill, Garrett Edward, 'Ralph Sutton, SC, called to the Bar, July 1948', *B.R.* 4:3 (1999)

Girard, Philip, *Lawyers and legal culture in British North America: Beamish Murdoch of Halifax* (Toronto, 2015)

Glazer, Penina Migdal and Miriam Slater, *Unequal colleagues: the entrance of women into the professions 1890–1940* (New Brunswick, 1987)

Godden-Rasul, Nikki, 'Portraits of women of the law: re-envisioning gender, law and the legal professions in law schools', *Legal Studies* 39:3 (2019)

Golding, G.M., *George Gavan Duffy 1882–1951* (Dublin, 1992)

Goldthorpe, Liz, 'First woman to practise as a barrister in Ireland and the (then) United Kingdom, Averil Deverell, 1921' in G. Rackley and R. Auchmuty (eds), *Women's legal landmarks* (Oxford, 2019)

Goulandris, Atalanta, *The enterprising barrister: organisation, culture and changing professionalism* (Oxford, 2020)

Grattan, Henry, *Memoirs of the life and times of the Rt Hon Henry Grattan* (London, 1839)

Hagan, John and Fiona Kay, *Gender in practice: a study of lawyers' lives* (New York, 1995)

Hale, Brenda, '100 years of women in the law: from Bertha Cave to Brenda Hale', delivered 20 Mar. 2019, King's College London: www.supremecourt.uk/docs/speech-190320.pdf

Hale, Leslie, *John Philpot Curran: his life and times* (London, 1958)

Hall, Eamonn G., *The superior courts of law: 'official' law reporting in Ireland, 1866–2006* (Dublin, 2007)

Hall, Eamonn G. and Daire Hogan, *The Law Society of Ireland, 1852–2002: portrait of a profession* (Dublin, 2002)

Hall, Eamonn G., 'The modern era: Blackhall Place, rights of audience and court dress, delays and reforms in the legal system' in Eamonn Hall and Daire Hogan (eds), *The Law Society of Ireland* (Dublin, 2002)

Hall, Eamonn, 'Mr Solicitor', *Law Society Gazette* 99:3 (April 2005)

Halpérin, Jean-Louise, 'For a renewed history of lawyers', *American Journal of Legal History* 56:1 (2016)

Hamilton, Liam, *Report of the tribunal of inquiry into the beef processing industry* (Dublin, 1994)

Hanna, Adam and Eugene McNulty (eds), *Law and literature: the Irish case* (Liverpool, 2022)

Hanna, Adam and Eugene McNulty, 'Introduction. Law and literature: the Irish case' in Hanna and McNulty (eds), *Law and literature* (Liverpool, 2022)

Hanna, Alan, *Poetry, politics, and the law in modern Ireland* (New York, 2022)

Hanna, J., 'The bench and Bar of Ireland in the nineteenth century', *American Bar Association Journal* 22:11 (1936)

Hardiman, Ann-Marie, 'Father of the Bar', *Bar Review* 27:5 (2022)

Harford, Judith (ed.), *Education for all?: the legacy of free post-primary education in Ireland* (Oxford, 2018)

Hargreaves-Mawdsley, William Norman, *A history of legal dress in Europe until the end of the eighteenth century* (Oxford, 1963)

Harman Akenson, Donald, 'The Irish, ethnic studies and the historiography of South Africa' in Donald Harman Akenson, *Occasional papers on the Irish in South Africa* (Grahamstown, SA, 1991)

Hart, A.R., 'The king's serjeants at law in Ireland: a short history' in Osborough (ed.), *Explorations in law and history* (Dublin, 1995)

Hart, A.R., *A history of the Bar and inn of court of Northern Ireland* (Belfast, 2013)

Hart, A.R., *A history of the king's serjeants at law in Ireland: honour rather than advantage?* (Dublin, 2000)

Harte, Liam (ed.), *A history of Irish autobiography* (Cambridge, 2018)

Harte, Liam, 'History, text, and society in Colm Tóibín's *The heather blazing*', *New Hibernia Review* 6:4 (Winter, 2002)

Healy, Maurice, *The old Munster Circuit: a book of memories and traditions* (Dublin, 1939)

Heaney, Seamus, *Writer and righter: fourth IHRC annual human rights lecture, 9 December 2009* (Dublin, 2010)

Hennessy, Dermot, 'How to use the internet effectively for legal research', *Irish Law Times* 15 (1997)

Heuston, R.V.F., 'Frances Elizabeth Moran', *Dublin University Law Journal* 11 (1989)

Hewitt, Alan, 'The regulation and education of the solicitors' profession in Northern Ireland, 1976–2002' in Daire Hogan and Colum Kenny (eds), *Changes in practice and law* (Dublin, 2013)

Hewitt, Alan, *The Law Society of Northern Ireland: a history* (Belfast, 2010)

Hill, Jacqueline, 'The legal profession and the decline of the ancien régime in Ireland, 1790–1840' in Hogan and Osborough (eds), *Brehons, serjeants and attorneys* (Dublin, 1990)

Hobsbawm, Eric and T. Ranger (eds), *The invention of tradition* (Cambridge, 1992)

Hogan, Daire and W.N. Osborough (eds), *Brehons, serjeants and attorneys: studies in the history of the Irish legal profession* (Dublin, 1990)

Hogan, Daire, *The legal profession in Ireland, 1789–1922* (Dublin, 1986)

Hogan, Daire, 'Arrows too sharply pointed: the relations of Lord Justice Christian and Lord O'Hagan, 1868–74' in J.F. McEldowney and P. O'Higgins (eds), *The common law tradition* (Dublin, 1990)

Hogan, Daire, 'Solicitors and the Four Courts' in Cardine Costello (ed.), *The Four Courts* (Dublin, 1996)

Hogan, Daire, 'The Society from independence to 1960' in Eamonn G. Hall and Daire Hogan (eds), *The law society of Ireland* (Dublin, 2002)

Hogan, Daire, *McCann Fitzgerald: origin and fifty years* (Dublin, 2016)

Hogan, Daire and Colum Kenny (eds), *Changes in practice and law: a selection of essays by members of the legal profession to mark twenty-five years of the Irish Legal History Society* (Dublin, 2013)

Hogan, Gerard, 'Hugh Kennedy, the Childers habeas corpus application and the return to the Four Courts' in Caroline Costello (ed.), *The Four Courts 200 years* (Dublin, 1996)

Holland, Ailsa C., 'The papers of Hugh Kennedy', *Irish Jurist* 24 (1989)

Hosier, Maeve, 'The legal profession in troikaland: before and after the Irish bailout', *International Journal of the Legal Professions* 22:2 (2015)

Howlin, Niamh, 'The Irish courts system and the court houses' in Colum O'Riordan, Paul Burns and Cíaran O'Connor (eds), *Ireland's court houses* (Dublin, 2019)

Hunter, Rosemary, 'Women in the legal profession: the Australian profile' in Ulrike Schultz and Gisela Shaw (eds), *Women in the world's legal professions* (Oxford, 2003)

Hunter, Rosemary, 'Discrimination against women barristers: evidence from a study of court appearances and briefing practices', *International Journal of the Legal Profession* 1 (2005)

Hutchinson, Emma, 'First woman professor of law in Ireland, Frances Moran, 1925' in E. Rackley and R. Auchmuty (eds), *Women's legal landmarks* (Oxford, 2019)

Inglis, Tom, *Truth, power and lies: Irish society and the case of the Kerry babies* (Dublin, 2003)

Johnson, Terry (ed.), *Professions and power* (London, 1972)

Jordan, Anthony J., *Seán MacBride: a biography* (Dublin, 1993)

Jordan, Eamon, *Justice in the plays and films of Martin McDonagh* (Cham, 2019)

Kathrani, Paresh, 'An "existential' shift? Technology and some questions for the legal profession', *Legal Ethics* 20:1 (2017)

Keane, Edward, Beryl P. Phair and Thomas U. Sadleir (eds), *King's Inns admission papers, 1607–1867* (Dublin, 1982)

Keane, Ronan, 'A mass of crumbling ruins: the destruction of the Four Courts in June 1922' in Cardine Costello (ed.), *The Four Courts: 200 years* (Dublin, 1996)

Keane, Ronan, 'Judges as lawmakers: the Irish experience', *Radharc* 4 (2003)

Keane, Ronan, 'Negligence of barristers', *Irish Jurist* 2:1 (1967)

Keane, Ronan, 'The future of the Irish Bar', *Studies: An Irish Quarterly Review* 54:216 (1965)

Keane, Ronan, 'The voice of the Gael: Chief Justice Kennedy and the emergence of the new Irish court system 1921–1936', *Irish Jurist* 31 (1996)

Keating, Barbara and Stephanie Keating, *Blood sisters* (London, 2005)

Keller, A., *A personal history of Whitney Moore and Keller solicitors: from 1882 to 1985* (Dublin, 1992)

Kelly, John, *The polling of the dead* (Dublin, 1993)

Kennedy, Brian, 'John Hearne and the Irish constitution', *Eire-Ireland* 24:2 (1989)

Kennedy, Greg, 'Buying a computer and other traumatic experiences', *Bar Review* 1:2 (1996)

Kennedy, Helena, 'Women at the Bar' in Robert Hazell (ed.), *The Bar on trial* (London, 1978)

Kennedy, Patrick C., *Hugh Kennedy: the great but neglected chief justice* (Limerick, 2005)

Kennedy, Hugh, 'The character and sources of the constitution of the Irish Free State', *American Bar Association Journal* 14:8 (Washington, 1928)

Kenny, Colum, 'Irish ambition and English preference in chancery appointments, 1827–1841: the fate of William Conyngham Plunkett' in W.N. Osborough (ed.), *Explorations in law and history* (Dublin, 1995)

Kenny, Colum, 'King's Inns and Henrietta Street chambers', *Dublin Historical Record* 47:2 (1994)

Kenny, Colum, 'Not every judge a phoenix: King's Inns under Cromwell' in Colman Dennehy (ed.), *Law and revolution in seventeenth-century Ireland* (Dublin, 2019)

Kenny, Colum, 'On holy ground: the benchers and the site of the present Four Courts before 1796' in C. Costello (ed.), *The Four Courts: 200 years* (Dublin, 1996)

Kenny, Colum, 'The exclusion of Catholics from the legal profession in Ireland, 1537–1829', *Irish Historical Studies* 25:100 (1987)

Kenny, Colum, 'The records of King's Inns, Dublin' in D. Hogan and W.N. Osborough (eds), *Brehons, serjeants and attorneys* (Dublin, 1990)

Kenny, Colum, 'You just have to get on with it: the advance of women in the legal profession, 1910–2012' in D. Hogan and C. Kenny (eds), *Changes in practice and law* (Dublin, 2013)

Kenny, Colum, *Battle of the books, 1972: cultural controversy at a Dublin library* (Dublin, 2002)

Kenny, Colum, *King's Inns and the kingdom of Ireland: the Irish 'inn of court' 1541–1800* (Dublin, 1992)

Kenny, Colum, *Midnight in London: the Anglo-Irish Treaty crisis, 1921* (Dublin, 2021)

Kenny, Colum, *The Honorable Society of King's Inns 1541–2016* (Dublin, 2016)

Kenny, Colum, *Tristram Kennedy and the revival of Irish legal training, 1835–1885* (Dublin, 1996)

Keogh, Dermot, *Jack Lynch: a biography* (Dublin, 2008)

Keogh, Dermot, *Jews in twentieth-century Ireland: refugees, anti-semitism and the Holocaust* (Cork, 1998)

Keogh, Dermot, *The Vatican, the bishops and Irish politics 1919–1939* (Cambridge, 1986)

Kerrigan, Gene, 'The Kerry babies case: an analysis of Mr Justice Lynch's report', *Magill* (Dublin, 1985)

Kerrigan, Gene, 'The Kerry babies scandal: scapegoats', *Magill* (Dublin, 1985)

Kerrigan, Gene, 'We still say the judge got it wrong', *Magill* (Dublin, 1986)

Kerwin, Hollie and Kim Rubenstein, 'Reading the life narrative of Valerie French, the first woman to sign the Western Australian Bar roll' in F. Davis, N. Musgrove and J. Smart (eds), *Founders, firsts and feminists: women leaders in twentieth-century Australia* (Melbourne, 2011)

Kissane, Bill, *The politics of the Irish Civil War* (Oxford, 2005)

Kissane, Bill, 'The geographical spread of state executions during the Irish Civil War, 1922–23', *Social Science History* 45:1 (2021)

Kissane, Bill, *New beginnings: constitutionalism and democracy in modern Ireland* (Dublin, 2011)

Kluttz, Daniel N. and Deirdre K. Mulligan, 'Automated decision support technologies and the legal profession', *Berkeley Technology Law Journal* 34:3 (2019)

Konntinen, Esa, '"Finland's route" of professionalisation and lawyer-officials' in W. Wesley Pue and David Sugarman (eds), *Lawyers and vampires: cultural histories of legal professions* (Oregon, 2003)

Kotsonouris, Mary, *Retreat from revolution: the Dáil Courts 1920–24* (Dublin, 1994)

Kotsonouris, Mary, *The winding-up of the Dáil Courts 1922–1925: an obvious duty* (Dublin, 2004)

Lachs, Phyllis S., 'A study of a professional elite: Anglo-Jewish barristers in the nineteenth century', *Jewish Social Studies* (1982) 44:2

Larkin, Felix M. and N.M. Dawson (eds), *Lawyers, the law and history* (Dublin, 2013)

Lee, Gerard A., *A memoir of the South-Western Circuit* (Dublin, 1990)

Lee, J.J., 'Foreword' in Judith Harford (ed.), *Education for all?: the legacy of free post-primary education in Ireland* (Oxford, 2018)

Lefroy, Thomas, *Memoir of Chief Justice Lefroy* (Dublin, 1871)

Lewis, Geoffrey, *Carson: the man who divided Ireland* (London, 2005)

Lindsay, Patrick J., *Memories* (Dublin, 1992)

Lobban, Michael, Joanne Begiato and Adrian Green, *Law, lawyers and litigants in early modern England: essays in memory of Christopher W. Brooks* (Cambridge, 2019)

Longson, Andrea, 'The advocates' library', *Legal Information Management* 9 (2009)

Lynch, Robert, *The partition of Ireland, 1918–1925* (Cambridge 2019)

Lysaght, Charles, 'The life of Cecil Lavery', *Bar Review* 17:4 (2012)

Mac an tSaoi, Máire, *The same age as the state* (Dublin, 2003)

Mac Cormaic, Ruadhán, *The Supreme Court* (Dublin, 2016)

MacColl, René, *Roger Casement: a new judgment* (London, 1956)

MacDermott, J.C., *An enriching life* (Belfast, 1980)

MacKenzie, Patrick, *Lawful occasions* (Dublin, 1992)

Mackey, Herbert O., *The life and times of Roger Casement* (Dublin, 1954)

Mackey, Noreen, *The secret ladder* (London, 2005)

Mackey, Rex, *Windward of the law* (1965, and 2nd ed 1991, Dublin)

Madon, Natasha S., 'Early departure: factors associated with the flight of women from the private practice of criminal law', *Criminal Law Quarterly* 65:3–4 (2018)

Magnus, S.W., 'The Foreign Compensation Commission', *International and Comparative Law Quarterly*, 37:4 (1988)

Maguire, Conor A., 'The republican courts', *Capuchin Annual* (1939)

Maguire, William Joseph, *Guide to the professions: barristers-at-law and solicitors* (Dublin, 1931)

Malatesta, Maria, *Professional men, professional women: the European professions from the 19th century until today* (tr. Adrian Belton, London, 2011)

Mannion, Patrick and Fearghal McGarry, *The Irish Revolution: a global history* (New York, 2022)

Marjoribanks, Edward, *The life of Lord Carson*, vol. 1 (London, 1932)

Marron, Maria B., 'Levels of professionalism and professional efficacy among journalists in Ireland', *Gazette* 56:1 (1996)

Marshall, Robert, 'Lieutenant W.E. Wylie KC: the soldiering lawyer of 1916' in Felix M. Larkin and N.M. Dawson (eds), *Lawyers, the law and history* (Dublin, 2013)

Marshall, T.H., 'The recent history of professionalism in relation to social structure and social policy', *Canadian Journal of Economics and Political Science* 5 (1939)

Mason, M., 'UK: room at the inns – the increased scope of regulation under the new Bar standards board handbook for England and Wales', *Legal Ethics* 17:1 (2014)

Matthew, Aidan Carl (ed.), *Immediate man: cuimhni ar Cearbhall Ó Dálaigh* (Dublin, 1983)

McCague, Eugene, *Arthur Cox, 1891–1965* (Dublin, 1994)

McCullagh, David, *The reluctant taoiseach: a biography of John A. Costello* (Dublin, 2011)

McDonnell Bodkin, M., *Recollections of an Irish judge: press, Bar and parliament, 1850–1933* (London, 1914)

McDonnell, A.D., *The life of Sir Denis Henry, Catholic unionist* (Belfast, 2000)

McDowell, R.B. and D.A. Webb, *Trinity College Dublin 15920–1952: an academic history* (Cambridge, 1982)

McEldowney, J.F. and P. O'Higgins (eds), *The common law tradition* (Dublin, 1990)

McGlynn, Clare, *The woman lawyer: making the difference* (London, 1998)

McLaren, James G., 'A brief history of wigs in the legal profession', *International Journal of the Legal Profession* 6:2 (1999)

McMahon, Bryan, *Judge or jury? The jury trial for personal injury cases in Ireland* (Cork, 1985)

McNulty, Eugene, 'Original intent: the limits of legal imagination in Colm Tóibín's *The heather blazing*', *Law and Literature* 32:3 (2019)

McParland, Edward, 'The old Four Courts, at Christ Church' in C. Costello (eds), *The Four Courts: 200 years* (Dublin, 1996)

Menkel-Meadow, Carrie, 'Portia in a different voice: speculation on a women's lawyering process', *Berkeley Women's Law Journal* 1 (1985)

Miller, Mark C., *The high priests of American politics: the role of lawyers in American political institutions* (Tennessee, 1995)

Millerson, Geoffrey, *The qualifying associations: a study in professionalisation* (London, 1964; 1998 ed.)

Modeer, Kjell A., 'From "rechtstaat" to "welfare-state": Swedish judicial culture in transition 1870–1970' in W. Wesley Pue and David Sugarman (eds), *Lawyers and vampires: cultural histories of legal professions* (Oregon, 2003)

Mohr, Thomas, 'British involvement in the creation of the constitution of the Irish Free State', *Dublin University Law Journal* 30 (2008)

Mohr, Thomas, 'Irish law journals and the emergence of the Irish state, 1916–22', *Journal of European Periodical Studies* 3:1 (2018)

Mohr, Thomas, 'Law and the foundation of the Irish state on 6 December 1922', *Irish Jurist* 59 (2018)

Mohr, Thomas, 'The influence of Chief Justice Hugh Kennedy on Irish legal scholarship and publishing', *Irish Jurist* 64 (2020)

Mohr, Thomas, 'The Anglo-Irish Treaty: legal interpretation, 1921–1925', *Irish Jurist* 66 (2021)

Mohr, Thomas, 'The strange fate of the Dáil decrees of revolutionary Ireland, 1919–22', *Statute Law Review* 43:1 (2022)

Molony, Thomas, 'Legal aid for poor persons', *Journal of the Statistical and Social Inquiry Society of Ireland* 15 (1930–7)

Moore, Peter, 'Irish lawyers and judges in South Australia, 1836–1914' in Susan Arthure et al. (eds), *Irish South Australia: new histories and insights* (Adelaide, 2019)

Morison, John and Philip Leith, *The barrister's world and the nature of law* (Berkshire, 1992)

Mortimer, John, *Rumpole of the Bailey* (ITV, 1978–94)

Mosca, Irene and Robert E. Wright, 'The long-term consequences of the Irish marriage bar', *Economy & Social Review* 51:1 (2020)

Mossman, Mary Jane, *The first women lawyers: a comparative study of gender, law and the legal profession* (Oxford, 2006)

Muldoon, J. Malachi, *A Trinity student: a comedy in four acts* (Dublin, 1913)

Muldoon, J. Malachi, *Children of the lost province: a play in three acts* (Dublin, 1930)

Muldoon, J. Malachi, *The red redeeming dawn: a national drama in three acts; being a sequel to 'The West's awake'* (Dublin, 1920)

Muldoon, J. Malachi, *The West's awake; or the dawn of freedom. A national play in three acts. Founded on a collection of historical facts* (Dublin, 1921)

Mulvagh, Conor, *Irish days, Indian memories: V.V. Giri and Indian law students at University College Dublin, 1913–1916* (Kildare, 2016)

Mungham, Geoff and Philip A. Thomas, 'Solicitors and clients: altruism or self-interest?' in Dingwall and Lewis (eds), *The sociology of the professions* (London, 1983)

Murray, Fiona and Eda Segarra, *The men and women of the Anglo-Irish Treaty delegations, 1921* (Dublin, 2021)

Murray, Georgina, 'New Zealand women lawyers at the end of the twentieth century' in Schultz and Shaw (eds), *Women in the judiciary* (London, 2012)

Nir, E., 'Approaching the bench: accessing elites on the judiciary for qualitative interviews', *International Journal of Social Research Methodology* 21:1 (2018)

Noyes, Alfred, *The accusing ghost: or justice for Roger Casement* (London, 1967)

Ó Síocháin, P.A., *Aran Islands of legend* (Dublin, 1962)

Ó Síocháin, P.A., *Dlína fianaise in Éirinn* (Dublin, 1962)

Ó Síocháin, P.A., *Ireland: a journey into lost time* (Dublin, 1983)

Ó Síocháin, P.A., *Ireland: journey to freedom* (Kells, 1990)

Ó Síocháin, P.A., *The criminal law of Ireland* (Dublin, 1940)

Ó Síocháin, P.A., *Dlí coiriúil na hÉireann* (Dublin, 1964)

O'Brien, Edna, *Down by the river* (London, 1996)

O'Connell, Mark, *A thread of violence* (London, 2023)

O'Connor, Frank, *Guests of the nation* (Dublin, 1931)

O'Connor, Frank, *In the train* (Dublin, 1937)

O'Donoghue, Tom and Judith Harford, *Piety and privilege: Catholic secondary schooling in Ireland and the theocratic state, 1922–1967* (Oxford, 2021)

O'Flaherty, Hugh, 'The independent Bar and the defence of human rights' in James O'Reilly (ed.), *Human rights and constitutional law: essays in honour of Brian Walsh* (Dublin, 1992)

O'Halloran, Stephen, 'Peek-a-boo I can sue you: barristers' immunity in the twenty-first century', parts I and II, *Irish Law Times* 26 (2008)

O'Higgins, T.F., *A double life* (Dublin, 1996)

O'Malley, Tom, 'Legal education and training in Europe: Ireland, *International Journal of the Legal Profession* 2 (1995)

O'Reilly, James (ed.), *Human rights and constitutional law: essays in honour of Brian Walsh* (Dublin, 1992)

O'Shea, Helen, 'Irish legal geographies in the era of emergency: independent Ireland, colonial Kenya, and the British colonial legal service', *Éire-Ireland* 51:1&2 (2016)

O'Shea, Helen, *Ireland and the end of the British empire: the republic and its role in the Cyprus emergency* (London, 2020)

O'Sullivan, Kevin, *Ireland, Africa and the end of empire: small state identity in the Cold War 1955–75* (Manchester, 2013)

Osborough, W.N., 'The regulation of the admission of attorneys and solicitors in Ireland, 1600–1866' in Daire Hogan and W.N. Osborough (eds), *Brehons, serjeants and attorneys* (Dublin, 1990)

Osborough, W.N., *The law school of University College Dublin* (Dublin, 2014)

Pakenham, Frank *Peace by ordeal: the negotiation of the Anglo-Irish Treaty, 1921* (London, 1935)

Pashigian, B. Peter, 'The market for lawyers: the determinants of the demand for the supply of lawyers', *Journal of Law and Economics* 20:1 (1977)

Paterson, Alan, 'Becoming a judge' in Robert Dingwall and Philip Lewis, *The sociology of the professions: lawyers, doctors and others* (London, 1983)

Pepitone, Ren, 'Gender, space, and ritual: women barristers, the inns of court, and the interwar press', *Journal of Women's History* 28:1 (2016)

Phillips, Barry, 'Getting the most from the internet', *Irish Law Times* 150 (1998)

Pirie, Fernanda and Justine Rogers, 'Pupillage: the shaping of a professional elite' in Jon Abbink and Tijo Salverda (eds), *The anthropology of elites: power, culture and the complexities of distinction* (New York, 2013)

Plunkett, Eric A., 'Attorneys and solicitors in Ireland' in Incorporated Law Society, *Record of the centenary of the charter of the Incorporated Law Society of Ireland, 1852–1952* (Dublin, 1952)

Polden, Patrick, 'Portia's progress: women at the Bar in England, 1919–1939', *International Journal of the Legal Profession* 12 (2005)

Power, T.P., 'Conversions among the legal profession in Ireland in the eighteenth century' in Daire Hogan and W.N. Osborough (eds), *Brehons, serjeants and attorneys* (Dublin, 1990)

Prest, Wilfred, *Lawyers in early modern Europe and America* (London, 1981)

Prest, Wilfred, *The rise of the barristers: a social history of the English Bar, 1590–1640* (Oxford, 1986)

Prices Advisory Committee (Motor Insurance), *Report of enquiry into the cost and methods of providing motor insurance* (Dublin, 1982)

Pringle, A.D., 'British Isles: Éire', *Journal of Comparative Legislation and International Law* 32:1 (1950)

Pue, W. Wesley and David Sugarman (eds), *Lawyers and vampires: cultural histories of legal professions* (Oregon, 2003)

Pue, W. Wesley, *Lawyers' empire: legal professions and cultural authority, 1780–1950* (Vancouver, 2016)

Pue, W. Wesley, 'The use of history in the development of lawyers' mythologies' in W. Wesley Pue, *Lawyers' empire: legal professions and cultural authority, 1780–1950* (Vancouver, 2016)

Qafisheh, Mutaz M., 'A century of the law profession in Palestine: quo vadis?', *International Journal of the Legal Profession* 25:2 (2018)

Quinn, A.P., *Wigs and guns: Irish barristers in the Great War* (Dublin, 2006)

Quinn, Antoinette, *Patrick Kavanagh: a biography* (Dublin, 2001)

Rackley, Erika and Rosemary Auchmuty (eds), *Women's legal landmarks: celebrating the history of women and law in the UK and Ireland* (Oxford, 2019)

Rackley, Erika and Rosemary Auchmuty, 'Women's legal landmarks: an introduction' in Rackley and Auchmuty (eds), *Women's legal landmarks* (Oxford, 2019)

Rackley, Erika, *Women, judging and judiciary: from difference to diversity* (London, 2013)

Redmond, Mary, 'The emergence of women in the solicitors' profession in Ireland' in Hogan and Hall (eds), *The law society of Ireland, 1852–2002* (Dublin, 2002)

Rhyne, Charles S., 'President's page', *American Bar Association Journal* 43:9 (1957)

Richie, Donald, *Doing oral history* (Oxford, 2014)

Rivlin, Ray, *Shalom Ireland: a social history of the Jews in modern Ireland* (Dublin, 2003)

Robinson, Mary, *Everybody matters: a memoir* (London, 2013)

Roche-Tiengo, Virginie, 'The judge and the human Hansard in Brian Friel's theatre' in Hanna and McNulty (eds), *Law and literature: the Irish case* (Liverpool, 2022)

Roffey, Jack, *Boyd Q.C.* (ITV, 1956–64)

Rogers, Justine, 'Representing the Bar: how the barristers' profession sells itself to prospective members', *Legal Studies* 32:2 (2012)

Ronayne, Jarlath, *First fleet to federation: Irish supremacy in colonial Australia* (Dublin, 2002)

Rosen, Sherwin, 'The market for lawyers', *Journal of Law and Economics* 35:2 (1992)

Ross, John, *The years of my pilgrimage. Random reminiscences* (London, 1924)

Ross, John, *Pilgrim scrip: more random reminiscences* (London, 1927)

Rueschemeyer, Dietrich, 'Professional autonomy and the social control of expertise' in Dingwall and Lewis (eds), *The sociology of the professions: lawyers, doctors and others* (London, 1983)

Ryan, Ray and Des Ryan, 'A Bar to recovery? barristers, public policy, and immunity from suit', *Bar Review* 10:6 (2005)

Sachs, Albie & Joan Hoff Wilson, *Sexism and the law: a study of male beliefs and legal bias in Britain and the United States* (Oxford, 1978)

Sagarra, Eda, *Kevin O'Shiel, Tyrone nationalist and state builder* (Dublin, 2013)

Sarfatti Larson, Magali, *The rise of professionalism: a sociological analysis* (Berkeley, 1977)

Schroeter, J., S.L. Smith and S. Cox, 'Advertising and competition in routine legal service markets: an empirical investigation', *Journal of Industrial Economics* 36 (1987)

Schultz, Ulrike and Gisela Shaw (eds), *Women in the world's legal professions* (Oxford, 2002)

Sheehy, Eugene, *May it please the court* (Dublin, 1951)

Sheil, Richard Lalor, *Sketches of the Irish Bar* (Dublin, 1854)

Shillman, Bernard, *The law relating to employers' liability and workmen's compensation in the Irish Free State* (Dublin, 1934)

Shinnick, E., F. Bruinsma, and C. Parker, 'Aspects of regulatory reform in the legal profession: Australia, Ireland and the Netherlands', *International Journal of the Legal Profession* 10:3 (2003)

Silvestri, Michael, 'British imperial intelligence and anticolonial revolutionaries during and after the Great War' in Patrick Mannion and Fearghal McGarry (eds), *The Irish Revolution: a global history* (New York, 2022)

Simms, Katharine, 'The brehons of later medieval Ireland' in Daire Hogan and W.N. Osborough (eds), *Brehons, serjeants and attorneys* (Dublin, 1990)

Small, Mario Luis, 'How many cases do I need? On science and the logic of case selection in field-based research', *Ethnography* 10:1 (2009)

Smith, George Hill, *The north-east Bar: a sketch, historical and reminiscent* (Belfast, 1910)

Smith, Katherine E, 'Problematising power relations in "elite" interviews', *Geoforum* 37 (2006)

Sommerlad, Hilary and Peter Sanderson, *Gender, choice and commitment: women solicitors in England and Wales and the struggle for equal status* (Aldershot, 1998)

Sommerlad, Hilary, '"A pit to put women in": professionalism, work intensification, sexualisation and work-life balance in the legal profession in England and Wales', *International Journal of the Legal Profession* 23:1 (2016)

Sommerlad, Hilary, 'The myth of feminisation: women and cultural change in the legal profession', *International Journal of the Legal Profession* 1 (1994)

Sommerlad, Hilary, Lisa Webley, Liz Duff, Daniel Muzio and Jennifer Tomlinson, *Diversity in the legal profession in England and Wales: a qualitative study of barriers and individual choices* (London, 2010)

Stigler, George J., 'The theory of economic regulation', *Bell Journal of Economics & Management Science* 2 (1971)

Stone, Jonathan, 'Our London meeting: an Englishman's impression', *American Bar Association Journal* 43:9 (1957)

Sullivan, A.M, 'The last forty years of the Irish Bar', *The Cambridge Law Journal* 3:3 (1929)

Sullivan, A.M., *Old Ireland: reminiscences of an Irish KC* (London, 1927)

Sullivan, A.M., *The last serjeant* (London, 1952)

Suresh, M., *Mapping and evaluating the formal and informal lesbian, gay and bisexual networks in the legal profession in England* (London, 2014)

Susskind, Richard E., *The future of law: facing the challenges of information technology* (Oxford, 1998)

The Law Society of Ireland, *Celebrating a century of equal opportunities legislation: the first 100 women solicitors* (Dublin, 2019)

Thornton, Margaret, *Dissonance and distrust: women in the legal profession* (Melbourne, 1996)

Tóibín, Colm, 'A brush with the law', *The Dublin Review* (Autumn 2007)

Trebilcock, Michael J., *Paradoxes of professional regulation: in search of regulatory principles* (Toronto, 2022)

Tubridy, Jean, *Pegged down: experiences of people in Ireland with significant physical disabilities* (Dublin, 1996)

Ungoed-Thomas, Jasper, *Jasper Wolfe of Skibbereen* (Cork, 2008)

Van Hoy, Jerry (ed.), *Legal professions: work, structure and organization* (Bradford, 2001)

Vaughan, Steven, '"Prefer not to say": diversity and diversity reporting at the Bar of England & Wales', *International Journal of the Legal Profession* 24:3 (2017)

Wakai, Nyo', *Under the broken scale of justice. The law and my times* (Cameroon, 2009)

Watkins, Jeff and Lynn Drury, 'The pressures on professional life in the 1990s', *International Journal of the Legal Profession* 1 (1994)

Weber, Max, *Economy and society* (Cambridge, 1969)

Weeks, Liam and Mícheál Ó Fathartaigh, *The Treaty: debating and establishing the Irish state* (Newbridge, 2018)

Whelan, Darius, 'Lawyers and the internet', *Irish Law Times* 14 (1996)

Winston, Jessica, *Lawyers at play: literature, law and politics at the early modern inns of court* (Oxford, 2016)

ONLINE DATABASES AND WEBSITES

Abbey Theatre Archive: https://www.abbeytheatre.ie/about/archive/

Courts Decade of Commemorations: www.courts.ie/acc/alfresco/7eea56a7–90ff–4782–9e22–56d7b2e87fd6/CourtsDecadeof CentenariesCommemorationsPosters.pdf/pdf#view=fitH

Dictionary of Irish biography: https://www.dib.ie/

Europeans in East Africa: www.europeansineastafrica.co.uk

First 100 years: https://first100years.org.uk/

Four Courts 100 Lecture series: https://courts.ie/four-courts–100-lecture-series

Hong Kong Court of Final Appeal former judges: www.hkcfa.hk/en/about/who/judges/former/

Law Library podcast: www.lawlibrary.ie/podcast/

'Legal lives': www.bl.uk/projects/national-life-stories-legal-lives

Law Society of Ontario, 'Oral history interviews': https://lso.ca/about-lso/osgoode-hall-and-ontario-legal-heritage/collections-and-research/online-resources-and-finding-aids/oral-history-interviews.

London School of Economics, 'Legal biography project; judicial interviews': www.lse.ac.uk/law/legal-biography-project/judicial-interviews/

Next 100 years: https://next100years.org.uk/

New South Wales Bar Association 'Oral history': https://nswbar.asn.au/the-bar-association/bar-history/oral-history#/

Oxford Centre for Socio-Legal Studies project, 'Enhancing democratic habits: an oral history of the law centres movement': https://gtr.ukri.org/projects?ref=AH%2 FT007710%2F1.

Oxford dictionary of national biography: https://www.oxforddnb.com/

Peter Sutherland UCD www.ucd.ie/newsandopinion/news/2018/january/07/peter sutherland25april19467january2018/

RTÉ Archives: www.rte.ie/archives/

'Trailblazers 1919-2019', online exhibition: www.lawlibrary.ie/about/history/trailblazers –1919–2019–100-years-of-women-at-the-bar/.

Victorian Bar, oral history: www.vicbar.com.au/public/about/about-victorian-bar/our-history

Index

Compiled by *Julitta Clancy*.
Note: footnotes are not included in the index;
page references in italics denote illustrations